COLLECTED WORKS OF
ANTHONY TROLLOPE

Copyright © 2008 BiblioBazaar
All rights reserved

COLLECTED WORKS OF ANTHONY TROLLOPE

Aaron Trow, Chateau of Prince Polignac, The Courtship of Susan Bell, George Walker at Suez, The House of Heine Brothers, John Bull on the Guadalquivir, The Man Who Kept His Money in a Box, La Mere Bauche, Miss Sarah Jack of Spanish Town, Jamaica, The Mistletoe Bough, Mrs. General Talboys, O'Conors of Castle Conor, The Parson's Daughter of Oxney Colne, Relics of General Chasse, Returning Home, A Ride Across Palestine, An Unprotected Female, and Victorian Short Stories: Stories of Courtship

BIBLIOBAZAAR

COLLECTED WORKS OF
ANTHONY TROLLOPE

CONTENTS

AARON TROW 9
THE CHATEAU OF PRINCE POLIGNAC 36
THE COURTSHIP OF SUSAN BELL 58
GEORGE WALKER AT SUEZ 88
THE HOUSE OF HEINE BROTHERS, IN MUNICH 106
JOHN BULL ON THE GUADALQUIVIR.
    FROM "TALES FROM ALL COUNTRIES" 131
THE MAN WHO KEPT HIS MONEY IN A BOX 154
LA MERE BAUCHE FROM "TALES FROM
    ALL COUNTRIES" 183
MISS SARAH JACK, OF SPANISH TOWN, JAMAICA 214
THE MISTLETOE BOUGH 238
MRS. GENERAL TALBOYS 261
MRS. GENERAL TALBOYS 283
THE O'CONORS OF CASTLE CONOR, COUNTY
    MAYO. FROM "TALES FROM ALL
    COUNTRIES" 305
THE PARSON'S DAUGHTER OF OXNEY COLNE 324
THE RELICS OF GENERAL CHASSE—
    A TALE OF ANTWERP 351
RETURNING HOME 371
A RIDE ACROSS PALESTINE 392
AN UNPROTECTED FEMALE AT THE PYRAMIDS 428
VICTORIAN SHORT STORIES:
    STORIES OF COURTSHIP 457

AARON TROW

I would wish to declare, at the beginning of this story, that I shall never regard that cluster of islets which we call Bermuda as the Fortunate Islands of the ancients. Do not let professional geographers take me up, and say that no one has so accounted them, and that the ancients have never been supposed to have gotten themselves so far westwards. What I mean to assert is this—that, had any ancient been carried thither by enterprise or stress of weather, he would not have given those islands so good a name. That the Neapolitan sailors of King Alonzo should have been wrecked here, I consider to be more likely. The vexed Bermoothes is a good name for them. There is no getting in or out of them without the greatest difficulty, and a patient, slow navigation, which is very heart-rending. That Caliban should have lived here I can imagine; that Ariel would have been sick of the place is certain; and that Governor Prospero should have been willing to abandon his governorship, I conceive to have been only natural. When one regards the present state of the place, one is tempted to doubt whether any of the governors have been conjurors since his days.

Bermuda, as all the world knows, is a British colony at which we maintain a convict establishment. Most of our outlying convict establishments have been sent back upon our hands from our colonies, but here one is still maintained. There is also in the islands a strong military fortress, though not a fortress looking magnificent to the eyes of civilians, as do Malta and Gibraltar. There are also here some six thousand white people and some six thousand black people, eating, drinking, sleeping, and dying.

The convict establishment is the most notable feature of Bermuda to a stranger, but it does not seem to attract much attention from the regular inhabitants of the place. There is no intercourse between the prisoners and the Bermudians. The convicts are rarely seen by them, and the convict islands are rarely visited. As to the prisoners themselves, of course it is not open to them—or should not be open to them—to have intercourse with any but the prison authorities.

There have, however, been instances in which convicts have escaped from their confinement, and made their way out among the islands. Poor wretches! As a rule, there is but little chance for any that can so escape. The whole length of the cluster is but twenty miles, and the breadth is under four. The prisoners are, of course, white men, and the lower orders of Bermuda, among whom alone could a runagate have any chance of hiding himself, are all negroes; so that such a one would be known at once. Their clothes are all marked. Their only chance of a permanent escape would be in the hold of an American ship; but what captain of an American or other ship would willingly encumber himself with an escaped convict? But, nevertheless, men have escaped; and in one instance, I believe, a convict got away, so that of him no farther tidings were ever heard.

For the truth of the following tale I will not by any means vouch. If one were to inquire on the spot one might probably find that the ladies all believe it, and the old men; that all the young men know exactly how much of it is false and how much true; and that the steady, middle-aged, well-to-do islanders are quite convinced that it is romance from beginning to end. My readers may range themselves with the ladies, the young men, or the steady, well-to-do, middle-aged islanders, as they please.

Some years ago, soon after the prison was first established on its present footing, three men did escape from it, and among them a certain notorious prisoner named Aaron Trow. Trow's antecedents in England had not been so villanously bad as those of many of his fellow-convicts, though the one offence for which he was punished had been of a deep dye: he had shed man's blood. At a period of great distress in a manufacturing town he had led men on to riot, and with his own hand had slain the first constable who had endeavoured to do his duty against him. There had been courage in the doing of the deed, and probably no malice; but the deed, let its moral blackness have been what it might, had sent him to Bermuda, with a sentence against him of penal servitude for life. Had he been then amenable to prison discipline,—even then, with such a sentence against him as that,—he might have won his way back, after the lapse of years, to the children, and perhaps, to the wife, that he had left behind him; but he was amenable to no rules—to no discipline. His heart was sore to death with an idea of injury, and he lashed himself against the bars of his cage with a feeling that it would be well if he could so lash himself till he might perish in his fury.

And then a day came in which an attempt was made by a large body of convicts, under his leadership, to get the better of the officers of the prison. It is hardly necessary to say that the attempt failed. Such attempts always fail. It failed on this occasion signally, and Trow, with two other men, were condemned to be scourged terribly, and then kept in solitary confinement for some lengthened term of months. Before, however, the day of scourging came, Trow and his two associates had escaped.

I have not the space to tell how this was effected, nor the power to describe the manner. They did escape from the establishment into the islands, and though two of them were taken after a single day's run at liberty, Aaron Trow had not been yet retaken even when a week was over. When a month was over he had not been retaken, and the officers of the prison began to say that he had got away from them in a vessel to the States. It was impossible, they said, that he should have remained in the islands and not been discovered. It was not impossible that he might have destroyed himself, leaving his body where it had not yet been found. But he could not have lived on in Bermuda during that month's search. So, at least, said the officers of the prison. There was, however, a report through the islands that he had been seen from time to time; that he had gotten bread from the negroes at night, threatening them with death if they told of his whereabouts; and that all the clothes of the mate of a vessel had been stolen while the man was bathing, including a suit of dark blue cloth, in which suit of clothes, or in one of such a nature, a stranger had been seen skulking about the rocks near St. George. All this the governor of the prison affected to disbelieve, but the opinion was becoming very rife in the islands that Aaron Trow was still there.

A vigilant search, however, is a task of great labour, and cannot be kept up for ever. By degrees it was relaxed. The warders and gaolers ceased to patrol the island roads by night, and it was agreed that Aaron Trow was gone, or that he would be starved to death, or that he would in time be driven to leave such traces of his whereabouts as must lead to his discovery; and this at last did turn out to be the fact.

There is a sort of prettiness about these islands which, though it never rises to the loveliness of romantic scenery, is nevertheless attractive in its way. The land breaks itself into little knolls, and the sea runs up, hither and thither, in a thousand creeks and inlets; and then, too, when the oleanders are in bloom, they give a wonderfully bright colour to the landscape. Oleanders seem to be the roses of Bermuda, and are cultivated round all the villages of the better class through the islands. There are two towns, St. George and Hamilton, and one main high-road, which connects them; but even this high-road is broken by a ferry, over which every vehicle going from St. George to Hamilton must be conveyed. Most of the locomotion in these parts is done by boats, and the residents look to the sea, with its narrow creeks, as their best highway from their farms to their best market. In those days—and those days were not very long since—the building of small ships was their chief trade, and they valued their land mostly for the small scrubby cedar-trees with which this trade was carried on.

As one goes from St. George to Hamilton the road runs between two seas; that to the right is the ocean; that on the left is an inland creek, which runs up through a large portion of the islands, so that the land on the other side of it is near to the traveller. For a considerable portion of the way there are no houses lying near the road, and, there is one residence, some way from the road, so secluded that no other house lies within a mile of it by land. By water it might probably be reached within half a mile. This place was called Crump Island, and here lived, and had lived for many years, an old gentleman, a native of Bermuda, whose business it had been to buy up cedar wood and sell it to the ship-builders at Hamilton. In our story we shall not have very much to do with old Mr. Bergen, but it will be necessary to say a word or two about his house.

It stood upon what would have been an island in the creek, had not a narrow causeway, barely broad enough for a road, joined it to that larger island on which stands the town of St. George. As the main road approaches the ferry it runs through some rough, hilly, open ground, which on the right side towards the ocean has never been cultivated. The distance from the ocean here may, perhaps, be a quarter of a mile, and the ground is for the most part covered with low furze. On the left of the road the land is cultivated in patches, and here, some half mile or more from the ferry, a path turns away to Crump Island. The house cannot be seen from the road, and, indeed, can hardly be seen at all, except from the sea. It lies, perhaps, three furlongs from the high road, and the path to it is but little used, as the passage to and from it is chiefly made by water.

Here, at the time of our story, lived Mr. Bergen, and here lived Mr. Bergen's daughter. Miss Bergen was well known at St. George's as a steady, good girl, who spent her time in looking after her father's household matters, in managing his two black maid-servants and the black gardener, and who did her duty in that sphere of life to which she had been called. She was a comely, well-shaped young woman, with a sweet countenance, rather large in size, and very quiet in demeanour. In her earlier years, when young girls usually first bud forth into womanly beauty, the neighbours had not thought much of Anastasia Bergen, nor had the young men of St. George been wont to stay their boats under the window of Crump Cottage in order that they might listen to her voice or feel the light of her eye; but slowly, as years went by, Anastasia Bergen became a woman that a man might well love; and a man learned to love her who was well worthy of a woman's heart. This was Caleb Morton, the Presbyterian minister of St. George; and Caleb Morton had been engaged to marry Miss Bergen for the last two years past, at the period of Aaron Trow's escape from prison.

Caleb Morton was not a native of Bermuda, but had been sent thither by the synod of his church from Nova Scotia. He was a tall, handsome man, at this time of some thirty years of age, of a presence which might almost have been called commanding. He was very strong, but of a temperament which did not often give him opportunity to put forth his strength; and his life had been such that neither he nor others knew of what nature might be his courage. The greater part of his life was spent in preaching to some few of the white people around him, and in teaching as many of the blacks as he could get to hear him. His days were very quiet, and had been altogether without excitement until he had met with

Anastasia Bergen. It will suffice for us to say that he did meet her, and that now, for two years past, they had been engaged as man and wife.

Old Mr. Bergen, when he heard of the engagement, was not well pleased at the information. In the first place, his daughter was very necessary to him, and the idea of her marrying and going away had hardly as yet occurred to him; and then he was by no means inclined to part with any of his money. It must not be presumed that he had amassed a fortune by his trade in cedar wood. Few tradesmen in Bermuda do, as I imagine, amass fortunes. Of some few hundred pounds he was possessed, and these, in the course of nature, would go to his daughter when he died; but he had no inclination to hand any portion of them over to his daughter before they did go to her in the course of nature. Now, the income which Caleb Morton earned as a Presbyterian clergyman was not large, and, therefore, no day had been fixed as yet for his marriage with Anastasia.

But, though the old man had been from the first averse to the match, his hostility had not been active. He had not forbidden Mr. Morton his house, or affected to be in any degree angry because his daughter had a lover. He had merely grumbled forth an intimation that those who marry in haste repent at leisure,—that love kept nobody warm if the pot did not boil; and that, as for him, it was as much as he could do to keep his own pot boiling at Crump Cottage. In answer to this Anastasia said nothing. She asked him for no money, but still kept his accounts, managed his household, and looked patiently forward for better days.

Old Mr. Bergen himself spent much of his time at Hamilton, where he had a woodyard with a couple of rooms attached to it. It was his custom to remain here three nights of the week, during which Anastasia was left alone at the cottage; and it happened by no means seldom that she was altogether alone, for the negro whom they called the gardener would go to her father's place at Hamilton, and the two black girls would crawl away up to the road, tired with the monotony of the sea at the cottage. Caleb had more than once told her that she was too much alone, but she had laughed at him, saying that solitude in Bermuda was not dangerous. Nor, indeed, was it; for the people are quiet and well-mannered, lacking much energy, but being, in the same degree, free from any propensity to violence.

"So you are going," she said to her lover, one evening, as he rose from the chair on which he had been swinging himself at the door of the cottage which looks down over the creek of the sea. He had sat there for an hour talking to her as she worked, or watching her as she moved about the place. It was a beautiful evening, and the sun had been falling to rest with almost tropical glory before his feet. The bright oleanders were red with their blossoms all around him, and he had thoroughly enjoyed his hour of easy rest. "So you are going," she said to him, not putting her work out of her hand as he rose to depart.

"Yes; and it is time for me to go. I have still work to do before I can get to bed. Ah, well; I suppose the day will come at last when I need not leave you as soon as my hour of rest is over."

"Come; of course it will come. That is, if your reverence should choose to wait for it another ten years or so."

"I believe you would not mind waiting twenty years."

"Not if a certain friend of mine would come down and see me of evenings when I'm alone after the day. It seems to me that I shouldn't mind waiting as long as I had that to look for."

"You are right not to be impatient," he said to her, after a pause, as he held her hand before he went. "Quite right. I only wish I could school myself to be as easy about it."

"I did not say I was easy," said Anastasia. "People are seldom easy in this world, I take it. I said I could be patient. Do not look in that way, as though you pretended that you were dissatisfied with me. You know that I am true to you, and you ought to be very proud of me."

"I am proud of you, Anastasia—" on hearing which she got up and courtesied to him. "I am proud of you; so proud of you that I feel you should not be left here all alone, with no one to help you if you were in trouble."

"Women don't get into trouble as men do, and do not want any one to help them. If you were alone in the house you would have to go to bed without your supper, because you could not make a basin of boiled milk ready for your own meal. Now, when your reverence has gone, I shall go to work and have my tea comfortably." And then he did go, bidding God bless her as he left her. Three hours after that he was disturbed in his own lodgings by one of the negro girls from the cottage rushing to his door, and begging him in Heaven's name to come down to the assistance of her mistress.

When Morton left her, Anastasia did not proceed to do as she had said, and seemed to have forgotten her evening meal. She had been working sedulously with her needle during all that last conversation; but when her lover was gone, she allowed the work to fall from her hands, and sat motionless for awhile, gazing at the last streak of colour left by the setting sun; but there was no longer a sign of its glory to be traced in the heavens around her. The twilight in Bermuda is not long and enduring as it is with us, though the daylight does not depart suddenly, leaving the darkness of night behind it without any intermediate time of warning, as is the case farther south, down among the islands of the tropics. But the soft, sweet light of the evening had waned and gone, and night had absolutely come upon her, while Anastasia was still seated before the cottage with her eyes fixed upon the white streak of motionless sea which was still visible through the gloom. She was thinking of him, of his ways of life, of his happiness, and of her duty towards him. She had told him, with her pretty feminine falseness, that she could wait without impatience; but now she said to herself that it would not be good for him to wait longer. He lived alone and without comfort, working very hard for his poor pittance, and she could see, and feel, and understand that a companion in his life was to him almost a necessity. She would tell her father that all this must be brought to an end. She would not ask him for money, but she would make him understand that her services must, at any rate in part, be transferred. Why should not she and Morton still live at the cottage when they were married? And so thinking, and at last resolving, she sat there till the dark night fell upon her.

She was at last disturbed by feeling a man's hand upon her shoulder. She jumped from her chair and faced him,—not screaming, for it was especially within her power to control herself, and to make no utterance except with forethought. Perhaps it might have been better for her had she screamed, and sent a shrill shriek down the shore of that inland sea. She was silent, however, and with awe-struck face and outstretched hands gazed into the face of him who still held her by the shoulder. The night was dark; but her eyes were now accustomed to the darkness, and she could see indistinctly something of his features. He was a low-sized man, dressed in a suit of sailor's blue clothing, with a rough cap of hair on his head, and a beard that had not been clipped for many weeks. His eyes were large, and hollow, and frightfully bright, so that she seemed to see nothing else of him; but she felt the strength of his fingers as he grasped her tighter and more tightly by the arm.

"Who are you?" she said, after a moment's pause.

"Do you know me?" he asked.

"Know you! No." But the words were hardly out of her mouth before it struck her that the man was Aaron Trow, of whom every one in Bermuda had been talking.

"Come into the house," he said, "and give me food." And he still held her with his hand as though he would compel her to follow him.

She stood for a moment thinking what she would say to him; for even then, with that terrible man standing close to her in the darkness, her presence of mind did not desert her. "Surely," she said, "I will give you food if you are hungry. But take your hand from me. No man would lay his hands on a woman."

"A woman!" said the stranger. "What does the starved wolf care for that? A woman's blood is as sweet to him as that of a man. Come into the house, I tell you." And then she preceded him through the open door into the narrow passage, and thence to the kitchen. There she saw that the back door, leading out on the other side of the house, was open, and she knew that he had come down from the road and entered on that side. She threw her eyes around, looking for the negro girls; but they were away, and she remembered that there was no human being within sound of her voice but this man who had told her that he was as a wolf thirsty after her blood!

"Give me food at once," he said.

"And will you go if I give it you?" she asked.

"I will knock out your brains if you do not," he replied, lifting from the grate a short, thick poker which lay there. "Do as I bid you at once. You also would be like a tiger if you had fasted for two days, as I have done."

She could see, as she moved across the kitchen, that he had already searched there for something that he might eat, but that he had searched in vain. With the close economy common among

17

his class in the islands, all comestibles were kept under close lock and key in the house of Mr. Bergen. Their daily allowance was given day by day to the negro servants, and even the fragments were then gathered up and locked away in safety. She moved across the kitchen to the accustomed cupboard, taking the keys from her pocket, and he followed close upon her. There was a small oil lamp hanging from the low ceiling which just gave them light to see each other. She lifted her hand to this to tare it from its hook, but he prevented her. "No, by Heaven!" he said, "you don't touch that till I've done with it. There's light enough for you to drag out your scraps."

She did drag out her scraps and a bowl of milk, which might hold perhaps a quart. There was a fragment of bread, a morsel of cold potato-cake, and the bone of a leg of kid. "And is that all?" said he. But as he spoke he fleshed his teeth against the bone as a dog would have done.

"It is the best I have," she said; "I wish it were better, and you should have had it without violence, as you have suffered so long from hunger."

"Bah! Better; yes! You would give the best no doubt, and set the hell hounds on my track the moment I am gone. I know how much I might expect from your charity."

"I would have fed you for pity's sake," she answered.

"Pity! Who are you, that you should dare to pity me! By—, my young woman, it is I that pity you. I must cut your throat unless you give me money. Do you know that?"

"Money! I have got no money."

"I'll make you have some before I go. Come; don't move till I have done." And as he spoke to her he went on tugging at the bone, and swallowing the lumps of stale bread. He had already finished the bowl of milk. "And, now," said he, "tell me who I am."

"I suppose you are Aaron Trow," she answered, very slowly. He said nothing on hearing this, but continued his meal, standing close to her so that she might not possibly escape from him out into the darkness. Twice or thrice in those few minutes she made up her mind to make such an attempt, feeling that it would be better to leave him in possession of the house, and make sure, if possible, of her own life. There was no money there; not a dollar! What money her father kept in his possession was locked up in his safe at Hamilton. And might he not keep to his threat, and murder her, when he found that she could give him nothing? She did not tremble outwardly, as she stood there watching him as he ate, but she thought how probable it might be that her last moments were very near. And yet she could scrutinise his features, form, and garments, so as to carry away in her mind a perfect picture of them. Aaron Trow—for of course it was the escaped convict—was not a man of frightful, hideous aspect. Had the world used him well, giving him when he was young ample wages and separating him from turbulent spirits, he also might have used the world well; and then women would have praised the brightness of his eye and the manly vigour of his brow. But things had not gone well with him. He had been separated from the wife he had loved, and the children who had been raised at his knee,—separated by his own violence; and now, as he had said of himself, he was a wolf rather than a man. As he stood there satisfying the craving of his appetite, breaking up the large morsels of food, he was an object very sad to be seen. Hunger had made him gaunt and yellow, he was squalid with the dirt of his hidden lair, and he had the look of a beast;—that look to which men fall when they live like the brutes of prey, as outcasts from their brethren. But still there was that about his brow which might have redeemed him,—which might have turned her horror into pity, had he been willing that it should be so.

"And now give me some brandy," he said.

There was brandy in the house,—in the sitting-room which was close at their hand, and the key of the little press which held it was in her pocket. It was useless, she thought, to refuse him; and so she told him that there was a bottle partly full, but that she must go to the next room to fetch it him.

"We'll go together, my darling," he said. "There's nothing like good company." And he again put his hand upon her arm as they passed into the family sitting-room.

"I must take the light," she said. But he unhooked it himself, and carried it in his own hand.

Again she went to work without trembling. She found the key of the side cupboard, and unlocking the door, handed him a bottle which might contain about half-a-pint of spirits. "And is that all?" he said.

"There is a full bottle here," she answered, handing him another; "but if you drink it, you will be drunk, and they will catch you."

"By Heavens, yes; and you would be the first to help them; would you not?"

"Look here," she answered. "If you will go now, I will not say a word to any one of your coming, nor set them on your track to follow you. There, take the full bottle with you. If you will go, you shall be safe from me."

"What, and go without money!"

"I have none to give you. You may believe me when I say so. I have not a dollar in the house."

Before he spoke again he raised the half empty bottle to his mouth, and drank as long as there was a drop to drink. "There," said he, putting the bottle down, "I am better after that. As to the other, you are right, and I will take it with me. And now, young woman, about the money?"

"I tell you that I have not a dollar."

"Look here," said he, and he spoke now in a softer voice, as though he would be on friendly terms with her. "Give me ten sovereigns, and I will go. I know you have it, and with ten sovereigns it is possible that I may save my life. You are good, and would not wish that a man should die so horrid a death. I know you are good. Come, give me the money." And he put his hands up, beseeching her, and looked into her face with imploring eyes.

"On the word of a Christian woman I have not got money to give you," she replied.

"Nonsense?" And as he spoke he took her by the arm and shook her. He shook her violently so that he hurt her, and her breath for a moment was all but gone from her. "I tell you you must make dollars before I leave you, or I will so handle you that it would have been better for you to coin your very blood."

"May God help me at my need," she said, "as I have not above a few penny pieces in the house."

"And you expect me to believe that! Look here! I will shake the teeth out of your head, but I will have it from you." And he did shake her again, using both his hands and striking her against the wall.

"Would you—murder me?" she said, hardly able now to utter the words.

"Murder you, yes; why not? I cannot be worse than I am, were I to murder you ten times over. But with money I may possibly be better."

"I have it not."

"Then I will do worse than murder you. I will make you such an object that all the world shall loathe to look on you." And so saying he took her by the arm and dragged her forth from the wall against which she had stood.

Then there came from her a shriek that was heard far down the shore of that silent sea, and away across to the solitary houses of those living on the other side,—a shriek, very sad, sharp, and prolonged,—which told plainly to those who heard it of woman's woe when in her extremest peril. That sound was spoken of in Bermuda for many a day after that, as something which had been terrible to hear. But then, at that moment, as it came wailing through the dark, it sounded as though it were not human. Of those who heard it, not one guessed from whence it came, nor was the hand of any brother put forward to help that woman at her need.

"Did you hear that?" said the young wife to her husband, from the far side of the arm of the sea.

"Hear it! Oh Heaven, yes! Whence did it come?" The young wife could not say from whence it came, but clung close to her husband's breast, comforting herself with the knowledge that that terrible sorrow was not hers.

But aid did come at last, or rather that which seemed as aid. Long and terrible was the fight between that human beast of prey and the poor victim which had fallen into his talons. Anastasia Bergen was a strong, well-built woman, and now that the time had come to her when a struggle was necessary, a struggle for life, for honour, for the happiness of him who was more to her than herself, she fought like a tigress attacked in her own lair. At such a moment as this she also could become wild and savage as the beast of the forest. When he pinioned her arms with one of his, as he pressed her down upon the floor, she caught the first joint of the forefinger of his other hand between her teeth till he yelled in agony, and another sound was heard across the silent water. And then, when one hand was loosed in the struggle, she twisted it through his long hair, and dragged back his head till his eyes were nearly starting from their sockets. Anastasia Bergen had hitherto been a sheer woman, all feminine in her nature. But now the foam came to her mouth, and fire sprang from her eyes, and the muscles of her body worked as though she had been trained to deeds of violence. Of violence, Aaron Trow had known much in his rough life, but never had he combated with harder antagonist than her whom he now held beneath his breast.

"By—I will put an end to you," he exclaimed, in his wrath, as he struck her violently across the face with his elbow. His hand was occupied, and he could not use it for a blow, but, nevertheless, the violence was so great that the blood gushed from her nostrils, while the back of her head was driven with violence against the floor. But she did not lose her hold of him. Her hand was still twined closely through his thick hair, and in every move he made she clung to him with all her might. "Leave go my hair," he shouted at her, but she still kept her hold, though he again dashed her head against the floor.

There was still light in the room, for when he first grasped her with both his hands, he had put the lamp down on a small table. Now they were rolling on the floor together, and twice he had essayed to kneel on her that he might thus crush the breath from her body, and deprive her altogether of her strength; but she had been too active for him, moving herself along the ground, though in doing so she dragged him with her. But by degrees he got one hand at liberty, and with that he pulled a clasp knife out of his pocket and opened it. "I will cut your head off if you do not let go my hair," he said. But still she held fast by him. He then stabbed at her arm, using his left hand and making short, ineffectual blows. Her dress partly saved her, and partly also the continual movement of all her limbs; but, nevertheless, the knife wounded her. It wounded her in several places about the arm, covering them both with blood;— but still she hung on. So close was her grasp in her agony, that, as she afterwards found, she cut the skin of her own hands with her own nails. Had the man's hair been less thick or strong, or her own tenacity less steadfast, he would have murdered her before any interruption could have saved her.

And yet he had not purposed to murder her, or even, in the first instance, to inflict on her any bodily harm. But he had been determined to get money. With such a sum of money as he had named, it might, he thought, be possible for him to win his way across to America. He might bribe men to hide him in the hold of a ship, and thus there might be for him, at any rate, a possibility of escape. That there must be money in the house he had still thought when first he laid hands on the poor woman; and then, when the struggle had once begun, when he had felt her muscles contending with his, the passion of the beast was aroused within him, and he strove against her as he would have striven against a dog. But yet, when the knife was in his hand, he had not driven it against her heart.

Then suddenly, while they were yet rolling on the floor, there was a sound of footsteps in the passage. Aaron Trow instantly leaped to his feet, leaving his victim on the ground, with huge lumps of his thick clotted hair in her hand. Thus, and thus only, could he have liberated himself from her grasp. He rushed at the door, and there he came against the two negro servant-girls who had returned down to their kitchen from the road on which they had been straying. Trow, as he half saw them in the dark, not knowing how many there might be, or whether there was a man among them, rushed through them, upsetting one scared girl in his passage. With the instinct and with the timidity of a beast, his impulse now was to escape, and he hurried away back to the road and to his lair, leaving the three women together in the cottage. Poor wretch! As he crossed the road, not skulking in his impotent haste, but running at his best, another pair of eyes saw him, and when the search became hot after him, it was known that his hiding-place was not distant.

It was some time before any of the women were able to act, and when some step was taken, Anastasia was the first to take it. She had not absolutely swooned, but the reaction, after the violence of her efforts, was so great, that for some minutes she had been unable to speak. She had risen from the floor when Trow left her, and had even followed him to the door; but since that she had fallen back into her father's old arm-chair, and there sat gasping not only for words, but for breath also.

At last she bade one of the girls to run into St. George, and beg Mr. Morton to come to her aid. The girl would not stir without her companion; and even then, Anastasia, covered as she was with blood, with dishevelled hair, and her clothes half torn from her body, accompanied them as far as the road. There they found a negro lad still hanging about the place, and he told them that he had seen the man cross the road, and run down over the open ground towards the rocks of the sea-coast. "He must be there," said the lad, pointing in the direction of a corner of the rocks; "unless he swim across the mouth of the ferry." But the mouth of that ferry is an arm of the sea, and it was not probable that a man would do that when he might have taken the narrow water by keeping on the other side of the road.

At about one that night Caleb Morton reached the cottage breathless with running, and before a word was spoken between them, Anastasia had fallen on his shoulder and had fainted. As soon as she was in the arms of her lover, all her power had gone from her. The spirit and passion of the tiger had gone, and she was again a weak woman shuddering at the thought of what she had suffered. She remembered that she had had the man's hand between her teeth, and by degrees she found his hair still clinging to her fingers; but even then she could hardly call to mind the nature of the struggle she had undergone. His hot breath close to her own cheek she did remember, and his glaring eyes, and even the roughness of his beard as he pressed his face against her own; but she could not say whence had come the blood, nor till her arm became stiff and motionless did she know that she had been wounded.

It was all joy with her now, as she sat motionless without speaking, while he administered to her wants and spoke words of love into her ears. She remembered the man's horrid threat, and knew that by God's mercy she had been saved. And he was there caressing her, loving her, comforting her! As she thought of the fate that had threatened her, of the evil that had been so imminent, she fell forward on her knees, and with incoherent sobs uttered her thanksgivings, while her head was still supported on his arms.

It was almost morning before she could induce herself to leave him and lie down. With him she seemed to be so perfectly safe; but the moment he was away she could see Aaron Trow's eyes gleaming at her across the room. At last, however, she slept; and when he saw that she was at rest, he told himself that his work must then begin. Hitherto Caleb Morton had lived in all respects the life of a man of peace; but now, asking himself no questions as to the propriety of what he would do, using no inward arguments as to this or that line of conduct, he girded the sword on his loins, and prepared himself for war. The wretch who had thus treated the woman whom he loved should be hunted down like a wild beast, as long as he had arms and legs with which to carry on the hunt. He would pursue the miscreant with any weapons that might come to his hands; and might Heaven help him at his need as he dealt forth punishment to that man, if he caught him within his grasp. Those who had hitherto known Morton in the island, could not recognise the man as he came forth on that day, thirsty after blood, and desirous to thrust himself into personal conflict with the wild ruffian who had injured him. The meek Presbyterian minister had been a preacher, preaching ways of peace, and living in accordance with his own doctrines. The world had been very quiet for him, and he had walked quietly in his appointed path. But now the world was quiet no longer, nor was there any preaching of peace. His cry was for blood; for the blood of the untamed savage brute who had come upon his young doe in her solitude, and striven with such brutal violence to tear her heart from her bosom.

He got to his assistance early in the morning some of the constables from St. George, and before the day was over, he was joined by two or three of the warders from the convict establishment. There was with him also a friend or two, and thus a party was formed, numbering together ten or twelve persons. They were of course all armed, and therefore it might be thought that there would be but small chance for the wretched man if they should come upon his track. At first they all searched together, thinking from the tidings which had reached them that he must be near to them; but gradually they spread themselves along the rocks between St. George and the ferry, keeping watchman on the road, so that he should not escape unnoticed into the island.

Ten times during the day did Anastasia send from the cottage up to Morton, begging him to leave the search to others, and come down to her. But not for a moment would he lose the scent of his prey. What! should it be said that she had been so treated, and that others had avenged her? He sent back to say that her father was with her now, and that he would come when his work was over.

And in that job of work the life-blood of Aaron Trow was counted up.

Towards evening they were all congregated on the road near to the spot at which the path turns off towards the cottage, when a voice was heard hallooing to them from the summit of a little hill which lies between the road and the sea on the side towards the ferry, and presently a boy came running down to them full of news. "Danny Lund has seen him," said the boy, "he has seen him plainly in among the rocks." And then came Danny Lund himself, a small negro lad about fourteen years of age, who was known in those parts as the idlest, most dishonest, and most useless of his race. On this occasion, however, Danny Lund became important, and every one listened to him. He had seen, he said, a pair of eyes moving down in a cave of the rocks which he well knew. He had been in the cave often, he said, and could get there again. But not now; not while that pair of eyes was moving at the bottom of it. And so they all went up over the hill, Morton leading the way with hot haste. In his waist-band he held a pistol, and his hand grasped a short iron bar with which he had armed himself. They ascended the top of the hill, and when there, the open sea was before them on two sides, and on the third was the narrow creek over which the ferry passed. Immediately beneath their feet were the broken rocks; for on that side, towards the sea, the earth and grass of the hill descended but a little way towards the water. Down among the rocks they all went, silently, Caleb Morton leading the way, and Danny Lund directing him from behind.

"Mr. Morton," said an elderly man from St. George, "had you not better let the warders of the gaol go first; he is a desperate man, and they will best understand his ways?"

In answer to this Morton said nothing, but he would let no one put a foot before him. He still pressed forward among the rocks, and at last came to a spot from whence he might have sprung at one leap into the ocean. It was a broken cranny on the sea-shore into which the sea beat, and surrounded on every side but the one by huge broken fragments of stone, which at first sight seemed as though they would have admitted of a path down among them to the water's edge; but which, when scanned more closely, were seen to be so large in size, that no man could climb from one to another.

It was a singularly romantic spot, but now well known to them all there, for they had visited it over and over again that morning.

"In there," said Danny Lund, keeping well behind Morton's body, and pointing at the same time to a cavern high up among the rocks, but quite on the opposite side of the little inlet of the sea. The mouth of the cavern was not twenty yards from where they stood, but at the first sight it seemed as though it must be impossible to reach it. The precipice on the brink of which they all now stood, ran down sheer into the sea, and the fall from the mouth of the cavern on the other side was as steep. But Danny solved the mystery by pointing upwards, and showing them how he had been used to climb to a projecting rock over their heads, and from thence creep round by certain vantages of the stone till he was able to let himself down into the aperture. But now, at the present moment, he was unwilling to make essay of his prowess as a cragsman. He had, he said, been up on that projecting rock thrice, and there had seen the eyes moving in the cavern. He was quite sure of that fact of the pair of eyes, and declined to ascend the rock again.

Traces soon became visible to them by which they knew that some one had passed in and out of the cavern recently. The stone, when examined, bore those marks of friction which passage and repassage over it will always give. At the spot from whence the climber left the platform and commenced his ascent, the side of the stone had been rubbed by the close friction of a man's body. A light boy like Danny Lund might find his way in and out without leaving such marks behind him, but no heavy man could do so. Thus before long they all were satisfied that Aaron Trow was in the cavern before them.

Then there was a long consultation as to what they would do to carry on the hunt, and how they would drive the tiger from his lair. That he should not again come out, except to fall into their hands, was to all of them a matter of course. They would keep watch and ward there, though it might be for days and nights. But that was a process which did not satisfy Morton, and did not indeed well satisfy any of them. It was not only that they desired to inflict punishment on the miscreant in accordance with the law, but also that they did not desire that the miserable man should die in a hole like a starved dog, and that then they should go after him to take out his wretched skeleton. There was something in that idea so horrid in every way, that all agreed that active steps must be taken. The warders of the prison felt that they would all be disgraced if they could not take their prisoner alive. Yet who would get round that perilous ledge in the face of such an adversary? A touch to any man while climbing there would send him headlong down among the wave! And then his fancy told to each what might be the nature of an embrace with such an animal as that, driven to despair, hopeless of life, armed, as they knew, at any rate, with a knife! If the first adventurous spirit should succeed in crawling round that ledge, what would be the reception which he might expect in the terrible depth of that cavern?

They called to their prisoner, bidding him come out, and telling him that they would fire in upon him if he did not show himself; but not a sound was heard. It was indeed possible that they should send their bullets to, perhaps, every corner of the cavern; and if so, in that way they might slaughter him; but even of this they were not sure. Who could tell that there might not be some protected nook in which he could lay secure? And who could tell when the man was struck, or whether he were wounded?

"I will get to him," said Morton, speaking with a low dogged voice, and so saying he clambered up to the rock to which Danny Lund had pointed. Many voices at once attempted to restrain him, and one or two put their hands upon him to keep him back, but he was too quick for them, and now stood upon the ledge of rock. "Can you see him?" they asked below.

"I can see nothing within the cavern," said Morton.

"Look down very hard, Massa," said Danny, "very hard indeed, down in deep dark hole, and then see him big eyes moving!"

Morton now crept along the ledge, or rather he was beginning to do so, having put forward his shoulders and arms to make a first step in advance from the spot on which he was resting, when a hand was put forth from one corner of the cavern's mouth,—a hand armed with a pistol;—and a shot was fired. There could be no doubt now but that Danny Lund was right, and no doubt now as to the whereabouts of Aaron Trow.

A hand was put forth, a pistol was fired, and Caleb Morton still clinging to a corner of the rock with both his arms was seen to falter. "He is wounded," said one of the voices from below; and then they all expected to see him fall into the sea. But he did not fall, and after a moment or two, he proceeded carefully to pick his steps along the ledge. The ball had touched him, grazing his cheek, and cutting through the light whiskers that he wore; but he had not felt it, though the blow had nearly knocked him from his perch. And then four or five shots were fired from the rocks into the mouth of the cavern. The man's arm had been seen, and indeed one or two declared that they had traced the dim outline of his figure. But no sound was heard to come from the cavern, except the sharp crack of the bullets against the rock, and the echo of the gunpowder. There had been no groan as of a man wounded, no sound of a body falling, no voice wailing in despair. For a few seconds all was dark with the smoke of the gunpowder, and then the empty mouth of the cave was again yawning before their eyes. Morton was now near it, still cautiously creeping. The first danger to which he was exposed was this; that his enemy within the recess might push him down from the rocks with a touch. But on the other hand, there were three or four men ready to fire, the moment that a hand should be put forth; and then Morton could swim,—was known to be a strong swimmer;—whereas of Aaron Trow it was already declared by the prison gaolers that he could not swim. Two of the warders had now followed Morton on the rocks, so that in the event of his making good his entrance into the cavern, and holding his enemy at bay for a minute, he would be joined by aid.

It was strange to see how those different men conducted themselves as they stood on the opposite platform watching the attack. The officers from the prison had no other thought but of their prisoner, and were intent on taking him alive or dead. To them it was little or nothing what became of Morton. It was their business to encounter peril, and they were ready to do so;— feeling, however, by no means sorry to have such a man as Morton in advance of them. Very little was said by them. They had their wits about them, and remembered that every word spoken for the guidance of their ally would be heard also by the escaped convict. Their prey was sure, sooner or later, and had not Morton been so eager in his pursuit, they would have waited till some plan had been devised of trapping him without danger. But the townsmen from St. George, of whom some dozen were now standing there, were quick and eager and loud in their counsels. "Stay where you are,

Mr. Morton,—stay awhile for the love of God—or he'll have you down." "Now's your time, Caleb; in on him now, and you'll have him." "Close with him, Morton, close with him at once; it's your only chance." "There's four of us here; we'll fire on him if he as much as shows a limb." All of which words as they were heard by that poor wretch within, must have sounded to him as the barking of a pack of hounds thirsting for his blood. For him at any rate there was no longer any hope in this world.

My reader, when chance has taken you into the hunting-field, has it ever been your lot to sit by on horseback, and watch the digging out of a fox? The operation is not an uncommon one, and in some countries it is held to be in accordance with the rules of fair sport. For myself, I think that when the brute has so far saved himself, he should be entitled to the benefit of his cunning; but I will not now discuss the propriety or impropriety of that practice in venery. I can never, however, watch the doing of that work without thinking much of the agonising struggles of the poor beast whose last refuge is being torn from over his head. There he lies within a few yards of his arch enemy, the huntsman. The thick breath of the hounds make hot the air within his hole. The sound of their voices is close upon his ears. His breast is nearly bursting with the violence of that effort which at last has brought him to his retreat. And then pickaxe and mattock are plied above his head, and nearer and more near to him press his foes,—his double foes, human and canine,— till at last a huge hand grasps him, and he is dragged forth among his enemies. Almost as soon as his eyes have seen the light the eager noses of a dozen hounds have moistened themselves in his entrails. Ah me! I know that he is vermin, the vermin after whom I have been risking my neck, with a bold ambition that I might ultimately witness his death-struggles; but, nevertheless, I would fain have saved him that last half hour of gradually diminished hope.

And Aaron Trow was now like a hunted fox, doomed to be dug out from his last refuge, with this addition to his misery, that these hounds when they caught their prey, would not put him at once out of his misery. When first he saw that throng of men coming down from the hill top and resting on the platform; he knew that his fate was come. When they called to him to surrender himself he was silent, but he knew that his silence was of no avail. To them who were so eager to be his captors the matter seemed to be still one of considerable difficulty; but, to his thinking, there was no difficulty. There were there some score of men, fully armed, within twenty yards of him. If he but showed a trace of his limbs he would become a mark for their bullets. And then if he were wounded, and no one would come to him! If they allowed him to lie there without food till he perished! Would it not be well for him to yield himself? Then they called again and he was still silent. That idea of yielding is very terrible to the heart of a man. And when the worst had come to the worst, did not the ocean run deep beneath his cavern's month?

But as they yelled at him and hallooed, making their preparations for his death, his presence of mind deserted the poor wretch. He had stolen an old pistol on one of his marauding expeditions, of which one barrel had been loaded. That in his mad despair he had fired; and now, as he lay near the mouth of the cavern, under the cover of the projecting stone, he had no weapon with him but his hands. He had had a knife, but that had dropped from him during the struggle on the floor of the cottage. He had now nothing but his hands, and was considering how he might best use them in ridding himself of the first of his pursuers. The man was near him, armed, with all the power and majesty of right on his side; whereas on his side, Aaron Trow had nothing,—not a hope. He raised his head that he might look forth, and a dozen voices shouted as his face appeared above the aperture. A dozen weapons were levelled at him, and he could see the gleaming of the muzzles of the guns. And then the foot of his pursuer was already on the corner stone at the cavern's mouth. "Now, Caleb, on him at once!" shouted a voice. Ah me! it was a moment in which to pity even such a man as Aaron Trow.

"Now, Caleb, at him at once!" shouted the voice. No, by heavens; not so, even yet! The sound of triumph in those words raised the last burst of energy in the breast of that wretched man; and he sprang forth, head foremost, from his prison house. Forth he came, manifest enough before the eyes of them all, and with head well down, and hands outstretched, but with his wide glaring eyes still turned towards his pursuers as he fell, he plunged down into the waves beneath him. Two of those who stood by, almost unconscious of what they did, fired at his body as it made its rapid way to the water; but, as they afterwards found, neither of the bullets struck him. Morton, when his prey thus leaped forth, escaping him for awhile, was already on the verge of the cavern,—had even then prepared his foot for that onward spring which should bring him to the throat of his foe. But he arrested himself, and for a moment stood there watching the body as it struck the water, and hid itself at once beneath the ripple. He stood there for a moment watching the deed and its effect, and then leaving his hold upon the rock, he once again followed his quarry. Down he went, head foremost, right on to the track in the waves which the other had made; and when the two rose to the surface together, each was struggling in the grasp of the other.

It was a foolish, nay, a mad deed to do. The poor wretch who had first fallen could not have escaped. He could not even swim, and had therefore flung himself to certain destruction when he took that leap from out of the cavern's mouth. It would have been sad to see him perish beneath the waves,—to watch him as he rose, gasping for breath, and then to see to him sinking again, to rise again, and then to go for ever. But his life had been fairly forfeit,— and why should one so much more precious have been flung after it? It was surely with no view of saving that pitiful life that Caleb Morton had leaped after his enemy. But the hound, hot with the chase, will follow the stag over the precipice and dash himself to pieces against the rocks. The beast thirsting for blood will rush in even among the weapons of men. Morton in his fury had felt but one desire, burned with but one passion. If the Fates would but grant him to fix his clutches in the throat of the man who had ill-used his love; for the rest it might all go as it would.

In the earlier part of the morning, while they were all searching for their victim, they had brought a boat up into this very inlet among the rocks; and the same boat had been at hand during the whole day. Unluckily, before they had come hither, it had been taken round the headland to a place among the rocks at which a government skiff is always moored. The sea was still so quiet that there was hardly a ripple on it, and the boat had been again sent for when first it was supposed that they had at last traced Aaron Trow to his hiding-place. Anxiously now were all eyes turned to the headland, but as yet no boat was there.

The two men rose to the surface, each struggling in the arms of the other. Trow, though he was in an element to which he was not used, though he had sprung thither as another suicide might spring to certain death beneath a railway engine, did not altogether lose his presence of mind. Prompted by a double instinct, he had clutched hold of Morton's body when he encountered it beneath the waters. He held on to it, as to his only protection, and he held on to him also as to his only enemy. If there was a chance for a life struggle, they would share that chance together; and if not, then together would they meet that other fate.

Caleb Morton was a very strong man, and though one of his arms was altogether encumbered by his antagonist, his other arm and his legs were free. With these he seemed to succeed in keeping his head above the water, weighted as he was with the body of his foe. But Trow's efforts were also used with the view of keeping himself above the water. Though he had purposed to destroy himself in taking that leap, and now hoped for nothing better than that they might both perish together, he yet struggled to keep his head above the waves. Bodily power he had none left to him, except that of holding on to Morton's arm and plunging with his legs; but he did hold on, and thus both their heads remained above the surface.

But this could not last long. It was easy to see that Trow's strength was nearly spent, and that when he went down Morton must go with him. If indeed they could be separated,—if Morton could once make himself free from that embrace into which he had been so anxious to leap,—then indeed there might be a hope. All round that little inlet the rock fell sheer down into the deep sea, so that there was no resting-place for a foot; it but round the headlands on either side, even within forty or fifty yards of that spot, Morton might rest on the rocks, till a boat should come to his assistance. To him that distance would have been nothing, if only his limbs had been at liberty.

Upon the platform of rocks they were all at their wits' ends. Many were anxious to fire at Trow; but even if they hit him, would Morton's position have been better? Would not the wounded man have still clung to him who was not wounded? And then there could be no certainty that any one of them would hit the right man. The ripple of the waves, though it was very slight, nevertheless sufficed to keep the bodies in motion; and then, too, there was not among them any marksman peculiar for his skill.

Morton's efforts in the water were too severe to admit of his speaking, but he could hear and understand the words which were addressed to him. "Shake him off, Caleb." "Strike him from you with your foot." "Swim to the right shore; swim for it, even if you take him with you." Yes; he could hear them all; but hearing and obeying were very different. It was not easy to shake off that dying man; and as for swimming with him, that was clearly impossible. It was as much as he could do to keep his head above water, let alone any attempt to move in one settled direction.

For some four or five minutes they lay thus battling on the waves before the head of either of them went down. Trow had been twice below the surface, but it was before he had succeeded in supporting himself by Morton's arm. Now it seemed as though he must sink again,—as though both must sink. His mouth was barely kept above the water, and as Morton shook him with his arm, the tide would pass over him. It was horrid to watch from the shore the glaring upturned eyes of the dying wretch, as his long streaming hair lay back upon the wave. "Now, Caleb, hold him down. Hold him under," was shouted in the voice of some eager friend. Rising up on the water, Morton made a last effort to do as he was bid. He did press the man's head down,—well down below the surface,—but still the hand clung to him, and as he struck out against the water, he was powerless against that grasp.

Then there came a loud shout along the shore, and all those on the platform, whose eyes had been fixed so closely on that terrible struggle beneath them, rushed towards the rocks on the other coast. The sound of oars was heard close to them,—an eager pressing stroke, as of men who knew well that they were rowing for the salvation of a life. On they came, close under the rocks, obeying with every muscle of their bodies the behests of those who called to them from the shore. The boat came with such rapidity,—was so recklessly urged, that it was driven somewhat beyond the inlet; but in passing, a blow was struck which made Caleb Morton once more the master of his own life. The two men had been carried out in their struggle towards the open sea; and as the boat curved in, so as to be as close as the rocks would allow, the bodies of the men were brought within the sweep of the oars. He in the bow—for there were four pulling in the boat—had raised his oar as he neared the rocks,—had raised it high above the water; and now, as they passed close by the struggling men, he let it fall with all its force on the upturned face of the wretched convict. It was a terrible, frightful thing to do,—thus striking one who was so stricken; but who shall say that the blow was not good and just? Methinks, however, that the eyes and face of that dying man will haunt for ever the dreams of him who carried that oar!

Trow never rose again to the surface. Three days afterwards his body was found at the ferry, and then they carried him to the convict island and buried him. Morton was picked up and taken into the boat. His life was saved; but it may be a question how the battle might have gone had not that friendly oar been raised in his behalf. As it was, he lay at the cottage for days before he was able to be moved, so as to receive the congratulations of those who had watched that terrible conflict from the shore. Nor did he feel that there had been anything in that day's work of which he could be proud;—much rather of which it behoved him to be thoroughly ashamed. Some six months after that he obtained the hand of Anastasia Bergen, but they did not remain long in Bermuda. "He went away, back to his own country," my informant told me; "because he could not endure to meet the ghost of Aaron Trow, at that point of the road which passes near the cottage." That the ghost of Aaron Trow may be seen there and round the little rocky inlet of the sea, is part of the creed of every young woman in Bermuda.

THE CHATEAU OF PRINCE POLIGNAC

Few Englishmen or Englishwomen are intimately acquainted with the little town of Le Puy. It is the capital of the old province of Le Velay, which also is now but little known, even to French ears, for it is in these days called by the imperial name of the Department of the Haute Loire. It is to the south-east of Auvergne, and is nearly in the centre of the southern half of France.

But few towns, merely as towns, can be better worth visiting. In the first place, the volcanic formation of the ground on which it stands is not only singular in the extreme, so as to be interesting to the geologist, but it is so picturesque as to be equally gratifying to the general tourist. Within a narrow valley there stand several rocks, rising up from the ground with absolute abruptness. Round two of these the town clusters, and a third stands but a mile distant, forming the centre of a faubourg, or suburb. These rocks appear to be, and I believe are, the harder particles of volcanic matter, which have not been carried away through successive ages by the joint agency of water and air.

When the tide of lava ran down between the hills the surface left was no doubt on a level with the heads of these rocks; but here and there the deposit became harder than elsewhere, and these harder points have remained, lifting up their steep heads in a line through the valley.

The highest of these is called the Rocher de Corneille. Round this and up its steep sides the town stands. On its highest summit there was an old castle; and there now is, or will be before these pages are printed, a colossal figure in bronze of the Virgin Mary, made from the cannon taken at Sebastopol. Half-way down the hill the cathedral is built, a singularly gloomy edifice,—Romanesque, as it is called, in its style, but extremely similar in its mode of architecture to what we know of Byzantine structures. But there has been no surface on the rock side large enough to form a resting-place for the church, which has therefore been built out on huge supporting piles, which form a porch below the west front; so that the approach is by numerous steps laid along the side of the wall below the church, forming a wondrous flight of stairs. Let all men who may find themselves stopping at Le Puy visit the top of these stairs at the time of the setting sun, and look down from thence through the framework of the porch on the town beneath, and at the hill-side beyond.

Behind the church is the seminary of the priests, with its beautiful walks stretching round the Rocher de Corneille, and overlooking the town and valley below.

Next to this rock, and within a quarter of a mile of it, is the second peak, called the Rock of the Needle. It rises narrow, sharp, and abrupt from the valley, allowing of no buildings on its sides. But on its very point has been erected a church sacred to St. Michael, that lover of rock summits, accessible by stairs cut from the stone. This, perhaps—this rock, I mean—is the most wonderful of the wonders which Nature has formed at La Puy.

Above this, at a mile's distance, is the rock of Espailly, formed in the same way, and almost equally precipitous. On its summit is a castle, having its own legend, and professing to have been the residence of Charles VII., when little of France belonged to its kings but the provinces of Berry, Auvergne, and Le Velay. Some three miles farther up there is another volcanic rock, larger, indeed, but equally sudden in its spring,—equally remarkable as rising abruptly from the valley,—on which stands the castle and old family residence of the house of Polignac. It was lost by them at the Revolution, but was repurchased by the minister of Charles X., and is still the property of the head of the race.

Le Puy itself is a small, moderate, pleasant French town, in which the language of the people has not the pure Parisian aroma, nor is the glory of the boulevards of the capital emulated in its streets. These are crooked, narrow, steep, and intricate, forming here and there excellent sketches for a lover of street picturesque beauty; but hurtful to the feet with their small, round-topped paving stones, and not always as clean as pedestrian ladies might desire.

And now I would ask my readers to join me at the morning table d'hote at the Hotel des Ambassadeurs. It will of course be understood that this does not mean a breakfast in the ordinary fashion of England, consisting of tea or coffee, bread and butter, and perhaps a boiled egg. It comprises all the requisites for a composite dinner, excepting soup; and as one gets farther south in France, this meal is called dinner. It is, however, eaten without any prejudice to another similar and somewhat longer meal at six or seven o'clock, which, when the above name is taken up by the earlier enterprise, is styled supper.

The dejeuner, or dinner, at the Hotel des Ambassadeurs, on the morning in question, though very elaborate, was not a very gay affair. There were some fourteen persons present, of whom half were residents in the town, men employed in some official capacity, who found this to be the cheapest, the most luxurious, and to them the most comfortable mode of living. They clustered together at the head of the table, and as they were customary guests at the house, they talked their little talk together—it was very little—and made the most of the good things before them. Then there were two or three commis-voyageurs, a chance traveller or two, and an English lady with a young daughter. The English lady sat next to one of the accustomed guests; but he, unlike the others, held converse with her rather than with them. Our story at present has reference only to that lady and to that gentleman.

Place aux dames. We will speak first of the lady, whose name was Mrs. Thompson. She was, shall I say, a young woman of about thirty-six. In so saying, I am perhaps creating a prejudice against her in the minds of some readers, as they will, not unnaturally, suppose her, after such an announcement, to be in truth over forty. Any such prejudice will be unjust. I would have it believed that thirty-six was the outside, not the inside of her age. She was good-looking, lady-like, and considering that she was an Englishwoman, fairly well dressed. She was inclined to be rather full in her person, but perhaps not more so than is becoming to ladies at her time of life. She had rings on her fingers and a brooch on her bosom which were of some value, and on the back of her head she wore a jaunty small lace cap, which seemed to tell, in conjunction with her other appointments, that her circumstances were comfortable.

The little girl who sat next to her was the youngest of her two daughters, and might be about thirteen years of age. Her name was Matilda, but infantine circumstances had invested her with the nickname of Mimmy, by which her mother always called her. A nice, pretty, playful little girl was Mimmy Thompson, wearing two long tails of plaited hair hanging, behind her head, and inclined occasionally to be rather loud in her sport.

Mrs. Thompson had another and an elder daughter, now some fifteen years old, who was at school in Le Puy; and it was with reference to her tuition that Mrs. Thompson had taken up a temporary residence at the Hotel des Ambassadeurs in that town. Lilian Thompson was occasionally invited down to dine or breakfast at the inn, and was visited daily at her school by her mother.

"When I'm sure that she'll do, I shall leave her there, and go back to England," Mrs. Thompson had said, not in the purest French, to the neighbour who always sat next to her at the table d'hote, the gentleman, namely, to whom we have above alluded. But still she had remained at Le Puy a month, and did not go; a circumstance which was considered singular, but by no means unpleasant, both by the innkeeper and by the gentleman in question.

The facts, as regarded Mrs. Thompson, were as follows:-She was the widow of a gentleman who had served for many years in the civil service of the East Indies, and who, on dying, had left her a comfortable income of—it matters not how many pounds, but constituting quite a sufficiency to enable her to live at her ease and educate her daughters.

Her children had been sent home to England before her husband's death, and after that event she had followed them; but there, though she was possessed of moderate wealth, she had no friends and few acquaintances, and after a little while she had found life to be rather dull. Her customs were not those of England, nor were her propensities English; therefore she had gone abroad, and having received some recommendation of this school at Le Puy, had made her way thither. As it appeared to her that she really enjoyed more consideration at Le Puy than had been accorded to her either at Torquay or Leamington, there she remained from day to day. The total payment required at the Hotel des Ambassadeurs was but six francs daily for herself and three and a half for her little girl; and where else could she live with a better junction of economy and comfort? And then the gentleman who always sat next to her was so exceedingly civil!

The gentleman's name was M. Lacordaire. So much she knew, and had learned to call him by his name very frequently. Mimmy, too, was quite intimate with M. Lacordaire; but nothing more than his name was known of him. But M. Lacordaire carried a general letter of recommendation in his face, manner, gait, dress, and tone of voice. In all these respects there was nothing left to be desired; and, in addition to this, he was decorated, and wore the little red ribbon of the Legion of Honour, ingeniously twisted into the shape of a small flower.

M. Lacordaire might be senior in age to Mrs. Thompson by about ten years, nor had he about him any of the airs or graces of a would-be young man. His hair, which he wore very short, was grizzled, as was also the small pretence of a whisker which came down about as far as the middle of his ear; but the tuft on his chin was still brown, without a gray hair. His eyes were bright and tender, his voice was low and soft, his hands were very white, his clothes were always new and well fitting, and a better-brushed hat could not be seen out of Paris, nor perhaps in it.

Now, during the weeks which Mrs. Thompson had passed at La Puy, the acquaintance which she had formed with M. Lacordaire had progressed beyond the prolonged meals in the salle a manger. He had occasionally sat beside her evening table as she took her English cup of tea in her own room, her bed being duly screened off in its distant niche by becoming curtains; and then he had occasionally walked beside her, as he civilly escorted her to the lions of the place; and he had once accompanied her, sitting on the back seat of a French voiture, when she had gone forth to see something of the surrounding country.

On all such occasions she had been accompanied by one of her daughters, and the world of Le Puy had had nothing material to say against her. But still the world of Le Puy had whispered a little, suggesting that M. Lacordaire knew very well what he was about. But might not Mrs. Thompson also know as well what she was about? At any rate, everything had gone on very pleasantly since the acquaintance had been made. And now, so much having been explained, we will go back to the elaborate breakfast at the Hotel des Ambassadeurs.

Mrs. Thompson, holding Mimmy by the hand, walked into the room some few minutes after the last bell had been rung, and took the place which was now hers by custom. The gentlemen who constantly frequented the house all bowed to her, but M. Lacordaire rose from his seat and offered her his hand.

"And how is Mees Meemy this morning?" said he; for 'twas thus he always pronounced her name.

Miss Mimmy, answering for herself, declared that she was very well, and suggested that M. Lacordaire should give her a fig from off a dish that was placed immediately before him on the table. This M. Lacordaire did, presenting it very elegantly between his two fingers, and making a little bow to the little lady as he did so.

"Fie, Mimmy!" said her mother; "why do you ask for the things before the waiter brings them round?"

"But, mamma," said Mimmy, speaking English, "M. Lacordaire always gives me a fig every morning."

"M. Lacordaire always spoils you, I think," answered Mrs. Thompson, in French. And then they went thoroughly to work at their breakfast. During the whole meal M. Lacordaire attended assiduously to his neighbour; and did so without any evil result, except that one Frenchman with a black moustache, at the head of the table, trod on the toe of another Frenchman with another black moustache—winking as he made the sign—just as M. Lacordaire, having selected a bunch of grapes, put it on Mrs. Thompson's plate with infinite grace. But who among us all is free from such impertinences as these?

"But madame really must see the chateau of Prince Polignac before she leaves Le Puy," said M. Lacordaire.

"The chateau of who?" asked Mimmy, to whose young ears the French words were already becoming familiar.

"Prince Polignac, my dear. Well, I really don't know, M. Lacordaire;—I have seen a great deal of the place already, and I shall be going now very soon; probably in a day or two," said Mrs. Thompson.

"But madame must positively see the chateau," said M. Lacordaire, very impressively; and then after a pause he added, "If madame will have the complaisance to commission me to procure a carriage for this afternoon, and will allow me the honour to be her guide, I shall consider myself one of the most fortunate of men."

"Oh, yes, mamma, do go," said Mimmy, clapping her hands. "And it is Thursday, and Lilian can go with us."

41

"Be quiet, Mimmy, do. Thank you, no, M. Lacordaire. I could not go today; but I am extremely obliged by your politeness."

M. Lacordaire still pressed the matter, and Mrs. Thompson still declined till it was time to rise from the table. She then declared that she did not think it possible that she should visit the chateau before she left Le Puy; but that she would give him an answer at dinner.

The most tedious time in the day to Mrs. Thompson were the two hours after breakfast. At one o'clock she daily went to the school, taking Mimmy, who for an hour or two shared her sister's lessons. This and her little excursions about the place, and her shopping, managed to make away with her afternoon. Then in the evening, she generally saw something of M. Lacordaire. But those two hours after breakfast were hard of killing.

On this occasion, when she gained her own room, she as usual placed Mimmy on the sofa with a needle. Her custom then was to take up a novel; but on this morning she sat herself down in her arm-chair, and resting her head upon her hand and elbow, began to turn over certain circumstances in her mind.

"Mamma," said Mimmy, "why won't you go with M. Lacordaire to that place belonging to the prince? Prince—Polly something, wasn't it?"

"Mind your work, my dear," said Mrs. Thompson.

"But I do so wish you'd go, mamma. What was the prince's name?"

"Polignac."

"Mamma, ain't princes very great people?"

"Yes, my dear; sometimes."

"Is Prince Polly-nac like our Prince Alfred?"

"No, my dear; not at all. At least, I suppose not."

"Is his mother a queen?"

"No, my dear."

"Then his father must be a king?"

"No, my dear. It is quite a different thing here. Here in France they have a great many princes."

"Well, at any rate I should like to see a prince's chateau; so I do hope you'll go." And then there was a pause. "Mamma, could it come to pass, here in France, that M. Lacordaire should ever be a prince?"

"M. Lacordaire a prince! No; don't talk such nonsense, but mind your work."

"Isn't M. Lacordaire a very nice man? Ain't you very fond of him?"

To this question Mrs. Thompson made no answer.

"Mamma," continued Mimmy, after a moment's pause, "won't you tell me whether you are fond of M. Lacordaire? I'm quite sure of this,—that he's very fond of you."

"What makes you think that?" asked Mrs. Thompson, who could not bring herself to refrain from the question.

"Because he looks at you in that way, mamma, and squeezes your hand."

"Nonsense, child," said Mrs. Thompson; "hold your tongue. I don't know what can have put such stuff into your head."

"But he does, mamma," said Mimmy, who rarely allowed her mother to put her down.

Mrs. Thompson made no further answer, but again sat with her head resting on her hand. She also, if the truth must be told, was thinking of M. Lacordaire and his fondness for herself. He had squeezed her hand and he had looked into her face. However much it may have been nonsense on Mimmy's part to talk of such things, they had not the less absolutely occurred. Was it really the fact that M. Lacordaire was in love with her?

And if so, what return should she, or could she make to such a passion? He had looked at her yesterday, and squeezed her hand today. Might it not be probable that he would advance a step further tomorrow? If so, what answer would she be prepared to make to him?

She did not think—so she said to herself—that she had any particular objection to marrying again. Thompson had been dead now for four years, and neither his friends, nor her friends, nor the world could say she was wrong on that score. And as to marrying a Frenchman, she could not say she felt within herself any absolute repugnance to doing that. Of her own country, speaking of England as such, she, in truth, knew but little—and perhaps cared less. She had gone to India almost as a child, and England had not been specially kind to her on her return. She had found it dull and cold, stiff, and almost ill-natured. People there had not smiled on her and been civil as M. Lacordaire had done. As far as

England and Englishmen were considered she saw no reason why she should not marry M. Lacordaire.

And then, as regarded the man; could she in her heart say that she was prepared to love, honour, and obey M. Lacordaire? She certainly knew no reason why she should not do so. She did not know much of him, she said to herself at first; but she knew as much, she said afterwards, as she had known personally of Mr. Thompson before their marriage. She had known, to be sure, what was Mr. Thompson's profession and what his income; or, if not, some one else had known for her. As to both these points she was quite in the dark as regarded M. Lacordaire.

Personally, she certainly did like him, as she said to herself more than once. There was a courtesy and softness about him which were very gratifying to her; and then, his appearance was so much in his favour. He was not very young, she acknowledged; but neither was she young herself. It was quite evident that he was fond of her children, and that he would be a kind and affectionate father to them. Indeed, there was kindness in all that he did.

Should she marry again,—and she put it to herself quite hypothetically,—she would look for no romance in such a second marriage. She would be content to sit down in a quiet home, to the tame dull realities of life, satisfied with the companionship of a man who would be kind and gentle to her, and whom she could respect and esteem. Where could she find a companion with whom this could be more safely anticipated than with M. Lacordaire?

And so she argued the question within her own breast in a manner not unfriendly to that gentleman. That there was as yet one great hindrance she at once saw; but then that might be remedied by a word. She did not know what was his income or his profession. The chambermaid, whom she had interrogated, had told her that he was a "marchand." To merchants, generally, she felt that she had no objection. The Barings and the Rothschilds were merchants, as was also that wonderful man at Bombay, Sir Hommajee Bommajee, who was worth she did no know how many thousand lacs of rupees.

That it would behove her, on her own account and that of her daughters, to take care of her own little fortune in contracting any such connection, that she felt strongly. She would never so commit herself as to put security in that respect out of her power. But then she did not think that M. Lacordaire would ever ask her to do so; at any rate, she was determined on this, that there should never be any doubt on that matter; and as she firmly resolved on this, she again took up her book, and for a minute or two made an attempt to read.

"Mamma," said Mummy, "will M. Lacordaire go up to the school to see Lilian when you go away from this?"

"Indeed, I cannot say, my dear. If Lilian is a good girl, perhaps he may do so now and then."

"And will he write to you and tell you how she is?"

"Lilian can write for herself; can she not?"

"Oh yes; I suppose she can; but I hope M. Lacordaire will write too. We shall come back here some day; shan't we, mamma?"

"I cannot say, my dear."

"I do so hope we shall see M. Lacordaire again. Do you know what I was thinking, mamma?"

"Little girls like you ought not to think," said Mrs. Thompson, walking slowly out of the room to the top of the stairs and back again; for she had felt the necessity of preventing Mimmy from disclosing any more of her thoughts. "And now, my dear, get yourself ready, and we will go up to the school."

Mrs. Thompson always dressed herself with care, though not in especially fine clothes, before she went down to dinner at the table d'hote; but on this occasion she was more than usually particular. She hardly explained to herself why she did this; but, nevertheless, as she stood before the glass, she did in a certain manner feel that the circumstances of her future life might perhaps depend on what might be said and done that evening. She had not absolutely decided whether or no she would go to the Prince's chateau; but if she did go——. Well, if she did; what then? She had sense enough, as she assured herself more than once, to regulate her own conduct with propriety in any such emergency.

During the dinner, M. Lacordaire conversed in his usual manner, but said nothing whatever about the visit to Polignac. He was very kind to Mimmy, and very courteous to her mother, but did not appear to be at all more particular than usual. Indeed, it might be a question whether he was not less so. As she had entered the room Mrs. Thompson had said to herself that, perhaps, after all, it would be better that there should be nothing more thought about it; but before the four of five courses were over, she was beginning to feel a little disappointed.

And now the fruit was on the table, after the consumption of which it was her practice to retire. It was certainly open to her to ask M. Lacordaire to take tea with her that evening, as she had done on former occasions; but she felt that she must not do this now, considering the immediate circumstances of the case. If any further steps were to be taken, they must be taken by him, and not by her;— or else by Mimmy, who, just as her mother was slowly consuming her last grapes, ran round to the back of M. Lacordaire's chair, and whispered something into his ear. It may be presumed that Mrs. Thompson did not see the intention of the movement in time to arrest it, for she did nothing till the whispering had been whispered; and then she rebuked the child, bade her not to be troublesome, and with more than usual austerity in her voice, desired her to get herself ready to go up stairs to their chamber.

As she spoke she herself rose from her chair, and made her final little bow to the table, and her other final little bow and smile to M. Lacordaire; but this was certain to all who saw it, that the smile was not as gracious as usual.

As she walked forth, M. Lacordaire rose from his chair—such being his constant practice when she left the table; but on this occasion he accompanied her to the door.

"And has madame decided," he asked, "whether she will permit me to accompany her to the chateau?"

"Well, I really don't know," said Mrs. Thompson.

"Mees Meemy," continued M. Lacordaire, "is very anxious to see the rock, and I may perhaps hope that Mees Lilian would be pleased with such a little excursion. As for myself—" and then M. Lacordaire put his hand upon his heart in a manner that seemed to speak more plainly than he had ever spoken.

"Well, if the children would really like it, and—as you are so very kind," said Mrs. Thompson; and so the matter was conceded.

"Tomorrow afternoon?" suggested M. Lacordaire. But Mrs. Thompson fixed on Saturday, thereby showing that she herself was in no hurry for the expedition.

"Oh, I am so glad!" said Mimmy, when they had re-entered their own room. "Mamma, do let me tell Lilian myself when I go up to the school tomorrow!"

But mamma was in no humour to say much to her child on this subject at the present moment. She threw herself back on her sofa in perfect silence, and began to reflect whether she would like to sign her name in future as Fanny Lacordaire, instead of Fanny Thompson. It certainly seemed as though things were verging towards such a necessity. A marchand! But a marchand of what? She had an instinctive feeling that the people in the hotel were talking about her and M. Lacordaire, and was therefore more than ever averse to asking any one a question.

As she went up to the school the next afternoon, she walked through more of the streets of Le Puy than was necessary, and in every street she looked at the names which she saw over the doors of the more respectable houses of business. But she looked in vain. It might be that M. Lacordaire was a marchand of so specially high a quality as to be under no necessity to put up his name at all. Sir Hommajee Bommajee's name did not appear over any door in Bombay;—at least, she thought not.

And then came the Saturday morning. "We shall be ready at two," she said, as she left the breakfast-table; "and perhaps you would not mind calling for Lilian on the way."

M. Lacordaire would be delighted to call anywhere for anybody on behalf of Mrs. Thompson; and then, as he got to the door of the salon, he offered her his hand. He did so with so much French courtesy that she could not refuse it, and then she felt that his purpose was more tender than ever it had been. And why not, if this was the destiny which Fate had prepared for her?

Mrs. Thompson would rather have got into the carriage at any other spot in Le Puy than at that at which she was forced to do so—the chief entrance, namely, of the Hotel des Ambassadeurs. And what made it worse was this, that an appearance of a special fate was given to the occasion. M. Lacordaire was dressed in more than his Sunday best. He had on new yellow kid gloves. His coat, if not new, was newer than any Mrs. Thompson had yet observed, and was lined with silk up to the very collar. He had on patent leather boots, which glittered, as Mrs. Thompson thought, much too conspicuously. And as for his hat, it was quite evident that it was fresh that morning from the maker's block.

In this costume, with his hat in his hand, he stood under the great gateway of the hotel, ready to hand Mrs. Thompson into the carriage. This would have been nothing if the landlord and landlady had not been there also, as well as the man-cook, and the four waiters, and the fille de chambre. Two or three other pair of eyes Mrs. Thompson also saw, as she glanced round, and then Mimmy walked across the yard in her best clothes with a fete-day air about her for which her mother would have liked to have whipped her.

But what did it matter? If it was written in the book that she should become Madame Lacordaire, of course the world would know that there must have been some preparatory love-making. Let them have their laugh; a good husband would not be dearly purchased at so trifling an expense. And so they sallied forth with already half the ceremony of a wedding.

Mimmy seated herself opposite to her mother, and M. Lacordaire also sat with his back to the horses, leaving the second place of honour for Lilian. "Pray make yourself comfortable, M. Lacordaire, and don't mind her," said Mrs. Thompson. But he was firm in his purpose of civility, perhaps making up his mind that when he should in truth stand in the place of papa to the young lady, then would be his time for having the back seat in the carnage.

Lilian, also in her best frock, came down the school-steps, and three of the school teachers came with her. It would have added to Mrs. Thompson's happiness at that moment if M. Lacordaire would have kept his polished boots out of sight, and put his yellow gloves into his pocket.

And then they started. The road from Le Puy to Polignac is nearly all up hill; and a very steep hill it is, so that there was plenty of time for conversation. But the girls had it nearly all to themselves. Mimmy thought that she had never found M. Lacordaire so stupid; and Lilian told her sister on the first safe opportunity that occurred, that it seemed very much as though they were all going to church.

"And do any of the Polignac people ever live at this place?" asked Mrs. Thompson, by way of making conversation; in answer to which M. Lacordaire informed madame that the place was at present only a ruin; and then there was again silence till they found themselves under the rock, and were informed by the driver that the rest of the ascent must be made on foot.

The rock now stood abrupt and precipitous above their heads. It was larger in its circumference and with much larger space on its summit than those other volcanic rocks in and close to the town; but then at the same time it was higher from the ground, and quite as inaccessible, except by the single path which led up to the chateau.

M. Lacordaire, with conspicuous gallantry, first assisted Mrs. Thompson from the carriage, and then handed down the two young ladies. No lady could have been so difficult to please as to complain of him, and yet Mrs. Thompson thought that he was not as agreeable as usual. Those horrid boots and those horrid gloves gave him such an air of holiday finery that neither could he be at his ease wearing them, nor could she, in seeing them worn.

They were soon taken in hand by the poor woman whose privilege it was to show the ruins. For a little distance they walked up the path in single file; not that it was too narrow to accommodate two, but M. Lacordaire's courage had not yet been screwed to a point which admitted of his offering his arm to the widow. For in France, it must be remembered, that this means more than it does in some other countries.

Mrs. Thompson felt that all this was silly and useless. If they were not to be dear friends this coming out feting together, those boots and gloves and new hat were all very foolish; and if they were, the sooner they understood each other the better. So Mrs. Thompson, finding that the path was steep and the weather warm, stood still for a while leaning against the wall, with a look of considerable fatigue in her face.

"Will madame permit me the honour of offering her my arm?" said M. Lacordaire. "The road is so extraordinarily steep for madame to climb."

Mrs. Thompson did permit him the honour, and so they went on till they reached the top.

The view from the summit was both extensive and grand, but neither Lilian nor Mimmy were much pleased with the place. The elder sister, who had talked over the matter with her school companions, expected a fine castle with turrets, battlements, and romance; and the other expected a pretty smiling house, such as princes, in her mind, ought to inhabit.

Instead of this they found an old turret, with steps so broken that M. Lacordaire did not care to ascend them, and the ruined walls of a mansion, in which nothing was to be seen but the remains of an enormous kitchen chimney.

"It was the kitchen of the family," said the guide.

"Oh," said Mrs. Thompson.

"And this," said the woman, taking them into the next ruined compartment, "was the kitchen of monsieur et madame."

"What! two kitchens?" exclaimed Lilian, upon which M. Lacordaire explained that the ancestors of the Prince de Polignac had been very great people, and had therefore required culinary performances on a great scale.

And then the woman began to chatter something about an oracle of Apollo. There was, she said, a hole in the rock, from which in past times, perhaps more than a hundred years ago, the oracle used to speak forth mysterious words.

"There," she said, pointing to a part of the rock at some distance, "was the hole. And if the ladies would follow her to a little outhouse which was just beyond, she would show them the huge stone mouth out of which the oracle used to speak."

Lilian and Mimmy both declared at once for seeing the oracle, but Mrs. Thompson expressed her determination to remain sitting where she was upon the turf. So the guide started off with the young ladies; and will it be thought surprising that M. Lacordaire should have remained alone by the side of Mrs. Thompson?

It must be now or never, Mrs. Thompson felt; and as regarded M. Lacordaire, he probably entertained some idea of the same kind. Mrs. Thompson's inclinations, though they had never been very strong in the matter, were certainly in favour of the "now." M. Lacordaire's inclinations were stronger. He had fully and firmly made up his mind in favour of matrimony; but then he was not so absolutely in favour of the "now." Mrs. Thompson's mind, if one could have read it, would have shown a great objection to shilly-shallying, as she was accustomed to call it. But M. Lacordaire, were it not for the danger which might thence arise, would have seen no objection to some slight further procrastination. His courage was beginning, perhaps, to ooze out from his fingers' ends.

"I declare that those girls have scampered away ever so far," said Mrs. Thompson.

"Would madame wish that I should call them back?" said M. Lacordaire, innocently.

"Oh, no, dear children! let them enjoy themselves; it will be a pleasure to them to run about the rock, and I suppose they will be safe with that woman?"

"Oh, yes, quite safe," said M. Lacordaire; and then there was another little pause.

Mrs. Thompson was sitting on a broken fragment of a stone just outside the entrance to the old family kitchen, and M. Lacordaire was standing immediately before her. He had in his hand a little cane with which he sometimes slapped his boots and sometimes poked about among the rubbish. His hat was not quite straight on his head, having a little jaunty twist to one side, with reference to which, by-the-bye, Mrs. Thompson then resolved that she would make a change, should ever the gentleman become her own property. He still wore his gloves, and was very smart; but it was clear to see that he was not at his ease.

"I hope the heat does not incommode you," he said after a few moments' silence. Mrs. Thompson declared that it did not, that she liked a good deal of heat, and that, on the whole, she was very well where she was. She was afraid, however, that she was detaining M. Lacordaire, who might probably wish to be moving about upon the rock. In answer to which M. Lacordaire declared that he never could be so happy anywhere as in her close vicinity.

"You are too good to me," said Mrs. Thompson, almost sighing. "I don't know what my stay here would have been without your great kindness."

"It is madame that has been kind to me," said M. Lacordaire, pressing the handle of his cane against his heart.

There was then another pause, after which Mrs. Thompson said that that was all his French politeness; that she knew that she had been very troublesome to him, but that she would now soon be gone; and that then, in her own country, she would never forget his great goodness.

"Ah, madame!" said M. Lacordaire; and, as he said it, much more was expressed in his face than in his words. But, then, you can neither accept nor reject a gentleman by what he says in his face. He blushed, too, up to his grizzled hair, and, turning round, walked a step or two away from the widow's seat, and back again.

Mrs. Thompson the while sat quite still. The displaced fragment, lying, as it did, near a corner of the building, made not an uncomfortable chair. She had only to be careful that she did not injure her hat or crush her clothes, and throw in a word here and there to assist the gentleman, should occasion permit it.

"Madame!" said M. Lacordaire, on his return from a second little walk.

"Monsieur!" replied Mrs. Thompson, perceiving that M. Lacordaire paused in his speech.

"Madame," he began again, and then, as he again paused, Mrs. Thompson looked up to him very sweetly; "madame, what I am going to say will, I am afraid, seem to evince by far too great audacity on my part."

Mrs. Thompson may, perhaps, have thought that, at the present moment, audacity was not his fault. She replied, however, that she was quite sure that monsieur would say nothing that was in any way unbecoming either for him to speak or for her to hear.

"Madame, may I have ground to hope that such may be your sentiments after I have spoken! Madame"—and now he went down, absolutely on his knees, on the hard stones; and Mrs. Thompson, looking about into the distance, almost thought that she saw the top of the guide's cap—"Madame, I have looked forward to this opportunity as one in which I may declare for you the greatest passion that I have ever yet felt. Madame, with all my heart and soul I love you. Madame, I offer to you the homage of my heart, my hand, the happiness of my life, and all that I possess in this world;" and then, taking her hand gracefully between his gloves, he pressed his lips against the tips of her fingers.

If the thing was to be done, this way of doing it was, perhaps, as good as any other. It was one, at any rate, which left no doubt whatever as to the gentleman's intentions. Mrs. Thompson, could she have had her own way, would not have allowed her lover of fifty to go down upon his knees, and would have spared him much of the romance of his declaration. So also would she have spared him his yellow gloves and his polished boots. But these were a part of the necessity of the situation, and therefore she wisely took them as matters to be passed over with indifference. Seeing, however, that M. Lacordaire still remained on his knees, it was necessary that she should take some step toward raising him, especially as her two children and the guide would infallibly be upon them before long.

"M. Lacordaire," she said, "you surprise me greatly; but pray get up."

"But will madame vouchsafe to give me some small ground for hope?"

"The girls will be here directly, M. Lacordaire; pray get up. I can talk to you much better if you will stand up, or sit down on one of these stones."

M. Lacordaire did as he was bid; he got up, wiped the knees of his pantaloons with his handkerchief, sat down beside her, and then pressed the handle of his cane to his heart.

"You really have so surprised me that I hardly know how to answer you," said Mrs. Thompson. "Indeed, I cannot bring myself to imagine that you are in earnest."

"Ah, madame, do not be so cruel! How can I have lived with you so long, sat beside you for so many days, without having received your image into my heart? I am in earnest! Alas! I fear too much in earnest!" And then he looked at her with all his eyes, and sighed with all his strength.

Mrs. Thompson's prudence told her that it would be well to settle the matter, in one way or the other, as soon as possible. Long periods of love-making were fit for younger people than herself and her future possible husband. Her object would be to make him comfortable if she could, and that he should do the same for her, if that also were possible. As for lookings and sighings and pressings of the hand, she had gone through all that some twenty years since in India, when Thompson had been young, and she was still in her teens.

"But, M. Lacordaire, there are so many things to be considered. There! I hear the children coming! Let us walk this way for a minute." And they turned behind a wall which placed them out of sight, and walked on a few paces till they reached a parapet, which stood on the uttermost edge of the high rock. Leaning upon this they continued their conversation.

"There are so many things to be considered," said Mrs. Thompson again.

"Yes, of course," said M. Lacordaire. "But my one great consideration is this;—that I love madame to distraction."

"I am very much flattered; of course, any lady would so feel. But, M. Lacordaire—"

"Madame, I am all attention. But, if you would deign to make me happy, say that one word, 'I love you!'" M. Lacordaire, as he uttered these words, did not look, as the saying is, at his best. But Mrs. Thompson forgave him. She knew that elderly gentlemen under such circumstances do not look at their best.

"But if I consented to—to—to such an arrangement, I could only do so on seeing that it would be beneficial—or, at any rate, not injurious—to my children; and that it would offer to ourselves a fair promise of future happiness."

"Ah, madame; it would be the dearest wish of my heart to be a second father to those two young ladies; except, indeed—" and then M. Lacordaire stopped the flow of his speech.

"In such matters it is so much the best to be explicit at once," said Mrs. Thompson.

"Oh, yes; certainly! Nothing can be more wise than madame."

"And the happiness of a household depends so much on money."

"Madame!"

"Let me say a word or two, Monsieur Lacordaire. I have enough for myself and my children; and, should I every marry again, I should not, I hope, be felt as a burden by my husband; but it would, of course, be my duty to know what were his circumstances before I accepted him. Of yourself, personally, I have seen nothing that I do not like."

"Oh, madame!"

"But as yet I know nothing of your circumstances."

M. Lacordaire, perhaps, did feel that Mrs. Thompson's prudence was of a strong, masculine description; but he hardly liked her the less on this account. To give him his due he was not desirous of marrying her solely for her money's sake. He also wished for a comfortable home, and proposed to give as much as he got; only he had been anxious to wrap up the solid cake of this business in a casing of sugar of romance. Mrs. Thompson would not have the sugar but the cake might not be the worse on that account.

"No, madame, not as yet; but they shall all be made open and at your disposal," said M. Lacordaire; and Mrs. Thompson bowed approvingly.

"I am in business," continued M. Lacordaire; "and my business gives me eight thousand francs a year."

"Four times eight are thirty-two," said Mrs. Thompson to herself; putting the francs into pounds sterling, in the manner that she had always found to be the readiest. Well, so far the statement was satisfactory. An income of three hundred and twenty pounds a year from business, joined to her own, might do very well. She did not in the least suspect M. Lacordaire of being false, and so far the matter sounded well.

"And what is the business?" she asked, in a tone of voice intended to be indifferent, but which nevertheless showed that she listened anxiously for an answer to her question.

They were both standing with their arms upon the wall, looking down upon the town of Le Puy; but they had so stood that each could see the other's countenance as they talked. Mrs. Thompson could now perceive that M. Lacordaire became red in the face, as he paused before answering her. She was near to him, and seeing his emotion gently touched his arm with her hand. This she did to reassure him, for she saw that he was ashamed of having to declare that he was a tradesman. As for herself, she had made up her mind to bear with this, if she found, as she felt sure she would find, that the trade was one which would not degrade either him or her. Hitherto, indeed,—in her early days,—she had looked down on trade; but of what benefit had her grand ideas been to her when she had returned to England? She had tried her hand at English genteel society, and no one had seemed to care for her. Therefore, she touched his arm lightly with her fingers that she might encourage him.

He paused for a moment, as I have said, and became red; and then feeling that he had shown some symptoms of shame—and feeling also, probably, that it was unmanly in him to do so, he shook himself slightly, raised his head up somewhat more proudly than was his wont, looked her full in the face with more strength of character than she had yet seen him assume; and then, declared his business.

"Madame," he said, in a very audible, but not in a loud voice, "madame—je suis tailleur." And having so spoken, he turned slightly from her and looked down over the valley towards Le Puy.

There was nothing more said upon the subject as they drove down from the rock of Polignac back to the town. Immediately on receiving the announcement, Mrs. Thompson found that she had no answer to make. She withdrew her hand—and felt at once that she had received a blow. It was not that she was angry with M. Lacordaire for being a tailor; nor was she angry with him in that, being a tailor, he had so addressed her. But she was surprised, disappointed, and altogether put beyond her ease. She had, at any rate, not expected this. She had dreamed of his being a banker; thought that, perhaps, he might have been a wine merchant; but her idea had never gone below a jeweller or watchmaker. When those words broke upon her ear, "Madame, je suis tailleur," she had felt herself to be speechless.

But the words had not been a minute spoken when Lilian and Mimmy ran up to their mother. "Oh, mamma," said Lilian, "we thought you were lost; we have searched for you all over the chateau."

"We have been sitting very quietly here, my dear, looking at the view," said Mrs. Thompson.

"But, mamma, I do wish you'd see the mouth of the oracle. It is so large, and so round, and so ugly. I put my arm into it all the way," said Mimmy.

But at the present moment her mamma felt no interest in the mouth of the oracle; and so they all walked down together to the carriage. And, though the way was steep, Mrs. Thompson managed to pick her steps without the assistance of an arm; nor did M. Lacordaire presume to offer it.

The drive back to town was very silent. Mrs. Thompson did make one or two attempts at conversation, but they were not effectual. M. Lacordaire could not speak at his ease till this matter was settled, and he already had begun to perceive that his business was against him. Why is it that the trade of a tailor should be less honourable than that of a haberdasher, or even a grocer?

They sat next each other at dinner, as usual; and here, as all eyes were upon them, they both made a great struggle to behave in their accustomed way. But even in this they failed. All the world of the Hotel des Ambassadeurs knew that M. Lacordaire had gone forth to make an offer to Mrs. Thompson, and all that world, therefore, was full of speculation. But all the world could make nothing of it. M. Lacordaire did look like a rejected man, but Mrs. Thompson did not look like the woman who had rejected him. That the offer had been made—in that everybody agreed, from the senior habitue of the house who always sat at the head of the table, down to the junior assistant garcon. But as to reading the riddle, there was no accord among them.

When the dessert was done, Mrs. Thompson, as usual, withdrew, and M. Lacordaire, as usual, bowed as he stood behind his own chair. He did not, however, attempt to follow her.

But when she reached the door she called him. He was at her side in a moment, and then she whispered in his ear—

"And I, also—I will be of the same business."

When M. Lacordaire regained the table the senior habitue, the junior garcon, and all the intermediate ranks of men at the Hotel des Ambassadeurs knew that they might congratulate him.

Mrs. Thompson had made a great struggle; but, speaking for myself, I am inclined to think that she arrived at last at a wise decision.

THE COURTSHIP OF SUSAN BELL

John Munroe Bell had been a lawyer in Albany, State of New York, and as such had thriven well. He had thriven well as long as thrift and thriving on this earth had been allowed to him. But the Almighty had seen fit to shorten his span.

Early in life he had married a timid, anxious, pretty, good little wife, whose whole heart and mind had been given up to do his bidding and deserve his love. She had not only deserved it but had possessed it, and as long as John Munroe Bell had lived, Henrietta Bell—Hetta as he called her—had been a woman rich in blessings. After twelve years of such blessings he had left her, and had left with her two daughters, a second Hetta, and the heroine of our little story, Susan Bell.

A lawyer in Albany may thrive passing well for eight or ten years, and yet not leave behind him any very large sum of money if he dies at the end of that time. Some small modicum, some few thousand dollars, John Bell had amassed, so that his widow and daughters were not absolutely driven to look for work or bread.

In those happy days when cash had begun to flow in plenteously to the young father of the family, he had taken it into his head to build for himself, or rather for his young female brood, a small neat house in the outskirts of Saratoga Springs. In doing so he was instigated as much by the excellence of the investment for his pocket as by the salubrity of the place for his girls. He furnished the house well, and then during some summer weeks his wife lived there, and sometimes he let it.

How the widow grieved when the lord of her heart and master of her mind was laid in the grave, I need not tell. She had already counted ten years of widowhood, and her children had grown to be young women beside her at the time of which I am now about to speak. Since that sad day on which they had left Albany they had lived together at the cottage at the Springs. In winter their life had been lonely enough; but as soon as the hot weather began to drive the fainting citizens out from New York, they had always received two or three boarders—old ladies generally, and occasionally an old gentleman—persons of very steady habits, with whose pockets the widow's moderate demands agreed better than the hotel charges. And so the Bells lived for ten years.

That Saratoga is a gay place in July, August, and September, the world knows well enough. To girls who go there with trunks full of muslin and crinoline, for whom a carriage and pair of horses is always waiting immediately after dinner, whose fathers' pockets are bursting with dollars, it is a very gay place. Dancing and flirtations come as a matter of course, and matrimony follows after with only too great rapidity. But the place was not very gay for Hetta or Susan Bell.

In the first place the widow was a timid woman, and among other fears feared greatly that she should be thought guilty of setting traps for husbands. Poor mothers! how often are they charged with this sin when their honest desires go no further than that their bairns may be "respectit like the lave." And then she feared flirtations; flirtations that should be that and nothing more, flirtations that are so destructive of the heart's sweetest essence. She feared love also, though she longed for that as well as feared it;—for her girls, I mean; all such feelings for herself were long laid under ground;—and then, like a timid creature as she was, she had other indefinite fears, and among them a great fear that those girls of hers would be left husbandless,—a phase of life which after her twelve years of bliss she regarded as anything but desirable. But the upshot was,—the upshot of so many fears and such small means,—that Hetta and Susan Bell had but a dull life of it.

Were it not that I am somewhat closely restricted in the number of my pages, I would describe at full the merits and beauties of Hetta and Susan Bell. As it is I can but say a few words. At our period of their lives Hetta was nearly one-and-twenty, and Susan was just nineteen. Hetta was a short, plump, demure young woman, with the softest smoothed hair, and the brownest brightest eyes. She was very useful in the house, good at corn cakes, and thought much, particularly in these latter months, of her religious duties. Her sister in the privacy of their own little room would sometimes twit her with the admiring patience with which she would listen to the lengthened eloquence of Mr. Phineas Beckard, the Baptist minister. Now Mr. Phineas Beckard was a bachelor.

Susan was not so good a girl in the kitchen or about the house as was her sister; but she was bright in the parlour, and if that motherly heart could have been made to give out its inmost secret—which however, it could not have been made to give out in any way painful to dear Hetta—perhaps it might have been found that Susan was loved with the closest love. She was taller than her sister, and lighter; her eyes were blue as were her mother's; her hair was brighter than Hetta's, but not always so singularly neat. She had a dimple on her chin, whereas Hetta had none; dimples on her cheeks too, when she smiled; and, oh, such a mouth! There; my allowance of pages permits no more.

One piercing cold winter's day there came knocking at the widow's door—a young man. Winter days, when the ice of January is refrozen by the wind of February, are very cold at Saratoga Springs. In these days there was not often much to disturb the serenity of Mrs. Bell's house; but on the day in question there came knocking at the door—a young man.

Mrs. Bell kept an old domestic, who had lived with them in those happy Albany days. Her name was Kate O'Brien, but though picturesque in name she was hardly so in person. She was a thick-set, noisy, good-natured old Irishwoman, who had joined her lot to that of Mrs. Bell when the latter first began housekeeping, and knowing when she was well off; had remained in the same place from that day forth. She had known Hetta as a baby, and, so to say, had seen Susan's birth.

"And what might you be wanting, sir?" said Kate O'Brien, apparently not quite pleased as she opened the door and let in all the cold air.

"I wish to see Mrs. Bell. Is not this Mrs. Bell's house?" said the young man, shaking the snow from out of the breast of his coat.

He did see Mrs. Bell, and we will now tell who he was, and why he had come, and how it came to pass that his carpet-bag was brought down to the widow's house and one of the front bedrooms was prepared for him, and that he drank tea that night in the widow's parlour.

His name was Aaron Dunn, and by profession he was an engineer. What peculiar misfortune in those days of frost and snow had befallen the line of rails which runs from Schenectady to Lake Champlain, I never quite understood. Banks and bridges had in some way come to grief, and on Aaron Dunn's shoulders was thrown the burden of seeing that they were duly repaired. Saratoga Springs was the centre of these mishaps, and therefore at Saratoga Springs it was necessary that he should take up his temporary abode.

Now there was at that time in New York city a Mr. Bell, great in railway matters—an uncle of the once thriving but now departed Albany lawyer. He was a rich man, but he liked his riches himself; or at any rate had not found himself called upon to share them with the widow and daughters of his nephew. But when it chanced to come to pass that he had a hand in despatching Aaron Dunn to Saratoga, he took the young man aside and recommended him to lodge with the widow. "There," said he, "show her my card." So much the rich uncle thought he might vouchsafe to do for the nephew's widow.

Mrs. Bell and both her daughters were in the parlour when Aaron Dunn was shown in, snow and all. He told his story in a rough, shaky voice, for his teeth chattered; and he gave the card, almost wishing that he had gone to the empty big hotel, for the widow's welcome was not at first quite warm.

The widow listened to him as he gave his message, and then she took the card and looked at it. Hetta, who was sitting on the side of the fireplace facing the door, went on demurely with her work. Susan gave one glance round—her back was to the stranger—and then another; and then she moved her chair a little nearer to the wall, so as to give the young man room to come to the fire, if he would. He did not come, but his eyes glanced upon Susan Bell; and he thought that the old man in New York was right, and that the big hotel would be cold and dull. It was a pretty face to look on that cold evening as she turned it up from the stocking she was mending.

"Perhaps you don't wish to take winter boarders, ma'am?" said Aaron Dunn.

"We never have done so yet, sir," said Mrs. Bell timidly. Could she let this young wolf in among her lamb-fold? He might be a wolf;—who could tell?

61

"Mr. Bell seemed to think it would suit," said Aaron.

Had he acquiesced in her timidity and not pressed the point, it would have been all up with him. But the widow did not like to go against the big uncle; and so she said, "Perhaps it may, sir."

"I guess it will, finely," said Aaron. And then the widow seeing that the matter was so far settled, put down her work and came round into the passage. Hetta followed her, for there would be housework to do. Aaron gave himself another shake, settled the weekly number of dollars—with very little difficulty on his part, for he had caught another glance at Susan's face; and then went after his bag. 'Twas thus that Aaron Dunn obtained an entrance into Mrs. Bell's house. "But what if he be a wolf?" she said to herself over and over again that night, though not exactly in those words. Ay, but there is another side to that question. What if he be a stalwart man, honest-minded, with clever eye, cunning hand, ready brain, broad back, and warm heart; in want of a wife mayhap; a man that can earn his own bread and another's;—half a dozen others' when the half dozen come? Would not that be a good sort of lodger? Such a question as that too did flit, just flit, across the widow's sleepless mind. But then she thought so much more of the wolf! Wolves, she had taught herself to think, were more common than stalwart, honest-minded, wife-desirous men.

"I wonder mother consented to take him," said Hetta, when they were in the little room together.

"And why shouldn't she?" said Susan. "It will be a help."

"Yes, it will be a little help," said Hetta. "But we have done very well hitherto without winter lodgers."

"But uncle Bell said she was to."

"What is uncle Bell to us?" said Hetta, who had a spirit of her own. And she began to surmise within herself whether Aaron Dunn would join the Baptist congregation, and whether Phineas Beckard would approve of this new move.

"He is a very well-behaved young man at any rate," said Susan, "and he draws beautifully. Did you see those things he was doing?"

"He draws very well, I dare say," said Hetta, who regarded this as but a poor warranty for good behaviour. Hetta also had some fear of wolves—not for herself perhaps; but for her sister.

Aaron Dunn's work—the commencement of his work—lay at some distance from the Springs, and he left every morning with a lot of workmen by an early train—almost before daylight. And every morning, cold and wintry as the mornings were, the widow got him his breakfast with her own hands. She took his dollars and would not leave him altogether to the awkward mercies of Kate O'Brien; nor would she trust her girls to attend upon the young man. Hetta she might have trusted; but then Susan would have asked why she was spared her share of such hardship.

In the evening, leaving his work when it was dark, Aaron always returned, and then the evening was passed together. But they were passed with the most demure propriety. These women would make the tea, cut the bread and butter, and then sew; while Aaron Dunn, when the cups were removed, would always go to his plans and drawings.

On Sundays they were more together; but even on this day there was cause of separation, for Aaron went to the Episcopalian church, rather to the disgust of Hetta. In the afternoon, however, they were together; and then Phineas Beckard came in to tea on Sundays, and he and Aaron got to talking on religion; and though they disagreed pretty much, and would not give an inch either one or the other, nevertheless the minister told the widow, and Hetta too probably, that the lad had good stuff in him, though he was so stiff-necked.

"But he should be more modest in talking on such matters with a minister," said Hetta.

The Rev. Phineas acknowledged that perhaps he should; but he was honest enough to repeat that the lad had stuff in him. "Perhaps after all he is not a wolf," said the widow to herself.

Things went on in this way for above a month. Aaron had declared to himself over and over again that that face was sweet to look upon, and had unconsciously promised to himself certain delights in talking and perhaps walking with the owner of it. But the walkings had not been achieved—nor even the talkings as yet. The truth was that Dunn was bashful with young women, though he could be so stiff-necked with the minister.

And then he felt angry with himself, inasmuch as he had advanced no further; and as he lay in his bed—which perhaps those pretty hands had helped to make—he resolved that he would be a thought bolder in his bearing. He had no idea of making love to Susan Bell; of course not. But why should he not amuse himself by talking to a pretty girl when she sat so near him, evening after evening?

"What a very quiet young man he is," said Susan to her sister.

"He has his bread to earn, and sticks to his work," said Hetta. "No doubt he has his amusement when he is in the city," added the elder sister, not wishing to leave too strong an impression of the young man's virtue.

They had all now their settled places in the parlour. Hetta sat on one side of the fire, close to the table, having that side to herself. There she sat always busy. She must have made every dress and bit of linen worn in the house, and hemmed every sheet and towel, so busy was she always. Sometimes, once in a week or so, Phineas Beckard would come in, and then place was made for him between Hetta's usual seat and the table. For when there he would read out loud. On the other side, close also to the table, sat the widow, busy, but not savagely busy as her elder daughter. Between Mrs. Bell and the wall, with her feet ever on the fender, Susan used to sit; not absolutely idle, but doing work of some slender pretty sort, and talking ever and anon to her mother. Opposite to them all, at the other side of the table, far away from the fire, would Aaron Dunn place himself with his plans and drawings before him.

"Are you a judge of bridges, ma'am?" said Aaron, the evening after he had made his resolution. 'Twas thus he began his courtship.

"Of bridges?" said Mrs. Bell—"oh dear no, sir." But she put out her hand to take the little drawing which Aaron handed to her.

"Because that's one I've planned for our bit of a new branch from Moreau up to Lake George. I guess Miss Susan knows something about bridges."

"I guess I don't," said Susan—"only that they oughtn't to tumble down when the frost comes."

"Ha, ha, ha; no more they ought. I'll tell McEvoy that." McEvoy had been a former engineer on the line. "Well, that won't burst with any frost, I guess."

"Oh my! how pretty!" said the widow, and then Susan of course jumped up to look over her mother's shoulder.

The artful dodger! he had drawn and coloured a beautiful little sketch of a bridge; not an engineer's plan with sections and measurements, vexatious to a woman's eye, but a graceful little bridge with a string of cars running under it. You could almost hear the bell going.

"Well; that is a pretty bridge," said Susan. "Isn't it, Hetta?"

"I don't know anything about bridges," said Hetta, to whose clever eyes the dodge was quite apparent. But in spite of her cleverness Mrs. Bell and Susan had soon moved their chairs round to the table, and were looking through the contents of Aaron's portfolio. "But yet he may be a wolf," thought the poor widow, just as she was kneeling down to say her prayers.

That evening certainly made a commencement. Though Hetta went on pertinaciously with the body of a new dress, the other two ladies did not put in another stitch that night. From his drawings Aaron got to his instruments, and before bedtime was teaching Susan how to draw parallel lines. Susan found that she had quite an aptitude for parallel lines, and altogether had a good time of it that evening. It is dull to go on week after week, and month after month, talking only to one's mother and sister. It is dull though one does not oneself recognise it to be so. A little change in such matters is so very pleasant. Susan had not the slightest idea of regarding Aaron as even a possible lover. But young ladies do like the conversation of young gentlemen. Oh, my exceedingly proper prim old lady, you who are so shocked at this as a general doctrine, has it never occurred to you that the Creator has so intended it?

Susan understanding little of the how and why, knew that she had had a good time, and was rather in spirits as she went to bed. But Hetta had been frightened by the dodge.

"Oh, Hetta, you should have looked at those drawings. He is so clever!" said Susan.

"I don't know that they would have done me much good," replied Hetta.

"Good! Well, they'd do me more good than a long sermon, I know," said Susan; "except on a Sunday, of course," she added apologetically. This was an ill-tempered attack both on Hetta and Hetta's admirer. But then why had Hetta been so snappish?

"I'm sure he's a wolf," thought Hetta as she went to bed.

"What a very clever young man he is!" thought Susan to herself as she pulled the warm clothes round about her shoulders and ears.

"Well that certainly was an improvement," thought Aaron as he went through the same operation, with a stronger feeling of self-approbation than he had enjoyed for some time past.

In the course of the next fortnight the family arrangements all altered themselves. Unless when Beckard was there Aaron would sit in the widow's place, the widow would take Susan's chair, and the two girls would be opposite. And then Dunn would read to them; not sermons, but passages from Shakspeare, and Byron, and Longfellow. "He reads much better than Mr. Beckard," Susan had said one night. "Of course you're a competent judge!" had been Hetta's retort. "I mean that I like it better," said Susan. "It's well that all people don't think alike," replied Hetta.

And then there was a deal of talking. The widow herself, as unconscious in this respect as her youngest daughter, certainly did find that a little variety was agreeable on those long winter nights; and talked herself with unaccustomed freedom. And Beckard came there oftener and talked very much. When he was there the two young men did all the talking, and they pounded each other immensely. But still there grew up a sort of friendship between them.

"Mr. Beckard seems quite to take to him," said Mrs. Bell to her eldest daughter.

"It is his great good nature, mother," replied Hetta.

It was at the end of the second month when Aaron took another step in advance—a perilous step. Sometimes on evenings he still went on with his drawing for an hour or so; but during three or four evenings he never asked any one to look at what he was doing. On one Friday he sat over his work till late, without any reading or talking at all; so late that at last Mrs. Bell said, "If you're going to sit much longer, Mr. Dunn, I'll get you to put out the candles." Thereby showing, had he known it or had she, that the mother's confidence in the young man was growing fast. Hetta knew all about it, and dreaded that the growth was too quick.

"I've finished now," said Aaron; and he looked carefully at the cardboard on which he had been washing in his water-colours. "I've finished now." He then hesitated a moment; but ultimately he put the card into his portfolio and carried it up to his bedroom. Who does not perceive that it was intended as a present to Susan Bell?

The question which Aaron asked himself that night, and which he hardly knew how to answer, was this. Should he offer the drawing to Susan in the presence of her mother and sister, or on some occasion when they two might be alone together? No such occasion had ever yet occurred, but Aaron thought that it might probably be brought about. But then he wanted to make no fuss about it. His first intention had been to chuck the drawing lightly across the table when it was completed, and so make nothing of it. But he had finished it with more care than he had at first intended; and then he had hesitated when he had finished it. It was too late now for that plan of chucking it over the table.

On the Saturday evening when he came down from his room, Mr. Beckard was there, and there was no opportunity that night. On the Sunday, in conformity with a previous engagement, he went to hear Mr. Beckard preach, and walked to and from meeting with the family. This pleased Mrs. Bell, and they were all very gracious that afternoon. But Sunday was no day for the picture.

On Monday the thing had become of importance to him. Things always do when they are kept over. Before tea that evening when he came down Mrs. Bell and Susan only were in the room. He knew Hetta for his foe, and therefore determined to use this occasion.

"Miss Susan," he said, stammering somewhat, and blushing too, poor fool! "I have done a little drawing which I want you to accept," and he put his portfolio down on the table.

"Oh! I don't know," said Susan, who had seen the blush.

Mrs. Bell had seen the blush also, and pursed her mouth up, and looked grave. Had there been no stammering and no blush, she might have thought nothing of it.

Aaron saw at once that his little gift was not to go down smoothly. He was, however, in for it now, so he picked it out from among the other papers in the case and brought it over to Susan. He endeavoured to hand it to her with an air of indifference, but I cannot say that he succeeded.

It was a very pretty, well-finished, water-coloured drawing, representing still the same bridge, but with more adjuncts. In

Susan's eyes it was a work of high art. Of pictures probably she had seen but little, and her liking for the artist no doubt added to her admiration. But the more she admired it and wished for it, the stronger was her feeling that she ought not to take it.

Poor Susan! she stood for a minute looking at the drawing, but she said nothing; not even a word of praise. She felt that she was red in the face, and uncourteous to their lodger; but her mother was looking at her and she did not know how to behave herself.

Mrs. Bell put out her hand for the sketch, trying to bethink herself as she did so in what least uncivil way she could refuse the present. She took a moment to look at it collecting her thoughts, and as she did so her woman's wit came to her aid.

"Oh dear, Mr. Dunn, it is very pretty; quite a beautiful picture. I cannot let Susan rob you of that. You must keep that for some of your own particular friends."

"But I did it for her," said Aaron innocently.

Susan looked down at the ground, half pleased at the declaration. The drawing would look very pretty in a small gilt frame put over her dressing-table. But the matter now was altogether in her mother's hands.

"I am afraid it is too valuable, sir, for Susan to accept."

"It is not valuable at all," said Aaron, declining to take it back from the widow's hand.

"Oh, I am quite sure it is. It is worth ten dollars at least—or twenty," said poor Mrs. Bell, not in the very best taste. But she was perplexed, and did not know how to get out of the scrape. The article in question now lay upon the table-cloth, appropriated by no one, and at this moment Hetta came into the room.

"It is not worth ten cents," said Aaron, with something like a frown on his brow. "But as we had been talking about the bridge, I thought Miss Susan would accept it."

"Accept what?" said Hetta. And then her eye fell upon the drawing and she took it up.

"It is beautifully done," said Mrs. Bell, wishing much to soften the matter; perhaps the more so that Hetta the demure was now present. "I am telling Mr. Dunn that we can't take a present of anything so valuable."

"Oh dear no," said Hetta. "It wouldn't be right."

It was a cold frosty evening in March, and the fire was burning brightly on the hearth. Aaron Dunn took up the drawing quietly—very quietly—and rolling it up, as such drawings are rolled, put it between the blazing logs. It was the work of four evenings, and his chef-d'oeuvre in the way of art.

Susan, when she saw what he had done, burst out into tears. The widow could very readily have done so also, but she was able to refrain herself, and merely exclaimed—"Oh, Mr. Dunn!"

"If Mr. Dunn chooses to burn his own picture, he has certainly a right to do so," said Hetta.

Aaron immediately felt ashamed of what he had done; and he also could have cried, but for his manliness. He walked away to one of the parlour-windows, and looked out upon the frosty night. It was dark, but the stars were bright, and he thought that he should like to be walking fast by himself along the line of rails towards Balston. There he stood, perhaps for three minutes. He thought it would be proper to give Susan time to recover from her tears.

"Will you please to come to your tea, sir?" said the soft voice of Mrs. Bell.

He turned round to do so, and found that Susan was gone. It was not quite in her power to recover from her tears in three minutes. And then the drawing had been so beautiful! It had been done expressly for her too! And there had been something, she knew not what, in his eye as he had so declared. She had watched him intently over those four evenings' work, wondering why he did not show it, till her feminine curiosity had become rather strong. It was something very particular, she was sure, and she had learned that all that precious work had been for her. Now all that precious work was destroyed. How was it possible that she should not cry for more than three minutes?

The others took their meal in perfect silence, and when it was over the two women sat down to their work. Aaron had a book which he pretended to read, but instead of reading he was bethinking himself that he had behaved badly. What right had he to throw them all into such confusion by indulging in his passion? He was ashamed of what he had done, and fancied that Susan would hate him. Fancying that, he began to find at the same time that he by no means hated her.

At last Hetta got up and left the room. She knew that her sister was sitting alone in the cold, and Hetta was affectionate. Susan had not been in fault, and therefore Hetta went up to console her.

"Mrs. Bell," said Aaron, as soon as the door was closed, "I beg your pardon for what I did just now."

"Oh, sir, I'm so sorry that the picture is burnt," said poor Mrs. Bell.

"The picture does not matter a straw," said Aaron. "But I see that I have disturbed you all,—and I am afraid I have made Miss Susan unhappy."

"She was grieved because your picture was burnt," said Mrs. Bell, putting some emphasis on the "your," intending to show that her daughter had not regarded the drawing as her own. But the emphasis bore another meaning; and so the widow perceived as soon as she had spoken.

"Oh, I can do twenty more of the same if anybody wanted them," said Aaron. "If I do another like it, will you let her take it, Mrs. Bell?—just to show that you have forgiven me, and that we are friends as we were before?"

Was he, or was he not a wolf? That was the question which Mrs. Bell scarcely knew how to answer. Hetta had given her voice, saying he was lupine. Mr. Beckard's opinion she had not liked to ask directly. Mr. Beckard she thought would probably propose to Hetta; but as yet he had not done so. And, as he was still a stranger in the family, she did not like in any way to compromise Susan's name. Indirectly she had asked the question, and, indirectly also, Mr. Beckard's answer had been favourable.

"But it mustn't mean anything, sir," was the widow's weak answer, when she had paused on the question for a moment.

"Oh no, of course not," said Aaron, joyously, and his face became radiant and happy. "And I do beg your pardon for burning it; and the young ladies' pardon too." And then he rapidly got out his cardboard, and set himself to work about another bridge. The widow, meditating many things in her heart, commenced the hemming of a handkerchief.

In about an hour the two girls came back to the room and silently took their accustomed places. Aaron hardly looked up, but went on diligently with his drawing. This bridge should be a better bridge than that other. Its acceptance was now assured. Of course it was to mean nothing. That was a matter of course. So he worked away diligently, and said nothing to anybody.

When they went off to bed the two girls went into the mother's room. "Oh, mother, I hope he is not very angry," said Susan.

"Angry!" said Hetta, "if anybody should be angry, it is mother. He ought to have known that Susan could not accept it. He should never have offered it."

"But he's doing another," said Mrs. Bell.

"Not for her," said Hetta.

"Yes he is," said Mrs. Bell, "and I have promised that she shall take it." Susan as she heard this sank gently into the chair behind her, and her eyes became full of tears. The intimation was almost too much for her.

"Oh, mother!" said Hetta.

"But I particularly said that it was to mean nothing."

"Oh, mother, that makes it worse."

Why should Hetta interfere in this way, thought Susan to herself. Had she interfered when Mr. Beckard gave Hetta a testament bound in Morocco? had not she smiled, and looked gratified, and kissed her sister, and declared that Phineas Beckard was a nice dear man, and by far the most elegant preacher at the Springs? Why should Hetta be so cruel?

"I don't see that, my dear," said the mother. Hetta would not explain before her sister, so they all went to bed.

On the Thursday evening the drawing was finished. Not a word had been said about it, at any rate in his presence, and he had gone on working in silence. "There," said he, late on the Thursday evening, "I don't know that it will be any better if I go on daubing for another hour. There, Miss Susan; there's another bridge. I hope that will neither burst with the frost, nor yet be destroyed by fire," and he gave it a light flip with his fingers and sent it skimming over the table.

Susan blushed and smiled, and took it up. "Oh, it is beautiful," she said. "Isn't it beautifully done, mother?" and then all the three got up to look at it, and all confessed that it was excellently done.

"And I am sure we are very much obliged to you," said Susan after a pause, remembering that she had not yet thanked him.

"Oh, it's nothing," said he, not quite liking the word "we." On the following day he returned from his work to Saratoga about noon. This he had never done before, and therefore no one expected that he would be seen in the house before the evening. On this occasion, however, he went straight thither, and as chance would have it, both the widow and her elder daughter were out. Susan was there alone in charge of the house.

He walked in and opened the parlour door. There she sat, with her feet on the fender, with her work unheeded on the table behind her, and the picture, Aaron's drawing, lying on her knees. She was gazing at it intently as he entered, thinking in her young heart that it possessed all the beauties which a picture could possess.

"Oh, Mr. Dunn," she said, getting up and holding the telltale sketch behind the skirt of her dress.

"Miss Susan, I have come here to tell your mother that I must start for New York this afternoon and be there for six weeks, or perhaps longer."

"Mother is out," said she; "I'm so sorry."

"Is she?" said Aaron.

"And Hetta too. Dear me. And you'll be wanting dinner. I'll go and see about it."

Aaron began to swear that he could not possibly eat any dinner. He had dined once, and was going to dine again;—anything to keep her from going.

"But you must have something, Mr. Dunn," and she walked towards the door.

But he put his back to it. "Miss Susan," said he, "I guess I've been here nearly two months."

"Yes, sir, I believe you have," she replied, shaking in her shoes, and not knowing which way to look.

"And I hope we have been good friends."

"Yes, sir," said Susan, almost beside herself as to what she was saying.

"I'm going away now, and it seems to be such a time before I'll be back."

"Will it, Sir?"

"Six weeks, Miss Susan!" and then he paused, looking into her eyes, to see what he could read there. She leant against the table, pulling to pieces a morsel of half-ravelled muslin which she held in her hand; but her eyes were turned to the ground, and he could hardly see them.

"Miss Susan," he continued, "I may as well speak out now as at another time." He too was looking towards the ground, and clearly did not know what to do with his hands. "The truth is just this. I—I love you dearly, with all my heart. I never saw any one I ever thought so beautiful, so nice, and so good;—and what's more, I never shall. I'm not very good at this sort of thing, I know; but I couldn't go away from Saratoga for six weeks and not tell you." And then he ceased. He did not ask for any love in return. His presumption had not got so far as that yet. He merely declared his passion, leaning against the door, and there he stood twiddling his thumbs.

Susan had not the slightest conception of the way in which she ought to receive such a declaration. She had never had a lover before; nor had she ever thought of Aaron absolutely as a lover, though something very like love for him had been crossing over her spirit. Now, at this moment, she felt that he was the beau-ideal of manhood, though his boots were covered with the railway mud, and though his pantaloons were tucked up in rolls round his ankles. He was a fine, well-grown, open-faced fellow, whose eye was bold and yet tender, whose brow was full and broad, and all his bearing manly. Love him! Of course she loved him. Why else had her heart melted with pleasure when her mother said that that second picture was to be accepted?

But what was she to say? Anything but the open truth; she well knew that. The open truth would not do at all. What would her mother say and Hetta if she were rashly to say that? Hetta, she knew, would be dead against such a lover, and of her mother's approbation she had hardly more hope. Why they should disapprove of Aaron as a lover she had never asked herself. There are many nice things that seem to be wrong only because they are so nice. Maybe that Susan regarded a lover as one of them. "Oh, Mr. Dunn, you shouldn't." That in fact was all that she could say.

"Should not I?" said he. "Well, perhaps not; but there's the truth, and no harm ever comes of that. Perhaps I'd better not ask you for an answer now, but I thought it better you should know it all. And remember this—I only care for one thing now in the world, and that is for your love." And then he paused, thinking possibly that in spite of what he had said he might perhaps get some sort of an answer, some inkling of the state of her heart's disposition towards him.

But Susan had at once resolved to take him at his word when he suggested that an immediate reply was not necessary. To say that she loved him was of course impossible, and to say that she did not was equally so. She determined therefore to close at once with the offer of silence.

When he ceased speaking there was a moment's pause, during which he strove hard to read what might be written on her downturned face. But he was not good at such reading. "Well, I guess I'll go and get my things ready now," he said, and then turned round to open the door.

"Mother will be in before you are gone, I suppose," said Susan.

"I have only got twenty minutes," said he, looking at his watch. "But, Susan, tell her what I have said to you. Goodbye." And he put out his hand. He knew he should see her again, but this had been his plan to get her hand in his.

"Goodbye, Mr. Dunn," and she gave him her hand.

He held it tight for a moment, so that she could not draw it away,—could not if she would. "Will you tell your mother?" he asked.

"Yes," she answered, quite in a whisper. "I guess I'd better tell her." And then she gave a long sigh. He pressed her hand again and got it up to his lips.

"Mr. Dunn, don't," she said. But he did kiss it. "God bless you, my own dearest, dearest girl! I'll just open the door as I come down. Perhaps Mrs. Bell will be here." And then he rushed up stairs.

But Mrs. Bell did not come in. She and Hetta were at a weekly service at Mr. Beckard's meeting-house, and Mr. Beckard it seemed had much to say. Susan, when left alone, sat down and tried to think. But she could not think; she could only love. She could use her mind only in recounting to herself the perfections of that demigod whose heavy steps were so audible overhead, as he walked to and fro collecting his things and putting them into his bag.

And then, just when he had finished, she bethought herself that he must be hungry. She flew to the kitchen, but she was too late. Before she could even reach at the loaf of bread he descended the stairs, with a clattering noise, and heard her voice as she spoke quickly to Kate O'Brien.

"Miss Susan," he said, "don't get anything for me, for I'm off."

"Oh, Mr. Dunn, I am so sorry. You'll be so hungry on your journey," and she came out to him in the passage.

"I shall want nothing on the journey, dearest, if you'll say one kind word to me."

Again her eyes went to the ground. "What do you want me to say, Mr. Dunn?"

"Say, God bless you, Aaron."

"God bless you, Aaron," said she; and yet she was sure that she had not declared her love. He however thought otherwise, and went up to New York with a happy heart.

Things happened in the next fortnight rather quickly. Susan at once resolved to tell her mother, but she resolved also not to tell Hetta. That afternoon she got her mother to herself in Mrs. Bell's own room, and then she made a clean breast of it.

"And what did you say to him, Susan?"

"I said nothing, mother."

"Nothing, dear!"

"No, mother; not a word. He told me he didn't want it." She forgot how she had used his Christian name in bidding God bless him.

"Oh dear!" said the widow.

"Was it very wrong?" asked Susan.

"But what do you think yourself, my child?" asked Mrs. Bell after a while. "What are your own feelings."

Mrs. Bell was sitting on a chair and Susan was standing opposite to her against the post of the bed. She made no answer, but moving from her place, she threw herself into her mother's arms, and hid her face on her mother's shoulder. It was easy enough to guess what were her feelings.

"But, my darling," said her mother, "you must not think that it is an engagement."

"No," said Susan, sorrowfully.

"Young men say those things to amuse themselves." Wolves, she would have said, had she spoken out her mind freely.

"Oh, mother, he is not like that."

The daughter contrived to extract a promise from the mother that Hetta should not be told just at present. Mrs. Bell calculated that she had six weeks before her; as yet Mr. Beckard had not spoken out, but there was reason to suppose that he would do so before those six weeks would be over, and then she would be able to seek counsel from him.

Mr. Beckard spoke out at the end of six days, and Hetta frankly accepted him. "I hope you'll love your brother-in-law," said she to Susan.

"Oh, I will indeed," said Susan; and in the softness of her heart at the moment she almost made up her mind to tell; but Hetta was full of her own affairs, and thus it passed off.

It was then arranged that Hetta should go and spend a week with Mr. Beckard's parents. Old Mr. Beckard was a farmer living near Utica, and now that the match was declared and approved, it was thought well that Hetta should know her future husband's family. So she went for a week, and Mr. Beckard went with her. "He will be back in plenty of time for me to speak to him before Aaron Dunn's six weeks are over," said Mrs. Bell to herself.

But things did not go exactly as she expected. On the very morning after the departure of the engaged couple, there came a letter from Aaron, saying that he would be at Saratoga that very evening. The railway people had ordered him down again for some days' special work; then he was to go elsewhere, and not to return to Saratoga till June. "But he hoped," so said the letter, "that Mrs. Bell would not turn him into the street even then, though the summer might have come, and her regular lodgers might be expected."

"Oh dear, oh dear!" said Mrs. Bell to herself, reflecting that she had no one of whom she could ask advice, and that she must decide that very day. Why had she let Mr. Beckard go without telling him? Then she told Susan, and Susan spent the day trembling. Perhaps, thought Mrs. Bell, he will say nothing about it. In such case, however, would it not be her duty to say something? Poor mother! She trembled nearly as much as Susan.

It was dark when the fatal knock came at the door. The tea-things were already laid, and the tea-cake was already baked; for it would at any rate be necessary to give Mr. Dunn his tea. Susan, when she heard the knock, rushed from her chair and took refuge up stairs. The widow gave a long sigh and settled her dress. Kate

O'Brien with willing step opened the door, and bade her old friend welcome.

"How are the ladies?" asked Aaron, trying to gather something from the face and voice of the domestic.

"Miss Hetta and Mr. Beckard be gone off to Utica, just man-and-wife like! and so they are, more power to them."

"Oh indeed; I'm very glad," said Aaron—and so he was; very glad to have Hetta the demure out of the way. And then he made his way into the parlour, doubting much, and hoping much.

Mrs. Bell rose from her chair, and tried to look grave. Aaron glancing round the room saw that Susan was not there. He walked straight up to the widow, and offered her his hand, which she took. It might be that Susan had not thought fit to tell, and in such case it would not be right for him to compromise her; so he said never a word.

But the subject was too important to the mother to allow of her being silent when the young man stood before her. "Oh, Mr. Dunn," said she, "what is this you have been saying to Susan?"

"I have asked her to be my wife," said he, drawing himself up and looking her full in the face. Mrs. Bell's heart was almost as soft as her daughter's, and it was nearly gone; but at the moment she had nothing to say but, "Oh dear, oh dear!"

"May I not call you mother?" said he, taking both her hands in his.

"Oh dear—oh dear! But will you be good to her? Oh, Aaron Dunn, if you deceive my child!"

In another quarter of an hour, Susan was kneeling at her mother's knee, with her face on her mother's lap; the mother was wiping tears out of her eyes; and Aaron was standing by holding one of the widow's hands.

"You are my mother too, now," said he. What would Hetta and Mr. Beckard say, when they came back? But then he surely was not a wolf!

There were four or five days left for courtship before Hetta and Mr. Beckard would return; four or five days during which Susan might be happy, Aaron triumphant, and Mrs. Bell nervous. Days I have said, but after all it was only the evenings that were so left. Every morning Susan got up to give Aaron his breakfast, but Mrs.

Bell got up also. Susan boldly declared her right to do so, and Mrs. Bell found no objection which she could urge.

But after that Aaron was always absent till seven or eight in the evening, when he would return to his tea. Then came the hour or two of lovers' intercourse.

But they were very tame, those hours. The widow still felt an undefined fear that she was wrong, and though her heart yearned to know that her daughter was happy in the sweet happiness of accepted love, yet she dreaded to be too confident. Not a word had been said about money matters; not a word of Aaron Dunn's relatives. So she did not leave them by themselves, but waited with what patience she could for the return of her wise counsellors.

And then Susan hardly knew how to behave herself with her accepted suitor. She felt that she was very happy; but perhaps she was most happy when she was thinking about him through the long day, assisting in fixing little things for his comfort, and waiting for his evening return. And as he sat there in the parlour, she could be happy then too, if she were but allowed to sit still and look at him,—not stare at him, but raise her eyes every now and again to his face for the shortest possible glance, as she had been used to do ever since he came there.

But he, unconscionable lover, wanted to hear her speak, was desirous of being talked to, and perhaps thought that he should by rights be allowed to sit by her, and hold her hand. No such privileges were accorded to him. If they had been alone together, walking side by side on the green turf, as lovers should walk, she would soon have found the use of her tongue,—have talked fast enough no doubt. Under such circumstances, when a girl's shyness has given way to real intimacy, there is in general no end to her power of chatting. But though there was much love between Aaron and Susan, there was as yet but little intimacy. And then, let a mother be ever so motherly—and no mother could have more of a mother's tenderness than Mrs. Bell—still her presence must be a restraint. Aaron was very fond of Mrs. Bell; but nevertheless he did sometimes wish that some domestic duty would take her out of the parlour for a few happy minutes. Susan went out very often, but Mrs. Bell seemed to be a fixture.

Once for a moment he did find his love alone, immediately as he came into the house. "My own Susan, you do love me? do say so to me once." And he contrived to slip his arm round her waist. "Yes," she whispered; but she slipped like an eel from his hands, and left him only preparing himself for a kiss. And then when she got to her room, half frightened, she clasped her hands together, and bethought herself that she did really love him with a strength and depth of love which filled her whole existence. Why could she not have told him something of all this?

And so the few days of his second sojourn at Saratoga passed away, not altogether satisfactorily. It was settled that he should return to New York on Saturday night, leaving Saratoga on that evening; and as the Beckards—Hetta was already regarded quite as a Beckard—were to be back to dinner on that day, Mrs. Bell would have an opportunity of telling her wondrous tale. It might be well that Mr. Beckard should see Aaron before his departure.

On that Saturday the Beckards did arrive just in time for dinner. It may be imagined that Susan's appetite was not very keen, nor her manner very collected. But all this passed by unobserved in the importance attached to the various Beckard arrangements which came under discussion. Ladies and gentlemen circumstanced as were Hetta and Mr. Beckard are perhaps a little too apt to think that their own affairs are paramount. But after dinner Susan vanished at once, and when Hetta prepared to follow her, desirous of further talk about matrimonial arrangements, her mother stopped her, and the disclosure was made.

"Proposed to her!" said Hetta, who perhaps thought that one marriage in a family was enough at a time.

"Yes, my love—and he did it, I must say, in a very honourable way, telling her not to make any answer till she had spoken to me;—now that was very nice; was it not, Phineas?" Mrs. Bell had become very anxious that Aaron should not be voted a wolf.

"And what has been said to him since?" asked the discreet Phineas.

"Why—nothing absolutely decisive." Oh, Mrs. Bell! "You see I know nothing as to his means."

"Nothing at all," said Hetta.

"He is a man that will always earn his bread," said Mr. Beckard; and Mrs. Bell blessed him in her heart for saying it.

"But has he been encouraged?" asked Hetta.

"Well; yes, he has," said the widow.

"Then Susan I suppose likes him?" asked Phineas.

"Well; yes, she does," said the widow. And the conference ended in a resolution that Phineas Beckard should have a conversation with Aaron Dunn, as to his worldly means and position; and that he, Phineas, should decide whether Aaron might, or might not be at once accepted as a lover, according to the tenor of that conversation. Poor Susan was not told anything of all this. "Better not," said Hetta the demure. "It will only flurry her the more." How would she have liked it, if without consulting her, they had left it to Aaron to decide whether or no she might marry Phineas?

They knew where on the works Aaron was to be found, and thither Mr. Beckard rode after dinner. We need not narrate at length the conference between the young men. Aaron at once declared that he had nothing but what he made as an engineer, and explained that he held no permanent situation on the line. He was well paid at that present moment, but at the end of summer he would have to look for employment.

"Then you can hardly marry quite at present," said the discreet minister.

"Perhaps not quite immediately."

"And long engagements are never wise," said the other.

"Three or four months," suggested Aaron. But Mr. Beckard shook his head.

The afternoon at Mrs. Bell's house was melancholy. The final decision of the three judges was as follows. There was to be no engagement; of course no correspondence. Aaron was to be told that it would be better that he should get lodgings elsewhere when he returned; but that he would be allowed to visit at Mrs. Bell's house,—and at Mrs. Beckard's, which was very considerate. If he should succeed in getting a permanent appointment, and if he and Susan still held the same mind, why then—&c. &c. Such was Susan's fate, as communicated to her by Mrs. Bell and Hetta. She sat still and wept when she heard it; but she did not complain. She had always felt that Hetta would be against her.

"Mayn't I see him, then?" she said through her tears.

Hetta thought she had better not. Mrs. Bell thought she might. Phineas decided that they might shake hands, but only in full conclave. There was to be no lovers' farewell. Aaron was to leave the house at half-past five; but before he went Susan should be called down. Poor Susan! She sat down and bemoaned herself; uncomplaining, but very sad.

Susan was soft, feminine, and manageable. But Aaron Dunn was not very soft, was especially masculine, and in some matters not easily manageable. When Mr. Beckard in the widow's presence— Hetta had retired in obedience to her lover—informed him of the court's decision, there came over his face the look which he had worn when he burned the picture. "Mrs. Bell," he said, "had encouraged his engagement; and he did not understand why other people should now come and disturb it."

"Not an engagement, Aaron," said Mrs. Bell piteously.

"He was able and willing to work," he said, "and knew his profession. What young man of his age had done better than he had?" and he glanced round at them with perhaps more pride than was quite becoming.

Then Mr. Beckard spoke out, very wisely no doubt, but perhaps a little too much at length. Sons and daughters, as well as fathers and mothers, will know very well what he said; so I need not repeat his words. I cannot say that Aaron listened with much attention, but he understood perfectly what the upshot of it was. Many a man understands the purport of many a sermon without listening to one word in ten. Mr. Beckard meant to be kind in his manner; indeed was so, only that Aaron could not accept as kindness any interference on his part.

"I'll tell you what, Mrs. Bell," said he. "I look upon myself as engaged to her. And I look on her as engaged to me. I tell you so fairly; and I believe that's her mind as well as mine."

"But, Aaron, you won't try to see her—or to write to her,— not in secret; will you?"

"When I try to see her, I'll come and knock at this door; and if I write to her, I'll write to her full address by the post. I never did and never will do anything in secret."

"I know you're good and honest," said the widow with her handkerchief to her eyes.

"Then why do you separate us?" asked he, almost roughly. "I suppose I may see her at any rate before I go. My time's nearly up now, I guess."

And then Susan was called for, and she and Hetta came down together. Susan crept in behind her sister. Her eyes were red with weeping, and her appearance was altogether disconsolate. She had had a lover for a week, and now she was to be robbed of him.

"Goodbye, Susan," said Aaron, and he walked up to her without bashfulness or embarrassment. Had they all been compliant and gracious to him he would have been as bashful as his love; but now his temper was hot. "Goodbye, Susan," and she took his hand, and he held hers till he had finished. "And remember this, I look upon you as my promised wife, and I don't fear that you'll deceive me. At any rate I shan't deceive you."

"Goodbye, Aaron," she sobbed.

"Goodbye, and God bless you, my own darling!" And then without saying a word to any one else, he turned his back upon them and went his way.

There had been something very consolatory, very sweet, to the poor girl in her lover's last words. And yet they had almost made her tremble. He had been so bold, and stern, and confident. He had seemed so utterly to defy the impregnable discretion of Mr. Beckard, so to despise the demure propriety of Hetta. But of this she felt sure, when she came to question her heart, that she could never, never, never cease to love him better than all the world beside. She would wait—patiently if she could find patience—and then, if he deserted her, she would die.

In another month Hetta became Mrs. Beckard. Susan brisked up a little for the occasion, and looked very pretty as bridesmaid. She was serviceable too in arranging household matters, hemming linen and sewing table-cloths; though of course in these matters she did not do a tenth of what Hetta did.

Then the summer came, the Saratoga summer of July, August, and September, during which the widow's house was full; and Susan's hands saved the pain of her heart, for she was forced into occupation. Now that Hetta was gone to her own duties, it was necessary that Susan's part in the household should be more prominent.

Aaron did not come back to his work at Saratoga. Why he did not they could not then learn. During the whole long summer they heard not a word of him nor from him; and then when the cold winter months came and their boarders had left them, Mrs. Beckard congratulated her sister in that she had given no further encouragement to a lover who cared so little for her. This was very hard to bear. But Susan did bear it.

That winter was very sad. They learned nothing of Aaron Dunn till about January; and then they heard that he was doing very well. He was engaged on the Erie trunk line, was paid highly, and was much esteemed. And yet he neither came nor sent! "He has an excellent situation," their informant told them. "And a permanent one?" asked the widow. "Oh, yes, no doubt," said the gentleman, "for I happen to know that they count greatly on him." And yet he sent no word of love.

After that the winter became very sad indeed. Mrs. Bell thought it to be her duty now to teach her daughter that in all probability she would see Aaron Dunn no more. It was open to him to leave her without being absolutely a wolf. He had been driven from the house when he was poor, and they had no right to expect that he would return, now that he had made some rise in the world. "Men do amuse themselves in that way," the widow tried to teach her.

"He is not like that, mother," she said again.

"But they do not think so much of these things as we do," urged the mother.

"Don't they?" said Susan, oh, so sorrowfully; and so through the whole long winter months she became paler and paler, and thinner and thinner.

And then Hetta tried to console her with religion, and that perhaps did not make things any better. Religious consolation is the best cure for all griefs; but it must not be looked for specially with regard to any individual sorrow. A religious man, should he become bankrupt through the misfortunes of the world, will find true consolation in his religion even for that sorrow. But a bankrupt, who has not thought much of such things, will hardly find solace by taking up religion for that special occasion.

And Hetta perhaps was hardly prudent in her attempts. She thought that it was wicked in Susan to grow thin and pale for love of Aaron Dunn, and she hardly hid her thoughts. Susan was not sure but that it might be wicked, but this doubt in no way tended to make her plump or rosy. So that in those days she found no comfort in her sister.

But her mother's pity and soft love did ease her sufferings, though it could not make them cease. Her mother did not tell her that she was wicked, or bid her read long sermons, or force her to go oftener to the meeting-house.

"He will never come again, I think," she said one day, as with a shawl wrapped around her shoulders, she leant with her head upon her mother's bosom.

"My own darling," said the mother, pressing her child closely to her side.

"You think he never will, eh, mother?" What could Mrs. Bell say? In her heart of hearts she did not think he ever would come again.

"No, my child. I do not think he will." And then the hot tears ran down, and the sobs came thick and frequent.

"My darling, my darling!" exclaimed the mother; and they wept together.

"Was I wicked to love him at the first," she asked that night.

"No, my child; you were not wicked at all. At least I think not."

"Then why—" Why was he sent away? It was on her tongue to ask that question; but she paused and spared her mother. This was as they were going to bed. The next morning Susan did not get up. She was not ill, she said; but weak and weary. Would her mother let her lie that day? And then Mrs. Bell went down alone to her room, and sorrowed with all her heart for the sorrow of her child. Why, oh why, had she driven away from her door-sill the love of an honest man?

On the next morning Susan again did not get up;—nor did she hear, or if she heard she did not recognise, the step of the postman who brought a letter to the door. Early, before the widow's breakfast, the postman came, and the letter which he brought was as follows:-

"MY DEAR MRS. BELL,

"I have now got a permanent situation on the Erie line, and the salary is enough for myself and a wife. At least I think so, and I hope you will too. I shall be down at Saratoga tomorrow evening, and I hope neither Susan nor you will refuse to receive me.

"Yours affectionately,

"AARON DUNN."

That was all. It was very short, and did not contain one word of love; but it made the widow's heart leap for joy. She was rather afraid that Aaron was angry, he wrote so curtly and with such a brusque business-like attention to mere facts; but surely he could have but one object in coming there. And then he alluded specially to a wife. So the widow's heart leapt with joy.

But how was she to tell Susan? She ran up stairs almost breathless with haste, to the bedroom door; but then she stopped; too much joy she had heard was as dangerous as too much sorrow; she must think it over for a while, and so she crept back again.

But after breakfast—that is, when she had sat for a while over her teacup—she returned to the room, and this time she entered it. The letter was in her hand, but held so as to be hidden;—in her left hand as she sat down with her right arm towards the invalid.

"Susan dear," she said, and smiled at her child, "you'll be able to get up this morning? eh, dear?"

"Yes, mother," said Susan, thinking that her mother objected to this idleness of her lying in bed. And so she began to bestir herself.

"I don't mean this very moment, love. Indeed, I want to sit with you for a little while," and she put her right arm affectionately round her daughter's waist.

"Dearest mother," said Susan.

"Ah! there's one dearer than me, I guess," and Mrs. Bell smiled sweetly, as she made the maternal charge against her daughter.

Susan raised herself quickly in the bed, and looked straight into her mother's face. "Mother, mother," she said, "what is it? You've something to tell. Oh, mother!" And stretching herself over, she struck her hand against the corner of Aaron's letter. "Mother, you've a letter. Is he coming, mother?" and with eager eyes and open lips, she sat up, holding tight to her mother's arm.

"Yes, love. I have got a letter."

"Is he—is he coming?"

How the mother answered, I can hardly tell; but she did answer, and they were soon lying in each other's arms, warm with each other's tears. It was almost hard to say which was the happier.

Aaron was to be there that evening—that very evening. "Oh, mother, let me get up," said Susan.

But Mrs. Bell said no, not yet; her darling was pale and thin, and she almost wished that Aaron was not coming for another week. What if he should come and look at her, and finding her beauty gone, vanish again and seek a wife elsewhere!

So Susan lay in bed, thinking of her happiness, dozing now and again, and fearing as she waked that it was a dream, looking constantly at that drawing of his, which she kept outside upon the bed, nursing her love and thinking of it, and endeavouring, vainly endeavouring, to arrange what she would say to him.

"Mother," she said, when Mrs. Bell once went up to her, "you won't tell Hetta and Phineas, will you? Not today, I mean?" Mrs. Bell agreed that it would be better not to tell them. Perhaps she thought that she had already depended too much on Hetta and Phineas in the matter.

Susan's finery in the way of dress had never been extensive, and now lately, in these last sad winter days, she had thought but little of the fashion of her clothes. But when she began to dress herself for the evening, she did ask her mother with some anxiety what she had better wear. "If he loves you he will hardly see what you have on," said the mother. But not the less was she careful to smooth her daughter's hair, and make the most that might be made of those faded roses.

How Susan's heart beat,—how both their hearts beat as the hands of the clock came round to seven! And then, sharp at seven, came the knock; that same short bold ringing knock which Susan had so soon learned to know as belonging to Aaron Dunn. "Oh mother, I had better go up stairs," she cried, starting from her chair.

"No dear; you would only be more nervous."

"I will, mother."

"No, no, dear; you have not time;" and then Aaron Dunn was in the room.

She had thought much what she would say to him, but had not yet quite made up her mind. It mattered however but very little. On whatever she might have resolved, her resolution would have vanished to the wind. Aaron Dunn came into the room, and in one second she found herself in the centre of a whirlwind, and his arms were the storms that enveloped her on every side.

"My own, own darling girl," he said over and over again, as he pressed her to his heart, quite regardless of Mrs. Bell, who stood by, sobbing with joy. "My own Susan."

"Aaron, dear Aaron," she whispered. But she had already recognised the fact that for the present meeting a passive part would become her well, and save her a deal of trouble. She had her lover there quite safe, safe beyond anything that Mr. or Mrs. Beckard might have to say to the contrary. She was quite happy; only that there were symptoms now and again that the whirlwind was about to engulf her yet once more.

"Dear Aaron, I am so glad you are come," said the innocent-minded widow, as she went up stairs with him, to show him his room; and then he embraced her also. "Dear, dear mother," he said.

On the next day there was, as a matter of course, a family conclave. Hetta and Phineas came down, and discussed the whole subject of the coming marriage with Mrs. Bell. Hetta at first was not quite certain;—ought they not to inquire whether the situation was permanent?

"I won't inquire at all," said Mrs. Bell, with an energy that startled both the daughter and son-in-law. "I would not part them now; no, not if—" and the widow shuddered as she thought of her daughter's sunken eyes, and pale cheeks.

"He is a good lad," said Phineas, "and I trust she will make him a sober steady wife;" and so the matter was settled.

During this time, Susan and Aaron were walking along the Balston road; and they also had settled the matter—quite as satisfactorily.

Such was the courtship of Susan Dunn.

GEORGE WALKER AT SUEZ

Of all the spots on the world's surface that I, George Walker, of Friday Street, London, have ever visited, Suez in Egypt, at the head of the Red Sea, is by far the vilest, the most unpleasant, and the least interesting. There are no women there, no water, and no vegetation. It is surrounded, and indeed often filled, by a world of sand. A scorching sun is always overhead; and one is domiciled in a huge cavernous hotel, which seems to have been made purposely destitute of all the comforts of civilised life. Nevertheless, in looking back upon the week of my life which I spent there I always enjoy a certain sort of triumph;—or rather, upon one day of that week, which lends a sort of halo not only to my sojourn at Suez, but to the whole period of my residence in Egypt.

I am free to confess that I am not a great man, and that, at any rate in the earlier part of my career, I had a hankering after the homage which is paid to greatness. I would fain have been a popular orator, feeding myself on the incense tendered to me by thousands; or failing that, a man born to power, whom those around him were compelled to respect, and perhaps to fear. I am not ashamed to acknowledge this, and I believe that most of my neighbours in Friday Street would own as much were they as candid and open-hearted as myself.

It is now some time since I was recommended to pass the first four months of the year in Cairo because I had a sore-throat. The doctor may have been right, but I shall never divest myself of the idea that my partners wished to be rid of me while they made certain changes in the management of the firm. They would not otherwise have shown such interest every time I blew my nose or relieved my huskiness by a slight cough;—they would not have been so intimate with that surgeon from St. Bartholomew's who dined with them twice at the Albion; nor would they have gone to work directly that my back was turned, and have done those very things which they could not have done had I remained at home. Be that as it may, I was frightened and went to Cairo, and while there I made a trip to Suez for a week.

I was not happy at Cairo, for I knew nobody there, and the people at the hotel were, as I thought, uncivil. It seemed to me as though I were allowed to go in and out merely by sufferance; and yet I paid my bill regularly every week. The house was full of company, but the company was made up of parties of twos and threes, and they all seemed to have their own friends. I did make attempts to overcome that terrible British exclusiveness, that noli me tangere with which an Englishman arms himself; and in which he thinks it necessary to envelop his wife; but it was in vain, and I found myself sitting down to breakfast and dinner, day after day, as much alone as I should do if I called for a chop at a separate table in the Cathedral Coffee-house. And yet at breakfast and dinner I made one of an assemblage of thirty or forty people. That I thought dull.

But as I stood one morning on the steps before the hotel, bethinking myself that my throat was as well as ever I remembered it to be, I was suddenly slapped on the back. Never in my life did I feel a more pleasant sensation, or turn round with more unaffected delight to return a friend's greeting. It was as though a cup of water had been handed to me in the desert. I knew that a cargo of passengers for Australia had reached Cairo that morning, and were to be passed on to Suez as soon as the railway would take them, and did not therefore expect that the greeting had come from any sojourner in Egypt. I should perhaps have explained that the even tenor of our life at the hotel was disturbed some four times a month by a flight through Cairo of a flock of travellers, who like locusts eat up all that there was eatable at the Inn for the day. They sat down at the same tables with us, never mixing with us, having their separate interests and hopes, and being often, as I thought, somewhat loud and almost selfish in the expression of them. These flocks consisted of passengers passing and repassing by the overland route to and from India and Australia; and had I nothing else to tell, I should delight to describe all that I watched of their habits and manners—the outward bound being so different in their traits from their brethren on their return. But I have to tell of my own triumph at Suez, and must therefore hasten on to say that on turning round quickly with my outstretched hand, I found it clasped by John Robinson.

"Well, Robinson, is this you?" "Holloa, Walker, what are you doing here?" That of course was the style of greeting. Elsewhere I should not have cared much to meet John Robinson, for he was a man who had never done well in the world. He had been in business and connected with a fairly good house in Sise Lane, but he had married early, and things had not exactly gone well with him. I don't think the house broke, but he did; and so he was driven to take himself and five children off to Australia. Elsewhere I should not have cared to come across him, but I was positively glad to be slapped on the back by anybody on that landing-place in front of Shepheard's Hotel at Cairo.

I soon learned that Robinson with his wife and children, and indeed with all the rest of the Australian cargo, were to be passed on to Suez that afternoon, and after a while I agreed to accompany their party. I had made up my mind, on coming out from England, that I would see all the wonders of Egypt, and hitherto I had seen nothing. I did ride on one day some fifteen miles on a donkey to see the petrified forest; but the guide, who called himself a dragoman, took me wrong or cheated me in some way. We rode half the day over a stony, sandy plain, seeing nothing, with a terrible wind that filled my mouth with grit, and at last the dragoman got off. "Dere," said he, picking up a small bit of stone, "Dis is de forest made of stone. Carry that home." Then we turned round and rode back to Cairo. My chief observation as to the country was this—that whichever way we went, the wind blew into our teeth. The day's work cost me five-and-twenty shillings, and since that I had not as yet made any other expedition. I was therefore glad of an opportunity of going to Suez, and of making the journey in company with an acquaintance.

At that time the railway was open, as far as I remember, nearly half the way from Cairo to Suez. It did not run four or five times a day, as railways do in other countries, but four or five times a month. In fact, it only carried passengers on the arrival of these flocks passing between England and her Eastern possessions. There were trains passing backwards and forwards constantly, as I perceived in walking to and from the station; but, as I learned, they carried nothing but the labourers working on the line, and the water sent into the Desert for their use. It struck me forcibly at the time that I should not have liked to have money in that investment.

Well; I went with Robinson to Suez. The journey, like everything else in Egypt, was sandy, hot, and unpleasant. The railway carriages were pretty fair, and we had room enough; but even in them the dust was a great nuisance. We travelled about ten miles an hour, and stopped about an hour at every ten miles. This was tedious, but we had cigars with us and a trifle of brandy and water; and in this manner the railway journey wore itself away. In the middle of the night, however, we were moved from the railway carriages into omnibuses, as they were called, and then I was not comfortable. These omnibuses were wooden boxes, placed each upon a pair of wheels, and supposed to be capable of carrying six passengers. I was thrust into one with Robinson, his wife and five children, and immediately began to repent of my good-nature in accompanying them. To each vehicle were attached four horses or mules, and I must acknowledge that as on the railway they went as slow as possible, so now in these conveyances, dragged through the sand, they went as fast as the beasts could be made to gallop. I remember the Fox Tally-ho coach on the Birmingham road when Boyce drove it, but as regards pace the Fox Tally-ho was nothing to these machines in Egypt. On the first going off I was jolted right on to Mrs. R. and her infant; and for a long time that lady thought that the child had been squeezed out of its proper shape; but at last we arrived at Suez, and the baby seemed to me to be all right when it was handed down into the boat at Suez.

The Robinsons were allowed time to breakfast at that cavernous hotel—which looked to me like a scheme to save the expense of the passengers' meal on board the ship—and then they were off. I shook hands with him heartily as I parted with him at the quay, and wished him well through all his troubles. A man who takes a wife and five young children out into a colony, and that with his pockets but indifferently lined, certainly has his troubles before him. So he has at home, no doubt; but, judging for myself, I should always prefer sticking to the old ship as long as there is a bag of biscuits in the locker. Poor Robinson! I have never heard a word of him or his since that day, and sincerely trust that the baby was none the worse for the little accident in the box.

And now I had the prospect of a week before me at Suez, and the Robinsons had not been gone half an hour before I began to feel that I should have been better off even at Cairo. I secured a bedroom at the hotel—I might have secured sixty bedrooms had I wanted them—and then went out and stood at the front door, or gate. It is a large house, built round a quadrangle, looking with one front towards the head of the Red Sea, and with the other into and on a sandy, dead-looking, open square. There I stood for ten minutes, and finding that it was too hot to go forth, returned to the long cavernous room in which we had breakfasted. In that long cavernous room I was destined to eat all my meals for the next six days. Now at Cairo I could, at any rate, see my fellow-creatures at their food. So I lit a cigar, and began to wonder whether I could survive the week. It was now clear to me that I had done a very rash thing in coming to Suez with the Robinsons.

Somebody about the place had asked me my name, and I had told it plainly—George Walker. I never was ashamed of my name yet, and never had cause to be. I believe at this day it will go as far in Friday Street as any other. A man may be popular, or he may not. That depends mostly on circumstances which are in themselves trifling. But the value of his name depends on the way in which he is known at his bank. I have never dealt in tea spoons or gravy spoons, but my name will go as far as another name. "George Walker," I answered, therefore, in a tone of some little authority, to the man who asked me, and who sat inside the gate of the hotel in an old dressing-gown and slippers.

That was a melancholy day with me, and twenty times before dinner did I wish myself back at Cairo. I had been travelling all night, and therefore hoped that I might get through some little time in sleeping, but the mosquitoes attacked me the moment I laid myself down. In other places mosquitoes torment you only at night, but at Suez they buzz around you, without ceasing, at all hours. A scorching sun was blazing overhead, and absolutely forbade me to leave the house. I stood for a while in the verandah, looking down at the few small vessels which were moored to the quay, but there was no life in them; not a sail was set, not a boatman or a sailor was to be seen, and the very water looked as though it were hot. I could fancy the glare of the sun was cracking the paint on the gunwales of the boats. I was the only visitor in the house, and during all the long hours of the morning it seemed as though the servants had deserted it.

I dined at four; not that I chose that hour, but because no choice was given to me. At the hotels in Egypt one has to dine at an hour fixed by the landlord, and no entreaties will suffice to obtain a meal at any other. So at four I dined, and after dinner was again reduced to despair.

I was sitting in the cavernous chamber almost mad at the prospect of the week before me, when I heard a noise as of various feet in the passage leading from the quadrangle. Was it possible that other human beings were coming into the hotel—Christian human beings at whom I could look, whose voices I could hear, whose words I could understand, and with whom I might possibly associate? I did not move, however, for I was still hot, and I knew that my chances might be better if I did not show myself over eager for companionship at the first moment. The door, however, was soon opened, and I saw that at least in one respect I was destined to be disappointed. The strangers who were entering the room were not Christians—if I might judge by the nature of the garments in which they were clothed.

The door had been opened by the man in an old dressing-gown and slippers, whom I had seen sitting inside the gate. He was the Arab porter of the hotel, and as he marshalled the new visitors into the room, I heard him pronounce some sound similar to my own name, and perceived that he pointed me out to the most prominent person of those who then entered the apartment. This was a stout, portly man, dressed from head to foot in Eastern costume of the brightest colours. He wore, not only the red fez cap which everybody wears—even I had accustomed myself to a fez cap—but a turban round it, of which the voluminous folds were snowy white. His face was fat, but not the less grave, and the lower part of it was enveloped in a magnificent beard, which projected round it on all sides, and touched his breast as he walked. It was a grand grizzled beard, and I acknowledged at a moment that it added a singular dignity to the appearance of the stranger. His flowing robe was of bright colours, and the under garment which fitted close round his breast, and then descended, becoming beneath his sash a pair of the loosest pantaloons—I might, perhaps, better describe them as bags—was a rich tawny silk. These loose pantaloons were tied close round his legs, above the ankle, and over a pair of scrupulously white stockings, and on his feet he wore a pair of yellow slippers. It was manifest to me at a glance that the Arab gentleman was got up in his best raiment, and that no expense had been spared on his suit.

And here I cannot but make a remark on the personal bearing of these Arabs. Whether they be Arabs or Turks, or Copts, it is always the same. They are a mean, false, cowardly race, I believe. They will bear blows, and respect the man who gives them. Fear goes further with them than love, and between man and man they understand nothing of forbearance. He who does not exact from them all that he can exact is simply a fool in their estimation, to the extent of that which he loses. In all this, they are immeasurably inferior to us who have had Christian teaching. But in one thing they beat us. They always know how to maintain their personal dignity.

Look at my friend and partner Judkins, as he stands with his hands in his trousers pockets at the door of our house in Friday Street. What can be meaner than his appearance? He is a stumpy, short, podgy man; but then so also was my Arab friend at Suez. Judkins is always dressed from head to foot in a decent black cloth suit; his coat is ever a dress coat, and is neither old nor shabby. On his head he carries a shining new silk hat, such as fashion in our metropolis demands. Judkins is rather a dandy than otherwise, piquing himself somewhat on his apparel. And yet how mean is his appearance, as compared with the appearance of that Arab;—how mean also is his gait, how ignoble his step! Judkins could buy that Arab out four times over, and hardly feel the loss; and yet were they to enter a room together, Judkins would know and acknowledge by his look that he was the inferior personage. Not the less, should a personal quarrel arise between them, would Judkins punch the Arab's head; ay, and reduce him to utter ignominy at his feet.

Judkins would break his heart in despair rather than not return a blow; whereas the Arab would put up with any indignity of that sort. Nevertheless Judkins is altogether deficient in personal dignity. I often thought, as the hours hung in Egypt, whether it might not be practicable to introduce an oriental costume in Friday Street.

At this moment, as the Arab gentleman entered the cavernous coffee-room, I felt that I was greatly the inferior personage. He was followed by four or five others, dressed somewhat as himself; though by no means in such magnificent colours, and by one gentleman in a coat and trousers. The gentleman in the coat and trousers came last, and I could see that he was one of the least of the number. As for myself, I felt almost overawed by the dignity of the stout party in the turban, and seeing that he came directly across the room to the place where I was seated, I got upon my legs and made him some sign of Christian obeisance.

I am a little man, and not podgy, as is Judkins, and I flatter myself that I showed more deportment, at any rate, than he would have exhibited.

I made, as I have said, some Christian obeisance. I bobbed my head, that is, rubbing my hands together the while, and expressed an opinion that it was a fine day. But if I was civil, as I hope I was, the Arab was much more so. He advanced till he was about six paces from me, then placed his right hand open upon his silken breast,-and inclining forward with his whole body, made to me a bow which Judkins never could accomplish. The turban and the flowing robe might be possible in Friday Street, but of what avail would be the outer garments and mere symbols, if the inner sentiment of personal dignity were wanting? I have often since tried it when alone, but I could never accomplish anything like that bow. The Arab with the flowing robe bowed, and the other Arabs all bowed also; and after that the Christian gentleman with the coat and trousers made a leg. I made a leg also, rubbing my hands again, and added to my former remarks that it was rather hot.

"Dat berry true," said the porter in the dirty dressing-gown, who stood by. I could see at a glance that the manner of that porter towards me was greatly altered, and I began to feel comforted in my wretchedness. Perhaps a Christian from Friday Street, with plenty of money in his pockets, would stand in higher esteem at Suez than at Cairo. If so, that alone would go far to atone for the apparent wretchedness of the place. At Cairo I had not received that attention which had certainly been due to me as the second partner in the flourishing Manchester house of Grimes, Walker, and Judkins.

But now, as my friend with the beard again bowed to me, I felt that this deficiency was to be made up. It was clear, however, that this new acquaintance, though I liked the manner of it, would be attended with considerable inconvenience, for the Arab gentleman commenced an address to me in French. It has always been to me a source of sorrow that my parents did not teach me the French language, and this deficiency on my part has given rise to an incredible amount of supercilious overbearing pretension on the part of Judkins—who after all can hardly do more than translate a correspondent's letter. I do not believe that he could have understood that Arab's oration, but at any rate I did not. He went on to the end, however, speaking for some three or four minutes, and then again he bowed. If I could only have learned that bow, I might still have been greater than Judkins with all his French.

"I am very sorry," said I, "but I don't exactly follow the French language when it is spoken."

"Ah! no French!" said the Arab in very broken English, "dat is one sorrow." How is it that these fellows learn all languages under the sun? I afterwards found that this man could talk Italian, and Turkish, and Armenian fluently, and say a few words in German, as he could also in English. I could not ask for my dinner in any other language than English, if it were to save me from starvation. Then he called to the Christian gentleman in the pantaloons, and, as far as I could understand, made over to him the duty of interpreting between us. There seemed, however, to be one difficulty in the way of this being carried on with efficiency. The Christian gentleman could not speak English himself. He knew of it perhaps something more than did the Arab, but by no means enough to enable us to have a fluent conversation.

And had the interpreter—who turned out to be an Italian from Trieste, attached to the Austrian Consulate at Alexandria—had the interpreter spoken English with the greatest ease, I should have had considerable difficulty in understanding and digesting in all its bearings, the proposition made to me. But before I proceed to the proposition, I must describe a ceremony which took place previous to its discussion. I had hardly observed, when first the procession entered the room, that one of my friend's followers—my friend's name, as I learned afterwards, was Mahmoud al Ackbar, and I will therefore call him Mahmoud—that one of Mahmoud's followers bore in his arms a bundle of long sticks, and that another carried an iron pot and a tray. Such was the case, and these two followers came forward to perform their services, while I, having been literally pressed down on to the sofa by Mahmoud, watched them in their progress. Mahmoud also sat down, and not a word was spoken while the ceremony went on. The man with the sticks first placed on the ground two little pans—one at my feet, and then one at the feet of his master. After that he loosed an ornamented bag which he carried round his neck, and producing from it tobacco, proceeded to fill two pipes. This he did with the utmost gravity, and apparently with very peculiar care. The pipes had been already fixed at one end of the stick, and to the other end the man had fastened two large yellow balls. These, as I afterwards perceived, were mouth-pieces made of amber. Then he lit the pipes, drawing up the difficult smoke by long painful suckings at the mouthpiece, and then, when the work had become apparently easy, he handed one pipe to me, and the other to his master. The bowls he had first placed in the little pans on the ground.

During all this time no word was spoken, and I was left altogether in the dark as to the cause which had produced this extraordinary courtesy. There was a stationary sofa—they called it there a divan—which was fixed into the corner of the room, and on one side of the angle sat Mahmoud al Ackbar, with his feet tucked under him, while I sat on the other. The remainder of the party stood around, and I felt so little master of the occasion, that I did not know whether it would become me to bid them be seated. I was not master of the entertainment. They were not my pipes. Nor was it my coffee, which I saw one of the followers preparing in a distant part of the room. And, indeed, I was much confused as to the management of the stick and amber mouth-piece with which I had been presented. With a cigar I am as much at home as any man in the City. I can nibble off the end of it, and smoke it to the last ash, when I am three parts asleep. But I had never before been invited to regale myself with such an instrument as this. What was I to do with that huge yellow ball? So I watched my new friend closely.

It had manifestly been a part of his urbanity not to commence till I had done so, but seeing my difficulty he at last raised the ball to his mouth and sucked at it. I looked at him and envied the gravity of his countenance, and the dignity of his demeanour. I sucked also, but I made a sputtering noise, and must confess that I did not enjoy it. The smoke curled gracefully from his mouth and nostrils as he sat there in mute composure. I was mute as regarded speech, but I coughed as the smoke came from me in convulsive puffs. And then the attendant brought us coffee in little tin cups—black coffee, without sugar and full of grit, of which the berries had been only bruised, not ground. I took the cup and swallowed the mixture, for I could not refuse, but I wish that I might have asked for some milk and sugar. Nevertheless there was something very pleasing in the whole ceremony, and at last I began to find myself more at home with my pipe.

When Mahmoud had exhausted his tobacco, and perceived that I also had ceased to puff forth smoke, he spoke in Italian to the interpreter, and the interpreter forthwith proceeded to explain to me the purport of this visit. This was done with much difficulty, for the interpreter's stock of English was very scanty—but after awhile I understood, or thought I understood, as follows:-At some previous period of my existence I had done some deed which had given infinite satisfaction to Mahmoud al Ackbar. Whether, however, I had done it myself, or whether my father had done it, was not quite clear to me. My father, then some time deceased, had been a wharfinger at Liverpool, and it was quite possible that Mahmoud might have found himself at that port. Mahmoud had heard of my arrival in Egypt, and had been given to understand that I was coming to Suez—to carry myself away in the ship, as the interpreter phrased it. This I could not understand, but I let it pass. Having heard these agreeable tidings—and Mahmoud, sitting in the corner, bowed low to me as this was said—he had prepared for my acceptance a slight refection for the morrow, hoping that I would not carry myself away in the ship till this had been eaten. On this subject I soon made him quite at ease, and he then proceeded to explain that as there was a point of interest at Suez, Mahmoud was anxious that I should partake of the refection somewhat in the guise of a picnic, at the Well of Moses, over in Asia, on the other side of the head of the Red Sea. Mahmoud would provide a boat to take across the party in the morning, and camels on which we would return after sunset. Or else we would go and return on camels, or go on camels and return in the boat. Indeed any arrangement would be made that I preferred. If I was afraid of the heat, and disliked the open boat, I could be carried round in a litter.

The provisions had already been sent over to the Well of Moses in the anticipation that I would not refuse this little request.

I did not refuse it. Nothing could have been more agreeable to me than this plan of seeing something of the sights and wonders of this land,—and of this seeing them in good company. I had not heard of the Well of Moses before, but now that I learned that it was in Asia,—in another quarter of the globe, to be reached by a transit of the Red Sea, to be returned from by a journey on camels' backs,—I burned with anxiety to visit its waters. What a story would this be for Judkins! This was, no doubt, the point at which the Israelites had passed. Of those waters had they drunk. I almost felt that I had already found one of Pharaoh's chariot wheels. I readily gave my assent, and then, with much ceremony and many low salaams, Mahmoud and his attendant left me. "I am very glad that I came to Suez," said I to myself.

I did not sleep much that night, for the mosquitoes of Suez are very persevering; but I was saved from the agonising despair which these animals so frequently produce, by my agreeable thoughts as to Mahmoud al Ackbar. I will put it to any of my readers who have travelled, whether it is not a painful thing to find one's-self regarded among strangers without any kindness or ceremonious courtesy. I had on this account been wretched at Cairo, but all this was to be made up to me at Suez. Nothing could be more pleasant than the whole conduct of Mahmoud al Ackbar, and I determined to take full advantage of it, not caring overmuch what might be the nature of those previous favours to which he had alluded. That was his look-out, and if he was satisfied, why should not I be so also?

On the following morning I was dressed at six, and, looking out of my bed-room, I saw the boat in which we were to be wafted into Asia being brought up to the quay close under my window. It had been arranged that we should start early, so as to avoid the midday sun, breakfast in the boat,—Mahmoud in this way engaged to provide me with two refections,—take our rest at noon in a pavilion which had been built close upon the well of the patriarch, and then eat our dinner, and return riding upon camels in the cool of the evening. Nothing could sound more pleasant than such a plan; and knowing as I did that the hampers of provisions had already been sent over, I did not doubt that the table arrangements would be excellent. Even now, standing at my window, I could see a basket laden with long-necked bottles going into the boat, and became aware that we should not depend altogether for our morning repast on that gritty coffee which my friend Mahmoud's followers prepared.

I had promised to be ready at six, and having carefully completed my toilet, and put a clean collar and comb into my pocket ready for dinner, I descended to the great gateway and walked slowly round to the quay. As I passed out, the porter greeted me with a low obeisance, and walking on, I felt that I stepped the ground with a sort of dignity of which I had before been ignorant. It is not, as a rule, the man who gives grace and honour to the position, but the position which confers the grace and honour upon the man. I have often envied the solemn gravity and grand demeanour of the Lord Chancellor, as I have seen him on the bench; but I almost think that even Judkins would look grave and dignified under such a wig. Mahmoud al Ackbar had called upon me and done me honour, and I felt myself personally capable of sustaining before the people of Suez the honour which he had done me.

As I walked forth with a proud step from beneath the portal, I perceived, looking down from the square along the street, that there was already some commotion in the town. I saw the flowing robes of many Arabs, with their backs turned towards me, and I thought that I observed the identical gown and turban of my friend Mahmoud on the back and head of a stout short man, who was hurrying round a corner in the distance. I felt sure that it was Mahmoud. Some of his servants had failed in their preparations, I said to myself, as I made my way round to the water's edge. This was only another testimony how anxious he was to do me honour.

I stood for a while on the edge of the quay looking into the boat, and admiring the comfortable cushions which were luxuriously arranged around the seats. The men who were at work did not know me, and I was unnoticed, but I should soon take my place upon the softest of those cushions. I walked slowly backwards and forwards on the quay, listening to a hum of voices that came to me from a distance. There was clearly something stirring in the town, and I felt certain that all the movement and all those distant voices were connected in some way with my expedition to the Well of Moses. At last there came a lad upon the walk dressed in Frank costume, and I asked him what was in the wind. He was a clerk attached to an English warehouse, and he told me that there had been an arrival from Cairo.

He knew no more than that, but he had heard that the omnibuses had just come in. Could it be possible that Mahmoud al Ackbar had heard of another old acquaintance, and had gone to welcome him also?

At first my ideas on the subject were altogether pleasant. I by no means wished to monopolise the delights of all those cushions, nor would it be to me a cause of sorrow that there should be some one to share with me the conversational powers of that interpreter. Should another guest be found, he might also be an Englishman, and I might thus form an acquaintance which would be desirable. Thinking of these things, I walked the quay for some minutes in a happy state of mind; but by degrees I became impatient, and by degrees also disturbed in my spirit. I observed that one of the Arab boatmen walked round from the vessel to the front of the hotel, and that on his return he looked at me—as I thought, not with courteous eyes. Then also I saw, or rather heard, some one in the verandah of the hotel above me, and was conscious that I was being viewed from thence. I walked and walked, and nobody came to me, and I perceived by my watch that it was seven o'clock. The noise, too, had come nearer and nearer, and I was now aware that wheels had been drawn up before the front door of the hotel, and that many voices were speaking there. It might be that Mahmoud should wait for some other friend, but why did he not send some one to inform me? And then, as I made a sudden turn at the end of the quay, I caught sight of the retreating legs of the Austrian interpreter, and I became aware that he had been sent down, and had gone away, afraid to speak to me. "What can I do?" said I to myself, "I can but keep my ground." I owned that I feared to go round to the front of the hotel. So I still walked slowly up and down the length of the quay, and began to whistle to show that I was not uneasy. The Arab sailors looked at me uncomfortably, and from time to time some one peered at me round the corner. It was now fully half-past seven, and the sun was becoming hot in the heavens. Why did we not hasten to place ourselves beneath the awning in that boat.

I had just made up my mind that I would go round to the front and penetrate this mystery, when, on turning, I saw approaching to me a man dressed at any rate like an English gentleman. As he came near to me, he raised his hat, and accosted me in our own language. "Mr. George Walker, I believe?" said he.

"Yes," said I, with some little attempt at a high demeanour,—"of the firm of Grimes, Walker, and Judkins, Friday Street, London."

"A most respectable house, I am sure," said he. "I am afraid there has been a little mistake here."

"No mistake as to the respectability of that house," said I. I felt that I was again alone in the world, and that it was necessary that I should support myself. Mahmoud al Ackbar had separated himself from me for ever. Of that I had no longer a doubt.

"Oh, none at all," said he. "But about this little expedition over the water;" and he pointed contemptuously to the boat. "There has been a mistake about that, Mr. Walker; I happen to be the English Vice-Consul here."

I took off my hat and bowed. It was the first time I had ever been addressed civilly by any English consular authority.

"And they have made me get out of bed to come down here and explain all this to you."

"All what?" said I.

"You are a man of the world, I know, and I'll just tell it you plainly. My old friend, Mahmoud al Ackbar, has mistaken you for Sir George Walker, the new Lieutenant-Governor of Pegu. Sir George Walker is here now; he has come this morning; and Mahmoud is ashamed to face you after what has occurred. If you won't object to withdraw with me into the hotel, I'll explain it all."

I felt as though a thunderbolt had fallen; and I must say, that even up to this day I think that the Consul might have been a little less abrupt. "We can get in here," said he, evidently in a hurry, and pointing to a small door which opened out from one corner of the house to the quay. What could I do but follow him? I did follow him, and in a few words learned the remainder of the story. When he had once withdrawn me from the public walk he seemed but little anxious about the rest, and soon left me again alone. The facts, as far as I could learn them, were simply these.

Sir George Walker, who was now going out to Pegu as Governor, had been in India before, commanding an army there. I had never heard of him before, and had made no attempt to pass myself off as his relative. Nobody could have been more innocent than I was—or have received worse usage. I have as much right to the name as he has. Well; when he was in India before, he had taken the city of Begum after a terrible siege—Begum, I think the Consul called it; and Mahmoud had been there, having been, it seems, a great man at Begum, and Sir George had spared him and his money; and in this way the whole thing had come to pass. There was no further explanation than that. The rest of it was all transparent. Mahmoud, having heard my name from the porter, had hurried down to invite me to his party. So far so good. But why had he been afraid to face me in the morning? And, seeing that the fault had all been his, why had he not asked me to join the expedition? Sir George and I may, after all, be cousins. But, coward as he was, he had been afraid of me. When they found that I was on the quay, they had been afraid of me, not knowing how to get rid of me. I wish that I had kept the quay all day, and stared them down one by one as they entered the boat. But I was down in the mouth, and when the Consul left me, I crept wearily back to my bedroom.

And the Consul did leave me almost immediately. A faint hope had, at one time, come upon me that he would have asked me to breakfast. Had he done so, I should have felt it as a full compensation for all that I had suffered. I am not an exacting man, but I own that I like civility. In Friday Street I can command it, and in Friday Street for the rest of my life will I remain. From this Consul I received no civility. As soon as he had got me out of the way and spoken the few words which he had to say, he again raised his hat and left me. I also again raised mine, and then crept up to my bed-room.

From my window, standing a little behind the white curtain, I could see the whole embarkation. There was Mahmoud al Ackbar, looking indeed a little hot, but still going through his work with all that excellence of deportment which had graced him on the preceding evening. Had his foot slipped, and had he fallen backwards into that shallow water, my spirit would, I confess, have been relieved. But, on the contrary, everything went well with him. There was the real Sir George, my namesake and perhaps my cousin, as fresh as paint, cool from the bath which he had been taking while I had been walking on that terrace. How is it that these governors and commanders-in-chief go through such a deal of work without fagging? It was not yet two hours since he was jolting about in that omnibus-box, and there he had been all night. I could not have gone off to the Well of Moses immediately on my arrival. It's the dignity of the position that does it. I have long known that the head of a firm must never count on a mere clerk to get through as much work as he could do himself. It's the interest in the matter that supports the man.

They went, and Sir George, as I was well assured, had never heard a word about me. Had he done so, is it probable that he would have requested my attendance?

But Mahmoud and his followers no doubt kept their own counsel as to that little mistake. There they went, and the gentle rippling breeze filled their sail pleasantly, as the boat moved away into the bay. I felt no spite against any of them but Mahmoud. Why had he avoided me with such cowardice? I could still see them when the morning tchibouk was handed to Sir George; and, though I wished him no harm, I did envy him as he lay there reclining luxuriously upon the cushions.

A more wretched day than that I never spent in my life. As I went in and out, the porter at the gate absolutely scoffed at me. Once I made up my mind to complain within the house. But what could I have said of the dirty Arab? They would have told me that it was his religion, or a national observance, or meant for a courtesy. What can a man do, in a strange country, when he is told that a native spits in his face by way of civility? I bore it, I bore it—like a man; and sighed for the comforts of Friday Street.

As to one matter, I made up my mind on that day, and I fully carried out my purpose on the next: I would go across to the Well of Moses in a boat. I would visit the coasts of Asia. And I would ride back into Africa on a camel. Though I did it alone, I would have my day's pleasuring. I had money in my pocket, and, though it might cost me 20 pounds, I would see all that my namesake had seen. It did cost me the best part of 20 pounds; and as for the pleasuring, I cannot say much for it.

I went to bed early that night, having concluded my bargain for the morrow with a rapacious Arab who spoke English. I went to bed early in order to escape the returning party, and was again on the quay at six the next morning. On this occasion, I stepped boldly into the boat the very moment that I came along the shore. There is nothing in the world like paying for what you use. I saw myself to the bottle of brandy and the cold meat, and acknowledged that a cigar out of my own case would suit me better than that long stick. The long stick might do very well for a Governor of Pegu, but would be highly inconvenient in Friday Street.

Well, I am not going to give an account of my day's journey here, though perhaps I may do so some day. I did go to the Well of Moses—if a small dirty pool of salt water, lying high above the sands, can be called a well; I did eat my dinner in the miserable ruined cottage which they graced by the name of a pavilion; and, alas for my poor bones! I did ride home upon a camel. If Sir George did so early, and started for Pegu the next morning—and I was informed such was the fact—he must have been made of iron. I laid in bed the whole day suffering greviously; but I was told that on such a journey I should have slakened my throat with oranges, and not with brandy.

I survived those four terrible days which remained to me at Suez, and after another month was once again in Friday Street. I suffered greatly on the occasion; but it is some consolation to me to reflect that I smoked a pipe of peace with Mahmoud al Ackbar; that I saw the hero of Begum while journeying out to new triumphs at Pegu; that I sailed into Asia in my own yacht—hired for the occasion; and that I rode back into Africa on a camel. Nor can Judkins, with all his ill-nature, rob me of these remembrances.

THE HOUSE OF HEINE BROTHERS, IN MUNICH

The house of Heine Brothers, in Munich, was of good repute at the time of which I am about to tell,—a time not long ago; and is so still, I trust. It was of good repute in its own way, seeing that no man doubted the word or solvency of Heine Brothers; but they did not possess, as bankers, what would in England be considered a large or profitable business. The operations of English bankers are bewildering in their magnitude. Legions of clerks are employed. The senior book-keepers, though only salaried servants, are themselves great men; while the real partners are inscrutable, mysterious, opulent beyond measure, and altogether unknown to their customers. Take any firm at random,—Brown, Jones, and Cox, let us say,—the probability is that Jones has been dead these fifty years, that Brown is a Cabinet Minister, and that Cox is master of a pack of hounds in Leicestershire. But it was by no means so with the house of Heine Brothers, of Munich. There they were, the two elderly men, daily to be seen at their dingy office in the Schrannen Platz; and if any business was to be transacted requiring the interchange of more than a word or two, it was the younger brother with whom the customer was, as a matter of course, brought into contact. There were three clerks in the establishment; an old man, namely, who sat with the elder brother and had no personal dealings with the public; a young Englishman, of whom we shall anon hear more; and a boy who ran messages, put the wood on to the stoves, and swept out the bank. Truly he house of Heine Brothers was of no great importance; but nevertheless it was of good repute.

The office, I have said, was in the Schrannen Platz, or old Market-place. Munich, as every one knows, is chiefly to be noted as a new town,—so new that many of the streets and most of the palaces look as though they had been sent home last night from the builders, and had only just been taken out of their bandboxes It is angular, methodical, unfinished, and palatial. But there is an old town; and, though the old town be not of surpassing interest, it is as dingy, crooked, intricate, and dark as other old towns in Germany. Here, in the old Market-place, up one long broad staircase, were situated the two rooms in which was held the bank of Heine Brothers.

Of the elder member of the firm we shall have something to say before this story be completed. He was an old bachelor, and was possessed of a bachelor's dwelling somewhere out in the suburbs of the city. The junior brother was a married man, with a wife some twenty years younger than himself, with two daughters, the elder of whom was now one-and-twenty, and one son. His name was Ernest Heine, whereas the senior brother was known as Uncle Hatto. Ernest Heine and his wife inhabited a portion of one of those new palatial residences at the further end of the Ludwigs Strasse; but not because they thus lived must it be considered that they were palatial people. By no means let it be so thought, as such an idea would altogether militate against whatever truth of character painting there may be in this tale. They were not palatial people, but the very reverse, living in homely guise, pursuing homely duties, and satisfied with homely pleasures. Up two pairs of stairs, however, in that street of palaces, they lived, having there a commodious suite of large rooms, furnished, after the manner of the Germans, somewhat gaudily as regarded their best salon, and with somewhat meagre comfort as regarded their other rooms. But, whether in respect of that which was meagre, or whether in respect of that which was gaudy, they were as well off as their neighbours; and this, as I take it, is the point of excellence which is desirable.

Ernest Heine was at this time over sixty; his wife was past forty; and his eldest daughter, as I have said, was twenty-one years of age. His second child, also a girl, was six years younger; and their third child, a boy, had not been born till another similar interval had elapsed. He was named Hatto after his uncle, and the two girls had been christened Isa and Agnes. Such, in number and mode of life, was the family of the Heines.

We English folk are apt to imagine that we are nearer akin to Germans than to our other continental neighbours. This may be so in blood, but, nevertheless, the difference in manners is so striking, that it could hardly be enhanced. An Englishman moving himself off to a city in the middle of Central America will find the customs to which he must adapt himself less strange to him there, than he would in many a German town. But in no degree of life is the difference more remarkable than among unmarried but marriageable young women. It is not my purpose at the present moment to attribute a superiority in this matter to either nationality. Each has its own charm, its own excellence, its own Heaven-given grace, whereby men are led up to purer thoughts and sweet desires; and each may possibly have its own defect. I will not here describe the excellence or defect of either; but will, if it be in my power, say a word as to this difference. The German girl of one-and-twenty,—our Isa's age,—is more sedate, more womanly, more meditative than her English sister. The world's work is more in her thoughts, and the world's amusements less so. She probably knows less of those things which women learn than the English girl, but that which she does know is nearer to her hand for use. She is not so much accustomed to society, but nevertheless she is more mistress of her own manner. She is not taught to think so much of those things which flurry and disturb the mind, and therefore she is seldom flurried and disturbed. To both of them, love,—the idea of love,—must be the thought of all the most absorbing; for is it not fated for them that the joys and sorrows of their future life must depend upon it? But the idea of the German girl is the more realistic, and the less romantic. Poetry and fiction she may have read, though of the latter sparingly; but they will not have imbued her with that hope for some transcendental paradise of affection which so often fills and exalts the hearts of our daughters here at home. She is moderate in her aspirations, requiring less excitement than an English girl; and never forgetting the solid necessities of life,—as they are so often forgotten here in England. In associating with young men, an English girl will always remember that in each one she so meets she may find an admirer whom she may possibly love, or an admirer whom she may probably be called on to repel. She is ever conscious of the fact of this position; and a romance is thus engendered which, if it may at times be dangerous, is at any rate always charming. But the German girl, in her simplicity, has no such consciousness. As you and I, my reader, might probably become dear friends were we to meet and know each other, so may the German girl learn to love the fair-haired youth with whom chance has for a time associated her; but to her mind there occurs no suggestive reason why it should be so,—no probability that the youth may regard her in such light, because that chance has come to pass. She can therefore give him her hand without trepidation, and talk with him for half an hour, when called on to do so, as calmly as she might do with his sister.

Such a one was Isa Heine at the time of which I am writing. We English, in our passion for daily excitement, might call her phlegmatic, but we should call her so unjustly. Life to her was a serious matter, of which the daily duties and daily wants were sufficient to occupy her thoughts. She was her mother's companion, the instructress of both her brother and her sister, and the charm of her father's vacant hours. With such calls upon her time, and so many realities around her, her imagination did not teach her to look for joys beyond those of her present life and home. When love and marriage should come to her, as come they probably might, she would endeavour to attune herself to a new happiness and a new sphere of duties. In the meantime she was contented to keep her mother's accounts, and look after her brother and sister up two pair of stairs in the Ludwigs Strasse. But change would certainly come, we may prophesy; for Isa Heine was a beautiful girl, tall and graceful, comely to the eye, and fit in every way to be loved and cherished as the partner of a man's home.

I have said that an English clerk made a part of that small establishment in the dingy banking-office in the Schrannen Platz, and I must say a word or two of Herbert Onslow. In his early career he had not been fortunate. His father, with means sufficiently moderate, and with a family more than sufficiently large, had sent him to a public school at which he had been very idle, and then to one of the universities, at which he had run into debt, and had therefore left without a degree. When this occurred, a family council of war had been held among the Onslows, and it was decided that Herbert should be sent off to the banking-house of Heines, at Munich, there being a cousinship between the families, and some existing connections of business.

It was, therefore, so settled; and Herbert, willing enough to see the world,—as he considered he should do by going to Munich,—started for his German home, with injunctions, very tender from his mother, and very solemn from his aggrieved father. But there was nothing bad at the heart about young Onslow, and if the solemn father had well considered it, he might perhaps have felt that those debts at Cambridge reflected more fault on him than on his son. When Herbert arrived at Munich, his cousins, the Heines,—faraway cousins though they were,—behaved kindly to him. They established him at first in lodgings, where he was boarded with many others, having heard somewhat of his early youth. But when Madame Heine, at the end of twelve months, perceived that he was punctual at the bank, and that his allowances, which, though moderate in England, were handsome in Munich, carried him on without debt, she opened her motherly arms and suggested to his mother and to himself, that he should live with them. In this way he also was domiciled up two pairs of stairs in the palatial residence in the Ludwigs Strasse.

But all this happened long ago. Isa Heine had been only seventeen when her cousin had first come to Munich, and had made acquaintance with him rather as a child than as a woman. And when, as she ripened into womanhood, this young man came more closely among them, it did not strike her that the change would affect her more powerfully than it would the others. Her uncle and father, she knew, had approved of Herbert at the bank; and Herbert had shown that he could be steady; therefore he was to be taken into their family, paying his annual subsidy, instead of being left with strangers at the boarding-house. All this was very simple to her. She assisted in mending his linen, as she did her father's; she visited his room daily, as she visited all the others; she took notice of his likings and dislikings as touching their table arrangement,—but by no means such notice as she did of her father's; and without any flutter, inwardly in her imagination or outwardly as regarded the world, she made him one of the family. So things went on for a year,—nay, so things went on for two years with her, after Herbert Onslow had come to the Ludwigs Strasse.

But the matter had been regarded in a very different light by Herbert himself. When the proposition had been made to him, his first idea had been that so close a connection with, a girl so very pretty would be delightful. He had blushed as he had given in his adhesion; but Madame Heine, when she saw the blush, had attributed it to anything but the true cause. When Isa had asked him as to his wants and wishes, he had blushed again, but she had been as ignorant as her mother. The father had merely stipulated that, as the young Englishman paid for his board, he should have the full value of his money, so that Isa and Agnes gave up their pretty front room, going into one that was inferior, and Hatto was put to sleep in the little closet that had been papa's own peculiar property. But nobody complained of this, for it was understood that the money was of service.

For the first year Herbert found that nothing especial happened. He always fancied that he was in love with Isa, and wrote some poetry about her. But the poetry was in English, and Isa could not read it, even had he dared to show it to her. During the second year he went home to England for three months, and by confessing a passion to one of his sisters, really brought himself to feel one. He returned to Munich resolved to tell Isa that the possibility of his remaining there depended upon her acceptance of his heart; but for months he did not find himself able to put his resolution in force. She was so sedate, so womanly, so attentive as regarded cousinly friendship, and so cold as regarded everything else, that he did not know how to speak to her. With an English girl whom he had met three times at a ball, he might have been much more able to make progress. He was alone with Isa frequently, for neither father, mother, nor Isa herself objected to such communion; but yet things so went between them that he could not take her by the hand and tell her that he loved her. And thus the third year of his life in Munich, and the second of his residence in the Ludwigs Strasse, went by him. So the years went by, and Isa was now past twenty. To Herbert, in his reveries, it seemed as though life, and the joys of life, were slipping away from him. But no such feeling disturbed any of the Heines. Life of course, was slipping away; but then is it not the destiny of man that life should slip away? Their wants were all satisfied, and for them, that, together with their close family affection, was happiness enough.

At last, however, Herbert so spoke, or so looked, that both Isa and her mother that his heart was touched. He still declared to himself that he had made no sign, and that he was an oaf, an ass, a coward, in that he had not done so. But he had made some sign, and the sign had been read. There was no secret,—no necessity for a secret on the subject between the mother and daughter, but yet it was not spoken of all at once. There was some little increase of caution between them as Herbert's name was mentioned, so that gradually each knew what the other thought; but for weeks, that was all. Then at last the mother spoke out.

"Isa," she said, "I think that Herbert Onslow is becoming attached to you."

"He has never said so, mamma."

"No; I am sure he has not. Had he done so, you would have told me. Nevertheless, is it not true?"

"Well, mamma, I cannot say. It may be so. Such an idea has occurred to me, but I have abandoned it as needless. If he has anything to say he will say it."

"And if he were to speak, how should you answer him?"

"I should take time to think. I do not at all know what means he has for a separate establishment." Then the subject was dropped between them for that time, and Isa, in her communications with her cousin, was somewhat more reserved than she had been.

"Isa, are you in love with Herbert?" Agnes asked her, as they were together in their room one night.

"In love with him? No; why should I be in love with him?"

"I think he is in love with you," said Agnes.

"That is quite another thing," said Isa, laughing. "But if so, he has not taken me into his confidence. Perhaps he has you."

"Oh no. He would not do that, I think. Not but what we are great friends, and I love him dearly. Would it not be nice for you and him to be betrothed?"

"That depends on many things, my dear."

"Oh yes, I know. Perhaps he has not got money enough. But you could live here, you know, and he has got some money, because he so often rides on horseback." And then the matter was dropped between the two sisters.

Herbert had given English lessons to the two girls, but the lessons had been found tedious, and had dwindled away. Isa, nevertheless, had kept up her exercises, duly translating German into English, and English into German; and occasionally she had shown them to her cousin. Now, however, she altogether gave over such showing of them, but, nevertheless, worked at the task with more energy than before.

"Isa," he said to her one day,—having with some difficulty found her alone in the parlour, "Isa, why should not we go on with our English?"

"Because it is troublesome,—to you I mean."

"Troublesome. Well; yes; it is troublesome. Nothing good is to be had without trouble. But I should like it if you would not mind."

"You know how sick you were of it before;—besides, I shall never be able to speak it."

"I shall not get sick of it now, Isa."

"Oh yes you would;—in two days."

"And I want you to speak it. I desire it especially."

"Why especially?" asked Isa. And even she, with all her tranquillity of demeanour, could hardly preserve her even tone and quiet look, as she asked the necessary question.

"I will tell you why," said Herbert; and as he spoke, he got up from his seat, and took a step or two over towards her, where she was sitting near the window. Isa, as she saw him, still continued her work, and strove hard to give to the stitches all that attention which they required. "I will tell you why I would wish you to talk my language. Because I love you, Isa, and would have you for my wife,—if that be possible."

She still continued her work, and the stitches, if not quite as perfect as usual, sufficed for their purpose.

"That is why I wish it. Now will you consent to learn from me again?"

"If I did, Herbert, that consent would include another."

"Yes; certainly it would. That is what I intend. And now will you learn from me again?"

"That is,—you mean to ask, will I marry you?"

"Will you love me? Can you learn to love me? Oh, Isa, I have thought of this so long! But you have seemed so cold that I have not dared to speak. Isa, can you love me?" And he sat himself close beside her. Now that the ice was broken, he was quite prepared to become an ardent lover,—if she would allow of such ardour. But as he sat down she rose.

"I cannot answer such a question on the sudden," she said. "Give me till tomorrow, Herbert, and then I will make you a reply;" whereupon she left him, and he stood alone in the room, having done the deed on which he had been meditating for the last two years. About half an hour afterwards he met her on the stairs as he was going to his chamber. "May I speak to your father about this," he said, hardly stopping her as he asked the question. "Oh yes; surely," she answered; and then again they parted. To him this last-accorded permission sounded as though it carried with it more weight than it in truth possessed. In his own country a reference to the lady's father is taken as indicating a full consent on the lady's part, should the stern paterfamilias raise no objection. But Isa had no such meaning. She had told him that she could not give her answer till the morrow. If, however, he chose to consult her father on the subject, she had no objection. It would probably be necessary that she should discuss the whole matter in family conclave, before she could bring herself to give any reply.

On that night, before he went to bed, he did speak to her father; and Isa also, before she went to rest, spoke to her mother. It was singular to him that there should appear to be so little privacy on the subject; that there should be held to be so little necessity for a secret. Had he made a suggestion that an extra room should be allotted to him at so much per annum, the proposition could not have been discussed with simpler ease. At last, after a three days' debate, the matter ended thus,—with by no means a sufficiency of romance for his taste. Isa had agreed to become his betrothed if certain pecuniary conditions should or could be fulfilled. It appeared now that Herbert's father had promised that some small modicum of capital should be forthcoming after a term of years, and that Heine Brothers had agreed that the Englishman should have a proportionate share in the bank when that promise should be brought to bear. Let it not be supposed that Herbert would thus become a millionaire. If all went well, the best would be that some three hundred a year would accrue to him from the bank, instead of the quarter of that income which he at present received. But three hundred a year goes a long way at Munich, and Isa's parents were willing that she should be Herbert's wife if such an income should be forthcoming.

But even of this there was much doubt. Application to Herbert's father could not be judiciously made for some months. The earliest period at which, in accordance with old Hatto Heine's agreement, young Onslow might be admitted to the bank, was still distant by four years; and the present moment was thought to be inopportune for applying to him for any act of grace. Let them wait, said papa and mamma Heine,—at any rate till New Year's Day, then ten months distant. Isa quietly said that she would wait till New Year's Day. Herbert fretted, fumed, and declared that he was ill-treated. But in the end he also agreed to wait. What else could he do?

"But we shall see each other daily, and be close to each other," he said to Isa, looking tenderly into her eyes. "Yes," she replied, "we shall see each other daily—of course. But, Herbert—"

Herbert looked up at her and paused for her to go on.

"I have promised mamma that there shall be no change between us,—in our manner to each other, I mean. We are not betrothed as yet, you know, and perhaps we may never be so."

"Isa!"

"It may not be possible, you know. And therefore we will go on as before. Of course we shall see each other, and of course we shall be friends."

Herbert Onslow again fretted and again fumed, but he did not have his way. He had looked forward to the ecstasies of a lover's life, but very few of those ecstasies were awarded to him. He rarely found himself alone with Isa, and when he did do so, her coldness overawed him. He could dare to scold her and sometimes did do so, but he could not dare to take the slightest liberty. Once, on that night when the qualified consent of papa and mamma Heine had first been given, he had been allowed to touch her lips with his own; but since that day there had been for him no such delight as that. She would not even allow her hand to remain in his. When they all passed their evenings together in the beer-garden, she would studiously manage that his chair should not be close to her own. Occasionally she would walk with him, but not more frequently now than of yore. Very few, indeed, of a lover's privileges did he enjoy. And in this way the long year wore itself out, and Isa Heine was one-and-twenty.

All those family details which had made it inexpedient to apply either to old Hatto or to Herbert's father before the end of the year need not be specially explained. Old Hatto, who had by far the greater share in the business, was a tyrant somewhat feared both by his brother and sister-in-law; and the elder Onslow, as was known to them all, was a man straitened in circumstances. But soon after New Year's Day the proposition was made in the Schrannen Platz, and the letter was written. On this occasion Madame Heine went down to the bank, and together with her husband, was closeted for an hour with old Hatto. Uncle Hatto's verdict was not favourable. As to the young people's marriage, that was his brother's affair, not his. But as to the partnership, that was a serious matter. Who ever heard of a partnership being given away merely because a man wanted to marry? He would keep to his promise, and if the stipulated moneys were forthcoming, Herbert Onslow should become a partner,—in four years. Nor was the reply from England more favourable. The alliance was regarded by all the Onslows very favourably. Nothing could be nicer than such a marriage! They already knew dear Isa so well by description! But as for the money,—that could not in any way be forthcoming till the end of the stipulated period.

"And what shall we do?" said Herbert to Papa Heine.

"You must wait," said he.

"For four years?" asked Herbert.

"You must wait,—as I did," said Papa Heine. "I was forty before I could marry." Papa Heine, however, should not have forgotten to say that his bride was only twenty, and that if he had waited, she had not.

"Isa," Herbert said to her, when all this had been fully explained to her, "what do you say now?"

"Of course it is all over," said she, very calmly.

"Oh, Isa, is that your love?"

"No, Herbert, that is not my love; that is my discretion;" and she even laughed with her mild low laughter, as she answered him. "You know you are too impatient to wait four years, and what else therefore can I say?"

"I wonder whether you love me?" said Herbert, with a grand look of injured sentiment.

"Well; in your sense of the word I do not think I do. I do not love you so that I need make every one around us unhappy because circumstances forbid me to marry you. That sort of love would be baneful."

"Ah no, you do not know what love means!"

"Not your boisterous, heartbreaking English love, Herbert. And, Herbert, sometimes I think you had better go home and look for a bride there. Though you fancy that you love me, in your heart you hardly approve of me."

"Fancy that I love you! Do you think, Isa, that a man can carry his heart round to one customer after another as the huckster carries his wares?"

"Yes; I think he can. I know that men do. What did your hero Waverley do with his heart in that grand English novel which you gave me to read? I am not Flora Mac Ivor, but you may find a Rose Bradwardine."

"And you really wish me to do so?"

"Look here, Herbert. It is bad to boast, but I will make this boast. I am so little selfish, that I desire above all that you should do that which may make you most happy and contented. I will be quite frank with you. I love you well enough to wait these four years with the hope of becoming your wife when they are over. But you will think but little of my love when I tell you that this waiting would not make me unhappy. I should go on as I do now, and be contented."

"Oh heavens!" sighed Herbert.

"But as I know that this would not suit you,—as I feel sure that such delay would gall you every day, as I doubt whether it would not make you sick of me long before the four years be over,—my advice is, that we should let this matter drop."

He now walked up to her and took her hand, and as he did so there was something in his gait and look and tone of voice that stirred her heart more sharply than it had yet been stirred. "And even that would not make you unhappy," he said.

She paused before she replied, leaving her hand in his, for he was contented to hold it without peculiar pressure. "I will not say so," she replied. "But, Herbert, I think that you press me too hard. Is it not enough that I leave you to be the arbiter of my destiny?"

"I would learn the very truth of your heart," he replied.

"I cannot tell you that truth more plainly. Methinks I have told it too plainly already. If you wish it, I will hold myself as engaged to you,—to be married to you when those four years are past. But, remember, I do not advise it. If you wish it, you shall have back your troth. And that I think will be the wiser course."

But neither alternative contented Herbert Onslow, and at the time he did not resolve on either. He had some little present income from home, some fifty pounds a year or so, and he would be satisfied to marry on that and on his salary as a clerk; but to this papa and mamma Heine would not consent;—neither would Isa.

"You are not a saving, close man," she said to him when he boasted of his economies. "No Englishmen are. You could not live comfortably in two small rooms, and with bad dinners."

"I do not care a straw about my dinners."

"Not now that you are a lover, but you would do when you were a husband. And you change your linen almost every day."

"Bah!"

"Yes; bah, if you please. But I know what these things cost. You had better go to England and fetch a rich wife. Then you will become a partner at once, and Uncle Hatto won't snub you. And you will be a grand man, and have a horse to ride on." Whereupon Herbert went away in disgust. Nothing in all this made him so unhappy as the feeling that Isa, under all their joint privations, would not be unhappy herself. As far as he could see, all this made no difference in Isa.

But, in truth, he had not yet read Isa's character very thoroughly. She had spoken truly in saying that she knew nothing of that boisterous love which was now tormenting him and making him gloomy; but nevertheless she loved him. She, in her short life, had learnt many lessons of self-denial; and now with reference to this half-promised husband she would again have practised such a lesson. Had he agreed at once to go from her, she would have balanced her own account within her own breast, and have kept to herself all her sufferings. There would have been no outward show of baffled love,—none even in the colour of her cheeks; for such was the nature of her temperament. But she did suffer for him. Day by day she began to think that his love, though boisterous as she had at first called it, was more deep-seated than she had believed. He made no slightest sign that he would accept any of those proffers which she had made him of release. Though he said so loudly that this waiting for four years was an impossibility, he spoke of no course that would be more possible,—except that evidently impossible course of an early marriage. And thus, while he with redoubled vehemence charged her with coolness and want of love, her love waxed warmer and warmer, and his happiness became the chief object of her thoughts. What could she do that he might no longer suffer?

And then he took a step which was very strange to them all. He banished himself altogether from the house, going away again into lodgings. "No," he said, on the morning of his departure, "I do not release you. I will never release you. You are mine, and I have a right so to call you. If you choose to release yourself, I cannot help it; but in doing so you will be forsworn."

"Nay, but, Herbert, I have sworn to nothing," said she, meaning that she had not been formally betrothed to him.

"You can do as you please; it is a matter of conscience; but I tell you what are my feelings. Here I cannot stay, for I should go mad; but I shall see you occasionally;—perhaps on Sundays."

"Oh, Herbert!"

"Well, what would you have? If you really cared to see me it would not be thus. All I ask of you now is this, that if you decide,— absolutely decide on throwing me over, you will tell me at once. Then I shall leave Munich."

"Herbert, I will never throw you over." So they parted, and Onslow went forth to his new lodgings.

Her promise that she would never throw him over was the warmest word of love that she had ever spoken, but even that was said in her own quiet, unimpassioned way. There was in it but very little show of love, though there might be an assurance of constancy. But her constancy he did not, in truth, much doubt. Four years,—fourteen,—or twenty-four, would be the same to her, he said, as he seated himself in the dull, cold room which he had chosen. While living in the Ludwigs Strasse he did not know how much had been daily done for his comfort by that hand which he had been so seldom allowed to press; but he knew that he was now cold and comfortless, and he wished himself back in the Ludwigs Strasse.

"Mamma," said Isa, when they were alone. "Is not Uncle Hatto rather hard on us? Papa said that he would ask this as a favour from his brother."

"So he did, my dear; and offered to give up more of his own time. But your Uncle Hatto is hard."

"He is rich, is he not?"

"Well; your father says not. Your father says that he spends all his income. Though he is hard and obstinate, he is not selfish. He is very good to the poor, but I believe he thinks that early marriages are very foolish."

"Mamma," said Isa again, when they had sat for some minutes in silence over their work.

"Well, my love?"

"Have you spoken to Uncle Hatto about this?"

"No, dear; not since that day when your papa and I first went to him. To tell the truth, I am almost afraid to speak to him; but, if you wish it, I will do so."

"I do wish it, mamma. But you must not think that I am discontented or impatient. I do not know that I have any right to ask my uncle for his money;—for it comes to that."

"I suppose it does, my dear."

"And as for myself, I am happy here with you and papa. I do not think so much of these four years."

"You would still be young, Isa;—quite young enough."

"And what if I were not young? What does it matter? But, mamma, there has been that between Herbert and me which makes me feel myself bound to think of him. As you and papa have sanctioned it, you are bound to think of him also. I know that he is unhappy, living there all alone."

"But why did he go, dear?"

"I think he was right to go. I could understand his doing that. He is not like us, and would have been fretful here, wanting that which I could not give him. He became worse from day to day, and was silent and morose. I am glad he went. But, mamma, for his sake I wish that this could be shortened."

Madame Heine told her daughter that she would, if Isa wished it, herself go to the Schrannen Platz, and see what could be done by talking to Uncle Hatto. "But," she added, "I fear that no good will come of it."

"Can harm come, mamma?"

"No, I do not think harm can come."

"I'll tell you what, mamma, I will go to Uncle Hatto myself, if you will let me. He is cross I know; but I shall not be afraid of him. I feel that I ought to do something." And so the matter was settled, Madame Heine being by no means averse to escape a further personal visit to the Head of the banking establishment.

Madame Heine well understood what her daughter meant, when she said she ought to do something, though Isa feared that she had imperfectly expressed her meaning. When he, Herbert, was willing to do so much to prove his love,—when he was ready to sacrifice all the little comforts of comparative wealth to which he had been accustomed, in order that she might be his companion and wife,—did it not behove her to give some proof of her love also? She could not be demonstrative as he was. Such exhibition of feeling would be quite contrary to her ideas of female delicacy, and to her very nature. But if called on to work for him, that she could do as long as strength remained to her. But there was no sacrifice which would be of service, nor any work which would avail. Therefore she was driven to think what she might do on his behalf, and at last she resolved to make her personal appeal to Uncle Hatto.

"Shall I tell papa?" Isa asked of her mother.

"I will do so," said Madame Heine. And then the younger member of the firm was informed as to the step which was to be taken; and he, though he said nothing to forbid the attempt, held out no hope that it would be successful.

Uncle Hatto was a little snuffy man, now full seventy years of age, who passed seven hours of every week-day of his life in the dark back chamber behind the banking-room of the firm, and he had so passed every week-day of his life for more years than any of the family could now remember. He had made the house what it was, and had taken his brother into partnership when that brother married. All the family were somewhat afraid of him, including even his partner. He rarely came to the apartments in the Ludwigs Strasse, as he himself lived in one of the older and shabbier suburbs on the other side of the town. Thither he always walked, starting punctually from the bank at four o'clock, and from thence he always walked in the morning, reaching the bank punctually at nine. His two nieces knew him well; for on certain stated days they were wont to attend on him at his lodgings, where they would be regaled with cakes, and afterwards go with him to some old-fashioned beer-garden in his neighbourhood. But these festivities were of a sombre kind; and if, on any occasion, circumstances prevented the fulfilment of the ceremony, neither of the girls would be loud in their lamentations.

In London, a visit paid by a niece to her uncle would, in all probability, be made at the uncle's private residence; but at Munich private and public matters were not so effectually divided. Isa therefore, having put on her hat and shawl, walked off by herself to the Schrannen Platz.

"Is Uncle Hatto inside?" she asked; and the answer was given to her by her own lover. Yes, he was within; but the old clerk was with him. Isa, however, signified her wish to see her uncle alone, and in a few minutes the ancient grey-haired servant of the house came out into the larger room.

"You can go in now, Miss Isa," he said. And Isa found herself in the presence of her uncle before she had been two minutes under the roof. In the mean time Ernest Heine, her father, had said not a word, and Herbert knew that something very special must be about to occur.

"Well, my bonny bird," said Uncle Hatto, "and what do you want at the bank?" Cheery words, such as these, were by no means uncommon with Uncle Hatto; but Isa knew very well that no presage could be drawn from them of any special good nature or temporary weakness on his part.

"Uncle Hatto," she began, rushing at once into the middle of her affair, "you know, I believe, that I am engaged to marry Herbert Onslow?"

"I know no such thing," said he. "I thought I understood your father specially to say that there had been no betrothal."

"No, Uncle Hatto, there has been no betrothal; that certainly is true; but, nevertheless, we are engaged to each other."

"Well," said Uncle Hatto, very sourly; and now there was no longer any cheery tone, or any calling of pretty names.

"Perhaps you may think all this very foolish," said Isa, who, spite of her resolves to do so, was hardly able to look up gallantly into her uncle's face as she thus talked of her own love affairs.

"Yes, I do," said Uncle Hatto. "I do think it foolish for young people to hold themselves betrothed before they have got anything to live on, and so I have told your father. He answered me by saying that you were not betrothed."

"Nor are we. Papa is quite right in that."

"Then, my dear, I would advise you to tell the young man that, as neither of you have means of your own, the thing must be at an end. It is the only step for you to take. If you agreed to wait, one of you might die, or his money might never be forth coming, or you might see somebody else that you liked better."

"I don't think I shall do that."

"You can't tell. And if you don't, the chances are ten to one that he will."

This little blow, which was intended to be severe, did not hit Isa at all hard. That plan of a Rose Bradwardine she herself had proposed in good faith, thinking that she could endure such a termination to the affair without flinching. She was probably wrong in this estimate of her power; but, nevertheless, her present object was his release from unhappiness and doubt, not her own.

"It might be so," she said.

"Take my word for it, it would. Look all around. There was Adelaide Schropner,—but that was before your time, and you would not remember." Considering that Adelaide Schropner had been for many years a grandmother, it was probable that Isa would not remember.

"But, Uncle Hatto, you have not heard me. I want to say something to you, if it will not take too much of your time." In answer to which, Uncle Hatto muttered something which was unheeded, to signify that Isa might speak.

"I also think that a long engagement is a foolish thing, and so does Herbert."

"But he wants to marry at once."

"Yes, he wants to marry—perhaps not at once, but soon."

"And I suppose you have come to say that you want the same thing."

Isa blushed ever so faintly as she commenced her answer. "Yes, uncle, I do wish the same thing. What he wishes, I wish."

"Very likely,—very likely."

"Don't be scornful to me, uncle. When two people love each other, it is natural that each should wish that which the other earnestly desires."

"Oh, very natural, my dear, that you should wish to get married!"

"Uncle Hatto, I did not think that you would be unkind to me, though I knew that you would be stern."

"Well, go on. What have you to say? I am not stern; but I have no doubt you will think me unkind. People are always unkind who do not do what they are asked."

"Papa says that Herbert Onslow is some day to become a partner in the bank."

"That depends on certain circumstances. Neither I nor your papa can say whether he will or no."

But Isa went on as though she had not heard the last reply. "I have come to ask you to admit him as a partner at once."

"Ah, I supposed so;—just as you might ask me to give you a new ribbon."

"But, uncle, I never did ask you to give me a new ribbon. I never asked you to give me anything for myself; nor do I ask this for myself."

"Do you think that if I could do it,—which of course I can't,—I would not sooner do it for you, who are my own flesh and blood, than for him, who is a stranger?"

"Nay; he is no stranger. He has sat at your desk and obeyed your orders for nearly four years. Papa says that he has done well in the bank."

"Humph! If every clerk that does well,—pretty well, that is,—wanted a partnership, where should we be, my dear? No, my dear, go home and tell him when you see him in the evening that all this must be at an end. Men's places in the world are not given away so easily as that. They must either be earned or purchased. Herbert Onslow has as yet done neither, and therefore he is not entitled to take a wife. I should have been glad to have had a wife at his age,—at least I suppose I should, but at any rate I could not afford it."

But Isa had by no means as yet done. So far the interview had progressed exactly as she had anticipated. She had never supposed it possible that her uncle would grant her so important a request as soon as she opened her mouth to ask it. She had not for a moment expected that things would go so easily with her. Indeed she had never expected that any success would attend her efforts; but, if any success were possible, the work which must achieve that success must now commence. It was necessary that she should first state her request plainly before she began to urge it with such eloquence as she had at her command.

"I can understand what you say, Uncle Hatto."

"I am glad of that, at any rate."

"And I know that I have no right to ask you for anything."

"I do not say that. Anything in reason, that a girl like you should ask of her old uncle, I would give you."

"I have no such reasonable request to make, uncle. I have never wanted new ribbons from you or gay toys. Even from my own mother I have not wanted them;—not wanted them faster than they seemed to come without any asking."

"No, no; you have been a good girl."

"I have been a happy girl; and quite happy with those I loved, and with what Providence had given me. I had nothing to ask for. But now I am no longer happy, nor can I be unless you do for me this which I ask of you. I have wanted nothing till now, and now in my need I come to you."

"And now you want a husband with a fortune!"

"No!" and that single word she spoke, not loudly, for her voice was low and soft, but with an accent which carried it sharply to his ear and to his brain. And then she rose from her seat as she went on. "Your scorn, uncle, is unjust,—unjust and untrue. I have ever acted maidenly, as has become my mother's daughter."

"Yes, yes, yes;—I believe that."

"And I can say more than that for myself. My thoughts have been the same, nor have my wishes even, ever gone beyond them. And when this young man came to me, telling me of his feelings, I gave him no answer till I had consulted my mother."

"She should have bade you not to think of him."

"Ah, you are not a mother, and cannot know. Why should I not think of him when he was good and kind, honest and hardworking? And then he had thought of me first. Why should I not think of him? Did not mamma listen to my father when he came to her?"

"But your father was forty years old, and had a business."

"You gave it him, Uncle Hatto. I have heard him say."

"And therefore I am to do as much for you. And then next year Agnes will come to me; and so before I die I shall see you all in want, with large families. No, Isa; I will not scorn you, but this thing I cannot do."

"But I have not told you all yet. You say that I want a husband."

"Well, well; I did not mean to say it harshly."

"I do want—to be married." And here her courage failed her a little, and for a moment her eye fell to the ground. "It is true, uncle. He has asked me whether I could love him, and I have told him I could. He has asked me whether I would be his wife, and I have given him a promise. After that, must not his happiness be my happiness, and his misery my misery? Am I not his wife already before God?"

"No, no," said Uncle Hatto, loudly.

"Ah, but I am. None feel the strength of the bonds but those who are themselves bound. I know my duty to my father and mother, and with God's help I will do it, but I am not the less bound to him. Without their approval I will not stand with him at the altar; but not the less is my lot joined to his for this world. Nothing could release me from that but his wish."

"And he will wish it in a month or two."

"Excuse me, Uncle Hatto, but in that I can only judge for myself as best I may. He has loved me now for two years—"

"Psha!"

"And whether it be wise or foolish, I have sanctioned it. I cannot now go back with honour, even if my own heart would let me. His welfare must be my welfare, and his sorrow my sorrow. Therefore I am bound to do for him anything that a girl may do for the man she loves; and, as I knew of no other resource, I come to you to help me."

"And he, sitting out there, knows what you are saying."

"Most certainly not. He knows no more than that he has seen me enter this room."

"I am glad of that, because I would not wish that he should be disappointed. In this matter, my dear, I cannot do anything for you."

"And that is your last answer, uncle?"

"Yes, indeed. When you come to think over this some twenty years hence, you will know then that I am right, and that your request was unreasonable.

"It may be so," she replied, "but I do not think it."

"It will be so. Such favours as you now ask are not granted in this world for light reasons."

"Light reasons! Well, uncle, I have had my say, and will not take up your time longer."

"Goodbye, my dear. I am sorry that I cannot oblige you;—that it is quite out of my power to oblige you."

Then she went, giving him her hand as she parted from him; and he, as she left the room looked anxiously at her, watching her countenance and her gait, and listening to the very fall of her footstep. "Ah," he said to himself; when he was alone, "the young people have the best of it. The sun shines for them; but why should they have all? Poor as he is, he is a happy dog,—a happy dog. But she is twice too good for him. Why did she not take to one of her own country?"

Isa, as she passed through the bank, smiled sweetly on her father, and then smiled sweetly at her lover, nodding to him with a pleasant kindly nod. If he could have heard all that had passed at that interview, how much more he would have known of her than he now knew, and how proud he would have been of her love. No word was spoken as she went out, and then she walked home with even step, as she had walked thither. It can hardly be said that she was disappointed, as she had expected nothing. But people hope who do not expect, and though her step was even and her face calm, yet her heart was sad.

"Mamma," she said, "there is no hope from Uncle Hatto."

"So I feared, my dear."

"But I thought it right to try—for Herbert's sake."

"I hope it will not do him an injury in the bank."

"Oh, mamma, do not put that into my head. If that were added to it all, I should indeed be wretched."

"No; he is too just for that. Poor young man! Sometimes I almost think it would be better that he should go back to England."

"Mamma, if he did, I should—break my heart."

"Isa!"

"Well, mamma! But do not suppose that I mean to complain, whatever happens."

"But I had been so sure that you had constrained your feelings!"

"So I had,—till I knew myself. Mamma, I could wait for years, if he were contented to wait by my side. If I could see him happy, I could watch him and love him, and be happy also. I do not want to have him kneeling to me, and making sweet speeches; but it has gone too far now,—and I could not bear to lose him." And thus to her mother she confessed the truth.

There was nothing more said between Isa and her mother on the subject, and for two days the matter remained as it then stood. Madame Heine had been deeply grieved at hearing those last words which her daughter had spoken. To her also that state of quiescence which Isa had so long affected seemed to be the proper state at which a maiden's heart should stand till after her marriage vows had been pronounced. She had watched her Isa, and had approved of everything,—of everything till this last avowal had been made. But now, though she could not approve, she expressed no disapproval in words. She pressed her daughter's hand and sighed, and then the two said no more upon the matter. In this way, for two days, there was silence in the apartments in the Ludwigs Strasse; for even when the father returned from his work, the whole circle felt that their old family mirth was for the present necessarily laid aside.

On the morning of the third day, about noon, Madame Heine returned home from the market with Isa, and as they reached the landing, Agnes met them with a packet. "Fritz brought it from the bank," said Agnes. Now Fritz was the boy who ran messages and swept out the office, and Madame Heine put out her hand for the parcel, thinking, not unnaturally, that it was for her. But Agnes would not give it to her mother, "It is for you, Isa," she said. Then Isa, looking at the address, recognised the handwriting of her uncle. "Mamma," she said, "I will come to you directly;" and then she passed quickly away into her own room.

The parcel was soon opened, and contained a note from her uncle, and a stiff, large document, looking as though it had come from the hands of a lawyer. Isa glanced at the document, and read some few of the words on the outer fold, but they did not carry home to her mind any clear perception of their meaning. She was flurried at the moment, and the words, perhaps, were not very plain. Then she took up her note, and that was plain enough. It was very short, and ran as follows:-

"My dear Niece,

You told me on Monday that I was stern, and harsh, and unjust. Perhaps I was. If so, I hope the enclosed will make amends, and that you will not think me such an old fool as I think myself.

"Your affectionate uncle,

"HATTO HEINE.

"I have told nobody yet, and the enclosed will require my brother's signature; but I suppose he will not object."

* * * * *

"But he does not know it, mamma," said Isa. "Who is to tell him? Oh, mamma, you must tell him."

"Nay, my dear; but it must be your own present to him."

"I could not give it him. It is Uncle Hatto's present Mamma, when I left him I thought that his eye was kind to me."

"His heart, at any rate, has been very kind." And then again they looked over the document, and talked of the wedding which must now be near at hand. But still they had not as yet decided how Herbert should be informed.

At last Isa resolved that she herself would write to him. She did write, and this was her letter:-

"Dear Herbert,

"Mamma and I wish to see you, and beg that you will come up to us this evening. We have tidings for you which I hope you will receive with joy. I may as well tell you at once, as I do not wish to flurry you. Uncle Hatto has sent to us a document which admits you as a partner into the bank. If, therefore, you wish to go on with our engagement, I suppose there is nothing now to cause any very great delay.

"ISA."

The letter was very simple, and Isa, when she had written it, subsided into all her customary quiescence. Indeed, when Herbert came to the Ludwigs Strasse, not in the evening as he was bidden to do, but instantly, leaving his own dinner uneaten, and coming upon the Heines in the midst of their dinner, she was more than usually tranquil. But his love was, as she had told him, boisterous. He could not contain himself, and embraced them all, and then scolded Isa because she was so calm.

"Why should I not be calm," said she, "now that I know you are happy?"

The house in the Schrannen Platz still goes by the name of Heine Brothers, but the mercantile world in Bavaria, and in some cities out of Bavaria, is well aware that the real pith and marrow of the business is derived from the energy of the young English partner.

JOHN BULL ON THE GUADALQUIVIR. FROM "TALES FROM ALL COUNTRIES"

I am an Englishman, living, as all Englishman should do, in England, and my wife would not, I think, be well pleased were any one to insinuate that she were other than an Englishwoman; but in the circumstances of my marriage I became connected with the south of Spain, and the narrative which I am to tell requires that I should refer to some of those details.

The Pomfrets and Daguilars have long been in trade together in this country, and one of the partners has usually resided at Seville for the sake of the works which the firm there possesses. My father, James Pomfret, lived there for ten years before his marriage; and since that and up to the present period, old Mr. Daguilar has always been on the spot. He was, I believe, born in Spain, but he came very early to England; he married an English wife, and his sons had been educated exclusively in England. His only daughter, Maria Daguilar, did not pass so large a proportion of her early life in this country, but she came to us for a visit at the age of seventeen, and when she returned I made up my mind that I most assuredly would go after her. So I did, and she is now sitting on the other side of the fireplace with a legion of small linen habiliments in a huge basket by her side.

I felt, at the first, that there was something lacking to make my cup of love perfectly delightful. It was very sweet, but there was wanting that flower of romance which is generally added to the heavenly draught by a slight admixture of opposition. I feared that the path of my true love would run too smooth. When Maria came to our house, my mother and elder sister seemed to be quite willing that I should be continually alone with her; and she had not been there ten days before my father, by chance, remarked that there was nothing old Mr. Daguilar valued so highly as a thorough feeling of intimate alliance between the two families which had been so long connected in trade. I was never told that Maria was to be my wife, but I felt that the same thing was done without words; and when, after six weeks of somewhat elaborate attendance upon her, I asked her to be Mrs. John Pomfret, I had no more fear of a refusal, or even of hesitation on her part, than I now have when I suggest to my partner some commercial transaction of undoubted advantage.

But Maria, even at that age, had about her a quiet sustained decision of character quite unlike anything I had seen in English girls. I used to hear, and do still hear, how much more flippant is the education of girls in France and Spain than in England; and I know that this is shown to be the result of many causes—the Roman Catholic religion being, perhaps, chief offender; but, nevertheless, I rarely see in one of our own young women the same power of a self-sustained demeanour as I meet on the Continent. It goes no deeper than the demeanour, people say. I can only answer that I have not found that shallowness in my own wife.

Miss Daguilar replied to me that she was not prepared with an answer; she had only known me six weeks, and wanted more time to think about it; besides, there was one in her own country with whom she would wish to consult. I knew she had no mother; and as for consulting old Mr. Daguilar on such a subject, that idea, I knew, could not have troubled her. Besides, as I afterwards learned, Mr. Daguilar had already proposed the marriage to his partner exactly as he would have proposed a division of assets. My mother declared that Maria was a foolish chit—in which by-the-bye she showed her entire ignorance of Miss Daguilar's character; my eldest sister begged that no constraint might he put on the young lady's inclinations—which provoked me to assert that the young lady's inclinations were by no means opposed to my own; and my father, in the coolest manner suggested that the matter might stand over for twelve months, and that I might then go to Seville, and see about it! Stand over for twelve months! Would not Maria, long before that time, have been snapped up and carried off by one of those inordinately rich Spanish grandees who are still to be met with occasionally in Andalucia?

My father's dictum, however, had gone forth; and Maria, in the calmest voice, protested that she thought it very wise. I should be less of a boy by that time, she said, smiling on me, but driving wedges between every fibre of my body as she spoke. "Be it so," I said, proudly. "At any rate, I am not so much of a boy that I shall forget you." "And, John, you still have the trade to learn," she added, with her deliciously foreign intonation—speaking very slowly, but with perfect pronunciation. The trade to learn! However, I said not a word, but stalked out of the room, meaning to see her no more before she went. But I could not resist attending on her in the hall as she started; and, when she took leave of us, she put her face up to be kissed by me, as she did by my father, and seemed to receive as much emotion from one embrace as from the other. "He'll go out by the packet of the 1st April," said my father, speaking of me as though I were a bale of goods. "Ah! that will be so nice," said Maria, settling her dress in the carriage; "the oranges will be ripe for him then!"

On the 17th April I did sail, and felt still very like a bale of goods. I had received one letter from her, in which she merely stated that her papa would have a room ready for me on my arrival; and, in answer to that, I had sent an epistle somewhat longer, and, as I then thought, a little more to the purpose. Her turn of mind was more practical than mine, and I must confess my belief that she did not appreciate my poetry.

I landed at Cadiz, and was there joined by an old family friend, one of the very best fellows that ever lived. He was to accompany me up as far as Seville; and, as he had lived for a year or two at Xeres, was supposed to be more Spanish almost than a Spaniard. His name was Johnson, and he was in the wine trade; and whether for travelling or whether for staying at home—whether for paying you a visit in your own house, or whether for entertaining you in his—there never was (and I am prepared to maintain there never will be) a stancher friend, choicer companion, or a safer guide than Thomas Johnson. Words cannot produce a eulogium sufficient for his merits. But, as I have since learned, he was not quite so Spanish as I had imagined. Three years among the bodegas of Xeres had taught him, no doubt, to appreciate the exact twang of a good, dry sherry; but not, as I now conceive, the exactest flavour of the true Spanish character. I was very lucky, however, in meeting such a friend, and now reckon him as one of the stanchest allies of the house of Pomfret, Daguilar, and Pomfret.

He met me at Cadiz, took me about the town, which appeared to me to be of no very great interest;—though the young ladies were all very well. But, in this respect, I was then a Stoic, till such time as I might be able to throw myself at the feet of her whom I was ready to proclaim the most lovely of all the Dulcineas of Andalucia. He carried me up by boat and railway to Xeres; gave me a most terrific headache, by dragging me out into the glare of the sun, after I had tasted some half a dozen different wines, and went through all the ordinary hospitalities. On the next day we returned to Puerto, and from thence getting across to St. Lucar and Bonanza, found ourselves on the banks of the Guadalquivir, and took our places in the boat for Seville. I need say but little to my readers respecting that far-famed river. Thirty years ago we in England generally believed that on its banks was to be found a pure elysium of pastoral beauty; that picturesque shepherds and lovely maidens here fed their flocks in fields of asphodel; that the limpid stream ran cool and crystal over bright stones and beneath perennial shade; and that every thing on the Guadalquivir was as lovely and as poetical as its name. Now, it is pretty widely known that no uglier river oozes down to its bourn in the sea through unwholesome banks of low mud. It is brown and dirty; ungifted by any scenic advantage; margined for miles upon miles by huge, flat, expansive fields, in which cattle are reared,—the bulls wanted for the bullfights among other; and birds of prey sit constant on the shore, watching for the carcases of such as die. Such are the charms of the golden Guadalquivir.

At first we were very dull on board that steamer. I never found myself in a position in which there was less to do. There was a nasty smell about the little boat which made me almost ill; every turn in the river was so exactly like the last, that we might have been standing still; there was no amusement except eating, and that, when once done, was not of a kind to make an early repetition desirable. Even Johnson was becoming dull, and I began to doubt whether I was so desirous as I once had been to travel the length and breadth of all Spain. But about noon a little incident occurred which did for a time remove some of our tedium. The boat had stopped to take in passengers on the river; and, among others, a man had come on board dressed in a fashion that, to my eyes, was equally strange and picturesque. Indeed, his appearance was so singular, that I could not but regard him with care, though I felt at first averse to stare at a fellow-passenger on account of his clothes. He was a man of about fifty, but as active apparently as though not more than twenty five; he was of low stature, but of admirable make; his hair was just becoming grizzled, but was short and crisp and well cared for; his face was prepossessing, having a look of good humour added to courtesy, and there was a pleasant, soft smile round his mouth which ingratiated one at the first sight. But it was his dress rather than his person which attracted attention. He wore the ordinary Andalucian cap—of which such hideous parodies are now making themselves common in England—but was not contented with the usual ornament of the double tuft. The cap was small, and jaunty; trimmed with silk velvet—as is common here with men careful to adorn their persons; but this man's cap was finished off with a jewelled button and golden filigree work. He was dressed in a short jacket with a stand up collar; and that also was covered with golden buttons and with golden button-holes. It was all gilt down the front, and all lace down the back. The rows of buttons were double; and those of the more backward row hung down in heavy pendules. His waistcoat was of coloured silk—very pretty to look at; and ornamented with a small sash, through which gold threads were worked. All the buttons of his breeches also were of gold; and there were gold tags to all the button-holes. His stockings were of the finest silk, and clocked with gold from the knee to the ankle.

Dress any Englishman in such a garb and he will at once give you the idea of a hog in armour. In the first place he will lack the proper spirit to carry it off, and in the next place the motion of his limbs will disgrace the ornaments they bear. "And so best," most Englishmen will say. Very likely; and, therefore, let no Englishman try it. But my Spaniard did not look at like a hog in armour. He walked slowly down the plank into the boat, whistling lowly but very clearly a few bars from a opera tune. It was plain to see that he was master of himself, of his ornaments, and of his limbs. He had no appearance of thinking that men were looking at him, or of feeling that he was beauteous in his attire;—nothing could be more natural than his foot-fall, or the quiet glance of his cheery gray eye. He walked up to the captain, who held the helm, and lightly raised his hand to his cap. The captain, taking one hand from the wheel, did the same, and then the stranger, turning his back to the stern of the vessel, and fronting down the river with his face, continued to whistle slowly, clearly, and in excellent time. Grand as were his clothes they were no burden on his mind.

"What is he?" said I, going up to my friend Johnson with a whisper.

"Well, I've been looking at him," said Johnson—which was true enough; "he's a—an uncommonly good-looking fellow, isn't he?"

"Particularly so," said I; "and got up quite irrespective of expense. Is he a—a—a gentleman, now, do you think?"

"Well, those things are so different in Spain that it's almost impossible to make an Englishman understand them. One learns to know all this sort of people by being with them in the country, but one can't explain."

"No; exactly. Are they real gold?"

"Yes, yes; I dare say they are. They sometimes have them silver gilt."

"It is quite a common thing, then, isn't it?" asked I.

"Well, not exactly; that—Ah! yes; I see! of course. He is a torero."

"A what?"

"A mayo. I will explain it all to you. You will see them about in all places, and you will get used to them."

"But I haven't seen one other as yet."

"No, and they are not all so gay as this, nor so new in their finery, you know."

"And what is a torero?"

"Well, a torero is a man engaged in bull-fighting."

"Oh! he is a matador, is he?" said I, looking at him with more than all my eyes.

"No, not exactly that;—not of necessity. He is probably a mayo. A fellow that dresses himself smart for fairs, and will be seen hanging about with the bull-fighters. What would be a sporting fellow in England—only he won't drink and curse like a low man on the turf there. Come, shall we go and speak to him?"

"I can't talk to him," said I, diffident of my Spanish. I had received lessons in England from Maria Daguilar; but six weeks is little enough for making love, let alone the learning of a foreign language.

"Oh! I'll do the talking. You'll find the language easy enough before long. It soon becomes the same as English to you, when you live among them." And then Johnson, walking up to the stranger, accosted him with that good-natured familiarity with which a thoroughly nice fellow always opens a conversation with his inferior. Of course I could not understand the words which were exchanged; but it was clear enough that the "mayo" took the address in good part, and was inclined to be communicative and social.

"They are all of pure gold," said Johnson, turning to me after a minute, making as he spoke a motion with his head to show the importance of the information.

"Are they indeed?" said I. "Where on earth did a fellow like that get them?" Whereupon Johnson again returned to his conversation with the man. After another minute he raised his hand, and began to finger the button on the shoulder; and to aid him in doing so, the man of the bull-ring turned a little on one side.

"They are wonderfully well made," said Johnson, talking to me, and still fingering the button. "They are manufactured, he says, at Osuna, and he tells me that they make them better there than anywhere else."

"I wonder what the whole set would cost?" said I. "An enormous deal of money for a fellow like him, I should think!"

"Over twelve ounces," said Johnson, having asked the question; "and that will be more than forty pounds."

"What an uncommon ass he must be!" said I.

As Johnson by this time was very closely scrutinising the whole set of ornaments I thought I might do so also, and going up close to our friend, I too began to handle the buttons and tags on the other side. Nothing could have been more good-humoured than he was—so much so that I was emboldened to hold up his arm that I might see the cut of his coat, to take off his cap and examine the make, to stuff my finger in beneath his sash, and at last to kneel down while I persuaded him to hold up his legs that I might look to the clocking. The fellow was thorough good-natured, and why should I not indulge my curiosity?

"You'll upset him if you don't take care," said Johnson; for I had got fast hold of him by one ankle, and was determined to finish the survey completely.

"Oh, no, I shan't," said I; "a bull-fighting chap can surely stand on one leg. But what I wonder at is, how on earth he can afford it!" Whereupon Johnson again began to interrogate him in Spanish.

"He says he has got no children," said Johnson, having received a reply, "and that as he has nobody but himself to look after, he is able to allow himself such little luxuries."

"Tell him that I say he would be better with a wife and couple of babies," said I—and Johnson interpreted.

"He says that he'll think of it some of these days, when he finds that the supply of fools in the world is becoming short," said Johnson.

We had nearly done with him now; but after regaining my feet, I addressed myself once more to the heavy pendules, which hung down almost under his arm. I lifted one of these, meaning to feel its weight between my fingers; but unfortunately I gave a lurch, probably through the motion of the boat, and still holding by the button, tore it almost off from our friend's coat.

"Oh, I am so sorry," I said, in broad English.

"It do not matter at all," he said, bowing, and speaking with equal plainness. And then, taking a knife from his pocket, he cut the pendule off, leaving a bit of torn cloth on the side of his jacket.

"Upon my word, I am quite unhappy," said I; "but I always am so awkward." Whereupon he bowed low.

"Couldn't I make it right?" said I, bringing out my purse.

He lifted his hand, and I saw that it was small and white; he lifted it and gently put it upon my purse, smiling sweetly as he did so. "Thank you, no, senor; thank you, no." And then, bowing to us both, he walked away down into the cabin.

"Upon my word he is a deuced well-mannered fellow," said I.

"You shouldn't have offered him money," said Johnson; "a Spaniard does not like it."

"Why, I thought you could do nothing without money in this country. Doesn't every one take bribes?"

"Ah! yes; that is a different thing; but not the price of a button. By Jove! he understood English, too. Did you see that?"

"Yes; and I called him an ass! I hope he doesn't mind it."

"Oh! no; he won't think anything about it," said Johnson. "That sort of fellows don't. I dare say we shall see him in the bull-ring next Sunday, and then we'll make all right with a glass of lemonade."

And so our adventure ended with the man of the gold ornaments. I was sorry that I had spoken English before him so heedlessly, and resolved that I would never be guilty of such gaucherie again. But, then, who would think that a Spanish bull-fighter would talk a foreign language? I was sorry, also, that I had torn his coat; it had looked so awkward; and sorry again that I had offered the man money. Altogether I was a little ashamed of myself; but I had too much to look forward to at Seville to allow any heaviness to remain long at my heart; and before I had arrived at the marvellous city I had forgotten both him and his buttons.

Nothing could be nicer than the way in which I was welcomed at Mr. Daguilar's house, or more kind—I may almost say affectionate—than Maria's manner to me. But it was too affectionate; and I am not sure that I should not have liked my reception better had she been more diffident in her tone, and less inclined to greet me with open warmth. As it was, she again gave me her cheek to kiss, in her father's presence, and called me dear John, and asked me specially after some rabbits which I had kept at home merely for a younger sister; and then it seemed as though she were in no way embarrassed by the peculiar circumstances of our position. Twelve months since I had asked her to be my wife, and now she was to give me an answer; and yet she was as assured in her gait, and as serenely joyous in her tone, as though I were a brother just returned from college. It could not be that she meant to refuse me, or she would not smile on me and be so loving; but I could almost have found it in my heart to wish that she would. "It is quite possible," said I to myself, "that I may not be found so ready for this family bargain. A love that is to be had like a bale of goods is not exactly the love to suit my taste." But then, when I met her again in the morning I could no more have quarrelled with her than I could have flown.

I was inexpressibly charmed with the whole city, and especially with the house in which Mr. Daguilar lived. It opened from the corner of a narrow, unfrequented street—a corner like an elbow—and, as seen from the exterior, there was nothing prepossessing to recommend it; but the outer door led by a short hall or passage to an inner door or grille, made of open ornamental iron-work, and through that we entered a court, or patio, as they I called it. Nothing could be more lovely or deliciously cool than was this small court. The building on each side was covered by trellis-work; and beautiful creepers, vines, and parasite flowers, now in the full magnificence of the early summer, grew up and clustered round the windows. Every inch of wall was covered, so that none of the glaring whitewash wounded the eye. In the four corners of the patio were four large orange-trees, covered with fruit. I would not say a word in special praise of these, remembering that childish promise she had made on my behalf. In the middle of the court there was a fountain, and round about on the marble floor there were chairs, and here and there a small table, as though the space were really a portion of the house. It was here that we used to take our cup of coffee and smoke our cigarettes, I and old Mr. Daguilar, while Maria sat by, not only approving, but occasionally rolling for me the thin paper round the fragrant weed with her taper fingers. Beyond the patio was an open passage or gallery, filled also with flowers in pots; and then, beyond this, one entered the drawing-room of the house. It was by no means a princely palace or mansion, fit for the owner of untold wealth. The rooms were not over large nor very numerous; but the most had been made of a small space, and everything had been done to relieve the heat of an almost tropical sun.

"It is pretty, is it not?" she said, as she took me through it.

"Very pretty," I said. "I wish we could live in such houses."

"Oh, they would not do at all for dear old fat, cold, cozy England. You are quite different, you know, in everything from us in the south; more phlegmatic, but then so much steadier. The men and the houses are all the same."

I can hardly tell why, but even this wounded me. It seemed to me as though she were inclined to put into one and the same category things English, dull, useful, and solid; and that she was disposed to show a sufficient appreciation for such necessaries of life, though she herself had another and inner sense—a sense keenly alive to the poetry of her own southern chime; and that I, as being English, was to have no participation in this latter charm. An English husband might do very well, the interests of the firm might make such an arrangement desirable, such a mariage de convenance—so I argued to myself—might be quite compatible with—with heaven only knows what delights of superterrestial romance, from which I, as being an English thick-headed lump of useful coarse mortality, was to be altogether debarred. She had spoken to me of oranges, and having finished the survey of the house, she offered me some sweet little cakes. It could not be that of such things were the thoughts which lay undivulged beneath the clear waters of those deep black eyes—undivulged to me, though no one else could have so good a right to read those thoughts! It could not be that that noble brow gave index of a mind intent on the trade of which she spoke so often! Words of other sort than any that had been vouchsafed to me must fall at times from the rich curves of that perfect month.

So felt I then, pining for something to make me unhappy. Ah, me! I know all about it now, and am content. But I wish that some learned pundit would give us a good definition of romance, would describe in words that feeling with which our hearts are so pestered when we are young, which makes us sigh for we know not what, and forbids us to be contented with what God sends us. We invest female beauty with impossible attributes, and are angry because our women have not the spiritualised souls of angels, anxious as we are that they should also be human in the flesh. A man looks at her he would love as at a distant landscape in a mountainous land. The peaks are glorious with more than the beauty of earth and rock and vegetation. He dreams of some mysterious grandeur of design which tempts him on under the hot sun, and over the sharp rock, till he has reached the mountain goal which he had set before him. But when there, he finds that the beauty is well-nigh gone, and as for that delicious mystery on which his soul had fed, it has vanished for ever.

I know all about it now, and am, as I said, content. Beneath those deep black eyes there lay a well of love, good, honest, homely love, love of father and husband and children that were to come—of that love which loves to see the loved ones prospering in honesty. That noble brow—for it is noble; I am unchanged in that opinion, and will go unchanged to my grave—covers thoughts as to the welfare of many, and an intellect fitted to the management of a household, of servants, namely, and children, and perchance a husband. That mouth can speak words of wisdom, of very useful wisdom—though of poetry it has latterly uttered little that was original. Poetry and romance! They are splendid mountain views seen in the distance. So let men be content to see them, and not attempt to tread upon the fallacious heather of the mystic hills.

In the first week of my sojourn in Seville I spoke no word of overt love to Maria, thinking, as I confess, to induce her thereby to alter her mode of conduct to myself. "She knows that I have come here to make love to her—to repeat my offer; and she will at any rate be chagrined if I am slow to do so." But it had no effect. At home my mother was rather particular about her table, and Maria's greatest efforts seemed to be used in giving me as nice dinners as we gave her. In those days I did not care a straw about my dinner, and so I took an opportunity of telling her. "Dear me," said she, looking at me almost with grief, "do you not? What a pity! And do you not like music either." "Oh, yes, I adore it," I replied. I felt sure at the time that had I been born in her own sunny clime, she would never have talked to me about eating. But that was my mistake.

I used to walk out with her about the city, seeing all that is there of beauty and magnificence. And in what city is there more that is worth the seeing? At first this was very delightful to me, for I felt that I was blessed with a privilege that would not be granted to any other man. But its value soon fell in my eyes, for others would accost her, and walk on the other side, talking to her in Spanish, as though I hardly existed, or were a servant there for her protection. And I was not allowed to take her arm, and thus to appropriate her, as I should have done in England. "No, John," she said, with the sweetest, prettiest smile, "we don't do that here; only when people are married." And she made this allusion to married life out, openly, with no slightest tremor on her tongue.

"Oh, I beg pardon," said I, drawing back my hand, and feeling angry with myself for not being fully acquainted with all the customs of a foreign country.

"You need not beg pardon," said she; "when we were in England we always walked so. It is just a custom, you know." And then I saw her drop her large dark eyes to the ground, and bow gracefully in answer to some salute.

I looked round, and saw that we had been joined by a young cavalier,—a Spanish nobleman, as I saw at once; a man with jet black hair, and a straight nose, and a black moustache, and patent leather boots, very slim and very tall, and—though I would not confess it then—uncommonly handsome. I myself am inclined to be stout, my hair is light, my nose broad, I have no hair on my upper lip, and my whiskers are rough and uneven. "I could punch your head though, my fine fellow," said I to myself, when I saw that he placed himself at Maria's side, "and think very little of the achievement."

The wretch went on with us round the plaza for some quarter of an hour talking Spanish with the greatest fluency, and she was every whit as fluent. Of course I could not understand a word that they said. Of all positions that a man can occupy, I think that that is about the most uncomfortable; and I cannot say that, even up to this day, I have quite forgiven her for that quarter of an hour.

"I shall go in," said I, unable to bear my feelings, and preparing to leave her. "The heat is unendurable."

"Oh dear, John, why did you not speak before?" she answered. "You cannot leave me here, you know, as I am in your charge; but I will go with you almost directly." And then she finished her conversation with the Spaniard, speaking with an animation she had never displayed in her conversations with me.

It had been agreed between us for two or three days before this, that we were to rise early on the following morning for the sake of ascending the tower of the cathedral, and visiting the Giralda, as the iron figure is called, which turns upon a pivot on the extreme summit. We had often wandered together up and down the long dark gloomy aisle of the stupendous building, and had, together, seen its treasury of art; but as yet we had not performed the task which has to be achieved by all visitors to Seville; and in order that we might have a clear view over the surrounding country, and not be tormented by the heat of an advanced sun, we had settled that we would ascend the Giralda before breakfast.

And now, as I walked away from the plaza towards Mr. Daguilar's house, with Maria by my side, I made up my mind that I would settle my business during this visit to the cathedral. Yes, and I would so manage the settlement that there should be no doubt left as to my intentions and my own ideas. I would not be guilty of shilly-shally conduct; I would tell her frankly what I felt and what I thought, and would make her understand that I did not desire her hand if I could not have her heart. I did not value the kindness of her manner, seeing that that kindness sprung from indifference rather than passion; and so I would declare to her. And I would ask her, also, who was this young man with whom she was intimate—for whom all her volubility and energy of tone seemed to be employed? She had told me once that it behoved her to consult a friend in Seville as to the expediency of her marriage with me. Was this the friend whom she had wished to consult? If so, she need not trouble herself. Under such circumstances I should decline the connection! And I resolved that I would find out how this might be. A man who proposes to take a woman to his bosom as his wife, has a right to ask for information—ay, and to receive it too. It flashed upon my mind at this moment that Donna Maria was well enough inclined to come to me as my wife, but—. I could hardly define the "buts" to myself, for there were three or four of them. Why did she always speak to me in a tone of childish affection, as though I were a schoolboy home for the holidays? I would have all this out with her on the tower on the following morning, standing under the Giralda.

On that morning we met together in the patio, soon after five o'clock, and started for the cathedral. She looked beautiful, with her black mantilla over her head, and with black gloves on, and her black morning silk dress—beautiful, composed, and at her ease, as though she were well satisfied to undertake this early morning walk from feelings of good nature—sustained, probably, by some under-current of a deeper sentiment. Well; I would know all about it before I returned to her father's house.

There hardly stands, as I think, on the earth, a building more remarkable than the cathedral of Seville, and hardly one more grand. Its enormous size; its gloom and darkness; the richness of ornamentation in the details, contrasted with the severe simplicity of the larger outlines; the variety of its architecture; the glory of its paintings; and the wondrous splendour of its metallic decoration, its altar-friezes, screens, rails, gates, and the like, render it, to my mind, the first in interest among churches. It has not the coloured glass of Chartres, or the marble glory of Milan, or such a forest of aisles as Antwerp, or so perfect a hue in stone as Westminster, nor in mixed beauty of form and colour does it possess anything equal to the choir of Cologne; but, for combined magnificence and awe-compelling grandeur, I regard it as superior to all other ecclesiastical edifices.

It is its deep gloom with which the stranger is so greatly struck on his first entrance. In a region so hot as the south of Spain, a cool interior is a main object with the architect, and this it has been necessary to effect by the exclusion of light; consequently the church is dark, mysterious, and almost cold. On the morning in question, as we entered, it seemed to be filled with gloom, and the distant sound of a slow footstep here and there beyond the transept inspired one almost with awe. Maria, when she first met me, had begun to talk with her usual smile, offering me coffee and a biscuit before I started. "I never eat biscuit," I said, with almost a severe tone, as I turned from her. That dark, horrid man of the plaza— would she have offered him a cake had she been going to walk with him in the gloom of the morning? After that little had been spoken between us. She walked by my side with her accustomed smile; but she had, as I flattered myself, begun to learn that I was not to be won by a meaningless good nature. "We are lucky in our morning for the view!" that was all she said, speaking with that peculiarly clear, but slow pronunciation which she had assumed in learning our language.

We entered the cathedral, and, walking the whole length of the aisle, left it again at the porter's porch at the farther end. Here we passed through a low door on to the stone flight of steps, and at once began to ascend. "There are a party of your countrymen up before us," said Maria; "the porter says that they went through the lodge half an hour since." "I hope they will return before we are on the top," said I, bethinking myself of the task that was before me. And indeed my heart was hardly at ease within me, for that which I had to say would require all the spirit of which I was master.

The ascent to the Giralda is very long and very fatiguing; and we had to pause on the various landings and in the singular belfry in order that Miss Daguilar might recruit her strength and breath. As we rested on one of these occasions, in a gallery which runs round the tower below the belfry, we heard a great noise of shouting, and a clattering of sticks among the bells. "It is the party of your countrymen who went up before us," said she. "What a pity that Englishmen should always make so much noise!" And then she spoke in Spanish to the custodian of the bells, who is usually to be found in a little cabin up there within the tower. "He says that they went up shouting like demons," continued Maria; and it seemed to me that she looked as though I ought to be ashamed of the name of an Englishman. "They may not be so solemn in their demeanour as Spaniards," I answered; "but, for all that, there may be quite as much in them."

We then again began to mount, and before we had ascended much farther we passed my three countrymen. They were young men, with gray coats and gray trousers, with slouched hats, and without gloves. They had fair faces and fair hair, and swung big sticks in their hands, with crooked handles. They laughed and talked loud, and, when we met them, seemed to be racing with each other; but nevertheless they were gentlemen. No one who knows by sight what an English gentleman is, could have doubted that; but I did acknowledge to myself that they should have remembered that the edifice they were treading was a church, and that the silence they were invading was the cherished property of a courteous people.

"They are all just the same as big boys," said Maria. The colour instantly flew into my face, and I felt that it was my duty to speak up for my own countrymen. The word "boys" especially wounded my ears. It was as a boy that she treated me; but, on looking at that befringed young Spanish Don—who was not, apparently, my elder in age—she had recognised a man. However, I said nothing further till I reached the summit. One cannot speak with manly dignity while one is out of breath on a staircase.

"There, John," she said, stretching her hands away over the fair plain of the Guadalquivir, as soon as we stood against the parapet; "is not that lovely?"

I would not deign to notice this. "Maria," I said, "I think that you are too hard upon my countrymen?"

"Too hard! no; for I love them. They are so good and industrious; and come home to their wives, and take care of their children. But why do they make themselves so—so—what the French call gauche?"

"Good and industrious, and come home to their wives!" thought I. "I believe you hardly understand us as yet," I answered. "Our domestic virtues are not always so very prominent; but, I believe, we know how to conduct ourselves as gentlemen: at any rate, as well as Spaniards." I was very angry—not at the faults, but at the good qualities imputed to us.

"In affairs of business, yes," said Maria, with a look of firm confidence in her own opinion—that look of confidence which she has never lost, and I pray that she may never lose it while I remain with her—"but in the little intercourses of the world, no! A Spaniard never forgets what is personally due either to himself or his neighbours. If he is eating an onion, he eats it as an onion should be eaten."

"In such matters as that he is very grand, no doubt," said I, angrily.

"And why should you not eat an onion properly, John? Now, I heard a story yesterday from Don—about two Englishmen, which annoyed me very much." I did not exactly catch the name of the Don in question but I felt through every nerve in my body that it was the man who had been talking to her on the plaza.

"And what have they done?" said I. "But it is the same everywhere. We are always abused; but, nevertheless, no people are so welcome. At any rate, we pay for the mischief we do." I was angry with myself the moment the words were out of my mouth, for, after all, there is no feeling more mean than that pocket-confidence with which an Englishman sometimes swaggers.

"There was no mischief done in this case," she answered. "It was simply that two men have made themselves ridiculous for ever. The story is all about Seville, and, of course, it annoys me that they should be Englishmen."

"And what did they do?"

"The Marquis D'Almavivas was coming up to Seville in the boat, and they behaved to him in the most outrageous manner. He is here now and is going to give a series of fetes. Of course he will not ask a single Englishman."

"We shall manage to live even though the Marquis D'Almavivas may frown upon us," said I, proudly.

"He is the richest, and also the best of our noblemen," continued Maria; "and I never heard of anything so absurd as what they did to him. It made me blush when Don—told me." Don Tomas, I thought she said.

"If he be the best of your noblemen, how comes it that he is angry because he has met two vulgar men? It is not to be supposed that every Englishman is a gentleman."

"Angry! Oh, no! he was not angry; he enjoyed the joke too much for that. He got completely the best of them, though they did not know it; poor fools! How would your Lord John Russell behave if two Spaniards in an English railway carriage were to pull him about and tear his clothes?"

"He would give them in charge to a policeman, of course," said I, speaking of such a matter with the contempt it deserved.

"If that were done here your ambassador would be demanding national explanations. But Almavivas did much better;—he laughed at them without letting them know it."

"But do you mean that they took hold of him violently, without any provocation? They must have been drunk."

"Oh, no, they were sober enough. I did not see it, so I do not quite know exactly how it was, but I understand that they committed themselves most absurdly, absolutely took hold of his coat and tore it, and—; but they did such ridiculous things that I cannot tell you." And yet Don Tomas, if that was the man's name, had been able to tell her, and she had been able to listen to him.

"What made them take hold of the marquis?" said I.

"Curiosity, I suppose," she answered. "He dresses somewhat fancifully, and they could not understand that any one should wear garments different from their own." But even then the blow did not strike home upon me.

"Is it not pretty to look down upon the quiet town?" she said, coming close up to me, so that the skirt of her dress pressed me, and her elbow touched my arm. Now was the moment I should have asked her how her heart stood towards me; but I was sore and uncomfortable, and my destiny was before me. She was willing enough to let these English faults pass without further notice, but I would not allow the subject I drop.

"I will find out who these men were," said I, "and learn the truth of it. When did it occur?"

"Last Thursday, I think he said."

"Why, that was the day we came up in the boat, Johnson and myself. There was no marquis there then, and we were the only Englishmen on board."

"It was on Thursday, certainly, because it was well known in Seville that he arrived on that day. You must have remarked him because he talks English perfectly—though by-the-bye, these men would go on chattering before him about himself as though it were impossible that a Spaniard should know their language. They are ignorant of Spanish, and they cannot bring themselves to believe that any one should be better educated than themselves."

Now the blow had fallen, and I straightway appreciated the necessity of returning immediately to Clapham where my family resided, and giving up for ever all idea of Spanish connections. I had resolved to assert the full strength of my manhood on that tower, and now words had been spoken which left me weak as a child. I felt that I was shivering, and did not dare to pronounce the truth which must be made known. As to speaking of love, and signifying my pleasure that Don Tomas should for the future be kept at a distance, any such effort was quite beyond me. Had Don Tomas been there, he might have walked off with her from before my face without a struggle on my part. "Now I remember about it," she continued, "I think he must have been in the boat on Thursday."

"And now that I remember," I replied, turning away to hide my embarrassment, "he was there. Your friend down below in the plaza seems to have made out a grand story. No doubt he is not fond of the English. There was such a man there, and I did take hold—"

"Oh, John, was it you?"

"Yes, Donna Maria, it was I; and if Lord John Russell were to dress himself in the same way—" But I had no time to complete my description of what might occur under so extravagantly impossible a combination of circumstances, for as I was yet speaking, the little door leading out on to the leads of the tower was opened and my friend, the mayo of the boat, still bearing gewgaws on his back, stepped up on to the platform. My eye instantly perceived that the one pendule was still missing from his jacket. He did not come alone, but three other gentlemen followed him, who, however, had no peculiarities in their dress. He saw me at once and bowed and smiled; and then observing Donna Maria, he lifted his cap from his head, and addressing himself to her in Spanish, began to converse with her as though she were an old friend.

"Senor," said Maria, after the first words of greeting had been spoken between them; "you must permit me to present to you my father's most particular friend, and my own,—Mr. Pomfret; John, this is the Marquis D'Almavivas."

I cannot now describe the grace with which this introduction was effected, or the beauty of her face as she uttered the word. There was a boldness about her as though she had said, "I know it all—the whole story. But, in spite of that you must take him on my representation, and be gracious to him in spite of what he has done. You must be content to do that; or in quarrelling with him you must quarrel with me also." And it was done at the spur of the moment—without delay. She, who not five minutes since had been loudly condemning the unknown Englishman for his rudeness, had already pardoned him, now that he was known to be her friend; and had determined that he should be pardoned by others also or that she would share his disgrace. I recognised the nobleness of this at the moment; but, nevertheless, I was so sore that I would almost have preferred that she should have disowned me.

The marquis immediately lifted his cap with his left hand while he gave me his right. "I have already had the pleasure of meeting this gentleman," he said; "we had some conversation in the boat together."

"Yes," said I, pointing to his rent, "and you still bear the marks of our encounter."

"Was it not delightful, Donna Maria," he continued, turning to her; "your friend's friend took me for a torero?"

"And it served you properly, senor," said Donna Maria, laughing, "you have no right to go about with all those rich ornaments upon you."

"Oh! quite properly; indeed, I make no complaint; and I must beg your friend to understand, and his friend also, how grateful I am for their solicitude as to my pecuniary welfare. They were inclined to be severe on me for being so extravagant in such trifles. I was obliged to explain that I had no wife at home kept without her proper allowance of dresses, in order that I might be gay."

"They are foreigners, and you should forgive their error," said she.

"And in token that I do so," said the marquis, "I shall beg your friend to accept the little ornament which attracted his attention." And so saying, he pulled the identical button out of his pocket, and gracefully proffered it to me.

"I shall carry it about with me always," said I, accepting it, "as a memento of humiliation. When I look at it, I shall ever remember the folly of an Englishman and the courtesy of a Spaniard;" and as I made the speech I could not but reflect whether it might, under any circumstances, be possible that Lord John Russell should be induced to give a button off his coat to a Spaniard.

There were other civil speeches made, and before we left the tower the marquis had asked me to his parties, and exacted from me an unwilling promise that I would attend them. "The senora," he said, bowing again to Maria, "would, he was sure, grace them. She had done so on the previous year; and as I had accepted his little present I was bound to acknowledge him as my friend." All this was very pretty, and of course I said that I would go, but I had not at that time the slightest intention of doing so. Maria had behaved admirably; she had covered my confusion, and shown herself not ashamed to own me, delinquent as I was; but, not the less, had she expressed her opinion, in language terribly strong, of the awkwardness of which I had been guilty, and had shown almost an aversion to my English character. I should leave Seville as quickly as I could, and should certainly not again put myself in the way of the Marquis D'Almavivas. Indeed, I dreaded the moment that I should be first alone with her, and should find myself forced to say something indicative of my feelings—to hear something also indicative of her feelings. I had come out this morning resolved to demand my rights and to exercise them—and now my only wish was to man away. I hated the marquis, and longed to be alone that I might cast his button from me. To think that a man should be so ruined by such a trifle!

We descended that prodigious flight without a word upon the subject, and almost without a word at all. She had carried herself well in the presence of Almavivas, and had been too proud to seem ashamed of her companion; but now, as I could well see, her feelings of disgust and contempt had returned. When I begged her not to hurry herself, she would hardly answer me; and when she did speak, her voice was constrained and unlike herself. And yet how beautiful she was! Well, my dream of Spanish love must be over. But I was sure of this; that having known her, and given her my heart, I could never afterwards share it with another.

We came out at last on the dark, gloomy aisle of the cathedral, and walked together without a word up along the side of the choir, till we came to the transept. There was not a soul near us, and not a sound was to be heard but the distant, low pattering of a mass, then in course of celebration at some far-off chapel in the cathedral. When we got to the transept Maria turned a little, as though she was going to the transept door, and then stopped herself. She stood still; and when I stood also, she made two steps towards me, and put her hand on my arm. "Oh, John!" she said.

"Well," said I; "after all it does not signify. You can make a joke of it when my back is turned."

"Dearest John!"—she had never spoken to me in that way before—"you must not be angry with me. It is better that we should explain to each other, is it not?"

"Oh, much better. I am very glad you heard of it at once. I do not look at it quite in the same light that you do; but nevertheless—"

"What do you mean? But I know you are angry with me. And yet you cannot think that I intended those words for you. Of course I know now that there was nothing rude in what passed."

"Oh, but there was."

"No, I am sure there was not. You could not be rude though you are so free hearted. I see it all now, and so does the marquis. You will like him so much when you come to know him. Tell me that you won't be cross with me for what I have said. Sometimes I think that I have displeased you, and yet my whole wish has been to welcome you to Seville, and to make you comfortable as an old friend. Promise me that you will not be cross with me."

Cross with her! I certainly had no intention of being cross, but I had begun to think that she would not care what my humour might be. "Maria," I said, taking hold of her hand.

"No, John, do not do that. It is in the church, you know."

"Maria, will you answer me a question?"

"Yes," she said, very slowly, looking dawn upon the stone slabs beneath our feet.

"Do you love me?"

"Love you!"

"Yes, do you love me? You were to give me an answer here, in Seville, and now I ask for it. I have almost taught myself to think that it is needless to ask; and now this horrid mischance—"

"What do you mean?" said she, speaking very quickly.

"Why this miserable blunder about the marquis's button! After that I suppose—"

"The marquis! Oh, John, is that to make a difference between you and me?—a little joke like that?"

"But does it not?"

"Make a change between us!—such a thing as that! Oh, John!"

"But tell me, Maria, what am I to hope? If you will say that you can love me, I shall care nothing for the marquis. In that case I can bear to be laughed at."

"Who will dare to laugh at you? Not the marquis, whom I am sure you will like."

"Your friend in this plaza, who told you of all this."

"What, poor Tomas!"

"I do not know about his being poor. I mean the gentleman who was with you last night."

"Yes, Tomas. You do not know who he is?"

"Not in the least."

"How droll! He is your own clerk—partly your own, now that you are one of the firm. And, John, I mean to make you do something for him; he is such a good fellow; and last year he married a young girl whom I love—oh, almost like a sister."

Do something for him! Of course I would. I promised, then and there, that I would raise his salary to any conceivable amount that a Spanish clerk could desire; which promise I have since kept, if not absolutely to the letter, at any rate, to an extent which has been considered satisfactory by the gentleman's wife.

"But, Maria—dearest Maria—"

"Remember, John, we are in the church; and poor papa will be waiting breakfast."

I need hardly continue the story further. It will be known to all that my love-suit throve in spite of my unfortunate raid on the button of the Marquis D'Almavivas, at whose series of fetes through that month I was, I may boast, an honoured guest. I have since that had the pleasure of entertaining him in my own poor house in England, and one of our boys bears his Christian name.

From that day in which I ascended the Giralda to this present day in which I write, I have never once had occasion to complain of a deficiency of romance either in Maria Daguilar or in Maria Pomfret.

THE MAN WHO KEPT
HIS MONEY IN A BOX

I first saw the man who kept his money in a box in the midst of the ravine of the Via Mala. I interchanged a few words with him or with his wife at the hospice, at the top of the Splugen; and I became acquainted with him in the courtyard of Conradi's hotel at Chiavenna. It was, however, afterwards at Bellaggio, on the lake of Como, that that acquaintance ripened into intimacy. A good many years have rolled by since then, and I believe this little episode in his life may be told without pain to the feelings of any one.

His name was—; let us for the present say that his name was Greene. How he learned that my name was Robinson I do not know, but I remember well that he addressed me by my name at Chiavenna. To go back, however, for a moment to the Via Mala;—I had been staying for a few days at the Golden Eagle at Tusis,—which, by-the-bye, I hold to be the best small inn in all Switzerland, and its hostess to be, or to have been, certainly the prettiest landlady,—and on the day of my departure southwards, I had walked on, into the Via Mala, so that the diligence might pick me up in the gorge. This pass I regard as one of the grandest spots to which my wandering steps have ever carried me, and though I had already lingered about it for many hours, I now walked thither again to take my last farewell of its dark towering rocks, its narrow causeway and roaring river, trusting to my friend the landlady to see that my luggage was duly packed upon the diligence. I need hardly say that my friend did not betray her trust.

As one goes out from Switzerland towards Italy, the road through the Via Mala ascends somewhat steeply, and passengers by the diligence may walk from the inn at Tusis into the gorge, and make their way through the greater part of the ravine before the vehicle will overtake them. This, however, Mr. Greene with his wife and daughter had omitted to do. When the diligence passed me in the defile, the horses trotting for a few yards over some level portion of the road, I saw a man's nose pressed close against the glass of the coupe window. I saw more of his nose than of any other part of his face, but yet I could perceive that his neck was twisted and his eye upturned, and that he was making a painful effort to look upwards to the summit of the rocks from his position inside the carriage.

There was such a roar of wind and waters at the spot that it was not practicable to speak to him, but I beckoned with my finger and then pointed to the road, indicating that he should have walked. He understood me, though I did not at the moment understand his answering gesture. It was subsequently, when I knew somewhat of his habits, that he explained to me that on pointing to his open mouth, he had intended to signify that he would be afraid of sore throat in exposing himself to the air of that damp and narrow passage.

I got up into the conductor's covered seat at the back of the diligence, and in this position encountered the drifting snow of the Splugen. I think it is coldest of all the passes. Near the top of the pass the diligence stops for awhile, and it is here, if I remember, that the Austrian officials demand the travellers' passports. At least in those days they did so. These officials have now retreated behind the Quadrilatere,—soon, as we hope, to make a further retreat,— and the district belongs to the kingdom of United Italy. There is a place of refreshment or hospice here, into which we all went for a few moments, and I then saw that my friend with the weak throat was accompanied by two ladies.

"You should not have missed the Via Mala," I said to him, as he stood warming his toes at the huge covered stove.

"We miss everything," said the elder of the two ladies, who, however, was very much younger than the gentleman, and not very much older than her companion.

"I saw it beautifully, mamma," said the younger one; whereupon mamma gave her head a toss, and made up her mind, as I thought, to take some little vengeance before long upon her step-daughter. I observed that Miss Greene always called her step-mother mamma on the first approach of any stranger, so that the nature of the connection between them might be understood. And I observed also that the elder lady always gave her head a toss when she was so addressed.

"We don't mean to enjoy ourselves till we get down to the lake of Como," said Mr. Greene. As I looked at him cowering over the stove, and saw how oppressed he was with great coats and warm wrappings for his throat, I quite agreed with him that he had not begun to enjoy himself as yet. Then we all got into our places again, and I saw no more of the Greenes till we were standing huddled together in the large courtyard of Conradi's hotel at Chiavenna.

Chiavenna is the first Italian town which the tourist reaches by this route, and I know no town in the North of Italy which is so closely surrounded by beautiful scenery. The traveller as he falls down to it from the Splugen road is bewildered by the loveliness of the valleys,—that is to say, if he so arranges that he can see them without pressing his nose against the glass of a coach window. And then from the town itself there are walks of two, three, and four hours, which I think are unsurpassed for wild and sometimes startling beauties. One gets into little valleys, green as emeralds, and surrounded on all sides by grey broken rocks, in which Italian Rasselases might have lived in perfect bliss; and then again one comes upon distant views up the river courses, bounded far away by the spurs of the Alps, which are perfect,—to which the fancy can add no additional charm. Conradi's hotel also is by no means bad; or was not in those days. For my part I am inclined to think that Italian hotels have received a worse name than they deserve; and I must profess that, looking merely to creature comforts, I would much sooner stay a week at the Golden Key at Chiavenna, than with mine host of the King's Head in the thriving commercial town of Muddleboro, on the borders of Yorkshire and Lancashire.

I am always rather keen about my room in travelling, and having secured a chamber looking out upon the mountains, had returned to the court-yard to collect my baggage before Mr. Greene had succeeded in realising his position, or understanding that he had to take upon himself the duties of settling his family for the night in the hotel by which he was surrounded. When I descended he was stripping off the outermost of three great coats, and four waiters around him were beseeching him to tell them what accommodation he would require. Mr. Greene was giving sundry very urgent instructions to the conductor respecting his boxes; but as these were given in English, I was not surprised to find that they were not accurately followed. The man, however, was much too courteous to say in any language that he did not understand every word that was said to him. Miss Greene was standing apart, doing nothing. As she was only eighteen years of age, it was of course her business to do nothing; and a very pretty little girl she was, by no means ignorant of her own beauty, and possessed of quite sufficient wit to enable her to make the most of it.

Mr. Greene was very leisurely in his proceedings, and the four waiters were almost reduced to despair.

"I want two bed-rooms, a dressing-room, and some dinner," he said at last, speaking very slowly, and in his own vernacular. I could not in the least assist him by translating it into Italian, for I did not speak a word of the language myself; but I suggested that the man would understand French. The waiter, however, had understood English. Waiters do understand all languages with a facility that is marvellous; and this one now suggested that Mrs. Greene should follow him up-stairs. Mrs. Greene, however, would not move till she had seen that her boxes were all right; and as Mrs. Greene was also a pretty woman, I found myself bound to apply myself to her assistance.

"Oh, thank you," said she. "The people are so stupid that one can really do nothing with them. And as for Mr. Greene, he is of no use at all. You see that box, the smaller one. I have four hundred pounds' worth of jewellery in that, and therefore I am obliged to look after it."

"Indeed," said I, rather startled at this amount of confidence on rather a short acquaintance. "In that case I do not wonder at your being careful. But is it not rather rash, perhaps—"

"I know what you are going to say. Well, perhaps it is rash. But when you are going to foreign courts, what are you to do? If you have got those sort of things you must wear them."

As I was not myself possessed of anything of that sort, and had no intention of going to any foreign court, I could not argue the matter with her. But I assisted her in getting together an enormous pile of luggage, among which there were seven large boxes covered with canvas, such as ladies not uncommonly carry with them when travelling. That one which she represented as being smaller than the others, and as holding jewellery, might be about a yard long by a foot and a half deep. Being ignorant in those matters, I should have thought it sufficient to carry all a lady's wardrobe for twelve months. When the boxes were collected together, she sat down upon the jewel-case and looked up into my face. She was a pretty woman, perhaps thirty years of age, with long light yellow hair, which she allowed to escape from her bonnet, knowing, perhaps, that it was not unbecoming to her when thus dishevelled. Her skin was very delicate, and her complexion good. Indeed her face would have been altogether prepossessing had there not been a want of gentleness in her eyes. Her hands, too, were soft and small, and on the whole she may be said to have been possessed of a strong battery of feminine attractions. She also well knew how to use them.

"Whisper," she said to me, with a peculiar but very proper aspiration on the h—"Wh-hisper," and both by the aspiration and the use of the word I knew at once from what island she had come. "Mr. Greene keeps all his money in this box also; so I never let it go out of my sight for a moment. But whatever you do, don't tell him that I told you so."

I laid my hand on my heart, and made a solemn asseveration that I would not divulge her secret. I need not, however, have troubled myself much on that head, for as I walked up stairs, keeping my eye upon the precious trunk, Mr. Greene addressed me.

"You are an Englishman, Mr. Robinson," said he. I acknowledged that I was.

"I am another. My wife, however, is Irish. My daughter,—by a former marriage,—is English also. You see that box there."

"Oh, yes," said I, "I see it." I began to be so fascinated by the box that I could not keep my eyes off it.

"I don't know whether or no it is prudent, but I keep all my money there; my money for travelling, I mean."

"If I were you, then," I answered, "I would not say anything about it to any one."

"Oh, no, of course not," said he; "I should not think of mentioning it. But those brigands in Italy always take away what you have about your person, but they don't meddle with the heavy luggage."

"Bills of exchange, or circular notes," I suggested.

"Ah, yes; and if you can't identify yourself, or happen to have a headache, you can't get them changed. I asked an old friend of mine, who has been connected with the Bank of England for the last fifty years, and he assured me that there was nothing like sovereigns."

"But you never get the value for them."

"Well, not quite. One loses a franc, or a franc and a half. But still, there's the certainty, and that's the great matter. An English sovereign will go anywhere," and he spoke these words with considerable triumph.

"Undoubtedly, if you consent to lose a shilling on each sovereign."

"At any rate, I have got three hundred and fifty in that box," he said. "I have them done up in rolls of twenty-five pounds each."

I again recommended him to keep this arrangement of his as private as possible,—a piece of counsel which I confess seemed to me to be much needed,—and then I went away to my own room, having first accepted an invitation from Mrs. Greene to join their party at dinner. "Do," said she; "we have been so dull, and it will be so pleasant."

I did not require to be much pressed to join myself to a party in which there was so pretty a girl as Miss Greene, and so attractive a woman as Mrs. Greene. I therefore accepted the invitation readily, and went away to make my toilet. As I did so I passed the door of Mr. Greene's room, and saw the long file of boxes being borne into the centre of it.

I spent a pleasant evening, with, however, one or two slight drawbacks. As to old Greene himself, he was all that was amiable; but then he was nervous, full of cares, and somewhat apt to be a bore. He wanted information on a thousand points, and did not seem to understand that a young man might prefer the conversation of his daughter to his own. Not that he showed any solicitude to prevent conversation on the part of his daughter. I should have been perfectly at liberty to talk to either of the ladies had he not wished to engross all my attention to himself. He also had found it dull to be alone with his wife and daughter for the last six weeks.

He was a small spare man, probably over fifty years of age, who gave me to understand that he had lived in London all his life, and had made his own fortune in the city. What he had done in the city to make his fortune he did not say. Had I come across him there I should no doubt have found him to be a sharp man of business, quite competent to teach me many a useful lesson of which I was as ignorant as an infant. Had he caught me on the Exchange, or at Lloyd's, or in the big room of the Bank of England, I should have been compelled to ask him everything. Now, in this little town under the Alps, he was as much lost as I should have been in Lombard Street, and was ready enough to look to me for information. I was by no means chary in giving him my counsel, and imparting to him my ideas on things in general in that part of the world;—only I should have preferred to be allowed to make myself civil to his daughter.

In the course of conversation it was mentioned by him that they intended to stay a few days at Bellaggio, which, as all the world knows, is a central spot on the lake of Como, and a favourite resting-place for travellers. There are three lakes which all meet here, and to all of which we give the name of Como. They are properly called the lakes of Como, Colico, and Lecco; and Bellaggio is the spot at which their waters join each other. I had half made up my mind to sleep there one night on my road into Italy, and now, on hearing their purpose, I declared that such was my intention.

"How very pleasant," said Mrs. Greene. "It will be quite delightful to have some one to show us how to settle ourselves, for really—"

"My dear, I'm sure you can't say that you ever have much trouble."

"And who does then, Mr. Greene? I am sure Sophonisba does not do much to help me."

"You won't let me," said Sophonisba, whose name I had not before heard. Her papa had called her Sophy in the yard of the inn. Sophonisba Greene! Sophonisba Robinson did not sound so badly in my ears, and I confess that I had tried the names together. Her papa had mentioned to me that he had no other child, and had mentioned also that he had made his fortune.

And then there was a little family contest as to the amount of travelling labour which fell to the lot of each of the party, during which I retired to one of the windows of the big front room in which we were sitting. And how much of this labour there is incidental to a tourist's pursuits! And how often these little contests do arise upon a journey! Who has ever travelled and not known them? I had taken up such a position at the window as might, I thought, have removed me out of hearing; but nevertheless from time to time a word would catch my ear about that precious box. "I have never taken MY eyes off it since I left England," said Mrs. Greene, speaking quick, and with a considerable brogue superinduced by her energy. "Where would it have been at Basle if I had not been looking after it?" "Quite safe," said Sophonisba; "those large things always are safe." "Are they, Miss? That's all you know about it. I suppose your bonnet-box was quite safe when I found it on the platform at—at—I forget the name of the place?"

"Freidrichshafen," said Sophonisba, with almost an unnecessary amount of Teutonic skill in her pronunciation. "Well, mamma, you have told me of that at least twenty times." Soon after that, the ladies took them to their own rooms, weary with the travelling of two days and a night, and Mr. Greene went fast asleep in the very comfortless chair in which he was seated.

At four o'clock on the next morning we started on our journey.

"Early to bed, and early to rise,
Is the way to be healthy, and wealthy, and wise."

We all know that lesson, and many of us believe in it; but if the lesson be true, the Italians ought to be the healthiest and wealthiest and wisest of all men and women. Three or four o'clock seems to them quite a natural hour for commencing the day's work. Why we should have started from Chiavenna at four o'clock in order that we might be kept waiting for the boat an hour and a half on the little quay at Colico, I don't know; but such was our destiny. There we remained an hour and a half; Mrs. Greene sitting pertinaciously on the one important box. She had designated it as being smaller than the others, and, as all the seven were now ranged in a row, I had an opportunity of comparing them. It was something smaller,—perhaps an inch less high, and an inch and a half shorter. She was a sharp woman, and observed my scrutiny. "I always know it," she said in a loud whisper, "by this little hole in the canvas," and she put her finger on a slight rent on one of the ends.

"As for Greene, if one of those Italian brigands were to walk off with it on his shoulders, before his eyes, he wouldn't be the wiser. How helpless you men are, Mr. Robinson!"

"It is well for us that we have women to look after us."

"But you have got no one to look after you;—or perhaps you have left her behind?"

"No, indeed. I'm all alone in the world as yet. But it's not my own fault. I have asked half a dozen."

"Now, Mr. Robinson!" And in this way the time passed on the quay at Colico, till the boat came and took us away. I should have preferred to pass my time in making myself agreeable to the younger lady; but the younger lady stood aloof, turning up her nose, as I thought, at her mamma.

I will not attempt to describe the scenery about Colico. The little town itself is one of the vilest places under the sun, having no accommodation for travellers, and being excessively unhealthy; but there is very little either north or south of the Alps,—and, perhaps, I may add, very little elsewhere,—to beat the beauty of the mountains which cluster round the head of the lake. When we had sat upon those boxes that hour and a half, we were taken on board the steamer, which had been lying off a little way from the shore, and then we commenced our journey. Of course there was a good deal of exertion and care necessary in getting the packages off from the shore on to the boat, and I observed that any one with half an eye in his head might have seen that the mental anxiety expended on that one box which was marked by the small hole in the canvas far exceeded that which was extended to all the other six boxes. "They deserve that it should be stolen," I said to myself, "for being such fools." And then we went down to breakfast in the cabin.

"I suppose it must be safe," said Mrs. Greene to me, ignoring the fact that the cabin waiter understood English, although she had just ordered some veal cutlets in that language.

"As safe as a church," I replied, not wishing to give much apparent importance to the subject.

"They can't carry it off here," said Mr. Greene. But he was innocent of any attempt at a joke, and was looking at me with all his eyes.

"They might throw it overboard," said Sophonisba. I at once made up my mind that she could not be a good-natured girl. The moment that breakfast was over, Mrs. Greene returned again upstairs, and I found her seated on one of the benches near the funnel, from which she could keep her eyes fixed upon the box. "When one is obliged to carry about one's jewels with one, one must be careful, Mr. Robinson," she said to me apologetically. But I was becoming tired of the box, and the funnel was hot and unpleasant, therefore I left her.

I had made up my mind that Sophonisba was ill-natured; but, nevertheless, she was pretty, and I now went through some little manoeuvres with the object of getting into conversation with her. This I soon did, and was surprised by her frankness. "How tired you must be of mamma and her box," she said to me. To this I made some answer, declaring that I was rather interested than otherwise in the safety of the precious trunk. "It makes me sick," said Sophonisba, "to hear her go on in that way to a perfect stranger. I heard what she said about her jewellery."

"It is natural she should be anxious," I said, "seeing that it contains so much that is valuable."

"Why did she bring them?" said Sophonisba. "She managed to live very well without jewels till papa married her, about a year since; and now she can't travel about for a month without lugging them with her everywhere. I should be so glad if some one would steal them."

"But all Mr. Greene's money is there also."

"I don't want papa to be bothered, but I declare I wish the box might be lost for a day or so. She is such a fool; don't you think so, Mr. Robinson?"

At this time it was just fourteen hours since I first had made their acquaintance in the yard of Conradi's hotel, and of those fourteen hours more than half had been passed in bed. I must confess that I looked upon Sophonisba as being almost more indiscreet than her mother-in-law. Nevertheless, she was not stupid, and I continued my conversation with her the greatest part of the way down the lake towards Bellaggio.

These steamers which run up and down the lake of Como and the Lago Maggiore, put out their passengers at the towns on the banks of the water by means of small rowing-boats, and the persons who are about to disembark generally have their own articles ready to their hands when their turn comes for leaving the steamer. As we came near to Bellaggio, I looked up my own portmanteau, and, pointing to the beautiful wood-covered hill that stands at the fork of the waters, told my friend Greene that he was near his destination. "I am very glad to hear it," said he, complacently, but he did not at the moment busy himself about the boxes. Then the small boat ran up alongside the steamer, and the passengers for Como and Milan crowded up the side.

"We have to go in that boat," I said to Greene.

"Nonsense!" he exclaimed.

"Oh, but we have."

"What! put our boxes into that boat," said Mrs. Greene. "Oh dear! Here, boatman! there are seven of these boxes, all in white like this," and she pointed to the one that had the hole in the canvas. "Make haste. And there are two bags, and my dressing case, and Mr. Greene's portmanteau. Mr. Greene, where is your portmanteau?"

The boatman whom she addressed, no doubt did not understand a word of English, but nevertheless he knew what she meant, and, being well accustomed to the work, got all the luggage together in an incredibly small number of moments.

"If you will get down into the boat," I said, "I will see that the luggage follows you before I leave the deck."

"I won't stir," she said, "till I see that box lifted down. Take care; you'll let it fall into the lake. I know you will."

"I wish they would," Sophonisba whispered into my ear.

Mr. Greene said nothing, but I could see that his eyes were as anxiously fixed on what was going on as were those of his wife. At last, however, the three Greens were in the boat, as also were all the packages. Then I followed them, my portmanteau having gone down before me, and we pushed off for Bellaggio. Up to this period most of the attendants around us had understood a word or two of English, but now it would be well if we could find some one to whose ears French would not be unfamiliar. As regarded Mr. Greene and his wife, they, I found, must give up all conversation, as they knew nothing of any language but their own. Sophonisba could make herself understood in French, and was quite at home, as she assured me, in German. And then the boat was beached on the shore at Bellaggio, and we all had to go again to work with the object of getting ourselves lodged at the hotel which overlooks the water.

I had learned before that the Greenes were quite free from any trouble in this respect, for their rooms had been taken for them before they left England. Trusting to this, Mrs. Greene gave herself no inconsiderable airs the moment her foot was on the shore, and ordered the people about as though she were the Lady Paramount of Bellaggio. Italians, however, are used to this from travellers of a certain description. They never resent such conduct, but simply put it down in the bill with the other articles. Mrs. Greene's words on this occasion were innocent enough, seeing that they were English; but had I been that head waiter who came down to the beach with his nice black shiny hair, and his napkin under his arm, I should have thought her manner very insolent.

Indeed, as it was, I did think so, and was inclined to be angry with her. She was to remain for some time at Bellaggio, and therefore it behoved her, as she thought, to assume the character of the grand lady at once. Hitherto she had been willing enough to do the work, but now she began to order about Mr. Greene and Sophonisba; and, as it appeared to me, to order me about also. I did not quite enjoy this; so leaving her still among her luggage and satellites, I walked up to the hotel to see about my own bed-room. I had some seltzer water, stood at the window for three or four minutes, and then walked up and down the room. But still the Greenes were not there. As I had put in at Bellaggio solely with the object of seeing something more of Sophonisba, it would not do for me to quarrel with them, or to allow them so to settle themselves in their private sitting-room, that I should be excluded. Therefore I returned again to the road by which they must come up, and met the procession near the house.

Mrs. Greene was leading it with great majesty, the waiter with the shiny hair walking by her side to point out to her the way. Then came all the luggage,—each porter carrying a white canvas-covered box. That which was so valuable no doubt was carried next to Mrs. Greene, so that she might at a moment's notice put her eye upon the well-known valuable rent. I confess that I did not observe the hole as the train passed by me, nor did I count the number of the boxes. Seven boxes, all alike, are very many; and then they were followed by three other men with the inferior articles,—Mr.

Greene's portmanteau, the carpetbag, &e., &c. At the tail of the line, I found Mr. Greene, and behind him Sophonisba. "All your fatigues will be over now," I said to the gentleman, thinking it well not to be too particular in my attentions to his daughter. He was panting beneath a terrible great-coat, having forgotten that the shores of an Italian lake are not so cold as the summits of the Alps, and did not answer me. "I'm sure I hope so," said Sophonisba. "And I shall advise papa not to go any farther unless he can persuade Mrs. Greene to send her jewels home." "Sophy, my dear," he said, "for Heaven's sake let us have a little peace since we are here." From all which I gathered that Mr. Green had not been fortunate in his second matrimonial adventure. We then made our way slowly up to the hotel, having been altogether distanced by the porters, and when we reached the house we found that the different packages were already being carried away through the house, some this way and some that. Mrs. Green, the meanwhile, was talking loudly at the door of her own sitting-room.

"Mr. Greene," she said, as soon as she saw her heavily oppressed spouse,—for the noonday sun was up,—"Mr. Greene, where are you?"

"Here, my dear," and Mr. Greene threw himself panting into the corner of a sofa.

"A little seltzer water and brandy," I suggested. Mr. Greene's inmost heart leaped at the hint, and nothing that his remonstrant wife could say would induce him to move, until he had enjoyed the delicious draught. In the mean time the box with the hole in the canvas had been lost.

Yes; when we came to look into matters, to count the packages, and to find out where we were, the box with the hole in the canvas was not there. Or, at any rate, Mrs. Greene said it was not there. I worked hard to look it up, and even went into Sophonisba's bed-room in my search. In Sophonisba's bed-room there was but one canvas-covered box. "That is my own," said she, "and it is all that I have, except this bag."

"Where on earth can it be?" said I, sitting down on the trunk in question. At the moment I almost thought that she had been instrumental in hiding it.

"How am I to know?" she answered; and I fancied that even she was dismayed. "What a fool that woman is!"

"The box must be in the house," I said.

"Do find it, for papa's sake; there's a good fellow. He will be so wretched without his money. I heard him say that he had only two pounds in his purse."

"Oh, I can let him have money to go on with," I answered grandly. And then I went off to prove that I was a good fellow, and searched throughout the house. Two white boxes had by order been left downstairs, as they would not be needed; and these two were in a large cupboard of the hall, which was used expressly for stowing away luggage. And then there were three in Mrs. Greene's bed-room, which had been taken there as containing the wardrobe which she would require while remaining at Bellaggio. I searched every one of these myself to see if I could find the hole in the canvas. But the hole in the canvas was not there. And let me count as I would, I could make out only six. Now there certainly had been seven on board the steamer, though I could not swear that I had seen the seven put into the small boat.

"Mr. Greene," said the lady standing in the middle of her remaining treasures, all of which were now open, "you are worth nothing when travelling. Were you not behind?" But Mr. Greene's mind was full, and he did not answer.

"It has been stolen before your very eyes," she continued.

"Nonsense, mamma," said Sophonisba. "If ever it came out of the steamer it certainly came into the house."

"I saw it out of the steamer," said Mrs. Greene, "and it certainly is not in the house. Mr. Robinson, may I trouble you to send for the police?—at once, if you please, sir."

I had been at Bellaggio twice before, but nevertheless I was ignorant of their system of police. And then, again, I did not know what was the Italian for the word.

"I will speak to the landlord," I said.

"If you will have the goodness to send for the police at once, I will be obliged to you." And as she thus reiterated her command, she stamped with her foot upon the floor.

"There are no police at Bellaggio," said Sophonisba.

"What on earth shall I do for money to go on with?" said Mr. Greene, looking piteously up to the ceiling, and shaking both his hands.

And now the whole house was in an uproar, including not only the landlord, his wife and daughters, and all the servants, but also every other visitor at the hotel. Mrs. Greene was not a lady who hid either her glories or her griefs under a bushel, and, though she spoke only in English, she soon made her protestations sufficiently audible. She protested loudly that she had been robbed, and that she had been robbed since she left the steamer. The box had come on shore; of that she was quite certain. If the landlord had any regard either for his own character or for that of his house, he would ascertain before an hour was over where it was, and who had been the thief. She would give him an hour. And then she sat herself down; but in two minutes she was up again, vociferating her wrongs as loudly as ever. All this was filtered through me and Sophonisba to the waiter in French, and from the waiter to the landlord; but the lady's gestures required no translation to make them intelligible, and the state of her mind on the matter was, I believe, perfectly well understood.

Mr. Greene I really did pity. His feelings of dismay seemed to be quite as deep, but his sorrow and solicitude were repressed into more decorum. "What am I to do for money?" he said. "I have not a shilling to go on with!" And he still looked up at the ceiling.

"You must send to England," said Sophonisba.

"It will take a month," he replied.

"Mr. Robinson will let you have what you want at present," added Sophonisba. Now I certainly had said so, and had meant it at the time. But my whole travelling store did not exceed forty or fifty pounds, with which I was going on to Venice, and then back to England through the Tyrol. Waiting a month for Mr. Greene's money from England might be even more inconvenient to me than to him. Then it occurred to me that the wants of the Greene family would be numerous and expensive, and that my small stock would go but a little way among so many. And what also if there had been no money and no jewels in that accursed box! I confess that at the moment such an idea did strike my mind. One hears of sharpers on every side committing depredations by means of most singular intrigues and contrivances. Might it not be possible that the whole batch of Greenes belonged to this order of society. It was a base idea, I own; but I confess that I entertained it for a moment.

I retired to my own room for a while that I might think over all the circumstances. There certainly had been seven boxes, and one had had a hole in the canvas. All the seven had certainly been on board the steamer. To so much I felt that I might safely swear. I had not counted the seven into the small boat, but on leaving the larger vessel I had looked about the deck to see that none of the Greene trappings were forgotten. If left on the steamer, it had been so left through an intent on the part of some one there employed. It was quite possible that the contents of the box had been ascertained through the imprudence of Mrs. Greene, and that it had been conveyed away so that it might be rifled at Como. As to Mrs. Greene's assertion that all the boxes had been put into the small boat, I thought nothing of it. The people at Bellaggio could not have known which box to steal, nor had there been time to concoct the plan in carrying the boxes up to the hotel. I came at last to this conclusion, that the missing trunk had either been purloined and carried on to Como,—in which case it would be necessary to lose no time in going after it; or that it had been put out of sight in some uncommonly clever way, by the Greenes themselves, as an excuse for borrowing as much money as they could raise and living without payment of their bills. With reference to the latter hypothesis, I declared to myself that Greene did not look like a swindler; but as to Mrs. Greene—! I confess that I did not feel so confident in regard to her.

Charity begins at home, so I proceeded to make myself comfortable in my room, feeling almost certain that I should not be able to leave Bellaggio on the following morning. I had opened my portmanteau when I first arrived, leaving it open on the floor as is my wont. Some people are always being robbed, and are always locking up everything; while others wander safe over the world and never lock up anything. For myself, I never turn a key anywhere, and no one ever purloins from me even a handkerchief. Cantabit vacuus—, and I am always sufficiently vacuus. Perhaps it is that I have not a handkerchief worth the stealing. It is your heavy-laden, suspicious, mal-adroit Greenes that the thieves attack. I now found out that the accommodating Boots, who already knew my ways, had taken my travelling gear into a dark recess which was intended to do for a dressing-room, and had there spread my portmanteau open upon some table or stool in the corner. It was a convenient arrangement, and there I left it during the whole period of my sojourn.

Mrs. Greene had given the landlord an hour to find the box, and during that time the landlord, the landlady, their three daughters, and all the servants in the house certainly did exert themselves to the utmost. Half a dozen times they came to my door, but I was luxuriating in a washing-tub, making up for that four-o'clock start from Chiavenna. I assured them, however, that the box was not there, and so the search passed by. At the end of the hour I went back to the Greenes according to promise, having resolved that some one must be sent on to Como to look after the missing article.

There was no necessity to knock at their sitting-room door, for it was wide open. I walked in, and found Mrs. Greene still engaged in attacking the landlord, while all the porters who had carried the luggage up to the house were standing round. Her voice was loud above the others, but, luckily for them all, she was speaking English. The landlord, I saw, was becoming sulky. He spoke in Italian, and we none of us understood him, but I gathered that he was declining to do anything further. The box, he was certain, had never come out of the steamer. The Boots stood by interpreting into French, and, acting as second interpreter, I put it into English.

Mr. Greene, who was seated on the sofa, groaned audibly, but said nothing. Sophonisba, who was sitting by him, beat upon the floor with both her feet.

"Do you hear, Mr. Greene?" said she, turning to him. "Do you mean to allow that vast amount of property to be lost without an effort? Are you prepared to replace my jewels?"

"Her jewels!" said Sophonisba, looking up into my face. "Papa had to pay the bill for every stitch she had when he married her." These last words were so spoken as to be audible only by me, but her first exclamation was loud enough. Were they people for whom it would be worth my while to delay my journey, and put myself to serious inconvenience with reference to money?

A few minutes afterwards I found myself with Greene on the terrace before the house. "What ought I to do?" said he.

"Go to Como," said I, "and look after your box. I will remain here and go on board the return steamer. It may perhaps be there."

"But I can't speak a word of Italian," said he.

"Take the Boots," said I.

"But I can't speak a word of French." And then it ended in my undertaking to go to Como. I swear that the thought struck me that I might as well take my portmanteau with me, and cut and run when I got there. The Greenes were nothing to me.

I did not, however, do this. I made the poor man a promise, and I kept it. I took merely a dressing-bag, for I knew that I must sleep at Como; and, thus resolving to disarrange all my plans, I started. I was in the midst of beautiful scenery, but I found it quite impossible to draw any enjoyment from it;—from that or from anything around me. My whole mind was given up to anathemas against this odious box, as to which I had undoubtedly heavy cause of complaint. What was the box to me? I went to Como by the afternoon steamer, and spent a long dreary evening down on the steamboat quays searching everywhere, and searching in vain. The boat by which we had left Colico had gone back to Colico, but the people swore that nothing had been left on board it. It was just possible that such a box might have gone on to Milan with the luggage of other passengers.

I slept at Como, and on the following morning I went on to Milan. There was no trace of the box to be found in that city. I went round to every hotel and travelling office, but could hear nothing of it. Parties had gone to Venice, and Florence, and Bologna, and any of them might have taken the box. No one, however, remembered it; and I returned back to Como, and thence to Bellaggio, reaching the latter place at nine in the evening, disappointed, weary, and cross.

"Has Monsieur found the accursed trunk?" said the Bellaggio Boots, meeting me on the quay.

"In the name of the—, no. Has it not turned up here?"

"Monsieur," said the Boots, "we shall all be mad soon. The poor master, he is mad already." And then I went up to the house.

"My jewels!" shouted Mrs. Greene, rushing to me with her arms stretched out as soon as she heard my step in the corridor. I am sure that she would have embraced me had I found the box. I had not, however, earned any such reward. "I can hear nothing of the box either at Como or Milan," I said.

"Then what on earth am I to do for my money?" said Mr. Greene.

I had had neither dinner nor supper, but the elder Greenes did not care for that. Mr. Greene sat silent in despair, and Mrs. Greene stormed about the room in her anger. "I am afraid you are very tired," said Sophonisba.

"I am tired, and hungry, and thirsty," said I. I was beginning to get angry, and to think myself ill used. And that idea as to a family of swindlers became strong again. Greene had borrowed ten napoleons from me before I started for Como, and I had spent above four in my fruitless journey to that place and Milan. I was beginning to fear that my whole purpose as to Venice and the Tyrol would be destroyed; and I had promised to meet friends at Innspruck, who,—who were very much preferable to the Greenes. As events turned out, I did meet them. Had I failed in this, the present Mrs. Robinson would not have been sitting opposite to me.

I went to my room and dressed myself, and then Sophonisba presided over the tea-table for me. "What are we to do?" she asked me in a confidential whisper.

"Wait for money from England."

"But they will think we are all sharpers," she said; "and upon my word I do not wonder at it from the way in which that woman goes on." She then leaned forward, resting her elbow on the table and her face on her hand, and told me a long history of all their family discomforts. Her papa was a very good sort of man, only he had been made a fool of by that intriguing woman, who had been left without a sixpence with which to bless herself. And now they had nothing but quarrels and misery. Papa did not always got the worst of it;—papa could rouse himself sometimes; only now he was beaten down and cowed by the loss of his money. This whispering confidence was very nice in its way, seeing that Sophonisba was a pretty girl; but the whole matter seemed to be full of suspicion.

"If they did not want to take you in in one way, they did in another," said the present Mrs. Robinson, when I told the story to her at Innspruck. I beg that it may be understood that at the time of my meeting the Greenes I was not engaged to the present Mrs. Robinson, and was open to make any matrimonial engagement that might have been pleasing to me.

On the next morning, after breakfast, we held a council of war. I had been informed that Mr. Greene had made a fortune, and was justified in presuming him to be a rich man. It seemed to me, therefore, that his course was easy. Let him wait at Bellaggio for more money, and when he returned home, let him buy Mrs. Greene more jewels. A poor man always presumes that a rich man is indifferent about his money. But in truth a rich man never is indifferent about his money, and poor Greene looked very blank at my proposition.

"Do you mean to say that it's gone for ever?" he asked.

"I'll not leave the country without knowing more about it," said Mrs. Greene.

"It certainly is very odd," said Sophonisba. Even Sophonisba seemed to think that I was too off-hand.

"It will be a month before I can get money, and my bill here will be something tremendous," said Greene.

"I wouldn't pay them a farthing till I got my box," said Mrs. Greene.

"That's nonsense," said Sophonisba. And so it was. "Hold your tongue, Miss!" said the step-mother.

"Indeed, I shall not hold my tongue," said the step-daughter. Poor Greene! He had lost more than his box within the last twelve months; for, as I had learned in that whispered conversation over the tea-table with Sophonisba; this was in reality her papa's marriage trip.

Another day was now gone, and we all went to bed. Had I not been very foolish I should have had myself called at five in the morning, and have gone away by the early boat, leaving my ten napoleons behind me. But, unfortunately, Sophonisba had exacted a promise from me that I would not do this, and thus all chance of spending a day or two in Venice was lost to me. Moreover, I was thoroughly fatigued, and almost glad of any excuse which would allow me to lie in bed on the following morning. I did lie in bed till nine o'clock, and then found the Greenes at breakfast.

"Let us go and look at the Serbelloni Gardens," said I, as soon as the silent meal was over; "or take a boat over to the Sommariva Villa."

"I should like it so much," said Sophonisba.

"We will do nothing of the kind till I have found my property," said Mrs. Greene. "Mr. Robinson, what arrangement did you make yesterday with the police at Como?"

"The police at Como?" I said. "I did not go to the police."

"Not go to the police? And do you mean to say that I am to be robbed of my jewels and no efforts made for redress? Is there no such thing as a constable in this wretched country? Mr. Greene, I do insist upon it that you at once go to the nearest British consul."

"I suppose I had better write home for money," said he.

"And do you mean to say that you haven't written yet?" said I, probably with some acrimony in my voice.

"You needn't scold papa," said Sophonisba.

"I don't know what I am to do," said Mr. Greene, and he began walking up and down the room; but still he did not call for pen and ink, and I began again to feel that he was a swindler. Was it possible that a man of business, who had made his fortune in London, should allow his wife to keep all her jewels in a box, and carry about his own money in the same?

"I don't see why you need be so very unhappy, papa," said Sophonisba. "Mr. Robinson, I'm sure, will let you have whatever money you may want at present." This was pleasant!

"And will Mr. Robinson return me my jewels which were lost, I must say, in a great measure, through his carelessness," said Mrs. Greene. This was pleasanter!

"Upon my word, Mrs. Greene, I must deny that," said I, jumping up. "What on earth could I have done more than I did do? I have been to Milan and nearly fagged myself to death."

"Why didn't you bring a policeman back with you?"

"You would tell everybody on board the boat what there was in it," said I.

"I told nobody but you," she answered.

"I suppose you mean to imply that I've taken the box," I rejoined. So that on this, the third or fourth day of our acquaintance, we did not go on together quite pleasantly.

But what annoyed me, perhaps, the most, was the confidence with which it seemed to be Mr. Greene's intention to lean upon my resources. He certainly had not written home yet, and had taken my ten napoleons, as one friend may take a few shillings from another when he finds that he has left his own silver on his dressing-table.

What could he have wanted of ten napoleons? He had alleged the necessity of paying the porters, but the few francs he had had in his pocket would have been enough for that. And now Sophonisba was ever and again prompt in her assurances that he need not annoy himself about money, because I was at his right hand. I went upstairs into my own room, and counting all my treasures, found that thirty-six pounds and some odd silver was the extent of my wealth. With that I had to go, at any rate, as far as Innspruck, and from thence back to London. It was quite impossible that I should make myself responsible for the Greenes' bill at Bellaggio.

We dined early, and after dinner, according to a promise made in the morning, Sophonisba ascended with me into the Serbelloni Gardens, and walked round the terraces on that beautiful hill which commands the view of the three lakes. When we started I confess that I would sooner have gone alone, for I was sick of the Greenes in my very soul. We had had a terrible day. The landlord had been sent for so often, that he refused to show himself again. The landlady—though Italians of that class are always courteous—had been so driven that she snapped her fingers in Mrs. Greene's face. The three girls would not show themselves. The waiters kept out of the way as much as possible; and the Boots, in confidence, abused them to me behind their back. "Monsieur," said the Boots, "do you think there ever was such a box?"

"Perhaps not," said I; and yet I knew that I had seen it.

I would, therefore, have preferred to walk without Sophonisba; but that now was impossible. So I determined that I would utilise the occasion by telling her of my present purpose. I had resolved to start on the following day, and it was now necessary to make my friends understand that it was not in my power to extend to them any further pecuniary assistance.

Sophonisba, when we were on the hill, seemed to have forgotten the box, and to be willing that I should forget it also. But this was impossible. When, therefore, she told me how sweet it was to escape from that terrible woman, and leaned on my arm with all the freedom of old acquaintance, I was obliged to cut short the pleasure of the moment.

"I hope your father has written that letter," said I.

"He means to write it from Milan. We know you want to get on, so we purpose to leave here the day after tomorrow."

"Oh!" said I thinking of the bill immediately, and remembering that Mrs. Greene had insisted on having champagne for dinner.

"And if anything more is to be done about the nasty box, it may be done there," continued Sophonisba.

"But I must go tomorrow," said I, "at 5 a.m."

"Nonsense," said Sophonisba. "Go tomorrow, when I,—I mean we,—are going on the next day!"

"And I might as well explain," said I, gently dropping the hand that was on my arm, "that I find,—I find it will be impossible for me—to—to—"

"To what?"

"To advance Mr. Greene any more money just at present." Then Sophonisba's arm dropped all at once, and she exclaimed, "Oh, Mr. Robinson!"

After all, there was a certain hard good sense about Miss Greene which would have protected her from my evil thoughts had I known all the truth. I found out afterwards that she was a considerable heiress, and, in spite of the opinion expressed by the present Mrs. Robinson when Miss Walker, I do not for a moment think she would have accepted me had I offered to her.

"You are quite right not to embarrass yourself," she said, when I explained to her my immediate circumstances; "but why did you make papa an offer which you cannot perform? He must remain here now till he hears from England. Had you explained it all at first, the ten napoleons would have carried us to Milan." This was all true, and yet I thought it hard upon me.

It was evident to me now, that Sophonisba was prepared to join her step-mother in thinking that I had ill-treated them, and I had not much doubt that I should find Mr. Greene to be of the same opinion. There was very little more said between us during the walk, and when we reached the hotel at seven or half-past seven o'clock, I merely remarked that I would go in and wish her father and mother goodbye. "I suppose you will drink tea with us," said Sophonisba, and to this I assented.

I went into my own room, and put all my things into my portmanteau, for according to the custom, which is invariable in Italy when an early start is premeditated, the Boots was imperative in his demand that the luggage should be ready over night. I then went to the Greene's sitting-room, and found that the whole party was now aware of my intentions.

"So you are going to desert us," said Mrs. Greene.

"I must go on upon my journey," I pleaded in a weak apologetic voice.

"Go on upon your journey, sir!" said Mrs. Greene. "I would not for a moment have you put yourself to inconvenience on our account." And yet I had already lost fourteen napoleons, and given up all prospect of going to Venice!

"Mr. Robinson is certainly right not to break his engagement with Miss Walker," said Sophonisba. Now I had said not a word about an engagement with Miss Walker, having only mentioned incidentally that she would be one of the party at Innspruck. "But," continued she, "I think he should not have misled us." And in this way we enjoyed our evening meal.

I was just about to shake hands with them all, previous to my final departure from their presence, when the Boots came into the room.

"I'll leave the portmanteau till tomorrow morning," said he.

"All right," said I.

"Because," said he, "there will be such a crowd of things in the hall. The big trunk I will take away now."

"Big trunk,—what big trunk?"

"The trunk with your rug over it, on which your portmanteau stood."

I looked round at Mr., Mrs., and Miss Greene, and saw that they were all looking at me. I looked round at them, and as their eyes met mine I felt that I turned as red as fire. I immediately jumped up and rushed away to my own room, hearing as I went that all their steps were following me. I rushed to the inner recess, pulled down the portmanteau, which still remained in its old place, tore away my own carpet rug which covered the support beneath it, and there saw—a white canvas-covered box, with a hole in the canvas on the side next to me!

"It is my box," said Mrs. Greene, pushing me away, as she hurried up and put her finger within the rent.

"It certainly does look like it," said Mr. Greene, peering over his wife's shoulder.

"There's no doubt about the box," said Sophonisba.

"Not the least in life," said I, trying to assume an indifferent look.

"Mon Dieu!" said the Boots.

"Corpo di Baccho!" exclaimed the landlord, who had now joined the party.

"Oh—h—h—h—!" screamed Mrs. Greene, and then she threw herself back on to my bed, and shrieked hysterically.

There was no doubt whatsoever about the fact. There was the lost box, and there it had been during all those tedious hours of unavailing search. While I was suffering all that fatigue in Milan, spending my precious zwanzigers in driving about from one hotel to another, the box had been safe, standing in my own room at Bellaggio, hidden by my own rug. And now that it was found everybody looked at me as though it were all my fault.

Mrs. Greene's eyes, when she had done being hysterical, were terrible, and Sophonisba looked at me as though I were a convicted thief.

"Who put the box here?" I said, turning fiercely upon the Boots.

"I did," said the Boots, "by Monsieur's express order."

"By my order?" I exclaimed.

"Certainly," said the Boots.

"Corpo di Baccho!" said the landlord, and he also looked at me as though I were a thief. In the mean time the landlady and the three daughters had clustered round Mrs. Greene, administering to her all manner of Italian consolation. The box, and the money, and the jewels were after all a reality; and much incivility can be forgiven to a lady who has really lost her jewels, and has really found them again.

There and then there arose a hurly-burly among us as to the manner in which the odious trunk found its way into my room. Had anybody been just enough to consider the matter coolly, it must have been quite clear that I could not have ordered it there. When I entered the hotel, the boxes were already being lugged about, and I had spoken a word to no one concerning them. That traitorous Boots had done it,—no doubt without malice prepense; but he had done it; and now that the Greenes were once more known as moneyed people, he turned upon me, and told me to my face, that I had desired that box to be taken to my own room as part of my own luggage!

"My dear," said Mr. Greene, turning to his wife, "you should never mention the contents of your luggage to any one."

"I never will again," said Mrs. Greene, with a mock repentant air, "but I really thought—"

"One never can be sure of sharpers," said Mr. Greene.

"That's true," said Mrs. Greene.

"After all, it may have been accidental," said Sophonisba, on hearing which good-natured surmise both papa and mamma Greene shook their suspicious heads.

I was resolved to say nothing then. It was all but impossible that they should really think that I had intended to steal their box; nor, if they did think so, would it have become me to vindicate myself before the landlord and all his servants. I stood by therefore in silence, while two of the men raised the trunk, and joined the procession which followed it as it was carried out of my room into that of the legitimate owner. Everybody in the house was there by that time, and Mrs. Greene, enjoying the triumph, by no means grudged them the entrance into her sitting-room. She had felt that she was suspected, and now she was determined that the world of Bellaggio should know how much she was above suspicion. The box was put down upon two chairs, the supporters who had borne it retiring a pace each. Mrs. Greene then advanced proudly with the selected key, and Mr. Greene stood by at her right shoulder, ready to receive his portion of the hidden treasure. Sophonisba was now indifferent, and threw herself on the sofa, while I walked up and down the room thoughtfully,—meditating what words I should say when I took my last farewell of the Greenes. But as I walked I could see what occurred. Mrs. Greene opened the box, and displayed to view the ample folds of a huge yellow woollen dressing-down. I could fancy that she would not willingly have exhibited this article of her toilet, had she not felt that its existence would speedily be merged in the presence of the glories which were to follow. This had merely been the padding at the top of the box. Under that lay a long papier-mache case, and in that were all her treasures. "Ah, they are safe," she said, opening the lid and looking upon her tawdry pearls and carbuncles.

Mr. Greene, in the mean time, well knowing the passage for his hand, had dived down to the very bottom of the box, and seized hold of a small canvas bag. "It is here," said he, dragging it up, "and as far as I can tell, as yet, the knot has not been untied." Whereupon he sat himself down by Sophonisba, and employing her to assist him in holding them, began to count his rolls. "They are all right," said he; and he wiped the perspiration from his brow.

I had not yet made up my mind in what manner I might best utter my last words among them so as to maintain the dignity of my character, and now I was standing over against Mr. Greene with my arms folded on my breast. I had on my face a frown of displeasure, which I am able to assume upon occasions, but I had not yet determined what words I would use. After all, perhaps, it might be as well that I should leave them without any last words.

"Greene, my dear," said the lady, "pay the gentleman his ten napoleons."

"Oh yes, certainly;" whereupon Mr. Greene undid one of the rolls and extracted eight sovereigns. "I believe that will make it right, sir," said he, handing them to me.

I took the gold, slipped it with an indifferent air into my waistcoat pocket, and then refolded my arms across my breast.

"Papa," said Sophonisba, in a very audible whisper, "Mr. Robinson went for you to Como. Indeed, I believe he says he went to Milan."

"Do not let that be mentioned," said I.

"By all means pay him his expenses," said Mrs. Greene; "I would not owe him anything for worlds."

"He should be paid," said Sophonisba.

"Oh, certainly," said Mr. Greene. And he at once extracted another sovereign, and tendered it to me in the face of the assembled multitude.

This was too much! "Mr. Greene," said I, "I intended to be of service to you when I went to Milan, and you are very welcome to the benefit of my intentions. The expense of that journey, whatever may be its amount, is my own affair." And I remained standing with my closed arms.

"We will be under no obligation to him," said Mrs. Greene; "and I shall insist on his taking the money."

"The servant will put it on his dressing-table," said Sophonisba. And she handed the sovereign to the Boots, giving him instructions.

"Keep it yourself, Antonio," I said. Whereupon the man chucked it to the ceiling with his thumb, caught it as it fell, and with a well-satisfied air, dropped it into the recesses of his pocket. The air of the Greenes was also well satisfied, for they felt that they had paid me in full for all my services.

And now, with many obsequious bows and assurances of deep respect, the landlord and his family withdrew from the room. "Was there anything else they could do for Mrs. Greene?" Mrs. Greene was all affability. She had shown her jewels to the girls, and allowed them to express their admiration in pretty Italian superlatives. There was nothing else she wanted tonight. She was very happy and liked Bellaggio. She would stay yet a week, and would make herself quite happy. And, though none of them understood a word that the other said, each understood that things were now rose-coloured, and so with scrapings, bows, and grinning smiles, the landlord and all his myrmidons withdrew. Mr. Greene was still counting his money, sovereign by sovereign, and I was still standing with my folded arms upon my bosom.

"I believe I may now go," said I.

"Good night," said Mrs. Greene.

"Adieu," said Sophonisba.

"I have the pleasure of wishing you goodbye," said Mr. Greene.

And then I walked out of the room. After all, what was the use of saying anything? And what could I say that would have done me any service? If they were capable of thinking me a thief,—which they certainly did,—nothing that I could say would remove the impression. Nor, as I thought, was it suitable that I should defend myself from such an imputation. What were the Greenes to me? So I walked slowly out of the room, and never again saw one of the family from that day to this.

As I stood upon the beach the next morning, while my portmanteau was being handed into the boat, I gave the Boots five zwanzigers. I was determined to show him that I did not condescend to feel anger against him.

He took the money, looked into my face, and then whispered to me, "Why did you not give me a word of notice beforehand?" he said, and winked his eye. He was evidently a thief, and took me to be another;—but what did it matter?

I went thence to Milan, in which city I had no heart to look at anything; thence to Verona, and so over the pass of the Brenner to Innspruck. When I once found myself near to my dear friends the Walkers I was again a happy man; and I may safely declare that, though a portion of my journey was so troublesome and unfortunate, I look back upon that tour as the happiest and the luckiest epoch of my life.

LA MERE BAUCHE FROM "TALES FROM ALL COUNTRIES"

The Pyreneean valley in which the baths of Vernet are situated is not much known to English, or indeed to any travellers. Tourists in search of good hotels and picturesque beauty combined, do not generally extend their journeys to the Eastern Pyrenees. They rarely get beyond Luchon; and in this they are right, as they thus end their peregrinations at the most lovely spot among these mountains, and are as a rule so deceived, imposed on, and bewildered by guides, innkeepers, and horse-owners, at this otherwise delightful place, as to become undesirous of further travel. Nor do invalids from distant parts frequent Vernet. People of fashion go to the Eaux Bonnes and to Luchon, and people who are really ill to Bareges and Cauterets. It is at these places that one meets crowds of Parisians, and the daughters and wives of rich merchants from Bordeaux, with an admixture, now by no means inconsiderable, of Englishmen and Englishwomen. But the Eastern Pyrenees are still unfrequented. And probably they will remain so; for though there are among them lovely valleys—and of all such the valley of Vernet is perhaps the most lovely—they cannot compete with the mountain scenery of other tourists-loved regions in Europe. At the Port de Venasquez and the Breche de Roland in the Western Pyrenees, or rather, to speak more truly, at spots in the close vicinity of these famous mountain entrances from France into Spain, one can make comparisons with Switzerland, Northern Italy, the Tyrol, and Ireland, which will not be injurious to the scenes then under view. But among the eastern mountains this can rarely be done. The hills do not stand thickly together so as to group themselves; the passes from one valley to another, though not wanting in altitude, are not close pressed together with overhanging rocks, and are deficient in grandeur as well as loveliness. And then, as a natural consequence of all this, the hotels—are not quite as good as they should be.

But there is one mountain among them which can claim to rank with the Pic du Midi or the Maledetta. No one can pooh-pooh the stern old Canigou, standing high and solitary, solemn and grand, between the two roads which run from Perpignan into Spain, the one by Prades and the other by Le Boulon. Under the Canigou, towards the west, lie the hot baths of Vernet, in a close secluded valley, which, as I have said before, is, as far as I know, the sweetest spot in these Eastern Pyrenees.

The frequenters of these baths were a few years back gathered almost entirely from towns not very far distant, from Perpignan, Narbonne, Carcassonne, and Bezieres, and the baths were not therefore famous, expensive, or luxurious; but those who believed in them believed with great faith; and it was certainly the fact that men and women who went thither worn with toil, sick with excesses, and nervous through over-care, came back fresh and strong, fit once more to attack the world with all its woes. Their character in latter days does not seem to have changed, though their circle of admirers may perhaps be somewhat extended.

In those days, by far the most noted and illustrious person in the village of Vernet was La Mere Bauche. That there had once been a Pere Bauche was known to the world, for there was a Fils Bauche who lived with his mother; but no one seemed to remember more of him than that he had once existed. At Vernet he had never been known. La Mere Bauche was a native of the village, but her married life had been passed away from it, and she had returned in her early widowhood to become proprietress and manager, or, as one may say, the heart and soul of the Hotel Bauche at Vernet.

This hotel was a large and somewhat rough establishment, intended for the accommodation of invalids who came to Vernet for their health. It was built immediately over one of the thermal springs, so that the water flowed from the bowels of the earth directly into the baths. There was accommodation for seventy people, and during the summer and autumn months the place was always full. Not a few also were to be found there during the winter and spring, for the charges of Madame Bauche were low, and the accommodation reasonably good.

And in this respect, as indeed in all others, Madame Bauche had the reputation of being an honest woman. She had a certain price, from which no earthly consideration would induce her to depart; and there were certain returns for this price in the shape of dejeuners and dinners, baths and beds, which she never failed to give in accordance with the dictates of a strict conscience. These were traits in the character of an hotel-keeper which cannot be praised too highly, and which had met their due reward in the custom of the public. But nevertheless there were those who thought that there was occasionally ground for complaint in the conduct even of Madame Bauche.

In the first place she was deficient in that pleasant smiling softness which should belong to any keeper of a house of public entertainment. In her general mode of life she was stern and silent with her guests, autocratic, authoritative and sometimes contradictory in her house, and altogether irrational and unconciliatory when any change even for a day was proposed to her, or when any shadow of a complaint reached her ears.

Indeed of complaint, as made against the establishment, she was altogether intolerant. To such she had but one answer. He or she who complained might leave the place at a moment's notice if it so pleased them. There were always others ready to take their places. The power of making this answer came to her from the lowness of her prices; and it was a power which was very dear to her.

The baths were taken at different hours according to medical advice, but the usual time was from five to seven in the morning. The dejeuner or early meal was at nine o'clock, the dinner was at four. After that, no eating or drinking was allowed in the Hotel Bauche. There was a cafe in the village, at which ladies and gentlemen could get a cup of coffee or a glass of eau sucre; but no such accommodation was to be had in the establishment. Not by any possible bribery or persuasion could any meal be procured at any other than the authorised hours. A visitor who should enter the salle a manger more than ten minutes after the last bell would be looked at very sourly by Madame Bauche, who on all occasions sat at the top of her own table. Should any one appear as much as half an hour late, he would receive only his share of what had not been handed round. But after the last dish had been so handed, it was utterly useless for any one to enter the room at all.

Her appearance at the period of our tale was perhaps not altogether in her favour. She was about sixty years of age and was very stout and short in the neck. She wore her own gray hair, which at dinner was always tidy enough; but during the 'whole day previous to that hour she might be seen with it escaping from under her cap in extreme disorder. Her eyebrows were large and bushy, but those alone would not have given to her face that look of indomitable sternness which it possessed. Her eyebrows were serious in their effect, but not so serious as the pair of green spectacles which she always wore under them. It was thought by those who had analysed the subject that the great secret of Madame Bauche's power lay in her green spectacles.

Her custom was to move about and through the whole establishment every day from breakfast till the period came for her to dress for dinner. She would visit every chamber and every bath, walk once or twice round the salle a manger, and very repeatedly round the kitchen; she would go into every hole and corner, and peer into everything through her green spectacles: and in these walks it was not always thought pleasant to meet her. Her custom was to move very slowly, with her hands generally clasped behind her back: she rarely spoke to the guests unless she was spoken to, and on such occasions she would not often diverge into general conversation. If any one had aught to say connected with the business of the establishment, she would listen, and then she would make her answers,—often not pleasant in the hearing.

And thus she walked her path through the world, a stern, hard, solemn old woman, not without gusts of passionate explosion; but honest withal, and not without some inward benevolence and true tenderness of heart. Children she had had many, some seven or eight. One or two had died, others had been married; she had sons settled far away from home, and at the time of which we are now speaking but one was left in any way subject to maternal authority.

Adolphe Bauche was the only one of her children of whom much was remembered by the present denizens and hangers-on of the hotel, he was the youngest of the number, and having been born only very shortly before the return of Madame Bauche to Vernet, had been altogether reared there. It was thought by the world of those parts, and rightly thought, that he was his mother's darling—more so than had been any of his brothers and sisters,—the very apple of her eye and gem of her life. At this time he was about twenty-five years of age, and for the last two years had been absent from Vernet—for reasons which will shortly be made to appear. He had been sent to Paris to see something of the world, and learn to talk French instead of the patois of his valley; and having left Paris had come down south into Languedoc, and remained there picking up some agricultural lore which it was thought might prove useful in the valley farms of Vernet. He was now expected home again very speedily, much to his mother's delight.

That she was kind and gracious to her favourite child does not perhaps give much proof of her benevolence; but she had also been kind and gracious to the orphan child of a neighbour; nay, to the orphan child of a rival innkeeper. At Vernet there had been more than one water establishment, but the proprietor of the second had died some few years after Madame Bauche had settled herself at the place. His house had not thrived, and his only child, a little girl, was left altogether without provision.

This little girl, Marie Clavert, La Mere Bauche had taken into her own house immediately after the father's death, although she had most cordially hated that father. Marie was then an infant, and Madame Bauche had accepted the charge without much thought, perhaps, as to what might be the child's ultimate destiny. But since then she had thoroughly done the duty of a mother by the little girl, who had become the pet of the whole establishment, the favourite plaything of Adolphe Bauche, and at last of course his early sweetheart.

And then and therefore there had come troubles at Vernet. Of course all the world of the valley had seen what was taking place and what was likely to take place, long before Madame Bauche knew anything about it. But at last it broke upon her senses that her son, Adolphe Bauche, the heir to all her virtues and all her riches, the first young man in that or any neighbouring valley, was absolutely contemplating the idea of marrying that poor little orphan, Marie Clavert!

That any one should ever fall in love with Marie Clavert had never occurred to Madame Bauche. She had always regarded the child as a child, as the object of her charity, and as a little thing to be looked on as poor Marie by all the world. She, looking through her green spectacles, had never seen that Marie Clavert was a beautiful creature, full of ripening charms, such as young men love to look on. Marie was of infinite daily use to Madame Bauche in a hundred little things about the house, and the old lady thoroughly recognised and appreciated her ability. But for this very reason she had never taught herself to regard Marie otherwise than as a useful drudge. She was very fond of her protegee—so much so that she would listen to her in affairs about the house when she would listen to no one else;—but Marie's prettiness and grace and sweetness as a girl had all been thrown away upon Maman Bauche, as Marie used to call her.

But unluckily it had not been thrown away upon Adolphe. He had appreciated, as it was natural that he should do, all that had been so utterly indifferent to his mother; and consequently had fallen in love. Consequently also he had told his love; and consequently also Marie had returned his love.

Adolphe had been hitherto contradicted but in few things, and thought that all difficulty would be prevented by his informing his mother that he wished to marry Marie Clavert. But Marie, with a woman's instinct, had known better. She had trembled and almost crouched with fear when she confessed her love; and had absolutely hid herself from sight when Adolphe went forth, prepared to ask his mother's consent to his marriage.

The indignation and passionate wrath of Madame Bauche were past and gone two years before the date of this story, and I need not therefore much enlarge upon that subject. She was at first abusive and bitter, which was bad for Marie; and afterwards bitter and silent, which was worse. It was of course determined that poor Marie should be sent away to some asylum for orphans or penniless paupers—in short anywhere out of the way. What mattered her outlook into the world, her happiness, or indeed her very existence? The outlook and happiness of Adolphe Bauche,—was not that to be considered as everything at Vernet?

But this terrible sharp aspect of affairs did not last very long. In the first place La Mere Bauche had under those green spectacles a heart that in truth was tender and affectionate, and after the first two days of anger she admitted that something must be done for Marie Clavert; and after the fourth day she acknowledged that the world of the hotel, her world, would not go as well without Marie Clavert as it would with her. And in the next place Madame Bauche had a friend whose advice in grave matters she would sometimes take. This friend had told her that it would be much better to send away Adolphe, since it was so necessary that there should be a sending away of some one; that he would be much benefited by passing some months of his life away from his native valley; and that an absence of a year or two would teach him to forget Marie, even if it did not teach Marie to forget him.

And we must say a word or two about this friend. At Vernet he was usually called M. le Capitaine, though in fact he had never reached that rank. He had been in the army, and having been wounded in the leg while still a sous-lieutenant, had been pensioned, and had thus been interdicted from treading any further the thorny path that leads to glory. For the last fifteen years he had resided under the roof of Madame Bauche, at first as a casual visitor, going and coming, but now for many years as constant there as she was herself.

He was so constantly called Le Capitaine that his real name was seldom heard. It may however as well be known to us that this was Theodore Campan. He was a tall, well-looking man; always dressed in black garments, of a coarse description certainly, but scrupulously clean and well brushed; of perhaps fifty years of age, and conspicuous for the rigid uprightness of his back—and for a black wooden leg.

This wooden leg was perhaps the most remarkable trait in his character. It was always jet black, being painted, or polished, or japanned, as occasion might require, by the hands of the capitaine himself. It was longer than ordinary wooden legs, as indeed the capitaine was longer than ordinary men; but nevertheless it never seemed in any way to impede the rigid punctilious propriety of his movements. It was never in his way as wooden legs usually are in the way of their wearers. And then to render it more illustrious it had round its middle, round the calf of the leg we may so say, a band of bright brass which shone like burnished gold.

It had been the capitaine's custom, now for some years past, to retire every evening at about seven o'clock into the sanctum sanctorum of Madame Bauche's habitation, the dark little private sitting-room in which she made out her bills and calculated her profits, and there regale himself in her presence—and indeed at her expense, for the items never appeared in the bill—with coffee and cognac. I have said that there was never eating or drinking at the establishment after the regular dinner-hours; but in so saying I spoke of the world at large. Nothing further was allowed in the way of trade; but in the way of friendship so much was now-a-days always allowed to the capitaine.

It was at these moments that Madame Bauche discussed her private affairs, and asked for and received advice. For even Madame Bauche was mortal; nor could her green spectacles without other aid carry her through all the troubles of life. It was now five years since the world of Vernet discovered that La Mere Bauche was going to marry the capitaine; and for eighteen months the world of Vernet had been full of this matter: but any amount of patience is at last exhausted, and as no further steps in that direction were ever taken beyond the daily cup of coffee, that subject died away—very much unheeded by La Mere Bauche.

But she, though she thought of no matrimony for herself, thought much of matrimony for other people; and over most of those cups of evening coffee and cognac a matrimonial project was discussed in these latter days. It has been seen that the capitaine pleaded in Marie's favour when the fury of Madame Bauche's indignation broke forth; and that ultimately Marie was kept at home, and Adolphe sent away by his advice.

"But Adolphe cannot always stay away," Madame Bauche had pleaded in her difficulty. The truth of this the capitaine had admitted; but Marie, he said, might be married to some one else before two years were over. And so the matter had commenced.

But to whom should she be married? To this question the capitaine had answered in perfect innocence of heart, that La Mere Bauche would be much better able to make such a choice than himself. He did not know how Marie might stand with regard to money. If madame would give some little "dot," the affair, the capitaine thought, would be more easily arranged.

All these things took months to say, during which period Marie went on with her work in melancholy listlessness. One comfort she had. Adolphe, before he went, had promised to her, holding in his hand as he did so a little cross which she had given him, that no earthly consideration should sever them;—that sooner or later he would certainly be her husband. Marie felt that her limbs could not work nor her tongue speak were it not for this one drop of water in her cup.

And then, deeply meditating, La Mere Bauche hit upon a plan, and herself communicated it to the capitaine over a second cup of coffee into which she poured a full teaspoonful more than the usual allowance of cognac. Why should not he, the capitaine himself, be the man to marry Marie Clavert?

It was a very startling proposal, the idea of matrimony for himself never having as yet entered into the capitaine's head at any period of his life; but La Mere Bauche did contrive to make it not altogether unacceptable. As to that matter of dowry she was prepared to be more than generous. She did love Marie well, and could find it in her heart to give her anything—any thing except her son, her own Adolphe. What she proposed was this. Adolphe, himself, would never keep the baths. If the capitaine would take Marie for his wife, Marie, Madame Bauche declared, should be the mistress after her death; subject of course to certain settlements as to Adolphe's pecuniary interests.

The plan was discussed a thousand times, and at last so far brought to bear that Marie was made acquainted with it—having been called in to sit in presence with La Mere Bauche and her future proposed husband. The poor girl manifested no disgust to the stiff ungainly lover whom they assigned to her,—who through his whole frame was in appearance almost as wooden as his own leg. On the whole, indeed, Marie liked the capitaine, and felt that he was her friend; and in her country such marriages were not uncommon. The capitaine was perhaps a little beyond the age at which a man might usually be thought justified in demanding the services of a young girl as his nurse and wife, but then Marie of herself had so little to give—except her youth, and beauty, and goodness.

But yet she could not absolutely consent; for was she not absolutely pledged to her own Adolphe? And therefore, when the great pecuniary advantages were, one by one, displayed before her, and when La Mere Bauche, as a last argument, informed her that as wife of the capitaine she would be regarded as second mistress in the establishment and not as a servant, she could only burst out into tears, and say that she did not know.

"I will be very kind to you," said the capitaine; "as kind as a man can be."

Marie took his hard withered hand and kissed it; and then looked up into his face with beseeching eyes which were not without avail upon his heart.

"We will not press her now," said the capitaine. "There is time enough."

But let his heart be touched ever so much, one thing was certain. It could not be permitted that she should marry Adolphe. To that view of the matter he had given in his unrestricted adhesion; nor could he by any means withdraw it without losing altogether his position in the establishment of Madame Bauche. Nor indeed did his conscience tell him that such a marriage should be permitted. That would be too much. If every pretty girl were allowed to marry the first young man that might fall in love with her, what would the world come to?

And it soon appeared that there was not time enough—that the time was growing very scant. In three months Adolphe would be back. And if everything was not arranged by that time, matters might still go astray.

And then Madame Bauche asked her final question: "You do not think, do you, that you can ever marry Adolphe?" And as she asked it the accustomed terror of her green spectacles magnified itself tenfold. Marie could only answer by another burst of tears.

The affair was at last settled among them. Marie said that she would consent to marry the capitaine when she should hear from Adolphe's own mouth that he, Adolphe, loved her no longer. She declared with many tears that her vows and pledges prevented her from promising more than this. It was not her fault, at any rate not now, that she loved her lover. It was not her fault—not now at least—that she was bound by these pledges. When she heard from his own mouth that he had discarded her, then she would marry the capitaine—or indeed sacrifice herself in any other way that La Mere Bauche might desire. What would anything signify then?

Madame Bauche's spectacles remained unmoved; but not her heart. Marie, she told the capitaine, should be equal to herself in the establishment, when once she was entitled to be called Madame Campan, and she should be to her quite as a daughter. She should have her cup of coffee every evening, and dine at the big table, and wear a silk gown at church, and the servants should all call her Madame; a great career should be open to her, if she would only give up her foolish girlish childish love for Adolphe. And all these great promises were repeated to Marie by the capitaine.

But nevertheless there was but one thing in the world which in Marie's eyes was of any value; and that one thing was the heart of Adolphe Bauche. Without that she would be nothing; with that,—with that assured, she could wait patiently till doomsday.

Letters were written to Adolphe during all these eventful doings; and a letter came from him saying that he greatly valued Marie's love, but that as it had been clearly proved to him that their marriage would be neither for her advantage, nor for his, he was willing to give it up. He consented to her marriage with the capitaine, and expressed his gratitude to his mother for the pecuniary advantages which she had held out to him. Oh, Adolphe, Adolphe! But, alas, alas! is not such the way of most men's hearts—and of the hearts of some women?

This letter was read to Marie, but it had no more effect upon her than would have had some dry legal document. In those days and in those places men and women did not depend much upon letters; nor when they were written, was there expressed in them much of heart or of feeling. Marie would understand, as she was well aware, the glance of Adolphe's eye and the tone of Adolphe's voice; she would perceive at once from them what her lover really meant, what he wished, what in the innermost corner of his heart he really desired that she should do. But from that stiff constrained written document she could understand nothing.

It was agreed therefore that Adolphe should return, and that she would accept her fate from his mouth. The capitaine, who knew more of human nature than poor Marie, felt tolerably sure of his bride. Adolphe, who had seen something of the world, would not care very much for the girl of his own valley. Money and pleasure, and some little position in the world, would soon wean him from his love; and then Marie would accept her destiny—as other girls in the same position had done since the French world began.

And now it was the evening before Adolphe's expected arrival. La Mere Bauche was discussing the matter with the capitaine over the usual cup of coffee. Madame Bauche had of late become rather nervous on the matter, thinking that they had been somewhat rash in acceding so much to Marie. It seemed to her that it was absolutely now left to the two young lovers to say whether or no they would have each other or not. Now nothing on earth could be further from Madame Bauche's intention than this. Her decree and resolve was to heap down blessings on all persons concerned—provided always that she could have her own way; but, provided she did not have her own way, to heap down,—anything but blessings. She had her code of morality in this matter. She would do good if possible to everybody around her. But she would not on any score be induced to consent that Adolphe should marry Marie Clavert. Should that be in the wind she would rid the house of Marie, of the capitaine, and even of Adolphe himself.

She had become therefore somewhat querulous, and self-opinionated in her discussions with her friend.

"I don't know," she said on the evening in question; "I don't know. It may be all right; but if Adolphe turns against me, what are we to do then?"

"Mere Bauche," said the capitaine, sipping his coffee and puffing out the smoke of his cigar, "Adolphe will not turn against us." It had been somewhat remarked by many that the capitaine was more at home in the house, and somewhat freer in his manner of talking with Madame Bauche, since this matrimonial alliance had been on the tapis than he had ever been before. La Mere herself observed it, and did not quite like it; but how could she prevent it now? When the capitaine was once married she would make him know his place, in spite of all her promises to Marie.

"But if he says he likes the girl?" continued Madame Bauche.

"My friend, you may be sure that he will say nothing of the kind. He has not been away two years without seeing girls as pretty as Marie. And then you have his letter."

"That is nothing, capitaine; he would eat his letter as quick as you would eat an omelet aux fines herbes."

Now the capitaine was especially quick over an omelet aux fines herbes.

"And, Mere Bauche, you also have the purse; he will know that he cannot eat that, except with your good will."

"Ah!" exclaimed Madame Bauche, "poor lad! He has not a sous in the world unless I give it to him." But it did not seem that this reflection was in itself displeasing to her.

"Adolphe will now be a man of the world," continued the capitaine. "He will know that it does not do to throw away everything for a pair of red lips. That is the folly of a boy, and Adolphe will be no longer a boy. Believe me, Mere Bauche, things will be right enough."

"And then we shall have Marie sick and ill and half dying on our hands," said Madame Bauche.

This was not flattering to the capitaine, and so he felt it. "Perhaps so, perhaps not," he said. "But at any rate she will get over it. It is a malady which rarely kills young women—especially when another alliance awaits them."

"Bah!" said Madame Bauche; and in saying that word she avenged herself for the too great liberty which the capitaine had lately taken. He shrugged his shoulders, took a pinch of snuff and uninvited helped himself to a teaspoonful of cognac. Then the conference ended, and on the next morning before breakfast Adolphe Bauche arrived.

On that morning poor Marie hardly knew how to bear herself. A month or two back, and even up to the last day or two, she had felt a sort of confidence that Adolphe would be true to her; but the nearer came that fatal day the less strong was the confidence of the poor girl. She knew that those two long-headed, aged counsellors were plotting against her happiness, and she felt that she could hardly dare hope for success with such terrible foes opposed to her. On the evening before the day Madame Bauche had met her in the passages, and kissed her as she wished her good night. Marie knew little about sacrifices, but she felt that it was a sacrificial kiss.

In those days a sort of diligence with the mails for Olette passed through Prades early in the morning, and a conveyance was sent from Vernet to bring Adolphe to the baths. Never was prince or princess expected with more anxiety. Madame Bauche was up and dressed long before the hour, and was heard to say five several times that she was sure he would not come. The capitaine was out and on the high road, moving about with his wooden leg, as perpendicular as a lamp-post and almost as black. Marie also was up, but nobody had seen her. She was up and had been out about the place before any of them were stirring; but now that the world was on the move she lay hidden like a hare in its form.

And then the old char-a-banc clattered up to the door, and Adolphe jumped out of it into his mother's arms. He was fatter and fairer than she had last seen him, had a larger beard, was more fashionably clothed, and certainly looked more like a man. Marie also saw him out of her little window, and she thought that he looked like a god. Was it probable, she said to herself, that one so godlike would still care for her?

The mother was delighted with her son, who rattled away quite at his ease. He shook hands very cordially with the capitaine—of whose intended alliance with his own sweetheart he had been informed, and then as he entered the house with his hand under his mother's arm, he asked one question about her. "And where is Marie?" said he. "Marie! oh upstairs; you shall see her after breakfast," said La Mere Bauche. And so they entered the house, and went in to breakfast among the guests. Everybody had heard something of the story, and they were all on the alert to see the young man whose love or want of love was considered to be of so much importance.

"You will see that it will be all right," said the capitaine, carrying his head very high.

"I think so, I think so," said La Mere Bauche, who, now that the capitaine was right, no longer desired to contradict him.

"I know that it will be all right," said the capitaine. "I told you that Adolphe would return a man; and he is a man. Look at him; he does not care this for Marie Clavert;" and the capitaine, with much eloquence in his motion, pitched over a neighbouring wall a small stone which he held in his hand.

And then they all went to breakfast with many signs of outward joy. And not without some inward joy; for Madame Bauche thought she saw that her son was cured of his love. In the mean time Marie sat up stairs still afraid to show herself.

"He has come," said a young girl, a servant in the house, running up to the door of Marie's room.

"Yes," said Marie; "I could see that he has come."

"And, oh, how beautiful he is!" said the girl, putting her hands together and looking up to the ceiling. Marie in her heart of hearts wished that he was not half so beautiful, as then her chance of having him might be greater.

"And the company are all talking to him as though he were the prefet," said the girl.

"Never mind who is talking to him," said Marie; "go away, and leave me—you are wanted for your work." Why before this was he not talking to her? Why not, if he were really true to her? Alas, it began to fall upon her mind that he would be false! And what then? What should she do then? She sat still gloomily, thinking of that other spouse that had been promised to her.

As speedily after breakfast as was possible Adolphe was invited to a conference in his mother's private room. She had much debated in her own mind whether the capitaine should be invited to this conference or no. For many reasons she would have wished to exclude him. She did not like to teach her son that she was unable to manage her own affairs, and she would have been well pleased to make the capitaine understand that his assistance was not absolutely necessary to her. But then she had an inward fear that her green spectacles would not now be as efficacious on Adolphe, as they had once been, in old days, before he had seen the world and become a man. It might be necessary that her son, being a man, should be opposed by a man. So the capitaine was invited to the conference.

What took place there need not be described at length. The three were closeted for two hours, at the end of which time they came forth together. The countenance of Madame Bauche was serene and comfortable; her hopes of ultimate success ran higher than ever. The face of the capitaine was masked, as are always the faces of great diplomatists; he walked placid and upright, raising his wooden leg with an ease and skill that was absolutely marvellous. But poor Adolphe's brow was clouded. Yes, poor Adolphe! for he was poor in spirit, he had pledged himself to give up Marie, and to accept the liberal allowance which his mother tendered him; but it remained for him now to communicate these tidings to Marie herself.

"Could not you tell her?" he had said to his mother, with very little of that manliness in his face on which his mother now so prided herself. But La Mere Bauche explained to him that it was a part of the general agreement that Marie was to hear his decision from his own mouth.

"But you need not regard it," said the capitaine, with the most indifferent air in the world. "The girl expects it. Only she has some childish idea that she is bound till you yourself release her. I don't think she will be troublesome." Adolphe at that moment did feel that he should have liked to kick the capitaine out of his mother's house.

And where should the meeting take place? In the hall of the bath-house, suggested Madame Bauche; because, as she observed, they could walk round and round, and nobody ever went there at that time of day. But to this Adolphe objected; it would be so cold and dismal and melancholy.

The capitaine thought that Mere Bauche's little parlour was the place; but La Mere herself did not like this. They might be overheard, as she well knew; and she guessed that the meeting would not conclude without some sobs that would certainly be bitter and might perhaps be loud.

"Send her up to the grotto, and I will follow her," said Adolphe. On this therefore they agreed. Now the grotto was a natural excavation in a high rock, which stood precipitously upright over the establishment of the baths. A steep zigzag path with almost never-ending steps had been made along the face of the rock from a little flower garden attached to the house which lay immediately under the mountain. Close along the front of the hotel ran a little brawling river, leaving barely room for a road between it and the door; over this there was a wooden bridge leading to the garden, and some two or three hundred yards from the bridge began the steps by which the ascent was made to the grotto.

When the season was full and the weather perfectly warm the place was much frequented. There was a green table in it, and four or five deal chairs; a green garden seat also was there, which however had been removed into the innermost back corner of the excavation, as its hinder legs were somewhat at fault. A wall about two feet high ran along the face of it, guarding its occupants from the precipice. In fact it was no grotto, but a little chasm in the rock, such as we often see up above our heads in rocky valleys, and which by means of these steep steps had been turned into a source of exercise and amusement for the visitors at the hotel.

Standing at the wall one could look down into the garden, and down also upon the shining slate roof of Madame Bauche's house; and to the left might be seen the sombre, silent, snow-capped top of stern old Canigou, king of mountains among those Eastern Pyrenees.

And so Madame Bauche undertook to send Marie up to the grotto, and Adolphe undertook to follow her thither. It was now spring; and though the winds had fallen and the snow was no longer lying on the lower peaks, still the air was fresh and cold, and there was no danger that any of the few guests at the establishment would visit the place.

"Make her put on her cloak, Mere Bauche," said the capitaine, who did not wish that his bride should have a cold in her head on their wedding-day. La Mere Bauche pished and pshawed, as though she were not minded to pay any attention to recommendations on such subjects from the capitaine. But nevertheless when Marie was seen slowly to creep across the little bridge about fifteen minutes after this time, she had a handkerchief on her head, and was closely wrapped in a dark brown cloak.

Poor Marie herself little heeded the cold fresh air, but she was glad to avail herself of any means by which she might hide her face. When Madame Bauche sought her out in her own little room, and with a smiling face and kind kiss bade her go to the grotto, she knew, or fancied that she knew that it was all over.

"He will tell you all the truth,—how it all is," said La Mere. "We will do all we can, you know, to make you happy, Marie. But you must remember what Monsieur le Cure told us the other day. In this vale of tears we cannot have everything; as we shall have some day, when our poor wicked souls have been purged of all their wickedness. Now go, dear, and take your cloak."

"Yes, maman."

"And Adolphe will come to you. And try and behave well, like a sensible girl."

"Yes, maman,"—and so she went, bearing on her brow another sacrificial kiss—and bearing in her heart such an unutterable load of woe!

Adolphe had gone out of the house before her; but standing in the stable yard, well within the gate so that she should not see him, he watched her slowly crossing the bridge and mounting the first flight of the steps. He had often seen her tripping up those stairs, and had, almost as often, followed her with his quicker feet. And she, when she would hear him, would run; and then he would catch her breathless at the top, and steal kisses from her when all power of refusing them had been robbed from her by her efforts at escape. There was no such running now, no such following, no thought of such kisses.

As for him, he would fain have skulked off and shirked the interview had he dared. But he did not dare; so he waited there, out of heart, for some ten minutes, speaking a word now and then to the bath-man, who was standing by, just to show that he was at his ease. But the bath-man knew that he was not at his ease. Such would-be lies as those rarely achieve deception;—are rarely believed. And then, at the end of the ten minutes, with steps as slow as Marie's had been, he also ascended to the grotto.

Marie had watched him from the top, but so that she herself should not be seen. He however had not once lifted up his head to look for her; but with eyes turned to the ground had plodded his way up to the cave. When he entered she was standing in the middle, with her eyes downcast and her hands clasped before her. She had retired some way from the wall, so that no eyes might possibly see her but those of her false lover. There she stood when he entered, striving to stand motionless, but trembling like a leaf in every limb.

It was only when he reached the top step that he made up his mind how he would behave. Perhaps after all, the capitaine was right; perhaps she would not mind it.

"Marie," said he, with a voice that attempted to be cheerful; "this is an odd place to meet in after such a long absence," and he held out his hand to her. But only his hand! He offered her no salute. He did not even kiss her cheek as a brother would have done! Of the rules of the outside world it must be remembered that poor Marie knew but little. He had been a brother to her before he had become her lover.

But Marie took his hand saying, "Yes, it has been very long."

"And now that I have come back," he went on to say, "it seems that we are all in a confusion together. I never knew such a piece of work. However, it is all for the best, I suppose."

"Perhaps so," said Marie, still trembling violently, and still looking upon the ground. And then there was silence between them for a minute or so.

"I tell you what it is, Marie," said Adolphe at last, dropping her hand and making a great effort to get through the work before him. "I am afraid we two have been very foolish. Don't you think we have now? It seems quite clear that we can never get ourselves married. Don't you see it in that light?"

Marie's head turned round and round with her, but she was not of the fainting order. She took three steps backwards and leant against the wall of the cave. She also was trying to think how she might best fight her battle. Was there no chance for her? Could no eloquence, no love prevail? On her own beauty she counted but little; but might not prayers do something, and a reference to those old vows which had been so frequent, so eager, so solemnly pledged between them?

"Never get ourselves married!" she said, repeating his words. "Never, Adolphe? Can we never be married?"

"Upon my word, my dear girl, I fear not. You see my mother is so dead against it."

"But we could wait; could we not?"

"Ah, but that's just it, Marie. We cannot wait. We must decide now,—today. You see I can do nothing without money from her—and as for you, you see she won't even let you stay in the house unless you marry old Campan at once. He's a very good sort of fellow though, old as he is. And if you do marry him, why you see you'll stay here, and have it all your own way in everything. As for me, I shall come and see you all from time to time, and shall be able to push my way as I ought to do."

"Then, Adolphe, you wish me to marry the capitaine?"

"Upon my honour I think it is the best thing you can do; I do indeed."

"Oh, Adolphe!"

"What can I do for you, you know? Suppose I was to go down to my mother and tell her that I had decided to keep you myself; what would come of it? Look at it in that light, Marie."

"She could not turn you out—you her own son!"

"But she would turn you out; and deuced quick, too, I can assure you of that; I can, upon my honour."

"I should not care that," and she made a motion with her hand to show how indifferent she would be to such treatment as regarded herself. "Not that—; if I still had the promise of your love."

"But what would you do?"

"I would work. There are other houses beside that one," and she pointed to the slate roof of the Bauche establishment.

"And for me—I should not have a penny in the world," said the young man.

She came up to him and took his right hand between both of hers and pressed it warmly, oh, so warmly. "You would have my love," said she; "my deepest, warmest best heart's love should want nothing more, nothing on earth, if I could still have yours." And she leaned against his shoulder and looked with all her eyes into his face.

"But, Marie, that's nonsense, you know."

"No, Adolphe, it is not nonsense. Do not let them teach you so. What does love mean, if it does not mean that? Oh, Adolphe, you do love me, you do love me, you do love me?"

"Yes;—I love you," he said slowly;—as though he would not have said it, if he could have helped it. And then his arm crept slowly round her waist, as though in that also he could not help himself.

"And do not I love you?" said the passionate girl. "Oh, I do, so dearly; with all my heart, with all my soul. Adolphe, I so love you, that I cannot give you up. Have I not sworn to be yours; sworn, sworn a thousand times? How can I marry that man! Oh Adolphe how can you wish that I should marry him?" And she clung to him, and looked at him, and besought him with her eyes.

"I shouldn't wish it;—only—" and then he paused. It was hard to tell her that he was willing to sacrifice her to the old man because he wanted money from his mother.

"Only what! But Adolphe, do not wish it at all! Have you not sworn that I should be your wife? Look here, look at this;" and she brought out from her bosom a little charm that he had given her in return for that cross. "Did you not kiss that when you swore before the figure of the Virgin that I should be your wife? And do you not remember that I feared to swear too, because your mother was so angry; and then you made me? After that, Adolphe! Oh, Adolphe! Tell me that I may have some hope. I will wait; oh, I will wait so patiently."

He turned himself away from her and walked backwards and forwards uneasily through the grotto. He did love her;—love her as such men do love sweet, pretty girls. The warmth of her hand, the affection of her touch, the pure bright passion of her tear-laden eye had re-awakened what power of love there was within him. But what was he to do? Even if he were willing to give up the immediate golden hopes which his mother held out to him, how was he to begin, and then how carry out this work of self-devotion? Marie would be turned away, and he would be left a victim in the hands of his mother, and of that stiff, wooden-legged militaire;—a penniless victim, left to mope about the place without a grain of influence or a morsel of pleasure.

"But what can we do?" he exclaimed again, as he once more met Marie's searching eye.

"We can be true and honest, and we can wait," she said, coming close up to him and taking hold of his arm. "I do not fear it; and she is not my mother, Adolphe. You need not fear your own mother."

"Fear! no, of course I don't fear. But I don't see how the very devil we can manage it."

"Will you let me tell her that I will not marry the capitaine; that I will not give up your promises; and then I am ready to leave the house?"

"It would do no good."

"It would do every good, Adolphe, if I had your promised word once more; if I could hear from your own voice one more tone of love. Do you not remember this place? It was here that you forced me to say that I loved you. It is here also that you will tell me that I have been deceived."

"It is not I that would deceive you," he said. "I wonder that you should be so hard upon me. God knows that I have trouble enough."

"Well, if I am a trouble to you, be it so. Be it as you wish," and she leaned back against the wall of the rock, and crossing her arms upon her breast looked away from him and fixed her eyes upon the sharp granite peaks of Canigou.

He again betook himself to walk backwards and forwards through the cave. He had quite enough of love for her to make him wish to marry her; quite enough now, at this moment, to make the idea of her marriage with the capitaine very distasteful to him; enough probably to make him become a decently good husband to her, should fate enable him to marry her; but not enough to enable him to support all the punishment which would be the sure effects of his mother's displeasure. Besides, he had promised his mother that he would give up Marie;—had entirely given in his adhesion to that plan of the marriage with the capitaine. He had owned that the path of life as marked out for him by his mother was the one which it behoved him, as a man, to follow. It was this view of his duties as a man which had I been specially urged on him with all the capitaine's eloquence. And old Campan had entirely succeeded. It is so easy to get the assent of such young men, so weak in mind and so weak in pocket, when the arguments are backed by a promise of two thousand francs a year.

"I'll tell you what I'll do," at last he said. "I'll get my mother by herself, and will ask her to let the matter remain as it is for the present."

"Not if it be a trouble, M. Adolphe;" and the proud girl still held her hands upon her bosom, and still looked towards the mountain.

"You know what I mean, Marie. You can understand how she and the capitaine are worrying me."

"But tell me, Adolphe, do you love me?"

"You know I love you, only."

"And you will not give me up?"

"I will ask my mother. I will try and make her yield."

Marie could not feel that she received much confidence from her lover's promise; but still, even that, weak and unsteady as it was, even that was better than absolute fixed rejection. So she thanked him, promised him with tears in her eyes that she would always, always be faithful to him, and then bade him go down to the house. She would follow, she said, as soon as his passing had ceased to be observed.

Then she looked at him as though she expected some sign of renewed love. But no such sign was vouchsafed to her. Now that she thirsted for the touch of his lip upon her cheek, it was denied to her. He did as she bade him; he went down, slowly loitering, by himself; and in about half an hour she followed him, and unobserved crept to her chamber.

Again we will pass over what took place between the mother and the son; but late in that evening, after the guests had gone to bed, Marie received a message, desiring her to wait on Madame Bauche in a small salon which looked out from one end of the house. It was intended as a private sitting-room should any special stranger arrive who required such accommodation, and therefore was but seldom used. Here she found La Mere Bauche sitting in an arm-chair behind a small table on which stood two candles; and on a sofa against the wall sat Adolphe. The capitaine was not in the room.

"Shut the door, Marie, and come in and sit down," said Madame Bauche. It was easy to understand from the tone of her voice that she was angry and stern, in an unbending mood, and resolved to carry out to the very letter all the threats conveyed by those terrible spectacles.

Marie did as she was bid. She closed the door and sat down on the chair that was nearest to her.

"Marie," said La Mere Bauche—and the voice sounded fierce in the poor girl's ears, and an angry fire glimmered through the green glasses—"what is all this about that I hear? Do you dare to say that you hold my son bound to marry you?" And then the august mother paused for an answer.

But Marie had no answer to give. See looked suppliantly towards her lover, as though beseeching him to carry on the fight for her. But if she could not do battle for herself, certainly he could not do it for her. What little amount of fighting he had had in him, had been thoroughly vanquished before her arrival.

"I will have an answer, and that immediately," said Madame Bauche. "I am not going to be betrayed into ignominy and disgrace by the object of my own charity. Who picked you out of the gutter, miss, and brought you up and fed you, when you would otherwise have gone to the foundling? And this is your gratitude for it all? You are not satisfied with being fed and clothed and cherished by me, but you must rob me of my son! Know this then, Adolphe shall never marry a child of charity such as you are."

Marie sat still, stunned by the harshness of these words. La Mere Bauche had often scolded her; indeed, she was given to much scolding; but she had scolded her as a mother may scold a child. And when this story of Marie's love first reached her ears, she had been very angry; but her anger had never brought her to such a pass as this. Indeed, Marie had not hitherto been taught to look at the matter in this light. No one had heretofore twitted her with eating the bread of charity. It had not occurred to her that on this account she was unfit to be Adolphe's wife. There, in that valley, they were all so nearly equal, that no idea of her own inferiority had ever pressed itself upon her mind. But now—!

When the voice ceased she again looked at him; but it was no longer a beseeching look. Did he also altogether scorn her? That was now the inquiry which her eyes were called upon to make. No; she could not say that he did. It seemed to her that his energies were chiefly occupied in pulling to pieces the tassel on the sofa cushion.

"And now, miss, let me know at once whether this nonsense is to be over or not," continued La Mere Bauche; "and I will tell you at once, I am not going to maintain you here, in my house, to plot against our welfare and happiness. As Marie Clavert you shall not stay here. Capitaine Campan is willing to marry you; and as his wife I will keep my word to you, though you little deserve it. If you refuse to marry him, you must go. As to my son, he is there; and he will tell you now, in my presence, that he altogether declines the honour you propose for him."

And then she ceased, waiting for an answer, drumming the table with a wafer stamp which happened to be ready to her hand; but Marie said nothing. Adolphe had been appealed to; but Adolphe had not yet spoken.

"Well, miss?" said La Mere Bauche

Then Marie rose from her seat, and walking round she touched Adolphe lightly on the shoulder. "Adolphe," she said, "it is for you to speak now. I will do as you bid me."

He gave a long sigh, looked first at Marie and then at his mother, shook himself slightly, and then spoke: "Upon my word, Marie, I think mother is right. It would never do for us to marry; it would not indeed."

"Then it is decided," said Marie, returning to her chair.

"And you will marry the capitaine?" said La Mere Bauche.

Marie merely bowed her head in token of acquiescence. "Then we are friends again. Come here, Marie, and kiss me. You must know that it is my duty to take care of my own son. But I don't want to be angry with you if I can help it; I don't indeed. When once you are Madame Campan, you shall be my own child; and you shall have any room in the house you like to choose—there!" And she once more imprinted a kiss on Marie's cold forehead.

How they all got out of the room, and off to their own chambers, I can hardly tell. But in five minutes from the time of this last kiss they were divided. La Mere Bauche had patted Marie, and smiled on her, and called her her dear good little Madame Campan, her young little Mistress of the Hotel Bauche; and had then got herself into her own room, satisfied with her own victory.

Nor must my readers be too severe on Madame Bauche. She had already done much for Marie Clavert; and when she found herself once more by her own bedside, she prayed to be forgiven for the cruelty which she felt that she had shown to the orphan. But in making this prayer, with her favourite crucifix in her hand and the little image of the Virgin before her, she pleaded her duty to her son. Was it not right, she asked the Virgin, that she should save her son from a bad marriage? And then she promised ever so much of recompense, both to the Virgin and to Marie; a new trousseau for each, with candles to the Virgin, with a gold watch and chain for Marie, as soon as she should be Marie Campan. She had been cruel; she acknowledged it. But at such a crisis was it not defensible? And then the recompense should be so full!

But there was one other meeting that night, very short indeed, but not the less significant. Not long after they had all separated, just so long as to allow of the house being quiet, Adolphe, still sitting in his room, meditating on what the day had done for him, heard a low tap at his door. "Come in," he said, as men always do say; and Marie opening the door, stood just within the verge of his chamber. She had on her countenance neither the soft look of entreating love which she had worn up there in the grotto, nor did she appear crushed and subdued as she had done before his mother. She carried her head somewhat more erect than usual, and looked boldly out at him from under her soft eyelashes. There might still be love there, but it was love proudly resolving to quell itself. Adolphe, as he looked at her, felt that he was afraid of her.

"It is all over then between us, M. Adolphe?" she said.

"Well, yes. Don't you think it had better be so, eh, Marie?"

"And this is the meaning of oaths and vows, sworn to each other so sacredly?"

"But, Marie, you heard what my mother said."

"Oh, sir! I have not come to ask you again to love me. Oh no! I am not thinking of that. But this, this would be a lie if I kept it now; it would choke me if I wore it as that man's wife. Take it back;" and she tendered to him the little charm which she had always worn round her neck since he had given it to her. He took it abstractedly, without thinking what he did, and placed it on his dressing-table.

"And you," she continued, "can you still keep that cross? Oh, no! you must give me back that. It would remind you too often of vows that were untrue."

"Marie," he said, "do not be so harsh to me."

"Harsh!" said she, "no; there has been enough of harshness. I would not be harsh to you, Adolphe. But give me the cross; it would prove a curse to you if you kept it."

He then opened a little box which stood upon the table, and taking out the cross gave it to her.

"And now goodbye," she said. "We shall have but little more to say to each other. I know this now, that I was wrong ever to have loved you. I should have been to you as one of the other poor girls in the house. But, oh! how was I to help it?" To this he made no answer, and she, closing the door softly, went back to her chamber. And thus ended the first day of Adolphe Bauche's return to his own house.

On the next morning the capitaine and Marie were formally betrothed. This was done with some little ceremony, in the presence of all the guests who were staying at the establishment, and with all manner of gracious acknowledgments of Marie's virtues. It seemed as though La Mere Bauche could not be courteous enough to her. There was no more talk of her being a child of charity; no more allusion now to the gutter. La Mere Bauche with her own hand brought her cake with a glass of wine after her betrothal was over, and patted her on the cheek, and called her her dear little Marie Campan. And then the capitaine was made up of infinite politeness, and the guests all wished her joy, and the servants of the house began to perceive that she was a person entitled to respect. How different was all this from that harsh attack that was made on her the preceding evening! Only Adolphe,—he alone kept aloof. Though he was present there he said nothing. He, and he only, offered no congratulations.

In the midst of all these gala doings Marie herself said little or nothing. La Mere Bauche perceived this, but she forgave it. Angrily as she had expressed herself at the idea of Marie's daring to love her son, she had still acknowledged within her own heart that such love had been natural. She could feel no pity for Marie as long as Adolphe was in danger; but now she knew how to pity her. So Marie was still petted and still encouraged, though she went through the day's work sullenly and in silence.

As to the capitaine it was all one to him. He was a man of the world. He did not expect that he should really be preferred, con amore, to a young fellow like Adolphe. But he did expect that Marie, like other girls, would do as she was bid; and that in a few days she would regain her temper and be reconciled to her life.

And then the marriage was fixed for a very early day; for as La Mere said, "What was the use of waiting? All their minds were made up now, and therefore the sooner the two were married the better. Did not the capitaine think so?"

The capitaine said that he did think so.

And then Marie was asked. It was all one to her, she said. Whatever Maman Bauche liked, that she would do; only she would not name a day herself. Indeed she would neither do nor say anything herself which tended in any way to a furtherance of these matrimonials. But then she acquiesced, quietly enough if not readily, in what other people did and said; and so the marriage was fixed for the day week after Adolphe's return.

The whole of that week passed much in the same way. The servants about the place spoke among themselves of Marie's perverseness, obstinacy, and ingratitude, because she would not look pleased, or answer Madame Bauche's courtesies with gratitude; but La Mere herself showed no signs of anger. Marie had yielded to her, and she required no more. And she remembered also the harsh words she had used to gain her purpose; and she reflected on all that Marie had lost. On these accounts she was forbearing and exacted nothing—nothing but that one sacrifice which was to be made in accordance to her wishes.

And it was made. They were married in the great salon, the dining-room, immediately after breakfast. Madame Bauche was dressed in a new puce silk dress, and looked very magnificent on the occasion. She simpered and smiled, and looked gay even in spite of her spectacles; and as the ceremony was being performed, she held fast clutched in her hand the gold watch and chain which were intended for Marie as soon as ever the marriage should be completed.

The capitaine was dressed exactly as usual, only that all his clothes were new. Madame Bauche had endeavoured to persuade him to wear a blue coat; but he answered that such a change would not, he was sure, be to Marie's taste. To tell the truth, Marie would hardly have known the difference had he presented himself in scarlet vestments.

Adolphe, however, was dressed very finely, but he did not make himself prominent on the occasion. Marie watched him closely, though none saw that she did so; and of his garments she could have given an account with much accuracy—of his garments, ay! and of every look. "Is he a man," she said at last to herself, "that he can stand by and see all this?"

She too was dressed in silk. They had put on her what they pleased, and she bore the burden of her wedding finery without complaint and without pride. There was no blush on her face as she walked up to the table at which the priest stood, nor hesitation in her low voice as she made the necessary answers. She put her hand into that of the capitaine when required to do so; and when the ring was put on her finger she shuddered, but ever so slightly. No one observed it but La Mere Bauche. "In one week she will be used to it, and then we shall all be happy," said La Mere to herself. "And I,—I will be so kind to her!"

And so the marriage was completed, and the watch was at once given to Marie. "Thank you, maman," said she, as the trinket was fastened to her girdle. Had it been a pincushion that had cost three sous, it would have affected her as much.

And then there was cake and wine and sweetmeats; and after a few minutes Marie disappeared. For an hour or so the capitaine was taken up with the congratulating of his friends, and with the efforts necessary to the wearing of his new honours with an air of ease; but after that time he began to be uneasy because his wife did not come to him. At two or three in the afternoon he went to La Mere Bauche to complain. "This lackadaisical nonsense is no good," he said. "At any rate it is too late now. Marie had better come down among us and show herself satisfied with her husband."

But Madame Bauche took Marie's part. "You must not be too hard on Marie," she said. "She has gone through a good deal this week past, and is very young; whereas, capitaine, you are not very young."

The capitaine merely shrugged his shoulders. In the mean time Mere Bauche went up to visit her protegee in her own room, and came down with a report that she was suffering from a headache. She could not appear at dinner, Madame Bauche said; but would make one at the little party which was to be given in the evening. With this the capitaine was forced to be content.

The dinner therefore went on quietly without her, much as it did on other ordinary days. And then there was a little time for vacancy, during which the gentlemen drank their coffee and smoked their cigars at the cafe, talking over the event that had taken place that morning, and the ladies brushed their hair and added some ribbon or some brooch to their usual apparel. Twice during this time did Madame Bauche go up to Marie's room with offers to assist her. "Not yet, maman; not quite yet," said Marie piteously through her tears, and then twice did the green spectacles leave the room, covering eyes which also were not dry. Ah! what had she done? What had she dared to take upon herself to do? She could not undo it now.

And then it became quite dark in the passages and out of doors, and the guests assembled in the salon. La Mere came in and out three or four times, uneasy in her gait and unpleasant in her aspect, and everybody began to see that things were wrong. "She is ill, I am afraid," said one. "The excitement has been too much," said a second; "and he is so old," whispered a third. And the capitaine stalked about erect on his wooden leg, taking snuff, and striving to look indifferent; but he also was uneasy in his mind.

Presently La Mere came in again, with a quicker step than before, and whispered something, first to Adolphe and then to the capitaine, whereupon they both followed her out of the room.

"Not in her chamber," said Adolphe.

"Then she must be in yours," said the capitaine.

"She is in neither," said La Mere Bauche, with her sternest voice; "nor is she in the house!"

And now there was no longer an affectation of indifference on the part of any of them. They were anything but indifferent. The capitaine was eager in his demands that the matter should still be kept secret from the guests. She had always been romantic, he said, and had now gone out to walk by the river side. They three and the old bath-man would go out and look for her.

"But it is pitch dark," said La Mere Bauche.

"We will take lanterns," said the capitaine. And so they sallied forth with creeping steps over the gravel, so that they might not be heard by those within, and proceeded to search for the young wife.

"Marie! Marie!" said La Mere Bauche, in piteous accents; "do come to me; pray do!"

"Hush!" said the capitaine. "They'll hear you if you call." He could not endure that the world should learn that a marriage with him had been so distasteful to Marie Clavert.

"Marie, dear Marie!" called Madame Bauche, louder than before, quite regardless of the capitaine' s feelings; but no Marie answered. In her innermost heart now did La Mere Bauche wish that this cruel marriage had been left undone.

Adolphe was foremost with his lamp, but he hardly dared to look in the spot where he felt that it was most likely that she should have taken refuge. How could he meet her again, alone, in that grotto? Yet he alone of the four was young. It was clearly for him to ascend. "Marie," he shouted, "are you there?" as he slowly began the long ascent of the steps.

But he had hardly begun to mount when a whirring sound struck his ear, and he felt that the air near him was moved; and then there was a crash upon the lower platform of rock, and a moan, repeated twice, but so faintly, and a rustle of silk, and a slight struggle somewhere as he knew within twenty paces of him; and then all was again quiet and still in the night air.

"What was that?" asked the capitaine in a hoarse voice. He made his way half across the little garden, and he also was within forty or fifty yards of the flat rock. But Adolphe was unable to answer him. He had fainted and the lamp had fallen from his hands and rolled to the bottom of the steps.

But the capitaine, though even his heart was all but quenched within him, had still strength enough to make his way up to the rock; and there, holding the lantern above his eyes, he saw all that was left for him to see of his bride.

As for La Mere Bauche, she never again sat at the head of that table,—never again dictated to guests,—never again laid down laws for the management of any one. A poor bedridden old woman, she lay there in her house at Vernet for some seven tedious years, and then was gathered to her fathers.

As for the capitaine—but what matters? He was made of sterner stuff. What matters either the fate of such a one as Adolphe Bauche?

MISS SARAH JACK, OF SPANISH TOWN, JAMAICA

There is nothing so melancholy as a country in its decadence, unless it be a people in their decadence. I am not aware that the latter misfortune can be attributed to the Anglo-Saxon race in any part of the world; but there is reason to fear that it has fallen on an English colony in the island of Jamaica.

Jamaica was one of those spots on which fortune shone with the full warmth of all her noonday splendour. That sun has set;— whether for ever or no none but a prophet can tell; but as far as a plain man may see, there are at present but few signs of a coming morrow, or of another summer.

It is not just or proper that one should grieve over the misfortunes of Jamaica with a stronger grief because her savannahs are so lovely, her forests so rich, her mountains so green, and he rivers so rapid; but it is so. It is piteous that a land so beautiful should be one which fate has marked for misfortune. Had Guiana, with its flat, level, unlovely soil, become poverty-stricken, one would hardly sorrow over it as one does sorrow for Jamaica.

As regards scenery she is the gem of the western tropics. It is impossible to conceive spots on the earth's surface more gracious to the eye than those steep green valleys which stretch down to the south-west from the Blue Mountain peak towards the sea; and but little behind these in beauty are the rich wooded hills which in the western part of the island divide the counties of Hanover and Westmoreland. The hero of the tale which I am going to tell was a sugar-grower in the latter district, and the heroine was a girl who lived under that Blue Mountain peak.

The very name of a sugar-grower as connected with Jamaica savours of fruitless struggle, failure, and desolation. And from his earliest growth fruitless struggle, failure, and desolation had been the lot of Maurice Cumming. At eighteen years of age he had been left by his father sole possessor of the Mount Pleasant estate, than which in her palmy days Jamaica had little to boast of that was more pleasant or more palmy. But those days had passed by before Roger Cumming, the father of our friend, had died.

These misfortunes coming on the head of one another, at intervals of a few years, had first stunned and then killed him. His slaves rose against him, as they did against other proprietors around him, and burned down his house and mills, his homestead and offices. Those who know the amount of capital which a sugar-grower must invest in such buildings will understand the extent of this misfortune. Then the slaves were emancipated. It is not perhaps possible that we, now-a-days, should regard this as a calamity; but it was quite impossible that a Jamaica proprietor of those days should not have done so. Men will do much for philanthropy, they will work hard, they will give the coat from their back;—nay the very shirt from their body; but few men will endure to look on with satisfaction while their commerce is destroyed.

But even this Mr. Cumming did bear after a while, and kept his shoulder to the wheel. He kept his shoulder to the wheel till that third misfortune came upon him—till the protection duty on Jamaica sugar was abolished. Then he turned his face to the wall and died.

His son at this time was not of age, and the large but lessening property which Mr. Cumming left behind him was for three years in the hands of trustees. But nevertheless Maurice, young as he was, managed the estate. It was he who grew the canes, and made the sugar;—or else failed to make it. He was the "massa" to whom the free negroes looked as the source from whence their wants should be supplied, notwithstanding that, being free, they were ill inclined to work for him, let his want of work be ever so sore.

Mount Pleasant had been a very large property. In addition to his sugar-canes Mr. Cumming had grown coffee; for his land ran up into the hills of Trelawney to that altitude which in the tropics seems necessary for the perfect growth of the coffee berry. But it soon became evident that labour for the double produce could not be had, and the coffee plantation was abandoned. Wild brush and the thick undergrowth of forest reappeared on the hill-sides which had been rich with produce. And the evil re-created and exaggerated itself. Negroes squatted on the abandoned property; and being able to live with abundance from their stolen gardens, were less willing than ever to work in the cane pieces.

And thus things went from bad to worse. In the good old times Mr. Cumming's sugar produce had spread itself annually over some three hundred acres; but by degrees this dwindle down to half that extent of land. And then in those old golden days they had always taken a full hogshead from the acre;—very often more. The estate had sometimes given four hundred hogsheads in the year. But in the days of which we now speak the crop had fallen below fifty.

At this time Maurice Cumming was eight-and-twenty, and it is hardly too much to say that misfortune had nearly crushed him. But nevertheless it had not crushed him. He, and some few like him, had still hoped against hope; had still persisted in looking forward to a future for the island which once was so generous with its gifts. When his father died he might still have had enough for the wants of life had he sold his property for what it would fetch. There was money in England, and the remains of large wealth. But he would not sacrifice Mount Pleasant or abandon Jamaica; and now after ten years' struggling he still kept Mount Pleasant, and the mill was still going; but all other property had parted from his hands.

By nature Maurice Cumming would have been gay and lively, a man with a happy spirit and easy temper; but struggling had made him silent if not morose, and had saddened if not soured his temper. He had lived alone at Mount Pleasant, or generally alone. Work or want of money, and the constant difficulty of getting labour for his estate, had left him but little time for a young man's ordinary amusements. Of the charms of ladies' society he had known but little. Very many of the estates around him had been absolutely abandoned, as was the case with his own coffee plantation, and from others men had sent away their wives and daughters. Nay, most of the proprietors had gone themselves, leaving an overseer to extract what little might yet be extracted out of the property. It too often happened that that little was not sufficient to meet the demands of the overseer himself.

The house at Mount Pleasant had been an irregular, low-roofed, picturesque residence, built with only one floor, and surrounded on all sides by large verandahs. In the old days it had always been kept in perfect order, but now this was far from being the case. Few young bachelors can keep a house in order, but no bachelor young or old can do so under such a doom as that of Maurice Cumming. Every shilling that Maurice Cumming could collect was spent in bribing negroes to work for him. But bribe as he would the negroes would not work. "No, massa: me pain here; me no workee today," and Sambo would lay his fat hand on his fat stomach.

I have said that he lived generally alone. Occasionally his house on Mount Pleasant was enlivened by visits of an aunt, a maiden sister of his mother, whose usual residence was at Spanish Town. It is or should be known to all men that Spanish Town was and is the seat of Jamaica legislature.

But Maurice was not over fond of his relative. In this he was both wrong and foolish, for Miss Sarah Jack—such was her name—was in many respects a good woman, and was certainly a rich woman. It is true that she was not a handsome woman, nor a fashionable woman, nor perhaps altogether an agreeable woman. She was tall, thin, ungainly, and yellow. Her voice, which she used freely, was harsh. She was a politician and a patriot. She regarded England as the greatest of countries, and Jamaica as the greatest of colonies. But much as she loved England she was very loud in denouncing what she called the perfidy of the mother to the brightest of her children. And much as she loved Jamaica she was equally severe in her taunts against those of her brother-islanders who would not believe that the island might yet flourish as it had flourished in her father's days.

"It is because you and men like you will not do your duty by your country," she had said some score of times to Maurice—not with much justice considering the laboriousness of his life.

But Maurice knew well what she meant. "What could I do there up at Spanish Town," he would answer, "among such a pack as there are there? Here I may do something."

And then she would reply with the full swing of her eloquence, "It is because you and such as you think only of yourself and not of Jamaica, that Jamaica has come to such a pass as this. Why is there a pack there as you call them in the honourable House of Assembly? Why are not the best men in the island to be found there, as the best men in England are to be found in the British

House of Commons? A pack, indeed! My father was proud of a seat in that house, and I remember the day, Maurice Cumming, when your father also thought it no shame to represent his own parish. If men like you, who have a stake in the country, will not go there, of course the house is filled with men who have no stake. If they are a pack, it is you who send them there;—you, and others like you."

All had its effect, though at the moment Maurice would shrug his shoulders and turn away his head from the torrent of the lady's discourse. But Miss Jack, though she was not greatly liked, was greatly respected. Maurice would not own that she convinced him; but at last he did allow his name to be put up as candidate for his own parish, and in due time he became a member of the honourable House of Assembly in Jamaica.

This honour entails on the holder of it the necessity of living at or within reach of Spanish Town for some ten weeks towards the chose of every year. Now on the whole face of the uninhabited globe there is perhaps no spot more dull to look at, more Lethean in its aspect, more corpse-like or more cadaverous than Spanish Town. It is the head-quarters of the government, the seat of the legislature, the residence of the governor;—but nevertheless it is, as it were, a city of the very dead.

Here, as we have said before, lived Miss Jack in a large forlorn ghost-like house in which her father and all her family had lived before her. And as a matter of course Maurice Cumming when he came up to attend to his duties as a member of the legislature took up his abode with her.

Now at the time of which we are specially speaking he had completed the first of these annual visits. He had already benefited his country by sitting out one session of the colonial parliament, and had satisfied himself that he did no other good than that of keeping away some person more objectionable than himself. He was however prepared to repeat this self-sacrifice in a spirit of patriotism for which he received a very meagre meed of eulogy from Miss Jack, and an amount of self-applause which was not much more extensive.

"Down at Mount Pleasant I can do something," he would say over and over again, "but what good can any man do up here?"

"You can do your duty," Miss Jack would answer, "as others did before you when the colony was made to prosper." And then they would run off into a long discussion about free labour and protective duties. But at the present moment Maurice Cumming had another vexation on his mind over and above that arising from his wasted hours at Spanish Town, and his fruitless labours at Mount Pleasant. He was in love, and was not altogether satisfied with the conduct of his lady-love.

Miss Jack had other nephews besides Maurice Cumming, and nieces also, of whom Marian Leslie was one. The family of the Leslies lived up near Newcastle—in the mountains, that is, which stand over Kingston—at a distance of some eighteen miles from Kingston, but in a climate as different from that of the town as the climate of Naples is from that of Berlin. In Kingston the heat is all but intolerable throughout the year, by day and by night, in the house and out of it. In the mountains round Newcastle, some four thousand feet above the sea, it is merely warm during the day, and cool enough at night to make a blanket desirable.

It is pleasant enough living up amongst those green mountains. There are no roads there for wheeled carriages, nor are there carriages with or without wheels. All journeys are made on horseback. Every visit paid from house to house is performed in this manner. Ladies young and old live before dinner in their riding-habits. The hospitality is free, easy, and unembarrassed. The scenery is magnificent. The tropical foliage is wild and luxuriant beyond measure. There may be enjoyed all that a southern climate has to offer of enjoyment, without the penalties which such enjoyments usually entail.

Mrs. Leslie was a half-sister of Miss Jack, and Miss Jack had been a half-sister also of Mrs. Cumming; but Mrs. Leslie and Mrs. Cumming had in no way been related. And it had so happened that up to the period of his legislative efforts Maurice Cumming had seen nothing of the Leslies. Soon after his arrival at Spanish Town he had been taken by Miss Jack to Shandy Hall, for so the residence of the Leslies was called, and having remained there for three days, had fallen in love with Marian Leslie. Now in the West Indies all young ladies flirt; it is the first habit of their nature—and few young ladies in the West Indies were more given to flirting, or understood the science better than Marian Leslie.

Maurice Cumming fell violently in love, and during his first visit at Shandy Hall found that Marian was perfection—for during this first visit her propensities were exerted altogether in his own favour. That little circumstance does make such a difference in a young man's judgment of a girl! He came back full of admiration, not altogether to Miss Jack's dissatisfaction; for Miss Jack was willing enough that both her nephew and her niece should settle down into married life.

But then Maurice met his fair one at a governor's ball—at a ball where red coats abounded, and aides-de-camp dancing in spurs, and narrow-waisted lieutenants with sashes or epaulettes! The aides-de-camp and narrow-waisted lieutenants waltzed better than he did; and as one after the other whisked round the ball-room with Marian firmly clasped in his arms, Maurice's feelings were not of the sweetest. Nor was this the worst of it. Had the whisking been divided equally among ten, he might have forgiven it; but there was one specially narrow-waisted lieutenant, who towards the end of the evening kept Marian nearly wholly to himself. Now to a man in love, who has had but little experience of either balls or young ladies, this is intolerable.

He only met her twice after that before his return to Mount Pleasant, and on the first occasion that odious soldier was not there. But a specially devout young clergyman was present, an unmarried, evangelical, handsome young curate fresh from England; and Marian's piety had been so excited that she had cared for no one else. It appeared moreover that the curate's gifts for conversion were confined, as regarded that opportunity, to Marion's advantage. "I will have nothing more to say to her," said Maurice to himself, scowling. But just as he went away Marian had given him her hand, and called him Maurice—for she pretended that they were cousins—and had looked into his eyes and declared that she did hope that the assembly at Spanish Town would soon be sitting again. Hitherto, she said, she had not cared one straw about it. Then poor Maurice pressed the little fingers which lay within his own, and swore that he would be at Shandy Hall on the day before his return to Mount Pleasant. So he was; and there he found the narrow-waisted lieutenant, not now bedecked with sash and epaulettes, but lolling at his ease on Mrs. Leslie's sofa in a white jacket, while Marian sat at his feet telling his fortune with a book about flowers.

"Oh, a musk rose, Mr. Ewing; you know what a musk rose means!" Then she got up and shook hands with Mr. Cumming; but her eyes still went away to the white jacket and the sofa. Poor Maurice had often been nearly broken-hearted in his efforts to manage his free black labourers; but even that was easier than managing such as Marion Leslie.

Marian Leslie was a Creole—as also were Miss Jack and Maurice Cumming—a child of the tropics; but by no means such a child as tropical children are generally thought to be by us in more northern latitudes. She was black-haired and black-eyed, but her lips were as red and her cheeks as rosy as though she had been born and bred in regions where the snow lies in winter. She was a small, pretty, beautifully made little creature, somewhat idle as regards the work of the world, but active and strong enough when dancing or riding were required from her. Her father was a banker, and was fairly prosperous in spite of the poverty of his country. His house of business was at Kingston, and he usually slept there twice a week; but he always resided at Shandy Hall, and Mrs. Leslie and her children knew but very little of the miseries of Kingston. For be it known to all men, that of all towns Kingston, Jamaica, is the most miserable.

I fear that I shall have set my readers very much against Marian Leslie;—much more so than I would wish to do. As a rule they will not know how thoroughly flirting is an institution in the West Indies—practised by all young ladies, and laid aside by them when they marry, exactly as their young-lady names and young-lady habits of various kinds are laid aside. All I would say of Marian Leslie is this, that she understood the working of the institution more thoroughly than others did. And I must add also in her favour that she did not keep her flirting for sly corners, nor did her admirers keep their distance till mamma was out of the way. It mattered not to her who was present. Had she been called on to make one at a synod of the clergy of the island, she would have flirted with the bishop before all his priests. And there have been bishops in the colony who would not have gainsayed her!

But Maurice Cumming did not rightly calculate all this; nor indeed did Miss Jack do so as thoroughly as she should have done, for Miss Jack knew more about such matters than did poor Maurice. "If you like Marion, why don't you marry her?"

Miss Jack had once said to him; and this coming from Miss Jack, who was made of money, was a great deal.

"She wouldn't have me," Maurice had answered.

"That's more than you know or I either," was Miss Jack's reply. "But if you like to try, I'll help you."

With reference to this, Maurice as he left Miss Jack's residence on his return to Mount Pleasant, had declared that Marian Leslie was not worth an honest man's love.

"Psha!" Miss Jack replied; "Marian will do like other girls. When you marry a wife I suppose you mean to be master?"

"At any rate I shan't marry her," said Maurice. And so he went his way back to Hanover with a sore heart. And no wonder, for that was the very day on which Lieutenant Ewing had asked the question about the musk rose.

But there was a dogged constancy of feeling about Maurice which could not allow him to disburden himself of his love. When he was again at Mount Pleasant among his sugar-canes and hogsheads he could not help thinking about Marian. It is true he always thought of her as flying round that ball-room in Ewing's arms, or looking up with rapt admiration into that young parson's face; and so he got but little pleasure from his thoughts. But not the less was he in love with her;—not the less, though he would swear to himself three times in the day that for no earthly consideration would he marry Marian Leslie.

The early months of the year from January to May are the busiest with a Jamaica sugar-grower, and in this year they were very busy months with Maurice Cumming. It seemed as though there were actually some truth in Miss Jack's prediction that prosperity would return to him if he attended to his country; for the prices of sugar had risen higher than they had ever been since the duty had been withdrawn, and there was more promise of a crop at Mount Pleasant than he had seen since his reign commenced. But then the question of labour? How he slaved in trying to get work from those free negroes; and alas! how often he slaved in vain! But it was not all in vain; for as things went on it became clear to him that in this year he would, for the first time since he commenced, obtain something like a return from his land. What if the turning-point had come, and things were now about to run the other way.

But then the happiness which might have accrued to him from this source was dashed by his thoughts of Marian Leslie. Why had he thrown himself in the way of that syren? Why had he left Mount Pleasant at all? He knew that on his return to Spanish Town his first work would be to visit Shandy Hall; and yet he felt that of all places in the island, Shandy Hall was the last which he ought to visit.

And then about the beginning of May, when he was hard at work turning the last of his canes into sugar and rum, he received his annual visit from Miss Jack. And whom should Miss Jack bring with her but Mr. Leslie.

"I'll tell you what it is," said Miss Jack; "I have spoken to Mr. Leslie about you and Marian."

"Then you had no business to do anything of the kind," said Maurice, blushing up to his ears.

"Nonsense," replied Miss Jack, "I understand what I am about. Of course Mr. Leslie will want to know something about the estate."

"Then he may go back as wise as he came, for he'll learn nothing from me. Not that I have anything to hide."

"So I told him. Now there are a large family of them, you see; and of course he can't give Marian much."

"I don't care a straw if he doesn't give her a shilling. If she cared for me, or I for her, I shouldn't look after her for her money."

"But a little money is not a bad thing, Maurice," said Miss Jack, who in her time had had a good deal, and had managed to take care of it.

"It is all one to me."

"But what I was going to say is this—hum—ha. I don't like to pledge myself for fear I should raise hopes which mayn't be fulfilled."

"Don't pledge yourself to anything, aunt, in which Marian Leslie and I are concerned."

"But what I was going to say is this; my money, what little I have, you know, must go some day either to you or to the Leslies."

"You may give all to them if you please."

"Of course I may, and I dare say I shall," said Miss Jack, who was beginning to be irritated. "But at any rate you might have the civility to listen to me when I am endeavouring to put you on your legs. I am sure I think about nothing else, morning, noon, and night, and yet I never get a decent word from you. Marian is too good for you; that's the truth."

But at length Miss Jack was allowed to open her budget, and to make her proposition; which amounted to this—that she had already told Mr. Leslie that she would settle the bulk of her property conjointly on Maurice and Marian if they would make a match of it. Now as Mr. Leslie had long been casting a hankering eye after Miss Jack's money, with a strong conviction however that Maurice Cumming was her favourite nephew and probable heir, this proposition was not unpalatable. So he agreed to go down to Mount Pleasant and look about him.

"But you may live for the next thirty years, my dear Miss Jack," Mr. Leslie had said.

"Yes, I may," Miss Jack replied, looking very dry.

"And I am sure I hope you will," continued Mr. Leslie. And then the subject was allowed to drop; for Mr. Leslie knew that it was not always easy to talk to Miss Jack on such matters.

Miss Jack was a person in whom I think we may say that the good predominated over the bad. She was often morose, crabbed, and self-opinionated. but then she knew her own imperfections, and forgave those she loved for evincing their dislike of them. Maurice Cumming was often inattentive to her, plainly showing that he was worried by her importunities and ill at ease in her company. But she loved her nephew with all her heart; and though she dearly liked to tyrannise over him, never allow herself to be really angry with him, though he so frequently refused to bow to her dictation. And she loved Marian Leslie also, though Marian was so sweet and lovely and she herself so harsh and ill-favoured. She loved Marian, though Marian would often be impertinent. She forgave the flirting, the light-heartedness, the love of amusement. Marian, she said to herself, was young and pretty. She, Miss Jack, had never known Marian's temptation. And so she resolved in her own mind that Marian should be made a good and happy woman;—but always as the wife of Maurice Cumming.

But Maurice turned a deaf ear to all these good tidings—or rather he turned to them an ear that seemed to be deaf. He dearly, ardently loved that little flirt; but seeing that she was a flirt, that she had flirted so grossly when he was by, he would not confess his love to a human being. He would not have it known that he was wasting his heart for a worthless little chit, to whom every man was the same—except that those were most eligible whose toes were the lightest and their outside trappings the brightest. That he did love her he could not help, but he would not disgrace himself by acknowledging it.

He was very civil to Mr. Leslie, but he would not speak a word that could be taken as a proposal for Marian. It had been part of Miss Jack's plan that the engagement should absolutely be made down there at Mount Pleasant, without any reference to the young lady; but Maurice could not be induced to break the ice. So he took Mr. Leslie through his mills and over his cane-pieces, talked to him about the laziness of the "niggers," while the "niggers" themselves stood by tittering, and rode with him away to the high grounds where the coffee plantation had been in the good old days; but not a word was said between them about Marian. And yet Marian was never out of his heart.

And then came the day on which Mr. Leslie was to go back to Kingston. "And you won't have her then?" said Miss Jack to her nephew early that morning. "You won't be said by me?"

"Not in this matter, aunt."

"Then you will live and die a poor man; you mean that, I suppose?"

"It's likely enough that I shall. There's this comfort, at any rate, I'm used to it." And then Miss Jack was silent again for a while.

"Very well, sir; that's enough," she said angrily. And then she began again. "But, Maurice, you wouldn't have to wait for my death, you know." And she put out her hand and touched his arm, entreating him as it were to yield to her. "Oh, Maurice," she said, "I do so want to make you comfortable. Let us speak to Mr. Leslie."

But Maurice would not. He took her hand and thanked her, but said that on this matter he must he his own master. "Very well, sir," she exclaimed, "I have done. In future you may manage for yourself. As for me, I shall go back with Mr. Leslie to Kingston." And so she did. Mr. Leslie returned that day, taking her with him. When he took his leave, his invitation to Maurice to come to Shandy Hall was not very pressing. "Mrs. Leslie and the children will always be glad to see you," said he.

"Remember me very kindly to Mrs. Leslie and the children," said Maurice. And so they parted.

"You have brought me down here on a regular fool's errand," said Mr. Leslie, on their journey back to town.

"It will all come right yet," replied Miss Jack. "Take my word for it he loves her."

"Fudge," said Mr. Leslie. But he could not afford to quarrel with his rich connection.

In spite of all that he had said and thought to the contrary, Maurice did look forward during the remainder of the summer to his return to Spanish Town with something like impatience, it was very dull work, being there alone at Mount Pleasant; and let him do what he would to prevent it, his very dreams took him to Shandy Hall. But at last the slow time made itself away, and he found himself once more in his aunt's house.

A couple of days passed and no word was said about the Leslies. On the morning of the third day he determined to go to Shandy Hall. Hitherto he had never been there without staying for the night; but on this occasion he made up his mind to return the same day. "It would not be civil of me not to go there," he said to his aunt.

"Certainly not," she replied, forbearing to press the matter further. "But why make such a terrible hard day's work of it?"

"Oh, I shall go down in the cool, before breakfast; and then I need not have the bother of taking a bag."

And in this way he started. Miss Jack said nothing further; but she longed in her heart that she might be at Marian's elbow unseen during the visit.

He found them all at breakfast, and the first to welcome him at the hall door was Marian. "Oh, Mr. Cumming, we are so glad to see you;" and she looked into his eyes with a way she had, that was enough to make a man's heart wild. But she not call him Maurice now.

Miss Jack had spoken to her sister, Mrs. Leslie, as well as to Mr. Leslie, about this marriage scheme. "Just let them alone," was Mrs. Leslie's advice. "You can't alter Marian by lecturing her. If they really love each other they'll come together; and if they don't, why then they'd better not."

"And you really mean that you're going back to Spanish Town today?" said Mrs. Leslie to her visitor.

"I'm afraid I must. Indeed I haven't brought my things with me." And then he again caught Marian's eye, and began to wish that his resolution had not been so sternly made.

"I suppose you are so fond of that House of Assembly," said Marian, "that you cannot tear yourself away for more than one day. You'll not be able, I suppose, to find time to come to our picnic next week?"

Maurice said he feared that he should not have time to go to a picnic.

"Oh, nonsense," said Fanny—one of the younger girls—"you must come. We can't do without him, can we?"

"Marian has got your name down the first on the list of the gentlemen," said another.

"Yes; and Captain Ewing's second," said Bell, the youngest.

"I'm afraid I must induce your sister to alter her list," said Maurice, in his sternest manner. "I cannot manage to go, and I'm sure she will not miss me."

Marion looked at the little girl who had so unfortunately mentioned the warrior's name, and the little girl knew that she had sinned.

"Oh, we cannot possibly do without you; can we, Marian?" said Fanny. "It's to be at Bingley's Dell, and we've got a bed for you at Newcastle; quite near, you know."

"And another for—" began Bell, but she stopped herself.

"Go away to your lessons, Bell," said Marion. "You know how angry mamma will be at your staying here all the morning;" and poor Bell with a sorrowful look left the room.

"We are all certainly very anxious that you should come; very anxious for a great many reasons," said Marian, in a voice that was rather solemn, and as though the matter were one of considerable import. "But if you really cannot, why of course there is no more to be said."

"There will be plenty without me, I am sure."

"As regards numbers, I dare say there will; for we shall have pretty nearly the whole of the two regiments;" and Marian as she alluded to the officers spoke in a tone which might lead one to think that she would much rather be without them; "but we counted on you as being one of ourselves; and as you had been away so long, we thought—we thought—," and then she turned away her face, and did not finish her speech. Before he could make up his mind as to his answer she had risen from her chair, and walked out of the room. Maurice almost thought that he saw a tear in her eye as she went.

He did ride back to Spanish Town that afternoon, after an early dinner; but before he went Marian spoke to him alone for one minute.

"I hope you are not offended with me," she said.

"Offended! oh no; how could I be offended with you?"

"Because you seem so stern. I am sure I would do anything I could to oblige you, if I knew how. It would be so shocking not to be good friends with a cousin like you."

"But there are so many different sorts of friends," said Maurice.

"Of course there are. There are a great many friends that one does not care a bit for,—people that one meets at balls and places like that—"

"And at picnics," said Maurice.

"Well, some of them there too; but we are not like that; are we?"

What could Maurice do but say, "no," and declare that their friendship was of a warmer description? And how could he resist promising to go to the picnic, though as he made the promise he knew that misery would be in store for him? He did promise, and then she gave him her hand and called him Maurice.

"Oh! I am so glad," she said. "It seemed so shocking that you should refuse to join us. And mind and be early, Maurice; for I shall want to explain it all. We are to meet, you know, at Clifton Gate at one o'clock, but do you be a little before that, and we shall be there."

Maurice Cumming resolved within his own breast as he rode back to Spanish Town, that if Marian behaved to him all that day at the picnic as she had done this day at Shandy Hall, he would ask her to be his wife before he left her.

And Miss Jack also was to be at the picnic.

"There is no need of going early," said she, when her nephew made a fuss about the starting. "People are never very punctual at such affairs as that; and then they are always quite long enough."

But Maurice explained that he was anxious to be early, and on this occasion he carried his point.

When they reached Clifton Gate the ladies were already there; not in carriages, as people go to picnics in other and tamer countries, but each on her own horse or her own pony. But they were not alone. Beside Miss Leslie was a gentleman, whom Maurice knew as Lieutenant Graham, of the flag-ship at Port Royal; and at a little distance which quite enabled him to join in the conversation was Captain Ewing, the lieutenant with the narrow waist of the previous year.

"We shall have a delightful day, Miss Leslie," said the lieutenant.

"Oh, charming, isn't it?" said Marian.

"But now to choose a place for dinner, Captain Ewing;—what do you say?"

"Will you commission me to select? You know I'm very well up in geometry, and all that?"

"But that won't teach you what sort of a place does for a picnic dinner;—will it, Mr. Cumming?" And then she shook hands with Maurice, but did not take any further special notice of him. "We'll all go together, if you please. The commission is too important to be left to one." And then Marian rode off, and the lieutenant and the captain rode with her.

It was open for Maurice to join them if he chose, but he did not choose. He had come there ever so much earlier than he need have done, dragging his aunt with him, because Marian had told him that his services would be specially required by her. And now as soon as she saw him she went away with the two officers!—went away without vouchsafing him a word. He made up his mind, there on the spot, that he would never think of her again—never speak to her otherwise than he might speak to the most indifferent of mortals.

And yet he was a man that could struggle right manfully with the world's troubles; one who had struggled with them from his boyhood, and had never been overcome. Now he was unable to conceal the bitterness of his wrath because a little girl had ridden off to look for a green spot for her tablecloth without asking his assistance!

Picnics are, I think, in general, rather tedious for the elderly people who accompany them. When the joints become a little stiff, dinners are eaten most comfortably with the accompaniment of chairs and tables, and a roof overhead is an agrement de plus. But, nevertheless, picnics cannot exist without a certain allowance of elderly people. The Miss Marians and Captains Ewing cannot go out to dine on the grass without some one to look after them. So the elderly people go to picnics, in a dull tame way, doing their duty, and wishing the day over. Now on the morning in question, when Marian rode off with Captain Ewing and lieutenant Graham, Maurice Cumming remained among the elderly people.

A certain Mr. Pomken, a great Jamaica agriculturist, one of the Council, a man who had known the good old times, got him by the button and held him fast, discoursing wisely of sugar and ruin, of Gadsden pans and recreant negroes, on all of which subjects Maurice Cumming was known to have an opinion of his own. But as Mr. Pomken's words sounded into one ear, into the other fell notes, listened to from afar,—the shrill laughing voice of Marian Leslie as she gave her happy order to her satellites around her, and ever and anon the bass haw-haw of Captain Ewing, who was made welcome as the chief of her attendants. That evening in a whisper to a brother councillor Mr. Pomken communicated his opinion that after all there was not so much in that young Cumming as some people said. But Mr. Pomken had no idea that that young Cumming was in love.

And then the dinner came, spread over half an acre. Maurice was among the last who seated himself; and when he did so it was in an awkward comfortless corner, behind Mr. Pomken's back, and far away from the laughter and mirth of the day. But yet from his comfortless corner he could see Marian as she sat in her pride of power, with her friend Julia Davis near her, a flirt as bad as herself, and her satellites around her, obedient to her nod, and happy in her smiles.

"Now I won't allow any more champagne," said Marian, "or who will there be steady enough to help me over the rocks to the grotto?"

"Oh, you have promised me!" cried the captain.

"Indeed, I have not; have I, Julia?"

"Miss Davis has certainly promised me," said the lieutenant.

"I have made no promise, and don't think I shall go at all," said Julia, who was sometimes inclined to imagine that Captain Ewing should be her own property.

All which and much more of the kind Maurice Cumming could not hear; but he could see—and imagine, which was worse. How innocent and inane are, after all, the flirtings of most young ladies, if all their words and doings in that line could be brought to paper! I do not know whether there be as a rule more vocal expression of the sentiment of love between a man and woman than there is between two thrushes! They whistle and call to each other, guided by instinct rather than by reason.

"You are going home with the ladies tonight, I believe," said Maurice to Miss Jack, immediately after dinner. Miss Jack acknowledged that such was her destination for the night.

"Then my going back to Spanish Town at once won't hurt any one—for, to tell the truth, I have had enough of this work."

"Why, Maurice, you were in such a hurry to come."

"The more fool I; and so now I am in a hurry to go away. Don't notice it to anybody."

Miss Jack looked in his face and saw that he was really wretched; and she knew the cause of his wretchedness.

"Don't go yet, Maurice," she said; and then added with a tenderness that was quite uncommon with her, "Go to her, Maurice, and speak to her openly and freely, once for all; you will find that she will listen then. Dear Maurice, do, for my sake."

He made no answer, but walked away, roaming sadly by himself among the trees. "Listen!" he exclaimed to himself. "Yes, she will alter a dozen times in as many hours. Who can care for a creature that can change as she changes?" And yet he could not help caring for her.

As he went on, climbing among rocks, he again came upon the sound of voices, and heard especially that of Captain Ewing. "Now, Miss Leslie, if you will take my hand you will soon be over all the difficulty." And then a party of seven or eight, scrambling over some stones, came nearly on the level on which he stood, in full view of him; and leading the others were Captain Ewing and Miss Leslie.

He turned on his heel to go away, when he caught the sound of a step following him, and a voice saying, "Oh, there is Mr.

Cumming, and I want to speak to him;" and in a minute a light hand was on his arm.

"Why are you running away from us?" said Marian.

"Because—oh, I don't know. I am not running away. You have your party made up, and I am not going to intrude on it."

"What nonsense! Do come now; we are going to this wonderful grotto. I thought it so ill-natured of you, not joining us at dinner. Indeed you know you had promised."

He did not answer her, but he looked at her—full in the face, with his sad eyes laden with love. She half understood his countenance, but only half understood it.

"What is the matter, Maurice?" she said. "Are you angry with me? Will you come and join us?"

"No, Marian, I cannot do that. But if you can leave them and come with me for half an hour, I will not keep you longer."

She stood hesitating a moment, while her companion remained on the spot where she had left him. "Come, Miss Leslie," called Captain Ewing. "You will have it dark before we can get down."

"I will come with you," whispered she to Maurice, "but wait a moment." And she tripped back, and in some five minutes returned after an eager argument with her friends. "There," she said, "I don't care about the grotto, one bit, and I will walk with you now;—only they will think it so odd." And so they started off together.

Before the tropical darkness had fallen upon them Maurice had told the tale of his love,—and had told it in a manner differing much from that of Marian's usual admirers, he spoke with passion and almost with violence; he declared that his heart was so full of her image that he could not rid himself of it for one minute; "nor would he wish to do so," he said, "if she would be his Marian, his own Marian, his very own. But if not—" and then he explained to her, with all a lover's warmth, and with almost more than a lover's liberty, what was his idea of her being "his own, his very own," and in doing so inveighed against her usual light-heartedness in terms which at any rate were strong enough.

But Marian here it all well. Perhaps she knew that the lesson was somewhat deserved; and perhaps she appreciated at its value the love of such a man as Maurice Cumming, weighing in her judgment the difference between him and the Ewings and the Grahams.

And then she answered him well and prudently, with words which startled him by their prudent seriousness as coming from her. She begged his pardon heartily, she said, for any grief which she had caused him; but yet how was she to he blamed, seeing that she had known nothing of his feelings? Her father and mother had said something to her of this proposed marriage; something, but very little; and she had answered by saying that she did not think Maurice had any warmer regard for her than of a cousin. After this answer neither father nor mother had pressed the matter further. As to her own feelings she could then say nothing, for she then knew nothing;—nothing but this, that she loved no one better than him, or rather that she loved no one else. She would ask herself if she could love him; but he must give her some little time for that. In the meantime—and she smiled sweetly at him as she made the promise—she would endeavour to do nothing that would offend him; and then she added that on that evening she would dance with him any dances that he liked. Maurice, with a self-denial that was not very wise, contented himself with engaging her for the first quadrille.

They were to dance that night in the mess-room of the officers at Newcastle. This scheme had been added on as an adjunct to the picnic, and it therefore became necessary that the ladies should retire to their own or their friends' houses at Newcastle to adjust their dresses. Marian Leslie and Julia Davis were there accommodated with the loan of a small room by the major's wife, and as they were brushing their hair, and putting on their dancing-shoes, something was said between them about Maurice Cumming.

"And so you are to be Mrs. C. of Mount Pleasant," said Julia. "Well; I didn't think it would come to that at last."

"But it has not come to that, and if it did why should I not be Mrs. C., as you call it?"

"The knight of the rueful countenance, I call him."

"I tell you what then, he is an excellent young man, and the fact is you don't know him."

"I don't like excellent young men with long faces. I suppose you won't be let to dance quick dances at all now."

"I shall dance whatever dances I like, as I have always done," said Marian, with some little asperity in her tone.

"Not you; or if you do, you'll lose your promotion. You'll never live to be my Lady Rue. And what will Graham say? You know you've given him half a promise."

"That's not true, Julia;—I never gave him the tenth part of a promise."

"Well, he says so;" and then the words between the young ladies became a little more angry. But, nevertheless, in due time they came forth with faces smiling as usual, with their hair brushed, and without any signs of warfare.

But Marian had to stand another attack before the business of the evening commenced, and this was from no less doughty an antagonist than her aunt, Miss Jack. Miss Jack soon found that Maurice had not kept his threat of going home; and though she did not absolutely learn from him that he had gone so far towards perfecting her dearest hopes as to make a formal offer to Marion, nevertheless she did gather that things were fast that way tending. If only this dancing were over! she said to herself, dreading the unnumbered waltzes with Ewing, and the violent polkas with Graham. So Miss Jack resolved to say one word to Marian—"A wise word in good season," said Miss Jack to herself, "how sweet a thing it is."

"Marian," said she. "Step here a moment, I want to say a word to you."

"Yes, aunt Sarah," said Marian, following her aunt into a corner, not quite in the best humour in the world; for she had a dread of some further interference.

"Are you going to dance with Maurice tonight?"

"Yes, I believe so,—the first quadrille."

"Well, what I was going to say is this. I don't want you to dance many quick dances tonight, for a reason I have;—that is, not a great many."

"Why, aunt, what nonsense!"

"Now my dearest, dearest girl, it is all for your own sake. Well, then, it must out. He does not like it, you know."

"What he?"

"Maurice."

"Well, aunt, I don't know that I'm bound to dance or not to dance just as Mr. Cumming may like. Papa does not mind my dancing. The people have come here to dance and you can hardly want to make me ridiculous by sitting still." And so that wise word did not appear to be very sweet.

And then the amusement of the evening commenced, and Marian stood up for a quadrille with her lover. She however was not in the very best humour. She had, as she thought, said and done enough for one day in Maurice's favour. And she had no idea, as she declared to herself, of being lectured by aunt Sarah.

"Dearest Marion," he said to her, as the quadrille came to a close, "it is an your power to make me so happy,—so perfectly happy."

"But then people have such different ideas of happiness," she replied. "They can't all see with the same eyes, you know." And so they parted.

But during the early part of the evening she was sufficiently discreet; she did waltz with Lieutenant Graham, and polk with Captain Ewing, but she did so in a tamer manner than was usual with her, and she made no emulous attempts to dance down other couples. When she had done she would sit down, and then she consented to stand up for two quadrilles with two very tame gentlemen, to whom no lover could object.

"And so, Marian, your wings are regularly clipped at last," said Julia Davis coming up to her.

"No more clipped than your own," said Marian.

"If Sir Rue won't let you waltz now, what will he require of you when you're married to him?"

"I am just as well able to waltz with whom I like as you are, Julia; and if you say so in that way, I shall think it's envy."

"Ha—ha—ha; I may have envied you some of your beaux before now; I dare say I have. But I certainly do not envy you Sir Rue." And then she went off to her partner.

All this was too much for Marian's weak strength, and before long she was again whirling round with Captain Ewing. "Come, Miss Leslie," said he, "let us see what we can do. Graham and Julia Davis have been saying that your waltzing days are over, but I think we can put them down."

Marian as she got up, and raised her arm in order that Ewing might put his round her waist, caught Maurice's eye as he leaned against a wall, and read in it a stern rebuke. "This is too bad," she said to herself. "He shall not make a slave of me, at any rate as yet." And away she went as madly, more madly than ever, and for the rest of the evening she danced with Captain Ewing and with him alone.

There is an intoxication quite distinct from that which comes from strong drink. When the judgment is altogether overcome by the spirits this species of drunkenness comes on, and in this way Marian Leslie was drunk that night. For two hours she danced with Captain Ewing, and ever and anon she kept saying to herself that she would teach the world to know—and of all the world Mr. Cumming especially—that she might be lead, but not driven.

Then about four o'clock she went home, and as she attempted to undress herself in her own room she burst into violent tears and opened her heart to her sister—"Oh, Fanny, I do love him, I do love him so dearly! and now he will never come to me again!"

Maurice stood still with his back against the wall, for the full two hours of Marian's exhibition, and then he said to his aunt before he left—"I hope you have now seen enough; you will hardly mention her name to me again." Miss Jack groaned from the bottom of her heart but she said nothing. She said nothing that night to any one; but she lay awake in her bed, thinking, till it was time to rise and dress herself. "Ask Miss Marian to come to me," she said to the black girl who came to assist her. But it was not till she had sent three times, that Miss Marian obeyed the summons.

At three o'clock on the following day Miss Jack arrived at her own hall door in Spanish Town. Long as the distance was she ordinarily rode it all, but on this occasion she had provided a carriage to bring her over as much of the journey as it was practicable for her to perform on wheels. As soon as she reached her own hall door she asked if Mr. Cumming was at home. "Yes," the servant said. "He was in the small book-room, at the back of the house, up stairs." Silently, as if afraid of being heard, she stepped up her own stairs into her own drawing-room; and very silently she was followed by a pair of feet lighter and smaller than her own.

Miss Jack was usually somewhat of a despot in her own house, but there was nothing despotic about her now as she peered into the book-room. This she did with her bonnet still on, looking round the half-opened door as though she were afraid to disturb her nephew, he sat at the window looking out into the verandah which ran behind the house, so intent on his thoughts that he did not hear her.

"Maurice," she said, "can I come in?"

"Come in? oh yes, of course;" and he turned round sharply at her. "I tell you what, aunt; I am not well here and I cannot stay out the session. I shall go back to Mount Pleasant."

"Maurice," and she walked close up to him as she spoke, "Maurice, I have brought some one with me to ask your pardon."

His face became red up to the roots of his hair as he stood looking at her without answering. "You would grant it certainly," she continued, "if you knew how much it would be valued."

"Whom do you mean? who is it?" he asked at last.

"One who loves you as well as you love her—and she cannot love you better. Come in, Marian." The poor girl crept in at the door, ashamed of what she was induced to do, but yet looking anxiously into her lover's face. "You asked her yesterday to be your wife," said Miss Jack, "and she did not then know her own mind. Now she has had a lesson. You will ask her once again; will you not, Maurice?"

What was he to say? how was he to refuse, when that soft little hand was held out to him; when those eyes laden with tears just ventured to look into his face?

"I beg your pardon if I angered you last night," she said.

In half a minute Miss Jack had left the room, and in the space of another thirty seconds Maurice had forgiven her. "I am your own now, you know," she whispered to him in the course of that long evening. "Yesterday, you know—," but the sentence was never finished.

It was in vain that Julia Davis was ill-natured and sarcastic, in vain that Ewing and Graham made joint attempt upon her constancy. From that night to the morning of her marriage—and the interval was only three months—Marian Leslie was never known to flirt.

THE MISTLETOE BOUGH

"Let the boys have it if they like it," said Mrs. Garrow, pleading to her only daughter on behalf of her two sons.

"Pray don't, mamma," said Elizabeth Garrow. "It only means romping. To me all that is detestable, and I am sure it is not the sort of thing that Miss Holmes would like."

"We always had it at Christmas when we were young."

"But, mamma, the world is so changed."

The point in dispute was one very delicate in its nature, hardly to be discussed in all its bearings, even in fiction, and the very mention of which between mother and daughter showed a great amount of close confidence between them. It was no less than this. Should that branch of mistletoe which Frank Garrow had brought home with him out of the Lowther woods be hung up on Christmas Eve in the dining-room at Thwaite Hall, according to his wishes; or should permission for such hanging be positively refused? It was clearly a thing not to be done after such a discussion, and therefore the decision given by Mrs. Garrow was against it.

I am inclined to think that Miss Garrow was right in saying that the world is changed as touching mistletoe boughs. Kissing, I fear, is less innocent now than it used to be when our grandmothers were alive, and we have become more fastidious in our amusements. Nevertheless, I think that she made herself fairly open to the raillery with which her brothers attacked her.

"Honi soit qui mal y pense," said Frank, who was eighteen.

"Nobody will want to kiss you, my lady Fineairs," said Harry, who was just a year younger.

"Because you choose to be a Puritan, there are to be no more cakes and ale in the house," said Frank.

"Still waters run deep; we all know that," said Harry.

The boys had not been present when the matter was decided between Mrs. Garrow and her daughter, nor had the mother been present when these little amenities had passed between the brothers and sister.

"Only that mamma has said it, and I wouldn't seem to go against her," said Frank, "I'd ask my father. He wouldn't give way to such nonsense, I know."

Elizabeth turned away without answering, and left the room. Her eyes were full of tears, but she would not let them see that they had vexed her. They were only two days home from school, and for the last week before their coming, all her thoughts had been to prepare for their Christmas pleasures. She had arranged their rooms, making everything warm and pretty. Out of her own pocket she had bought a shot-belt for one, and skates for the other. She had told the old groom that her pony was to belong exclusively to Master Harry for the holidays, and now Harry told her that still waters ran deep. She had been driven to the use of all her eloquence in inducing her father to purchase that gun for Frank, and now Frank called her a Puritan. And why? She did not choose that a mistletoe bough should be hung in her father's hall, when Godfrey Holmes was coming to visit him. She could not explain this to Frank, but Frank might have had the wit to understand it. But Frank was thinking only of Patty Coverdale, a blue-eyed little romp of sixteen, who, with her sister Kate, was coming from Penrith to spend the Christmas at Thwaite Hall. Elizabeth left the room with her slow, graceful step, hiding her tears,—hiding all emotion, as latterly she had taught herself that it was feminine to do. "There goes my lady Fineairs," said Harry, sending his shrill voice after her.

Thwaite Hall was not a place of much pretension. It was a moderate-sized house, surrounded by pretty gardens and shrubberies, close down upon the river Eamont, on the Westmoreland side of the river, looking over to a lovely wooded bank in Cumberland. All the world knows that the Eamont runs out of Ulleswater, dividing the two counties, passing under Penrith Bridge and by the old ruins of Brougham Castle, below which it joins the Eden. Thwaite Hall nestled down close upon the clear rocky stream about half way between Ulleswater and Penrith, and had been built just at a bend of the river. The windows of the dining-parlour and of the drawing-room stood at right angles to each other, and yet each commanded a reach of the stream. Immediately from a side of the house steps were cut down through the red rock to the water's edge, and here a small boat was always moored to a chain. The chain was stretched across the river, fixed to the staples driven into the rock on either side, and the boat was pulled backwards and forwards over the stream without aid from oars or paddles. From the opposite side a path led through the woods and across the fields to Penrith, and this was the route commonly used between Thwaite Hall and the town.

Major Garrow was a retired officer of Engineers, who had seen service in all parts of the world, and who was now spending the evening of his days on a small property which had come to him from his father. He held in his own hands about twenty acres of land, and he was the owner of one small farm close by, which was let to a tenant. That, together with his half-pay, and the interest of his wife's thousand pounds, sufficed to educate his children and keep the wolf at a comfortable distance from his door. He himself was a spare thin man, with quiet, lazy, literary habits. He had done the work of life, but had so done it as to permit of his enjoying that which was left to him. His sole remaining care was the establishment of his children; and, as far as he could see, he had no ground for anticipating disappointment. They were clever, good-looking, well-disposed young people, and upon the whole it may be said that the sun shone brightly on Thwaite Hall. Of Mrs. Garrow it may suffice to say that she always deserved such sunshine.

For years past it had been the practice of the family to have some sort of gathering at Thwaite Hall during Christmas. Godfrey Holmes had been left under the guardianship of Major Garrow, and, as he had always spent his Christmas holidays with his guardian, this, perhaps, had given rise to the practice. Then the Coverdales were cousins of the Garrows, and they had usually been there as children. At the Christmas last past the custom had been broken, for young Holmes had been abroad. Previous to that, they had all been children, excepting him. But now that they were to meet again, they were no longer children. Elizabeth, at any rate, was not so, for she had already counted nineteen winters. And Isabella Holmes was coming. Now Isabella was two years older than Elizabeth, and had been educated in Brussels; moreover she was comparatively a stranger at Thwaite Hall, never having been at those early Christmas meetings.

And now I must take permission to begin my story by telling a lady's secret. Elizabeth Garrow had already been in love with Godfrey Holmes, or perhaps it might be more becoming to say that Godfrey Holmes had already been in love with her. They had already been engaged; and, alas! they had already agreed that that engagement should be broken off!

Young Holmes was now twenty-seven years of age, and was employed in a bank at Liverpool, not as a clerk, but as assistant-manager, with a large salary. He was a man well to do in the world, who had money also of his own, and who might well afford to marry. Some two years since, on the eve of leaving Thwaite Hall, he had with low doubting whisper told Elizabeth that he loved her, and she had flown trembling to her mother. "Godfrey, my boy," the father said to him, as he parted with him the next morning, "Bessy is only a child, and too young to think of this yet." At the next Christmas Godfrey was in Italy, and the thing was gone by,—so at least the father and mother said to each other. But the young people had met in the summer, and one joyful letter had come from the girl home to her mother. "I have accepted him. Dearest, dearest mamma, I do love him. But don't tell papa yet, for I have not quite accepted him. I think I am sure, but I am not quite sure. I am not quite sure about him."

And then, two days after that, there had come a letter that was not at all joyful. "Dearest Mamma,—It is not to be. It is not written in the book. We have both agreed that it will not do. I am so glad that you have not told dear papa, for I could never make him understand. You will understand, for I shall tell you everything, down to his very words. But we have agreed that there shall be no quarrel. It shall be exactly as it was, and he will come at Christmas all the same. It would never do that he and papa should be separated, nor could we now put off Isabella. It is better so in every way, for there is and need be no quarrel. We still like each other. I am sure I like him, but I know that I should not make him happy as his wife. He says it is my fault. I, at any rate, have never told him that I thought it his." From all which it will be seen that the confidence between the mother and daughter was very close.

Elizabeth Garrow was a very good girl, but it might almost be a question whether she was not too good. She had learned, or thought that she had learned, that most girls are vapid, silly, and useless,—given chiefly to pleasure-seeking and a hankering after lovers; and she had resolved that she would not be such a one.

Industry, self-denial, and a religious purpose in life, were the tasks which she set herself; and she went about the performance of them with much courage. But such tasks, though they are excellently well adapted to fit a young lady for the work of living, may also be carried too far, and thus have the effect of unfitting her for that work. When Elizabeth Garrow made up her mind that the finding of a husband was not the only purpose of life, she did very well. It is very well that a young lady should feel herself capable of going through the world happily without one. But in teaching herself this she also taught herself to think that there was a certain merit in refusing herself the natural delight of a lover, even though the possession of the lover were compatible with all her duties to herself, her father and mother, and the world at large. It was not that she had determined to have no lover. She made no such resolve, and when the proper lover came he was admitted to her heart. But she declared to herself unconsciously that she must put a guard upon herself, lest she should be betrayed into weakness by her own happiness. She had resolved that in loving her lord she would not worship him, and that in giving her heart she would only so give it as it should be given to a human creature like herself. She had acted on these high resolves, and hence it had come to pass,—not unnaturally,—that Mr. Godfrey Holmes had told her that it was "her fault."

She was a pretty, fair girl, with soft dark-brown hair, and soft long dark eyelashes. Her grey eyes, though quiet in their tone, were tender and lustrous. Her face was oval, and the lines of her cheek and chin perfect in their symmetry. She was generally quiet in her demeanour, but when moved she could rouse herself to great energy, and speak with feeling and almost with fire. Her fault was a reverence for martyrdom in general, and a feeling, of which she was unconscious, that it became a young woman to be unhappy in secret;—that it became a young woman, I might rather say, to have a source of unhappiness hidden from the world in general, and endured without any detriment to her outward cheerfulness.

We know the story of the Spartan boy who held the fox under his tunic. The fox was biting into him,—into the very entrails; but the young hero spake never a word. Now Bessy Garrow was inclined to think that it was a good thing to have a fox always biting, so that the torment caused no ruffling to her outward smiles. Now at this moment the fox within her bosom was biting her sore enough, but she bore it without flinching.

"If you would rather that he should not come I will have it arranged," her mother had said to her.

"Not for worlds," she had answered. "I should never think well of myself again."

Her mother had changed her own mind more than once as to the conduct in this matter which might be best for her to follow, thinking solely of her daughter's welfare. "If he comes they will be reconciled, and she will be happy," had been her first idea. But then there was a stern fixedness of purpose in Bessy's words when she spoke of Mr. Holmes, which had expelled this hope, and Mrs. Garrow had for a while thought it better that the young man should not come. But Bessy would not permit this. It would vex her father, put out of course the arrangements of other people, and display weakness on her own part. He should come, and she would endure without flinching while the fox gnawed at her.

That battle of the mistletoe had been fought on the morning before Christmas-day, and the Holmeses came on Christmas-eve. Isabella was comparatively a stranger, and therefore received at first the greater share of attention. She and Elizabeth had once seen each other, and for the last year or two had corresponded, but personally they had never been intimate. Unfortunately for the latter, that story of Godfrey's offer and acceptance had been communicated to Isabella, as had of course the immediately subsequent story of their separation. But now it would be almost impossible to avoid the subject in conversation. "Dearest Isabella, let it be as though it had never been," she had said in one of her letters. But sometimes it is very difficult to let things be as though they had never been.

The first evening passed over very well. The two Coverdale girls were there, and there had been much talking and merry laughter, rather juvenile in its nature, but on the whole none the worse for that. Isabella Holmes was a fine, tall, handsome girl; good-humoured, and well disposed to be pleased; rather Frenchified in her manners, and quite able to take care of herself. But she was not above round games, and did not turn up her nose at the boys. Godfrey behaved himself excellently, talking much to the Major, but by no means avoiding Miss Garrow. Mrs. Garrow, though she had known him since he was a boy, had taken an aversion to him since he had quarrelled with her daughter; but there was no room on this first night for showing such aversion, and everything went off well.

"Godfrey is very much improved," the Major said to his wife that night.

"Do you think so?"

"Indeed I do. He has filled out and become a fine man."

"In personal appearance, you mean. Yes, he is well-looking enough."

"And in his manner, too. He is doing uncommonly well in Liverpool, I can tell you; and if he should think of Bessy—"

"There is nothing of that sort," said Mrs. Garrow.

"He did speak to me, you know,—two years ago. Bessy was too young then, and so indeed was he. But if she likes him—"

"I don't think she does."

"Then there's an end of it." And so they went to bed.

"Frank," said the sister to her elder brother, knocking at his door when they had all gone up stairs, "may I come in,—if you are not in bed?"

"In bed," said he, looking up with some little pride from his Greek book; "I've one hundred and fifty lines to do before I can get to bed. It'll be two, I suppose. I've got to mug uncommon hard these holidays. I have only one more half, you know, and then—"

"Don't overdo it, Frank."

"No; I won't overdo it. I mean to take one day a week, and work eight hours a day on the other five. That will be forty hours a week, and will give me just two hundred hours for the holidays. I have got it all down here on a table. That will be a hundred and five for Greek play, forty for Algebra—" and so he explained to her the exact destiny of all his long hours of proposed labour. He had as yet been home a day and a half, and had succeeded in drawing out with red lines and blue figures the table which he showed her. "If I can do that, it will be pretty well; won't it?"

"But, Frank, you have come home for your holidays,—to enjoy yourself?"

"But a fellow must work now-a-days."

"Don't overdo it, dear; that's all. But, Frank, I could not rest if I went to bed without speaking to you. You made me unhappy today."

"Did I, Bessy?"

"You called me a Puritan, and then you quoted that ill-natured French proverb at me. Do you really believe your sister thinks evil, Frank?" and as she spoke she put her arm caressingly round his neck.

"Of course I don't."

"Then why say so? Harry is so much younger and so thoughtless that I can bear what he says without so much suffering. But if you and I are not friends I shall be very wretched. If you knew how I have looked forward to your coming home!"

"I did not mean to vex you, and I won't say such things again."

"That's my own Frank. What I said to mamma, I said because I thought it right; but you must not say that I am a Puritan. I would do anything in my power to make your holidays bright and pleasant. I know that boys require so much more to amuse them than girls do. Good night, dearest; pray don't overdo yourself with work, and do take care of your eyes."

So saying she kissed him and went her way. In twenty minutes after that, he had gone to sleep over his book; and when he woke up to find the candle guttering down, he resolved that he would not begin his measured hours till Christmas-day was fairly over.

The morning of Christmas-day passed very quietly. They all went to church, and then sat round the fire chatting until the four o'clock dinner was ready. The Coverdale girls thought it was rather more dull than former Thwaite Hall festivities, and Frank was seen to yawn. But then everybody knows that the real fun of Christmas never begins till the day itself be passed. The beef and pudding are ponderous, and unless there be absolute children in the party, there is a difficulty in grafting any special afternoon amusements on the Sunday pursuits of the morning. In the evening they were to have a dance; that had been distinctly promised to Patty Coverdale; but the dance would not commence till eight. The beef and pudding were ponderous, but with due efforts they were overcome and disappeared. The glass of port was sipped, the almonds and raisins were nibbled, and then the ladies left the room. Ten minutes after that Elizabeth found herself seated with Isabella Holmes over the fire in her father's little book-room. It was not by her that this meeting was arranged, for she dreaded such a constrained confidence; but of course it could not be avoided, and perhaps it might be as well now as hereafter.

"Bessy," said the elder girl, "I am dying to be alone with you for a moment."

"Well, you shall not die; that is, if being alone with me will save you."

"I have so much to say to you. And if you have any true friendship in you, you also will have so much to say to me."

Miss Garrow perhaps had no true friendship in her at that moment, for she would gladly have avoided saying anything, had that been possible. But in order to prove that she was not deficient in friendship, she gave her friend her hand.

"And now tell me everything about Godfrey," said Isabella.

"Dear Bella, I have nothing to tell;—literally nothing."

"That is nonsense. Stop a moment, dear, and understand that I do not mean to offend you. It cannot be that you have nothing to tell, if you choose to tell it. You are not the girl to have accepted Godfrey without loving him, nor is he the man to have asked you without loving you. When you write me word that you have changed your mind, as you might about a dress, of course I know you have not told me all. Now I insist upon knowing it,—that is, if we are to be friends. I would not speak a word to Godfrey till I had seen you, in order that I might hear your story first."

"Indeed, Bella, there is no story to tell."

"Then I must ask him."

"If you wish to play the part of a true friend to me, you will let the matter pass by and say nothing. You must understand that, circumstanced as we are, your brother's visit here,—what I mean is, that it is very difficult for me to act and speak exactly as I should do, and a few unfortunate words spoken may make my position unendurable."

"Will you answer me one question?"

"I cannot tell. I think I will."

"Do you love him?" For a moment or two Bessy remained silent, striving to arrange her words so that they should contain no falsehood, and yet betray no truth. "Ah, I see you do," continued Miss Holmes. "But of course you do. Why else did you accept him?"

"I fancied that I did, as young ladies do sometimes fancy."

"And will you say that you do not, now?" Again Bessy was silent, and then her friend rose from her seat. "I see it all," she said. "What a pity it was that you both had not some friend like me by you at the time! But perhaps it may not be too late."

I need not repeat at length all the protestations which upon this were poured forth with hot energy by poor Bessy. She endeavoured to explain how great had been the difficulty of her position. This Christmas visit had been arranged before that unhappy affair at Liverpool had occurred. Isabella's visit had been partly one of business, it being necessary that certain money affairs should be arranged between her, her brother, and the Major. "I determined," said Bessy, "not to let my feelings stand in the way; and hoped that things might settle down to their former friendly footing. I already fear that I have been wrong, but it will be ungenerous in you to punish me." Then she went on to say that if anybody attempted to interfere with her, she should at once go away to her mother's sister, who lived at Hexham, in Northumberland.

Then came the dance, and the hearts of Kate and Patty Coverdale were at last happy. But here again poor Bessy was made to understand how terribly difficult was this experiment of entertaining on a footing of friendship a lover with whom she had quarrelled only a month or two before. That she must as a necessity become the partner of Godfrey Holmes she had already calculated, and so much she was prepared to endure. Her brothers would of course dance with the Coverdale girls, and her father would of course stand up with Isabella. There was no other possible arrangement, at any rate as a beginning.

She had schooled herself, too, as to the way in which she would speak to him on the occasion, and how she would remain mistress of herself and of her thoughts. But when the time came the difficulty was almost too much for her.

"You do not care much for dancing, if I remember?" said he.

"Oh yes, I do. Not as Patty Coverdale does. It's a passion with her. But then I am older than Patty Coverdale." After that he was silent for a minute or two.

"It seems so odd to me to be here again," he said. It was odd;—she felt that it was odd. But he ought not to have said so.

"Two years make a great difference. The boys have grown so much."

"Yes, and there are other things," said he.

"Bella was never here before; at least not with you."

"No. But I did not exactly mean that. All that would not make the place so strange. But your mother seems altered to me. She used to be almost like my own mother."

"I suppose she finds that you are a more formidable person as you grow older. It was all very well scolding you when you were a clerk in the bank, but it does not do to scold the manager. These are the penalties men pay for becoming great."

"It is not my greatness that stands in my way, but—"

"Then I'm sure I cannot say what it is. But Patty will scold you if you do not mind the figure, though you were the whole Board of Directors packed into one. She won't respect you if you neglect your present work."

When Bessy went to bed that night she began to feel that she had attempted too much. "Mamma," she said, "could I not make some excuse and go away to Aunt Mary?"

"What now?"

"Yes, mamma; now; tomorrow. I need not say that it will make me very unhappy to be away at such a time, but I begin to think that it will be better."

"What will papa say?"

"You must tell him all."

"And Aunt Mary must be told also. You would not like that. Has he said anything?"

"No, nothing;—very little, that is. But Bella has spoken to me. Oh, mamma, I think we have been very wrong in this. That is, I have been wrong. I feel as though I should disgrace myself, and turn the whole party here into a misfortune."

It would be dreadful, that telling of the story to her father and to her aunt, and such a necessity must, if possible, be avoided. Should such a necessity actually come, the former task would, no doubt, be done by her mother, but that would not lighten the load materially. After a fortnight she would again meet her father, and would be forced to discuss it. "I will remain if it be possible," she said; "but, mamma, if I wish to go, you will not stop me?" Her mother promised that she would not stop her, but strongly advised her to stand her ground.

On the following morning, when she came down stairs before breakfast, she found Frank standing in the hall with his gun, of which he was trying the lock. "It is not loaded, is it, Frank?" said she.

"Oh dear, no; no one thinks of loading now-a-days till he has got out of the house. Directly after breakfast I am going across with Godfrey to the back of Greystock, to see after some moor-fowl. He asked me to go, and I couldn't well refuse."

"Of course not. Why should you?"

"It will be deuced hard work to make up the time. I was to have been up at four this morning, but that alarum went off and never woke me. However, I shall be able to do something tonight."

"Don't make a slavery of your holidays, Frank. What's the good of having a new gun if you're not to use it?"

"It's not the new gun. I'm not such a child as that comes to. But, you see, Godfrey is here, and one ought to be civil to him. I'll tell you what I want you girls to do, Bessy. You must come and meet us on our way home. Come over in the boat and along the path to the Patterdale road. We'll be there under the hill about five."

"And if you are not, we are to wait in the snow?"

"Don't make difficulties, Bessy. I tell you we will be there. We are to go in the cart, and so shall have plenty of time."

"And how do you know the other girls will go?"

"Why, to tell you the truth, Patty Coverdale has promised. As for Miss Holmes, if she won't, why you must leave her at home with mamma. But Kate and Patty can't come without you."

"Your discretion has found that out, has it?"

"They say so. But you will come; won't you, Bessy? As for waiting, it's all nonsense. Of course you can walk on. But we'll be at the stile by five. I've got my watch, you know." And then Bessy promised him. What would she not have done for him that was in her power to do?

"Go! Of course I'll go," said Miss Holmes. "I'm up to anything. I'd have gone with them this morning, and have taken a gun if they'd asked me. But, by-the-bye, I'd better not."

"Why not?" said Patty, who was hardly yet without fear lest something should mar the expedition.

"What will three gentlemen do with four ladies?"

"Oh, I forgot," said Patty innocently.

"I'm sure I don't care," said Kate; "you may have Harry if you like."

"Thank you for nothing," said Miss Holmes. "I want one for myself. It's all very well for you to make the offer, but what should I do if Harry wouldn't have me? There are two sides, you know, to every bargain."

"I'm sure he isn't anything to me," said Kate. "Why, he's not quite seventeen years old yet!"

"Poor boy! What a shame to dispose of him so soon. We'll let him off for a year or two; won't we, Miss Coverdale? But as there seems by acknowledgment to be one beau with unappropriated services—"

"I'm sure I have appropriated nobody," said Patty, "and didn't intend."

"Godfrey, then, is the only knight whose services are claimed," said Miss Holmes, looking at Bessy. Bessy made no immediate answer with either her eyes or tongue; but when the Coverdales were gone, she took her new friend to task.

"How can you fill those young girls' heads with such nonsense?"

"Nature has done that, my dear."

"But nature should be trained; should it not? You will make them think that those foolish boys are in love with them."

"The foolish boys, as you call them, will look after that themselves. It seems to me that the foolish boys know what they are about better than some of their elders." And then, after a moment's pause, she added, "As for my brother, I have no patience with him."

"Pray do not discuss your brother," said Bessy. "And, Bella, unless you wish to drive me away, pray do not speak of him and me together as you did just now."

"Are you so bad as that,—that the slightest commonplace joke upsets you? Would not his services be due to you as a matter of course? If you are so sore about it, you will betray your own secret."

"I have no secret,—none at least from you, or from mamma; and, indeed, none from him. We were both very foolish, thinking that we knew each other and our own hearts, when we knew neither."

"I hate to hear people talk of knowing their hearts. My idea is, that if you like a young man, and he asks you to marry him, you ought to have him. That is, if there is enough to live on. I don't know what more is wanted. But girls are getting to talk and think as though they were to send their hearts through some fiery furnace of trial before they may give them up to a husband's keeping. I am not at all sure that the French fashion is not the best, and that these things shouldn't be managed by the fathers and mothers, or perhaps by the family lawyers. Girls who are so intent upon knowing their own hearts generally end by knowing nobody's heart but their own; and then they die old maids."

"Better that than give themselves to the keeping of those they don't know and cannot esteem."

"That's a matter of taste. I mean to take the first that comes, so long as he looks like a gentleman, and has not less than eight hundred a year. Now Godfrey does look like a gentleman, and has double that. If I had such a chance I shouldn't think twice about it."

"But I have no such chance."

"That's the way the wind blows; is it?"

"No, no. Oh, Bella, pray, pray leave me alone. Pray do not interfere. There is no wind blowing in any way. All that I want is your silence and your sympathy."

"Very well. I will be silent and sympathetic as the grave. Only don't imagine that I am cold as the grave also. I don't exactly appreciate your ideas; but if I can do no good, I will at any rate endeavour to do no harm."

After lunch, at about three, they started on their walk, and managed to ferry themselves over the river. "Oh, do let me, Bessy," said Kate Coverdale. "I understand all about it. Look here, Miss Holmes. You pull the chain through your hands—"

"And inevitably tear your gloves to pieces," said Miss Holmes. Kate certainly had done so, and did not seem to be particularly well pleased with the accident. "There's a nasty nail in the chain," she said. "I wonder those stupid boys did not tell us."

Of course they reached the trysting-place much too soon, and were very tired of walking up and down to keep their feet warm, before the sportsmen came up. But this was their own fault, seeing that they had reached the stile half an hour before the time fixed.

"I never will go anywhere to meet gentlemen again," said Miss Holmes. "It is most preposterous that ladies should be left in the snow for an hour. Well, young men, what sport have you had?"

"I shot the big black cock," said Harry.

"Did you indeed?" said Kate Coverdale.

"And here are the feathers out of his tail for you. He dropped them in the water, and I had to go in after them up to my middle. But I told you that I would, so I was determined to get them."

"Oh, you silly, silly boy," said Kate. "But I'll keep them for ever. I will indeed." This was said a little apart, for Harry had managed to draw the young lady aside before he presented the feathers.

Frank had also his trophies for Patty, and the tale to tell of his own prowess. In that he was a year older than his brother, he was by a year's growth less ready to tender his present to his lady-love, openly in the presence of them all. But he found his opportunity, and then he and Patty went on a little in advance. Kate also was deep in her consolations to Harry for his ducking; and therefore the four disposed of themselves in the manner previously suggested by Miss Holmes. Miss Holmes, therefore, and her brother, and Bessy Garrow, were left together in the path, and discussed the performances of the day in a manner that elicited no very ecstatic interest. So they walked for a mile, and by degrees the conversation between them dwindled down almost to nothing.

"There is nothing I dislike so much as coming out with people younger than myself," said Miss Holmes. "One always feels so old and dull. Listen to those children there; they make me feel as though I were an old maiden aunt, brought out with them to do propriety."

"Patty won't at all approve if she hears you call her a child."

"Nor shall I approve, if she treats me like an old woman," and then she stepped on and joined the children. "I wouldn't spoil even their sport if I could help it," she said to herself. "But with them I shall only be a temporary nuisance; if I remain behind I shall become a permanent evil." And thus Bessy and her old lover were left by themselves.

"I hope you will get on well with Bella," said Godfrey, when they had remained silent for a minute or two.

"Oh, yes. She is so good-natured and light-spirited that everybody must like her. She has been used to so much amusement and active life, that I know she must find it very dull here."

"She is never dull anywhere,—even at Liverpool, which, for a young lady, I sometimes think the dullest place on earth. I know it is for a man."

"A man who has work to do can never be dull; can he?"

"Indeed he can; as dull as death. I am so often enough. I have never been very bright there, Bessy, since you left us."

There was nothing in his calling her Bessy, for it had become a habit with him since they were children; and they had formerly agreed that everything between them should be as it had been before that foolish whisper of love had been spoken and received. Indeed, provision had been made by them specially on this point, so that there need be no awkwardness in this mode of addressing each other. Such provision had seemed to be very prudent, but it hardly had the desired effect on the present occasion.

"I hardly know what you mean by brightness," she said, after a pause. "Perhaps it is not intended that people's lives should be what you call bright."

"Life ought to be as bright as we can make it."

"It all depends on the meaning of the word. I suppose we are not very bright here at Thwaite Hall, but yet we think ourselves very happy."

"I am sure you are," said Godfrey. "I very often think of you here."

"We always think of places where we have been when we were young," said Bessy; and then again they walked on for some way in silence, and Bessy began to increase her pace with the view of catching the children. The present walk to her was anything but bright, and she bethought herself with dismay that there were still two miles before she reached the Ferry.

"Bessy," Godfrey said at last. And then he stopped as though he were doubtful how to proceed. She, however, did not say a word, but walked on quickly, as though her only hope was in catching the party before her. But they also were walking quickly, for Bella was determined that she would not be caught.

"Bessy, I must speak to you once of what passed between us at Liverpool."

"Must you?" said she.

"Unless you positively forbid it."

"Stop, Godfrey," she said. And they did stop in the path, for now she no longer thought of putting an end to her embarrassment by overtaking her companions. "If any such words are necessary for your comfort, it would hardly become me to forbid them. Were I to speak so harshly you would accuse me afterwards in your own heart. It must be for you to judge whether it is well to reopen a wound that is nearly healed."

"But with me it is not nearly healed. The wound is open always."

"There are some hurts," she said, "which do not admit of an absolute and perfect cure, unless after long years." As she said so, she could not but think how much better was his chance of such perfect cure than her own. With her,—so she said to herself,— such curing was all but impossible; whereas with him, it was as impossible that the injury should last.

"Bessy," he said, and he again stopped her on the narrow path, standing immediately before her on the way, "you remember all the circumstances that made us part?"

"Yes; I think I remember them."

"And you still think that we were right to part?"

She paused for a moment before she answered him; but it was only for a moment, and then she spoke quite firmly. "Yes, Godfrey, I do; I have thought about it much since then. I have thought, I fear, to no good purpose about aught else. But I have never thought that we had been unwise in that."

"And yet I think you loved me."

"I am bound to confess I did so, as otherwise I must confess myself a liar. I told you at the time that I loved you, and I told you so truly. But it is better, ten times better, that those who love should part, even though they still should love, than that two should be joined together who are incapable of making each other happy. Remember what you told me."

"I do remember."

"You found yourself unhappy in your engagement, and you said it was my fault."

"Bessy, there is my hand. If you have ceased to love me, there is an end of it. But if you love me still, let all that be forgotten."

"Forgotten, Godfrey! How can it be forgotten? You were unhappy, and it was my fault. My fault, as it would be if I tried to solace a sick child with arithmetic, or feed a dog with grass. I had no right to love you, knowing you as I did; and knowing also that my ways would not be your ways. My punishment I understand, and it is not more than I can bear; but I had hoped that your punishment would have been soon over."

"You are too proud, Bessy."

"That is very likely. Frank says that I am a Puritan, and pride was the worst of their sins."

"Too proud and unbending. In marriage should not the man and woman adapt themselves to each other?"

"When they are married, yes. And every girl who thinks of marrying should know that in very much she must adapt herself to her husband. But I do not think that a woman should be the ivy, to take the direction of every branch of the tree to which she clings. If she does so, what can be her own character? But we must go on, or we shall be too late."

"And you will give me no other answer?"

"None other, Godfrey. Have you not just now, at this very moment, told me that I was too proud? Can it be possible that you should wish to tie yourself for life to female pride? And if you tell me that now, at such a moment as this, what would you tell me in the close intimacy of married life, when the trifles of every day would have worn away the courtesies of guest and lover?"

There was a sharpness of rebuke in this which Godfrey Holmes could not at the moment overcome. Nevertheless he knew the girl, and understood the workings of her heart and mind. Now, in her present state, she could be unbending, proud, and almost rough. In that she had much to lose in declining the renewed offer which he made her, she would, as it were, continually prompt herself to be harsh and inflexible. Had he been poor, had she not loved him, had not all good things seemed to have attended the promise of such a marriage, she would have been less suspicious of herself in receiving the offer, and more gracious in replying to it. Had he lost all his money before he came back to her, she would have taken him at once; or had he been deprived of an eye, or become crippled in his legs, she would have done so. But, circumstanced as he was, she had no motive to tenderness. There was an organic defect in her character, which no doubt was plainly marked by its own bump in her cranium,—the bump of philomartyrdom, it might properly be called. She had shipwrecked her own happiness in rejecting Godfrey Holmes; but it seemed to her to be the proper thing that a well-behaved young lady should shipwreck her own happiness. For the last month or two she had been tossed about by the waters and was nearly drowned. Now there was beautiful land again close to her, and a strong pleasant hand stretched out to save her. But though she had suffered terribly among the waves, she still thought it wrong to be saved. It would be so pleasant to take that hand, so sweet, so joyous, that it surely must be wrong. That was her doctrine; and Godfrey Holmes, though he hardly analysed the matter, partly understood that it was so. And yet, if once she were landed on that green island, she would be so happy. She spoke with scorn of a woman clinging to a tree like ivy; and yet, were she once married, no woman would cling to her husband with sweeter feminine tenacity than Bessy Garrow. He spoke no further word to her as he walked home, but in handing her down to the ferry-boat he pressed her hand. For a second it seemed as though she had returned this pressure. If so, the action was involuntary, and her hand instantly resumed its stiffness to his touch.

It was late that night when Major Garrow went to his bedroom, but his wife was still up, waiting for him. "Well," said she, "what has he said to you? He has been with you above an hour."

"Such stories are not very quickly told; and in this case it was necessary to understand him very accurately. At length I think I do understand him."

It is not necessary to repeat at length all that was said on that night between Major and Mrs. Garrow, as to the offer which had now for a third time been made to their daughter. On that evening, after the ladies had gone, and when the two boys had taken themselves off, Godfrey Holmes told his tale to his host, and had honestly explained to him what he believed to be the state of his daughter's feelings. "Now you know all," said he. "I do believe that she loves me, and if she does, perhaps she may still listen to you." Major Garrow did not feel sure that he "knew it all." But when he had fully discussed the matter that night with his wife, then he thought that perhaps he had arrived at that knowledge.

On the following morning Bessy learned from the maid, at an early hour, that Godfrey Holmes had left Thwaite Hall and gone back to Liverpool. To the girl she said nothing on the subject, but she felt obliged to say a word or two to Bella. "It is his coming that I regret," she said;—"that he should have had the trouble and annoyance for nothing. I acknowledge that it was my fault, and I am very sorry."

"It cannot be helped," said Miss Holmes, somewhat gravely. "As to his misfortunes, I presume that his journeys between here and Liverpool are not the worst of them."

After breakfast on that day Bessy was summoned into her father's book-room, and found him there, and her mother also. "Bessy," said he, "sit down, my dear. You know why Godfrey has left us this morning?"

Bessy walked round the room, so that in sitting she might be close to her mother and take her mother's hand in her own. "I suppose I do, papa," she said.

"He was with me late last night, Bessy; and when he told me what had passed between you I agreed with him that he had better go."

"It was better that he should go, papa."

"But he has left a message for you."

"A message, papa?"

"Yes, Bessy. And your mother agrees with me that it had better be given to you. It is this,—that if you will send him word to come again, he will be here by Twelfth-night. He came before on my invitation, but if he returns it must be on yours."

"Oh, papa, I cannot."

"I do not say that you can, but think of it calmly before you altogether refuse. You shall give me your answer on New Year's morning."

"Mamma knows that it would be impossible," said Bessy.

"Not impossible, dearest."

"In such a matter you should do what you believe to be right," said her father.

"If I were to ask him here again, it would be telling him that I would—"

"Exactly, Bessy. It would be telling him that you would be his wife. He would understand it so, and so would your mother and I. It must be so understood altogether."

"But, papa, when we were at Liverpool—"

"I have told him everything, dearest," said Mrs. Garrow.

"I think I understand the whole," said the Major; "and in such a matter as this I will not give you counsel on either side. But you must remember that in making up your mind, you must think of him as well as of yourself. If you do not love him;—if you feel that as his wife you should not love him, there is not another word to be said. I need not explain to my daughter that under such circumstances she would be wrong to encourage the visits of a suitor. But your mother says you do love him."

"I will not ask you. But if you do;—if you have so told him, and allowed him to build up an idea of his life-happiness on such telling, you will, I think, sin greatly against him by allowing a false feminine pride to mar his happiness. When once a girl has confessed to a man that she loves him, the confession and the love together put upon her the burden of a duty towards him, which she cannot with impunity throw aside." Then he kissed her, and bidding her give him a reply on the morning of the new year, left her with her mother.

She had four days for consideration, and they went past her by no means easily. Could she have been alone with her mother, the struggle would not have been so painful; but there was the necessity that she should talk to Isabella Holmes, and the necessity also that she should not neglect the Coverdales. Nothing could have been kinder than Bella. She did not speak on the subject till the morning of the last day, and then only in a very few words. "Bessy," she said, "as you are great, be merciful."

"But I am not great, and it would not be mercy."

"As to that," said Bella, "he has surely a right to his own opinion."

On that evening she was sitting alone in her room when her mother came to her, and her eyes were red with weeping. Pen and paper were before her, as though she were resolved to write, but hitherto no word had been written.

"Well, Bessy," said her mother, sitting down close beside her; "is the deed done?"

"What deed, mamma? Who says that I am to do it?"

"The deed is not the writing, but the resolution to write. Five words will be sufficient,—if only those five words may be written."

"It is for one's whole life, mamma. For his life, as well as my own."

"True, Bessy;—that is quite true. But equally true whether you bid him come or allow him to remain away. That task of making up one's mind for life, must at last be done in some special moment of that life."

"Mamma, mamma; tell me what I should do."

But this Mrs. Garrow would not do. "I will write the words for you if you like," she said, "but it is you who must resolve that they shall be written. I cannot bid my darling go away and leave me for another home;—I can only say that in my heart I do believe that home would be a happy one."

It was morning before the note was written, but when the morning came Bessy had written it and brought it to her mother.

"You must take it to papa," she said. Then she went and hid herself from all eyes till the noon had passed. "Dear Godfrey," the letter ran, "Papa says that you will return on Wednesday if I write to ask you. Do come back to us,—if you wish it. Yours always, Bessy."

"It is as good as though she had filled the sheet," said the Major. But in sending it to Godfrey Holmes, he did not omit a few accompanying remarks of his own.

An answer came from Godfrey by return of post; and on the afternoon of the sixth of January, Frank Garrow drove over to the station at Penrith to meet him. On their way back to Thwaite Hall there grew up a very close confidence between the two future brothers-in-law, and Frank explained with great perspicuity a little plan which he had arranged himself. "As soon as it is dark, so that she won't see it, Harry will hang it up in the dining-room," he said, "and mind you go in there before you go anywhere else."

"I am very glad you have come back, Godfrey," said the Major, meeting him in the hall.

"God bless you, dear Godfrey," said Mrs. Garrow, "you will find Bessy in the dining-room," she whispered; but in so whispering she was quite unconscious of the mistletoe bough.

And so also was Bessy, nor do I think that she was much more conscious when that introduction was over. Godfrey had made all manner of promises to Frank, but when the moment arrived, he had found the moment too important for any special reference to the little bough above his head. Not so, however, Patty Coverdale. "It's a shame," said she, bursting out of the room, "and if I'd known what you had done, nothing on earth should have induced me to go in. I won't enter the room till I know that you have taken it out." Nevertheless her sister Kate was bold enough to solve the mystery before the evening was over.

MRS. GENERAL TALBOYS

Why Mrs. General Talboys first made up her mind to pass the winter of 1859 at Rome I never clearly understood. To myself she explained her purposes, soon after her arrival at the Eternal City, by declaring, in her own enthusiastic manner, that she was inspired by a burning desire to drink fresh at the still living fountains of classical poetry and sentiment. But I always thought that there was something more than this in it. Classical poetry and sentiment were doubtless very dear to her; but so also, I imagine, were the substantial comforts of Hardover Lodge, the General's house in Berkshire; and I do not think that she would have emigrated for the winter had there not been some slight domestic misunderstanding. Let this, however, be fully made clear,—that such misunderstanding, if it existed, must have been simply an affair of temper. No impropriety of conduct has, I am very sure, ever been imputed to the lady. The General, as all the world knows, is hot; and Mrs. Talboys, when the sweet rivers of her enthusiasm are unfed by congenial waters, can, I believe, make herself disagreeable.

But be this as it may, in November, 1859, Mrs. Talboys came among us English at Rome, and soon succeeded in obtaining for herself a comfortable footing in our society. We all thought her more remarkable for her mental attributes than for physical perfection; but, nevertheless, she was, in her own way, a sightly woman. She had no special brilliance, either of eye or complexion, such as would produce sudden flames in susceptible hearts; nor did she seem to demand instant homage by the form and step of a goddess; but we found her to be a good-looking woman of some thirty or thirty-three years of age, with soft, peach-like cheeks,—rather too like those of a cherub, with sparkling eyes which were hardly large enough, with good teeth, a white forehead, a dimpled chin and a full bust. Such, outwardly, was Mrs. General Talboys.

The description of the inward woman is the purport to which these few pages will be devoted.

There are two qualities to which the best of mankind are much subject, which are nearly related to each other, and as to which the world has not yet decided whether they are to be classed among the good or evil attributes of our nature. Men and women are under the influence of them both, but men oftenest undergo the former, and women the latter. They are ambition and enthusiasm. Now Mrs. Talboys was an enthusiastic woman.

As to ambition, generally as the world agrees with Mark Antony in stigmatising it as a grievous fault, I am myself clear that it is a virtue; but with ambition at present we have no concern. Enthusiasm also, as I think, leans to virtue's side; or, at least, if it be a fault, of all faults it is the prettiest. But then, to partake at all of virtue, or even to be in any degree pretty, the enthusiasm must be true.

Bad coin is known from good by the ring of it; and so is bad enthusiasm. Let the coiner be ever so clever at his art, in the coining of enthusiasm the sound of true gold can never be imparted to the false metal. And I doubt whether the cleverest she in the world can make false enthusiasm palatable to the taste of man. To the taste of any woman the enthusiasm of another woman is never very palatable.

We understood at Home that Mrs. Talboys had a considerable family,—four or five children, we were told; but she brought with her only one daughter, a little girl about twelve years of age. She had torn herself asunder, as she told me, from the younger nurslings of her heart, and had left them to the care of a devoted female attendant, whose love was all but maternal. And then she said a word or two about the General, in terms which made me almost think that this quasi-maternal love extended itself beyond the children. The idea, however, was a mistaken one, arising from the strength of her language, to which I was then unaccustomed. I have since become aware that nothing can be more decorous than old Mrs. Upton, the excellent head-nurse at Hardover Lodge; and no gentleman more discreet in his conduct than General Talboys.

And I may as well here declare, also, that there could be no more virtuous woman than the General's wife. Her marriage vow was to her paramount to all other vows and bonds whatever. The

General's honour was quite safe when he sent her off to Rome by herself; and he no doubt knew that it was so. Illi robur et aes triplex, of which I believe no weapons of any assailant could get the better. But, nevertheless, we used to fancy that she had no repugnance to impropriety in other women,—to what the world generally calls impropriety. Invincibly attached herself to the marriage tie, she would constantly speak of it as by no means necessarily binding on others; and, virtuous herself as any griffin of propriety, she constantly patronised, at any rate, the theory of infidelity in her neighbours. She was very eager in denouncing the prejudices of the English world, declaring that she had found existence among them to be no longer possible for herself. She was hot against the stern unforgiveness of British matrons, and equally eager in reprobating the stiff conventionalities of a religion in which she said that none of its votaries had faith, though they all allowed themselves to be enslaved.

We had at that time a small set at Rome, consisting chiefly of English and Americans, who habitually met at each other's rooms, and spent many of our evening hours in discussing Italian politics. We were, most of us, painters, poets, novelists, or sculptors;— perhaps I should say would-be painters, poets, novelists, and sculptors,—aspirants hoping to become some day recognised; and among us Mrs. Talboys took her place, naturally enough, on account of a very pretty taste she had for painting.

I do not know that she ever originated anything that was grand; but she made some nice copies, and was fond, at any rate, of art conversation. She wrote essays, too, which she showed in confidence to various gentlemen, and had some idea of taking lessons in modelling.

In all our circle Conrad Mackinnon, an American, was, perhaps, the person most qualified to be styled its leader. He was one who absolutely did gain his living, and an ample living too, by his pen, and was regarded on all sides as a literary lion, justified by success in roaring at any tone he might please. His usual roar was not exactly that of a sucking-dove or a nightingale; but it was a good-humoured roar, not very offensive to any man, and apparently acceptable enough to some ladies. He was a big burly man, near to fifty as I suppose, somewhat awkward in his gait, and somewhat loud in his laugh. But though nigh to fifty, and thus ungainly, he liked to be smiled on by pretty women, and liked, as some said, to be flattered by them also. If so, he should have been happy, for the ladies at Rome at that time made much of Conrad Mackinnon.

Of Mrs. Mackinnon no one did make very much, and yet she was one of the sweetest, dearest, quietest, little creatures that ever made glad a man's fireside. She was exquisitely pretty, always in good humour, never stupid, self-denying to a fault, and yet she was generally in the background. She would seldom come forward of her own will, but was contented to sit behind her teapot and hear Mackinnon do his roaring. He was certainly much given to what the world at Rome called flirting, but this did not in the least annoy her. She was twenty years his junior, and yet she never flirted with any one. Women would tell her—good-natured friends—how Mackinnon went on; but she received such tidings as an excellent joke, observing that he had always done the same, and no doubt always would until he was ninety. I do believe that she was a happy woman; and yet I used to think that she should have been happier. There is, however, no knowing the inside of another man's house, or reading the riddles of another man's joy and sorrow.

We had also there another lion,—a lion cub,—entitled to roar a little, and of him also I must say something. Charles O'Brien was a young man, about twenty-five years of age, who had sent out from his studio in the preceding year a certain bust, supposed by his admirers to be unsurpassed by any effort of ancient or modern genius. I am no judge of sculpture, and will not, therefore, pronounce an opinion; but many who considered themselves to be judges, declared that it was a "goodish head and shoulders," and nothing more. I merely mention the fact, as it was on the strength of that head and shoulders that O'Brien separated himself from a throng of others such as himself in Rome, walked solitary during the days, and threw himself at the feet of various ladies when the days were over. He had ridden on the shoulders of his bust into a prominent place in our circle, and there encountered much feminine admiration—from Mrs. General Talboys and others.

Some eighteen or twenty of us used to meet every Sunday evening in Mrs. Mackinnon's drawing-room. Many of us, indeed, were in the habit of seeing each other daily, and of visiting together the haunts in Rome which are best loved by art-loving strangers; but here, in this drawing-room, we were sure to come together, and here before the end of November, Mrs. Talboys might always be found, not in any accustomed seat, but moving about the room as the different male mental attractions of our society might chance to move themselves. She was at first greatly taken by Mackinnon,— who also was, I think, a little stirred by her admiration, though he stoutly denied the charge. She became, however, very dear to us all before she left us, and certainly we owed to her our love, for she added infinitely to the joys of our winter.

"I have come here to refresh myself," she said to Mackinnon one evening—to Mackinnon and myself; for we were standing together.

"Shall I get you tea?" said I.

"And will you have something to eat?" Mackinnon asked.

"No, no, no;" she answered. "Tea, yes; but for Heaven's sake let nothing solid dispel the associations of such a meeting as this!"

"I thought you might have dined early," said Mackinnon. Now Mackinnon was a man whose own dinner was very dear to him. I have seen him become hasty and unpleasant, even under the pillars of the Forum, when he thought that the party were placing his fish in jeopardy by their desire to linger there too long.

"Early! Yes. No; I know not when it was. One dines and sleeps in obedience to that dull clay which weighs down so generally the particle of our spirit. But the clay may sometimes be forgotten. Here I can always forget it."

"I thought you asked for refreshment," I said. She only looked at me, whose small attempts at prose composition had, up to that time, been altogether unsuccessful, and then addressed herself in reply to Mackinnon.

"It is the air which we breathe that fills our lungs and gives us life and light. It is that which refreshes us if pure, or sinks us into stagnation if it be foul. Let me for awhile inhale the breath of an invigorating literature. Sit down, Mr. Mackinnon; I have a question that I must put to you." And then she succeeded in carrying him off into a corner. As far as I could see he went willingly enough at that time, though he soon became averse to any long retirement in company with Mrs. Talboys.

We none of us quite understood what were her exact ideas on the subject of revealed religion. Somebody, I think, had told her that there were among us one or two whose opinions were not exactly orthodox according to the doctrines of the established English church. If so, she was determined to show us that she also was advanced beyond the prejudices of an old and dry school of theology. "I have thrown down all the barriers of religion," she said to poor Mrs. Mackinnon, "and am looking for the sentiments of a pure Christianity."

"Thrown down all the barriers of religion!" said Mrs. Mackinnon, in a tone of horror which was not appreciated.

"Indeed, yes," said Mrs. Talboys, with an exulting voice. "Are not the days for such trammels gone by?"

"But yet you hold by Christianity?"

"A pure Christianity, unstained by blood and perjury, by hypocrisy and verbose genuflection. Can I not worship and say my prayers among the clouds?" And she pointed to the lofty ceiling and the handsome chandelier.

"But Ida goes to church," said Mrs. Mackinnon. Ida Talboys was her daughter. Now, it may be observed, that many who throw down the barriers of religion, so far as those barriers may affect themselves, still maintain them on behalf of their children. "Yes," said Mrs. Talboys; "dear Ida! her soft spirit is not yet adapted to receive the perfect truth. We are obliged to govern children by the strength of their prejudices." And then she moved away, for it was seldom that Mrs. Talboys remained long in conversation with any lady.

Mackinnon, I believe, soon became tired of her. He liked her flattery, and at first declared that she was clever and nice; but her niceness was too purely celestial to satisfy his mundane tastes. Mackinnon himself can revel among the clouds in his own writings, and can leave us sometimes in doubt whether he ever means to come back to earth; but when his foot is on terra firma, he loves to feel the earthly substratum which supports his weight. With women he likes a hand that can remain an unnecessary moment within his own, an eye that can glisten with the sparkle of champagne, a heart weak enough to make its owner's arm tremble within his own beneath the moonlight gloom of the Coliseum arches. A dash of sentiment the while makes all these things the sweeter; but the sentiment alone will not suffice for him. Mrs. Talboys did, I believe, drink her glass of champagne, as do other ladies; but with her it had no such pleasing effect. It loosened only her tongue, but never her eye. Her arm, I think, never trembled, and her hand never lingered. The General was always safe, and happy, perhaps, in his solitary safety.

It so happened that we had unfortunately among us two artists who had quarrelled with their wives. O'Brien, whom I have before mentioned, was one of them. In his case, I believe him to have been almost as free from blame as a man can be whose marriage was in itself a fault. However, he had a wife in Ireland some ten years older than himself; and though he might sometimes almost forget the fact, his friends and neighbours were well aware of it. In the other case the whole fault probably was with the husband. He was an ill-tempered, bad-hearted man, clever enough, but without principle; and he was continually guilty of the great sin of speaking evil of the woman whose name he should have been anxious to protect. In both cases our friend Mrs. Talboys took a warm interest, and in each of them she sympathised with the present husband against the absent wife.

Of the consolation which she offered in the latter instance we used to hear something from Mackinnon. He would repeat to his wife, and to me and my wife, the conversations which she had with him. "Poor Brown;" she would say, "I pity him, with my very heart's blood."

"You are aware that he has comforted himself in his desolation," Mackinnon replied.

"I know very well to what you allude. I think I may say that I am conversant with all the circumstances of this heart-blighting sacrifice." Mrs. Talboys was apt to boast of the thorough confidence reposed in her by all those in whom she took an interest. "Yes, he has sought such comfort in another love as the hard cruel world would allow him."

"Or perhaps something more than that," said Mackinnon. "He has a family here in Rome, you know; two little babies."

"I know it, I know it," she said. "Cherub angels!" and as she spoke she looked up into the ugly face of Marcus Aurelius; for they were standing at the moment under the figure of the great horseman on the Campidoglio. "I have seen them, and they are the children of innocence. If all the blood of all the Howards ran in their veins it could not make their birth more noble!"

"Not if the father and mother of all the Howards had never been married," said Mackinnon.

"What; that from you, Mr. Mackinnon!" said Mrs. Talboys, turning her back with energy upon the equestrian statue, and looking up into the faces, first of Pollux and then of Castor, as though from them she might gain some inspiration on the subject which Marcus Aurelius in his coldness had denied to her. "From you, who have so nobly claimed for mankind the divine attributes of free action! From you, who have taught my mind to soar above the petty bonds which one man in his littleness contrives for the subjection of his brother. Mackinnon! you who are so great!" And she now looked up into his face. "Mackinnon, unsay those words."

"They ARE illegitimate," said he; "and if there was any landed property—"

"Landed property! and that from an American!"

"The children are English, you know."

"Landed property! The time will shortly come—ay, and I see it coming—when that hateful word shall be expunged from the calendar; when landed property shall be no more. What! shall the free soul of a God-born man submit itself for ever to such trammels as that? Shall we never escape from the clay which so long has manacled the subtler particles of the divine spirit? Ay, yes, Mackinnon;" and then she took him by the arm, and led him to the top of the huge steps which lead down from the Campidoglio into the streets of modern Rome. "Look down upon that countless multitude." Mackinnon looked down, and saw three groups of French soldiers, with three or four little men in each group; he saw, also, a couple of dirty friars, and three priests very slowly beginning the side ascent to the church of the Ara Coeli. "Look down upon that countless multitude," said Mrs. Talboys, and she stretched her arms out over the half-deserted city. "They are escaping now from these trammels,—now, now,—now that I am speaking."

"They have escaped long ago from all such trammels as that of landed property," said Mackinnon.

"Ay, and from all terrestrial bonds," she continued, not exactly remarking the pith of his last observation; "from bonds quasi-terrestrial and quasi-celestial. The full-formed limbs of the present age, running with quick streams of generous blood, will no longer bear the ligatures which past times have woven for the decrepit.

Look down upon that multitude, Mackinnon; they shall all be free." And then, still clutching him by the arm, and still standing at the top of those stairs, she gave forth her prophecy with the fury of a Sybil.

"They shall all be free. Oh, Rome, thou eternal one! thou who hast bowed thy neck to imperial pride and priestly craft; thou who hast suffered sorely, even to this hour, from Nero down to Pio Nono,—the days of thine oppression are over. Gone from thy enfranchised ways for ever is the clang of the Praetorian cohorts and the more odious drone of meddling monks!" And yet, as Mackinnon observed, there still stood the dirty friars and the small French soldiers; and there still toiled the slow priests, wending their tedious way up to the church of the Ara Coeli. But that was the mundane view of the matter,—a view not regarded by Mrs. Talboys in her ecstasy. "O Italia," she continued, "O Italia una, one and indivisible in thy rights, and indivisible also in thy wrongs! to us is it given to see the accomplishment of thy glory. A people shall arise around thine altars greater in the annals of the world than thy Scipios, thy Gracchi, or thy Caesars. Not in torrents of blood, or with screams of bereaved mothers, shall thy new triumphs be stained. But mind shall dominate over matter; and doomed, together with Popes and Bourbons, with cardinals, diplomatists, and police spies, ignorance and prejudice shall be driven from thy smiling terraces. And then Rome shall again become the fair capital of the fairest region of Europe. Hither shall flock the artisans of the world, crowding into thy marts all that God and man can give. Wealth, beauty, and innocence shall meet in thy streets—"

"There will be a considerable change before that takes place," said Mackinnon.

"There shall be a considerable change," she answered. "Mackinnon, to thee it is given to read the signs of the time; and hast thou not read? Why have the fields of Magenta and Solferino been piled with the corpses of dying heroes? Why have the waters of the Mincio ran red with the blood of martyrs? That Italy might be united and Rome immortal. Here, standing on the Capitolium of the ancient city, I say that it shall be so; and thou, Mackinnon, who hearest me, knowest that my words are true."

There was not then in Rome,—I may almost say there was not in Italy, an Englishman or an American who did not wish well to the cause for which Italy was and is still contending; as also there is hardly one who does not now regard that cause as well-nigh triumphant; but, nevertheless, it was almost impossible to sympathise with Mrs. Talboys. As Mackinnon said, she flew so high that there was no comfort in flying with her.

"Well," said he, "Brown and the rest of them are down below. Shall we go and join them?"

"Poor Brown! How was it that, in speaking of his troubles, we were led on to this heart-stirring theme? Yes, I have seen them, the sweet angels; and I tell you also that I have seen their mother. I insisted on going to her when I heard her history from him."

"And what is she like, Mrs. Talboys?"

"Well; education has done more for some of us than for others; and there are those from whose morals and sentiments we might thankfully draw a lesson, whose manners and outward gestures are not such as custom has made agreeable to us. You, I know, can understand that. I have seen her, and feel sure that she is pure in heart and high in principle. Has she not sacrificed herself; and is not self-sacrifice the surest guarantee for true nobility of character? Would Mrs. Mackinnon object to my bringing them together?"

Mackinnon was obliged to declare that he thought his wife would object; and from that time forth he and Mrs. Talboys ceased to be very close in their friendship. She still came to the house every Sunday evening, still refreshed herself at the fountains of his literary rills; but her special prophecies from henceforth were poured into other ears. And it so happened that O'Brien now became her chief ally. I do not remember that she troubled herself much further with the cherub angels or with their mother; and I am inclined to think that, taking up warmly, as she did, the story of O'Brien's matrimonial wrongs, she forgot the little history of the Browns. Be that as it may, Mrs. Talboys and O'Brien now became strictly confidential, and she would enlarge by the half-hour together on the miseries of her friend's position, to any one whom she could get to hear her.

"I'll tell you what, Fanny," Mackinnon said to his wife one day,—to his wife and to mine, for we were all together; "we shall have a row in the house if we don't take care. O'Brien will be making love to Mrs. Talboys."

"Nonsense," said Mrs. Mackinnon. "You are always thinking that somebody is going to make love to some one."

"Somebody always is," said he.

"She's old enough to be his mother," said Mrs. Mackinnon.

"What does that matter to an Irishman?" said Mackinnon. "Besides, I doubt if there is more than five years' difference between them."

"There must be more than that," said my wife. "Ida Talboys is twelve, I know, and I am not quite sure that Ida is the eldest."

"If she had a son in the Guards it would make no difference," said Mackinnon. "There are men who consider themselves bound to make love to a woman under certain circumstances, let the age of the lady be what it may. O'Brien is such a one; and if she sympathises with him much oftener, he will mistake the matter, and go down on his knees. You ought to put him on his guard," he said, addressing himself to his wife.

"Indeed, I shall do no such thing," said she; "if they are two fools, they must, like other fools, pay the price of their folly." As a rule there could be no softer creature than Mrs. Mackinnon; but it seemed to me that her tenderness never extended itself in the direction of Mrs. Talboys.

Just at this time, towards the end, that is, of November, we made a party to visit the tombs which lie along the Appian Way, beyond that most beautiful of all sepulchres, the tomb of Cecilia Metella. It was a delicious day, and we had driven along this road for a couple of miles beyond the walls of the city, enjoying the most lovely view which the neighbourhood of Rome affords,—looking over the wondrous ruins of the old aqueducts, up towards Tivoli and Palestrina. Of all the environs of Rome this is, on a fair clear day, the most enchanting; and here perhaps, among a world of tombs, thoughts and almost memories of the old, old days come upon one with the greatest force. The grandeur of Rome is best seen and understood from beneath the walls of the Coliseum, and its beauty among the pillars of the Forum and the arches of the Sacred Way; but its history and fall become more palpable to the mind, and more clearly realised, out here among the tombs, where the eyes rest upon the mountains whose shades were cool to the old Romans as to us,—than anywhere within the walls of the city. Here we look out at the same Tivoli and the same Praeneste, glittering in the sunshine, embowered among the far-off valleys, which were dear to them; and the blue mountains have not crumbled away into ruins. Within Rome itself we can see nothing as they saw it.

Our party consisted of some dozen or fifteen persons, and as a hamper with luncheon in it had been left on the grassy slope at the base of the tomb of Cecilia Metella, the expedition had in it something of the nature of a picnic. Mrs. Talboys was of course with us, and Ida Talboys. O'Brien also was there. The hamper had been prepared in Mrs. Mackinnon's room, under the immediate eye of Mackinnon himself, and they therefore were regarded as the dominant spirits of the party. My wife was leagued with Mrs. Mackinnon, as was usually the case; and there seemed to be a general opinion among those who were closely in confidence together, that something would happen in the O'Brien-Talboys matter. The two had been inseparable on the previous evening, for Mrs. Talboys had been urging on the young Irishman her counsels respecting his domestic troubles. Sir Cresswell Cresswell, she had told him, was his refuge. "Why should his soul submit to bonds which the world had now declared to be intolerable? Divorce was not now the privilege of the dissolute rich. Spirits which were incompatible need no longer be compelled to fret beneath the same cobbles." In short, she had recommended him to go to England and get rid of his wife, as she would, with a little encouragement, have recommended any man to get rid of anything. I am sure that, had she been skilfully brought on to the subject, she might have been induced to pronounce a verdict against such ligatures for the body as coats, waistcoats, and trowsers. Her aspirations for freedom ignored all bounds, and, in theory, there were no barriers which she was not willing to demolish.

Poor O'Brien, as we all now began to see, had taken the matter amiss. He had offered to make a bust of Mrs. Talboys, and she had consented, expressing a wish that it might find a place among those who had devoted themselves to the enfranchisement of their fellow-creatures. I really think she had but little of a woman's customary personal vanity. I know she had an idea that her eye was lighted up in her warmer moments by some special fire, that sparks of liberty shone round her brow, and that her bosom heaved with glorious aspirations; but all these feelings had reference to her inner genius, not to any outward beauty. But O'Brien misunderstood the woman, and thought it necessary to gaze into her face, and sigh as though his heart were breaking. Indeed he declared to a young friend that Mrs. Talboys was perfect in her style of beauty, and began the bust with this idea. It was gradually becoming clear to us all that he would bring himself to grief; but in such a matter who can caution a man?

Mrs. Mackinnon had contrived to separate them in making the carriage arrangements on this day, but this only added fuel to the fire which was now burning within O'Brien's bosom. I believe that he really did love her, in his easy, eager, susceptible Irish way. That he would get over the little episode without any serious injury to his heart no one doubted; but then, what would occur when the declaration was made? How would Mrs. Talboys bear it?

"She deserves it," said Mrs. Mackinnon.

"And twice as much," my wife added. Why is it that women are so spiteful to each other?

Early in the day Mrs. Talboys clambered up to the top of a tomb, and made a little speech, holding a parasol over her head. Beneath her feet, she said, reposed the ashes of some bloated senator, some glutton of the empire, who had swallowed into his maw the provision necessary for a tribe. Old Rome had fallen through such selfishness as that; but new Rome would not forget the lesson. All this was very well, and then O'Brien helped her down; but after this there was no separating them. For her own part she would sooner have had Mackinnon at her elbow. But Mackinnon now had found some other elbow.

"Enough of that was as good as a feast," he had said to his wife. And therefore Mrs. Talboys, quite unconscious of evil, allowed herself to be engrossed by O'Brien.

And then, about three o'clock, we returned to the hamper. Luncheon under such circumstances always means dinner, and we arranged ourselves for a very comfortable meal. To those who know the tomb of Cecilia Metella no description of the scene is necessary, and to those who do not, no description will convey a fair idea of its reality. It is itself a large low tower of great diameter, but of beautiful proportion, standing far outside the city, close on to the side of the old Roman way. It has been embattled on the top by some latter-day baron, in order that it might be used for protection to the castle, which has been built on and attached to it. If I remember rightly, this was done by one of the Frangipani, and a very lovely ruin he has made of it. I know no castellated old tumble-down residence in Italy more picturesque than this baronial adjunct to the old Roman tomb, or which better tallies with the ideas engendered within our minds by Mrs. Radcliffe and the Mysteries of Udolpho. It lies along the road, protected on the side of the city by the proud sepulchre of the Roman matron, and up to the long ruined walls of the back of the building stretches a grassy slope, at the bottom of which are the remains of an old Roman circus. Beyond that is the long, thin, graceful line of the Claudian aqueduct, with Soracte in the distance to the left, and Tivoli, Palestine, and Frascati lying among the hills which bound the view. That Frangipani baron was in the right of it, and I hope he got the value of his money out of the residence which he built for himself. I doubt, however, that he did but little good to those who lived in his close neighbourhood.

We had a very comfortable little banquet seated on the broken lumps of stone which lie about under the walls of the tomb. I wonder whether the shade of Cecilia Metella was looking down upon us. We have heard much of her in these latter days, and yet we know nothing about her, nor can conceive why she was honoured with a bigger tomb than any other Roman matron. There were those then among our party who believed that she might still come back among us, and with due assistance from some cognate susceptible spirit, explain to us the cause of her widowed husband's liberality. Alas, alas! if we may judge of the Romans by ourselves, the true reason for such sepulchral grandeur would redound little to the credit of the lady Cecilia Metella herself, or to that of Crassus, her bereaved and desolate lord.

She did not come among us on the occasion of this banquet, possibly because we had no tables there to turn in preparation for her presence; but, had she done so, she could not have been more eloquent of things of the other world than was Mrs. Talboys. I have said that Mrs. Talboys' eye never glanced more brightly after a glass of champagne, but I am inclined to think that on this occasion it may have done so. O'Brien enacted Ganymede, and was, perhaps, more liberal than other latter-day Ganymedes, to whose services Mrs. Talboys had been accustomed. Let it not, however, be suspected by any one that she exceeded the limits of a discreet joyousness. By no means! The generous wine penetrated, perhaps, to some inner cells of her heart, and brought forth thoughts in sparkling words, which otherwise might have remained concealed; but there was nothing in what she thought or spoke calculated to give umbrage either to an anchorite or to a vestal. A word or two she said or sung about the flowing bowl, and once she called for Falernian; but beyond this her converse was chiefly of the rights of man and the weakness of women; of the iron ages that were past, and of the golden time that was to come.

She called a toast and drank to the hopes of the latter historians of the nineteenth century. Then it was that she bade O'Brien "Fill high the bowl with Samian wine." The Irishman took her at her word, and she raised the bumper, and waved it over her head before she put it to her lips. I am bound to declare that she did not spill a drop. "The true 'Falernian grape,'" she said, as she deposited the empty beaker on the grass beneath her elbow. Viler champagne I do not think I ever swallowed; but it was the theory of the wine, not its palpable body present there, as it were, in the flesh, which inspired her. There was really something grand about her on that occasion, and her enthusiasm almost amounted to reality.

Mackinnon was amused, and encouraged her, as, I must confess, did I also. Mrs. Mackinnon made useless little signs to her husband, really fearing that the Falernian would do its good offices too thoroughly. My wife, getting me apart as I walked round the circle distributing viands, remarked that "the woman was a fool, and would disgrace herself." But I observed that after the disposal of that bumper she worshipped the rosy god in theory only, and therefore saw no occasion to interfere. "Come, Bacchus," she said; "and come, Silenus, if thou wilt; I know that ye are hovering round the graves of your departed favourites. And ye, too, nymphs of Egeria," and she pointed to the classic grove which was all but close to us as we sat there. "In olden days ye did not always despise the abodes of men. But why should we invoke the presence of the gods,—we, who can become godlike ourselves! We ourselves are the deities of the present age. For us shall the tables be spread with ambrosia; for us shall the nectar flow."

Upon the whole it was very good fooling,—for awhile; and as soon as we were tired of it we arose from our seats, and began to stroll about the place. It was beginning to be a little dusk, and somewhat cool, but the evening air was pleasant, and the ladies, putting on their shawls, did not seem inclined at once to get into the carriages.

At any rate, Mrs. Talboys was not so inclined, for she started down the hill towards the long low wall of the old Roman circus at the bottom; and O'Brien, close at her elbow, started with her.

"Ida, my dear, you had better remain here," she said to her daughter; "you will be tired if you come as far as we are going."

"Oh, no, mamma, I shall not," said Ida. "You get tired much quicker than I do."

"Oh, yes, you will; besides I do not wish you to come." There was an end of it for Ida, and Mrs. Talboys and O'Brien walked off together, while we all looked into each other's faces.

"It would be a charity to go with them," said Mackinnon.

"Do you be charitable, then," said his wife.

"It should be a lady," said he.

"It is a pity that the mother of the spotless cherubim is not here for the occasion," said she. "I hardly think that any one less gifted will undertake such a self sacrifice." Any attempt of the kind would, however, now have been too late, for they were already at the bottom of the hill. O'Brien had certainly drunk freely of the pernicious contents of those long-necked bottles; and though no one could fairly accuse him of being tipsy, nevertheless that which might have made others drunk had made him bold, and he dared to do— perhaps more than might become a man. If under any circumstances he could be fool enough to make an avowal of love to Mrs. Talboys, he might be expected, as we all thought, to do it now.

We watched them as they made for a gap in the wall which led through into the large enclosed space of the old circus. It had been an arena for chariot games, and they had gone down with the avowed purpose of searching where might have been the meta, and ascertaining how the drivers could have turned when at their full speed. For awhile we had heard their voices,—or rather her voice especially. "The heart of a man, O'Brien, should suffice for all emergencies," we had heard her say. She had assumed a strange habit of calling men by their simple names, as men address each other. When she did this to Mackinnon, who was much older than herself, we had been all amused by it, and, other ladies of our party had taken to call him "Mackinnon" when Mrs. Talboys was not by; but we had felt the comedy to be less safe with O'Brien, especially when, on one occasion, we heard him address her as Arabella. She did not seem to be in any way struck by his doing so, and we supposed, therefore, that it had become frequent between them. What reply he made at the moment about the heart of a man I do not know;—and then in a few minutes they disappeared through the gap in the wall.

None of us followed them, though it would have seemed the most natural thing in the world to do so had nothing out of the way been expected. As it was we remained there round the tomb quizzing the little foibles of our dear friend, and hoping that O'Brien would be quick in what he was doing. That he would undoubtedly get a slap in the face—metaphorically—we all felt certain, for none of us doubted the rigid propriety of the lady's intentions. Some of us strolled into the buildings, and some of us got out on to the road; but we all of us were thinking that O'Brien was very slow a considerable time before we saw Mrs. Talboys reappear through the gap.

At last, however, she was there, and we at once saw that she was alone. She came on, breasting the hill with quick steps, and when she drew near we could see that there was a frown as of injured majesty on her brow. Mackinnon and his wife went forward to meet her. If she were really in trouble it would be fitting in some way to assist her; and of all women Mrs. Mackinnon was the last to see another woman suffer from ill-usage without attempting to aid her. "I certainly never liked her," Mrs. Mackinnon said afterwards; "but I was bound to go and hear her tale, when she really had a tale to tell."

And Mrs. Talboys now had a tale to tell,—if she chose to tell it. The ladies of our party declared afterwards that she would have acted more wisely had she kept to herself both O'Brien's words to her and her answer. "She was well able to take care of herself," Mrs. Mackinnon said; "and, after all, the silly man had taken an answer when he got it." Not, however, that O'Brien had taken his answer quite immediately, as far as I could understand from what we heard of the matter afterwards.

At the present moment Mrs. Talboys came up the rising ground all alone, and at a quick pace. "The man has insulted me," she said aloud, as well as her panting breath would allow her, and as soon as she was near enough to Mrs. Mackinnon to speak to her.

"I am sorry for that," said Mrs. Mackinnon. "I suppose he has taken a little too much wine."

"No; it was a premeditated insult. The base-hearted churl has failed to understand the meaning of true, honest sympathy."

"He will forget all about it when he is sober," said Mackinnon, meaning to comfort her.

"What care I what he remembers or what he forgets!" she said, turning upon poor Mackinnon indignantly. "You men grovel so in your ideas—" "And yet," as Mackinnon said afterwards, "she had been telling me that I was a fool for the last three weeks."— "You men grovel so in your ideas, that you cannot understand the feelings of a true-hearted woman. What can his forgetfulness or his remembrance be to me? Must not I remember this insult? Is it possible that I should forget it?"

Mr. and Mrs. Mackinnon only had gone forward to meet her; but, nevertheless, she spoke so loud that all heard her who were still clustered round the spot on which we had dined.

"What has become of Mr. O'Brien?" a lady whispered to me.

I had a field-glass with me, and, looking round, I saw his hat as he was walking inside the walls of the circus in the direction towards the city. "And very foolish he must feel," said the lady.

"No doubt he is used to it," said another.

"But considering her age, you know," said the first, who might have been perhaps three years younger than Mrs. Talboys, and who was not herself averse to the excitement of a moderate flirtation. But then why should she have been averse, seeing that she had not as yet become subject to the will of any imperial lord?

"He would have felt much more foolish," said the third, "if she had listened to what he said to her."

"Well I don't know," said the second; "nobody would have known anything about it then, and in a few weeks they would have gradually become tired of each other in the ordinary way."

But in the meantime Mrs. Talboys was among us. There had been no attempt at secresy, and she was still loudly inveighing against the grovelling propensities of men. "That's quite true, Mrs. Talboys," said one of the elder ladies; "but then women are not always so careful as they should be. Of course I do not mean to say that there has been any fault on your part."

"Fault on my part! Of course there has been fault on my part. No one can make any mistake without fault to some extent. I took him to be a man of sense, and he is a fool. Go to Naples indeed!"

"Did he want you to go to Naples?" asked Mrs. Mackinnon.

"Yes; that was what he suggested. We were to leave by the train for Civita Vecchia at six tomorrow morning and catch the steamer which leaves Leghorn tonight. Don't tell me of wine. He was prepared for it!" And she looked round about on us with an air of injured majesty in her face which was almost insupportable.

"I wonder whether he took the tickets over-night," said Mackinnon.

"Naples!" she said, as though now speaking exclusively to herself; "the only ground in Italy which has as yet made no struggle on behalf of freedom;—a fitting residence for such a dastard!"

"You would have found it very pleasant at this season," said the unmarried lady, who was three years her junior.

My wife had taken Ida out of the way when the first complaining note from Mrs. Talboys had been heard ascending the hill. But now, when matters began gradually to become quiescent, she brought her back, suggesting, as she did so, that they might begin to think of returning.

"It is getting very cold, Ida, dear, is it not?" said she.

"But where is Mr. O'Brien?" said Ida.

"He has fled,—as poltroons always fly," said Mrs. Talboys. I believe in my heart that she would have been glad to have had him there in the middle of the circle, and to have triumphed over him publicly among us all. No feeling of shame would have kept her silent for a moment.

"Fled!" said Ida, looking up into her mother's face.

"Yes, fled, my child." And she seized her daughter in her arms, and pressed her closely to her bosom. "Cowards always fly."

"Is Mr. O'Brien a coward?" Ida asked.

"Yes, a coward, a very coward! And he has fled before the glance of an honest woman's eye. Come, Mrs. Mackinnon, shall we go back to the city? I am sorry that the amusement of the day should have received this check." And she walked forward to the carriage and took her place in it with an air that showed that she was proud of the way in which she had conducted herself.

"She is a little conceited about it after all," said that unmarried lady. "If poor Mr. O'Brien had not shown so much premature anxiety with reference to that little journey to Naples, things might have gone quietly after all."

But the unmarried lady was wrong in her judgment. Mrs. Talboys was proud and conceited in the matter,—but not proud of having excited the admiration of her Irish lover. She was proud of her own subsequent conduct, and gave herself credit for coming out strongly as a noble-minded matron. "I believe she thinks," said Mrs. Mackinnon, "that her virtue is quite Spartan and unique; and if she remains in Rome she'll boast of it through the whole winter."

"If she does, she may be certain that O'Brien will do the same," said Mackinnon. "And in spite of his having fled from the field, it is upon the cards that he may get the best of it. Mrs. Talboys is a very excellent woman. She has proved her excellence beyond a doubt. But, nevertheless, she is susceptible of ridicule."

We all felt a little anxiety to hear O'Brien's account of the matter, and after having deposited the ladies at their homes, Mackinnon and I went off to his lodgings. At first he was denied to us, but after awhile we got his servant to acknowledge that he was at home, and then we made our way up to his studio. We found him seated behind a half-formed model, or rather a mere lump of clay punched into something resembling the shape of a head, with a pipe in his mouth and a bit of stick in his hand. He was pretending to work, though we both knew that it was out of the question that he should do anything in his present frame of mind.

"I think I heard my servant tell you that I was not at home," said he.

"Yes, he did," said Mackinnon, "and would have sworn to it too if we would have let him. Come, don't pretend to be surly."

"I am very busy, Mr. Mackinnon."

"Completing your head of Mrs. Talboys, I suppose, before you start for Naples."

"You don't mean to say that she has told you all about it," and he turned away from his work, and looked up into our faces with a comical expression, half of fun and half of despair.

"Every word of it," said I. "When you want a lady to travel with you, never ask her to get up so early in winter."

"But, O'Brien, how could you be such an ass?" said Mackinnon. "As it has turned out, there is no very great harm done. You have insulted a respectable middle-aged woman, the mother of a family, and the wife of a general officer, and there is an end of it;—unless, indeed, the general officer should come out from England to call you to account."

"He is welcome," said O'Brien, haughtily.

"No doubt, my dear fellow," said Mackinnon; "that would be a dignified and pleasant ending to the affair. But what I want to know is this;—what would you have done if she had agreed to go?"

"He never calculated on the possibility of such a contingency," said I.

"By heavens, then, I thought she would like it," said he.

"And to oblige her you were content to sacrifice yourself," said Mackinnon.

"Well, that was just it. What the deuce is a fellow to do when a woman goes on in that way. She told me down there, upon the old race course you know, that matrimonial bonds were made for fools and slaves. What was I to suppose that she meant by that? But to make all sure, I asked her what sort of a fellow the General was. 'Dear old man,' she said, clasping her hands together. 'He might, you know, have been my father.' 'I wish he were,' said I, 'because then you'd be free.' 'I am free,' said she, stamping on the ground, and looking up at me as much as to say that she cared for no one. 'Then,' said I, 'accept all that is left of the heart of Wenceslaus O'Brien,' and I threw myself before her in her path. 'Hand,' said I, 'I have none to give, but the blood which runs red through my veins is descended from a double line of kings.' I said that because she is always fond of riding a high horse. I had gotten close under the wall, so that none of you should see me from the tower."

"And what answer did she make?" said Mackinnon.

"Why she was pleased as Punch;—gave me both her hands, and declared that we would be friends for ever. It is my belief, Mackinnon, that that woman never heard anything of the kind before. The General, no doubt, did it by letter."

"And how was it that she changed her mind?"

"Why; I got up, put my arm round her waist, and told her that we would be off to Naples. I'm blest if she didn't give me a knock in the ribs that nearly sent me backwards. She took my breath away, so that I couldn't speak to her."

"And then—"

"Oh, there was nothing more. Of course I saw how it was. So she walked off one way and I the other. On the whole I consider that I am well out of it."

"And so do I," said Mackinnon, very gravely. "But if you will allow me to give you my advice, I would suggest that it would be well to avoid such mistakes in future."

"Upon my word," said O'Brien, excusing himself, "I don't know what a man is to do under such circumstances. I give you my honour that I did it all to oblige her."

We then decided that Mackinnon should convey to the injured lady the humble apology of her late admirer. It was settled that no detailed excuses should be made. It should be left to her to consider whether the deed which had been done might have been occasioned by wine, or by the folly of a moment,—or by her own indiscreet enthusiasm. No one but the two were present when the message was given, and therefore we were obliged to trust to Mackinnon's accuracy for an account of it.

She stood on very high ground indeed, he said, at first refusing to hear anything that he had to say on the matter. "The foolish young man," she declared, "was below her anger and below her contempt."

"He is not the first Irishman that has been made indiscreet by beauty," said Mackinnon.

"A truce to that," she replied, waving her hand with an air of assumed majesty. "The incident, contemptible as it is, has been unpleasant to me. It will necessitate my withdrawal from Rome."

"Oh, no, Mrs. Talboys; that will be making too much of him."

"The greatest hero that lives," she answered, "may have his house made uninhabitable by a very small insect." Mackinnon swore that those were her own words. Consequently a sobriquet was attached to O'Brien of which he by no means approved. And from that day we always called Mrs. Talboys "the hero."

Mackinnon prevailed at last with her, and she did not leave Rome. She was even induced to send a message to O'Brien, conveying her forgiveness. They shook hands together with great eclat in Mrs. Mackinnon's drawing-room; but I do not suppose that she ever again offered to him sympathy on the score of his matrimonial troubles.

MRS. GENERAL TALBOYS

Why Mrs. General Talboys first made up her mind to pass the winter of 1859 at Rome I never clearly understood. To myself she explained her purposes, soon after her arrival at the Eternal City, by declaring, in her own enthusiastic manner, that she was inspired by a burning desire to drink fresh at the still living fountains of classical poetry and sentiment. But I always thought that there was something more than this in it. Classical poetry and sentiment were doubtless very dear to her; but so also, I imagine, were the substantial comforts of Hardover Lodge, the General's house in Berkshire; and I do not think that she would have emigrated for the winter had there not been some slight domestic misunderstanding. Let this, however, be fully made clear,—that such misunderstanding, if it existed, must have been simply an affair of temper. No impropriety of conduct has, I am very sure, ever been imputed to the lady. The General, as all the world knows, is hot; and Mrs. Talboys, when the sweet rivers of her enthusiasm are unfed by congenial waters, can, I believe, make herself disagreeable.

But be this as it may, in November, 1859, Mrs. Talboys came among us English at Rome, and soon succeeded in obtaining for herself a comfortable footing in our society. We all thought her more remarkable for her mental attributes than for physical perfection; but, nevertheless, she was, in her own way, a sightly woman. She had no special brilliance, either of eye or complexion, such as would produce sudden flames in susceptible hearts; nor did she seem to demand instant homage by the form and step of a goddess; but we found her to be a good-looking woman of some thirty or thirty-three years of age, with soft, peach-like cheeks,—rather too like those of a cherub, with sparkling eyes which were hardly large enough, with good teeth, a white forehead, a dimpled chin and a full bust. Such, outwardly, was Mrs. General Talboys.

The description of the inward woman is the purport to which these few pages will be devoted.

There are two qualities to which the best of mankind are much subject, which are nearly related to each other, and as to which the world has not yet decided whether they are to be classed among the good or evil attributes of our nature. Men and women are under the influence of them both, but men oftenest undergo the former, and women the latter. They are ambition and enthusiasm. Now Mrs. Talboys was an enthusiastic woman.

As to ambition, generally as the world agrees with Mark Antony in stigmatising it as a grievous fault, I am myself clear that it is a virtue; but with ambition at present we have no concern. Enthusiasm also, as I think, leans to virtue's side; or, at least, if it be a fault, of all faults it is the prettiest. But then, to partake at all of virtue, or even to be in any degree pretty, the enthusiasm must be true.

Bad coin is known from good by the ring of it; and so is bad enthusiasm. Let the coiner be ever so clever at his art, in the coining of enthusiasm the sound of true gold can never be imparted to the false metal. And I doubt whether the cleverest she in the world can make false enthusiasm palatable to the taste of man. To the taste of any woman the enthusiasm of another woman is never very palatable.

We understood at Home that Mrs. Talboys had a considerable family,—four or five children, we were told; but she brought with her only one daughter, a little girl about twelve years of age. She had torn herself asunder, as she told me, from the younger nurslings of her heart, and had left them to the care of a devoted female attendant, whose love was all but maternal. And then she said a word or two about the General, in terms which made me almost think that this quasi-maternal love extended itself beyond the children. The idea, however, was a mistaken one, arising from the strength of her language, to which I was then unaccustomed. I have since become aware that nothing can be more decorous than old Mrs. Upton, the excellent head-nurse at Hardover Lodge; and no gentleman more discreet in his conduct than General Talboys.

And I may as well here declare, also, that there could be no more virtuous woman than the General's wife. Her marriage vow was to her paramount to all other vows and bonds whatever. The

General's honour was quite safe when he sent her off to Rome by herself; and he no doubt knew that it was so. Illi robur et aes triplex, of which I believe no weapons of any assailant could get the better. But, nevertheless, we used to fancy that she had no repugnance to impropriety in other women,—to what the world generally calls impropriety. Invincibly attached herself to the marriage tie, she would constantly speak of it as by no means necessarily binding on others; and, virtuous herself as any griffin of propriety, she constantly patronised, at any rate, the theory of infidelity in her neighbours. She was very eager in denouncing the prejudices of the English world, declaring that she had found existence among them to be no longer possible for herself. She was hot against the stern unforgiveness of British matrons, and equally eager in reprobating the stiff conventionalities of a religion in which she said that none of its votaries had faith, though they all allowed themselves to be enslaved.

We had at that time a small set at Rome, consisting chiefly of English and Americans, who habitually met at each other's rooms, and spent many of our evening hours in discussing Italian politics. We were, most of us, painters, poets, novelists, or sculptors;— perhaps I should say would-be painters, poets, novelists, and sculptors,—aspirants hoping to become some day recognised; and among us Mrs. Talboys took her place, naturally enough, on account of a very pretty taste she had for painting.

I do not know that she ever originated anything that was grand; but she made some nice copies, and was fond, at any rate, of art conversation. She wrote essays, too, which she showed in confidence to various gentlemen, and had some idea of taking lessons in modelling.

In all our circle Conrad Mackinnon, an American, was, perhaps, the person most qualified to be styled its leader. He was one who absolutely did gain his living, and an ample living too, by his pen, and was regarded on all sides as a literary lion, justified by success in roaring at any tone he might please. His usual roar was not exactly that of a sucking-dove or a nightingale; but it was a good-humoured roar, not very offensive to any man, and apparently acceptable enough to some ladies. He was a big burly man, near to fifty as I suppose, somewhat awkward in his gait, and somewhat loud in his laugh. But though nigh to fifty, and thus ungainly, he liked to be smiled on by pretty women, and liked, as some said, to be flattered by them also. If so, he should have been happy, for the ladies at Rome at that time made much of Conrad Mackinnon.

Of Mrs. Mackinnon no one did make very much, and yet she was one of the sweetest, dearest, quietest, little creatures that ever made glad a man's fireside. She was exquisitely pretty, always in good humour, never stupid, self-denying to a fault, and yet she was generally in the background. She would seldom come forward of her own will, but was contented to sit behind her teapot and hear Mackinnon do his roaring. He was certainly much given to what the world at Rome called flirting, but this did not in the least annoy her. She was twenty years his junior, and yet she never flirted with any one. Women would tell her—good-natured friends—how Mackinnon went on; but she received such tidings as an excellent joke, observing that he had always done the same, and no doubt always would until he was ninety. I do believe that she was a happy woman; and yet I used to think that she should have been happier. There is, however, no knowing the inside of another man's house, or reading the riddles of another man's joy and sorrow.

We had also there another lion,—a lion cub,—entitled to roar a little, and of him also I must say something. Charles O'Brien was a young man, about twenty-five years of age, who had sent out from his studio in the preceding year a certain bust, supposed by his admirers to be unsurpassed by any effort of ancient or modern genius. I am no judge of sculpture, and will not, therefore, pronounce an opinion; but many who considered themselves to be judges, declared that it was a "goodish head and shoulders," and nothing more. I merely mention the fact, as it was on the strength of that head and shoulders that O'Brien separated himself from a throng of others such as himself in Rome, walked solitary during the days, and threw himself at the feet of various ladies when the days were over. He had ridden on the shoulders of his bust into a prominent place in our circle, and there encountered much feminine admiration—from Mrs. General Talboys and others.

Some eighteen or twenty of us used to meet every Sunday evening in Mrs. Mackinnon's drawing-room. Many of us, indeed, were in the habit of seeing each other daily, and of visiting together the haunts in Rome which are best loved by art-loving strangers; but here, in this drawing-room, we were sure to come together, and here before the end of November, Mrs. Talboys might always be found, not in any accustomed seat, but moving about the room as the different male mental attractions of our society might chance to move themselves. She was at first greatly taken by Mackinnon,— who also was, I think, a little stirred by her admiration, though he stoutly denied the charge. She became, however, very dear to us all before she left us, and certainly we owed to her our love, for she added infinitely to the joys of our winter.

"I have come here to refresh myself," she said to Mackinnon one evening—to Mackinnon and myself; for we were standing together.

"Shall I get you tea?" said I.

"And will you have something to eat?" Mackinnon asked.

"No, no, no;" she answered. "Tea, yes; but for Heaven's sake let nothing solid dispel the associations of such a meeting as this!"

"I thought you might have dined early," said Mackinnon. Now Mackinnon was a man whose own dinner was very dear to him. I have seen him become hasty and unpleasant, even under the pillars of the Forum, when he thought that the party were placing his fish in jeopardy by their desire to linger there too long.

"Early! Yes. No; I know not when it was. One dines and sleeps in obedience to that dull clay which weighs down so generally the particle of our spirit. But the clay may sometimes be forgotten. Here I can always forget it."

"I thought you asked for refreshment," I said. She only looked at me, whose small attempts at prose composition had, up to that time, been altogether unsuccessful, and then addressed herself in reply to Mackinnon.

"It is the air which we breathe that fills our lungs and gives us life and light. It is that which refreshes us if pure, or sinks us into stagnation if it be foul. Let me for awhile inhale the breath of an invigorating literature. Sit down, Mr. Mackinnon; I have a question that I must put to you." And then she succeeded in carrying him off into a corner. As far as I could see he went willingly enough at that time, though he soon became averse to any long retirement in company with Mrs. Talboys.

We none of us quite understood what were her exact ideas on the subject of revealed religion. Somebody, I think, had told her that there were among us one or two whose opinions were not exactly orthodox according to the doctrines of the established English church. If so, she was determined to show us that she also was advanced beyond the prejudices of an old and dry school of theology. "I have thrown down all the barriers of religion," she said to poor Mrs. Mackinnon, "and am looking for the sentiments of a pure Christianity."

"Thrown down all the barriers of religion!" said Mrs. Mackinnon, in a tone of horror which was not appreciated.

"Indeed, yes," said Mrs. Talboys, with an exulting voice. "Are not the days for such trammels gone by?"

"But yet you hold by Christianity?"

"A pure Christianity, unstained by blood and perjury, by hypocrisy and verbose genuflection. Can I not worship and say my prayers among the clouds?" And she pointed to the lofty ceiling and the handsome chandelier.

"But Ida goes to church," said Mrs. Mackinnon. Ida Talboys was her daughter. Now, it may be observed, that many who throw down the barriers of religion, so far as those barriers may affect themselves, still maintain them on behalf of their children. "Yes," said Mrs. Talboys; "dear Ida! her soft spirit is not yet adapted to receive the perfect truth. We are obliged to govern children by the strength of their prejudices." And then she moved away, for it was seldom that Mrs. Talboys remained long in conversation with any lady.

Mackinnon, I believe, soon became tired of her. He liked her flattery, and at first declared that she was clever and nice; but her niceness was too purely celestial to satisfy his mundane tastes. Mackinnon himself can revel among the clouds in his own writings, and can leave us sometimes in doubt whether he ever means to come back to earth; but when his foot is on terra firma, he loves to feel the earthly substratum which supports his weight. With women he likes a hand that can remain an unnecessary moment within his own, an eye that can glisten with the sparkle of champagne, a heart weak enough to make its owner's arm tremble within his own beneath the moonlight gloom of the Coliseum arches. A dash of sentiment the while makes all these things the sweeter; but the sentiment alone will not suffice for him. Mrs. Talboys did, I believe, drink her glass of champagne, as do other ladies; but with her it had no such pleasing effect. It loosened only her tongue, but never her eye. Her arm, I think, never trembled, and her hand never lingered. The General was always safe, and happy, perhaps, in his solitary safety.

It so happened that we had unfortunately among us two artists who had quarrelled with their wives. O'Brien, whom I have before mentioned, was one of them. In his case, I believe him to have been almost as free from blame as a man can be whose marriage was in itself a fault. However, he had a wife in Ireland some ten years older than himself; and though he might sometimes almost forget the fact, his friends and neighbours were well aware of it. In the other case the whole fault probably was with the husband. He was an ill-tempered, bad-hearted man, clever enough, but without principle; and he was continually guilty of the great sin of speaking evil of the woman whose name he should have been anxious to protect. In both cases our friend Mrs. Talboys took a warm interest, and in each of them she sympathised with the present husband against the absent wife.

Of the consolation which she offered in the latter instance we used to hear something from Mackinnon. He would repeat to his wife, and to me and my wife, the conversations which she had with him. "Poor Brown;" she would say, "I pity him, with my very heart's blood."

"You are aware that he has comforted himself in his desolation," Mackinnon replied.

"I know very well to what you allude. I think I may say that I am conversant with all the circumstances of this heart-blighting sacrifice." Mrs. Talboys was apt to boast of the thorough confidence reposed in her by all those in whom she took an interest. "Yes, he has sought such comfort in another love as the hard cruel world would allow him."

"Or perhaps something more than that," said Mackinnon. "He has a family here in Rome, you know; two little babies."

"I know it, I know it," she said. "Cherub angels!" and as she spoke she looked up into the ugly face of Marcus Aurelius; for they were standing at the moment under the figure of the great horseman on the Campidoglio. "I have seen them, and they are the children of innocence. If all the blood of all the Howards ran in their veins it could not make their birth more noble!"

"Not if the father and mother of all the Howards had never been married," said Mackinnon.

"What; that from you, Mr. Mackinnon!" said Mrs. Talboys, turning her back with energy upon the equestrian statue, and looking up into the faces, first of Pollux and then of Castor, as though from them she might gain some inspiration on the subject which Marcus Aurelius in his coldness had denied to her. "From you, who have so nobly claimed for mankind the divine attributes of free action! From you, who have taught my mind to soar above the petty bonds which one man in his littleness contrives for the subjection of his brother. Mackinnon! you who are so great!" And she now looked up into his face. "Mackinnon, unsay those words."

"They ARE illegitimate," said he; "and if there was any landed property—"

"Landed property! and that from an American!"

"The children are English, you know."

"Landed property! The time will shortly come—ay, and I see it coming—when that hateful word shall be expunged from the calendar; when landed property shall be no more. What! shall the free soul of a God-born man submit itself for ever to such trammels as that? Shall we never escape from the clay which so long has manacled the subtler particles of the divine spirit? Ay, yes, Mackinnon;" and then she took him by the arm, and led him to the top of the huge steps which lead down from the Campidoglio into the streets of modern Rome. "Look down upon that countless multitude." Mackinnon looked down, and saw three groups of French soldiers, with three or four little men in each group; he saw, also, a couple of dirty friars, and three priests very slowly beginning the side ascent to the church of the Ara Coeli. "Look down upon that countless multitude," said Mrs. Talboys, and she stretched her arms out over the half-deserted city. "They are escaping now from these trammels,—now, now,—now that I am speaking."

"They have escaped long ago from all such trammels as that of landed property," said Mackinnon.

"Ay, and from all terrestrial bonds," she continued, not exactly remarking the pith of his last observation; "from bonds quasi-terrestrial and quasi-celestial. The full-formed limbs of the present age, running with quick streams of generous blood, will no longer bear the ligatures which past times have woven for the decrepit.

Look down upon that multitude, Mackinnon; they shall all be free." And then, still clutching him by the arm, and still standing at the top of those stairs, she gave forth her prophecy with the fury of a Sybil.

"They shall all be free. Oh, Rome, thou eternal one! thou who hast bowed thy neck to imperial pride and priestly craft; thou who hast suffered sorely, even to this hour, from Nero down to Pio Nono,—the days of thine oppression are over. Gone from thy enfranchised ways for ever is the clang of the Praetorian cohorts and the more odious drone of meddling monks!" And yet, as Mackinnon observed, there still stood the dirty friars and the small French soldiers; and there still toiled the slow priests, wending their tedious way up to the church of the Ara Coeli. But that was the mundane view of the matter,—a view not regarded by Mrs. Talboys in her ecstasy. "O Italia," she continued, "O Italia una, one and indivisible in thy rights, and indivisible also in thy wrongs! to us is it given to see the accomplishment of thy glory. A people shall arise around thine altars greater in the annals of the world than thy Scipios, thy Gracchi, or thy Caesars. Not in torrents of blood, or with screams of bereaved mothers, shall thy new triumphs be stained. But mind shall dominate over matter; and doomed, together with Popes and Bourbons, with cardinals, diplomatists, and police spies, ignorance and prejudice shall be driven from thy smiling terraces. And then Rome shall again become the fair capital of the fairest region of Europe. Hither shall flock the artisans of the world, crowding into thy marts all that God and man can give. Wealth, beauty, and innocence shall meet in thy streets—"

"There will be a considerable change before that takes place," said Mackinnon.

"There shall be a considerable change," she answered. "Mackinnon, to thee it is given to read the signs of the time; and hast thou not read? Why have the fields of Magenta and Solferino been piled with the corpses of dying heroes? Why have the waters of the Mincio ran red with the blood of martyrs? That Italy might be united and Rome immortal. Here, standing on the Capitolium of the ancient city, I say that it shall be so; and thou, Mackinnon, who hearest me, knowest that my words are true."

There was not then in Rome,—I may almost say there was not in Italy, an Englishman or an American who did not wish well to the cause for which Italy was and is still contending; as also there is hardly one who does not now regard that cause as well-nigh triumphant; but, nevertheless, it was almost impossible to sympathise with Mrs. Talboys. As Mackinnon said, she flew so high that there was no comfort in flying with her.

"Well," said he, "Brown and the rest of them are down below. Shall we go and join them?"

"Poor Brown! How was it that, in speaking of his troubles, we were led on to this heart-stirring theme? Yes, I have seen them, the sweet angels; and I tell you also that I have seen their mother. I insisted on going to her when I heard her history from him."

"And what is she like, Mrs. Talboys?"

"Well; education has done more for some of us than for others; and there are those from whose morals and sentiments we might thankfully draw a lesson, whose manners and outward gestures are not such as custom has made agreeable to us. You, I know, can understand that. I have seen her, and feel sure that she is pure in heart and high in principle. Has she not sacrificed herself; and is not self-sacrifice the surest guarantee for true nobility of character? Would Mrs. Mackinnon object to my bringing them together?"

Mackinnon was obliged to declare that he thought his wife would object; and from that time forth he and Mrs. Talboys ceased to be very close in their friendship. She still came to the house every Sunday evening, still refreshed herself at the fountains of his literary rills; but her special prophecies from henceforth were poured into other ears. And it so happened that O'Brien now became her chief ally. I do not remember that she troubled herself much further with the cherub angels or with their mother; and I am inclined to think that, taking up warmly, as she did, the story of O'Brien's matrimonial wrongs, she forgot the little history of the Browns. Be that as it may, Mrs. Talboys and O'Brien now became strictly confidential, and she would enlarge by the half-hour together on the miseries of her friend's position, to any one whom she could get to hear her.

"I'll tell you what, Fanny," Mackinnon said to his wife one day,—to his wife and to mine, for we were all together; "we shall have a row in the house if we don't take care. O'Brien will be making love to Mrs. Talboys."

"Nonsense," said Mrs. Mackinnon. "You are always thinking that somebody is going to make love to some one."

"Somebody always is," said he.

"She's old enough to be his mother," said Mrs. Mackinnon.

"What does that matter to an Irishman?" said Mackinnon. "Besides, I doubt if there is more than five years' difference between them."

"There must be more than that," said my wife. "Ida Talboys is twelve, I know, and I am not quite sure that Ida is the eldest."

"If she had a son in the Guards it would make no difference," said Mackinnon. "There are men who consider themselves bound to make love to a woman under certain circumstances, let the age of the lady be what it may. O'Brien is such a one; and if she sympathises with him much oftener, he will mistake the matter, and go down on his knees. You ought to put him on his guard," he said, addressing himself to his wife.

"Indeed, I shall do no such thing," said she; "if they are two fools, they must, like other fools, pay the price of their folly." As a rule there could be no softer creature than Mrs. Mackinnon; but it seemed to me that her tenderness never extended itself in the direction of Mrs. Talboys.

Just at this time, towards the end, that is, of November, we made a party to visit the tombs which lie along the Appian Way, beyond that most beautiful of all sepulchres, the tomb of Cecilia Metella. It was a delicious day, and we had driven along this road for a couple of miles beyond the walls of the city, enjoying the most lovely view which the neighbourhood of Rome affords,—looking over the wondrous ruins of the old aqueducts, up towards Tivoli and Palestrina. Of all the environs of Rome this is, on a fair clear day, the most enchanting; and here perhaps, among a world of tombs, thoughts and almost memories of the old, old days come upon one with the greatest force. The grandeur of Rome is best seen and understood from beneath the walls of the Coliseum, and its beauty among the pillars of the Forum and the arches of the Sacred Way; but its history and fall become more palpable to the mind, and more clearly realised, out here among the tombs, where the eyes rest upon the mountains whose shades were cool to the old Romans as to us,—than anywhere within the walls of the city. Here we look out at the same Tivoli and the same Praeneste, glittering in the sunshine, embowered among the far-off valleys, which were dear to them; and the blue mountains have not crumbled away into ruins. Within Rome itself we can see nothing as they saw it.

Our party consisted of some dozen or fifteen persons, and as a hamper with luncheon in it had been left on the grassy slope at the base of the tomb of Cecilia Metella, the expedition had in it something of the nature of a picnic. Mrs. Talboys was of course with us, and Ida Talboys. O'Brien also was there. The hamper had been prepared in Mrs. Mackinnon's room, under the immediate eye of Mackinnon himself, and they therefore were regarded as the dominant spirits of the party. My wife was leagued with Mrs. Mackinnon, as was usually the case; and there seemed to be a general opinion among those who were closely in confidence together, that something would happen in the O'Brien-Talboys matter. The two had been inseparable on the previous evening, for Mrs. Talboys had been urging on the young Irishman her counsels respecting his domestic troubles. Sir Cresswell Cresswell, she had told him, was his refuge. "Why should his soul submit to bonds which the world had now declared to be intolerable? Divorce was not now the privilege of the dissolute rich. Spirits which were incompatible need no longer be compelled to fret beneath the same cobbles." In short, she had recommended him to go to England and get rid of his wife, as she would, with a little encouragement, have recommended any man to get rid of anything. I am sure that, had she been skilfully brought on to the subject, she might have been induced to pronounce a verdict against such ligatures for the body as coats, waistcoats, and trowsers. Her aspirations for freedom ignored all bounds, and, in theory, there were no barriers which she was not willing to demolish.

Poor O'Brien, as we all now began to see, had taken the matter amiss. He had offered to make a bust of Mrs. Talboys, and she had consented, expressing a wish that it might find a place among those who had devoted themselves to the enfranchisement of their fellow-creatures. I really think she had but little of a woman's customary personal vanity. I know she had an idea that her eye was lighted up in her warmer moments by some special fire, that sparks of liberty shone round her brow, and that her bosom heaved with glorious aspirations; but all these feelings had reference to her inner genius, not to any outward beauty. But O'Brien misunderstood the woman, and thought it necessary to gaze into her face, and sigh as though his heart were breaking. Indeed he declared to a young friend that Mrs. Talboys was perfect in her style of beauty, and began the bust with this idea. It was gradually becoming clear to us all that he would bring himself to grief; but in such a matter who can caution a man?

Mrs. Mackinnon had contrived to separate them in making the carriage arrangements on this day, but this only added fuel to the fire which was now burning within O'Brien's bosom. I believe that he really did love her, in his easy, eager, susceptible Irish way. That he would get over the little episode without any serious injury to his heart no one doubted; but then, what would occur when the declaration was made? How would Mrs. Talboys bear it?

"She deserves it," said Mrs. Mackinnon.

"And twice as much," my wife added. Why is it that women are so spiteful to each other?

Early in the day Mrs. Talboys clambered up to the top of a tomb, and made a little speech, holding a parasol over her head. Beneath her feet, she said, reposed the ashes of some bloated senator, some glutton of the empire, who had swallowed into his maw the provision necessary for a tribe. Old Rome had fallen through such selfishness as that; but new Rome would not forget the lesson. All this was very well, and then O'Brien helped her down; but after this there was no separating them. For her own part she would sooner have had Mackinnon at her elbow. But Mackinnon now had found some other elbow.

"Enough of that was as good as a feast," he had said to his wife. And therefore Mrs. Talboys, quite unconscious of evil, allowed herself to be engrossed by O'Brien.

And then, about three o'clock, we returned to the hamper. Luncheon under such circumstances always means dinner, and we arranged ourselves for a very comfortable meal. To those who know the tomb of Cecilia Metella no description of the scene is necessary, and to those who do not, no description will convey a fair idea of its reality. It is itself a large low tower of great diameter, but of beautiful proportion, standing far outside the city, close on to the side of the old Roman way. It has been embattled on the top by some latter-day baron, in order that it might be used for protection to the castle, which has been built on and attached to it. If I remember rightly, this was done by one of the Frangipani, and a very lovely ruin he has made of it. I know no castellated old tumble-down residence in Italy more picturesque than this baronial adjunct to the old Roman tomb, or which better tallies with the ideas engendered within our minds by Mrs. Radcliffe and the Mysteries of Udolpho. It lies along the road, protected on the side of the city by the proud sepulchre of the Roman matron, and up to the long ruined walls of the back of the building stretches a grassy slope, at the bottom of which are the remains of an old Roman circus. Beyond that is the long, thin, graceful line of the Claudian aqueduct, with Soracte in the distance to the left, and Tivoli, Palestine, and Frascati lying among the hills which bound the view. That Frangipani baron was in the right of it, and I hope he got the value of his money out of the residence which he built for himself. I doubt, however, that he did but little good to those who lived in his close neighbourhood.

We had a very comfortable little banquet seated on the broken lumps of stone which lie about under the walls of the tomb. I wonder whether the shade of Cecilia Metella was looking down upon us. We have heard much of her in these latter days, and yet we know nothing about her, nor can conceive why she was honoured with a bigger tomb than any other Roman matron. There were those then among our party who believed that she might still come back among us, and with due assistance from some cognate susceptible spirit, explain to us the cause of her widowed husband's liberality. Alas, alas! if we may judge of the Romans by ourselves, the true reason for such sepulchral grandeur would redound little to the credit of the lady Cecilia Metella herself, or to that of Crassus, her bereaved and desolate lord.

She did not come among us on the occasion of this banquet, possibly because we had no tables there to turn in preparation for her presence; but, had she done so, she could not have been more eloquent of things of the other world than was Mrs. Talboys. I have said that Mrs. Talboys' eye never glanced more brightly after a glass of champagne, but I am inclined to think that on this occasion it may have done so. O'Brien enacted Ganymede, and was, perhaps, more liberal than other latter-day Ganymedes, to whose services Mrs. Talboys had been accustomed. Let it not, however, be suspected by any one that she exceeded the limits of a discreet joyousness. By no means! The generous wine penetrated, perhaps, to some inner cells of her heart, and brought forth thoughts in sparkling words, which otherwise might have remained concealed; but there was nothing in what she thought or spoke calculated to give umbrage either to an anchorite or to a vestal. A word or two she said or sung about the flowing bowl, and once she called for Falernian; but beyond this her converse was chiefly of the rights of man and the weakness of women; of the iron ages that were past, and of the golden time that was to come.

She called a toast and drank to the hopes of the latter historians of the nineteenth century. Then it was that she bade O'Brien "Fill high the bowl with Samian wine." The Irishman took her at her word, and she raised the bumper, and waved it over her head before she put it to her lips. I am bound to declare that she did not spill a drop. "The true 'Falernian grape,'" she said, as she deposited the empty beaker on the grass beneath her elbow. Viler champagne I do not think I ever swallowed; but it was the theory of the wine, not its palpable body present there, as it were, in the flesh, which inspired her. There was really something grand about her on that occasion, and her enthusiasm almost amounted to reality.

Mackinnon was amused, and encouraged her, as, I must confess, did I also. Mrs. Mackinnon made useless little signs to her husband, really fearing that the Falernian would do its good offices too thoroughly. My wife, getting me apart as I walked round the circle distributing viands, remarked that "the woman was a fool, and would disgrace herself." But I observed that after the disposal of that bumper she worshipped the rosy god in theory only, and therefore saw no occasion to interfere. "Come, Bacchus," she said; "and come, Silenus, if thou wilt; I know that ye are hovering round the graves of your departed favourites. And ye, too, nymphs of Egeria," and she pointed to the classic grove which was all but close to us as we sat there. "In olden days ye did not always despise the abodes of men. But why should we invoke the presence of the gods,—we, who can become godlike ourselves! We ourselves are the deities of the present age. For us shall the tables be spread with ambrosia; for us shall the nectar flow."

Upon the whole it was very good fooling,—for awhile; and as soon as we were tired of it we arose from our seats, and began to stroll about the place. It was beginning to be a little dusk, and somewhat cool, but the evening air was pleasant, and the ladies, putting on their shawls, did not seem inclined at once to get into the carriages. At any rate, Mrs. Talboys was not so inclined, for she started down the hill towards the long low wall of the old Roman circus at the bottom; and O'Brien, close at her elbow, started with her.

"Ida, my dear, you had better remain here," she said to her daughter; "you will be tired if you come as far as we are going."

"Oh, no, mamma, I shall not," said Ida. "You get tired much quicker than I do."

"Oh, yes, you will; besides I do not wish you to come." There was an end of it for Ida, and Mrs. Talboys and O'Brien walked off together, while we all looked into each other's faces.

"It would be a charity to go with them," said Mackinnon.

"Do you be charitable, then," said his wife.

"It should be a lady," said he.

"It is a pity that the mother of the spotless cherubim is not here for the occasion," said she. "I hardly think that any one less gifted will undertake such a self sacrifice." Any attempt of the kind would, however, now have been too late, for they were already at the bottom of the hill. O'Brien had certainly drunk freely of the pernicious contents of those long-necked bottles; and though no one could fairly accuse him of being tipsy, nevertheless that which might have made others drunk had made him bold, and he dared to do— perhaps more than might become a man. If under any circumstances he could be fool enough to make an avowal of love to Mrs. Talboys, he might be expected, as we all thought, to do it now.

We watched them as they made for a gap in the wall which led through into the large enclosed space of the old circus. It had been an arena for chariot games, and they had gone down with the avowed purpose of searching where might have been the meta, and ascertaining how the drivers could have turned when at their full speed. For awhile we had heard their voices,—or rather her voice especially. "The heart of a man, O'Brien, should suffice for all emergencies," we had heard her say. She had assumed a strange habit of calling men by their simple names, as men address each other. When she did this to Mackinnon, who was much older than herself, we had been all amused by it, and, other ladies of our party had taken to call him "Mackinnon" when Mrs. Talboys was not by; but we had felt the comedy to be less safe with O'Brien, especially when, on one occasion, we heard him address her as Arabella. She did not seem to be in any way struck by his doing so, and we supposed, therefore, that it had become frequent between them. What reply he made at the moment about the heart of a man I do not know;—and then in a few minutes they disappeared through the gap in the wall.

None of us followed them, though it would have seemed the most natural thing in the world to do so had nothing out of the way been expected. As it was we remained there round the tomb quizzing the little foibles of our dear friend, and hoping that O'Brien would be quick in what he was doing. That he would undoubtedly get a slap in the face—metaphorically—we all felt certain, for none of us doubted the rigid propriety of the lady's intentions. Some of us strolled into the buildings, and some of us got out on to the road; but we all of us were thinking that O'Brien was very slow a considerable time before we saw Mrs. Talboys reappear through the gap.

At last, however, she was there, and we at once saw that she was alone. She came on, breasting the hill with quick steps, and when she drew near we could see that there was a frown as of injured majesty on her brow. Mackinnon and his wife went forward to meet her. If she were really in trouble it would be fitting in some way to assist her; and of all women Mrs. Mackinnon was the last to see another woman suffer from ill-usage without attempting to aid her. "I certainly never liked her," Mrs. Mackinnon said afterwards; "but I was bound to go and hear her tale, when she really had a tale to tell."

And Mrs. Talboys now had a tale to tell,—if she chose to tell it. The ladies of our party declared afterwards that she would have acted more wisely had she kept to herself both O'Brien's words to her and her answer. "She was well able to take care of herself," Mrs. Mackinnon said; "and, after all, the silly man had taken an answer when he got it." Not, however, that O'Brien had taken his answer quite immediately, as far as I could understand from what we heard of the matter afterwards.

At the present moment Mrs. Talboys came up the rising ground all alone, and at a quick pace. "The man has insulted me," she said aloud, as well as her panting breath would allow her, and as soon as she was near enough to Mrs. Mackinnon to speak to her.

"I am sorry for that," said Mrs. Mackinnon. "I suppose he has taken a little too much wine."

"No; it was a premeditated insult. The base-hearted churl has failed to understand the meaning of true, honest sympathy."

"He will forget all about it when he is sober," said Mackinnon, meaning to comfort her.

"What care I what he remembers or what he forgets!" she said, turning upon poor Mackinnon indignantly. "You men grovel so in your ideas—" "And yet," as Mackinnon said afterwards, "she had been telling me that I was a fool for the last three weeks."— "You men grovel so in your ideas, that you cannot understand the feelings of a true-hearted woman. What can his forgetfulness or his remembrance be to me? Must not I remember this insult? Is it possible that I should forget it?"

Mr. and Mrs. Mackinnon only had gone forward to meet her; but, nevertheless, she spoke so loud that all heard her who were still clustered round the spot on which we had dined.

"What has become of Mr. O'Brien?" a lady whispered to me.

I had a field-glass with me, and, looking round, I saw his hat as he was walking inside the walls of the circus in the direction towards the city. "And very foolish he must feel," said the lady.

"No doubt he is used to it," said another.

"But considering her age, you know," said the first, who might have been perhaps three years younger than Mrs. Talboys, and who was not herself averse to the excitement of a moderate flirtation. But then why should she have been averse, seeing that she had not as yet become subject to the will of any imperial lord?

"He would have felt much more foolish," said the third, "if she had listened to what he said to her."

"Well I don't know," said the second; "nobody would have known anything about it then, and in a few weeks they would have gradually become tired of each other in the ordinary way."

But in the meantime Mrs. Talboys was among us. There had been no attempt at secresy, and she was still loudly inveighing against the grovelling propensities of men. "That's quite true, Mrs. Talboys," said one of the elder ladies; "but then women are not always so careful as they should be. Of course I do not mean to say that there has been any fault on your part."

"Fault on my part! Of course there has been fault on my part. No one can make any mistake without fault to some extent. I took him to be a man of sense, and he is a fool. Go to Naples indeed!"

"Did he want you to go to Naples?" asked Mrs. Mackinnon.

"Yes; that was what he suggested. We were to leave by the train for Civita Vecchia at six tomorrow morning and catch the steamer which leaves Leghorn tonight. Don't tell me of wine. He was prepared for it!" And she looked round about on us with an air of injured majesty in her face which was almost insupportable.

"I wonder whether he took the tickets over-night," said Mackinnon.

"Naples!" she said, as though now speaking exclusively to herself; "the only ground in Italy which has as yet made no struggle on behalf of freedom;—a fitting residence for such a dastard!"

"You would have found it very pleasant at this season," said the unmarried lady, who was three years her junior.

My wife had taken Ida out of the way when the first complaining note from Mrs. Talboys had been heard ascending the hill. But now, when matters began gradually to become quiescent, she brought her back, suggesting, as she did so, that they might begin to think of returning.

"It is getting very cold, Ida, dear, is it not?" said she.

"But where is Mr. O'Brien?" said Ida.

"He has fled,—as poltroons always fly," said Mrs. Talboys. I believe in my heart that she would have been glad to have had him there in the middle of the circle, and to have triumphed over him publicly among us all. No feeling of shame would have kept her silent for a moment.

"Fled!" said Ida, looking up into her mother's face.

"Yes, fled, my child." And she seized her daughter in her arms, and pressed her closely to her bosom. "Cowards always fly."

"Is Mr. O'Brien a coward?" Ida asked.

"Yes, a coward, a very coward! And he has fled before the glance of an honest woman's eye. Come, Mrs. Mackinnon, shall we go back to the city? I am sorry that the amusement of the day should have received this check." And she walked forward to the carriage and took her place in it with an air that showed that she was proud of the way in which she had conducted herself.

"She is a little conceited about it after all," said that unmarried lady. "If poor Mr. O'Brien had not shown so much premature anxiety with reference to that little journey to Naples, things might have gone quietly after all."

But the unmarried lady was wrong in her judgment. Mrs. Talboys was proud and conceited in the matter,—but not proud of having excited the admiration of her Irish lover. She was proud of her own subsequent conduct, and gave herself credit for coming out strongly as a noble-minded matron. "I believe she thinks," said Mrs. Mackinnon, "that her virtue is quite Spartan and unique; and if she remains in Rome she'll boast of it through the whole winter."

"If she does, she may be certain that O'Brien will do the same," said Mackinnon. "And in spite of his having fled from the field, it is upon the cards that he may get the best of it. Mrs. Talboys is a very excellent woman. She has proved her excellence beyond a doubt. But, nevertheless, she is susceptible of ridicule."

We all felt a little anxiety to hear O'Brien's account of the matter, and after having deposited the ladies at their homes, Mackinnon and I went off to his lodgings. At first he was denied to us, but after awhile we got his servant to acknowledge that he was at home, and then we made our way up to his studio. We found him seated behind a half-formed model, or rather a mere lump of clay punched into something resembling the shape of a head, with a pipe in his mouth and a bit of stick in his hand. He was pretending to work, though we both knew that it was out of the question that he should do anything in his present frame of mind.

"I think I heard my servant tell you that I was not at home," said he.

"Yes, he did," said Mackinnon, "and would have sworn to it too if we would have let him. Come, don't pretend to be surly."

"I am very busy, Mr. Mackinnon."

"Completing your head of Mrs. Talboys, I suppose, before you start for Naples."

"You don't mean to say that she has told you all about it," and he turned away from his work, and looked up into our faces with a comical expression, half of fun and half of despair.

"Every word of it," said I. "When you want a lady to travel with you, never ask her to get up so early in winter."

"But, O'Brien, how could you be such an ass?" said Mackinnon. "As it has turned out, there is no very great harm done. You have insulted a respectable middle-aged woman, the mother of a family, and the wife of a general officer, and there is an end of it;—unless, indeed, the general officer should come out from England to call you to account."

"He is welcome," said O'Brien, haughtily.

"No doubt, my dear fellow," said Mackinnon; "that would be a dignified and pleasant ending to the affair. But what I want to know is this;—what would you have done if she had agreed to go?"

"He never calculated on the possibility of such a contingency," said I.

"By heavens, then, I thought she would like it," said he.

"And to oblige her you were content to sacrifice yourself," said Mackinnon.

"Well, that was just it. What the deuce is a fellow to do when a woman goes on in that way. She told me down there, upon the old race course you know, that matrimonial bonds were made for fools and slaves. What was I to suppose that she meant by that? But to make all sure, I asked her what sort of a fellow the General was. 'Dear old man,' she said, clasping her hands together. 'He might, you know, have been my father.' 'I wish he were,' said I, 'because then you'd be free.' 'I am free,' said she, stamping on the ground, and looking up at me as much as to say that she cared for no one. 'Then,' said I, 'accept all that is left of the heart of Wenceslaus O'Brien,' and I threw myself before her in her path. 'Hand,' said I, 'I have none to give, but the blood which runs red through my veins is descended from a double line of kings.' I said that because she is always fond of riding a high horse. I had gotten close under the wall, so that none of you should see me from the tower."

"And what answer did she make?" said Mackinnon.

"Why she was pleased as Punch;—gave me both her hands, and declared that we would be friends for ever. It is my belief, Mackinnon, that that woman never heard anything of the kind before. The General, no doubt, did it by letter."

"And how was it that she changed her mind?"

"Why; I got up, put my arm round her waist, and told her that we would be off to Naples. I'm blest if she didn't give me a knock in the ribs that nearly sent me backwards. She took my breath away, so that I couldn't speak to her."

"And then—"

"Oh, there was nothing more. Of course I saw how it was. So she walked off one way and I the other. On the whole I consider that I am well out of it."

"And so do I," said Mackinnon, very gravely. "But if you will allow me to give you my advice, I would suggest that it would be well to avoid such mistakes in future."

"Upon my word," said O'Brien, excusing himself, "I don't know what a man is to do under such circumstances. I give you my honour that I did it all to oblige her."

We then decided that Mackinnon should convey to the injured lady the humble apology of her late admirer. It was settled that no detailed excuses should be made. It should be left to her to consider whether the deed which had been done might have been occasioned by wine, or by the folly of a moment,—or by her own indiscreet enthusiasm. No one but the two were present when the message was given, and therefore we were obliged to trust to Mackinnon's accuracy for an account of it.

She stood on very high ground indeed, he said, at first refusing to hear anything that he had to say on the matter. "The foolish young man," she declared, "was below her anger and below her contempt."

"He is not the first Irishman that has been made indiscreet by beauty," said Mackinnon.

"A truce to that," she replied, waving her hand with an air of assumed majesty. "The incident, contemptible as it is, has been unpleasant to me. It will necessitate my withdrawal from Rome."

"Oh, no, Mrs. Talboys; that will be making too much of him."

"The greatest hero that lives," she answered, "may have his house made uninhabitable by a very small insect." Mackinnon swore that those were her own words. Consequently a sobriquet was attached to O'Brien of which he by no means approved. And from that day we always called Mrs. Talboys "the hero."

Mackinnon prevailed at last with her, and she did not leave Rome. She was even induced to send a message to O'Brien, conveying her forgiveness. They shook hands together with great eclat in Mrs. Mackinnon's drawing-room; but I do not suppose that she ever again offered to him sympathy on the score of his matrimonial troubles.

THE O'CONORS OF CASTLE CONOR, COUNTY MAYO. FROM "TALES FROM ALL COUNTRIES"

I shall never forget my first introduction to country life in Ireland, my first day's hunting there, or the manner in which I passed the evening afterwards. Nor shall I ever cease to be grateful for the hospitality which I received from the O'Conors of Castle Conor. My acquaintance with the family was first made in the following manner. But before I begin my story, let me inform my reader that my name is Archibald Green.

I had been for a fortnight in Dublin, and was about to proceed into county Mayo on business which would occupy me there for some weeks. My head-quarters would, I found, be at the town of Ballyglass; and I soon learned that Ballyglass was not a place in which I should find hotel accommodation of a luxurious kind, or much congenial society indigenous to the place itself.

"But you are a hunting man, you say," said old Sir P-C-; "and in that case you will soon know Tom O'Conor. Tom won't let you be dull. I'd write you a letter to Tom, only he'll certainly make you out without my taking the trouble."

I did think at the time that the old baronet might have written the letter for me, as he had been a friend of my father's in former days; but he did not, and I started for Ballyglass with no other introduction to any one in the county than that contained in Sir P-'s promise that I should soon know Mr. Thomas O'Conor.

I had already provided myself with a horse, groom, saddle and bridle, and these I sent down, en avant, that the Ballyglassians might know that I was somebody. Perhaps, before I arrived Tom O'Conor might learn that a hunting man was coming into the neighbourhood, and I might find at the inn a polite note intimating that a bed was at my service at Castle Conor. I had heard so much of the free hospitality of the Irish gentry as to imagine that such a thing might be possible.

But I found nothing of the kind. Hunting gentlemen in those days were very common in county Mayo, and one horse was no great evidence of a man's standing in the world. Men there as I learnt afterwards, are sought for themselves quite as much as they are elsewhere; and though my groom's top-boots were neat, and my horse a very tidy animal, my entry into Ballyglass created no sensation whatever.

In about four days after my arrival, when I was already infinitely disgusted with the little Pot-house in which I was forced to stay, and had made up my mind that the people in county Mayo were a churlish set, I sent my horse on to a meet of the fox-hounds, and followed after myself on an open car.

No one but an erratic fox-hunter such as I am,—a fox-hunter, I mean, whose lot it has been to wander about from one pack of hounds to another,—can understand the melancholy feeling which a man has when he first intrudes himself, unknown by any one, among an entirely new set of sportsmen. When a stranger falls thus as it were out of the moon into a hunt, it is impossible that men should not stare at him and ask who he is. And it is so disagreeable to be stared at, and to have such questions asked! This feeling does not come upon a man in Leicestershire or Gloucestershire where the numbers are large, and a stranger or two will always be overlooked, but in small hunting fields it is so painful that a man has to pluck up much courage before he encounters it.

We met on the morning in question at Bingham's Grove. There were not above twelve or fifteen men out, all of whom, or nearly all were cousins to each other. They seemed to be all Toms, and Pats, and Larrys, and Micks. I was done up very knowingly in pink, and thought that I looked quite the thing, but for two or three hours nobody noticed me.

I had my eyes about me, however, and soon found out which of them was Tom O'Conor. He was a fine-looking fellow, thin and tall, but not largely made, with a piercing gray eye, and a beautiful voice for speaking to a hound. He had two sons there also, short, slight fellows, but exquisite horsemen. I already felt that I had a kind of acquaintance with the father, but I hardly knew on what ground to put in my claim.

We had no sport early in the morning. It was a cold bleak February day, with occasional storms of sleet. We rode from cover to cover, but all in vain. "I am sorry, sir, that we are to have such a bad day, as you are a stranger here," said one gentleman to me. This was Jack O'Conor, Tom's eldest son, my bosom friend for many a year after. Poor Jack! I fear that the Encumbered Estates Court sent him altogether adrift upon the world.

"We may still have a run from Poulnaroe, if the gentleman chooses to come on," said a voice coming from behind with a sharp trot. It was Tom O'Conor.

"Wherever the hounds go, I'll follow," said I.

"Then come on to Poulnaroe," said Mr. O'Conor. I trotted on quickly by his side, and before we reached the cover had managed to slip in something about Sir P. C.

"What the deuce!" said he. "What! a friend of Sir P-'s? Why the deuce didn't you tell me so? What are you doing down here? Where are you staying?" &c. &c. &c.

At Poulnaroe we found a fox, but before we did so Mr. O'Conor had asked me over to Castle Conor. And this he did in such a way that there was no possibility of refusing him—or, I should rather say, of disobeying him. For his invitation came quite in the tone of a command.

"You'll come to us of course when the day is over—and let me see; we're near Ballyglass now, but the run will be right away in our direction. Just send word for them to send your things to Castle Conor."

"But they're all about, and unpacked," said I.

"Never mind. Write a note and say what you want now, and go and get the rest tomorrow yourself. Here, Patsey!—Patsey! run into Ballyglass for this gentleman at once. Now don't be long, for the chances are we shall find here." And then, after giving some further hurried instructions he left me to write a line in pencil to the innkeeper's wife on the back of a ditch.

This I accordingly did. "Send my small portmanteau," I said, "and all my black dress clothes, and shirts, and socks, and all that, and above all my dressing things which are on the little table, and the satin neck-handkerchief, and whatever you do, mind you send my PUMPS;" and I underscored the latter word; for Jack O'Conor, when his father left me, went on pressing the invitation. "My sisters are going to get up a dance," said he; "and if you are fond of that kind of things perhaps we can amuse you." Now in those days I was very fond of dancing—and very fond of young ladies too, and therefore glad enough to learn that Tom O'Conor had daughters as well as sons. On this account I was very particular in underscoring the word pumps.

"And hurry, you young divil," Jack O'Conor said to Patsey.

"I have told him to take the portmanteau over on a car," said I.

"All right; then you'll find it there on our arrival."

We had an excellent run, in which I may make bold to say that I did not acquit myself badly. I stuck very close to the hounds, as did the whole of the O'Conor brood; and when the fellow contrived to earth himself, as he did, I received those compliments on my horse, which is the most approved praise which one fox-hunter ever gives to another.

"We'll buy that fellow of you before we let you go," said Peter, the youngest son.

"I advise you to look sharp after your money if you sell him to my brother," said Jack.

And then we trotted slowly off to Castle Conor, which, however, was by no means near to us. "We have ten miles to go;—good Irish miles," said the father. "I don't know that I ever remember a fox from Poulnaroe taking that line before."

"He wasn't a Poulnaroe fox," said Peter.

"I don't know that;" said Jack; and then they debated that question hotly.

Our horses were very tired, and it was late before we reached Mr. O'Conor's house. That getting home from hunting with a thoroughly weary animal, who has no longer sympathy or example to carry him on, is very tedious work. In the present instance I had company with me; but when a man is alone, when his horse toes at every ten steps, when the night is dark and the rain pouring, and there are yet eight miles of road to be conquered,—at such time a man is almost apt to swear that he will give up hunting.

At last we were in the Castle Conor stable yard;—for we had approached the house by some back way; and as we entered the house by a door leading through a wilderness of back passages, Mr. O'Conor said out loud, "Now, boys, remember I sit down to dinner in twenty minutes." And then turning expressly to me, he laid his hand kindly upon my shoulder and said, "I hope you will make yourself quite at home at Castle Conor, and whatever you do, don't keep us waiting for dinner. You can dress in twenty minutes, I suppose?"

"In ten!" said I, glibly.

"That's well. Jack and Peter will show you your room," and so he turned away and left us.

My two young friends made their way into the great hall, and thence into the drawing-room, and I followed them. We were all dressed in pink, and had waded deep through bog and mud. I did not exactly know whither I was being led in this guise, but I soon found myself in the presence of two young ladies, and of a girl about thirteen years of age.

"My sisters," said Jack, introducing me very laconically; "Miss O'Conor, Miss Kate O'Conor, Miss Tizzy O'Conor."

"My name is not Tizzy," said the younger; "it's Eliza. How do you do, sir? I hope you had a fine hunt! Was papa well up, Jack?"

Jack did not condescend to answer this question, but asked one of the elder girls whether anything had come, and whether a room had been made ready for me.

"Oh yes!" said Miss O'Conor; "they came, I know, for I saw them brought into the house; and I hope Mr. Green will find everything comfortable." As she said this I thought I saw a slight smile steal across her remarkably pretty mouth.

They were both exceedingly pretty girls. Fanny the elder wore long glossy curls,—for I write, oh reader, of bygone days, as long ago as that, when ladies wore curls if it pleased them so to do, and gentlemen danced in pumps, with black handkerchiefs round their necks,—yes, long black, or nearly black silken curls; and then she had such eyes;—I never knew whether they were most wicked or most bright; and her face was all dimples, and each dimple was laden with laughter and laden with love. Kate was probably the prettier girl of the two, but on the whole not so attractive. She was fairer than her sister, and wore her hair in braids; and was also somewhat more demure in her manner.

In spite of the special injunctions of Mr. O'Conor senior, it was impossible not to loiter for five minutes over the drawing-room fire talking to these houris—more especially as I seemed to know them intimately by intuition before half of the five minutes was over. They were so easy, so pretty, so graceful, so kind, they seemed to take it so much as a matter of course that I should stand there talking in my red coat and muddy boots.

"Well; do go and dress yourselves," at last said Fanny, pretending to speak to her brothers but looking more especially a me. "You know how mad papa will be. And remember Mr. Green, we expect great things from your dancing tonight. Your coming just at this time is such a Godsend." And again that soupcon of a smile passed over her face.

I hurried up to my room, Peter and Jack coming with me to the door. "Is everything right?" said Peter, looking among the towels and water-jugs. "They've given you a decent fire for a wonder," said Jack, stirring up the red hot turf which blazed in the grate. "All right as a trivet," said I. "And look alive like a good fellow," said Jack. We had scowled at each other in the morning as very young men do when they are strangers; and now, after a few hours, we were intimate friends.

I immediately turned to my work, and was gratified to find that all my things were laid out ready for dressing; my portmanteau had of course come open, as my keys were in my pocket, and therefore some of the excellent servants of the house had been able to save me all the trouble of unpacking. There was my shirt hanging before the fire; my black clothes were spread upon the bed, my socks and collar and handkerchief beside them; my brushes were on the toilet table, and everything prepared exactly as though my own man had been there. How nice!

I immediately went to work at getting off my spurs and boots, and then proceeded to loosen the buttons at my knees. In doing this I sat down in the arm-chair which had been drawn up for me, opposite the fire. But what was the object on which my eyes then fell;—the objects I should rather say!

Immediately in front of my chair was placed, just ready for may feet, an enormous pair of shooting-boots—half-boots made to lace up round the ankles, with thick double leather soles, and each bearing half a stone of iron in the shape of nails and heel-pieces. I had superintended the making of these shoes in Burlington Arcade with the greatest diligence. I was never a good shot; and, like some other sportsmen, intended to make up for my deficiency in performance by the excellence of my shooting apparel. "Those nails are not large enough," I had said; "nor nearly large enough." But when the boots came home they struck even me as being too heavy, too metalsome. "He, he, he," laughed the boot boy as he turned them up for me to look at. It may therefore be imagined of what nature were the articles which were thus set out for the evening's dancing.

And then the way in which they were placed! When I saw this the conviction flew across my mind like a flash of lightning that the preparation had been made under other eyes than those of the servant. The heavy big boots were placed so prettily before the chair, and the strings of each were made to dangle down at the sides, as though just ready for tying! They seemed to say, the boots did, "Now, make haste. We at any rate are ready—you cannot say that you were kept waiting for us." No mere servant's hand had ever enabled a pair of boots to laugh at one so completely.

But what was I to do? I rushed at the small portmanteau, thinking that my pumps also might be there. The woman surely could not have been such a fool as to send me those tons of iron for my evening wear! But, alas, alas! no pumps were there. There was nothing else in the way of covering for my feet; not even a pair of slippers.

And now what was I to do? The absolute magnitude of my misfortune only loomed upon me by degrees. The twenty minutes allowed by that stern old paterfamilias were already gone and I had done nothing towards dressing. And indeed it was impossible that I should do anything that would be of avail. I could not go down to dinner in my stocking feet, nor could I put on my black dress trousers, over a pair of mud-painted top-boots. As for those iron-soled horrors—; and then I gave one of them a kick with the side of my bare foot which sent it half way under the bed.

But what was I to do? I began washing myself and brushing my hair with this horrid weight upon my mind. My first plan was to go to bed, and send down word that I had been taken suddenly ill in the stomach; then to rise early in the morning and get away unobserved. But by such a course of action I should lose all chance of any further acquaintance with those pretty girls! That they were already aware of the extent of my predicament, and were now enjoying it—of that I was quite sure.

What if I boldly put on the shooting-boots, and clattered down to dinner in them? What if I took the bull by the horns, and made, myself, the most of the joke? This might be very well for the dinner, but it would be a bad joke for me when the hour for dancing came. And, alas! I felt that I lacked the courage. It is not every man that can walk down to dinner, in a strange house full of ladies, wearing such boots as those I have described.

Should I not attempt to borrow a pair? This, all the world will say, should have been my first idea. But I have not yet mentioned that I am myself a large-boned man, and that my feet are especially well developed. I had never for a moment entertained a hope that I should find any one in that house whose boot I could wear. But at last I rang the bell. I would send for Jack, and if everything failed, I would communicate my grief to him.

I had to ring twice before anybody came. The servants, I well knew, were putting the dinner on the table. At last a man entered the room, dressed in rather shabby black, whom I afterwards learned to be the butler.

"What is your name, my friend?" said I, determined to make an ally of the man.

"My name? Why Larry sure, yer honer. And the masther is out of his sinses in a hurry, becase yer honer don't come down."

"Is he though? Well now, Larry; tell me this; which of all the gentlemen in the house has got the largest foot?"

"Is it the largest foot, yer honer?" said Larry, altogether surprised by my question.

"Yes; the largest foot," and then I proceeded to explain to him my misfortune. He took up first my top-boot, and then the shooting-boot—in looking at which he gazed with wonder at the nails;—and then he glanced at my feet, measuring them with his eye; and after this he pronounced his opinion.

"Yer honer couldn't wear a morsel of leather belonging to ere a one of 'em, young or ould. There niver was a foot like that yet among the O'Conors."

"But are there no strangers staying here?"

"There's three or four on 'em come in to dinner; but they'll be wanting their own boots I'm thinking. And there's young Misther Dillon; he's come to stay. But Lord love you—" and he again looked at the enormous extent which lay between the heel and the toe of the shooting apparatus which he still held in his hand. "I niver see such a foot as that in the whole barony," he said, "barring my own."

Now Larry was a large man, much larger altogether than myself, and as he said this I looked down involuntarily at his feet; or rather at his foot, for as he stood I could only see one. And then a sudden hope filled my heart. On that foot there glittered a shoe—not indeed such as were my own which were now resting ingloriously at Ballyglass while they were so sorely needed at Castle Conor; but one which I could wear before ladies, without shame—and in my present frame of mind with infinite contentment.

"Let me look at that one of your own," said I to the man, as though it were merely a subject for experimental inquiry. Larry, accustomed to obedience, took off the shoe and handed it to me.

My own foot was immediately in it, and I found that it fitted me like a glove.

"And now the other," said I—not smiling, for a smile would have put him on his guard; but somewhat sternly, so that that habit of obedience should not desert him at this perilous moment. And then I stretched out my hand.

"But yer honer can't keep 'em, you know," said he. "I haven't the ghost of another shoe to my feet." But I only looked more sternly than before, and still held out my hand. Custom prevailed. Larry stooped down slowly, looking at me the while, and pulling off the other slipper handed it to me with much hesitation. Alas! as I put it to my foot I found that it was old, and worn, and irredeemably down at heel;—that it was in fact no counterpart at all to that other one which was to do duty as its fellow. But nevertheless I put my foot into it, and felt that a descent to the drawing-room was now possible.

"But yer honer will give 'em back to a poor man?" said Larry almost crying. "The masther's mad this minute becase the dinner's not up. Glory to God, only listhen to that!" And as he spoke a tremendous peal rang out from some bell down stairs that had evidently been shaken by an angry hand.

"Larry," said I—and I endeavoured to assume a look of very grave importance as I spoke—"I look to you to assist me in this matter."

"Och—wirra sthrue then, and will you let me go? just listhen to that," and another angry peal rang out, loud and repeated.

"If you do as I ask you," I continued, "you shall be well rewarded. Look here; look at these boots," and I held up the shooting-shoes new from Burlington Arcade. "They cost thirty shillings—thirty shillings! and I will give them to you for the loan of this pair of slippers."

"They'd be no use at all to me, yer honer; not the laist use in life."

"You could do with them very well for tonight, and then you could sell them. And here are ten shillings besides," and I held out half a sovereign which the poor fellow took into his hand.

I waited no further parley but immediately walked out of the room. With one foot I was sufficiently pleased. As regarded that I felt that I had overcome my difficulty. But the other was not so satisfactory. Whenever I attempted to lift it from the ground the horrid slipper would fall off, or only just hang by the toe. As for dancing, that would be out of the question.

"Och, murther, murther," sang out Larry, as he heard me going down stairs. "What will I do at all? Tare and 'ounds; there, he's at it agin, as mad as blazes." This last exclamation had reference to another peal which was evidently the work of the master's hand.

I confess I was not quite comfortable as I walked down stairs. In the first place I was nearly half an hour late, and I knew from the vigour of the peals that had sounded that my slowness had already been made the subject of strong remarks. And then my left shoe went flop, flop, on every alternate step of the stairs. By no exertion of my foot in the drawing up of my toe could I induce it to remain permanently fixed upon my foot. But over and above and worse than all this was the conviction strong upon my mind that I should become a subject of merriment to the girls as soon as I entered the room. They would understand the cause of my distress, and probably at this moment were expecting to hear me clatter through the stone hall with those odious metal boots.

However, I hurried down and entered the drawing-room, determined to keep my position near the door, so that I might have as little as possible to do on entering and as little as possible in going out. But I had other difficulties in store for me. I had not as yet been introduced to Mrs. O'Conor; nor to Miss O'Conor, the squire's unmarried sister.

"Upon my word I thought you were never coming," said Mr. O'Conor as soon as he saw me. "It is just one hour since we entered the house. Jack, I wish you would find out what has come to that fellow Larry," and again he rang the bell. He was too angry, or it might be too impatient to go through the ceremony of introducing me to anybody.

I saw that the two girls looked at me very sharply, but I stood at the back of an arm-chair so that no one could see my feet. But that little imp Tizzy walked round deliberately, looked at my heels, and then walked back again. It was clear that she was in the secret.

There were eight or ten people in the room, but I was too much fluttered to notice well who they were.

"Mamma," said Miss O'Conor, "let me introduce Mr. Green to you."

It luckily happened that Mrs. O'Conor was on the same side of the fire as myself, and I was able to take the hand which she offered me without coming round into the middle of the circle. Mrs. O'Conor was a little woman, apparently not of much importance in the world, but, if one might judge from first appearance, very good-natured.

"And my aunt Die, Mr. Green," said Kate, pointing to a very straight-backed, grim-looking lady, who occupied a corner of a sofa, on the opposite side of the hearth. I knew that politeness required that I should walk across the room and make acquaintance with her. But under the existing circumstances how was I to obey the dictates of politeness? I was determined therefore to stand my ground, and merely bowed across the room at Miss O'Conor. In so doing I made an enemy who never deserted me during the whole of my intercourse with the family. But for her, who knows who might have been sitting opposite to me as I now write?

"Upon my word, Mr. Green, the ladies will expect much from an Adonis who takes so long over his toilet," said Tom O'Conor in that cruel tone of banter which he knew so well how to use.

"You forget, father, that men in London can't jump in and out of their clothes as quick as we wild Irishmen," said Jack.

"Mr. Green knows that we expect a great deal from him this evening. I hope you polk well, Mr. Green," said Kate.

I muttered something about never dancing, but I knew that that which I said was inaudible.

"I don't think Mr. Green will dance," said Tizzy; "at least not much." The impudence of that child was, I think, unparalleled by any that I have ever witnessed.

"But in the name of all that's holy, why don't we have dinner?" And Mr. O'Conor thundered at the door. "Larry, Larry, Larry!" he screamed.

"Yes, yer honer, it'll be all right in two seconds," answered Larry, from some bottomless abyss. "Tare an' ages; what'll I do at all," I heard him continuing, as he made his way into the hall. Oh what a clatter he made upon the pavement,—for it was all stone! And how the drops of perspiration stood upon my brow as I listened to him!

And then there was a pause, for the man had gone into the dining-room. I could see now that Mr. O'Conor was becoming very angry, and Jack the eldest son—oh, how often he and I have laughed over all this since—left the drawing-room for the second time. Immediately afterwards Larry's footsteps were again heard, hurrying across the hall, and then there was a great slither, and an exclamation, and the noise of a fall—and I could plainly hear poor Larry's head strike against the stone floor.

"Ochone, ochone!" he cried at the top of his voice—"I'm murthered with 'em now intirely; and d—'em for boots—St. Peter be good to me."

There was a general rush into the hall, and I was carried with the stream. The poor fellow who had broken his head would be sure to tell how I had robbed him of his shoes. The coachman was already helping him up, and Peter good-naturedly lent a hand.

"What on earth is the matter?" said Mr. O'Conor.

"He must be tipsy," whispered Miss O'Conor, the maiden sister.

"I aint tipsy at all thin," said Larry, getting up and rubbing the back of his head, and sundry other parts of his body. "Tipsy indeed!" And then he added when he was quite upright, "The dinner is sarved—at last."

And he bore it all without telling! "I'll give that fellow a guinea tomorrow morning," said I to myself—"if it's the last that I have in the world."

I shall never forget the countenance of the Miss O'Conors as Larry scrambled up cursing the unfortunate boots—"What on earth has he got on?" said Mr. O'Conor.

"Sorrow take 'em for shoes," ejaculated Larry. But his spirit was good and he said not a word to betray me.

We all then went in to dinner how we best could. It was useless for us to go back into the drawing-room, that each might seek his own partner. Mr. O'Conor "the masther," not caring much for the girls who were around him, and being already half beside himself with the confusion and delay, led the way by himself. I as a stranger should have given my arm to Mrs. O'Conor; but as it was I took her eldest daughter instead, and contrived to shuffle along into the dining-room without exciting much attention, and when there I found myself happily placed between Kate and Fanny.

"I never knew anything so awkward," said Fanny; "I declare I can't conceive what has come to our old servant Larry. He's generally the most precise person in the world, and now he is nearly an hour late—and then he tumbles down in the hall."

"I am afraid I am responsible for the delay," said I.

"But not for the tumble I suppose," said Kate from the other side. I felt that I blushed up to the eyes, but I did not dare to enter into explanations.

"Tom," said Tizzy, addressing her father across the table, "I hope you had a good run today." It did seem odd to me that young lady should call her father Tom, but such was the fact.

"Well; pretty well," said Mr. O'Conor.

"And I hope you were up with the hounds."

"You may ask Mr. Green that. He at any rate was with them, and therefore he can tell you."

"Oh, he wasn't before you, I know. No Englishman could get before you;—I am quite sure of that."

"Don't you be impertinent, miss," said Kate. "You can easily see, Mr. Green, that papa spoils my sister Eliza."

"Do you hunt in top-boots, Mr. Green?" said Tizzy.

To this I made no answer. She would have drawn me into a conversation about my feet in half a minute, and the slightest allusion to the subject threw me into a fit of perspiration.

"Are you fond of hunting, Miss O'Conor?" asked I, blindly hurrying into any other subject of conversation.

Miss O'Conor owned that she was fond of hunting—just a little; only papa would not allow it. When the hounds met anywhere within reach of Castle Conor, she and Kate would ride out to look at them; and if papa was not there that day,—an omission of rare occurrence,—they would ride a few fields with the hounds.

"But he lets Tizzy keep with them the whole day," said she, whispering.

"And has Tizzy a pony of her own?"

"Oh yes, Tizzy has everything. She's papa's pet, you know."

"And whose pet are you?" I asked.

"Oh—I am nobody's pet, unless sometimes Jack makes a pet of me when he's in a good humour. Do you make pets of your sisters, Mr. Green?"

"I have none. But if I had I should not make pets of them."

"Not of your own sisters?"

"No. As for myself, I'd sooner make a pet of my friend's sister; a great deal."

"How very unnatural," said Miss O'Conor, with the prettiest look of surprise imaginable.

"Not at all unnatural I think," said I, looking tenderly and lovingly into her face. Where does one find girls so pretty, so easy, so sweet, so talkative as the Irish girls? And then with all their talking and all their ease who ever hears of their misbehaving? They certainly love flirting, as they also love dancing. But they flirt without mischief and without malice.

I had now quite forgotten my misfortune, and was beginning to think how well I should like to have Fanny O'Conor for my wife. In this frame of mind I was bending over towards her as a servant took away a plate from the other side, when a sepulchral note sounded in my ear. It was like the memento mori of the old Roman;—as though some one pointed in the midst of my bliss to the sword hung over my head by a thread. It was the voice of Larry, whispering in his agony just above my head—

"They's disthroying my poor feet intirely, intirely; so they is! I can't bear it much longer, yer honer." I had committed murder like Macbeth; and now my Banquo had come to disturb me at my feast.

"What is it he says to you?" asked Fanny.

"Oh nothing," I answered, once more in my misery.

"There seems to be some point of confidence between you and our Larry," she remarked.

"Oh no," said I, quite confused; "not at all."

"You need not be ashamed of it. Half the gentlemen in the county have their confidences with Larry;—and some of the ladies too, I can tell you. He was born in this house, and never lived anywhere else; and I am sure he has a larger circle of acquaintance than any one else in it."

I could not recover my self-possession for the next ten minutes. Whenever Larry was on our side of the table I was afraid he was coming to me with another agonised whisper. When he was opposite, I could not but watch him as he hobbled in his misery. It was evident that the boots were too tight for him, and had they been made throughout of iron they could not have been less capable of yielding to the feet. I pitied him from the bottom of my heart. And I pitied myself also, wishing that I was well in bed upstairs with some feigned malady, so that Larry might have had his own again.

And then for a moment I missed him from the room. He had doubtless gone to relieve his tortured feet in the servants' hall, and as he did so was cursing my cruelty. But what mattered it? Let him curse. If he would only stay away and do that, I would appease his wrath when we were alone together with pecuniary satisfaction.

But there was no such rest in store for me. "Larry, Larry," shouted Mr. O'Conor, "where on earth has the fellow gone to?" They were all cousins at the table except myself, and Mr. O'Conor was not therefore restrained by any feeling of ceremony. "There is something wrong with that fellow today; what is it, Jack?"

"Upon my word, sir, I don't know," said Jack.

"I think he must be tipsy," whispered Miss O'Conor, the maiden sister, who always sat at her brother's left hand. But a whisper though it was, it was audible all down the table.

"No, ma'am; it aint dhrink at all," said the coachman. "It is his feet as does it."

"His feet!" shouted Tom O'Conor.

"Yes; I know it's his feet," said that horrid Tizzy. "He's got on great thick nailed shoes. It was that that made him tumble down in the hall."

I glanced at each side of me, and could see that there was a certain consciousness expressed in the face of each of my two neighbours;—on Kate's mouth there was decidedly a smile, or rather, perhaps, the slightest possible inclination that way; whereas on Fanny's part I thought I saw something like a rising sorrow at my distress. So at least I flattered myself.

"Send him back into the room immediately," said Tom, who looked at me as though he had some consciousness that I had introduced all this confusion into his household. What should I do? Would it not be best for me to make clean breast of it before them all? But alas! I lacked the courage.

The coachman went out, and we were left for five minutes without any servant, and Mr. O'Conor the while became more and more savage. I attempted to say a word to Fanny, but failed. Vox faucibus haesit.

"I don't think he has got any others," said Tizzy—"at least none others left."

On the whole I am glad I did not marry into the family, as I could not have endured that girl to stay in my house as a sister-in-law.

"Where the d—has that other fellow gone to?" said Tom. "Jack, do go out and see what is the matter. If anybody is drunk send for me."

"Oh, there is nobody drunk," said Tizzy.

Jack went out, and the coachman returned; but what was done and said I hardly remember. The whole room seemed to swim round and round, and as far as I can recollect the company sat mute, neither eating nor drinking. Presently Jack returned.

"It's all right," said he. I always liked Jack. At the present moment he just looked towards me and laughed slightly.

"All right?" said Tom. "But is the fellow coming?"

"We can do with Richard, I suppose," said Jack.

"No—I can't do with Richard," said the father. "And will know what it all means. Where is that fellow Larry?"

Larry had been standing just outside the door, and now he entered gently as a mouse. No sound came from his footfall, nor was there in his face that look of pain which it had worn for the last fifteen minutes. But he was not the less abashed, frightened and unhappy.

"What is all this about, Larry?" said his master, turning to him. "I insist upon knowing."

"Och thin, Mr. Green, yer honer, I wouldn't be afther telling agin yer honer; indeed I wouldn't thin, av' the masther would only let me hould my tongue." And he looked across at me, deprecating my anger.

"Mr. Green!" said Mr. O'Conor.

"Yes, yer honer. It's all along of his honer's thick shoes;" and Larry, stepping backwards towards the door, lifted them up from some corner, and coming well forward, exposed them with the soles uppermost to the whole table.

"And that's not all, yer honer; but they've squoze the very toes of me into a jelly."

There was now a loud laugh, in which Jack and Peter and Fanny and Kate and Tizzy all joined; as too did Mr. O'Conor—and I also myself after a while.

"Whose boots are they?" demanded Miss O'Conor senior, with her severest tone and grimmest accent.

"'Deed then and the divil may have them for me, Miss," answered Larry. "They war Mr. Green's, but the likes of him won't wear them agin afther the likes of me—barring he wanted them very particular," added he, remembering his own pumps.

I began muttering something, feeling that the time had come when I must tell the tale. But Jack with great good nature, took up the story and told it so well, that I hardly suffered in the telling.

"And that's it," said Tom O'Conor, laughing till I thought he would have fallen from his chair. "So you've got Larry's shoes on—"

"And very well he fills them," said Jack.

"And it's his honer that's welcome to 'em," said Larry, grinning from ear to ear now that he saw that "the masther" was once more in a good humour.

"I hope they'll be nice shoes for dancing," said Kate.

"Only there's one down at the heel I know," said Tizzy.

"The servant's shoes!" This was an exclamation made by the maiden lady, and intended apparently only for her brother's ear. But it was clearly audible by all the party.

"Better that than no dinner," said Peter.

"But what are you to do about the dancing?" said Fanny, with an air of dismay on her face which flattered me with an idea that she did care whether I danced or no.

In the mean time Larry, now as happy as an emperor, was tripping round the room without any shoes to encumber him as he withdrew the plates from the table.

"And it's his honer that's welcome to 'em," said he again, as he pulled off the table-cloth with a flourish. "And why wouldn't he, and he able to folly the hounds betther nor any Englishman that iver war in these parts before,—anyways so Mick says!"

Now Mick was the huntsman, and this little tale of eulogy from Larry went far towards easing my grief. I had ridden well to the hounds that day, and I knew it.

There was nothing more said about the shoes, and I was soon again at my ease, although Miss O'Conor did say something about the impropriety of Larry walking about in his stocking feet. The ladies however soon withdrew,—to my sorrow, for I was getting on swimmingly with Fanny; and then we gentlemen gathered round the fire and filled our glasses.

In about ten minutes a very light tap was heard, the door was opened to the extent of three inches, and a female voice which I readily recognised called to Jack.

Jack went out, and in a second or two put his head back into the room and called to me—"Green," he said, "just step here moment, there's a good fellow." I went out, and there I found Fanny standing with her brother.

"Here are the girls at their wits' ends," said he, "about your dancing. So Fanny has put a boy upon one of the horse and proposes that you should send another line to Mrs. Meehan at Ballyglass. It's only ten miles, and he'll be back in two hours."

I need hardly say that I acted in conformity with this advice, I went into Mr. O'Conor's book room, with Jack and his sister, and there scribbled a note. I was delightful to feel how intimate I was with them, and how anxious they were to make me happy.

"And we won't begin till they come," said Fanny.

"Oh, Miss O'Conor, pray don't wait," said I.

"Oh, but we will," she answered. "You have your wine to drink, and then there's the tea; and then we'll have a song two. I'll spin it out; see if I don't." And so we went to the front door where the boy was already on his horse—her own nag as I afterwards found.

"And Patsey," said she, "ride for your life; and Patsey, whatever you do, don't come back without Mr. Green's pumps—his dancing-shoes you know."

And in about two hours the pumps did arrive; and I don't think I ever spent a pleasanter evening or got more satisfaction out of a pair of shoes. They had not been two minutes on my feet before Larry was carrying a tray of negus across the room in those which I had worn at dinner.

"The Dillon girls are going to stay here," said Fanny as I wished her good night at two o'clock. "And we'll have dancing every evening as long as you remain."

"But I shall leave tomorrow," said I.

"Indeed you won't. Papa will take care of that."

And so he did. "You had better go over to Ballyglass yourself tomorrow," said he, "and collect your own things. There's no knowing else what you may have to borrow of Larry."

I stayed there three weeks, and in the middle of the third I thought that everything would be arranged between me and Fanny. But the aunt interfered; and in about a twelvemonth after my adventures she consented to make a more fortunate man happy for his life.

THE PARSON'S DAUGHTER OF OXNEY COLNE

The prettiest scenery in all England—and if I am contradicted in that assertion, I will say in all Europe—is in Devonshire, on the southern and south-eastern skirts of Dartmoor, where the rivers Dart, and Avon, and Teign form themselves, and where the broken moor is half cultivated, and the wild-looking upland fields are half moor. In making this assertion I am often met with much doubt, but it is by persons who do not really know the locality. Men and women talk to me on the matter, who have travelled down the line of railway from Exeter to Plymouth, who have spent a fortnight at Torquay, and perhaps made an excursion from Tavistock to the convict prison on Dartmoor. But who knows the glories of Chagford? Who has walked through the parish of Manaton? Who is conversant with Lustleigh Cleeves and Withycombe in the moor? Who has explored Holne Chase? Gentle reader, believe me that you will be rash in contradicting me, unless you have done these things.

There or thereabouts—I will not say by the waters of which little river it is washed—is the parish of Oxney Colne. And for those who wish to see all the beauties of this lovely country, a sojourn in Oxney Colne would be most desirable, seeing that the sojourner would then be brought nearer to all that he would wish to visit, than at any other spot in the country. But there in an objection to any such arrangement. There are only two decent houses in the whole parish, and these are—or were when I knew the locality—small and fully occupied by their possessors. The larger and better is the parsonage, in which lived the parson and his daughter; and the smaller is a freehold residence of a certain Miss Le Smyrger, who owned a farm of a hundred acres, which was rented by one Farmer

Cloysey, and who also possessed some thirty acres round her own house, which she managed herself; regarding herself to be quite as great in cream as Mr. Cloysey, and altogether superior to him in the article of cyder. "But yeu has to pay no rent, Miss," Farmer Cloysey would say, when Miss Le Smyrger expressed this opinion of her art in a manner too defiant. "Yeu pays no rent, or yeu couldn't do it." Miss Le Smyrger was an old maid, with a pedigree and blood of her own, a hundred and thirty acres of fee-simple land on the borders of Dartmoor, fifty years of age, a constitution of iron, and an opinion of her own on every subject under the sun.

And now for the parson and his daughter. The parson's name was Woolsworthy—or Woolathy, as it was pronounced by all those who lived around him—the Rev. Saul Woolsworthy; and his daughter was Patience Woolsworthy, or Miss Patty, as she was known to the Devonshire world of those parts. That name of Patience had not been well chosen for her, for she was a hot-tempered damsel, warm in her convictions, and inclined to express them freely. She had but two closely intimate friends in the world, and by both of them this freedom of expression had now been fully permitted to her since she was a child. Miss Le Smyrger and her father were well accustomed to her ways, and on the whole well satisfied with them. The former was equally free and equally warm-tempered as herself, and as Mr. Woolsworthy was allowed by his daughter to be quite paramount on his own subject—for he had a subject—he did not object to his daughter being paramount on all others. A pretty girl was Patience Woolsworthy at the time of which I am writing, and one who possessed much that was worthy of remark and admiration, had she lived where beauty meets with admiration, or where force of character is remarked. But at Oxney Colne, on the borders of Dartmoor, there were few to appreciate her, and it seemed as though she herself had but little idea of carrying her talent further afield, so that it might not remain for ever wrapped in a blanket.

She was a pretty girl, tall end slender, with dark eyes and black hair. Her eyes were perhaps too round for regular beauty, and her hair was perhaps too crisp; her mouth was large and expressive; her nose was finely formed, though a critic in female form might have declared it to be somewhat broad. But her countenance altogether was wonderfully attractive—if only it might be seen without that resolution for dominion which occasionally marred it, though sometimes it even added to her attractions.

It must be confessed on behalf of Patience Woolsworthy, that the circumstances of her life had peremptorily called upon her to exercise dominion. She had lost her mother when she was sixteen, and had had neither brother nor sister. She had no neighbours near her fit either from education or rank to interfere in the conduct of her life, excepting always Miss La Smyrger. Miss Le Smyrger would have done anything for her, including the whole management of her morals and of the parsonage household, had Patience been content with such an arrangement. But much as Patience had ever loved Miss Le Smyrger, she was not content with this, and therefore she had been called on to put forth a strong hand of her own. She had put forth this strong hand early, and hence had come the character which I am attempting to describe. But I must say on behalf of this girl, that it was not only over others that she thus exercised dominion. In acquiring that power she had also acquired the much greater power of exercising rule over herself.

But why should her father have been ignored in these family arrangements? Perhaps it may almost suffice to say, that of all living men her father was the man best conversant with the antiquities of the county in which he lived. He was the Jonathan Oldbuck of Devonshire, and especially of Dartmoor, without that decision of character which enabled Oldbuck to keep his womenkind in some kind of subjection, and probably enabled him also to see that his weekly bills did not pass their proper limits. Our Mr. Oldbuck, of Oxney Colne, was sadly deficient in these. As a parish pastor with but a small cure, he did his duty with sufficient energy, to keep him, at any rate, from reproach. He was kind and charitable to the poor, punctual in his services, forbearing with the farmers around him, mild with his brother clergymen, and indifferent to aught that bishop or archdeacon might think or say of him. I do not name this latter attribute as a virtue, but as a fact. But all these points were as nothing in the known character of Mr. Woolsworthy, of Oxney Colne. He was the antiquarian of Dartmoor. That was his line of life. It was in that capacity that he was known to the Devonshire world; it was as such that he journeyed about with his humble carpet-bag, staying away from his parsonage a night or two at a time; it was in that character that he received now and again stray visitors in the single spare bedroom—not friends asked to see him and his girl because of their friendship—but men who knew something as to this buried stone, or that old land-mark. In all these things his daughter let him have his own way, assisting and encouraging him. That was his line of life, and therefore she respected it. But in all other matters she chose to be paramount at the parsonage.

Mr. Woolsworthy was a little man, who always wore, except on Sundays, grey clothes—clothes of so light a grey that they would hardly have been regarded as clerical in a district less remote. He had now reached a goodly age, being full seventy years old; but still he was wiry and active, and showed but few symptoms of decay. His head was bald, and the few remaining locks that surrounded it were nearly white. But there was a look of energy about his mouth, and a humour in his light grey eye, which forbade those who knew him to regard him altogether as an old man. As it was, he could walk from Oxney Colne to Priestown, fifteen long Devonshire miles across the moor; and he who could do that could hardly be regarded as too old for work.

But our present story will have more to do with his daughter than with him. A pretty girl, I have said, was Patience Woolsworthy; and one, too, in many ways remarkable. She had taken her outlook into life, weighing the things which she had and those which she had not, in a manner very unusual, and, as a rule, not always desirable for a young lady. The things which she had not were very many. She had not society; she had not a fortune; she had not any assurance of future means of livelihood; she had not high hope of procuring for herself a position in life by marriage; she had not that excitement and pleasure in life which she read of in such books as found their way down to Oxney Colne Parsonage. It would be easy to add to the list of the things which she had not; and this list against herself she made out with the utmost vigour. The things which she had, or those rather which she assured herself of having, were much more easily counted. She had the birth and education of a lady, the strength of a healthy woman, and a will of her own. Such was the list as she made it out for herself, and I protest that I assert no more than the truth in saying that she never added to it either beauty, wit, or talent.

I began these descriptions by saying that Oxney Colne would, of all places, be the best spot from which a tourist could visit those parts of Devonshire, but for the fact that he could obtain there none of the accommodation which tourists require. A brother antiquarian might, perhaps, in those days have done so, seeing that there was, as I have said, a spare bedroom at the parsonage. Any intimate friend of Miss Le Smyrger's might be as fortunate, for she was equally well provided at Oxney Combe, by which name her house was known. But Miss Le Smyrger was not given to extensive hospitality, and it was only to those who were bound to her, either by ties of blood or of very old friendship, that she delighted to open her doors. As her old friends were very few in number, as those few lived at a distance, and as her nearest relations were higher in the world than she was, and were said by herself to look down upon her, the visits made to Oxney Combe were few and far between.

But now, at the period of which I am writing, such a visit was about to be made. Miss Le Smyrger had a younger sister, who had inherited a property in the parish of Oxney Colne equal to that of the lady who now lived there; but this the younger sister had inherited beauty also, and she therefore, in early life, had found sundry lovers, one of whom became her husband. She had married a man even then well to do in the world, but now rich and almost mighty; a Member of Parliament, a lord of this and that board, a man who had a house in Eaton Square, and a park in the north of England; and in this way her course of life had been very much divided from that of our Miss Le Smyrger. But the Lord of the Government Board had been blessed with various children; and perhaps it was now thought expedient to look after Aunt Penelope's Devonshire acres. Aunt Penelope was empowered to leave them to whom she pleased; and though it was thought in Eaton Square that she must, as a matter of course, leave them to one of the family, nevertheless a little cousinly intercourse might make the thing more certain. I will not say that this was the sole cause of such a visit, but in these days a visit was to be made by Captain Broughton to his aunt. Now Captain John Broughton was the second son of Alfonso Broughton, of Clapham Park and Eaton Square, Member of Parliament, and Lord of the aforesaid Government Board.

"And what do you mean to do with him?" Patience Woolsworthy asked of Miss Le Smyrger when that lady walked over from the Combe to say that her nephew John was to arrive on the following morning.

"Do with him? Why I shall bring him over here to talk to your father."

"He'll be too fashionable for that; and papa won't trouble his head about him if he finds that he doesn't care for Dartmoor."

"Then he may fall in love with you, my dear."

"Well, yes; there's that resource at any rate, and for your sake I dare say I should be more civil to him than papa. But he'll soon get tired of making love, and what you'll do then I cannot imagine."

That Miss Woolsworthy felt no interest in the coming of the Captain I will not pretend to say. The advent of any stranger with whom she would be called on to associate must be matter of interest to her in that secluded place; and she was not so absolutely unlike other young ladies that the arrival of an unmarried young man would be the same to her as the advent of some patriarchal paterfamilias. In taking that outlook into life of which I have spoken, she had never said to herself that she despised those things from which other girls received the excitement, the joys, and the disappointment of their lives. She had simply given herself to understand that very little of such things would come her way, and that it behoved her to live—to live happily if such might be possible—without experiencing the need of them. She had heard, when there was no thought of any such visit to Oxney Colne, that John Broughton was a handsome, clever man—one who thought much of himself, and was thought much of by others—that there had been some talk of his marrying a great heiress, which marriage, however, had not taken place through unwillingness on his part, and that he was on the whole a man of more mark in the world than the ordinary captain of ordinary regiments.

Captain Broughton came to Oxney Combe, stayed there a fortnight,—the intended period for his projected visit having been fixed at three or four days,—and then went his way. He went his way back to his London haunts, the time of the year then being the close of the Easter holidays; but as he did so he told his aunt that he should assuredly return to her in the autumn.

"And assuredly I shall be happy to see you, John—if you come with a certain purpose. If you have no such purpose, you had better remain away."

"I shall assuredly come," the Captain had replied, and then he had gone on his journey.

The summer passed rapidly by, and very little was said between Miss Le Smyrger and Miss Woolsworthy about Captain Broughton. In many respects—nay, I may say, as to all ordinary matters, no two women could well be more intimate with each other than they were,—and more than that, they had the courage each to talk to the other with absolute truth as to things concerning themselves—a courage in which dear friends often fail. But nevertheless, very little was said between them about Captain John Broughton. All that was said may be here repeated.

"John says that he shall return here in August," Miss Le Smyrger said, as Patience was sitting with her in the parlour at Oxney Combe, on the morning after that gentleman's departure.

"He told me so himself," said Patience; and as she spoke her round dark eyes assumed a look of more than ordinary self-will. If Miss Le Smyrger had intended to carry the conversation any further, she changed her mind as she looked at her companion. Then, as I said, the summer ran by, and towards the close of the warm days of July, Miss Le Smyrger, sitting in the same chair in the same room, again took up the conversation.

"I got a letter from John this morning. He says that he shall be here on the third."

"Does he?"

"He is very punctual to the time he named."

"Yes; I fancy that he is a punctual man," said Patience.

"I hope that you will be glad to see him," said Miss Le Smyrger.

"Very glad to see him," said Patience, with a bold clear voice; and then the conversation was again dropped, and nothing further was said till after Captain Broughton's second arrival in the parish.

Four months had then passed since his departure, and during that time Miss Woolsworthy had performed all her usual daily duties in their accustomed course. No one could discover that she had been less careful in her household matters than had been her wont, less willing to go among her poor neighbours, or less assiduous in her attentions to her father. But not the less was there a feeling in the minds of those around her that some great change had come upon her. She would sit during the long summer evenings on a certain spot outside the parsonage orchard, at the top of a small sloping field in which their solitary cow was always pastured, with a book on her knees before her, but rarely reading. There she would sit, with the beautiful view down to the winding river below her, watching the setting sun, and thinking, thinking, thinking—thinking of something of which she had never spoken. Often would Miss Le Smyrger come upon her there, and sometimes would pass by her even without a word; but never—never once did she dare to ask her of the matter of her thoughts. But she knew the matter well enough. No confession was necessary to inform her that Patience Woolsworthy was in love with John Broughton—ay, in love, to the full and entire loss of her whole heart.

On one evening she was so sitting till the July sun had fallen and hidden himself for the night, when her father came upon her as he returned from one of his rambles on the moor. "Patty," he said, "you are always sitting there now. Is it not late? Will you not be cold?"

"No, papa," said she, "I shall not be cold."

"But won't you come to the house? I miss you when you come in so late that there's no time to say a word before we go to bed."

She got up and followed him into the parsonage, and when they were in the sitting-room together, and the door was closed, she came up to him and kissed him. "Papa," she said, "would it make you very unhappy if I were to leave you?"

"Leave me!" he said, startled by the serious and almost solemn tone of her voice. "Do you mean for always?"

"If I were to marry, papa?"

"Oh, marry! No; that would not make me unhappy. It would make me very happy, Patty, to see you married to a man you would love—very, very happy; though my days would be desolate without you."

"That is it, papa. What would you do if I went from you?"

"What would it matter, Patty? I should be free, at any rate, from a load which often presses heavy on me now. What will you do when I shall leave you? A few more years and all will be over with me. But who is it, love? Has anybody said anything to you?"

"It was only an idea, papa. I don't often think of such a thing; but I did think of it then." And so the subject was allowed to pass by. This had happened before the day of the second arrival had been absolutely fixed and made known to Miss Woolsworthy.

And then that second arrival took place. The reader may have understood from the words with which Miss Le Smyrger authorised her nephew to make his second visit to Oxney Combe that Miss Woolsworthy's passion was not altogether unauthorised. Captain Broughton had been told that he was not to come unless he came with a certain purpose; and having been so told, he still persisted in coming. There can be no doubt but that he well understood the purport to which his aunt alluded. "I shall assuredly come," he had said. And true to his word, he was now there.

Patience knew exactly the hour at which he must arrive at the station at Newton Abbot, and the time also which it would take to travel over those twelve uphill miles from the station to Oxney. It need hardly he said that she paid no visit to Miss Le Smyrger's house on that afternoon; but she might have known something of Captain Broughton's approach without going thither. His road to the Combe passed by the parsonage-gate, and had Patience sat even at her bedroom window she must have seen him. But on such a morning she would not sit at her bedroom window—she would do nothing which would force her to accuse herself of a restless longing for her lover's coming. It was for him to seek her. If he chose to do so, he knew the way to the parsonage.

Miss Le Smyrger—good, dear, honest, hearty Miss Le Smyrger, was in a fever of anxiety on behalf of her friend. It was not that she wished her nephew to marry Patience—or rather that she had entertained any such wish when he first came,—among them. She was not given to match-making, and moreover thought, or had thought within herself, that they of Oxney Colne could do very well without any admixture from Eaton Square. Her plan of life had been that, when old Mr. Woolsworthy was taken away from Dartmoor, Patience should live with her; and that when she also shuffled off her coil, then Patience Woolsworthy should be the maiden mistress of Oxney Combe—of Oxney Combe and Mr. Cloysey's farm—to the utter detriment of all the Broughtons. Such had been her plan before nephew John had come among them—a plan not to be spoken of till the coming of that dark day which should make Patience an orphan. But now her nephew had been there, and all was to be altered. Miss Le Smyrger's plan would have provided a companion for her old age; but that had not been her chief object. She had thought more of Patience than of herself, and now it seemed that a prospect of a higher happiness was opening for her friend.

"John," she said, as soon as the first greetings were over, "do you remember the last words that I said to you before you went away?" Now, for myself, I much admire Miss Le Smyrger's heartiness, but I do not think much of her discretion. It would have been better, perhaps, had she allowed things to take their course.

"I can't say that I do," said the Captain. At the same time the Captain did remember very well what those last words had been.

"I am so glad to see you, so delighted to see you, if—if—if—," and then she paused, for with all her courage she hardly dared to ask her nephew whether he had come there with the express purpose of asking Miss Woolsworthy to marry him.

To tell the truth, for there is no room for mystery within the limits of this short story,—to tell, I say, at a word the plain and simple truth, Captain Broughton had already asked that question. On the day before he left Oxney Come, he had in set terms proposed to the parson's daughter, and indeed the words, the hot and frequent words, which previously to that had fallen like sweetest honey into the ears of Patience Woolsworthy, had made it imperative on him to do so. When a man in such a place as that has talked to a girl of love day after day, must not he talk of it to some definite purpose on the day on which he leaves her? Or if he do not, must he not submit to be regarded as false, selfish, and almost fraudulent? Captain Broughton, however, had asked the question honestly and truly. He had done so honestly and truly, but in words, or, perhaps, simply with a tone, that had hardly sufficed to satisfy the proud spirit of the girl he loved. She by that time had confessed to herself that she loved him with all her heart; but she had made no such confession to him. To him she had spoken no word, granted no favour, that any lover might rightfully regard as a token of love returned. She had listened to him as he spoke, and bade him keep such sayings for the drawing-rooms of his fashionable friends. Then he had spoken out and had asked for that hand,—not, perhaps, as a suitor tremulous with hope,—but as a rich man who knows that he can command that which he desires to purchase.

"You should think more of this," she had said to him at last. "If you would really have me for your wife, it will not be much to you to return here again when time for thinking of it shall have passed by." With these words she had dismissed him, and now he had again come back to Oxney Colne. But still she would not place herself at the window to look for him, nor dress herself in other than her simple morning country dress, nor omit one item of her daily work. If he wished to take her at all, he should wish to take her as she really was, in her plain country life, but he should take her also with full observance of all those privileges which maidens are allowed to claim from their lovers. He should contract no ceremonious observance because she was the daughter of a poor country parson who would come to him without a shilling, whereas he stood high in the world's books. He had asked her to give him all that she had, and that all she was ready to give, without stint. But the gift must be valued before it could be given or received, he also was to give her as much, and she would accept it as beyond all price. But she would not allow that that which was offered to her was in any degree the more precious because of his outward worldly standing.

She would not pretend to herself that she thought he would come to her that day, and therefore she busied herself in the kitchen and about the house, giving directions to her two maids as though the afternoon would pass as all other days did pass in that household. They usually dined at four, and she rarely in these summer months went far from the house before that hour. At four precisely she sat down with her father, and then said that she was going up as far as Helpholme after dinner. Helpholme was a solitary farmhouse in another parish, on the border of the moor, and Mr. Woolsworthy asked her whether he should accompany her.

"Do, papa," she said, "if you are not too tired." And yet she had thought how probable it might be that she should meet John Broughton on her walk. And so it was arranged; but just as dinner was over, Mr. Woolsworthy remembered himself.

"Gracious me," he said, "how my memory is going. Gribbles, from Ivybridge, and old John Poulter, from Bovey, are coming to meet here by appointment. You can't put Helpholme off till tomorrow?"

Patience, however, never put off anything, and therefore at six o'clock, when her father had finished his slender modicum of toddy, she tied on her hat and went on her walk. She started with a quick step, and left no word to say by which route she would go.

As she passed up along the little lane which led towards Oxney Combe, she would not even look to see if he was coming towards her; and when she left the road, passing over a stone stile into a little path which ran first through the upland fields, and then across the moor ground towards Helpholme, she did not look back once, or listen for his coming step.

She paid her visit, remaining upwards of an hour with the old bedridden mother of the tenant of Helpholme. "God bless you, my darling!" said the old woman as she left her; "and send you some one to make your own path bright and happy through the world." These words were still ringing in her ears with all their significance as she saw John Broughton waiting for her at the first stile which she had to pass after leaving the farmer's haggard.

"Patty," he said, as he took her hand, and held it close within both his own, "what a chase I have had after you!"

"And who asked you, Captain Broughton?" she answered, smiling. "If the journey was too much for your poor London strength, could you not have waited till tomorrow morning, when you would have found me at the parsonage?" But she did not draw her hand away from him, or in any way pretend that he had not a right to accost her as a lover.

"No, I could not wait. I am more eager to see those I love than you seem to be."

"How do you know whom I love, or how eager I might be to see them? There is an old woman there whom I love, and I have thought nothing of this walk with the object of seeing her." And now, slowly drawing her hand away from him, she pointed to the farmhouse which she had left.

"Patty," he said, after a minute's pause, during which she had looked full into his face with all the force of her bright eyes; "I have come from London today, straight down here to Oxney, and from my aunt's house close upon your footsteps after you, to ask you that one question—Do you love me?"

"What a Hercules!" she said, again laughing. "Do you really mean that you left London only this morning? Why, you must have been five hours in a railway carriage and two in a postchaise, not to talk of the walk afterwards. You ought to take more care of yourself, Captain Broughton!"

He would have been angry with her—for he did not like to be quizzed—had she not put her hand on his arm as she spoke, and the softness of her touch had redeemed the offence of her words.

"All that I have done," said he, "that I may hear one word from you."

"That any word of mine should have such potency! But let us walk on, or my father will take us for some of the standing stones of the moor. How have you found your aunt? If you only knew the cares that have sat on her dear shoulders for the last week past, in order that your high mightiness might have a sufficiency to eat and drink in these desolate half-starved regions!"

"She might have saved herself such anxiety. No one can care less for such things than I do."

"And yet I think I have heard you boast of the cook of your club." And then again there was silence for a minute or two.

"Patty," said he, stopping again in the path; "answer my question. I have a right to demand an answer. Do you love me?"

"And what if I do? What if I have been so silly as to allow your perfections to be too many for my weak heart? What then, Captain Broughton?"

"It cannot be that you love me, or you would not joke now."

"Perhaps not, indeed," she said. It seemed as though she were resolved not to yield an inch in her own humour. And then again they walked on.

"Patty," he said once more, "I shall get an answer from you tonight,—this evening; now, during this walk, or I shall return tomorrow, and never revisit this spot again."

"Oh, Captain Broughton, how should we ever manage to live without you?"

"Very well," he said; "up to the end of this walk I can hear it all;—and one word spoken then will mend it all."

During the whole of this time she felt that she was ill-using him. She knew that she loved him with all her heart; that it would nearly kill her to part with him; that she had heard his renewed offer with an ecstacy of joy. She acknowledged to herself that he was giving proof of his devotion as strong as any which a girl could receive from her lover. And yet she could hardly bring herself to say the word he longed to hear. That word once said, and then she knew that she must succumb to her love for ever! That word once said, and there would be nothing for her but to spoil him with her idolatry! That word once said, and she must continue to repeat it into his ears, till perhaps he might be tired of hearing it! And now he had threatened her, and how could she speak after that? She certainly would not speak it unless he asked her again without such threat. And so they walked on in silence.

"Patty," he said at last. "By the heavens above us you shall answer me. Do you love me?"

She now stood still, and almost trembled as she looked up into his face. She stood opposite to him for a moment, and then placing her two hands on his shoulders, she answered him. "I do, I do, I do," she said, "with all my heart; with all my heart—with all my heart and strength." And then her head fell upon his breast.

* * * * *

Captain Broughton was almost as much surprised as delighted by the warmth of the acknowledgment made by the eager-hearted passionate girl whom he now held within his arms. She had said it now; the words had been spoken; and there was nothing for her but to swear to him over and over again with her sweetest oaths, that those words were true—true as her soul. And very sweet was the walk down from thence to the parsonage gate. He spoke no more of the distance of the ground, or the length of his day's journey. But he stopped her at every turn that he might press her arm the closer to his own, that he might look into the brightness of her eyes, and prolong his hour of delight. There were no more gibes now on her tongue, no raillery at his London finery, no laughing comments on his coming and going. With downright honesty she told him everything: how she had loved him before her heart was warranted in such a passion; how, with much thinking, she had resolved that it would be unwise to take him at his first word, and had thought it better that he should return to London, and then think over it; how she had almost repented of her courage when she had feared, during those long summer days, that he would forget her; and how her heart had leapt for joy when her old friend had told her that he was coming.

"And yet," said he, "you were not glad to see me!"

"Oh, was I not glad? You cannot understand the feelings of a girl who has lived secluded as I have done. Glad is no word for the joy I felt. But it was not seeing you that I cared for so much. It was the knowledge that you were near me once again. I almost wish now that I had not seen you till tomorrow." But as she spoke she pressed his arm, and this caress gave the lie to her last words.

"No, do not come in tonight," she said, when she reached the little wicket that led up to the parsonage. "Indeed, you shall not. I could not behave myself properly if you did."

"But I don't want you to behave properly."

"Oh! I am to keep that for London, am I? But, nevertheless, Captain Broughton, I will not invite you either to tea or to supper tonight."

"Surely I may shake hands with your father."

"Not tonight—not till—John, I may tell him, may I not? I must tell him at once."

"Certainly," said he.

"And then you shall see him tomorrow. Let me see—at what hour shall I bid you come?"

"To breakfast."

"No, indeed. What on earth would your aunt do with her broiled turkey and the cold pie? I have got no cold pie for you."

"I hate cold pie."

"What a pity! But, John, I should be forced to leave you directly after breakfast. Come down—come down at two, or three; and then I will go back with you to Aunt Penelope. I must see her tomorrow;" and so at last the matter was settled, and the happy Captain, as he left her, was hardly resisted in his attempt to press her lips to his own.

When she entered the parlour in which her father was sitting, there still were Gribbles and Poulter discussing some knotty point of Devon lore. So Patience took off her hat, and sat herself down, waiting till they should go. For full an hour she had to wait, and then Gribbles and Poulter did go. But it was not in such matters as this that Patience Woolsworthy was impatient. She could wait, and wait, and wait, curbing herself for weeks and months, while the thing waited for was in her eyes good; but she could not curb her hot thoughts or her hot words when things came to be discussed which she did not think to be good.

"Papa," she said, when Gribbles' long-drawn last word had been spoken at the door. "Do you remember how I asked you the other day what you would say if I were to leave you?"

"Yes, surely," he replied, looking up at her in astonishment.

"I am going to leave you now," she said. "Dear, dearest father, how am I to go from you?"

"Going to leave me," said he, thinking of her visit to Helpholme, and thinking of nothing else.

Now, there had been a story about Helpholme. That bedridden old lady there had a stalwart son, who was now the owner of the Helpholme pastures. But though owner in fee of all those wild acres, and of the cattle which they supported, he was not much above the farmers around him, either in manners or education. He had his merits, however; for he was honest, well-to-do in the world, and modest withal. How strong love had grown up, springing from neighbourly kindness, between our Patience and his mother, it needs not here to tell; but rising from it had come another love—or an ambition which might have grown to love. The young man, after much thought, had not dared to speak to Miss Woolsworthy, but he had sent a message by Miss Le Smyrger. If there could be any hope for him, he would present himself as a suitor—on trial. He did not owe a shilling in the world, and had money by him—saved. He wouldn't ask the parson for a shilling of fortune. Such had been the tenor of his message, and Miss Le Smyrger had delivered it faithfully. "He does not mean it," Patience had said with her stern voice. "Indeed he does, my dear. You may be sure he is in earnest," Miss Le Smyrger had replied; "and there is not an honester man in these parts."

"Tell him," said Patience, not attending to the latter portion of her friend's last speech, "that it cannot be—make him understand, you know—and tell him also that the matter shall be thought of no more." The matter had, at any rate, been spoken of no more, but the young farmer still remained a bachelor, and Helpholme still wanted a mistress. But all this came back upon the parson's mind when his daughter told him that she was about to leave him.

"Yes, dearest," she said; and as she spoke she now knelt at his knees. "I have been asked in marriage, and I have given myself away."

"Well, my love, if you will be happy—"

"I hope I shall; I think I shall. But you, papa?"

"You will not be far from us."

"Oh, yes; in London."

"In London?"

"Captain Broughton lives in London generally."

"And has Captain Broughton asked you to marry him?"

"Yes, papa—who else? Is he not good? Will you not love him? Oh, papa, do not say that I am wrong to love him?"

He never told her his mistake, or explained to her that he had not thought it possible that the high-placed son of the London great man should have fallen in love with his undowered daughter; but he embraced her, and told her, with all his enthusiasm, that he rejoiced in her joy, and would be happy in her happiness. "My own Patty," he said, "I have ever known that you were too good for this life of ours here." And then the evening wore away into the night, with many tears, but still with much happiness.

Captain Broughton, as he walked back to Oxney Combe, made up his mind that he would say nothing on the matter to his aunt till the next morning. He wanted to think over it all, and to think it over, if possible, by himself. He had taken a step in life, the most important that a man is ever called on to take, and he had to reflect whether or no he had taken it with wisdom.

"Have you seen her?" said Miss Le Smyrger, very anxiously, when he came into the drawing-room.

"Miss Woolsworthy you mean," said he. "Yes, I've seen her. As I found her out, I took a long walk, and happened to meet her. Do you know, aunt, I think I'll go to bed; I was up at five this morning, and have been on the move ever since."

Miss Le Smyrger perceived that she was to hear nothing that evening, so she handed him his candlestick and allowed him to go to his room.

But Captain Broughton did not immediately retire to bed, nor when he did so was he able to sleep at once. Had this step that he had taken been a wise one? He was not a man who, in worldly matters, had allowed things to arrange themselves for him, as is the case with so many men. He had formed views for himself, and had a theory of life. Money for money's sake he had declared to himself to be bad. Money, as a concomitant to things which were in themselves good, he had declared to himself to be good also. That concomitant in this affair of his marriage, he had now missed. Well; he had made up his mind to that, and would put up with the loss. He had means of living of his own, the means not so extensive as might have been desirable. That it would be well for him to become a married man, looking merely to the state of life as opposed to his present state, he had fully resolved. On that point, therefore, there was nothing to repent. That Patty Woolsworthy was good, affectionate, clever, and beautiful, he was sufficiently satisfied. It would be odd indeed if he were not so satisfied now, seeing that for the last four months he had so declared to himself daily with many inward asseverations. And yet though he repeated, now again, that he was satisfied, I do not think that he was so fully satisfied of it as he had been throughout the whole of those four months. It is sad to say so, but I fear—I fear that such was the case. When you have your plaything, how much of the anticipated pleasure vanishes, especially if it be won easily.

He had told none of his family what were his intentions in this second visit to Devonshire, and now he had to bethink himself whether they would be satisfied. What would his sister say, she who had married the Honourable Augustus Gumbleton, gold-stick-in-waiting to Her Majesty's Privy Council? Would she receive Patience with open arms, and make much of her about London? And then how far would London suit Patience, or would Patience suit London? There would be much for him to do in teaching her, and it would be well for him to set about the lesson without loss of time. So far he got that night, but when the morning came he went a step further, and began mentally to criticise her manner to himself. It had been very sweet, that warm, that full, that ready declaration of love. Yes; it had been very sweet; but—but—; when, after her little jokes, she did confess her love, had she not been a little too free for feminine excellence? A man likes to be told that he is loved, but he hardly wishes that the girl he is to marry should fling herself at his head!

Ah me! yes; it was thus he argued to himself as on that morning he went through the arrangements of his toilet. "Then he was a brute," you say, my pretty reader. I have never said that he was not a brute. But this I remark, that many such brutes are to be met with in the beaten paths of the world's highway. When Patience Woolsworthy had answered him coldly, bidding him go back to London and think over his love; while it seemed from her manner that at any rate as yet she did not care for him; while he was absent from her, and, therefore, longing for her, the possession of her charms, her talent and bright honesty of purpose had seemed to him a thing most desirable. Now they were his own. They had, in fact, been his own from the first. The heart of this country-bred girl had fallen at the first word from his mouth. Had she not so confessed to him? She was very nice—very nice indeed. He loved her dearly. But had he not sold himself too cheaply?

I by no means say that he was not a brute. But whether brute or no, he was an honest man, and had no remotest dream, either then, on that morning, or during the following days on which such thoughts pressed more quickly on his mind—of breaking away from his pledged word. At breakfast on that morning he told all to Miss Le Smyrger, and that lady, with warm and gracious intentions, confided to him her purpose regarding her property. "I have always regarded Patience as my heir," she said, "and shall do so still."

"Oh, indeed," said Captain Broughton.

"But it is a great, great pleasure to me to think that she will give back the little property to my sister's child. You will have your mother's, and thus it will all come together again."

"Ah!" said Captain Broughton. He had his own ideas about property, and did not, even under existing circumstances, like to hear that his aunt considered herself at liberty to leave the acres away to one who was by blood quite a stranger to the family.

"Does Patience know of this?" he asked.

"Not a word," said Miss Le Smyrger. And then nothing more was said upon the subject.

On that afternoon he went down and received the parson's benediction and congratulations with a good grace. Patience said very little on the occasion, and indeed was absent during the greater part of the interview. The two lovers then walked up to Oxney Combe, and there were more benedictions and more congratulations. "All went merry as a marriage bell," at any rate as far as Patience was concerned. Not a word had yet fallen from that dear mouth, not a look had yet come over that handsome face, which tended in any way to mar her bliss. Her first day of acknowledged love was a day altogether happy, and when she prayed for him as she knelt beside her bed there was no feeling in her mind that any fear need disturb her joy.

I will pass over the next three or four days very quickly, merely saying that Patience did not find them so pleasant as that first day after her engagement. There was something in her lover's manner—something which at first she could not define—which by degrees seemed to grate against her feelings.

He was sufficiently affectionate, that being a matter on which she did not require much demonstration; but joined to his affection there seemed to be—; she hardly liked to suggest to herself a harsh word, but could it be possible that he was beginning to think that she was not good enough for him? And then she asked herself the question—was she good enough for him? If there were doubt about that, the match should be broken off, though she tore her own heart out in the struggle. The truth, however, was this—that he had begun that teaching which he had already found to be so necessary. Now, had any one essayed to teach Patience German or mathematics, with that young lady's free consent, I believe that she would have been found a meek scholar. But it was not probable that she would be meek when she found a self-appointed tutor teaching her manners and conduct without her consent.

So matters went on for four or five days, and on the evening of the fifth day Captain Broughton and his aunt drank tea at the parsonage. Nothing very especial occurred; but as the parson and Miss La Smyrger insisted on playing backgammon with devoted perseverance during the whole evening, Broughton had a good opportunity of saying a word or two about those changes in his lady-love which a life in London would require—and some word he said also—some single slight word as to the higher station in life to which he would exalt his bride. Patience bore it—for her father and Miss La Smyrger were in the room—she bore it well, speaking no syllable of anger, and enduring, for the moment, the implied scorn of the old parsonage. Then the evening broke up, and Captain Broughton walked back to Oxney Combe with his aunt. "Patty," her father said to her before they went to bed, "he seems to me to be a most excellent young man." "Dear papa," she answered, kissing him. "And terribly deep in love," said Mr. Woolsworthy. "Oh, I don't know about that," she answered, as she left him with her sweetest smile. But though she could thus smile at her father's joke, she had already made up her mind that there was still something to be learned as to her promised husband before she could place herself altogether in his hands. She would ask him whether he thought himself liable to injury from this proposed marriage; and though he should deny any such thought, she would know from the manner of his denial what his true feelings were.

And he, too, on that night, during his silent walk with Miss Le Smyrger, had entertained some similar thoughts. "I fear she is obstinate," he said to himself; and then he had half accused her of being sullen also. "If that be her temper, what a life of misery I have before me!"

"Have you fixed a day yet?" his aunt asked him as they came near to her house.

"No, not yet; I don't know whether it will suit me to fix it before I leave."

"Why, it was but the other day you were in such a hurry."

"Ah—yes—I have thought more about it since then."

"I should have imagined that this would depend on what Patty thinks," said Miss Le Smyrger, standing up for the privileges of her sex. "It is presumed that the gentleman is always ready as soon as the lady will consent."

"Yes, in ordinary cases it is so; but when a girl is taken out of her own sphere—"

"Her own sphere! Let me caution you, Master John, not to talk to Patty about her own sphere."

"Aunt Penelope, as Patience is to be my wife and not yours, I must claim permission to speak to her on such subjects as may seem suitable to me." And then they parted—not in the best humour with each other.

On the following day Captain Broughton and Miss Woolsworthy did not meet till the evening. She had said, before those few ill-omened words had passed her lover's lips, that she would probably be at Miss Le Smyrger's house on the following morning. Those ill-omened words did pass her lover's lips, and then she remained at home. This did not come from sullenness, nor even from anger, but from a conviction that it would be well that she should think much before she met him again. Nor was he anxious to hurry a meeting. His thought—his base thought—was this; that she would be sure to come up to the Combe after him; but she did not come, and therefore in the evening he went down to her, and asked her to walk with him.

They went away by the path that led to Helpholme, and little was said between them till they had walked some mile together.

Patience, as she went along the path, remembered almost to the letter the sweet words which had greeted her ears as she came down that way with him on the night of his arrival; but he remembered nothing of that sweetness then. Had he not made an ass of himself during these last six months? That was the thought which very much had possession of his mind.

"Patience," he said at last, having hitherto spoken only an indifferent word now and again since they had left the parsonage, "Patience, I hope you realise the importance of the step which you and I are about to take?"

"Of course I do," she answered. "What an odd question that is for you to ask!"

"Because," said he, "sometimes I almost doubt it. It seems to me as though you thought you could remove yourself from here to your new home with no more trouble than when you go from home up to the Combe."

"Is that meant for a reproach, John?"

"No, not for a reproach, but for advice. Certainly not for a reproach."

"I am glad of that."

"But I should wish to make you think how great is the leap in the world which you are about to take." Then again they walked on for many steps before she answered him.

"Tell me, then, John," she said, when she had sufficiently considered what words she should speak; and as she spoke a bright colour suffused her face, and her eyes flashed almost with anger. "What leap do you mean? Do you mean a leap upwards?"

"Well, yes; I hope it will be so."

"In one sense, certainly, it would be a leap upwards. To be the wife of the man I loved; to have the privilege of holding his happiness in my hand; to know that I was his own—the companion whom he had chosen out of all the world—that would, indeed, be a leap upwards; a leap almost to heaven, if all that were so. But if you mean upwards in any other sense—"

"I was thinking of the social scale."

"Then, Captain Broughton, your thoughts were doing me dishonour."

"Doing you dishonour!"

"Yes, doing me dishonour. That your father is, in the world's esteem, a greater man than mine is doubtless true enough. That you, as a man, are richer than I am as a woman, is doubtless also true. But you dishonour me, and yourself also, if these things can weigh with you now."

"Patience,—I think you can hardly know what words you are saying to me."

"Pardon me, but I think I do. Nothing that you can give me—no gifts of that description—can weigh aught against that which I am giving you. If you had all the wealth and rank of the greatest lord in the land, it would count as nothing in such a scale. If—as I have not doubted—if in return for my heart you have given me yours, then—then—then you have paid me fully. But when gifts such as those are going, nothing else can count even as a make-weight."

"I do not quite understand you," he answered, after a pause. "I fear you are a little high-flown." And then, while the evening was still early, they walked back to the parsonage almost without another word.

Captain Broughton at this time had only one full day more to remain at Oxney Colne. On the afternoon following that he was to go as far as Exeter, and thence return to London. Of course, it was to be expected that the wedding day would be fixed before he went, and much had been said about it during the first day or two of his engagement. Then he had pressed for an early time, and Patience, with a girl's usual diffidence, had asked for some little delay. But now nothing was said on the subject; and how was it probable that such a matter could be settled after such a conversation as that which I have related? That evening, Miss Le Smyrger asked whether the day had been fixed. "No," said Captain Broughton, harshly; "nothing has been fixed." "But it will be arranged before you go?" "Probably not," he said; and then the subject was dropped for the time.

"John," she said, just before she went to bed, "if there be anything wrong between you and Patience, I conjure you to tell me."

"You had better ask her," he replied. "I can tell you nothing."

On the following morning he was much surprised by seeing Patience on the gravel path before Miss Le Smyrger's gate immediately after breakfast. He went to the door to open it for her, and she, as she gave him her hand, told him that she came up to speak to him. There was no hesitation in her manner, nor any look of anger in her face. But there was in her gait and form, in her voice and countenance, a fixedness of purpose which he had never seen before, or at any rate had never acknowledged.

"Certainly," said he. "Shall I come out with you, or will you come up stairs?"

"We can sit down in the summer-house," she said; and thither they both went.

"Captain Broughton," she said—and she began her task the moment that they were both seated—"you and I have engaged ourselves as man and wife, but perhaps we have been over rash."

"How so?" said he.

"It may be—and indeed I will say more—it is the case that we have made this engagement without knowing enough of each other's character."

"I have not thought so."

"The time will perhaps come when you will so think, but for the sake of all that we most value, let it come before it is too late. What would be our fate—how terrible would be our misery—if such a thought should come to either of us after we have linked our lots together."

There was a solemnity about her as she thus spoke which almost repressed him,—which for a time did prevent him from taking that tone of authority which on such a subject he would choose to adopt. But he recovered himself. "I hardly think that this comes well from you," he said.

"From whom else should it come? Who else can fight my battle for me; and, John, who else can fight that same battle on your behalf? I tell you this, that with your mind standing towards me as it does stand at present, you could not give me your hand at the altar with true words and a happy conscience. Am I not true? You have half repented of your bargain already. Is it not so?"

He did not answer her; but getting up from his seat walked to the front of the summer-house, and stood there with his back turned upon her. It was not that he meant to be ungracious, but in truth he did not know how to answer her. He had half repented of his bargain.

"John," she said, getting up and following him, so that she could put her hand upon his arm, "I have been very angry with you."

"Angry with me!" he said, turning sharp upon her.

"Yes, angry with you. You would have treated me like a child. But that feeling has gone now. I am not angry now. There is my hand;—the hand of a friend. Let the words that have been spoken between us be as though they had not been spoken. Let us both be free."

"Do you mean it?"

"Certainly I mean it." As she spoke these words her eyes filled with tears, in spite of all the efforts she could make; but he was not looking at her, and her efforts had sufficed to prevent any sob from being audible.

"With all my heart," he said; and it was manifest from his tone that he had no thought of her happiness as he spoke. It was true that she had been angry with him—angry, as she had herself declared; but nevertheless, in what she had said and what she had done, she had thought more of his happiness than of her own. Now she was angry once again.

"With all your heart, Captain Broughton! Well, so be it. If with all your heart, then is the necessity so much the greater. You go tomorrow. Shall we say farewell now?"

"Patience, I am not going to be lectured."

"Certainly not by me. Shall we say farewell now?"

"Yes, if you are determined."

"I am determined. Farewell, Captain Broughton. You have all my wishes for your happiness." And she held out her hand to him.

"Patience!" he said. And he looked at her with a dark frown, as though he would strive to frighten her into submission. If so, he might have saved himself any such attempt.

"Farewell, Captain Broughton. Give me your hand, for I cannot stay." He gave her his hand, hardly knowing why he did so. She lifted it to her lips and kissed it, and then, leaving him, passed from the summer-house down through the wicket-gate, and straight home to the parsonage.

During the whole of that day she said no word to any one of what had occurred. When she was once more at home she went about her household affairs as she had done on that day of his arrival. When she sat down to dinner with her father he observed nothing to make him think that she was unhappy; nor during the evening was there any expression in her face, or any tone in her voice, which excited his attention. On the following morning Captain Broughton called at the parsonage, and the servant-girl brought word to her mistress that he was in the parlour. But she would not see him. "Laws, miss, you ain't a quarrelled with your beau?" the poor girl said. "No, not quarrelled," she said; "but give him that." It was a scrap of paper, containing a word or two in pencil. "It is better that we should not meet again. God bless you." And from that day to this, now more than ten years, they never have met.

"Papa," she said to her father that afternoon, "dear papa, do not be angry with me. It is all over between me and John Broughton. Dearest, you and I will not be separated." It would be useless here to tell how great was the old man's surprise and how true his sorrow. As the tale was told to him no cause was given for anger with any one. Not a word was spoken against the suitor who had on that day returned to London with a full conviction that now at least he was relieved from his engagement. "Patty, my darling child," he said, "may God grant that it be for the best!

"It is for the best," she answered stoutly. "For this place I am fit; and I much doubt whether I am fit for any other."

On that day she did not see Miss Le Smyrger, but on the following morning, knowing that Captain Broughton had gone off, having heard the wheels of the carriage as they passed by the parsonage gate on his way to the station,—she walked up to the Combe.

"He has told you, I suppose?" said she.

"Yes," said Miss Le Smyrger. "And I will never see him again unless he asks your pardon on his knees. I have told him so. I would not even give him my hand as he went."

"But why so, thou kindest one? The fault was mine more than his."

"I understand. I have eyes in my head," said the old maid. "I have watched him for the last four or five days. If you could have kept the truth to yourself and bade him keep off from you, he would have been at your feet now, licking the dust from your shoes."

"But, dear friend, I do not want a man to lick dust from my shoes."

"Ah, you are a fool. You do not know the value of your own wealth."

"True; I have been a fool. I was a fool to think that one coming from such a life as he has led could be happy with such as I am. I know the truth now. I have bought the lesson dearly,—but perhaps not too dearly, seeing that it will never be forgotten."

There was but little more said about the matter between our three friends at Oxney Colne. What, indeed, could be said? Miss Le Smyrger for a year or two still expected that her nephew would return and claim his bride; but he has never done so, nor has there been any correspondence between them. Patience Woolsworthy had learned her lesson dearly. She had given her whole heart to the man; and, though she so bore herself that no one was aware of the violence of the struggle, nevertheless the struggle within her bosom was very violent. She never told herself that she had done wrong; she never regretted her loss; but yet—yet—the loss was very hard to bear. He also had loved her, but he was not capable of a love which could much injure his daily peace. Her daily peace was gone for many a day to come.

Her father is still living; but there is a curate now in the parish. In conjunction with him and with Miss Le Smyrger she spends her time in the concerns of the parish. In her own eyes she is a confirmed old maid; and such is my opinion also. The romance of her life was played out in that summer. She never sits now lonely on the hill-side thinking how much she might do for one whom she really loved. But with a large heart she loves many, and, with no romance, she works hard to lighten the burdens of those she loves.

As for Captain Broughton, all the world know that he did marry that great heiress with whom his name was once before connected, and that he is now a useful member of Parliament, working on committees three or four days a week with a zeal that is indefatigable. Sometimes, not often, as he thinks of Patience Woolsworthy, a gratified smile comes across his face.

THE RELICS OF GENERAL CHASSE—
A TALE OF ANTWERP

That Belgium is now one of the European kingdoms, living by its own laws, resting on its own bottom, with a king and court, palaces and parliament of its own, is known to all the world. And a very nice little kingdom it is; full of old towns, fine Flemish pictures, and interesting Gothic churches. But in the memory of very many of us who do not think ourselves old men, Belgium, as it is now called—in those days it used to be Flanders and Brabant—was a part of Holland; and it obtained its own independence by a revolution. In that revolution the most important military step was the siege of Antwerp, which was defended on the part of the Dutch by General Chasse, with the utmost gallantry, but nevertheless ineffectually.

After the siege Antwerp became quite a show place; and among the visitors who flocked there to talk of the gallant general, and to see what remained of the great effort which he had made to defend the place, were two Englishmen. One was the hero of this little history; and the other was a young man of considerably less weight in the world. The less I say of the latter the better; but it is necessary that I should give some description of the former.

The Rev. Augustus Horne was, at the time of my narrative, a beneficed clergyman of the Church of England. The profession which he had graced sat easily on him. Its external marks and signs were as pleasing to his friends as were its internal comforts to himself. He was a man of much quiet mirth, full of polished wit, and on some rare occasions he could descend to the more noisy hilarity of a joke. Loved by his friends he loved all the world. He had known no care and seen no sorrow. Always intended for holy orders he had entered them without a scruple, and remained within their pale without a regret. At twenty-four he had been a deacon, at twenty-seven a priest, at thirty a rector, and at thirty-five a prebendary; and as his rectory was rich and his prebendal stall well paid, the Rev. Augustus Horne was called by all, and called himself, a happy man. His stature was about six feet two, and his corpulence exceeded even those bounds which symmetry would have preferred as being most perfectly compatible even with such a height. But nevertheless Mr. Horne was a well-made man; his hands and feet were small; his face was handsome, frank, and full of expression; his bright eyes twinkled with humour; his finely-cut mouth disclosed two marvellous rows of well-preserved ivory; and his slightly aquiline nose was just such a projection as one would wish to see on the face of a well-fed good-natured dignitary of the Church of England. When I add to all this that the reverend gentleman was as generous as he was rich—and the kind mother in whose arms he had been nurtured had taken care that he should never want—I need hardly say that I was blessed with a very pleasant travelling companion.

I must mention one more interesting particular. Mr. Horne was rather inclined to dandyism, in an innocent way. His clerical starched neckcloth was always of the whitest, his cambric handkerchief of the finest, his bands adorned with the broadest border; his sable suit never degenerated to a rusty brown; it not only gave on all occasions glossy evidence of freshness, but also of the talent which the artisan had displayed in turning out a well-dressed clergyman of the Church of England. His hair was ever brushed with scrupulous attention, and showed in its regular waves the guardian care of each separate bristle. And all this was done with that ease and grace which should be the characteristics of a dignitary of the established English Church.

I had accompanied Mr. Horne to the Rhine; and we had reached Brussels on our return, just at the close of that revolution which ended in affording a throne to the son-in-law of George the Fourth. At that moment General Chasse's name and fame were in every man's mouth, and, like other curious admirers of the brave, Mr. Horne determined to devote two days to the scene of the late events at Antwerp. Antwerp, moreover, possesses perhaps the finest spire, and certainly one of the three or four finest pictures, in the world. Of General Chasse, of the cathedral, and of the Rubens, I had heard much, and was therefore well pleased that such should be his resolution. This accomplished we were to return to Brussels; and thence, via Ghent, Ostend, and Dover, I to complete my legal studies in London, and Mr. Horne to enjoy once more the peaceful retirement of Ollerton rectory. As we were to be absent from Brussels but one night we were enabled to indulge in the gratification of travelling without our luggage. A small sac-de-nuit was prepared; brushes, combs, razors, strops, a change of linen, &c. &c., were carefully put up; but our heavy baggage, our coats, waistcoats, and other wearing apparel were unnecessary. It was delightful to feel oneself so light-handed. The reverend gentleman, with my humble self by his side, left the portal of the Hotel de Belle Vue at 7 a.m., in good humour with all the world. There were no railroads in those days; but a cabriolet, big enough to hold six persons, with rope traces and corresponding appendages, deposited us at the Golden Fleece in something less than six hours. The inward man was duly fortified, and we started for the castle.

It boots not here to describe the effects which gunpowder and grape-shot had had on the walls of Antwerp. Let the curious in these matters read the horrors of the siege of Troy, or the history of Jerusalem taken by Titus. The one may be found in Homer, and the other in Josephus. Or if they prefer doings of a later date there is the taking of Sebastopol, as narrated in the columns of the "Times" newspaper. The accounts are equally true, instructive, and intelligible. In the mean time allow the Rev. Augustus Horne and myself to enter the private chambers of the renowned though defeated general.

We rambled for a while through the covered way, over the glacis and along the counterscarp, and listened to the guide as he detailed to us, in already accustomed words, how the siege had gone. Then we got into the private apartments of the general, and, having dexterously shaken off our attendant, wandered at large among the deserted rooms.

"It is clear that no one ever comes here," said I.

"No," said the Rev. Augustus; "it seems not; and to tell the truth, I don't know why any one should come. The chambers in themselves are not attractive."

What he said was true. They were plain, ugly, square, unfurnished rooms, here a big one, and there a little one, as is usual in most houses;—unfurnished, that is, for the most part. In one place we did find a table and a few chairs, in another a bedstead, and so on. But to me it was pleasant to indulge in those ruminations which any traces of the great or unfortunate create in softly sympathising minds. For a time we communicated our thoughts to each other as we roamed free as air through the apartments; and then I lingered for a few moments behind, while Mr. Horne moved on with a quicker step.

At last I entered the bedchamber of the general, and there I overtook my friend. He was inspecting, with much attention, an article of the great man's wardrobe which he held in his hand. It was precisely that virile habiliment to which a well-known gallant captain alludes in his conversation with the posthumous appearance of Miss Bailey, as containing a Bank of England 5 pound note.

"The general must have been a large man, George, or he would hardly have filled these," said Mr. Horne, holding up to the light the respectable leathern articles in question. "He must have been a very large man,—the largest man in Antwerp, I should think; or else his tailor has done him more than justice."

They were certainly large, and had about them a charming regimental military appearance. They were made of white leather, with bright metal buttons at the knees and bright metal buttons at the top. They owned no pockets, and were, with the exception of the legitimate outlet, continuous in the circumference of the waistband. No dangling strings gave them an appearance of senile imbecility. Were it not for a certain rigidity, sternness, and mental inflexibility,—we will call it military ardour,—with which they were imbued, they would have created envy in the bosom of a fox-hunter.

Mr. Horne was no fox-hunter, but still he seemed to be irresistibly taken with the lady-like propensity of wishing to wear them. "Surely, George," he said, "the general must have been a stouter man than I am"—and he contemplated his own proportions with complacency—"these what's-the-names are quite big enough for me."

I differed in opinion, and was obliged to explain that I thought he did the good living of Ollerton insufficient justice.

"I am sure they are large enough for me," he repeated, with considerable obstinacy. I smiled incredulously; and then to settle the matter he resolved that he would try them on. Nobody had been in these rooms for the last hour, and it appeared as though they were never visited. Even the guide had not come on with us, but was employed in showing other parties about the fortifications. It was clear that this portion of the building was left desolate, and that the experiment might be safely made. So the sportive rector declared that he would for a short time wear the regimentals which had once contained the valorous heart of General Chassé.

With all decorum the Rev. Mr. Horne divested himself of the work of the London artist's needle, and, carefully placing his own garments beyond the reach of dust, essayed to fit himself in military garb.

At that important moment—at the critical instant of the attempt—the clatter of female voices was heard approaching the chamber. They must have suddenly come round some passage corner, for it was evident by the sound that they were close upon us before we had any warning of their advent. At this very minute Mr. Horne was somewhat embarrassed in his attempts, and was not fully in possession of his usual active powers of movement, nor of his usual presence of mind. He only looked for escape; and seeing a door partly open, he with difficulty retreated through it, and I followed him. We found that we were in a small dressing-room; and as by good luck the door was defended by an inner bolt, my friend was able to protect himself.

"There shall be another siege, at any rate as stout as the last, before I surrender," said he.

As the ladies seemed inclined to linger in the room it became a matter of importance that the above-named articles should fit, not only for ornament but for use. It was very cold, and Mr. Horne was altogether unused to move in a Highland sphere of life. But alas, alas! General Chassé had not been nurtured in the classical retirement of Ollerton. The ungiving leather would stretch no point to accommodate the divine, though it had been willing to minister to the convenience of the soldier. Mr. Horne was vexed and chilled; and throwing the now hateful garments into a corner, and protecting himself from the cold as best he might by standing with his knees together and his body somewhat bent so as to give the skirts of his coat an opportunity of doing extra duty, he begged me to see if those jabbering females were not going to leave him in peace to recover his own property. I accordingly went to the door, and opening it to a small extent I peeped through.

Who shall describe my horror at the sight which I then saw? The scene, which had hitherto been tinted with comic effect, was now becoming so decidedly tragic that I did not dare at once to acquaint my worthy pastor with that which was occurring,—and, alas! had already occurred.

Five country-women of our own—it was easy to know them by their dress and general aspect—were standing in the middle of the room; and one of them, the centre of the group, the senior harpy of the lot, a maiden lady—I could have sworn to that—with a red nose, held in one hand a huge pair of scissors, and in the other— the already devoted goods of my most unfortunate companion! Down from the waistband, through that goodly expanse, a fell gash had already gone through and through; and in useless, unbecoming disorder the broadcloth fell pendant from her arm on this side and on that. At that moment I confess that I had not the courage to speak to Mr. Horne,—not even to look at him.

I must describe that group. Of the figure next to me I could only see the back. It was a broad back done up in black silk not of the newest. The whole figure, one may say, was dumpy. The black silk was not long, as dresses now are worn, nor wide in its skirts. In every way it was skimpy, considering the breadth it had to cover; and below the silk I saw the heels of two thick shoes, and enough to swear by of two woollen stockings. Above the silk was a red and blue shawl; and above that a ponderous, elaborate brown bonnet, as to the materials of which I should not wish to undergo an examination. Over and beyond this I could only see the backs of her two hands. They were held up as though in wonder at that which the red-nosed holder of the scissors had dared to do.

Opposite to this lady, and with her face fully turned to me, was a kindly-looking, fat motherly woman, with light-coloured hair, not in the best order. She was hot and scarlet with exercise, being perhaps too stout for the steep steps of the fortress; and in one hand she held a handkerchief, with which from time to time she wiped her brow. In the other hand she held one of the extremities of my friend's property, feeling—good, careful soul!—what was the texture of the cloth. As she did so, I could see a glance of approbation pass across her warm features. I liked that lady's face, in spite of her untidy hair, and felt that had she been alone my friend would not have been injured.

On either side of her there stood a flaxen-haired maiden, with long curls, large blue eyes, fresh red cheeks, an undefined lumpy nose, and large good-humoured mouth. They were as like as two peas, only that one was half an inch taller than the other; and there was no difficulty in discovering, at a moment's glance, that they were the children of that over-heated matron who was feeling the web of my friend's cloth.

But the principal figure was she who held the centre place in the group. She was tall and thin, with fierce-looking eyes, rendered more fierce by the spectacles which she wore; with a red nose as I said before; and about her an undescribable something which quite convinced me that she had never known—could never know—aught of the comforts of married life. It was she who held the scissors and the black garments. It was she who had given that unkind cut. As I looked at her she whisked herself quickly round from one companion to the other, triumphing in what she had done, and ready to triumph further in what she was about to do. I immediately conceived a deep hatred for that Queen of the Harpies.

"Well, I suppose they can't be wanted again," said the mother, rubbing her forehead.

"Oh dear no!" said she of the red nose. "They are relics!" I thought to leap forth; but for what purpose should I have leaped? The accursed scissors had already done their work; and the symmetry, nay, even the utility of the vestment was destroyed.

"General Chassé wore a very good article;—I will say that for him," continued the mother.

"Of course he did!" said the Queen Harpy. "Why should he not, seeing that the country paid for it for him? Well, ladies, who's for having a bit?"

"Oh my! you won't go for to cut them up," said the stout back.

"Won't I," said the scissors; and she immediately made another incision. "Who's for having a bit? Don't all speak at once."

"I should like a morsel for a pincushion," said flaxen-haired Miss No. 1, a young lady about nineteen, actuated by a general affection for all sword-bearing, fire-eating heroes. "I should like to have something to make me think of the poor general!"

Snip, snip went the scissors with professional rapidity, and a round piece was extracted from the back of the calf of the left leg. I shuddered with horror; and so did the Rev. Augustus Horne with cold.

"I hardly think it's proper to cut them up," said Miss No. 2.

"Oh isn't it?" said the harpy. "Then I'll do what's improper!" And she got her finger and thumb well through the holes in the scissors' handles. As she spoke resolution was plainly marked on her brow.

"Well, if they are to be cut up, I should certainly like a bit for a pen-wiper," said No. 2. No. 2 was a literary young lady with a periodical correspondence, a journal, and an album. Snip, snip went the scissors again, and the broad part of the upper right division afforded ample materials for a pen-wiper.

Then the lady with the back, seeing that the desecration of the article had been completed, plucked up heart of courage and put in her little request; "I think I might have a needle-case out of it," said she, "just as a suvneer of the poor general"—and a long fragment cut rapidly out of the waistband afforded her unqualified delight.

Mamma, with the hot face and untidy hair, came next. "Well, girls," she said, "as you are all served, I don't see why I'm to be left out. Perhaps, Miss Grogram"—she was an old maid, you see—"perhaps, Miss Grogram, you could get me as much as would make a decent-sized reticule."

There was not the slightest difficulty in doing this. The harpy in the centre again went to work, snip, snip, and extracting from that portion of the affairs which usually sustained the greater portion of Mr. Horne's weight two large round pieces of cloth, presented them to the well-pleased matron. "The general knew well where to get a bit of good broadcloth, certainly," said she, again feeling the pieces.

"And now for No. 1," said she whom I so absolutely hated; "I think there is still enough for a pair of slippers. There's nothing so nice for the house as good black cloth slippers that are warm to the feet and don't show the dirt." And so saying, she spread out on the floor the lacerated remainders.

"There's a nice bit there," said young lady No. 2, poking at one of the pockets with the end of her parasol.

"Yes," said the harpy, contemplating her plunder. "But I'm thinking whether I couldn't get leggings as well. I always wear leggings in the thick of the winter." And so she concluded her operations, and there was nothing left but a melancholy skeleton of seams and buttons.

All this having been achieved, they pocketed their plunder and prepared to depart. There are people who have a wonderful appetite for relics. A stone with which Washington had broken a window when a boy—with which he had done so or had not, for there is little difference; a button that was on a coat of Napoleon's, or on that of one of his lackeys; a bullet said to have been picked up at Waterloo or Bunker's Hill; these, and suchlike things are great treasures. And their most desirable characteristic is the ease with which they are attained. Any bullet or any button does the work. Faith alone is necessary. And now these ladies had made themselves happy and glorious with "Relics" of General Chassé cut from the ill-used habiliments of an elderly English gentleman!

They departed at last, and Mr. Horne, for once in an ill humour, followed me into the bedroom. Here I must be excused if I draw a veil over his manly sorrow at discovering what fate had done for him. Remember what was his position, unclothed in the Castle of Antwerp! The nearest suitable change for those which had been destroyed was locked up in his portmanteau at the Hotel de Belle Rue in Brussels! He had nothing left to him—literally nothing, in that Antwerp world. There was no other wretched being wandering then in that Dutch town so utterly denuded of the goods of life. For what is a man fit,—for what can he be fit,—when left in such a position? There are some evils which seem utterly to crush a man; and if there be any misfortune to which a man may be allowed to succumb without imputation on his manliness, surely it is such as this. How was Mr. Horne to return to his hotel without incurring the displeasure of the municipality? That was my first thought.

He had a cloak, but it was at the inn; and I found that my friend was oppressed with a great horror at the idea of being left alone; so that I could not go in search of it. There is an old saying, that no man is a hero to his valet de chambre, the reason doubtless being this, that it is customary for his valet to see the hero divested of those trappings in which so much of the heroic consists. Who reverences a clergyman without his gown, or a warrior without his sword and sabre-tasche? What would even Minerva be without her helmet?

I do not wish it to be understood that I no longer reverenced Mr. Horne because he was in an undress; but he himself certainly lost much of his composed, well-sustained dignity of demeanour. He was fearful and querulous, cold, and rather cross. When, forgetting his size, I offered him my own, he thought that I was laughing at him. He began to be afraid that the story would get abroad, and he then and there exacted a promise that I would never tell it during his lifetime. I have kept my word; but now my old friend has been gathered to his fathers, full of years.

At last I got him to the hotel. It was long before he would leave the castle, cloaked though he was;—not, indeed, till the shades of evening had dimmed the outlines of men and things, and made indistinct the outward garniture of those who passed to and fro in the streets. Then, wrapped in his cloak, Mr. Horne followed me along the quays and through the narrowest of the streets; and at length, without venturing to return the gaze of any one in the hotel court, he made his way up to his own bedroom.

Dinnerless and supperless he went to his couch. But when there he did consent to receive some consolation in the shape of mutton cutlets and fried potatoes, a savory omelet, and a bottle of claret. The mutton cutlets and fried potatoes at the Golden Fleece at Antwerp are—or were then, for I am speaking now of well-nigh thirty years since—remarkably good; the claret, also, was of the best; and so, by degrees, the look of despairing dismay passed from his face, and some scintillations of the old fire returned to his eyes.

"I wonder whether they find themselves much happier for what they have got?" said he.

"A great deal happier," said I. "They'll boast of those things to all their friends at home, and we shall doubtless see some account of their success in the newspapers."

"It would be delightful to expose their blunder,—to show them up. Would it not, George? To turn the tables on them?"

"Yes," said I, "I should like to have the laugh against them."

"So would I, only that I should compromise myself by telling the story. It wouldn't do at all to have it told at Oxford with my name attached to it."

To this also I assented. To what would I not have assented in my anxiety to make him happy after his misery?

But all was not over yet. He was in bed now, but it was necessary that he should rise again on the morrow. At home, in England, what was required might perhaps have been made during the night; but here, among the slow Flemings, any such exertion would have been impossible. Mr. Horne, moreover, had no desire to be troubled in his retirement by a tailor.

Now the landlord of the Golden Fleece was a very stout man,—a very stout man indeed. Looking at him as he stood with his hands in his pockets at the portal of his own establishment, I could not but think that he was stouter even than Mr. Horne. But then he was certainly much shorter, and the want of due proportion probably added to his unwieldy appearance. I walked round him once or twice wishfully, measuring him in my eye, and thinking of what texture might be the Sunday best of such a man. The clothes which he then had on were certainly not exactly suited to Mr. Horne's tastes.

He saw that I was observing him, and appeared uneasy and offended. I had already ascertained that he spoke a little English. Of Flemish I knew literally nothing, and in French, with which probably he was also acquainted, I was by no means voluble. The business which I had to transact was intricate, and I required the use of my mother-tongue.

It was intricate and delicate, and difficult withal. I began by remarking on the weather, but he did not take my remarks kindly. I am inclined to fancy that he thought I was desirous of borrowing money from him. At any rate he gave me no encouragement in my first advances.

"Vat misfortune?" at last he asked, when I had succeeded in making him understand that a gentleman up stairs required his assistance.

"He has lost these things," and I took hold of my own garments. "It's a long story, or I'd tell you how; but he has not a pair in the world till he gets back to Brussels,—unless you can lend him one."

"Lost hees br-?" and he opened his eyes wide, and looked at me with astonishment.

"Yes, yes, exactly so," said I, interrupting him. "Most astonishing thing, isn't it? But it's quite true."

"Vas hees money in de pocket?" asked my auspicious landlord.

"No, no, no. It's not so bad as that, his money is all right. I had the money, luckily."

"Ah! dat is better. But he have lost hees b-?"

"Yes, yes;" I was now getting rather impatient. "There is no mistake about it. He has lost them as sure as you stand there." And then I proceeded to explain that as the gentleman in question was very stout, and as he, the landlord, was stoat also, he might assist us in this great calamity by a loan from his own wardrobe.

When he found that the money was not in the pocket, and that his bill therefore would be paid, he was not indisposed to be gracious. He would, he said, desire his servant to take up what was required to Mr. Horne's chamber. I endeavoured to make him understand that a sombre colour would be preferable; but he only answered that he would put the best that he had at the gentleman's disposal. He could not think of offering anything less than his best on such an occasion. And then he turned his back and went his way, muttering as he went something in Flemish, which I believed to be an exclamation of astonishment that any man should, under any circumstances, lose such an article.

It was now getting late; so when I had taken a short stroll by myself, I went to bed without disturbing Mr. Horne again that night. On the following morning I thought it best not to go to him unless he sent for me; so I desired the boots to let him know that I had ordered breakfast in a private room, and that I would await him there unless he wished to see me. He sent me word back to say that he would be with me very shortly.

He did not keep me waiting above half an hour, but I confess that that half hour was not pleasantly spent. I feared that his temper would be tried in dressing, and that he would not be able to eat his breakfast in a happy state of mind. So that when I heard his heavy footstep advancing along the passage my heart did misgive me, and I felt that I was trembling.

That step was certainly slower and more ponderous than usual. There was always a certain dignity in the very sound of his movements, but now this seemed to have been enhanced. To judge merely by the step one would have said that a bishop was coming that way instead of a prebendary.

And then he entered. In the upper half of his august person no alteration was perceptible. The hair was as regular and as graceful as ever, the handkerchief as white, the coat as immaculate; but below his well-filled waistcoat a pair of red plush began to shine in unmitigated splendour, and continued from thence down to within an inch above his knee; nor, as it appeared, could any pulling induce them to descend lower. Mr. Horne always wore black silk stockings,—at least so the world supposed, but it was now apparent that the world had been wrong in presuming him to be guilty of such extravagance. Those, at any rate, which he exhibited on the present occasion were more economical. They were silk to the calf, but thence upwards they continued their career in white cotton. These then followed the plush; first two snowy, full-sized pillars of white, and then two jet columns of flossy silk. Such was the appearance, on that well-remembered morning, of the Rev. Augustus Horne, as he entered the room in which his breakfast was prepared.

I could see at a glance that a dark frown contracted his eyebrows, and that the compressed muscles of his upper lip gave a strange degree of austerity to his open face. He carried his head proudly on high, determined to be dignified in spite of his misfortunes, and advanced two steps into the room without a remark, as though he were able to show that neither red plush nor black cloth could disarrange the equal poise of his mighty mind!

And after all what are a man's garments but the outward husks in which the fruit is kept, duly tempered from the wind?

"The rank is but the guinea stamp,
The man's the gowd for a' that."

And is not the tailor's art as little worthy, as insignificant as that of the king who makes

"A marquis, duke, and a' that"?

Who would be content to think that his manly dignity depended on his coat and waistcoat, or his hold on the world's esteem on any other garment of usual wear? That no such weakness soiled his mind Mr. Horne was determined to prove; and thus he entered the room with measured tread, and stern dignified demeanour.

Having advanced two steps his eye caught mine. I do not know whether he was moved by some unconscious smile on my part;—for in truth I endeavoured to seem as indifferent as himself to the nature of his dress;—or whether he was invincibly tickled by some inward fancy of his own, but suddenly his advancing step ceased, a broad flash of comic humour spread itself over his features, he retreated with his back against the wall, and then burst out into an immoderate roar of loud laughter.

And I—what else could I then do but laugh? He laughed, and I laughed. He roared, and I roared. He lifted up his vast legs to view till the rays of the morning sun shone through the window on the bright hues which he displayed; and he did not sit down to his breakfast till he had in every fantastic attitude shown off to the best advantage the red plush of which he had so recently become proud.

An Antwerp private cabriolet on that day reached the yard of the Hotel de Belle Vue at about 4 p.m., and four waiters, in a frenzy of astonishment, saw the Reverend Augustus Horne descend from the vehicle and seek his chamber dressed in the garments which I have described. But I am inclined to think that he never again favoured any of his friends with such a sight.

It was on the next evening after this that I went out to drink tea with two maiden ladies, relatives of mine, who kept a seminary for English girls at Brussels. The Misses Macmanus were very worthy women, and earned their bread in an upright, painstaking manner. I would not for worlds have passed through Brussels without paying them this compliment. They were, however, perhaps a little dull, and I was aware that I should not probably meet in their drawing-room many of the fashionable inhabitants of the city. Mr. Horne had declined to accompany me; but in doing so he was good enough to express a warm admiration for the character of my worthy cousins.

The elder Miss Macmanus, in her little note, had informed me that she would have the pleasure of introducing me to a few of my "compatriots." I presumed she meant Englishmen; and as I was in the habit of meeting such every day of my life at home, I cannot say that I was peculiarly elevated by the promise. When, however, I entered the room, there was no Englishman there;—there was no man of any kind. There were twelve ladies collected together with the view of making the evening pass agreeably to me, the single virile being among them all. I felt as though I were a sort of Mohammed in Paradise; but I certainly felt also that the Paradise was none of my own choosing.

In the centre of the amphitheatre which the ladies formed sat the two Misses Macmanus;—there, at least, they sat when they had completed the process of shaking hands with me. To the left of them, making one wing of the semicircle, were arranged the five pupils by attending to whom the Misses Macmanus earned their living; and the other wing consisted of the five ladies who had furnished themselves with relics of General Chasse. They were my "compatriots."

I was introduced to them all, one after the other; but their names did not abide in my memory one moment. I was thinking too much of the singularity of the adventure, and could not attend to such minutiae. That the red-rosed harpy was Miss Grogram, that I remembered;—that, I may say, I shall never forget. But whether the motherly lady with the somewhat blowsy hair was Mrs. Jones, or Mrs. Green, or Mrs. Walker, I cannot now say. The dumpy female with the broad back was always called Aunt Sally by the young ladies.

Too much sugar spoils one's tea; I think I have heard that even prosperity will cloy when it comes in overdoses; and a schoolboy has been known to be overdone with jam. I myself have always been peculiarly attached to ladies' society, and have avoided bachelor parties as things execrable in their very nature. But on this special occasion I felt myself to be that schoolboy;—I was literally overdone with jam. My tea was all sugar, so that I could not drink it. I was one among twelve. What could I do or say? The proportion of alloy was too small to have any effect in changing the nature of the virgin silver, and the conversation became absolutely feminine.

I must confess also that my previous experience as to these compatriots of mine had not prejudiced me in their favour. I regarded them with,—I am ashamed to say so, seeing that they were ladies,—but almost with loathing. When last I had seen them their occupation had reminded me of some obscene feast of harpies, or almost of ghouls. They had brought down to the verge of desperation the man whom of all men I most venerated. On these accounts I was inclined to be taciturn with reference to them;—and then what could I have to say to the Misses Macmanus's five pupils?

My cousin at first made an effort or two in my favour, but these efforts were fruitless. I soon died away into utter unrecognised insignificance, and the conversation, as I have before said, became feminine. And indeed that horrid Miss Grogram, who was, as it were, the princess of the ghouls, nearly monopolised the whole of it. Mamma Jones—we will call her Jones for the occasion—put in a word now and then, as did also the elder and more energetic Miss Macmanus. The dumpy lady with the broad back ate tea-cake incessantly; the two daughters looked scornful, as though they were above their company with reference to the five pupils; and the five pupils themselves sat in a row with the utmost propriety, each with her hands crossed on her lap before her.

Of what they were talking at last I became utterly oblivious. They had ignored me, going into realms of muslin, questions of maid-servants, female rights, and cheap under-clothing; and I therefore had ignored them. My mind had gone back to Mr. Horne and his garments. While they spoke of their rights, I was thinking of his wrongs; when they mentioned the price of flannel, I thought of that of broadcloth.

But of a sudden my attention was arrested. Miss Macmanus had said something of the black silks of Antwerp, when Miss Grogram replied that she had just returned from that city and had there enjoyed a great success. My cousin had again asked something about the black silks, thinking, no doubt, that Miss Grogram had achieved some bargain, but that lady had soon undeceived her.

"Oh no," said Miss Grogram, "it was at the castle. We got such beautiful relics of General Chassé! Didn't we, Mrs. Jones?"

"Indeed we did," said Mrs. Jones, bringing out from beneath the skirts of her dress and ostensibly displaying a large black bag.

"And I've got such a beautiful needle-case," said the broad-back, displaying her prize. "I've been making it up all the morning." And she handed over the article to Miss Macmanus.

"And only look at this duck of a pen-wiper," simpered flaxen-hair No. 2. "Only think of wiping one's pens with relics of General Chassé!" and she handed it over to the other Miss Macmanus.

"And mine's a pin-cushion," said No. 1, exhibiting the trophy.

"But that's nothing to what I've got," said Miss Grogram. "In the first place, there's a pair of slippers,—a beautiful pair;—they're not made up yet, of course; and then—"

The two Misses Macmanus and their five pupils were sitting open-eared, open-eyed, and open-mouthed. How all these sombre-looking articles could be relics of General Chassé did not at first appear clear to them.

"What are they, Miss Grogram?" said the elder Miss Macmanus, holding the needle-case in one hand and Mrs. Jones's bag in the other. Miss Macmanus was a strong-minded female, and I reverenced my cousin when I saw the decided way in which she intended to put down the greedy arrogance of Miss Grogram.

"They are relics."

"But where do they come from, Miss Grogram?"

"Why, from the castle, to be sure;—from General Chassé's own rooms."

"Did anybody sell them to you?"

"No."

"Or give them to you?"

"Why, no;—at least not exactly give."

"There they were, and she took 'em," said the broad-back. Oh, what a look Miss Grogram gave her! "Took them! of course I took them. That is, you took them as much as I did. They were things that we found lying about."

"What things?" asked Miss Macmanus, in a peculiarly strong-minded tone.

Miss Grogram seemed to be for a moment silenced. I had been ignored, as I have said, and my existence forgotten; but now I observed that the eyes of the culprits were turned towards me,—the eyes, that is, of four of them. Mrs. Jones looked at me from beneath her fan; the two girls glanced at me furtively, and then their eyes fell to the lowest flounces of their frocks.

Miss Grogram turned her spectacles right upon me, and I fancied that she nodded her head at me as a sort of answer to Miss Macmanus. The five pupils opened their mouths and eyes wider; but she of the broad back was nothing abashed. It would have been nothing to her had there been a dozen gentlemen in the room.

"We just found a pair of black—." The whole truth was told in the plainest possible language.

"Oh, Aunt Sally!" "Aunt Sally, how can you?" "Hold your tongue, Aunt Sally!"

"And then Miss Grogram just cut them up with her scissors," continued Aunt Sally, not a whit abashed, "and gave us each a bit, only she took more than half for herself." It was clear to me that there had been some quarrel, some delicious quarrel, between Aunt Sally and Miss Grogram. Through the whole adventure I had rather respected Aunt Sally. "She took more than half for herself," continued Aunt Sally. "She kept all the—"

"Jemima," said the elder Miss Macmanus, interrupting the speaker and addressing her sister, "it is time, I think, for the young ladies to retire. Will you be kind enough to see them to their rooms?" The five pupils thereupon rose from their seats—and courtesied. They then left the room in file, the younger Miss Macmanus showing them the way.

"But we haven't done any harm, have we?" asked Mrs. Jones, with some tremulousness in her voice.

"Well, I don't know," said Miss Macmanus. "What I'm thinking of now is this;—to whom, I wonder, did the garments properly belong? Who had been the owner and wearer of them?"

"Why, General Chassé of course," said Miss Grogram.

"They were the general's," repeated the two young ladies; blushing, however, as they alluded to the subject.

"Well, we thought they were the general's, certainly; and a very excellent article they were," said Mrs. Jones.

"Perhaps they were the butler's?" said Aunt Sally. I certainly had not given her credit for so much sarcasm.

"Butler's!" exclaimed Miss Grogram, with a toss of her head.

"Oh, Aunt Sally, Aunt Sally! how can you?" shrieked the two young ladies.

"Oh laws!" ejaculated Mrs. Jones.

"I don't think that they could have belonged to the butler," said Miss Macmanus, with much authority, "seeing that domestics in this country are never clad in garments of that description; so far my own observation enables me to speak with certainty. But it is equally sure that they were never the property of the general lately in command at Antwerp. Generals, when they are in full dress, wear ornamental lace upon their—their regimentals; and when—" So much she said, and something more, which it may be unnecessary that I should repeat; but such were her eloquence and logic that no doubt would have been left on the mind of any impartial hearer. If an argumentative speaker ever proved anything, Miss Macmanus proved that General Chassé had never been the wearer of the article in question.

"But I know very well they were his!" said Miss Grogram, who was not an impartial hearer. "Of course they were; whose else's should they be?"

"I'm sure I hope they were his," said one of the young ladies, almost crying.

"I wish I'd never taken it," said the other.

"Dear, dear, dear!" said Mrs. Jones.

"I'll give you my needle-case, Miss Grogram," said Aunt Sally.

I had sat hitherto silent during the whole scene, meditating how best I might confound the red-nosed harpy. Now, I thought, was the time for me to strike in.

"I really think, ladies, that there has been some mistake," said I.

"There has been no mistake at all, sir!" said Miss Grogram.

"Perhaps not," I answered, very mildly; "very likely not. But some affair of a similar nature was very much talked about in Antwerp yesterday."

"Oh laws!" again ejaculated Mrs. Jones.

"The affair I allude to has been talked about a good deal, certainly," I continued. "But perhaps it may be altogether a different circumstance."

"And what may be the circumstance to which you allude?" asked Miss Macmanus, in the same authoritative tone.

"I dare say it has nothing to do with these ladies," said I; "but an article of dress, of the nature they have described, was cut up in the Castle of Antwerp on the day before yesterday. It belonged to a gentleman who was visiting the place; and I was given to understand that he is determined to punish the people who have wronged him."

"It can't be the same," said Miss Grogram; but I could see that she was trembling.

"Oh laws! what will become of us?" said Mrs. Jones.

"You can all prove that I didn't touch them, and that I warned her not," said Aunt Sally. In the mean time the two young ladies had almost fainted behind their fans.

"But how had it come to pass," asked Miss Macmanus, "that the gentleman had—"

"I know nothing more about it, cousin," said I; "only it does seem that there is an odd coincidence."

Immediately after this I took my leave. I saw that I had avenged my friend, and spread dismay in the hearts of these who had injured him. I had learned in the course of the evening at what hotel the five ladies were staying; and in the course of the next morning I sauntered into the hall, and finding one of the porters alone, asked if they were still there. The man told me that they had started by the earliest diligence. "And," said he, "if you are a friend of theirs, perhaps you will take charge of these things, which they have left behind them?" So saying, he pointed to a table at the back of the hall, on which were lying the black bag, the black needle-case, the black pin cushion, and the black pen-wiper. There was also a heap of fragments of cloth which I well knew had been intended by Miss Grogram for the comfort of her feet and ancles.

I declined the commission, however. "They were no special friends of mine," I said; and I left all the relics still lying on the little table in the back hall.

"Upon the whole, I am satisfied!" said the Rev. Augustus Horne, when I told him the finale of the story.

RETURNING HOME

It is generally supposed that people who live at home,—good domestic people, who love tea and their arm-chairs, and who keep the parlour hearth-rug ever warm,—it is generally supposed that these are the people who value home the most, and best appreciate all the comforts of that cherished institution. I am inclined to doubt this. It is, I think, to those who live farthest away from home, to those who find the greatest difficulty in visiting home, that the word conveys the sweetest idea. In some distant parts of the world it may be that an Englishman acknowledges his permanent resting place; but there are many others in which he will not call his daily house, his home. He would, in his own idea, desecrate the word by doing so. His home is across the blue waters, in the little northern island, which perhaps he may visit no more; which he has left, at any rate, for half his life; from which circumstances, and the necessity of living, have banished him. His home is still in England, and when he speaks of home his thoughts are there.

No one can understand the intensity of this feeling who has not seen or felt the absence of interest in life which falls to the lot of many who have to eat their bread on distant soils. We are all apt to think that a life in strange countries will be a life of excitement, of stirring enterprise, and varied scenes;—that in abandoning the comforts of home, we shall receive in exchange more of movement and of adventure than would come in our way in our own tame country; and this feeling has, I am sure, sent many a young man roaming. Take any spirited fellow of twenty, and ask him whether he would like to go to Mexico for the next ten years! Prudence and his father may ultimately save him from such banishment, but he will not refuse without a pang of regret.

Alas! it is a mistake. Bread may be earned, and fortunes, perhaps, made in such countries; and as it is the destiny of our race to spread itself over the wide face of the globe, it is well that there should be something to gild and paint the outward face of that lot which so many are called upon to choose. But for a life of daily excitement, there is no life like life in England; and the farther that one goes from England the more stagnant, I think, do the waters of existence become.

But if it be so for men, it is ten times more so for women. An Englishman, if he be at Guatemala or Belize, must work for his bread, and that work will find him in thought and excitement. But what of his wife? Where will she find excitement? By what pursuit will she repay herself for all that she has left behind her at her mother's fireside? She will love her husband. Yes; that at least! If there be not that, there will be a hell, indeed. Then she will nurse her children, and talk of her—home. When the time shall come that her promised return thither is within a year or two of its accomplishment, her thoughts will all be fixed on that coming pleasure, as are the thoughts of a young girl on her first ball for the fortnight before that event comes off.

On the central plain of that portion of Central America which is called Costa Rica stands the city of San Jose. It is the capital of the Republic,—for Costa Rica is a Republic,—and, for Central America, is a town of some importance. It is in the middle of the coffee district, surrounded by rich soil on which the sugar-cane is produced, is blessed with a climate only moderately hot, and the native inhabitants are neither cut-throats nor cannibals. It may be said, therefore, that by comparison with some other spots to which Englishmen and others are congregated for the gathering together of money, San Jose may be considered as a happy region; but, nevertheless, a life there is not in every way desirable. It is a dull place, with little to interest either the eye or the ear. Although the heat of the tropics is but little felt there on account of its altitude, men and women become too lifeless for much enterprise. There is no society. There are a few Germans and a few Englishmen in the place, who see each other on matters of business during the day; but, sombre as life generally is, they seem to care little for each other's company on any other footing. I know not to what point the aspirations of the Germans may stretch themselves, but to the English the one idea that gives salt to life is the idea of home. On some day, however distant it may be, they will once more turn their faces towards the little northern island, and then all will be well with them.

To a certain Englishman there, and to his dear little wife, this prospect came some few years since somewhat suddenly. Events and tidings, it matters not which or what, brought it about that they resolved between themselves that they would start immediately;—almost immediately. They would pack up and leave San José within four months of the day on which their purpose was first formed. At San José a period of only four months for such a purpose was immediately. It creates a feeling of instant excitement, a necessity for instant doing, a consciousness that there was in those few weeks ample work both for the hands and thoughts,—work almost more than ample. The dear little wife, who for the last two years had been so listless, felt herself flurried.

"Harry," she said to her husband, "how shall we ever be ready?" And her pretty face was lighted up with unusual brightness at the happy thought of so much haste with such an object. "And baby's things too," she said, as she thought of all the various little articles of dress that would be needed. A journey from San José to Southampton cannot in truth be made as easily as one from London to Liverpool. Let us think of a month to be passed without any aid from the washerwoman, and the greatest part of that month amidst the sweltering heats of the West Indian tropics!

In the first month of her hurry and flurry Mrs. Arkwright was a happy woman. She would see her mother again and her sisters. It was now four years since she had left them on the quay at Southampton, while all their hearts were broken at the parting. She was a young bride then, going forth with her new lord to meet the stern world. He had then been home to look for a wife, and he had found what he looked for in the younger sister of his partner. For he, Henry Arkwright, and his wife's brother, Abel Ring, had established themselves together in San José. And now, she thought, how there would be another meeting on those quays at which there should be no broken hearts; at which there should be love without sorrow, and kisses, sweet with the sweetness of welcome, not bitter with the bitterness of parting. And people told her,—the few neighbours around her,—how happy, how fortunate she was to get home thus early in her life. They had been out some ten,—some twenty years, and still the day of their return was distant. And then she pressed her living baby to her breast, and wiped away a tear as she thought of the other darling whom she would leave beneath that distant sod.

And then came the question as to the route home. San Jose stands in the middle of the high plain of Costa Rica, half way between the Pacific and the Atlantic. The journey thence down to the Pacific is, by comparison, easy. There is a road, and the mules on which the travellers must ride go steadily and easily down to Punta Arenas, the port on that ocean. There are inns, too, on the way,—places of public entertainment at which refreshment may be obtained, and beds, or fair substitutes for beds. But then by this route the traveller must take a long additional sea voyage. He must convey himself and his weary baggage down to that wretched place on the Pacific, there wait for a steamer to take him to Panama, cross the isthmus, and reship himself in the other waters for his long journey home. That terrible unshipping and reshipping is a sore burden to the unaccustomed traveller. When it is absolutely necessary,—then indeed it is done without much thought; but in the case of the Arkwrights it was not absolutely necessary. And there was another reason which turned Mrs. Arkwright's heart against that journey by Punt' Arenas. The place is unhealthy, having at certain seasons a very bad name;—and here on their outward journey her husband had been taken ill. She had never ceased to think of the fortnight she had spent there among uncouth strangers, during a portion of which his life had trembled in the balance. Early, therefore, in those four months she begged that she might not be taken round by Punt' Arenas. There was another route. "Harry, if you love me, let me go by the Serapiqui." As to Harry's loving her, there was no doubt about that, as she well knew.

There was this other route by the Serapiqui river, and by Greytown. Greytown, it is true, is quite as unhealthy as Punt' Arenas, and by that route one's baggage must be shipped and unshipped into small boats. There are all manner of difficulties attached to it. Perhaps no direct road to and from any city on the world's surface is subject to sharper fatigue while it lasts. Journeying by this route also, the traveller leaves San Jose mounted on his mule, and so mounted he makes his way through the vast primeval forests down to the banks of the Serapiqui river. That there is a track for him is of course true; but it is simply a track, and during nine months of the twelve is so deep in mud that the mules sink in it to their bellies. Then, when the river has been reached, the traveller seats him in his canoe, and for two days is paddled down,—down along the Serapiqui, into the San Juan River, and down along the San Juan till he reaches Greytown, passing one night at some hut on the river side. At Greytown he waits for the steamer which will carry him his first stage on his road towards Southampton. He must be a connoisseur in disagreeables of every kind who can say with any precision whether Greytown or Punt' Arenas is the better place for a week's sojourn.

For a full month Mr. Arkwright would not give way to his wife. At first he all but conquered her by declaring that the Serapiqui journey would be dangerous for the baby; but she heard from some one that it could be made less fatiguing for the baby than the other route. A baby had been carried down in a litter strapped on to a mule's back. A guide at the mule's head would be necessary, and that was all. When once in her boat the baby would be as well as in her cradle. What purpose cannot a woman gain by perseverance? Her purpose in this instance Mrs. Arkwright did at last gain by persevering.

And then their preparations for the journey went on with much flurrying and hot haste. To us at home, who live and feel our life every day, the manufacture of endless baby-linen and the packing of mountains of clothes does not give an idea of much pleasurable excitement; but at San Jose, where there was scarcely motion enough in existence to prevent its waters from becoming foul with stagnation, this packing of baby-linen was delightful, and for a month or so the days went by with happy wings.

But by degrees reports began to reach both Arkwright and his wife as to this new route, which made them uneasy. The wet season had been prolonged, and even though they might not be deluged by rain themselves, the path would be in such a state of mud as to render the labour incessant. One or two people declared that the road was unfit at any time for a woman,—and then the river would be much swollen. These tidings did not reach Arkwright and his wife together, or at any rate not till late amidst their preparations, or a change might still have been made. As it was, after all her entreaties, Mrs. Arkwright did not like to ask him again to alter his plans; and he, having altered them once, was averse to change them again. So things went on till the mules and the boats had been hired, and things had gone so far that no change could then be made without much cost and trouble.

During the last ten days of their sojourn at San Jose, Mrs. Arkwright had lost all that appearance of joy which had cheered up her sweet face during the last few months. Terror at that terrible journey obliterated in her mind all the happiness which had arisen from the hope of being soon at home. She was thoroughly cowed by the danger to be encountered, and would gladly have gone down to Punt' Arenas, had it been now possible that she could so arrange it. It rained, and rained, and still rained, when there was now only a week from the time they started. Oh! if they could only wait for another month! But this she said to no one. After what had passed between her and her husband, she had not the heart to say such words to him. Arkwright himself was a man not given to much talking, a silent thoughtful man, stern withal in his outward bearing, but tender-hearted and loving in his nature. The sweet young wife who had left all, and come with him out to that dull distant place, was very dear to him,—dearer than she herself was aware, and in these days he was thinking much of her coming troubles. Why had he given way to her foolish prayers? Ah, why indeed? And thus the last few days of their sojourn in San Jose passed away from them. Once or twice during these days she did speak out, expressing her fears. Her feelings were too much for her, and she could not restrain herself. "Poor mamma," she said, "I shall never see her!" And then again, "Harry, I know I shall never reach home alive."

"Fanny, my darling, that is nonsense." But in order that his spoken word might not sound stern to her, he took her in his arms and kissed her.

"You must behave well, Fanny," he said to her the day before they started. Though her heart was then very low within her, she promised him that she would do her best, and then she made a great resolution. Though she should be dying on the road, she would not complain beyond the absolute necessity of her nature. She fully recognised his thoughtful tender kindness, for though he thus cautioned her, he never told her that the dangers which she feared were the result of her own choice. He never threw in her teeth those prayers which she had made, in yielding to which he knew that he had been weak.

Then came the morning of their departure. The party of travellers consisted of four besides the baby. There was Mr. Arkwright, his wife, and an English nurse, who was going to England with them, and her brother, Abel Ring, who was to accompany them as far as the Serapiqui River. When they had reached that, the real labour of the journey would be over.

They had eight mules; four for the four travellers, one for the baby, a spare mule laden simply with blankets, so that Mrs. Arkwright might change in order that she should not be fatigued by the fatigue of her beast, and two for their luggage. The portion of their baggage had already been sent off by Punt' Arenas, and would meet them at the other side of the Isthmus of Panama.

For the last four days the rain had ceased,—had ceased at any rate at San Jose. Those who knew the country well, would know that it might still be raining over those vast forests; but now as the matter was settled, they would hope for the best. On that morning on which they started the sun shone fairly, and they accepted this as an omen of good. Baby seemed to lay comfortably on her pile of blankets on the mule's back, and the face of the tall Indian guide who took his place at that mule's head pleased the anxious mother.

"Not leave him ever," he said in Spanish, laying his hand on the cord which was fastened to the beast's head; and not for one moment did he leave his charge, though the labour of sticking close to him was very great.

They had four attendants or guides, all of whom made the journey on foot. That they were all men of mixed race was probable; but three of them would have been called Spaniards, Spaniards, that is, of Costa Rica, and the other would be called an Indian. One of the Spaniards was the leader, or chief man of the party, but the others seemed to stand on an equal footing with each other; and indeed the place of greatest care had been given to the Indian.

For the first four or five miles their route lay along the high road which leads from San Jose to Punt' Arenas, and so far a group of acquaintances followed them, all mounted on mules. Here, where the ways forked, their road leading through the great forests to the Atlantic, they separated, and many tears were shed on each side. What might be the future life of the Arkwrights had not been absolutely fixed, but there was a strong hope on their part that they might never be forced to return to Costa Rica. Those from whom they now parted had not seemed to be dear to them in any especial degree while they all lived together in the same small town, seeing each other day by day; but now,—now that they might never meet again, a certain love sprang up for the old familiar faces, and women kissed each other who hitherto had hardly cared to enter each other's houses.

And then the party of the Arkwrights again started, and its steady work began. In the whole of the first day the way beneath their feet was tolerably good, and the weather continued fine. It was one long gradual ascent from the plain where the roads parted, but there was no real labour in travelling. Mrs. Arkwright rode beside her baby's mule, at the head of which the Indian always walked, and the two men went together in front. The husband had found that his wife would prefer this, as long as the road allowed of such an arrangement. Her heart was too full to admit of much speaking, and so they went on in silence.

The first night was passed in a hut by the roadside, which seemed to be deserted,—a hut or rancho as it is called in that country. Their food they had, of course, brought with them; and here, by common consent, they endeavoured in some sort to make themselves merry.

"Fanny," Arkwright said to her, "it is not so bad after all; eh, my darling?"

"No," she answered; "only that the mule tires one so. Will all the days be as long as that?"

He had not the heart to tell her that as regarded hours of work, that first day must of necessity be the shortest. They had risen to a considerable altitude, and the night was very cold; but baby was enveloped among a pile of coloured blankets, and things did not go very badly with them; only this, that when Fanny Arkwright rose from her hard bed, her limbs were more weary and much more stiff than they had been when Arkwright had lifted her from her mule.

On the second morning they mounted before the day had quite broken, in order that they might breakfast on the summit of the ridge which separates the two oceans. At this spot the good road comes to an end, and the forest track begins; and here also, they would, in truth, enter the forest, though their path had for some time been among straggling trees and bushes. And now, again, they rode two and two, up to this place of halting, Arkwright and Ring well knowing that from hence their labours would in truth commence.

Poor Mrs. Arkwright, when she reached this resting-place, would fain have remained there for the rest of the day. One word, in her low, plaintive voice, she said, asking whether they might not sleep in the large shed which stands there. But this was manifestly impossible. At such a pace they would never reach Greytown; and she spoke no further word when he told her that they must go on.

At about noon that day the file of travellers formed itself into the line which it afterwards kept during the whole of the journey, and then started by the narrow path into the forest. First walked the leader of the guides, then another man following him; Abel Ring came next, and behind him the maid-servant; then the baby's mule, with the Indian ever at its head; close at his heels followed Mrs. Arkwright, so that the mother's eye might be always on her child; and after her her husband; then another guide on foot completed the number of the travellers. In this way they went on and on, day after day, till they reached the banks of the Serapiqui, never once varying their places in the procession. As they started in the morning, so they went on till their noon-day's rest, and so again they made their evening march. In that journey there was no idea of variety, no searching after the pleasures of scenery, no attempts at conversation with any object of interest or amusement. What words were spoken were those simply needful, or produced by sympathy for suffering. So they journeyed, always in the same places, with one exception. They began their work with two guides leading them, but before the first day was over one of them had fallen back to the side of Mrs. Arkwright, for she was unable to sit on her mule without support.

Their daily work was divided into two stages, so as to give some hours for rest in the middle of the day. It had been arranged that the distance for each day should not be long,—should be very short as was thought by them all when they talked it over at San Jose; but now the hours which they passed in the saddle seemed to be endless. Their descent began from that ridge of which I have spoken, and they had no sooner turned their faces down upon the mountain slopes looking towards the Atlantic, than that passage of mud began to which there was no cessation till they found themselves on the banks of the Serapiqui river. I doubt whether it be possible to convey in words an adequate idea of the labour of riding over such a path. It is not that any active exertion is necessary,—that there is anything which requires doing. The traveller has before him the simple task of sitting on his mule from hour to hour, and of seeing that his knees do not get themselves jammed against the trees; but at every step the beast he rides has to drag his legs out from the deep clinging mud, and the body of the rider never knows one moment of ease. Why the mules do not die on the road, I cannot say. They live through it, and do not appear to suffer. They have their own way in everything, for no exertion on the rider's part will make them walk either faster or slower than is their wont.

On the day on which they entered the forest,—that being the second of their journey,—Mrs. Arkwright had asked for mercy, for permission to escape that second stage. On the next she allowed herself to be lifted into her saddle after her mid-day rest without a word. She had tried to sleep, but in vain; and had sat within a little hut, looking out upon the desolate scene before her, with her baby in her lap. She had this one comfort, that of all the travellers, she, the baby, suffered the least. They had now left the high grounds, and the heat was becoming great, though not as yet intense. And then, the Indian guide, looking out slowly over the forest, saw that the rain was not yet over. He spoke a word or two to one of his companions in a low voice and in a patois which Mrs. Arkwright did not understand, and then going after the husband, told him that the heavens were threatening.

"We have only two leagues," said Arkwright, "and it may perhaps hold up."

"It will begin in an hour," said the Indian, "and the two leagues are four hours."

"And tomorrow," asked Arkwright.

"Tomorrow, and tomorrow, and tomorrow it will still rain," said the guide, looking as he spoke up over the huge primeval forest.

"Then we had better start at once," said Arkwright, "before the first falling drops frighten the women." So the mules were brought out, and he lifted his uncomplaining wife on to the blankets which formed her pillion. The file again formed itself, and slowly they wound their way out from the small enclosure by which the hut was surrounded;—out from the enclosure on to a rough scrap of undrained pasture ground from which the trees had been cleared. In a few minutes they were once more struggling through the mud.

The name of the spot which our travellers had just left is Carablanco. There they found a woman living all alone. Her husband was away, she told them, at San Jose, but would be back to her when the dry weather came, to look up the young cattle which were straying in the forest. What a life for a woman! Nevertheless, in talking with Mrs. Arkwright she made no complaint of her own lot, but had done what little she could to comfort the poor lady who was so little able to bear the fatigues of her journey.

"Is the road very bad?" Mrs. Arkwright asked her in a whisper.

"Ah, yes; it is a bad road."

"And when shall we be at the river?"

"It took me four days," said the woman.

"Then I shall never see my mother again," and as she spoke Mrs. Arkwright pressed her baby to her bosom. Immediately after that her husband came in, and they started.

Their path now led away across the slope of a mountain which seemed to fall from the very top of that central ridge in an unbroken descent down to the valley at its foot. Hitherto, since they had entered the forest, they had had nothing before their eyes but the trees and bushes which grew close around them. But now a prospect of unrivalled grandeur was opened before them, if only had they been able to enjoy it. At the bottom of the valley ran a river, which, so great was the depth, looked like a moving silver cord; and on the other side of this there arose another mountain, steep but unbroken like that which they were passing,—unbroken, so that the eye could stretch from the river up to the very summit. Not a spot on that mountain side or on their side either was left uncovered by thick forest, which had stood there untouched by man since nature first produced it.

But all this was nothing to our travellers, nor was the clang of the macaws anything, or the roaring of the little congo ape. Nothing was gained by them from beautiful scenery, nor was there any fear from the beasts of prey. The immediate pain of each step of the journey drove all other feelings from them, and their thoughts were bounded by an intense desire for the evening halt.

And then, as the guide had prophesied, the rain began. At first it came in such small soft drops that it was found to be refreshing, but the clouds soon gathered and poured forth their collected waters as though it had not rained for months among those mountains. Not that it came in big drops, or with the violence which wind can give it, beating hither and thither, breaking branches from the trees, and rising up again as it pattered against the ground. There was no violence in the rain. It fell softly in a long, continuous, noiseless stream, sinking into everything that it touched, converting the deep rich earth on all sides into mud.

Not a word was said by any of them as it came on. The Indian covered the baby with her blanket, closer than she was covered before, and the guide who walked by Mrs. Arkwright's side drew her cloak around her knees. But such efforts were in vain. There is a rain that will penetrate everything, and such was the rain which fell upon them now. Nevertheless, as I have said, hardly a word was spoken. The poor woman, finding that the heat of her cloak increased her sufferings, threw it open again.

"Fanny," said her husband, "you had better let him protect you as well as he can."

She answered him merely by an impatient wave of her hand, intending to signify that she could not speak, but that in this matter she must have her way.

After that her husband made no further attempt to control her. He could see, however, that ever and again she would have slipped forward from her mule and fallen, had not the man by her side steadied her with his hand. At every tree he protected her knees and feet, though there was hardly room for him to move between the beast and the bank against which he was thrust.

And then, at last, that day's work was also over, and Fanny Arkwright slipped from her pillion down into her husband's arms at the door of another rancho in the forest. Here there lived a large family adding from year to year to the patch of ground which they had rescued from the wood, and valiantly doing their part in the extension of civilisation. Our party was but a few steps from the door when they left their mules, but Mrs. Arkwright did not now as heretofore hasten to receive her baby in her arms. When placed upon the ground, she still leaned against the mule, and her husband saw that he must carry her into the hut. This he did, and then, wet, mud-laden, dishevelled as she was, she laid herself down upon the planks that were to form her bed, and there stretched out her arms for her infant. On that evening they undressed and tended her like a child; and then when she was alone with her husband, she repeated to him her sad foreboding.

"Harry," she said, "I shall never see my mother again."

"Oh, yes, Fanny, you will see her and talk over all these troubles with pleasure. It is very bad, I know; but we shall live through it yet."

"You will, of course; and you will take baby home to her."

"And face her without you! No, my darling. Three more days' riding, or rather two and a half, will bring us to the river, and then your trouble will be over. All will be easy after that."

"Ah, Harry, you do not know."

"I do know that it is very bad, my girl, but you must cheer up. We shall be laughing at all this in a month's time."

On the following morning she allowed herself to be lifted up, speaking no word of remonstrance. Indeed she was like a child in their hands, having dropped all the dignity and authority of a woman's demeanour. It rained again during the whole of this day, and the heat was becoming oppressive as every hour they were descending nearer and nearer to the sea level. During this first stage hardly a word was spoken by any one; but when she was again taken from her mule she was in tears. The poor servant-girl, too, was almost prostrate with fatigue, and absolutely unable to wait upon her mistress, or even to do anything for herself. Nevertheless they did make the second stage, seeing that their mid-day resting place had been under the trees of the forest. Had there been any hut there, they would have remained for the night.

On the following day they rested altogether, though the place at which they remained had but few attractions. It was another forest hut inhabited by an old Spanish couple who were by no means willing to give them room, although they paid for their accommodation at exorbitant rates. It is one singularity of places strange and out of the way like such forest tracks as these, that money in small sums is hardly valued. Dollars there were not appreciated as sixpences are in this rich country. But there they stayed for a day, and the guides employed themselves in making a litter with long poles so that they might carry Mrs. Arkwright over a portion of the ground. Poor fellows! When once she had thus changed her mode of conveyance, she never again was lifted on to the mule.

There was strong reason against this day's delay. They were to go down the Serapiqui along with the post, which would overtake them on its banks. But if the post should pass them before they got there, it could not wait; and then they would be deprived of the best canoe on the water. Then also it was possible, if they encountered further delay, that the steamer might sail from Greytown without them, and a month's residence at that frightful place be thus made necessary.

The day's rest apparently did little to relieve Mrs. Arkwright's sufferings. On the following day she allowed herself to be put upon the mule, but after the first hour the beasts were stopped and she was taken off it. During that hour they had travelled hardly over half a league. At that time she so sobbed and moaned that Arkwright absolutely feared that she would perish in the forest, and he implored the guides to use the poles which they had prepared. She had declared to him over and over again that she felt sure that she should die, and, half-delirious with weariness and suffering, had begged him to leave her at the last hut. They had not yet come to the flat ground over which a litter might be carried with comparative ease; but nevertheless the men yielded, and she was placed in a recumbent position upon blankets, supported by boughs of trees. In this way she went through that day with somewhat less of suffering than before, and without that necessity for self-exertion which had been worse to her than any suffering.

There were places between that and the river at which one would have said that it was impossible that a litter should be carried, or even impossible that a mule should walk with a load on his back. But still they went on, and the men carried their burden without complaining. Not a word was said about money, or extra pay;— not a word, at least by them; and when Arkwright was profuse in his offer, their leader told him that they would not have done it for money. But for the poor suffering Senora they would make exertions which no money would have bought from them.

On the next day about noon the post did pass them, consisting of three strong men carrying great weights on their backs, suspended by bands from their foreheads. They travelled much quicker than our friends, and would reach the banks of the river that evening. In their ordinary course they would start down the river close upon daybreak on the following day; but, after some consultation with the guides, they agreed to wait till noon. Poor Mrs. Arkwright knew nothing of hours or of any such arrangements now, but her husband greatly doubted their power of catching this mail despatch. However, it did not much depend on their exertions that afternoon. Their resting-place was marked out for them, and they could not go beyond it, unless indeed they could make the whole journey, which was impossible.

But towards evening matters seemed to improve with them. They had now got on to ground which was more open, and the men who carried the litter could walk with greater ease. Mrs. Arkwright also complained less, and when they reached their resting-place on that night, said nothing of a wish to be left there to her fate. This was a place called Padregal, a cacao plantation, which had been cleared in the forest with much labour. There was a house here containing three rooms, and some forty or fifty acres round it had been stripped of the forest trees. But nevertheless the adventure had not been a prosperous one, for the place was at that time deserted. There were the cacao plants, but there was no one to pick the cacao. There was a certain melancholy beauty about the place. A few grand trees had been left standing near the house, and the grass around was rich and park-like. But it was deserted, and nothing was heard but the roaring of the congos. Ah me! Indeed it was a melancholy place as it was seen by some of that party afterwards.

On the following morning they were astir very early, and Mrs. Arkwright was so much better that she offered to sit again upon her mule. The men, however, declared that they would finish their task, and she was placed again upon the litter. And then with slow and weary step they did make their way to the river bank. It was not yet noon when they saw the mud fort which stands there, and as they drew into the enclosure round a small house which stands close by the river side, they saw the three postmen still busy about their packages.

"Thank God!" said Arkwright.

"Thank God, indeed!" said his brother. "All will be right with you now."

"Well, Fanny," said her husband, as he took her very gently from the litter and seated her on a bench which stood outside the door. "It is all over now,—is it not?"

She answered him by a shower of tears, but they were tears which brought her relief. He was aware of this, and therefore stood by her, still holding her by both her hands while her head rested against his side. "You will find the motion of the boat very gentle," he said; "indeed there will be no motion, and you and baby will sleep all the way down to Greytown." She did not answer him in words, but she looked up into his face, and he could see that her spirit was recovering itself.

There was almost a crowd of people collected on the spot, preparatory to the departure of the canoes. In the first place there was the commandant of the fort, to whom the small house belonged. He was looking to the passports of our friends, and with due diligence endeavouring to make something of the occasion, by discovering fatal legal impediments to the further prosecution of their voyage, which impediments would disappear on the payment of certain dollars. And then there were half a dozen Costa Rican soldiers, men with coloured caps and old muskets, ready to support the dignity and authority of the commandant. There were the guides taking payment from Abel Ring for their past work, and the postmen preparing their boats for the further journey. And then there was a certain German there, with a German servant, to whom the boats belonged. He also was very busy preparing for the river voyage. He was not going down with them, but it was his business to see them well started. A singular looking man was he, with a huge shaggy beard, and shaggy uncombed hair, but with bright blue eyes, which gave to his face a remarkable look of sweetness. He was an uncouth man to the eye, and yet a child would have trusted herself with him in a forest.

At this place they remained some two hours. Coffee was prepared here, and Mrs. Arkwright refreshed herself and her child. They washed and arranged their clothes, and when she stepped down the steep bank, clinging to her husband's arm as she made her way towards the boat, she smiled upon him as he looked at her.

"It is all over now,—is it not, my girl?"—he said, encouraging her.

"Oh, Harry, do not talk about it," she answered, shuddering.

"But I want you to say a word to me to let me know that you are better."

"I am better,—much better."

"And you will see your mother again; will you not; and give baby to her yourself?"

To this she made no immediate answer, for she was on a level with the river, and the canoe was close at her feet. And then she had to bid farewell to her brother. He was now the unfortunate one of the party, for his destiny required that he should go back to San Jose alone,—go back and remain there perhaps some ten years longer before he might look for the happiness of home.

"God bless you, dearest Abel," she said, kissing him and sobbing as she spoke.

"Goodbye, Fanny," he said, "and do not let them forget me in England. It is a great comfort to think that the worst of your troubles are over."

"Oh,—she's all right now," said Arkwright. "Goodbye, old boy,"—and the two brothers-in-law grasped each other's hands heartily. "Keep up your spirits, and we'll have you home before long."

"Oh, I'm all right," said the other. But from the tone of the voices, it was clear that poor Ring was despondent at the thoughts of his coming solitude, and that Arkwright was already triumphing in his emancipation.

And then, with much care, Fanny Arkwright was stowed away in the boat. There was a great contest about the baby, but at last it was arranged, that at any rate for the first few hours she should be placed in the boat with the servant. The mother was told that by this plan she would feel herself at liberty to sleep during the heat of the day, and then she might hope to have strength to look to the child when they should be on shore during the night. In this way therefore they prepared to start, while Abel Ring stood on the bank looking at them with wishful eyes. In the first boat were two Indians paddling, and a third man steering with another paddle. In the middle there was much luggage, and near the luggage so as to be under shade, was the baby's soft bed. If nothing evil happened to the boat, the child could not be more safe in the best cradle that was ever rocked. With her was the maid-servant and some stranger who was also going down to Greytown.

In the second boat were the same number of men to paddle, the Indian guide being one of them, and there were the mails placed. Then there was a seat arranged with blankets, cloaks, and cushions, for Mrs. Arkwright, so that she might lean back and sleep without fatigue, and immediately opposite to her her husband placed himself. "You all look very comfortable," said poor Abel from the bank.

"We shall do very well now," said Arkwright.

"And I do think I shall see mamma again," said his wife.

"That's right, old girl;—of course you will see her. Now then,—we are all ready." And with some little assistance from the German on the bank, the first boat was pushed off into the stream.

The river in this place is rapid, because the full course of the water is somewhat impeded by a bank of earth jutting out from the opposite side of the river into the stream; but it is not so rapid as to make any recognised danger in the embarkation. Below this bank, which is opposite to the spot at which the boats were entered, there were four or five broken trees in the water, some of the shattered boughs of which showed themselves above the surface. These are called snags, and are very dangerous if they are met with in the course of the stream; but in this instance no danger was apprehended from them, as they lay considerably to the left of the passage which the boats would take. The first canoe was pushed off by the German, and went rapidly away. The waters were strong with rain, and it was pretty to see with what velocity the boat was carried on some hundred of yards in advance of the other by the force of the first effort of the paddle. The German, however, from the bank holloaed to the first men in Spanish, bidding them relax their efforts for awhile; and then he said a word or two of caution to those who were now on the point of starting.

The boat then was pushed steadily forward, the man at the stern keeping it with his paddle a little farther away from the bank at which they had embarked. It was close under the land that the stream ran the fastest, and in obedience to the directions given to him he made his course somewhat nearer to the sunken trees. It was but one turn of his hand that gave the light boat its direction, but that turn of the hand was too strong. Had the anxious master of the canoes been but a thought less anxious, all might have been well; but, as it was, the prow of the boat was caught by some slight hidden branch which impeded its course and turned it round in the rapid river. The whole lengths of the canoe was thus brought against the sunken tree, and in half a minute the five occupants of the boat were struggling in the stream.

Abel Ring and the German were both standing on the bank close to the water when this happened, and each for a moment looked into the other's face. "Stand where you are," shouted the German, "so that you may assist them from the shore. I will go in." And then, throwing from him his boots and coat, he plunged into the river.

The canoe had been swept round so as to be brought by the force of the waters absolutely in among the upturned roots and broken stumps of the trees which impeded the river, and thus, when the party was upset, they were at first to be seen scrambling among the branches. But unfortunately there was much more wood below the water than above it, and the force of the stream was so great, that those who caught hold of the timber were not able to support themselves by it above the surface. Arkwright was soon to be seen some forty yards down, having been carried clear of the trees, and here he got out of the river on the farther bank. The distance to him was not above forty yards, but from the nature of the ground he could not get up towards his wife, unless he could have forced his way against the stream.

The Indian who had had charge of the baby rose quickly to the surface, was carried once round in the eddy, with his head high above the water, and then was seen to throw himself among the broken wood. He had seen the dress of the poor woman, and made his effort to save her. The other two men were so caught by the fragments of the boughs, that they could not extricate themselves so as to make any exertions; ultimately, however, they also got out on the further bank.

Mrs. Arkwright had sunk at once on being precipitated into the water, but the buoyancy of her clothes had brought her for a moment again to the surface. She had risen for a moment, and then had again gone down, immediately below the forked trunk of a huge tree;—had gone down, alas, alas! never to rise again with life within her bosom. The poor Indian made two attempts to save her, and then came up himself, incapable of further effort.

It was then that the German, the owner of the canoes, who had fought his way with great efforts across the violence of the waters, and indeed up against the stream for some few yards, made his effort to save the life of that poor frail creature. He had watched the spot at which she had gone down, and even while struggling across the river, had seen how the Indian had followed her and had failed. It was now his turn. His life was in his hand, and he was prepared to throw it away in that attempt. Having succeeded in placing himself a little above the large tree, he turned his face towards the bottom of the river, and dived down among the branches. And he also, after that, was never again seen with the life-blood flowing round his heart.

When the sun set that night, the two swollen corpses were lying in the Commandant's hut, and Abel Ring and Arkwright were sitting beside them. Arkwright had his baby sleeping in his arms, but he sat there for hours,—into the middle of the long night,—without speaking a word to any one.

"Harry," said his brother at last, "come away and lay down. It will be good for you to sleep."

"Nothing ever will be good again for me," said he.

"You must bear up against your sorrow as other men do," said Ring.

"Why am I not sleeping with her as the poor German sleeps? Why did I let another man take my place in dying for her?" And then he walked away that the other might not see the tears on his face.

It was a sad night,—that at the Commandant's hut, and a sad morning followed upon it. It must be remembered that they had there none of those appurtenances which are so necessary to make woe decent and misfortune comfortable. They sat through the night in the small hut, and in the morning they came forth with their clothes still wet and dirty, with their haggard faces, and weary stiff limbs, encumbered with the horrid task of burying that loved body among the forest trees. And then, to keep life in them till it was done, the brandy flask passed from hand to hand; and after that, with slow but resolute efforts, they reformed the litter on which the living woman had been carried thither, and took her body back to the wild plantation at Padregal. There they dug for her her grave, and repeating over her some portion of the service for the dead, left her to sleep the sleep of death. But before they left her, they erected a pallisade of timber round the grave, so that the beasts of the forest should not tear the body from its resting-place.

When that was done Arkwright and his brother made their slow journey back to San Jose. The widowed husband could not face his darling's mother with such a tale upon his tongue as that.

A RIDE ACROSS PALESTINE

Circumstances took me to the Holy Land without a companion, and compelled me to visit Bethany, the Mount of Olives, and the Church of the Sepulchre alone. I acknowledge myself to be a gregarious animal, or, perhaps, rather one of those which nature has intended to go in pairs. At any rate I dislike solitude, and especially travelling solitude, and was, therefore, rather sad at heart as I sat one night at Z-'s hotel, in Jerusalem, thinking over my proposed wanderings for the next few days. Early on the following morning I intended to start, of course on horseback, for the Dead Sea, the banks of Jordan, Jericho, and those mountains of the wilderness through which it is supposed that Our Saviour wandered for the forty days when the devil tempted him. I would then return to the Holy City, and remaining only long enough to refresh my horse and wipe the dust from my hands and feet, I would start again for Jaffa, and there catch a certain Austrian steamer which would take me to Egypt. Such was my programme, and I confess that I was but ill contented with it, seeing that I was to be alone during the time.

I had already made all my arrangements, and though I had no reason for any doubt as to my personal security during the trip, I did not feel altogether satisfied with them. I intended to take a French guide, or dragoman, who had been with me for some days, and to put myself under the peculiar guardianship of two Bedouin Arabs, who were to accompany me as long as I should remain east of Jerusalem. This travelling through the desert under the protection of Bedouins was, in idea, pleasant enough; and I must here declare that I did not at all begrudge the forty shillings which I was told by our British consul that I must pay them for their trouble, in accordance with the established tariff. But I did begrudge the fact of the tariff. I would rather have fallen in with my friendly Arabs, as it were by chance, and have rewarded their fidelity at the end of our joint journeyings by a donation of piastres to be settled by myself, and which, under such circumstances, would certainly have been as agreeable to them as the stipulated sum. In the same way I dislike having waiters put down in my bill. I find that I pay them twice over, and thus lose money; and as they do not expect to be so treated, I never have the advantage of their civility. The world, I fear, is becoming too fond of tariffs.

"A tariff!" said I to the consul, feeling that the whole romance of my expedition would be dissipated by such an arrangement. "Then I'll go alone; I'll take a revolver with me."

"You can't do it, sir," said the consul, in a dry and somewhat angry tone. "You have no more right to ride through that country without paying the regular price for protection, than you have to stop in Z-'s hotel without settling the bill."

I could not contest the point, so I ordered my Bedouins for the appointed day, exactly as I would send for a ticket-porter at home, and determined to make the best of it. The wild unlimited sands, the desolation of the Dead Sea, the rushing waters of Jordan, the outlines of the mountains of Moab;—those things the consular tariff could not alter, nor deprive them of the glories of their association.

I had submitted, and the arrangements had been made. Joseph, my dragoman, was to come to me with the horses and an Arab groom at five in the morning, and we were to encounter our Bedouins outside the gate of St. Stephen, down the hill, where the road turns, close to the tomb of the Virgin.

I was sitting alone in the public room at the hotel, filling my flask with brandy,—for matters of primary importance I never leave to servant, dragoman, or guide,—when the waiter entered, and said that a gentleman wished to speak with me. The gentleman had not sent in his card or name; but any gentleman was welcome to me in my solitude, and I requested that the gentleman might enter. In appearance the gentleman certainly was a gentleman, for I thought that I had never before seen a young man whose looks were more in his favour, or whose face and gait and outward bearing seemed to betoken better breeding. He might be some twenty or twenty-one years of age, was slight and well made, with very black hair, which he wore rather long, very dark long bright eyes, a straight nose, and teeth that were perfectly white. He was dressed throughout in grey tweed clothing, having coat, waistcoat, and trousers of the same; and in his hand he carried a very broad-brimmed straw hat.

"Mr. Jones, I believe," he said, as he bowed to me. Jones is a good travelling name, and, if the reader will allow me, I will call myself Jones on the present occasion.

"Yes," I said, pausing with the brandy-bottle in one hand, and the flask in the other. "That's my name; I'm Jones. Can I do anything for you, sir?"

"Why, yes, you can," said he. "My name is Smith,—John Smith."

"Pray sit down, Mr. Smith," I said, pointing to a chair. "Will you do anything in this way?" and I proposed to hand the bottle to him. "As far as I can judge from a short stay, you won't find much like that in Jerusalem."

He declined the Cognac, however, and immediately began his story. "I hear, Mr. Jones," said he, "that you are going to Moab tomorrow."

"Well," I replied, "I don't know whether I shall cross the water. It's not very easy, I take it, at all times; but I shall certainly get as far as Jordan. Can I do anything for you in those parts?"

And then he explained to me what was the object of his visit. He was quite alone in Jerusalem, as I was myself; and was staying at H-'s hotel. He had heard that I was starting for the Dead Sea, and had called to ask if I objected to his joining me. He had found himself, he said, very lonely; and as he had heard that I also was alone, he had ventured to call and make his proposition. He seemed to be very bashful, and half ashamed of what he was doing; and when he had done speaking he declared himself conscious that he was intruding, and expressed a hope that I would not hesitate to say so if his suggestion were from any cause disagreeable to me.

As a rule I am rather shy of chance travelling English friends. It has so frequently happened to me that I have had to blush for the acquaintances whom I have selected, that I seldom indulge in any close intimacies of this kind. But, nevertheless, I was taken with John Smith, in spite of his name. There was so much about him that was pleasant, both to the eye and to the understanding! One meets constantly with men from contact with whom one revolts without knowing the cause of such dislike. The cut of their beard is displeasing, or the mode in which they walk or speak. But, on the other hand, there are men who are attractive, and I must confess that I was attracted by John Smith at first sight. I hesitated, however, for a minute; for there are sundry things of which it behoves a traveller to think before he can join a companion for such a journey as that which I was about to make. Could the young man rise early, and remain in the saddle for ten hours together? Could he live upon hard-boiled eggs and brandy-and-water? Could he take his chance of a tent under which to sleep, and make himself happy with the bare fact of being in the desert? He saw my hesitation, and attributed it to a cause which was not present in my mind at the moment, though the subject was one of the greatest importance when strangers consent to join themselves together for a time, and agree to become no strangers on the spur of the moment.

"Of course I will take half the expense," said he, absolutely blushing as he mentioned the matter.

"As to that there will be very little. You have your own horse, of course?"

"Oh, yes."

"My dragoman and groom-boy will do for both. But you'll have to pay forty shillings to the Arabs! There's no getting over that. The consul won't even look after your dead body, if you get murdered, without going through that ceremony."

Mr. Smith immediately produced his purse, which he tendered to me. "If you will manage it all," said he, "it will make it so much the easier, and I shall be infinitely obliged to you." This of course I declined to do. I had no business with his purse, and explained to him that if we went together we could settle that on our return to Jerusalem. "But could he go through really hard work?" I asked. He answered me with an assurance that he would and could do anything in that way that it was possible for man to perform. As for eating and drinking he cared nothing about it, and would undertake to be astir at any hour of the morning that might be named. As for sleeping accommodation, he did not care if he kept his clothes on for a week together. He looked slight and weak; but he spoke so well, and that without boasting, that I ultimately agreed to his proposal, and in a few minutes he took his leave of me, promising to be at Z-'s door with his horse at five o'clock on the following morning.

"I wish you'd allow me to leave my purse with you," he said again.

"I cannot think of it. There is no possible occasion for it," I said again. "If there is anything to pay, I'll ask you for it when the journey is over. That forty shillings you must fork out. It's a law of the Medes and Persians."

"I'd better give it you at once," he said again, offering me money. But I would not have it. It would be quite time enough for that when the Arabs were leaving us.

"Because," he added, "strangers, I know, are sometimes suspicious about money; and I would not, for worlds, have you think that I would put you to expense." I assured him that I did not think so, and then the subject was dropped.

He was, at any rate, up to his time, for when I came down on the following morning I found him in the narrow street, the first on horseback. Joseph, the Frenchman, was strapping on to a rough pony our belongings, and was staring at Mr. Smith. My new friend, unfortunately, could not speak a word of French, and therefore I had to explain to the dragoman how it had come to pass that our party was to be enlarged.

"But the Bedouins will expect full pay for both," said he, alarmed. Men in that class, and especially Orientals, always think that every arrangement of life, let it be made in what way it will, is made with the intention of saving some expense, or cheating somebody out of some money. They do not understand that men can have any other object, and are ever on their guard lest the saving should be made at their cost, or lest they should be the victims of the fraud.

"All right," said I.

"I shall be responsible, Monsieur," said the dragoman, piteously.

"It shall be all right," said I, again. "If that does not satisfy you, you may remain behind."

"If Monsieur says it is all right, of course it is so;" and then he completed his strapping. We took blankets with us, of which I had to borrow two out of the hotel for my friend Smith, a small hamper of provisions, a sack containing forage for the horses, and a large empty jar, so that we might supply ourselves with water when leaving the neighbourhood of wells for any considerable time.

"I ought to have brought these things for myself," said Smith, quite unhappy at finding that he had thrown on me the necessity of catering for him. But I laughed at him, saying that it was nothing; he should do as much for me another time. I am prepared to own that I do not willingly rush up-stairs and load myself with blankets out of strange rooms for men whom I do not know; nor, as a rule, do I make all the Smiths of the world free of my canteen. But, with reference to this fellow I did feel more than ordinarily good-natured and unselfish. There was something in the tone of his voice which was satisfactory; and I should really have felt vexed had anything occurred at the last moment to prevent his going with me.

Let it be a rule with every man to carry an English saddle with him when travelling in the East. Of what material is formed the nether man of a Turk I have never been informed, but I am sure that it is not flesh and blood. No flesh and blood,—simply flesh and blood,—could withstand the wear and tear of a Turkish saddle. This being the case, and the consequences being well known to me, I was grieved to find that Smith was not properly provided. He was seated on one of those hard, red, high-pointed machines, in which the shovels intended to act as stirrups are attached in such a manner, and hang at such an angle, as to be absolutely destructive to the leg of a Christian. There is no part of the Christian body with which the Turkish saddle comes in contact that does not become more or less macerated. I have sat in one for days, but I left it a flayed man; and, therefore, I was sorry for Smith.

I explained this to him, taking hold of his leg by the calf to show how the leather would chafe him; but it seemed to me that he did not quite like my interference. "Never mind," said he, twitching his leg away, "I have ridden in this way before."

"Then you must have suffered the very mischief?"

"Only a little, and I shall be used to it now. You will not hear me complain."

"By heavens, you might have heard me complain a mile off when I came to the end of a journey I once took. I roared like a bull when I began to cool. Joseph, could you not get a European saddle for Mr. Smith?" But Joseph did not seem to like Mr. Smith, and declared such a thing to be impossible. No European in Jerusalem would think of lending so precious an article, except to a very dear friend. Joseph himself was on an English saddle, and I made up my mind that after the first stage, we would bribe him to make an exchange. And then we started.

The Bedouins were not with us, but we were to meet them, as I have said before, outside St. Stephen's gate. "And if they are not there," said Joseph, "we shall be sure to come across them on the road."

"Not there!" said I. "How about the consul's tariff, if they don't keep their part of the engagement?" But Joseph explained to me that their part of the engagement really amounted to this,—that we should ride into their country without molestation, provided that such and such payments were made.

It was the period of Easter, and Jerusalem was full of pilgrims. Even at that early hour of the morning we could hardly make our way through the narrow streets. It must be understood that there is no accommodation in the town for the fourteen or fifteen thousand strangers who flock to the Holy Sepulchre at this period of the year. Many of them sleep out in the open air, lying on low benches which run along the outside walls of the houses, or even on the ground, wrapped in their thick hoods and cloaks. Slumberers such as these are easily disturbed, nor are they detained long at their toilets. They shake themselves like dogs, and growl and stretch themselves, and then they are ready for the day.

We rode out of the town in a long file. First went the groom-boy; I forget his proper Syrian appellation, but we used to call him Mucherry, that sound being in some sort like the name. Then followed the horse with the forage and blankets, and next to him my friend Smith in the Turkish saddle. I was behind him, and Joseph brought up the rear. We moved slowly down the Via Dolorosa, noting the spot at which our Saviour is said to have fallen while bearing his cross; we passed by Pilate's house, and paused at the gate of the Temple,—the gate which once was beautiful,—looking down into the hole of the pool in which the maimed and halt were healed whenever the waters moved. What names they are! And yet there at Jerusalem they are bandied to and fro with as little reverence as are the fanciful appellations given by guides to rocks and stones and little lakes in all countries overrun by tourists.

"For those who would still fain believe,—let them stay at home," said my friend Smith.

"For those who cannot divide the wheat from the chaff, let THEM stay at home," I answered. And then we rode out through St. Stephen's gate, having the mountain of the men of Galilee directly before us, and the Mount of Olives a little to our right, and the Valley of Jehoshaphat lying between us and it. "Of course you know all these places now?" said Smith. I answered that I did know them well.

"And was it not better for you when you knew them only in Holy Writ?" he asked.

"No, by Jove," said I. "The mountains stand where they ever stood. The same valleys are still green with the morning dew, and the water-courses are unchanged. The children of Mahomet may build their tawdry temple on the threshing-floor which David bought that there might stand the Lord's house. Man may undo what man did, even though the doer was Solomon. But here we have God's handiwork and His own evidences."

At the bottom of the steep descent from the city gate we came to the tomb of the Virgin; and by special agreement made with Joseph we left our horses here for a few moments, in order that we might descend into the subterranean chapel under the tomb, in which mass was at this moment being said. There is something awful in that chapel, when, as at the present moment, it is crowded with Eastern worshippers from the very altar up to the top of the dark steps by which the descent is made. It must be remembered that Eastern worshippers are not like the churchgoers of London, or even of Rome or Cologne. They are wild men of various nations and races,—Maronites from Lebanon Roumelians, Candiotes, Copts from Upper Egypt, Russians from the Crimea, Armenians and Abyssinians. They savour strongly of Oriental life and of Oriental dirt. They are clad in skins or hairy cloaks with huge hoods. Their heads are shaved, and their faces covered with short, grisly, fierce beards. They are silent mostly, looking out of their eyes ferociously, as though murder were in their thoughts, and rapine. But they never slouch, or cringe in their bodies, or shuffle in their gait. Dirty, fierce-looking, uncouth, repellent as they are, there is always about them a something of personal dignity which is not compatible with an Englishman's ordinary hat and pantaloons.

As we were about to descend, preparing to make our way through the crowd, Smith took hold of my arm. "That will never do, my dear fellow," said I, "the job will be tough enough for a single file, but we should never cut our way two and two. I'm broad-shouldered and will go first." So I did, and gradually we worked our way into the body of the chapel. How is it that Englishmen can push themselves anywhere? These men were fierce-looking, and had murder and rapine, as I have said, almost in their eyes. One would have supposed that they were not lambs or doves, capable of being thrust here or there without anger on their part; and they, too, were all anxious to descend and approach the altar. Yet we did win our way through them, and apparently no man was angry with us. I doubt, after all, whether a ferocious eye and a strong smell and dirt are so efficacious in creating awe and obedience in others, as an open brow and traces of soap and water. I know this, at least,—that a dirty Maronite would make very little progress, if he attempted to shove his way unfairly through a crowd of Englishmen at the door of a London theatre. We did shove unfairly, and we did make progress, till we found ourselves in the centre of the dense crowd collected in the body of the chapel.

Having got so far, our next object was to get out again. The place was dark, mysterious, and full of strange odours; but darkness, mystery, and strange odours soon lose their charms when men have much work before them. Joseph had made a point of being allowed to attend mass before the altar of the Virgin, but a very few minutes sufficed for his prayers. So we again turned round and pushed our way back again, Smith still following in my wake. The men who had let us pass once let us pass again without opposition or show of anger. To them the occasion was very holy. They were stretching out their hands in every direction, with long tapers, in order that they might obtain a spark of the sacred fire which was burning on one of the altars. As we made our way out we passed many who, with dumb motions, begged us to assist them in their object. And we did assist them, getting lights for their tapers, handing them to and fro, and using the authority with which we seemed to be invested. But Smith, I observed, was much more courteous in this way to the women than to the men, as I did not forget to remind him when we were afterwards on our road together.

Remounting our horses we rode slowly up the winding ascent of the Mount of Olives, turning round at the brow of the hill to look back over Jerusalem. Sometimes I think that of all spots in the world this one should be the spot most cherished in the memory of Christians. It was there that He stood when He wept over the city. So much we do know, though we are ignorant, and ever shall be so, of the site of His cross and of the tomb. And then we descended on the eastern side of the hill, passing through Bethany, the town of Lazarus and his sisters, and turned our faces steadily towards the mountains of Moab.

Hitherto we had met no Bedouins, and I interrogated my dragoman about them more than once; but he always told me that it did not signify; we should meet them, he said, before any danger could arise. "As for danger," said I, "I think more of this than I do of the Arabs," and I put my hand on my revolver. "But as they agreed to be here, here they ought to be. Don't you carry a revolver, Smith?"

Smith said that he never had done so, but that he would take the charge of mine if I liked. To this, however, I demurred. "I never part with my pistol to any one," I said, rather drily. But he explained that he only intended to signify that if there were danger to be encountered, he would be glad to encounter it; and I fully believed him. "We shan't have much fighting," I replied; "but if there be any, the tool will come readiest to the hand of its master. But if you mean to remain here long I would advise you to get one. These Orientals are a people with whom appearances go a long way, and, as a rule, fear and respect mean the same thing with them. A pistol hanging over your loins is no great trouble to you, and looks as though you could bite. Many a dog goes through the world well by merely showing his teeth."

And then my companion began to talk of himself. "He did not," he said, "mean to remain in Syria very long."

"Nor I either," said I. "I have done with this part of the world for the present, and shall take the next steamer from Jaffa for Alexandria. I shall only have one night in Jerusalem on my return."

After this he remained silent for a few moments and then declared that that also had been his intention. He was almost ashamed to say so, however, because it looked as though he had resolved to hook himself on to me. So he answered, expressing almost regret at the circumstance.

"Don't let that trouble you," said I; "I shall be delighted to have your company. When you know me better, as I hope you will do, you will find that if such were not the case I should tell you so as frankly. I shall remain in Cairo some little time; so that beyond our arrival in Egypt, I can answer for nothing."

He said that he expected letters at Alexandria which would govern his future movements. I thought he seemed sad as he said so, and imagined, from his manner, that he did not expect very happy tidings. Indeed I had made up my mind that he was by no means free from care or sorrow. He had not the air of a man who could say of himself that he was "totus teres atque rotundus." But I had no wish to inquire, and the matter would have dropped had he not himself added—"I fear that I shall meet acquaintances in Egypt whom it will give me no pleasure to see."

"Then," said I, "if I were you, I would go to Constantinople instead;—indeed, anywhere rather than fall among friends who are not friendly. And the nearer the friend is, the more one feels that sort of thing. To my way of thinking, there is nothing on earth so pleasant as a pleasant wife; but then, what is there so damnable as one that is unpleasant?"

"Are you a married man?" he inquired. All his questions were put in a low tone of voice which seemed to give to them an air of special interest, and made one almost feel that they were asked with some special view to one's individual welfare. Now the fact is, that I am a married man with a family; but I am not much given to talk to strangers about my domestic concerns, and, therefore, though I had no particular object in view, I denied my obligations in this respect. "No," said I; "I have not come to that promotion yet. I am too frequently on the move to write myself down as Paterfamilias."

"Then you know nothing about that pleasantness of which you spoke just now?"

"Nor of the unpleasantness, thank God; my personal experiences are all to come,—as also are yours, I presume?"

It was possible that he had hampered himself with some woman, and that she was to meet him at Alexandria. Poor fellow! thought I. But his unhappiness was not of that kind. "No," said he; "I am not married; I am all alone in the world."

"Then I certainly would not allow myself to be troubled by unpleasant acquaintances."

It was now four hours since we had left Jerusalem, and we had arrived at the place at which it was proposed that we should breakfast. There was a large well there, and shade afforded by a rock under which the water sprung; and the Arabs had constructed a tank out of which the horses could drink, so that the place was ordinarily known as the first stage out of Jerusalem.

Smith had said not a word about his saddle, or complained in any way of discomfort, so that I had in truth forgotten the subject. Other matters had continually presented themselves, and I had never even asked him how he had fared. I now jumped from my horse, but I perceived at once that he was unable to do so. He smiled faintly, as his eye caught mine, but I knew that he wanted assistance. "Ah," said I, "that confounded Turkish saddle has already galled your skin. I see how it is; I shall have to doctor you with a little brandy,—externally applied, my friend." But I lent him my shoulder, and with that assistance he got down, very gently and slowly.

We ate our breakfast with a good will; bread and cold fowl and brandy-and-water, with a hard-boiled egg by way of a final delicacy; and then I began to bargain with Joseph for the loan of his English saddle. I saw that Smith could not get through the journey with that monstrous Turkish affair, and that he would go on without complaining till he fainted or came to some other signal grief. But the Frenchman, seeing the plight in which we were, was disposed to drive a very hard bargain. He wanted forty shillings, the price of a pair of live Bedouins, for the accommodation, and declared that, even then, he should make the sacrifice only out of consideration to me.

"Very well," said I. "I'm tolerably tough myself; and I'll change with the gentleman. The chances are that I shall not be in a very liberal humour when I reach Jaffa with stiff limbs and a sore skin. I have a very good memory, Joseph."

"I'll take thirty shillings, Mr. Jones; though I shall have to groan all the way like a condemned devil."

I struck a bargain with him at last for five-and-twenty, and set him to work to make the necessary change on the horses. "It will be just the same thing to him," I said to Smith. "I find that he is as much used to one as to the other."

"But how much money are you to pay him?" he asked. "Oh, nothing," I replied. "Give him a few piastres when you part with him at Jaffa." I do not know why I should have felt thus inclined to pay money out of my pocket for this Smith,—a man whom I had only seen for the first time on the preceding evening, and whose temperament was so essentially different from my own; but so I did. I would have done almost anything in reason for his comfort; and yet he was a melancholy fellow, with good inward pluck as I believed, but without that outward show of dash and hardihood which I confess I love to see. "Pray tell him that I'll pay him for it," said he. "We'll make that all right," I answered; and then we remounted,—not without some difficulty on his part. "You should have let me rub in that brandy," I said. "You can't conceive how efficaciously I would have done it." But he made me no answer.

At noon we met a caravan of pilgrims coming up from Jordan. There might be some three or four hundred, but the number seemed to be treble that, from the loose and straggling line in which they journeyed. It was a very singular sight, as they moved slowly along the narrow path through the sand, coming out of a defile among the hills, which was perhaps a quarter of a mile in front of us, passing us as we stood still by the wayside, and then winding again out of sight on the track over which we had come. Some rode on camels,—a whole family, in many cases, being perched on the same animal. I observed a very old man and a very old woman slung in panniers over a camel's back,—not such panniers as might be befitting such a purpose, but square baskets, so that the heads and heels of each of the old couple hung out of the rear and front. "Surely the journey will be their death," I said to Joseph. "Yes it will," he replied, quite coolly; "but what matter how soon they die now that they have bathed in Jordan?" Very many rode on donkeys; two, generally, on each donkey; others, who had command of money, on horses; but the greater number walked, toiling painfully from Jerusalem to Jericho on the first day, sleeping there in tents and going to bathe on the second day, and then returning from Jericho to Jerusalem on the third. The pilgrimage is made throughout in accordance with fixed rules, and there is a tariff for the tent accommodation at Jericho,—so much per head per night, including the use of hot water.

Standing there, close by the wayside, we could see not only the garments and faces of these strange people, but we could watch their gestures and form some opinion of what was going on within their thoughts. They were much quieter,—tamer, as it were,—than Englishmen would be under such circumstances. Those who were carried seemed to sit on their beasts in passive tranquillity, neither enjoying nor suffering anything. Their object had been to wash in Jordan,—to do that once in their lives;—and they had washed in Jordan. The benefit expected was not to be immediately spiritual. No earnest prayerfulness was considered necessary after the ceremony. To these members of the Greek Christian Church it had been handed down from father to son that washing in Jordan once during life was efficacious towards salvation. And therefore the journey had been made at terrible cost and terrible risk; for these people had come from afar, and were from their habits but little capable of long journeys. Many die under the toil; but this matters not if they do not die before they have reached Jordan. Some few there are, undoubtedly, more ecstatic in this great deed of their religion. One man I especially noticed on this day. He had bound himself to make the pilgrimage from Jerusalem to the river with one foot bare. He was of a better class, and was even nobly dressed, as though it were a part of his vow to show to all men that he did this deed, wealthy and great though he was. He was a fine man, perhaps thirty years of age, with a well-grown beard descending on his breast, and at his girdle he carried a brace of pistols.

But never in my life had I seen bodily pain so plainly written in a man's face. The sweat was falling from his brow, and his eyes were strained and bloodshot with agony. He had no stick, his vow, I presume, debarring him from such assistance, and he limped along, putting to the ground the heel of the unprotected foot. I could see it, and it was a mass of blood, and sores, and broken skin. An Irish girl would walk from Jerusalem to Jericho without shoes, and be not a penny the worse for it. This poor fellow clearly suffered so much that I was almost inclined to think that in the performance of his penance he had done something to aggravate his pain. Those around him paid no attention to him, and the dragoman seemed to think nothing of the affair whatever. "Those fools of Greeks do not understand the Christian religion," he said, being himself a Latin or Roman Catholic.

At the tail of the line we encountered two Bedouins, who were in charge of the caravan, and Joseph at once addressed them. The men were mounted, one on a very sorry-looking jade, but the other on a good stout Arab barb. They had guns slung behind their backs, coloured handkerchiefs on their heads, and they wore the striped bernouse. The parley went on for about ten minutes, during which the procession of pilgrims wound out of sight; and it ended in our being accompanied by the two Arabs, who thus left their greater charge to take care of itself back to the city. I understood afterwards that they had endeavoured to persuade Joseph that we might just as well go on alone, merely satisfying the demand of the tariff. But he had pointed out that I was a particular man, and that under such circumstances the final settlement might be doubtful. So they turned and accompanied us; but, as a matter of fact, we should have been as well without them.

The sun was beginning to fall in the heavens when we reached the actual margin of the Dead Sea. We had seen the glitter of its still waters for a long time previously, shining under the sun as though it were not real. We have often heard, and some of us have seen, how effects of light and shade together will produce so vivid an appearance of water where there is no water, as to deceive the most experienced. But the reverse was the case here. There was the lake, and there it had been before our eyes for the last two hours; and yet it looked, then and now, as though it were an image of a lake, and not real water. I had long since made up my mind to bathe in it, feeling well convinced that I could do so without harm to myself, and I had been endeavouring to persuade Smith to accompany me; but he positively refused. He would bathe, he said, neither in the Dead Sea nor in the river Jordan. He did not like bathing, and preferred to do his washing in his own room. Of course I had nothing further to say, and begged that, under these circumstances, he would take charge of my purse and pistols while I was in the water. This he agreed to do; but even in this he was strange and almost uncivil. I was to bathe from the farthest point of a little island, into which there was a rough causeway from the land made of stones and broken pieces of wood, and I exhorted him to go with me thither; but he insisted on remaining with his horse on the mainland at some little distance from the island. He did not feel inclined to go down to the water's edge, he said.

I confess that at this moment I almost suspected that he was going to play me foul, and I hesitated. He saw in an instant what was passing through my mind. "You had better take your pistol and money with you; they will be quite safe on your clothes." But to have kept the things now would have shown suspicion too plainly, and as I could not bring myself to do that, I gave them up. I have sometimes thought that I was a fool to do so.

I went away by myself to the end of the island, and then I did bathe. It is impossible to conceive anything more desolate than the appearance of the place. The land shelves very gradually away to the water, and the whole margin, to the breadth of some twenty or thirty feet, is strewn with the debris of rushes, bits of timber, and old white withered reeds. Whence these bits of timber have come it seems difficult to say. The appearance is as though the water had receded and left them there. I have heard it said that there is no vegetation near the Dead Sea; but such is not the case, for these rushes do grow on the bank. I found it difficult enough to get into the water, for the ground shelves down very slowly, and is rough with stones and large pieces of half-rotten wood; moreover, when I was in nearly up to my hips the water knocked me down; indeed, it did so when I had gone as far as my knees, but I recovered myself; and by perseverance did proceed somewhat farther. It must not be imagined that this knocking down was effected by the movement of the water. There is no such movement. Everything is perfectly still, and the fluid seems hardly to be displaced by the entrance of the body; but the effect is that one's feet are tripped up, and that one falls prostrate on to the surface. The water is so strong and buoyant, that, when above a few feet in depth has to be encountered, the strength and weight of the bather are not sufficient to keep down his feet and legs. I then essayed to swim; but I could not do this in the ordinary way, as I was unable to keep enough of my body below the surface; so that my head and face seemed to be propelled down upon it.

I turned round and floated, but the glare of the sun was so powerful that I could not remain long in that position. However, I had bathed in the Dead Sea, and was so far satisfied.

Anything more abominable to the palate than this water, if it be water, I never had inside my mouth. I expected it to be extremely salt, and no doubt, if it were analysed, such would be the result;

but there is a flavour in it which kills the salt. No attempt can be made at describing this taste. It may be imagined that I did not drink heartily, merely taking up a drop or two with my tongue from the palm of my hand; but it seemed to me as though I had been drenched with it. Even brandy would not relieve me from it. And then my whole body was in a mess, and I felt as though I had been rubbed with pitch. Looking at my limbs, I saw no sign on them of the fluid. They seemed to dry from this as they usually do from any other water; but still the feeling remained. However, I was to ride from hence to a spot on the banks of Jordan, which I should reach in an hour, and at which I would wash; so I clothed myself, and prepared for my departure.

Seated in my position in the island I was unable to see what was going on among the remainder of the party, and therefore could not tell whether my pistols and money was safe. I dressed, therefore, rather hurriedly, and on getting again to the shore, found that Mr. John Smith had not levanted. He was seated on his horse at some distance from Joseph and the Arabs, and had no appearance of being in league with those, no doubt, worthy guides. I certainly had suspected a ruse, and now was angry with myself that I had done so; and yet, in London, one would not trust one's money to a stranger whom one had met twenty-four hours since in a coffee-room! Why, then, do it with a stranger whom one chanced to meet in a desert?

"Thanks," I said, as he handed me my belongings. "I wish I could have induced you to come in also. The Dead Sea is now at your elbow, and, therefore, you think nothing of it; but in ten or fifteen years' time, you would be glad to be able to tell your children that you had bathed in it."

"I shall never have any children to care for such tidings," he replied.

The river Jordan, for some miles above the point at which it joins the Dead Sea, runs through very steep banks,—banks which are almost precipitous,—and is, as it were, guarded by the thick trees and bushes which grow upon its sides. This is so much the case, that one may ride, as we did, for a considerable distance along the margin, and not be able even to approach the water. I had a fancy for bathing in some spot of my own selection, instead of going to the open shore frequented by all the pilgrims; but I was baffled in this. When I did force my way down to the river side, I found that the water ran so rapidly, and that the bushes and boughs of trees grew so far over and into the stream, as to make it impossible for me to bathe. I could not have got in without my clothes, and having got in, I could not have got out again. I was, therefore obliged to put up with the open muddy shore to which the bathers descend, and at which we may presume that Joshua passed when he came over as one of the twelve spies to spy out the land. And even here I could not go full into the stream as I would fain have done, lest I should be carried down, and so have assisted to whiten the shores of the Dead Sea with my bones. As to getting over to the Moabitish side of the river, that was plainly impossible; and, indeed, it seemed to be the prevailing opinion that the passage of the river was not practicable without going up as far as Samaria. And yet we know that there, or thereabouts, the Israelites did cross it.

I jumped from my horse the moment I got to the place, and once more gave my purse and pistols to my friend. "You are going to bathe again?" he said. "Certainly," said I; "you don't suppose that I would come to Jordan and not wash there, even if I were not foul with the foulness of the Dead Sea!" "You'll kill yourself, in your present state of heat;" he said, remonstrating just as one's mother or wife might do. But even had it been my mother or wife I could not have attended to such remonstrance then; and before he had done looking at me with those big eyes of his, my coat and waistcoat and cravat were on the ground, and I was at work at my braces; whereupon he turned from me slowly, and strolled away into the wood. On this occasion I had no base fears about my money.

And then I did bathe,—very uncomfortably. The shore was muddy with the feet of the pilgrims, and the river so rapid that I hardly dared to get beyond the mud. I did manage to take a plunge in, head-foremost, but I was forced to wade out through the dirt and slush, so that I found it difficult to make my feet and legs clean enough for my shoes and stockings; and then, moreover, the flies plagued me most unmercifully. I should have thought that the filthy flavour from the Dead Sea would have saved me from that nuisance; but the mosquitoes thereabouts are probably used to it. Finding this process of bathing to be so difficult, I inquired as to the practice of the pilgrims. I found that with them, bathing in

Jordan has come to be much the same as baptism has with us. It does not mean immersion. No doubt they do take off their shoes and stockings; but they do not strip, and go bodily into the water.

As soon as I was dressed I found that Smith was again at my side with purse and pistols. We then went up a little above the wood, and sat down together on the long sandy grass. It was now quite evening, so that the short Syrian twilight had commenced, and the sun was no longer hot in the heavens. It would be night as we rode on to the tents at Jericho; but there was no difficulty as to the way, and therefore we did not hurry the horses, who were feeding on the grass. We sat down together on a spot from which we could see the stream,—close together, so that when I stretched myself out in my weariness, as I did before we started, my head rested on his legs. Ah, me! one does not take such liberties with new friends in England. It was a place which led one on to some special thoughts. The mountains of Moab were before us, very plain in their outline.

"Moab is my wash-pot, and over Edom will I cast out my shoe!" There they were before us, very visible to the eye, and we began naturally to ask questions of each other. Why was Moab the wash-pot, and Edom thus cursed with indignity? Why had the right bank of the river been selected for such great purposes, whereas the left was thus condemned? Was there, at that time, any special fertility in this land of promise which has since departed from it? We are told of a bunch of grapes which took two men to carry it; but now there is not a vine in the whole country side. Now-a-days the sandy plain round Jericho is as dry and arid as are any of the valleys of Moab. The Jordan was running beneath our feet,—the Jordan in which the leprous king had washed, though the bright rivers of his own Damascus were so much nearer to his hand. It was but a humble stream to which he was sent; but the spot probably was higher up, above the Sea of Galilee, where the river is narrow. But another also had come down to this river, perhaps to this very spot on its shores, and submitted Himself to its waters;—as to whom, perhaps, it will be better that I should not speak much in this light story.

The Dead Sea was on our right, still glittering in the distance, and behind us lay the plains of Jericho and the wretched collection of huts which still bears the name of the ancient city. Beyond that, but still seemingly within easy distance of us, were the mountains of the wilderness. The wilderness! In truth, the spot was one which did lead to many thoughts.

We talked of these things, as to many of which I found that my friend was much more free in his doubts and questionings than myself; and then our words came back to ourselves, the natural centre of all men's-thoughts and words. "From what you say," I said, "I gather that you have had enough of this land?"

"Quite enough," he said. "Why seek such spots as these, if they only dispel the associations and veneration of one's childhood?"

"But with me such associations and veneration are riveted the stronger by seeing the places, and putting my hand upon the spots. I do not speak of that fictitious marble slab up there; but here, among the sandhills by this river, and at the Mount of Olives over which we passed, I do believe."

He paused a moment, and then replied: "To me it is all nothing,—absolutely nothing. But then do we not know that our thoughts are formed, and our beliefs modelled, not on the outward signs or intrinsic evidences of things,—as would be the case were we always rational,—but by the inner workings of the mind itself? At the present turn of my life I can believe in nothing that is gracious."

"Ah, you mean that you are unhappy. You have come to grief in some of your doings or belongings, and therefore find that all things are bitter to the taste. I have had my palate out of order too; but the proper appreciation of flavours has come back to me. Bah,—how noisome was that Dead Sea water!"

"The Dead Sea waters are noisome," he said; "and I have been drinking of them by long draughts."

"Long draughts!" I answered, thinking to console him. "Draughts have not been long which can have been swallowed in your years. Your disease may be acute, but it cannot yet have become chronic. A man always thinks at the moment of each misfortune that that special misery will last his lifetime; but God is too good for that. I do not know what ails you; but this day twelvemonth will see you again as sound as a roach."

We then sat silent for a while, during which I was puffing at a cigar. Smith, among his accomplishments, did not reckon that of smoking,—which was a grief to me; for a man enjoys the tobacco doubly when another is enjoying it with him.

"No, you do not know what ails me," he said at last, "and, therefore, cannot judge."

"Perhaps not, my dear fellow. But my experience tells me that early wounds are generally capable of cure; and, therefore, I surmise that yours may be so. The heart at your time of life is not worn out, and has strength and soundness left wherewith to throw off its maladies. I hope it may be so with you."

"God knows. I do not mean to say that there are none more to be pitied than I am; but at the present moment, I am not—not light-hearted."

"I wish I could ease your burden, my dear fellow."

"It is most preposterous in me thus to force myself upon you, and then trouble you with my cares. But I had been alone so long, and I was so weary of it!"

"By Jove, and so had I. Make no apology. And let me tell you this,—though perhaps you will not credit me,—that I would sooner laugh with a comrade than cry with him is true enough; but, if occasion demands, I can do the latter also."

He then put out his hand to me, and I pressed it in token of my friendship. My own hand was hot and rough with the heat and sand; but his was soft and cool almost as a woman's. I thoroughly hate an effeminate man; but, in spite of a certain womanly softness about this fellow, I could not hate him. "Yes," I continued, "though somewhat unused to the melting mood, I also sometimes give forth my medicinal gums. I don't want to ask you any questions, and, as a rule, I hate to be told secrets, but if I can be of any service to you in any matter I will do my best. I don't say this with reference to the present moment, but think of it before we part."

I looked round at him and saw that he was in tears. "I know that you will think that I am a weak fool," he said, pressing his handkerchief to his eyes.

"By no means. There are moments in a man's life when it becomes him to weep like a woman; but the older he grows the more seldom those moments come to him. As far as I can see of men, they never cry at that which disgraces them."

"It is left for women to do that," he answered.

"Oh, women! A woman cries for everything and for nothing. It is the sharpest arrow she has in her quiver,—the best card in her hand. When a woman cries, what can you do but give her all she asks for?"

"Do you—dislike women?"

"No, by Jove! I am never really happy unless one is near me, or more than one. A man, as a rule, has an amount of energy within him which he cannot turn to profit on himself alone. It is good for him to have a woman by him that he may work for her, and thus have exercise for his limbs and faculties. I am very fond of women. But I always like those best who are most helpless."

We were silent again for a while, and it was during this time that I found myself lying with my head in his lap. I had slept, but it could have been but for a few minutes, and when I woke I found his hand upon my brow. As I started up he said that the flies had been annoying me, and that he had not chosen to waken me as I seemed weary. "It has been that double bathing," I said, apologetically; for I always feel ashamed when I am detected sleeping in the day. "In hot weather the water does make one drowsy. By Jove, it's getting dark; we had better have the horses."

"Stay half a moment," he said, speaking very softly, and laying his hand upon my arm, "I will not detain you a minute."

"There is no hurry in life," I said.

"You promised me just now you would assist me."

"If it be in my power, I will."

"Before we part at Alexandria I will endeavour to tell you the story of my troubles, and then if you can aid me—" It struck me as he paused that I had made a rash promise, but nevertheless I must stand by it now—with one or two provisoes. The chances were that the young man was short of money, or else that he had got into a scrape about a girl. In either case I might give him some slight assistance; but, then, it behoved me to make him understand that I would not consent to become a participator in mischief. I was too old to get my head willingly into a scrape, and this I must endeavour to make him understand.

"I will, if it be in my power," I said. "I will ask no questions now; but if your trouble be about some lady—"

"It is not," said he.

"Well; so be it. Of all troubles those are the most troublesome. If you are short of cash—"

"No, I am not short of cash."

"You are not. That's well too; for want of money is a sore trouble also." And then I paused before I came to the point. "I do not suspect anything bad of you, Smith. Had I done so, I should not have spoken as I have done. And if there be nothing bad—"

"There is nothing disgraceful," he said.

"That is just what I mean; and in that case I will do anything for you that may be within my power. Now let us look for Joseph and the mucherry-boy, for it is time that we were at Jericho."

I cannot describe at length the whole of our journey from thence to our tents at Jericho, nor back to Jerusalem, nor even from Jerusalem to Jaffa. At Jericho we did sleep in tents, paying so much per night, according to the tariff. We wandered out at night, and drank coffee with a family of Arabs in the desert, sitting in a ring round their coffee-kettle. And we saw a Turkish soldier punished with the bastinado,—a sight which did not do me any good, and which made Smith very sick. Indeed after the first blow he walked away. Jericho is a remarkable spot in that pilgrim week, and I wish I had space to describe it. But I have not, for I must hurry on, back to Jerusalem and thence to Jaffa. I had much to tell also of those Bedouins; how they were essentially true to us, but teased us almost to frenzy by their continual begging. They begged for our food and our drink, for our cigars and our gunpowder, for the clothes off our backs, and the handkerchiefs out of our pockets. As to gunpowder I had none to give them, for my charges were all made up in cartridges; and I learned that the guns behind their backs were a mere pretence, for they had not a grain of powder among them.

We slept one night in Jerusalem, and started early on the following morning. Smith came to my hotel so that we might be ready together for the move. We still carried with us Joseph and the mucherry-boy; but for our Bedouins, who had duly received their forty shillings a piece, we had no further use. On our road down to Jerusalem we had much chat together, but only one adventure. Those pilgrims, of whom I have spoken, journey to Jerusalem in the greatest number by the route which we were now taking from it, and they come in long droves, reaching Jaffa in crowds by the French and Austrian steamers from Smyrna, Damascus, and

Constantinople. As their number confers security in that somewhat insecure country, many travellers from the west of Europe make arrangements to travel with them. On our way down we met the last of these caravans for the year, and we were passing it for more than two hours. On this occasion I rode first, and Smith was immediately behind me; but of a sudden I observed him to wheel his horse round, and to clamber downwards among bushes and stones towards a river that ran below us. "Hallo, Smith," I cried, "you will destroy your horse, and yourself too." But he would not answer me, and all I could do was to draw up in the path and wait. My confusion was made the worse, as at that moment a long string of pilgrims was passing by. "Good morning, sir," said an old man to me in good English. I looked up as I answered him, and saw a grey-haired gentleman, of very solemn and sad aspect. He might be seventy years of age, and I could see that he was attended by three or four servants. I shall never forget the severe and sorrowful expression of his eyes, over which his heavy eyebrows hung low. "Are there many English in Jerusalem?" he asked. "A good many," I replied; "there always are at Easter." "Can you tell me anything of any of them?" he asked. "Not a word," said I, for I knew no one; "but our consul can." And then we bowed to each other and he passed on.

I got off my horse and scrambled down on foot after Smith. I found him gathering berries and bushes as though his very soul were mad with botany; but as I had seen nothing of this in him before, I asked what strange freak had taken him.

"You were talking to that old man," he said.

"Well, yes, I was."

"That is the relation of whom I have spoken to you."

"The d—he is!"

"And I would avoid him, if it be possible."

I then learned that the old gentleman was his uncle. He had no living father or mother, and he now supposed that his relative was going to Jerusalem in quest of him. "If so," said I, "you will undoubtedly give him leg bail, unless the Austrian boat is more than ordinarily late. It is as much as we shall do to catch it, and you may be half over Africa, or far gone on your way to India, before he can be on your track again."

"I will tell you all about it at Alexandria," he replied; and then he scrambled up again with his horse, and we went on. That night we slept at the Armenian convent at Ramlath, or Ramath. This place is supposed to stand on the site of Arimathea, and is marked as such in many of the maps. The monks at this time of the year are very busy, as the pilgrims all stay here for one night on their routes backwards and forwards, and the place on such occasions is terribly crowded. On the night of our visit it was nearly empty, as a caravan had left it that morning; and thus we were indulged with separate cells, a point on which my companion seemed to lay considerable stress.

On the following day, at about noon, we entered Jaffa, and put up at an inn there which is kept by a Pole. The boat from Beyrout, which touches at Jaffa on its way to Alexandria, was not yet in, nor even sighted; we were therefore amply in time. "Shall we sail tonight?" I asked of the agent. "Yes, in all probability," he replied. "If the signal be seen before three we shall do so. If not, then not;" and so I returned to the hotel.

Smith had involuntarily shown signs of fatigue during the journey, but yet he had borne up well against it. I had never felt called on to grant any extra indulgence as to time because the work was too much for him. But now he was a good deal knocked up, and I was a little frightened fearing that I had over-driven him under the heat of the sun. I was alarmed lest he should have fever, and proposed to send for the Jaffa doctor. But this he utterly refused. He would shut himself for an hour or two in his room, he said, and by that time he trusted the boat would be in sight. It was clear to me that he was very anxious on the subject, fearing that his uncle would be back upon his heels before he had started.

I ordered a serious breakfast for myself, for with me, on such occasions, my appetite demands more immediate attention than my limbs. I also acknowledge that I become fatigued, and can lay myself at length during such idle days and sleep from hour to hour; but the desire to do so never comes till I have well eaten and drunken. A bottle of French wine, three or four cutlets of goats' flesh, an omelet made out of the freshest eggs, and an enormous dish of oranges, was the banquet set before me; and though I might have found fault with it in Paris or London, I thought that it did well enough in Jaffa. My poor friend could not join me, but had a cup of coffee in his room. "At any rate take a little brandy in it," I said to him, as I stood over his bed. "I could not swallow it," said he, looking at me with almost beseeching eyes. "Beshrew the fellow," I said to myself as I left him, carefully closing the door, so that the sound should not shake him; "he is little better than a woman, and yet I have become as fond of him as though he were my brother."

I went out at three, but up to that time the boat had not been signalled. "And we shall not get out tonight?" "No, not tonight," said the agent. "And what time tomorrow?" "If she comes in this evening, you will start by daylight. But they so manage her departure from Beyrout, that she seldom is here in the evening." "It will be noon tomorrow then?" "Yes," the man said, "noon tomorrow." I calculated, however, that the old gentleman could not possibly be on our track by that time. He would not have reached Jerusalem till late in the day on which we saw him, and it would take him some time to obtain tidings of his nephew. But it might be possible that messengers sent by him should reach Jaffa by four or five on the day after his arrival. That would be this very day which we were now wasting at Jaffa. Having thus made my calculations, I returned to Smith to give him such consolation as it might be in my power to afford.

He seemed to be dreadfully afflicted by all this. "He will have traced me to Jerusalem, and then again away; and will follow me immediately."

"That is all very well," I said; "but let even a young man do the best he can, and he will not get from Jerusalem to Jaffa in less than twelve hours. Your uncle is not a young man, and could not possibly do the journey under two days."

"But he will send. He will not mind what money he spends."

"And if he does send, take off your hat to his messengers, and bid them carry your complaints back. You are not a felon whom he can arrest."

"No, he cannot arrest me; but, ah! you do not understand;" and then he sat up on the bed, and seemed as though he were going to wring his hands in despair.

I waited for some half hour in his room, thinking that he would tell me this story of his. If he required that I should give him my aid in the presence either of his uncle or of his uncle's myrmidons, I must at any rate know what was likely to be the dispute between them. But as he said nothing I suggested that he should stroll out with me among the orange-groves by which the town is surrounded. In answer to this he looked up piteously into my face as though begging me to be merciful to him. "You are strong," said he, "and cannot understand what it is to feel fatigue as I do." And yet he had declared on commencing his journey that he would not be found to complain? Nor had he complained by a single word till after that encounter with his uncle. Nay, he had borne up well till this news had reached us of the boat being late. I felt convinced that if the boat were at this moment lying in the harbour all that appearance of excessive weakness would soon vanish. What it was that he feared I could not guess; but it was manifest to me that some great terror almost overwhelmed him.

"My idea is," said I, and I suppose that I spoke with something less of good-nature in my tone than I had assumed for the last day or two, "that no man should, under any circumstances, be so afraid of another man, as to tremble at his presence,—either at his presence or his expected presence."

"Ah, now you are angry with me; now you despise me!"

"Neither the one nor the other. But if I may take the liberty of a friend with you, I should advise you to combat this feeling of horror. If you do not, it will unman you. After all, what can your uncle do to you? He cannot rob you of your heart and soul. He cannot touch your inner self."

"You do not know," he said.

"Ah but, Smith, I do know that. Whatever may be this quarrel between you and him, you should not tremble at the thought of him; unless indeed—"

"Unless what?"

"Unless you had done aught that should make you tremble before every honest man." I own I had begun to have my doubts of him, and to fear that he had absolutely disgraced himself. Even in such case I,—I individually,—did not wish to be severe on him; but I should be annoyed to find that I had opened my heart to a swindler or a practised knave.

"I will tell you all tomorrow," said he; "but I have been guilty of nothing of that sort."

In the evening he did come out, and sat with me as I smoked my cigar. The boat, he was told, would almost undoubtedly come in by daybreak on the following morning, and be off at nine; whereas it was very improbable that any arrival from Jerusalem would be so early as that. "Beside," I reminded him, "your uncle will hardly hurry down to Jaffa, because he will have no reason to think but what you have already started. There are no telegraphs here, you know."

In the evening he was still very sad, though the paroxysm of his terror seemed to have passed away. I would not bother him, as he had himself chosen the following morning for the telling of his story. So I sat and smoked, and talked to him about our past journey, and by degrees the power of speech came back to him, and I again felt that I loved him! Yes, loved him! I have not taken many such fancies into my head, at so short a notice; but I did love him, as though he were a younger brother. I felt a delight in serving him, and though I was almost old enough to be his father, I ministered to him as though he had been an old man, or a woman.

On the following morning we were stirring at daybreak, and found that the vessel was in sight. She would be in the roads off the town in two hours' time, they said, and would start at eleven or twelve. And then we walked round by the gate of the town, and sauntered a quarter of a mile or so along the way that leads towards Jerusalem. I could see that his eye was anxiously turned down the road, but he said nothing. We saw no cloud of dust, and then we returned to breakfast.

"The steamer has come to anchor," said our dirty Polish host to us in execrable English. "And we may be off on board," said Smith. "Not yet," he said; "they must put their cargo out first." I saw, however, that Smith was uneasy, and I made up my mind to go off to the vessel at once. When they should see an English portmanteau making an offer to come up the gangway, the Austrian sailors would not stop it. So I called for the bill, and ordered that the things should be taken down to the wretched broken heap of rotten timber which they called a quay. Smith had not told me his story, but no doubt he would as soon as he was on board.

I was in the act of squabbling with the Pole over the last demand for piastres, when we heard a noise in the gateway of the inn, and I saw Smith's countenance become pale. It was an Englishman's voice asking if there were any strangers there; so I went into the courtyard, closing the door behind me, and turning

419

the key upon the landlord and Smith. "Smith," said I to myself, "will keep the Pole quiet if he have any wit left."

The man who had asked the question had the air of an upper English servant, and I thought that I recognised one of those whom I had seen with the old gentleman on the road; but the matter was soon put at rest by the appearance of that gentleman himself. He walked up into the courtyard, looked hard at me from under those bushy eyebrows, just raised his hat, and then—said, "I believe I am speaking to Mr. Jones."

"Yes," said I, "I am Mr. Jones. Can I have the honour of serving you?"

There was something peculiarly unpleasant about this man's face. At the present moment I examined it closely, and could understand the great aversion which his nephew felt towards him. He looked like a gentleman and like a man of talent, nor was there anything of meanness in his face; neither was he ill-looking, in the usual acceptation of the word; but one could see that he was solemn, austere, and overbearing; that he would be incapable of any light enjoyment, and unforgiving towards all offences. I took him to be a man who, being old himself, could never remember that he had been young, and who, therefore, hated the levities of youth. To me such a character is specially odious; for I would fain, if it be possible, be young even to my grave. Smith, if he were clever, might escape from the window of the room, which opened out upon a terrace, and still get down to the steamer. I would keep the old man in play for some time; and, even though I lost my passage, would be true to my friend. There lay our joint luggage at my feet in the yard. If Smith would venture away without his portion of it, all might yet be right.

"My name, sir, is Sir William Weston," he began. I had heard of the name before, and knew him to be a man of wealth, and family, and note. I took off my hat, and said that I had much honour in meeting Sir William Weston.

"And I presume you know the object with which I am now here," he continued.

"Not exactly," said I. "Nor do I understand how I possibly should know it, seeing that, up to this moment, I did not even know your name, and have heard nothing concerning either your movements or your affairs."

"Sir," said he, "I have hitherto believed that I might at any rate expect from you the truth."

"Sir," said I, "I am bold to think that you will not dare to tell me, either now, or at any other time, that you have received, or expect to receive, from me anything that is not true."

He then stood still, looking at me for a moment or two, and I beg to assert that I looked as fully at him. There was, at any rate, no cause why I should tremble before him. I was not his nephew, nor was I responsible for his nephew's doings towards him. Two of his servants were behind him, and on my side there stood a boy and girl belonging to the inn. They, however, could not understand a word of English. I saw that he was hesitating, but at last he spoke out. I confess, now, that his words, when they were spoken, did, at the first moment, make me tremble.

"I have to charge you," said he, "with eloping with my niece, and I demand of you to inform me where she is. You are perfectly aware that I am her guardian by law."

I did tremble;—not that I cared much for Sir William's guardianship, but I saw before me so terrible an embarrassment! And then I felt so thoroughly abashed in that I had allowed myself to be so deceived! It all came back upon me in a moment, and covered me with a shame that even made me blush. I had travelled through the desert with a woman for days, and had not discovered her, though she had given me a thousand signs. All those signs I remembered now, and I blushed painfully. When her hand was on my forehead I still thought that she was a man! I declare that at this moment I felt a stronger disinclination to face my late companion than I did to encounter her angry uncle.

"Your niece!" I said, speaking with a sheepish bewilderment which should have convinced him at once of my innocence. She had asked me, too, whether I was a married man, and I had denied it. How was I to escape from such a mess of misfortunes? I declare that I began to forget her troubles in my own.

"Yes, my niece,—Miss Julia Weston. The disgrace which you have brought upon me must be wiped out; but my first duty is to save that unfortunate young woman from further misery."

"If it be as you say," I exclaimed, "by the honour of a gentleman—"

"I care nothing for the honour of a gentleman till I see it proved. Be good enough to inform me, sir, whether Miss Weston is in this house."

For a moment I hesitated; but I saw at once that I should make myself responsible for certain mischief, of which I was at any rate hitherto in truth innocent, if I allowed myself to become a party to concealing a young lady. Up to this period I could at any rate defend myself, whether my defence were believed or not believed. I still had a hope that the charming Julia might have escaped through the window, and a feeling that if she had done so I was not responsible. When I turned the lock I turned it on Smith.

For a moment I hesitated, and then walked slowly across the yard and opened the door. "Sir William," I said, as I did so, "I travelled here with a companion dressed as a man; and I believed him to be what he seemed till this minute."

"Sir!" said Sir William, with a look of scorn in his face which gave me the lie in my teeth as plainly as any words could do. And then he entered the room. The Pole was standing in one corner, apparently amazed at what was going on, and Smith,—I may as well call her Miss Weston at once, for the baronet's statement was true,—was sitting on a sort of divan in the corner of the chamber hiding her face in her hands. She had made no attempt at an escape, and a full explanation was therefore indispensable. For myself I own that I felt ashamed of my part in the play,—ashamed even of my own innocency. Had I been less innocent I should certainly have contrived to appear much less guilty. Had it occurred to me on the banks of the Jordan that Smith was a lady, I should not have travelled with her in her gentleman's habiliments from Jerusalem to Jaffa. Had she consented to remain under my protection, she must have done so without a masquerade.

The uncle stood still and looked at his niece. He probably understood how thoroughly stern and disagreeable was his own face, and considered that he could punish the crime of his relative in no severer way than by looking at her. In this I think he was right. But at last there was a necessity for speaking. "Unfortunate young woman!" he said, and then paused.

"We had better get rid of the landlord," I said, "before we come to any explanation." And I motioned to the man to leave the room. This he did very unwillingly, but at last he was gone.

"I fear that it is needless to care on her account who may hear the story of her shame," said Sir William. I looked at Miss Weston, but she still sat hiding her face. However, if she did not defend herself, it was necessary that I should defend both her and me.

"I do not know how far I may be at liberty to speak with reference to the private matters of yourself or of your—your niece, Sir William Weston. I would not willingly interfere—"

"Sir," said he, "your interference has already taken place. Will you have the goodness to explain to me what are your intentions with regard to that lady?"

My intentions! Heaven help me! My intentions, of course, were to leave her in her uncle's hands. Indeed, I could hardly be said to have formed any intention since I had learned that I had been honoured by a lady's presence. At this moment I deeply regretted that I had thoughtlessly stated to her that I was an unmarried man. In doing so I had had no object. But at that time "Smith" had been quite a stranger to me, and I had not thought it necessary to declare my own private concerns. Since that I had talked so little of myself that the fact of my family at home had not been mentioned. "Will you have the goodness to explain what are your intentions with regard to that lady?" said the baronet.

"Oh, Uncle William!" exclaimed Miss Weston, now at length raising her head from her hands.

"Hold your peace, madam," said he. "When called upon to speak, you will find your words with difficulty enough. Sir, I am waiting for an answer from you."

"But, uncle, he is nothing to me;—the gentleman is nothing to me!"

"By the heavens above us, he shall be something, or I will know the reason why! What! he has gone off with you; he has travelled through the country with you, hiding you from your only natural friend; he has been your companion for weeks—"

"Six days, sir," said I.

"Sir!" said the baronet, again giving me the lie. "And now," he continued, addressing his niece, "you tell me that he is nothing to you. He shall give me his promise that he will make you his wife at the consulate at Alexandria, or I will destroy him. I know who he is."

"If you know who I am," said I, "you must know—"

But he would not listen to me. "And as for you, madam, unless he makes me that promise—" And then he paused in his threat, and, turning round, looked me in the face. I saw that she also was looking at me, though not openly as he did; and some flattering devil that was at work round my heart, would have persuaded that she also would have heard a certain answer given without dismay,—would even have received comfort in her agony from such an answer. But the reader knows how completely that answer was out of my power.

"I have not the slightest ground for supposing," said I, "that the lady would accede to such an arrangement,—if it were possible. My acquaintance with her has been altogether confined to—. To tell the truth, I have not been in Miss Weston's confidence, and have only taken her for that which she has seemed to be."

"Sir!" said the baronet, again looking at me as though he would wither me on the spot for my falsehood.

"It is true!" said Julia, getting up from her seat, and appealing with clasped hands to her uncle—"as true as Heaven."

"Madam!" said he, "do you both take me for a fool?"

"That you should take me for one," said I, "would be very natural. The facts are as we state to you. Miss Weston,—as I now learn that she is,—did me the honour of calling at my hotel, having heard—" And then it seemed to me as though I were attempting to screen myself by telling the story against her, so I was again silent. Never in my life had I been in a position of such extraordinary difficulty. The duty which I owed to Julia as a woman, and to Sir William as a guardian, and to myself as the father of a family, all clashed with each other. I was anxious to be generous, honest, and prudent, but it was impossible; so I made up my mind to say nothing further.

"Mr. Jones," said the baronet, "I have explained to you the only arrangement which under the present circumstances I can permit to pass without open exposure and condign punishment. That you are a gentleman by birth, education, and position I am aware,"—whereupon I raised my hat, and then he continued: "That lady has three hundred a year of her own—"

"And attractions, personal and mental, which are worth ten times the money," said I, and I bowed to my fair friend, who looked at me the while with sad beseeching eyes. I confess that the mistress of my bosom, had she known my thoughts at that one moment, might have had cause for anger.

"Very well," continued he. "Then the proposal which I name, cannot, I imagine, but be satisfactory. If you will make to her and to me the only amends which it is in your power as a gentleman to afford, I will forgive all. Tell me that you will make her your wife on your arrival in Egypt."

I would have given anything not to have looked at Miss Weston at this moment, but I could not help it. I did turn my face half round to her before I answered, and then felt that I had been cruel in doing so. "Sir William," said I, "I have at home already a wife and family of my own."

"It is not true!" said he, retreating a step, and staring at me with amazement.

"There is something, sir," I replied, "in the unprecedented circumstances of this meeting, and in your position with regard to that lady, which, joined to your advanced age, will enable me to regard that useless insult as unspoken. I am a married man. There is the signature of my wife's last letter," and I handed him one which I had received as I was leaving Jerusalem.

But the coarse violent contradiction which Sir William had given me was nothing compared with the reproach conveyed in Miss Weston's countenance. She looked at me as though all her anger were now turned against me. And yet, methought, there was more of sorrow than of resentment in her countenance. But what cause was there for either? Why should I be reproached, even by her look? She did not remember at the moment that when I answered her chance question as to my domestic affairs, I had answered it as to a man who was a stranger to me, and not as to a beautiful woman, with whom I was about to pass certain days in close and intimate society. To her, at the moment, it seemed as though I had cruelly deceived her. In truth, the one person really deceived had been myself.

And here I must explain, on behalf of the lady, that when she first joined me she had no other view than that of seeing the banks of the Jordan in that guise which she had chosen to assume, in order to escape from the solemnity and austerity of a disagreeable relative. She had been very foolish, and that was all. I take it that she had first left her uncle at Constantinople, but on this point I never got certain information. Afterwards, while we were travelling together, the idea had come upon her, that she might go on as far as Alexandria with me. And then I know nothing further of the lady's intentions, but I am certain that her wishes were good and pure. Her uncle had been intolerable to her, and she had fled from him. Such had been her offence, and no more.

"Then, sir," said the baronet, giving me back my letter, "you must be a double-dyed villain."

"And you, sir," said I—. But here Julia Weston interrupted me.

"Uncle, you altogether wrong this gentleman," she said. "He has been kind to me beyond my power of words to express; but, till told by you, he knew nothing of my secret. Nor would he have known it," she added, looking down upon the ground. As to that latter assertion, I was at liberty to believe as much as I pleased.

The Pole now came to the door, informing us that any who wished to start by the packet must go on board, and therefore, as the unreasonable old gentleman perceived, it was necessary that we should all make our arrangements. I cannot say that they were such as enable me to look back on them with satisfaction. He did seem now at last to believe that I had been an unconscious agent in his niece's stratagem, but he hardly on that account became civil to me. "It was absolutely necessary," he said, "that he and that unfortunate young woman," as he would call her, "should depart at once,—by this ship now going." To this proposition of course I made no opposition. "And you, Mr. Jones," he continued, "will at once perceive that you, as a gentleman, should allow us to proceed on our journey without the honour of your company."

This was very dreadful, but what could I say; or, indeed, what could I do? My most earnest desire in the matter was to save Miss Weston from annoyance; and under existing circumstances my presence on board could not but be a burden to her. And then, if I went,—if I did go, in opposition to the wishes of the baronet, could I trust my own prudence? It was better for all parties that I should remain.

"Sir William," said I, after a minute's consideration, "if you will apologise to me for the gross insults you have offered me, it shall be as you say."

"Mr. Jones," said Sir William, "I do apologise for the words which I used to you while I was labouring under a very natural misconception of the circumstances." I do not know that I was much the better for the apology, but at the moment I regarded it sufficient.

Their things were then hurried down to the strand, and I accompanied them to the ruined quay. I took off my hat to Sir William as he was first let down into the boat. He descended first, so that he might receive his niece,—for all Jaffa now knew that it was a lady,—and then I gave her my hand for the last time. "God bless you, Miss Weston," I said, pressing it closely. "God bless you, Mr. Jones," she replied. And from that day to this I have neither spoken to her nor seen her.

I waited a fortnight at Jaffa for the French boat, eating cutlets of goat's flesh, and wandering among the orange groves. I certainly look back on that fortnight as the most miserable period of my life. I had been deceived, and had failed to discover the deceit, even though the deceiver had perhaps wished that I should do so. For that blindness I have never forgiven myself.

AN UNPROTECTED FEMALE
AT THE PYRAMIDS

In the happy days when we were young, no description conveyed to us so complete an idea of mysterious reality as that of an Oriental city. We knew it was actually there, but had such vague notions of its ways and looks! Let any one remember his early impressions as to Bagdad or Grand Cairo, and then say if this was not so. It was probably taken from the "Arabian Nights," and the picture produced was one of strange, fantastic, luxurious houses; of women who were either very young and very beautiful, or else very old and very cunning; but in either state exercising much more influence in life than women in the East do now; of good-natured, capricious, though sometimes tyrannical monarchs; and of life full of quaint mysteries, quite unintelligible in every phasis, and on that account the more picturesque.

And perhaps Grand Cairo has thus filled us with more wonder even than Bagdad. We have been in a certain manner at home at Bagdad, but have only visited Grand Cairo occasionally. I know no place which was to me, in early years, so delightfully mysterious as Grand Cairo.

But the route to India and Australia has changed all this. Men from all countries going to the East, now pass through Cairo, and its streets and costumes are no longer strange to us. It has become also a resort for invalids, or rather for those who fear that they may become invalids if they remain in a cold climate during the winter months. And thus at Cairo there is always to be found a considerable population of French, Americans, and of English. Oriental life is brought home to us, dreadfully diluted by western customs, and the delights of the "Arabian Nights" are shorn of half their value. When we have seen a thing it is never so magnificent to us as when it was half unknown.

It is not much that we deign to learn from these Orientals,—we who glory in our civilisation. We do not copy their silence or their abstemiousness, nor that invariable mindfulness of his own personal dignity which always adheres to a Turk or to an Arab. We chatter as much at Cairo as elsewhere, and eat as much and drink as much, and dress ourselves generally in the same old ugly costume. But we do usually take upon ourselves to wear red caps, and we do ride on donkeys.

Nor are the visitors from the West to Cairo by any means confined to the male sex. Ladies are to be seen in the streets quite regardless of the Mahommedan custom which presumes a veil to be necessary for an appearance in public; and, to tell the truth, the Mahommedans in general do not appear to be much shocked by their effrontery.

A quarter of the town has in this way become inhabited by men wearing coats and waistcoats, and by women who are without veils; but the English tongue in Egypt finds its centre at Shepheard's Hotel. It is here that people congregate who are looking out for parties to visit with them the Upper Nile, and who are generally all smiles and courtesy; and here also are to be found they who have just returned from this journey, and who are often in a frame of mind towards their companions that is much less amiable. From hence, during the winter, a cortege proceeds almost daily to the pyramids, or to Memphis, or to the petrified forest, or to the City of the Sun. And then, again, four or five times a month the house is filled with young aspirants going out to India, male and female, full of valour and bloom; or with others coming home, no longer young, no longer aspiring, but laden with children and grievances.

The party with whom we are at present concerned is not about to proceed further than the Pyramids, and we shall be able to go with them and return in one and the same day.

It consisted chiefly of an English family, Mr. and Mrs. Damer, their daughter, and two young sons;—of these chiefly, because they were the nucleus to which the others had attached themselves as adherents; they had originated the journey, and in the whole management of it Mr. Damer retarded himself as the master.

The adherents were, firstly, M. Delabordeau, a Frenchman, now resident in Cairo, who had given out that he was in some way concerned in the canal about to be made between the

Mediterranean and the Red Sea. In discussion on this subject he had become acquainted with Mr. Damer; and although the latter gentleman, true to English interests, perpetually declared that the canal would never be made, and thus irritated M. Delabordeau not a little—nevertheless, some measure of friendship had grown up between them.

There was also an American gentleman, Mr. Jefferson Ingram, who was comprising all countries and all nations in one grand tour, as American gentlemen so often do. He was young and good-looking, and had made himself especially agreeable to Mr. Damer, who had declared, more than once, that Mr. Ingram was by far the most rational American he had ever met. Mr. Ingram would listen to Mr. Damer by the half-hour as to the virtue of the British Constitution, and had even sat by almost with patience when Mr. Damer had expressed a doubt as to the good working of the United States' scheme of policy,—which, in an American, was most wonderful. But some of the sojourners at Shepheard's had observed that Mr. Ingram was in the habit of talking with Miss Damer almost as much as with her father, and argued from that, that fond as the young man was of politics, he did sometimes turn his mind to other things also.

And then there was Miss Dawkins. Now Miss Dawkins was an important person, both as to herself and as to her line of life, and she must be described. She was, in the first place, an unprotected female of about thirty years of age. As this is becoming an established profession, setting itself up as it were in opposition to the old world idea that women, like green peas, cannot come to perfection without supporting-sticks, it will be understood at once what were Miss Dawkins's sentiments. She considered—or at any rate so expressed herself—that peas could grow very well without sticks, and could not only grow thus unsupported, but could also make their way about the world without any incumbrance of sticks whatsoever. She did not intend, she said, to rival Ida Pfeiffer, seeing that she was attached in a moderate way to bed and board, and was attached to society in a manner almost more than moderate; but she had no idea of being prevented from seeing anything she wished to see because she had neither father, nor husband, nor brother available for the purpose of escort. She was a human creature, with arms and legs, she said; and she intended to use them. And this was all very well; but nevertheless she had a strong inclination to use the arms and legs of other people when she could make them serviceable.

In person Miss Dawkins was not without attraction. I should exaggerate if I were to say that she was beautiful and elegant; but she was good looking, and not usually ill mannered. She was tall, and gifted with features rather sharp and with eyes very bright. Her hair was of the darkest shade of brown, and was always worn in bandeaux, very neatly. She appeared generally in black, though other circumstances did not lead one to suppose that she was in mourning; and then, no other travelling costume is so convenient! She always wore a dark broad-brimmed straw hat, as to the ribbons on which she was rather particular. She was very neat about her gloves and boots; and though it cannot be said that her dress was got up without reference to expense, there can be no doubt that it was not effected without considerable outlay,—and more considerable thought.

Miss Dawkins—Sabrina Dawkins was her name, but she seldom had friends about her intimate enough to use the word Sabrina—was certainly a clever young woman. She could talk on most subjects, if not well, at least well enough to amuse. If she had not read much, she never showed any lamentable deficiency; she was good-humoured, as a rule, and could on occasions be very soft and winning. People who had known her long would sometimes say that she was selfish; but with new acquaintance she was forbearing and self-denying.

With what income Miss Dawkins was blessed no one seemed to know. She lived like a gentlewoman, as far as outward appearance went, and never seemed to be in want; but some people would say that she knew very well how many sides there were to a shilling, and some enemy had once declared that she was an "old soldier." Such was Miss Dawkins.

She also, as well as Mr. Ingram and M. Delabordeau, had laid herself out to find the weak side of Mr. Damer. Mr. Damer, with all his family, was going up the Nile, and it was known that he had room for two in his boat over and above his own family. Miss Dawkins had told him that she had not quite made up her mind to undergo so great a fatigue, but that, nevertheless, she had a longing of the soul to see something of Nubia. To this Mr. Damer had answered nothing but "Oh!" which Miss Dawkins had not found to be encouraging.

But she had not on that account despaired. To a married man there are always two sides, and in this instance there was Mrs. Damer as well as Mr. Damer. When Mr. Damer said "Oh!" Miss Dawkins sighed, and said, "Yes, indeed!" then smiled, and betook herself to Mrs. Damer.

Now Mrs. Damer was soft-hearted, and also somewhat old-fashioned. She did not conceive any violent affection for Miss Dawkins, but she told her daughter that "the single lady by herself was a very nice young woman, and that it was a thousand pities she should have to go about so much alone like."

Miss Damer had turned up her pretty nose, thinking, perhaps, how small was the chance that it ever should be her own lot to be an unprotected female. But Miss Dawkins carried her point at any rate as regarded the expedition to the Pyramids.

Miss Damer, I have said, had a pretty nose. I may also say that she had pretty eyes, mouth, and chin, with other necessary appendages, all pretty. As to the two Master Damers, who were respectively of the ages of fifteen and sixteen, it may be sufficient to say that they were conspicuous for red caps and for the constancy with which they raced their donkeys.

And now the donkeys, and the donkey boys, and the dragomans were all standing at the steps of Shepheard's Hotel. To each donkey there was a donkey-boy, and to each gentleman there was a dragoman, so that a goodly cortege was assembled, and a goodly noise was made. It may here be remarked, perhaps with some little pride, that not half the noise is given in Egypt to persons speaking any other language that is bestowed on those whose vocabulary is English.

This lasted for half an hour. Had the party been French the donkeys would have arrived only fifteen minutes before the appointed time. And then out came Damer pere and Damer mere, Damer fille, and Damer fils. Damer mere was leaning on her husband, as was her wont. She was not an unprotected female, and had no desire to make any attempts in that line. Damer fille was attended sedulously by Mr. Ingram, for whose demolishment, however, Mr. Damer still brought up, in a loud voice, the fag ends of certain political arguments which he would fain have poured direct into the ears of his opponent, had not his wife been so persistent in claiming her privileges. M. Delabordeau should have followed with Miss Dawkins, but his French politeness, or else his fear of the unprotected female, taught him to walk on the other side of the mistress of the party.

Miss Dawkins left the house with an eager young Damer yelling on each side of her; but nevertheless, though thus neglected by the gentlemen of the party, she was all smiles and prettiness, and looked so sweetly on Mr. Ingram when that gentleman stayed a moment to help her on to her donkey, that his heart almost misgave him for leaving her as soon as she was in her seat.

And then they were off. In going from the hotel to the Pyramids our party had not to pass through any of the queer old narrow streets of the true Cairo—Cairo the Oriental. They all lay behind them as they went down by the back of the hotel, by the barracks of the Pasha and the College of the Dervishes, to the village of old Cairo and the banks of the Nile.

Here they were kept half an hour while their dragomans made a bargain with the ferryman, a stately reis, or captain of a boat, who declared with much dignity that he could not carry them over for a sum less than six times the amount to which he was justly entitled; while the dragomans, with great energy on behalf of their masters, offered him only five times that sum.

As far as the reis was concerned, the contest might soon have been at an end, for the man was not without a conscience; and would have been content with five times and a half; but then the three dragomans quarrelled among themselves as to which should have the paying of the money, and the affair became very tedious.

"What horrid, odious men!" said Miss Dawkins, appealing to Mr. Damer. "Do you think they will let us go over at all?"

"Well, I suppose they will; people do get over generally, I believe. Abdallah! Abdallah! why don't you pay the man? That fellow is always striving to save half a piastre for me."

"I wish he wasn't quite so particular," said Mrs. Damer, who was already becoming rather tired; "but I'm sure he's a very honest man in trying to protect us from being robbed."

"That he is," said Miss Dawkins. "What a delightful trait of national character it is to see these men so faithful to their employers." And then at last they got over the ferry, Mr. Ingram having descended among the combatants, and settled the matter in dispute by threats and shouts, and an uplifted stick.

They crossed the broad Nile exactly at the spot where the nilometer, or river guage, measures from day to day, and from year to year, the increasing or decreasing treasures of the stream, and landed at a village where thousands of eggs are made into chickens by the process of artificial incubation.

Mrs. Damer thought that it was very hard upon the maternal hens—the hens which should have been maternal—that they should be thus robbed of the delights of motherhood.

"So unnatural, you know," said Miss Dawkins; "so opposed to the fostering principles of creation. Don't you think so, Mr. Ingram?"

Mr. Ingram said he didn't know. He was again seating Miss Damer on her donkey, and it must be presumed that he performed this feat clumsily; for Fanny Damer could jump on and off the animal with hardly a finger to help her, when her brother or her father was her escort; but now, under the hands of Mr. Ingram, this work of mounting was one which required considerable time and care. All which Miss Dawkins observed with precision.

"It's all very well talking," said Mr. Damer, bringing up his donkey nearly alongside that of Mr. Ingram, and ignoring his daughter's presence, just as he would have done that of his dog; "but you must admit that political power is more equally distributed in England than it is in America."

"Perhaps it is," said Mr. Ingram; "equally distributed among, we will say, three dozen families," and he made a feint as though to hold in his impetuous donkey, using the spur, however, at the same time on the side that was unseen by Mr. Damer. As he did so, Fanny's donkey became equally impetuous, and the two cantered on in advance of the whole party. It was quite in vain that Mr. Damer, at the top of his voice, shouted out something about "three dozen corruptible demagogues." Mr. Ingram found it quite impossible to restrain his donkey so as to listen to the sarcasm.

"I do believe papa would talk politics," said Fanny, "if he were at the top of Mont Blanc, or under the Falls of Niagara. I do hate politics, Mr. Ingram."

"I am sorry for that, very," said Mr. Ingram, almost sadly.

"Sorry, why? You don't want me to talk politics, do you?"

"In America we are all politicians, more or less; and, therefore, I suppose you will hate us all."

"Well, I rather think I should," said Fanny; "you would be such bores." But there was something in her eye, as she spoke, which atoned for the harshness of her words.

"A very nice young man is Mr. Ingram; don't you think so?" said Miss Dawkins to Mrs. Damer. Mrs. Damer was going along upon her donkey, not altogether comfortably. She much wished to have her lord and legitimate protector by her side, but he had left her to the care of a dragoman whose English was not intelligible to her, and she was rather cross.

"Indeed, Miss Dawkins, I don't know who are nice and who are not. This nasty donkey stumbles at ever step. There! I know I shall be down directly."

"You need not be at all afraid of that; they are perfectly safe, I believe, always," said Miss Dawkins, rising in her stirrup, and handling her reins quite triumphantly. "A very little practice will make you quite at home."

"I don't know what you mean by a very little practice. I have been here six weeks. Why did you put me on such a bad donkey as this?" and she turned to Abdallah, the dragoman.

"Him berry good donkey, my lady; berry good,—best of all. Call him Jack in Cairo. Him go to Pyramid and back, and mind noting."

"What does he say, Miss Dawkins?"

"He says that that donkey is one called Jack. If so I've had him myself many times, and Jack is a very good donkey."

"I wish you had him now with all my heart," said Mrs. Damer. Upon which Miss Dawkins offered to change; but those perils of mounting and dismounting were to Mrs. Damer a great deal too severe to admit of this.

"Seven miles of canal to be carried out into the sea, at a minimum depth of twenty-three feet, and the stone to be fetched from Heaven knows where! All the money in France wouldn't do it." This was addressed by Mr. Damer to M. Delabordeau, whom he had caught after the abrupt flight of Mr. Ingram.

"Den we will borrow a leetle from England," said M. Delabordeau.

"Precious little, I can tell you. Such stock would not hold its price in our markets for twenty-four hours. If it were made, the freights would be too heavy to allow of merchandise passing through. The heavy goods would all go round; and as for passengers and mails, you don't expect to get them, I suppose, while there is a railroad ready made to their hand?"

"Ye vill carry all your ships through vidout any transportation. Think of that, my friend."

"Pshaw! You are worse than Ingram. Of all the plans I ever heard of it is the most monstrous, the most impracticable, the most—" But here he was interrupted by the entreaties of his wife, who had, in absolute deed and fact, slipped from her donkey, and was now calling lustily for her husband's aid. Whereupon Miss Dawkins allied herself to the Frenchman, and listened with an air of strong conviction to those arguments which were so weak in the ears of Mr. Damer. M. Delabordeau was about to ride across the Great Desert to Jerusalem, and it might perhaps be quite as well to do that with him, as to go up the Nile as far as the second cataract with the Damers.

"And so, M. Delabordeau, you intend really to start for Mount Sinai?"

"Yes, mees; ve intend to make one start on Monday week."

"And so on to Jerusalem. You are quite right. It would be a thousand pities to be in these countries, and to return without going over such ground as that. I shall certainly go to Jerusalem myself by that route."

"Vot, mees! you? Would you not find it too much fatigante?"

"I care nothing for fatigue, if I like the party I am with,— nothing at all, literally. You will hardly understand me, perhaps, M. Delabordeau; but I do not see any reason why I, as a young woman, should not make any journey that is practicable for a young man."

"Ah! dat is great resolution for you, mees."

"I mean as far as fatigue is concerned. You are a Frenchman, and belong to the nation that is at the head of all human civilisation—"

M. Delabordeau took off his hat and bowed low, to the peak of his donkey saddle. He dearly loved to hear his country praised, as Miss Dawkins was aware.

"And I am sure you must agree with me," continued Miss Dawkins, "that the time is gone by for women to consider themselves helpless animals, or to be so considered by others."

"Mees Dawkins vould never be considered, not in any times at all, to be one helpless animal," said M. Delabordeau civilly.

"I do not, at any rate, intend to be so regarded," said she. "It suits me to travel alone; not that I am averse to society; quite the contrary; if I meet pleasant people I am always ready to join them. But it suits me to travel without any permanent party, and I do not see why false shame should prevent my seeing the world as thoroughly as though I belonged to the other sex. Why should it, M. Delabordeau?"

M. Delabordeau declared that he did not see any reason why it should.

"I am passionately anxious to stand upon Mount Sinai," continued Miss Dawkins; "to press with my feet the earliest spot in sacred history, of the identity of which we are certain; to feel within me the awe-inspiring thrill of that thrice sacred hour!"

The Frenchman looked as though he did not quite understand her, but he said that it would be magnifique.

"You have already made up your party I suppose, M. Delabordeau?"

M. Delabordeau gave the names of two Frenchmen and one Englishman who were going with him.

"Upon my word it is a great temptation to join you," said Miss Dawkins, "only for that horrid Englishman."

"Vat, Mr. Stanley?"

"Oh, I don't mean any disrespect to Mr. Stanley. The horridness I speak of does not attach to him personally, but to his stiff, respectable, ungainly, well-behaved, irrational, and uncivilised country. You see I am not very patriotic."

"Not quite so much as my friend, Mr. Damer."

"Ha! ha! ha! an excellent creature, isn't he? And so they all are, dear creatures. But then they are so backward. They are most anxious that I should join them up the Nile, but—," and then Miss Dawkins shrugged her shoulders gracefully, and, as she flattered herself, like a Frenchwoman. After that they rode on in silence for a few moments.

"Yes, I must see Mount Sinai," said Miss Dawkins, and then sighed deeply. M. Delabordeau, notwithstanding that his country does stand at the head of all human civilisation, was not courteous enough to declare that if Miss Dawkins would join his party across the desert, nothing would be wanting to make his beatitude in this world perfect.

Their road from the village of the chicken-hatching ovens lay up along the left bank of the Nile, through an immense grove of lofty palm-trees, looking out from among which our visitors could ever and anon see the heads of the two great Pyramids;—that is, such of them could see it as felt any solicitude in the matter.

It is astonishing how such things lose their great charm as men find themselves in their close neighbourhood. To one living in New York or London, how ecstatic is the interest inspired by these huge structures. One feels that no price would be too high to pay for seeing them as long as time and distance, and the world's inexorable task-work, forbid such a visit. How intense would be the delight of climbing over the wondrous handiwork of those wondrous architects so long since dead; how thrilling the awe with which one would penetrate down into their interior caves—those caves in which lay buried the bones of ancient kings, whose very names seem to have come to us almost from another world!

But all these feelings become strangely dim, their acute edges wonderfully worn, as the subjects which inspired them are brought near to us. "Ah! so those are the Pyramids, are they?" says the traveller, when the first glimpse of them is shown to him from the window of a railway carriage. "Dear me; they don't look so very high, do they? For Heaven's sake put the blind down, or we shall be destroyed by the dust." And then the ecstasy and keen delight of the Pyramids has vanished for ever.

Our friends, therefore, who for weeks past had seen from a distance, though they had not yet visited them, did not seem to have any strong feeling on the subject as they trotted through the grove of palm-trees. Mr. Damer had not yet escaped from his wife, who was still fretful from the result of her little accident.

"It was all the chattering of that Miss Dawkins," said Mrs. Damer. "She would not let me attend to what I was doing."

"Miss Dawkins is an ass," said her husband.

"It is a pity she has no one to look after her," said Mrs. Damer. M. Delabordeau was still listening to Miss Dawkins's raptures about Mount Sinai. "I wonder whether she has got any money," said M. Delabordeau to himself. "It can't be much," he went on thinking, "or she would not be left in this way by herself." And the result of his thoughts was that Miss Dawkins, if undertaken, might probably become more plague than profit. As to Miss Dawkins herself, though she was ecstatic about Mount Sinai—which was not present—she seemed to have forgotten the poor Pyramids, which were then before her nose.

The two lads were riding races along the dusty path, much to the disgust of their donkey-boys. Their time for enjoyment was to come. There were hampers to be opened; and then the absolute climbing of the Pyramids would actually be a delight to them.

As for Miss Damer and Mr. Ingram, it was clear that they had forgotten palm-trees, Pyramids, the Nile, and all Egypt. They had escaped to a much fairer paradise.

"Could I bear to live among Republicans?" said Fanny, repeating the last words of her American lover, and looking down from her donkey to the ground as she did so. "I hardly know what Republicans are, Mr. Ingram."

"Let me teach you," said he.

"You do talk such nonsense. I declare there is that Miss Dawkins looking at us as though she had twenty eyes. Could you not teach her, Mr. Ingram?"

And so they emerged from the palm-tree grove, through a village crowded with dirty, straggling Arab children, on to the cultivated plain, beyond which the Pyramids stood, now full before them; the two large Pyramids, a smaller one, and the huge sphynx's head all in a group together.

"Fanny," said Bob Damer, riding up to her, "mamma wants you; so toddle back."

"Mamma wants me! What can she want me for now?" said Fanny, with a look of anything but filial duty in her face.

"To protect her from Miss Dawkins, I think. She wants you to ride at her side, so that Dawkins mayn't get at her. Now, Mr. Ingram, I'll bet you hall-a-crown I'm at the top of the big Pyramid before you."

Poor Fanny! She obeyed, however; doubtless feeling that it would not do as yet to show too plainly that she preferred Mr. Ingram to her mother. She arrested her donkey, therefore, till Mrs. Damer overtook her; and Mr. Ingram, as he paused for a moment with her while she did so, fell into the hands of Miss Dawkins.

"I cannot think, Fanny, how you get on so quick," said Mrs. Damer. "I'm always last; but then my donkey is such a very nasty one. Look there, now; he's always trying to get me off."

"We shall soon be at the Pyramids now, mamma."

"How on earth I am ever to get back again I cannot think. I am so tired now that I can hardly sit."

"You'll be better, mamma, when you get your luncheon and a glass of wine."

"How on earth we are to eat and drink with those nasty Arab people around us, I can't conceive. They tell me we shall be eaten up by them. But, Fanny, what has Mr. Ingram been saying to you all the day?"

"What has he been saying, mamma? Oh! I don't know;—a hundred things, I dare say. But he has not been talking to me all the time."

"I think he has, Fanny, nearly, since we crossed the river. Oh, dear! oh, dear! this animal does hurt me so! Every time he moves he flings his head about, and that gives me such a bump." And then Fanny commiserated her mother's sufferings, and in her commiseration contrived to elude any further questionings as to Mr. Ingram's conversation.

"Majestic piles, are they not?" said Miss Dawkins, who, having changed her companion, allowed her mind to revert from Mount Sinai to the Pyramids. They were now riding through cultivated ground, with the vast extent of the sands of Libya before them. The two Pyramids were standing on the margin of the sand, with the head of the recumbent sphynx plainly visible between them. But no idea can be formed of the size of this immense figure till it is visited much more closely. The body is covered with sand, and the head and neck alone stand above the surface of the ground. They were still two miles distant, and the sphynx as yet was but an obscure mount between the two vast Pyramids.

"Immense piles!" said Miss Dawkins, repeating her own words.

"Yes, they are large," said Mr. Ingram, who did not choose to indulge in enthusiasm in the presence of Miss Dawkins.

"Enormous! What a grand idea!—eh, Mr. Ingram? The human race does not create such things as those nowadays!"

"No, indeed," he answered; "but perhaps we create better things."

"Better! You do not mean to say, Mr. Ingram, that you are an utilitarian. I do, in truth, hope better things of you than that. Yes! steam mills are better, no doubt, and mechanics' institutes and penny newspapers. But is nothing to be valued but what is useful?" And Miss Dawkins, in the height of her enthusiasm, switched her donkey severely over the shoulder.

"I might, perhaps, have said also that we create more beautiful things," said Mr. Ingram.

"But we cannot create older things."

"No, certainly; we cannot do that."

"Nor can we imbue what we do create with the grand associations which environ those piles with so intense an interest. Think of the mighty dead, Mr. Ingram, and of their great homes when living. Think of the hands which it took to raise those huge blocks—"

"And of the lives which it cost."

"Doubtless. The tyranny and invincible power of the royal architects add to the grandeur of the idea. One would not wish to have back the kings of Egypt."

"Well, no; they would be neither useful nor beautiful."

"Perhaps not; and I do not wish to be picturesque at the expense of my fellow-creatures."

"I doubt, even, whether they would be picturesque."

"You know what I mean, Mr. Ingram. But the associations of such names, and the presence of the stupendous works with which they are connected, fill the soul with awe. Such, at least, is the effect with mine."

"I fear that my tendencies, Miss Dawkins, are more realistic than your own."

"You belong to a young country, Mr. Ingram, and are naturally prone to think of material life. The necessity of living looms large before you."

"Very large, indeed, Miss Dawkins."

"Whereas with us, with some of us at least, the material aspect has given place to one in which poetry and enthusiasm prevail. To such among us the associations of past times are very dear. Cheops, to me, is more than Napoleon Bonaparte."

"That is more than most of your countrymen can say, at any rate, just at present."

"I am a woman," continued Miss Dawkins.

Mr. Ingram took off his hat in acknowledgment both of the announcement and of the fact.

"And to us it is not given—not given as yet—to share in the great deeds of the present. The envy of your sex has driven us from the paths which lead to honour. But the deeds of the past are as much ours as yours."

"Oh, quite as much."

"'Tis to your country that we look for enfranchisement from this thraldom. Yes, Mr. Ingram, the women of America have that strength of mind which has been wanting to those of Europe. In the United States woman will at last learn to exercise her proper mission."

Mr. Ingram expressed a sincere wish that such might be the case; and then wondering at the ingenuity with which Miss Dawkins had travelled round from Cheops and his Pyramid to the rights of women in America, he contrived to fall back, under the pretence of asking after the ailments of Mrs. Damer.

And now at last they were on the sand, in the absolute desert, making their way up to the very foot of the most northern of the two Pyramids. They were by this time surrounded by a crowd of Arab guides, or Arabs professing to be guides, who had already ascertained that Mr. Damer was the chief of the party, and were accordingly driving him almost to madness by the offers of their services, and their assurance that he could not possibly see the outside or the inside of either structure, or even remain alive upon the ground, unless he at once accepted their offers made at their own prices.

"Get away, will you?" said he. "I don't want any of you, and I won't have you! If you take hold of me I'll shoot you!" This was said to one specially energetic Arab, who, in his efforts to secure his prey, had caught hold of Mr. Damer by the leg.

"Yes, yes, I say! Englishmen always take me;—me—me, and then no break him leg. Yes—yes—yes;—I go. Master, say yes. Only one leetle ten shillings!"

"Abdallah!" shouted Mr. Damer, "why don't you take this man away? Why don't you make him understand that if all the Pyramids depended on it, I would not give him sixpence!"

And then Abdallah, thus invoked, came up, and explained to the man in Arabic that he would gain his object more surely if he would behave himself a little more quietly; a hint which the man took for one minute, and for one minute only.

And then poor Mrs. Damer replied to an application for backsheish by the gift of a sixpence. Unfortunate woman! The word backsheish means, I believe, a gift; but it has come in Egypt to signify money, and is eternally dinned into the ears of strangers by Arab suppliants. Mrs. Damer ought to have known better, as, during the last six weeks she had never shown her face out of Shepheard's Hotel without being pestered for backsheish; but she was tired and weak, and foolishly thought to rid herself of the man who was annoying her.

No sooner had the coin dropped from her hand into that of the Arab, than she was surrounded by a cluster of beggars, who loudly made their petitions as though they would, each of them, individually be injured if treated with less liberality than that first comer. They took hold of her donkey, her bridle, her saddle, her legs, and at last her arms and hands, screaming for backsheish in voices that were neither sweet nor mild.

In her dismay she did give away sundry small coins—all, probably, that she had about her; but this only made the matter worse. Money was going, and each man, by sufficient energy, might hope to get some of it. They were very energetic, and so frightened the poor lady that she would certainly have fallen, had she not been kept on her seat by the pressure around her.

"Oh, dear! oh, dear! get away," she cried. "I haven't got any more; indeed I haven't. Go away, I tell you! Mr. Damer! oh, Mr. Damer!" and then, in the excess of her agony, she uttered one loud, long, and continuous shriek.

Up came Mr. Damer; up came Abdallah; up came M. Delabordeau; up came Mr. Ingram, and at last she was rescued.

"You shouldn't go away and leave me to the mercy of these nasty people. As to that Abdallah, he is of no use to anybody."

"Why you bodder de good lady, you dem blackguard?" said Abdallah, raising his stick, as though he were going to lay them all low with a blow. "Now you get noting, you tief!"

The Arabs for a moment retired to a little distance, like flies driven from a sugar-bowl; but it was easy to see that, like the flies, they would return at the first vacant moment.

And now they had reached the very foot of the Pyramids and proceeded to dismount from their donkeys. Their intention was first to ascend to the top, then to come down to their banquet, and after that to penetrate into the interior. And all this would seem to be easy of performance. The Pyramid is undoubtedly high, but it is so constructed as to admit of climbing without difficulty. A lady mounting it would undoubtedly need some assistance, but any man possessed of moderate activity would require no aid at all.

But our friends were at once imbued with the tremendous nature of the task before them. A sheikh of the Arabs came forth, who communicated with them through Abdallah. The work could be done, no doubt, he said; but a great many men would be wanted to assist. Each lady must have four Arabs, and each gentlemen three; and then, seeing that the work would be peculiarly severe on this special day, each of these numerous Arabs must be remunerated by some very large number of piastres.

Mr. Damer, who was by no means a close man in his money dealings, opened his eyes with surprise, and mildly expostulated; M. Delabordeau, who was rather a close man in his reckonings, immediately buttoned up his breeches pocket and declared that he should decline to mount the Pyramid at all at that price; and then Mr. Ingram descended to the combat.

The protestations of the men were fearful. They declared, with loud voices, eager actions, and manifold English oaths, that an attempt was being made to rob them. They had a right to demand the sums which they were charging, and it was a shame that English gentlemen should come and take the bread out of their mouths. And so they screeched, gesticulated, and swore, and frightened poor Mrs. Damer almost into fits.

But at last it was settled and away they started, the sheikh declaring that the bargain had been made at so low a rate as to leave him not one piastre for himself. Each man had an Arab on each side of him, and Miss Dawkins and Miss Damer had each, in addition, one behind. Mrs. Damer was so frightened as altogether to have lost all ambition to ascend. She sat below on a fragment of stone, with the three dragomans standing around her as guards; but even with the three dragomans the attacks on her were so frequent, and as she declared afterwards she was so bewildered, that she never had time to remember that she had come there from England to see the Pyramids, and that she was now immediately under them.

The boys, utterly ignoring their guides, scrambled up quicker than the Arabs could follow them. Mr. Damer started off at a pace which soon brought him to the end of his tether, and from that point was dragged up by the sheer strength of his assistants; thereby accomplishing the wishes of the men, who induce their victims to start as rapidly as possible, in order that they may soon find themselves helpless from want of wind. Mr. Ingram endeavoured to attach himself to Fanny, and she would have been nothing loth to have him at her right hand instead of the hideous brown, shrieking, one-eyed Arab who took hold of her. But it was soon found that any such arrangement was impossible. Each guide felt that if he lost his own peculiar hold he would lose his prey, and held on, therefore, with invincible tenacity. Miss Dawkins looked, too, as though she had thought to be attended to by some Christian cavalier, but no Christian cavalier was forthcoming. M. Delabordeau was the wisest, for he took the matter quietly, did as he was bid, and allowed the guides nearly to carry him to the top of the edifice.

"Ha! so this is the top of the Pyramid, is it?" said Mr. Damer, bringing out his words one by one, being terribly out of breath. "Very wonderful, very wonderful, indeed!"

"It is wonderful," said Miss Dawkins, whose breath had not failed her in the least, "very wonderful, indeed! Only think, Mr. Damer, you might travel on for days and days, till days became months, through those interminable sands, and yet you would never come to the end of them. Is it not quite stupendous?"

"Ah, yes, quite,—puff, puff"—said Mr. Damer striving to regain his breath.

Mr. Damer was now at her disposal; weak and worn with toil and travel, out of breath, and with half his manhood gone; if ever she might prevail over him so as to procure from his mouth an assent to that Nile proposition, it would be now. And after all, that Nile proposition was the best one now before her. She did not quite like the idea of starting off across the Great Desert without any lady, and was not sure that she was prepared to be fallen in love with by M. Delabordeau, even if there should ultimately be any readiness on the part of that gentleman to perform the role of lover. With Mr. Ingram the matter was different, nor was she so diffident of her own charms as to think it altogether impossible that she might succeed, in the teeth of that little chit, Fanny Damer. That Mr. Ingram would join the party up the Nile she had very little doubt; and then there would be one place left for her. She would thus, at any rate, become commingled with a most respectable family, who might be of material service to her.

Thus actuated she commenced an earnest attack upon Mr. Damer.

"Stupendous!" she said again, for she was fond of repeating favourite words. "What a wondrous race must have been those Egyptian kings of old!"

"I dare say they were," said Mr. Damer, wiping his brow as he sat upon a large loose stone, a fragment lying on the flat top of the Pyramid, one of those stones with which the complete apex was once made, or was once about to be made.

"A magnificent race! so gigantic in their conceptions! Their ideas altogether overwhelm us poor, insignificant, latter-day mortals. They built these vast Pyramids; but for us, it is task enough to climb to their top."

"Quite enough," ejaculated Mr. Damer.

But Mr. Damer would not always remain weak and out of breath, and it was absolutely necessary for Miss Dawkins to hurry away from Cheops and his tomb, to Thebes and Karnac.

"After seeing this it is impossible for any one with a spark of imagination to leave Egypt without going farther a-field."

Mr. Damer merely wiped his brow and grunted. This Miss Dawkins took as a signal of weakness, and went on with her task perseveringly.

"For myself, I have resolved to go up, at any rate, as far as Asouan and the first cataract. I had thought of acceding to the wishes of a party who are going across the Great Desert by Mount Sinai to Jerusalem; but the kindness of yourself and Mrs. Damer is so great, and the prospect of joining in your boat is so pleasurable, that I have made up my mind to accept your very kind offer."

This, it will be acknowledged, was bold on the part of Miss Dawkins; but what will not audacity effect? To use the slang of modern language, cheek carries everything nowadays. And whatever may have been Miss Dawkins's deficiencies, in this virtue she was not deficient.

"I have made up my mind to accept your very kind offer," she said, shining on Mr. Damer with her blandest smile.

What was a stout, breathless, perspiring, middle-aged gentleman to do under such circumstances? Mr. Damer was a man who, in most matters, had his own way. That his wife should have given such an invitation without consulting him, was, he knew, quite impossible. She would as soon have thought of asking all those Arab guides to accompany them. Nor was it to be thought of that he should allow himself to be kidnapped into such an arrangement by the impudence of any Miss Dawkins. But there was, he felt, a difficulty in answering such a proposition from a young lady with a direct negative, especially while he was so scant of breath. So he wiped his brow again, and looked at her.

"But I can only agree to this on one understanding," continued Miss Dawkins, "and that is, that I am allowed to defray my own full share of the expense of the journey."

Upon hearing this Mr. Damer thought that he saw his way out of the wood. "Wherever I go, Miss Dawkins, I am always the paymaster myself," and this he contrived to say with some sternness, palpitating though he still was; and the sternness which was deficient in his voice he endeavoured to put into his countenance.

But he did not know Miss Dawkins. "Oh, Mr. Damer," she said, and as she spoke her smile became almost blander than it was before; "oh, Mr. Damer, I could not think of suffering you to be so liberal; I could not, indeed. But I shall be quite content that you should pay everything, and let me settle with you in one sum afterwards."

Mr. Damer's breath was now rather more under his own command. "I am afraid, Miss Dawkins," he said, "that Mrs. Damer's weak state of health will not admit of such an arrangement."

"What, about the paying?"

"Not only as to that, but we are a family party, Miss Dawkins; and great as would be the benefit of your society to all of us, in Mrs. Damer's present state of health, I am afraid—in short, you would not find it agreeable.—And therefore—" this he added, seeing that she was still about to persevere—"I fear that we must forego the advantage you offer."

And then, looking into his face, Miss Dawkins did perceive that even her audacity would not prevail.

"Oh, very well," she said, and moving from the stone on which she had been sitting, she walked off, carrying her head very high, to a corner of the Pyramid from which she could look forth alone towards the sands of Libya.

In the mean time another little overture was being made on the top of the same Pyramid,—an overture which was not received quite in the same spirit. While Mr. Damer was recovering his breath for the sake of answering Miss Dawkins, Miss Damer had walked to the further corner of the square platform on which they were placed, and there sat herself down with her face turned towards Cairo. Perhaps it was not singular that Mr. Ingram should have followed her.

This would have been very well if a dozen Arabs had not also followed them. But as this was the case, Mr. Ingram had to play his game under some difficulty. He had no sooner seated himself beside her than they came and stood directly in front of the seat, shutting out the view, and by no means improving the fragrance of the air around them.

"And this, then, Miss Damer, will be our last excursion together," he said, in his tenderest, softest tone.

"De good Englishman will gib de poor Arab one little backsheish," said an Arab, putting out his hand and shaking Mr. Ingram's shoulder.

"Yes, yes, yes; him gib backsheish," said another.

"Him berry good man," said a third, putting up his filthy hand, and touching Mr. Ingram's face.

"And young lady berry good, too; she give backsheish to poor Arab."

"Yes," said a fourth, preparing to take a similar liberty with Miss Damer.

This was too much for Mr. Ingram. He had already used very positive language in his endeavour to assure his tormentors that they would not get a piastre from him. But this only changed their soft persuasions into threats. Upon hearing which, and upon seeing what the man attempted to do in his endeavour to get money from Miss Damer, he raised his stick, and struck first one and then the other as violently as he could upon their heads.

Any ordinary civilised men would have been stunned by such blows, for they fell on the bare foreheads of the Arabs; but the objects of the American's wrath merely skulked away; and the others, convinced by the only arguments which they understood, followed in pursuit of victims who might be less pugnacious.

It is hard for a man to be at once tender and pugnacious—to be sentimental, while he is putting forth his physical strength with all the violence in his power. It is difficult, also, for him to be gentle instantly after having been in a rage. So he changed his tactics at the moment, and came to the point at once in a manner befitting his present state of mind.

"Those vile wretches have put me in such a heat," he said, "that I hardly know what I am saying. But the fact is this, Miss Damer, I cannot leave Cairo without knowing—. You understand what I mean, Miss Damer."

"Indeed I do not, Mr. Ingram; except that I am afraid you mean nonsense."

"Yes, you do; you know that I love you. I am sure you must know it. At any rate you know it now."

"Mr. Ingram, you should not talk in such a way."

"Why should I not? But the truth is, Fanny, I can talk in no other way. I do love you dearly. Can you love me well enough to go and be my wife in a country far away from your own?"

Before she left the top of the Pyramid Fanny Damer had said that she would try.

Mr. Ingram was now a proud and happy man, and seemed to think the steps of the Pyramid too small for his elastic energy. But Fanny feared that her troubles were to come. There was papa—that terrible bugbear on all such occasions. What would papa say? She was sure her papa would not allow her to marry and go so far away from her own family and country. For herself, she liked the Americans—always had liked them; so she said;—would desire nothing better than to live among them. But papa! And Fanny sighed as she felt that all the recognised miseries of a young lady in love were about to fall upon her.

Nevertheless, at her lover's instance, she promised, and declared, in twenty different loving phrases, that nothing on earth should ever make her false to her love or to her lover.

"Fanny, where are you? Why are you not ready to come down?" shouted Mr. Damer, not in the best of tempers. He felt that he had almost been unkind to an unprotected female, and his heart misgave him. And yet it would have misgiven him more had he allowed himself to be entrapped by Miss Dawkins.

"I am quite ready, papa," said Fanny, running up to him—for it may be understood that there is quite room enough for a young lady to run on the top of the Pyramid.

"I am sure I don't know where you have been all the time," said Mr. Damer; "and where are those two boys?"

Fanny pointed to the top of the other Pyramid, and there they were, conspicuous with their red caps.

"And M. Delabordeau?"

"Oh! he has gone down, I think;—no, he is there with Miss Dawkins." And in truth Miss Dawkins was leaning on his arm most affectionately, as she stooped over and looked down upon the ruins below her.

"And where is that fellow, Ingram?" said Mr. Damer, looking about him. "He is always out of the way when he's wanted."

To this Fanny said nothing. Why should she? She was not Mr. Ingram's keeper.

And then they all descended, each again with his proper number of Arabs to hurry and embarrass him; and they found Mr. Damer at the bottom, like a piece of sugar covered with flies. She was heard to declare afterwards that she would not go to the Pyramids again, not if they were to be given to her for herself, as ornaments for her garden.

The picnic lunch among the big stones at the foot of the Pyramid was not a very gay affair. Miss Dawkins talked more than any one else, being determined to show that she bore her defeat gallantly. Her conversation, however, was chiefly addressed to M. Delabordeau, and he seemed to think more of his cold chicken and ham than he did of her wit and attention.

Fanny hardly spoke a word. There was her father before her and she could not eat, much less talk, as she thought of all that she would have to go through. What would he say to the idea of having an American for a son-in-law?

Nor was Mr. Ingram very lively. A young man when he has been just accepted, never is so. His happiness under the present circumstances was, no doubt, intense, but it was of a silent nature.

And then the interior of the building had to be visited. To tell the truth none of the party would have cared to perform this feat had it not been for the honour of the thing. To have come from Paris, New York, or London, to the Pyramids, and then not to have visited the very tomb of Cheops, would have shown on the part of all of them an indifference to subjects of interest which would have been altogether fatal to their character as travellers. And so a party for the interior was made up.

Miss Damer when she saw the aperture through which it was expected that she should descend, at once declared for staying with her mother. Miss Dawkins, however, was enthusiastic for the journey. "Persons with so very little command over their nerves might really as well stay at home," she said to Mr. Ingram, who glowered at her dreadfully for expressing such an opinion about his Fanny.

This entrance into the Pyramids is a terrible task, which should be undertaken by no lady. Those who perform it have to creep down, and then to be dragged up, through infinite dirt, foul smells, and bad air; and when they have done it, they see nothing. But they do earn the gratification of saying that they have been inside a Pyramid.

"Well, I've done that once," said Mr. Damer, coming out, "and I do not think that any one will catch me doing it again. I never was in such a filthy place in my life."

"Oh, Fanny! I am so glad you did not go; I am sure it is not fit for ladies," said poor Mrs. Damer, forgetful of her friend Miss Dawkins.

"I should have been ashamed of myself," said Miss Dawkins, bristling up, and throwing back her head as she stood, "if I had allowed any consideration to have prevented my visiting such a spot. If it be not improper for men to go there, how can it be improper for women?"

"I did not say improper, my dear," said Mrs. Damer, apologetically.

"And as for the fatigue, what can a woman be worth who is afraid to encounter as much as I have now gone through for the sake of visiting the last resting-place of such a king as Cheops?" And Miss Dawkins, as she pronounced the last words, looked round her with disdain upon poor Fanny Damer.

"But I meant the dirt," said Mrs. Damer.

"Dirt!" ejaculated Miss Dawkins, and then walked away. Why should she now submit her high tone of feeling to the Damers, or why care longer for their good opinion? Therefore she scattered contempt around her as she ejaculated the last word, "dirt."

And then the return home! "I know I shall never get there," said Mrs. Damer, looking piteously up into her husband's face.

"Nonsense, my dear; nonsense; you must get there." Mrs. Damer groaned, and acknowledged in her heart that she must,— either dead or alive.

"And, Jefferson," said Fanny, whispering—for there had been a moment since their descent in which she had been instructed to call him by his Christian name—"never mind talking to me going home. I will ride by mamma. Do you go with papa and put him in good humour; and it he says anything about the lords and the bishops, don't you contradict him, you know."

What will not a man do for love? Mr. Ingram promised.

And in this way they started; the two boys led the van; then came Mr. Damer and Mr. Ingram, unusually and unpatriotically acquiescent as to England's aristocratic propensities; then Miss Dawkins riding, alas! alone; after her, M. Delabordeau, also alone,—the ungallant Frenchman! And the rear was brought up by Mrs. Damer and her daughter, flanked on each side by a dragoman, with a third dragoman behind them.

And in this order they went back to Cairo, riding their donkeys, and crossing the ferry solemnly, and, for the most part, silently. Mr. Ingram did talk, as he had an important object in view,—that of putting Mr. Damer into a good humour.

In this he succeeded so well that by the time they had remounted, after crossing the Nile, Mr. Damer opened his heart to his companion on the subject that was troubling him, and told him all about Miss Dawkins.

"I don't see why we should have a companion that we don't like for eight or ten weeks, merely because it seems rude to refuse a lady."

"Indeed, I agree with you," said Mr. Ingram; "I should call it weak-minded to give way in such a case."

"My daughter does not like her at all," continued Mr. Damer.

"Nor would she be a nice companion for Miss Damer; not according to my way of thinking," said Mr. Ingram.

"And as to my having asked her, or Mrs. Damer having asked her! Why, God bless my soul, it is pure invention on the woman's part!"

"Ha! ha! ha!" laughed Mr. Ingram; "I must say she plays her game well; but then she is an old soldier, and has the benefit of experience." What would Miss Dawkins have said had she known that Mr. Ingram called her an old soldier?

"I don't like the kind of thing at all," said Mr. Damer, who was very serious upon the subject. "You see the position in which I am placed. I am forced to be very rude, or—"

"I don't call it rude at all."

"Disobliging, then; or else I must have all my comfort invaded and pleasure destroyed by, by, by—" And Mr. Damer paused, being at a loss for an appropriate name for Miss Dawkins.

"By an unprotected female," suggested Mr. Ingram.

"Yes, just so. I am as fond of pleasant company as anybody; but then I like to choose it myself."

"So do I," said Mr. Ingram, thinking of his own choice.

"Now, Ingram, if you would join us, we should be delighted."

"Upon my word, sir, the offer is too flattering," said Ingram, hesitatingly; for he felt that he could not undertake such a journey until Mr. Damer knew on what terms he stood with Fanny.

"You are a terrible democrat," said Mr. Damer, laughing; "but then, on that matter, you know, we could agree to differ."

"Exactly so," said Mr. Ingram, who had not collected his thoughts or made up his mind as to what he had better say and do, on the spur of the moment.

"Well, what do you say to it?" said Mr. Damer, encouragingly. But Ingram paused before he answered.

"For Heaven's sake, my dear fellow, don't have the slightest hesitation in refusing, if you don't like the plan."

"The fact is, Mr. Damer, I should like it too well."

"Like it too well?"

"Yes, sir, and I may as well tell you now as later. I had intended this evening to have asked for your permission to address your daughter."

"God bless my soul!" said Mr. Damer, looking as though a totally new idea had now been opened to him.

"And under these circumstances, I will now wait and see whether or no you will renew your offer."

"God bless my soul!" said Mr. Damer, again. It often does strike an old gentleman as very odd that any man should fall in love with his daughter, whom he has not ceased to look upon as a child. The case is generally quite different with mothers. They seem to think that every young man must fall in love with their girls.

"And have you said anything to Fanny about this?" asked Mr. Damer.

"Yes, sir, I have her permission to speak to you."

"God bless my soul!" said Mr. Damer; and by this time they had arrived at Shepheard's Hotel.

"Oh, mamma," said Fanny, as soon as she found herself alone with her mother that evening, "I have something that I must tell you."

"Oh, Fanny, don't tell me anything tonight, for I am a great deal too tired to listen."

"But oh, mamma, pray;—you must listen to this; indeed you must." And Fanny knelt down at her mother's knee, and looked beseechingly up into her face.

"What is it, Fanny? You know that all my bones are sore, and I am so tired that I am almost dead."

"Mamma, Mr. Ingram has—"

"Has what, my dear? has he done anything wrong?"

"No, mamma: but he has;—he has proposed to me." And Fanny, bursting into tears, hid her face in her mother's lap.

And thus the story was told on both sides of the house. On the next day, as a matter of course, all the difficulties and dangers of such a marriage as that which was now projected were insisted on by both father and mother. It was improper; it would cause a severing of the family not to be thought of; it would be an alliance of a dangerous nature, and not at all calculated to insure happiness; and, in short, it was impossible. On that day, therefore, they all went to bed very unhappy. But on the next day, as was also a matter of course, seeing that there were no pecuniary difficulties, the mother and father were talked over, and Mr. Ingram was accepted as a son-in-law. It need hardly be said that the offer of a place in Mr. Damer's boat was again made, and that on this occasion it was accepted without hesitation.

There was an American Protestant clergyman resident in Cairo, with whom, among other persons, Miss Dawkins had become acquainted. Upon this gentleman or upon his wife Miss Dawkins called a few days after the journey to the Pyramid, and finding him in his study, thus performed her duty to her neighbour,—

"You know your countryman Mr. Ingram, I think?" said she.

"Oh, yes; very intimately."

"If you have any regard for him, Mr. Burton," such was the gentleman's name, "I think you should put him on his guard."

"On his guard against what?" said Mr. Burton with a serious air, for there was something serious in the threat of impending misfortune as conveyed by Miss Dawkins.

"Why," said she, "those Damers, I fear, are dangerous people."

"Do you mean that they will borrow money of him?"

"Oh, no; not that, exactly; but they are clearly setting their cap at him."

"Setting their cap at him?"

"Yes; there is a daughter, you know; a little chit of a thing; and I fear Mr. Ingram may be caught before he knows where he is. It would be such a pity, you know. He is going up the river with them, I hear. That, in his place, is very foolish. They asked me, but I positively refused."

Mr. Burton remarked that "In such a matter as that Mr. Ingram would be perfectly able to take care of himself."

"Well, perhaps so; but seeing what was going on, I thought it my duty to tell you." And so Miss Dawkins took her leave.

Mr. Ingram did go up the Nile with the Damers, as did an old friend of the Damers who arrived from England. And a very pleasant trip they had of it. And, as far as the present historian knows, the two lovers were shortly afterwards married in England.

Poor Miss Dawkins was left in Cairo for some time on her beam ends. But she was one of those who are not easily vanquished. After an interval of ten days she made acquaintance with an Irish family—having utterly failed in moving the hard heart of M. Delabordeau—and with these she proceeded to Constantinople. They consisted of two brothers and a sister, and were, therefore, very convenient for matrimonial purposes. But nevertheless, when I last heard of Miss Dawkins, she was still an unprotected female.

VICTORIAN SHORT STORIES

Stories of Courtship

ANGELA

An Inverted Love Story
By William Schwenk Gilbert

I am a poor paralysed fellow who, for many years past, has been confined to a bed or a sofa. For the last six years I have occupied a small room, giving on to one of the side canals of Venice, and having no one about me but a deaf old woman, who makes my bed and attends to my food; and there I eke out a poor income of about thirty pounds a year by making water-colour drawings of flowers and fruit (they are the cheapest models in Venice), and these I send to a friend in London, who sells them to a dealer for small sums. But, on the whole, I am happy and content.

It is necessary that I should describe the position of my room rather minutely. Its only window is about five feet above the water of the canal, and above it the house projects some six feet, and overhangs the water, the projecting portion being supported by stout piles driven into the bed of the canal. This arrangement has the disadvantage (among others) of so limiting my upward view that I am unable to see more than about ten feet of the height of the house immediately opposite to me, although, by reaching as far out of the window as my infirmity will permit, I can see for a considerable distance up and down the canal, which does not exceed fifteen feet in width. But, although I can see but little of the material house opposite, I can see its reflection upside down in the canal, and I take a good deal of inverted interest in such of its inhabitants as show themselves from time to time (always upside down) on its balconies and at its windows.

When I first occupied my room, about six years ago, my attention was directed to the reflection of a little girl of thirteen or so (as nearly as I could judge), who passed every day on a balcony just above the upward range of my limited field of view. She had a glass of flowers and a crucifix on a little table by her side; and as she sat there, in fine weather, from early morning until dark, working assiduously all the time, I concluded that she earned her living by needle-work. She was certainly an industrious little girl, and, as far as I could judge by her upside-down reflection, neat in her dress and pretty. She had an old mother, an invalid, who, on warm days, would sit on the balcony with her, and it interested me to see the little maid wrap the old lady in shawls, and bring pillows for her chair, and a stool for her feet, and every now and again lay down her work and kiss and fondle the old lady for half a minute, and then take up her work again.

Time went by, and as the little maid grew up, her reflection grew down, and at last she was quite a little woman of, I suppose, sixteen or seventeen. I can only work for a couple of hours or so in the brightest part of the day, so I had plenty of time on my hands in which to watch her movements, and sufficient imagination to weave a little romance about her, and to endow her with a beauty which, to a great extent, I had to take for granted. I saw—or fancied that I could see—that she began to take an interest in *my* reflection (which, of course, she could see as I could see hers); and one day, when it appeared to me that she was looking right at it—that is to say when her reflection appeared to be looking right at me—I tried the desperate experiment of nodding to her, and to my intense delight her reflection nodded in reply. And so our two reflections became known to one another.

It did not take me very long to fall in love with her, but a long time passed before I could make up my mind to do more than nod to her every morning, when the old woman moved me from my bed to the sofa at the window, and again in the evening, when the little maid left the balcony for that day. One day, however, when I saw her reflection looking at mine, I nodded to her, and threw a flower into the canal. She nodded several times in return, and I saw her direct her mother's attention to the incident. Then every morning

I threw a flower into the water for 'good morning', and another in the evening for 'goodnight', and I soon discovered that I had not altogether thrown them in vain, for one day she threw a flower to join mine, and she laughed and clapped her hands when she saw the two flowers join forces and float away together. And then every morning and every evening she threw her flower when I threw mine, and when the two flowers met she clapped her hands, and so did I; but when they were separated, as they sometimes were, owing to one of them having met an obstruction which did not catch the other, she threw up her hands in a pretty affectation of despair, which I tried to imitate but in an English and unsuccessful fashion. And when they were rudely run down by a passing gondola (which happened not unfrequently) she pretended to cry, and I did the same. Then, in pretty pantomime, she would point downwards to the sky to tell me that it was Destiny that had caused the shipwreck of our flowers, and I, in pantomime, not nearly so pretty, would try to convey to her that Destiny would be kinder next time, and that perhaps tomorrow our flowers would be more fortunate—and so the innocent courtship went on. One day she showed me her crucifix and kissed it, and thereupon I took a little silver crucifix that always stood by me, and kissed that, and so she knew that we were one in religion.

One day the little maid did not appear on her balcony, and for several days I saw nothing of her; and although I threw my flowers as usual, no flower came to keep it company. However, after a time, she reappeared, dressed in black, and crying often, and then I knew that the poor child's mother was dead, and, as far as I knew, she was alone in the world. The flowers came no more for many days, nor did she show any sign of recognition, but kept her eyes on her work, except when she placed her handkerchief to them. And opposite to her was the old lady's chair, and I could see that, from time to time, she would lay down her work and gaze at it, and then a flood of tears would come to her relief. But at last one day she roused herself to nod to me, and then her flower came, day by day, and my flower went forth to join it, and with varying fortunes the two flowers sailed away as of yore.

But the darkest day of all to me was when a good-looking young gondolier, standing right end uppermost in his gondola (for I could see *him* in the flesh), worked his craft alongside the house, and stood talking to her as she sat on the balcony. They seemed to speak as old friends—indeed, as well as I could make out, he held her by the hand during the whole of their interview which lasted quite half an hour. Eventually he pushed off, and left my heart heavy within me. But I soon took heart of grace, for as soon as he was out of sight, the little maid threw two flowers growing on the same stem—an allegory of which I could make nothing, until it broke upon me that she meant to convey to me that he and she were brother and sister, and that I had no cause to be sad. And thereupon I nodded to her cheerily, and she nodded to me, and laughed aloud, and I laughed in return, and all went on again as before.

Then came a dark and dreary time, for it became necessary that I should undergo treatment that confined me absolutely to my bed for many days, and I worried and fretted to think that the little maid and I should see each other no longer, and worse still, that she would think that I had gone away without even hinting to her that I was going. And I lay awake at night wondering how I could let her know the truth, and fifty plans flitted through my brain, all appearing to be feasible enough at night, but absolutely wild and impracticable in the morning. One day—and it was a bright day indeed for me—the old woman who tended me told me that a gondolier had inquired whether the English signor had gone away or had died; and so I learnt that the little maid had been anxious about me, and that she had sent her brother to inquire, and the brother had no doubt taken to her the reason of my protracted absence from the window.

From that day, and ever after during my three weeks of bed-keeping, a flower was found every morning on the ledge of my window, which was within easy reach of anyone in a boat; and when at last a day came when I could be moved, I took my accustomed place on my sofa at the window, and the little maid saw me, and stood on her head (so to speak) and clapped her hands upside down with a delight that was as eloquent as my right-end-up delight could be. And so the first time the gondolier passed my window I beckoned to him, and he pushed alongside, and told me, with many bright smiles, that he was glad indeed to see me well again. Then I thanked him and his sister for their many kind thoughts about me during my retreat, and I then learnt from him that her name was

Angela, and that she was the best and purest maiden in all Venice, and that anyone might think himself happy indeed who could call her sister, but that he was happier even than her brother, for he was to be married to her, and indeed they were to be married the next day.

Thereupon my heart seemed to swell to bursting, and the blood rushed through my veins so that I could hear it and nothing else for a while. I managed at last to stammer forth some words of awkward congratulation, and he left me, singing merrily, after asking permission to bring his bride to see me on the morrow as they returned from church.

'For', said he, 'my Angela has known you very long—ever since she was a child, and she has often spoken to me of the poor Englishman who was a good Catholic, and who lay all day long for years and years on a sofa at a window, and she had said over and over again how dearly she wished she could speak to him and comfort him; and one day, when you threw a flower into the canal, she asked me whether she might throw another, and I told her yes, for he would understand that it meant sympathy for one sorely afflicted.'

And so I learned that it was pity, and not love, except indeed such love as is akin to pity, that prompted her to interest herself in my welfare, and there was an end of it all.

For the two flowers that I thought were on one stem were two flowers tied together (but I could not tell that), and they were meant to indicate that she and the gondolier were affianced lovers, and my expressed pleasure at this symbol delighted her, for she took it to mean that I rejoiced in her happiness.

And the next day the gondolier came with a train of other gondoliers, all decked in their holiday garb, and on his gondola sat Angela, happy, and blushing at her happiness. Then he and she entered the house in which I dwelt, and came into my room (and it was strange indeed, after so many years of inversion, to see her with her head above her feet!), and then she wished me happiness and a speedy restoration to good health (which could never be); and I in broken words and with tears in my eyes, gave her the little silver crucifix that had stood by my bed or my table for so many years. And Angela took it reverently, and crossed herself, and kissed it, and so departed with her delighted husband.

And as I heard the song of the gondoliers as they went their way—the song dying away in the distance as the shadows of the sundown closed around me—I felt that they were singing the requiem of the only love that had ever entered my heart.

THE PARSON'S DAUGHTER OF OXNEY COLNE

By Anthony Trollope

The prettiest scenery in all England—and if I am contradicted in that assertion, I will say in all Europe—is in Devonshire, on the southern and southeastern skirts of Dartmoor, where the rivers Dart and Avon and Teign form themselves, and where the broken moor is half cultivated, and the wild-looking uplands fields are half moor. In making this assertion I am often met with much doubt, but it is by persons who do not really know the locality. Men and women talk to me on the matter who have travelled down the line of railway from Exeter to Plymouth, who have spent a fortnight at Torquay, and perhaps made an excursion from Tavistock to the convict prison on Dartmoor. But who knows the glories of Chagford? Who has walked through the parish of Manaton? Who is conversant with Lustleigh Cleeves and Withycombe in the moor? Who has explored Holne Chase? Gentle reader, believe me that you will be rash in contradicting me unless you have done these things.

There or thereabouts—I will not say by the waters of which little river it is washed—is the parish of Oxney Colne. And for those who would wish to see all the beauties of this lovely country a sojourn in Oxney Colne would be most desirable, seeing that the sojourner would then be brought nearer to all that he would delight to visit, than at any other spot in the country. But there is an objection to any such arrangement. There are only two decent houses in the whole parish, and these are—or were when I knew the locality—small and fully occupied by their possessors. The larger and better is the parsonage in which lived the parson and his daughter; and the smaller is the freehold residence of a certain Miss Le Smyrger, who owned a farm of a hundred acres which was rented by one Farmer Cloysey, and who also possessed some thirty acres round her own house which she managed herself, regarding herself to be quite as great in cream as Mr. Cloysey, and altogether superior to him in the article of cider. 'But yeu has to pay no rent, Miss,' Farmer Cloysey would say, when Miss Le Smyrger expressed this opinion of her art in a manner too defiant. 'Yeu pays no rent, or yeu couldn't do it.' Miss Le Smyrger was an old maid, with a pedigree and blood of her own, a hundred and thirty acres of fee-simple land on the borders of Dartmoor, fifty years of age, a constitution of iron, and an opinion of her own on every subject under the sun.

And now for the parson and his daughter. The parson's name was Woolsworthy—or Woolathy as it was pronounced by all those who lived around him—the Rev. Saul Woolsworthy; and his daughter was Patience Woolsworthy, or Miss Patty, as she was known to the Devonshire world of those parts. That name of Patience had not been well chosen for her for she was a hot-tempered damsel, warm in her convictions, and inclined to express them freely. She had but two closely intimate friends in the world, and by both of them this freedom of expression had been fully permitted to her since she was a child. Miss Le Smyrger and her father were well accustomed to her ways, and on the whole well satisfied with them. The former was equally free and equally warm-tempered as herself, and as Mr. Woolsworthy was allowed by his daughter to be quite paramount on his own subject—for he had a subject—he did not object to his daughter being paramount on all others. A pretty girl was Patience Woolsworthy at the time of which I am writing, and one who possessed much that was worthy of remark and admiration had she lived where beauty meets with admiration, or where force of character is remarked. But at Oxney Colne, on the borders of Dartmoor, there were few to appreciate her, and it seemed as though she herself had but little idea of carrying her talent further afield, so that it might not remain for ever wrapped in a blanket.

She was a pretty girl, tall and slender, with dark eyes and black hair. Her eyes were perhaps too round for regular beauty, and her hair was perhaps too crisp; her mouth was large and expressive; her nose was finely formed, though a critic in female form might have declared it to be somewhat broad. But her countenance altogether was very attractive—if only it might be seen without that resolution for dominion which occasionally marred it, though sometimes it even added to her attractions.

It must be confessed on behalf of Patience Woolsworthy that the circumstances of her life had peremptorily called upon her to exercise dominion. She had lost her mother when she was sixteen, and had had neither brother nor sister. She had no neighbours near her fit either from education or rank to interfere in the conduct of her life, excepting always Miss Le Smyrger. Miss Le Smyrger would have done anything for her, including the whole management of her morals and of the parsonage household, had Patience been content with such an arrangement. But much as Patience had ever loved Miss Le Smyrger, she was not content with this, and therefore she had been called on to put forth a strong hand of her own. She had put forth this strong hand early, and hence had come the character which I am attempting to describe. But I must say on behalf of this girl that it was not only over others that she thus exercised dominion. In acquiring that power she had also acquired the much greater power of exercising rule over herself.

But why should her father have been ignored in these family arrangements? Perhaps it may almost suffice to say, that of all living men her father was the man best conversant with the antiquities of the county in which he lived. He was the Jonathan Oldbuck of Devonshire, and especially of Dartmoor,—but without that decision of character which enabled Oldbuck to keep his womenkind in some kind of subjection, and probably enabled him also to see that his weekly bill did not pass their proper limits. Our Mr. Oldbuck, of Oxney Colne, was sadly deficient in these respects. As a parish pastor with but a small cure he did his duty with sufficient energy to keep him, at any rate, from reproach. He was kind and charitable to the poor, punctual in his services, forbearing with the farmers around him, mild with his brother clergymen, and indifferent to aught that bishop or archdeacon might think or say of him. I do not name this latter attribute as a virtue, but as a fact. But all these points were as nothing in the known character of Mr. Woolsworthy, of Oxney Colne. He was the antiquarian of Dartmoor. That was his line of life. It was in that capacity that he was known to the Devonshire world; it was as such that he journeyed about with his humble carpetbag, staying away from his parsonage a night or two at a time; it was in that character that he received now and again stray visitors in the single spare bedroom—not friends asked to see him and his girl because of their friendship—but men who knew something as to this buried stone, or that old land-mark. In all these things his daughter let him have his own way, assisting and encouraging him. That was his line of life, and therefore she respected it. But in all other matters she chose to be paramount at the parsonage.

Mr. Woolsworthy was a little man, who always wore, except on Sundays, grey clothes—clothes of so light a grey that they would hardly have been regarded as clerical in a district less remote. He had now reached a goodly age, being full seventy years old; but still he was wiry and active, and shewed but few symptoms of decay. His head was bald, and the few remaining locks that surrounded it were nearly white. But there was a look of energy about his mouth, and a humour in his light grey eye, which forbade those who knew him to regard him altogether as an old man. As it was, he could walk from Oxney Colne to Priestown, fifteen long Devonshire miles across the moor; and he who could do that could hardly be regarded as too old for work.

But our present story will have more to do with his daughter than with him. A pretty girl, I have said, was Patience Woolsworthy; and one, too, in many ways remarkable. She had taken her outlook into life, weighing the things which she had and those which she had not, in a manner very unusual, and, as a rule, not always desirable for a young lady. The things which she had not were very many. She had not society; she had not a fortune; she had not any assurance of future means of livelihood; she had not high hope of procuring for herself a position in life by marriage; she had not that excitement and pleasure in life which she read of in such books as found their way down to Oxney Colne Parsonage. It would be easy to add to the list of the things which she had not; and this list against herself she made out with the utmost vigour. The things which she had, or those rather which she assured herself of having, were much more easily counted. She had the birth and education of a lady, the strength of a healthy woman, and a will of her own. Such was the list as she made it out for herself, and I protest that I assert no more than the truth in saying that she never added to it either beauty, wit, or talent.

I began these descriptions by saying that Oxney Colne would, of all places, be the best spot from which a tourist could visit those parts of Devonshire, but for the fact that he could obtain there none of the accommodation which tourists require. A brother antiquarian might, perhaps, in those days have done so, seeing that there was, as I have said, a spare bedroom at the parsonage. Any intimate friend of Miss Le Smyrger's might be as fortunate, for she was also so provided at Oxney Colne, by which name her house was known. But Miss Le Smyrger was not given to extensive hospitality, and it was only to those who were bound to her, either by ties of blood or of very old friendship, that she delighted to open her doors. As her old friends were very few in number, as those few lived at a distance, and as her nearest relations were higher in the world than she was, and were said by herself to look down upon her, the visits made to Oxney Colne were few and far between.

But now, at the period of which I am writing, such a visit was about to be made. Miss Le Smyrger had a younger sister who had inherited a property in the parish of Oxney Colne equal to that of the lady who lived there; but this younger sister had inherited beauty also, and she therefore, in early life, had found sundry lovers, one of whom became her husband. She had married a man even then well to do in the world, but now rich and almost mighty; a Member of Parliament, a Lord of this and that board, a man who had a house in Eaton Square, and a park in the north of England; and in this way her course of life had been very much divided from that of our Miss Le Smyrger. But the Lord of the Government board had been blessed with various children, and perhaps it was now thought expedient to look after Aunt Penelope's Devonshire acres. Aunt Penelope was empowered to leave them to whom she pleased; and though it was thought in Eaton Square that she must, as a matter of course, leave them to one of the family, nevertheless a little cousinly intercourse might make the thing more certain. I will not say that this was the sole cause for such a visit, but in these days a visit was to be made by Captain Broughton to his aunt. Now Captain John Broughton was the second son of Alfonso Broughton, of Clapham Park and Eaton Square, Member of Parliament, and Lord of the aforesaid Government Board.

And what do you mean to do with him? Patience Woolsworthy asked of Miss Le Smyrger when that lady walked over from the Colne to say that her nephew John was to arrive on the following morning.

'Do with him? Why, I shall bring him over here to talk to your father.'

'He'll be too fashionable for that, and papa won't trouble his head about him if he finds that he doesn't care for Dartmoor.'

'Then he may fall in love with you, my dear.'

'Well, yes; there's that resource at any rate, and for your sake I dare say I should be more civil to him than papa. But he'll soon get tired of making love to me, and what you'll do then I cannot imagine.'

That Miss Woolsworthy felt no interest in the coming of the Captain I will not pretend to say. The advent of any stranger with whom she would be called on to associate must be matter of interest to her in that secluded place; and she was not so absolutely unlike other young ladies that the arrival of an unmarried young man would be the same to her as the advent of some patriarchal pater-familias. In taking that outlook into life of which I have spoken she had never said to herself that she despised those things from which other girls received the excitement, the joys, and the disappointment of their lives. She had simply given herself to understand that very little of such things would come in her way, and that it behoved her to live—to live happily if such might be possible—without experiencing the need of them. She had heard, when there was no thought of any such visit to Oxney Colne, that John Broughton was a handsome clever man—one who thought much of himself and was thought much of by others—that there had been some talk of his marrying a great heiress, which marriage, however had not taken place through unwillingness on his part, and that he was on the whole a man of more mark in the world than the ordinary captains of ordinary regiments.

Captain Broughton came to Oxney Colne, stayed there a fortnight—the intended period for his projected visit having been fixed at three or four days—and then went his way. He went his way back to his London haunts, the time of the year then being the close of the Easter holy-days; but as he did so he told his aunt that he should assuredly return to her in the autumn.

'And assuredly I shall be happy to see you, John—if you come with a certain purpose. If you have no such purpose, you had better remain away.'

'I shall assuredly come,' the Captain had replied, and then he had gone on his journey.

The summer passed rapidly by, and very little was said between Miss Le Smyrger and Miss Woolsworthy about Captain Broughton. In many respects—nay, I may say, as to all ordinary matters,—no two women could well be more intimate with each other than they were; and more than that, they had the courage each to talk to the other with absolute truth as to things concerning themselves—a courage in which dear friends often fail. But, nevertheless, very little was said between them about Captain John Broughton. All that was said may be here repeated.

'John says that he shall return here in August,' Miss Le Smyrger said as Patience was sitting with her in the parlour at Oxney Colne, on the morning after that gentleman's departure.

'He told me so himself,' said Patience; and as she spoke her round dark eyes assumed a look of more than ordinary self-will. If Miss Le Smyrger had intended to carry the conversation any further she changed her mind as she looked at her companion. Then, as I said, the summer ran by, and towards the close of the warm days of July, Miss Le Smyrger, sitting in the same chair in the same room, again took up the conversation.

'I got a letter from John this morning. He says that he shall be here on the third.'

'Does he?'

'He is very punctual to the time he named.'

'Yes; I fancy that he is a punctual man,' said Patience.

'I hope that you will be glad to see him,' said Miss Le Smyrger.

'Very glad to see him,' said Patience, with a bold clear voice; and then the conversation was again dropped, and nothing further was said till after Captain Broughton's second arrival in the parish.

Four months had then passed since his departure, and during that time Miss Woolsworthy had performed all her usual daily duties in their accustomed course. No one could discover that she had been less careful in her household matters than had been her wont, less willing to go among her poor neighbours, or less assiduous in her attentions to her father. But not the less was there a feeling in the minds of those around her that some great change had come upon her. She would sit during the long summer evenings on a certain spot outside the parsonage orchard, at the top of a small sloping field in which their solitary cow was always pastured, with a book on her knees before her, but rarely reading. There she would sit, with the beautiful view down to the winding river below her, watching the setting sun, and thinking, thinking, thinking—thinking of something of which she had never spoken. Often would Miss Le Smyrger come upon her there, and sometimes would pass her even without a word; but never—never once did she dare to ask of the matter of her thoughts. But she knew the matter well enough. No confession was necessary to inform her that Patience Woolsworthy was in love with John Broughton—ay, in love, to the full and entire loss of her whole heart.

On one evening she was so sitting till the July sun had fallen and hidden himself for the night, when her father came upon her as he returned from one of his rambles on the moor. 'Patty,' he said, 'you are always sitting there now. Is it not late? Will you not be cold?'

'No papa,' she said, 'I shall not be cold.'

'But won't you come to the house? I miss you when you come in so late that there's no time to say a word before we go to bed.'

She got up and followed him into the parsonage, and when they were in the sitting-room together, and the door was closed, she came up to him and kissed him. 'Papa,' she said, 'would it make you very unhappy if I were to leave you?'

'Leave me!' he said, startled by the serious and almost solemn tone of her voice. 'Do you mean for always?'

'If I were to marry, papa?'

'Oh, marry! No; that would not make me unhappy. It would make me very happy, Patty, to see you married to a man you would love;—very, very happy; though my days would be desolate without you.'

'That is it, papa. What would you do if I went from you?'

'What would it matter, Patty? I should be free, at any rate, from a load which often presses heavy on me now. What will you do when I shall leave you? A few more years and all will be over with me. But who is it, love? Has anybody said anything to you?'

'It was only an idea, papa. I don't often think of such a thing; but I did think of it then.' And so the subject was allowed to pass by. This had happened before the day of the second arrival had been absolutely fixed and made known to Miss Woolsworthy.

And then that second arrival took place. The reader may have understood from the words with which Miss Le Smyrger authorized her nephew to make his second visit to Oxney Colne that Miss Woolsworthy's passion was not altogether unauthorized. Captain Broughton had been told that he was not to come unless he came with a certain purpose; and having been so told, he still persisted in coming. There can be no doubt but that he well understood the purport to which his aunt alluded. 'I shall assuredly come,' he had said. And true to his word, he was now there.

Patience knew exactly the hour at which he must arrive at the station at Newton Abbot, and the time also which it would take to travel over those twelve up-hill miles from the station to Oxney. It need hardly be said that she paid no visit to Miss Le Smyrger's house on that afternoon; but she might have known something of Captain Broughton's approach without going thither. His road to the Colne passed by the parsonage-gate, and had Patience sat even at her bedroom window she must have seen him. But on such an evening she would not sit at her bedroom window;—she would do nothing which would force her to accuse herself of a restless longing for her lover's coming. It was for him to seek her. If he chose to do so, he knew the way to the parsonage.

Miss Le Smyrger—good, dear, honest, hearty Miss Le Smyrger, was in a fever of anxiety on behalf of her friend. It was not that she wished her nephew to marry Patience,—or rather that she had entertained any such wish when he first came among them. She was not given to match-making, and moreover thought, or had thought within herself, that they of Oxney Colne could do very well without any admixture from Eaton Square. Her plan of life had been that when old Mr. Woolsworthy was taken away from Dartmoor, Patience should live with her, and that when she also shuffled off her coil, then Patience Woolsworthy should be the maiden-mistress of Oxney Colne—of Oxney Colne and of Mr. Cloysey's farm—to the utter detriment of all the Broughtons. Such had been her plan before nephew John had come among them—a plan not to be spoken of till the coming of that dark day which should make Patience an orphan. But now her nephew had been there, and all was to be altered. Miss Le Smyrger's plan would have provided a companion for her old age; but that had not been her chief object. She had thought more of Patience than of herself, and now it seemed that a prospect of a higher happiness was opening for her friend.

'John,' she said, as soon as the first greetings were over, 'do you remember the last words that I said to you before you went away?' Now, for myself, I much admire Miss Le Smyrger's heartiness, but I do not think much of her discretion. It would have been better, perhaps, had she allowed things to take their course.

'I can't say that I do,' said the Captain. At the same time the Captain did remember very well what those last words had been.

'I am so glad to see you, so delighted to see you, if—if—if—,' and then she paused, for with all her courage she hardly dared to ask her nephew whether he had come there with the express purport of asking Miss Woolsworthy to marry him.

To tell the truth—for there is no room for mystery within the limits of this short story,—to tell, I say, at a word the plain and simple truth, Captain Broughton had already asked that question. On the day before he left Oxney Colne he had in set terms proposed to the parson's daughter, and indeed the words, the hot and frequent words, which previously to that had fallen like sweetest honey into the ears of Patience Woolsworthy, had made it imperative on him to do so. When a man in such a place as that has talked to a girl of love day after day, must not he talk of it to some definite purpose on the day on which he leaves her? Or if he do not, must he not submit to be regarded as false, selfish, and almost fraudulent? Captain Broughton, however, had asked the question honestly and truly. He had done so honestly and truly, but in words, or, perhaps, simply with a tone, that had hardly sufficed to satisfy the proud spirit of the girl he loved. She by that time had confessed to herself that she loved him with all her heart; but she had made no such confession to him. To him she had spoken no word, granted no favour, that any lover might rightfully regard as a token of love returned. She had listened to him as he spoke, and bade him keep such sayings for the drawing-rooms of his fashionable friends. Then he had spoken out and had asked for that hand,—not, perhaps, as a suitor tremulous with hope,—but as a rich man who knows that he can command that which he desires to purchase.

'You should think more of this,' she had said to him at last. 'If you would really have me for your wife, it will not be much to you to return here again when time for thinking of it shall have passed by.' With these words she had dismissed him, and now he had again come back to Oxney Colne. But still she would not place herself at the window to look for him, nor dress herself in other than her simple morning country dress, nor omit one item of her daily work. If he wished to take her at all, he should wish to take her as she really was, in her plain country life, but he should take her also with full observance of all those privileges which maidens are allowed to claim from their lovers. He should curtail no ceremonious observance because she was the daughter of a poor country parson who would come to him without a shilling, whereas he stood high in the world's books. He had asked her to give him all that she had, and that all she was ready to give, without stint. But the gift must be valued before it could be given or received. He also was to give her as much, and she would accept it as being beyond all price. But she would not allow that that which was offered to her was in any degree the more precious because of his outward worldly standing.

She would not pretend to herself that she thought he would come to her that afternoon, and therefore she busied herself in the kitchen and about the house, giving directions to her two maids as though the day would pass as all other days did pass in that household. They usually dined at four, and she rarely, in these summer months, went far from the house before that hour. At four precisely she sat down with her father, and then said that she was going up as far as Helpholme after dinner. Helpholme was a solitary farmhouse in another parish, on the border of the moor, and Mr. Woolsworthy asked her whether he should accompany her.

'Do, papa,' she said, 'if you are not too tired.' And yet she had thought how probable it might be that she should meet John Broughton on her walk. And so it was arranged; but, just as dinner was over, Mr. Woolsworthy remembered himself.

'Gracious me,' he said, 'how my memory is going! Gribbles, from Ivybridge, and old John Poulter, from Bovey, are coming to meet here by appointment. You can't put Helpholme off till tomorrow?'

Patience, however, never put off anything, and therefore at six o'clock, when her father had finished his slender modicum of toddy, she tied on her hat and went on her walk. She started forth with a quick step, and left no word to say by which route she would go. As she passed up along the little lane which led towards Oxney Colne she would not even look to see if he was coming towards her; and when she left the road, passing over a stone stile into a little path which ran first through the upland fields, and then across the moor ground towards Helpholme, she did not look back once, or listen for his coming step.

She paid her visit, remaining upwards of an hour with the old bedridden mother of the farmer of Helpholme. 'God bless you, my darling!' said the old lady as she left her; 'and send you someone to make your own path bright and happy through the world.' These words were still ringing in her ears with all their significance as she saw John Broughton waiting for her at the first stile which she had to pass after leaving the farmer's haggard.

'Patty,' he said, as he took her hand, and held it close within both his own, 'what a chase I have had after you!'

'And who asked you, Captain Broughton?' she answered, smiling. 'If the journey was too much for your poor London strength, could you not have waited till tomorrow morning, when you would have found me at the parsonage?' But she did not draw her hand away from him, or in any way pretend that he had not a right to accost her as a lover.

'No, I could not wait. I am more eager to see those I love than you seem to be.'

'How do you know whom I love, or how eager I might be to see them? There is an old woman there whom I love, and I have thought nothing of this walk with the object of seeing her.' And now, slowly drawing her hand away from him, she pointed to the farmhouse which she had left.

'Patty,' he said, after a minute's pause, during which she had looked full into his face with all the force of her bright eyes; 'I have come from London today, straight down here to Oxney, and from my aunt's house close upon your footsteps after you to ask you that one question. Do you love me?'

'What a Hercules?' she said, again laughing. 'Do you really mean that you left London only this morning? Why, you must have been five hours in a railway carriage and two in a post-chaise, not to talk of the walk afterwards. You ought to take more care of yourself, Captain Broughton!'

He would have been angry with her,—for he did not like to be quizzed,—had she not put her hand on his arm as she spoke, and the softness of her touch had redeemed the offence of her words.

'All that have I done,' said he, 'that I may hear one word from you.'

'That any word of mine should have such potency! But, let us walk on, or my father will take us for some of the standing stones of the moor. How have you found your aunt? If you only knew the cares that have sat on her dear shoulders for the last week past, in order that your high mightyness might have a sufficiency to eat and drink in these desolate half-starved regions.'

'She might have saved herself such anxiety. No one can care less for such things than I do.'

'And yet I think I have heard you boast of the cook of your club.' And then again there was silence for a minute or two.

'Patty,' said he, stopping again in the path; 'answer my question. I have a right to demand an answer. Do you love me?'

'And what if I do? What if I have been so silly as to allow your perfections to be too many for my weak heart? What then, Captain Broughton?'

'It cannot be that you love me, or you would not joke now.'

'Perhaps not, indeed,' she said. It seemed as though she were resolved not to yield an inch in her own humour. And then again they walked on.

'Patty,' he said once more, 'I shall get an answer from you tonight,—this evening; now, during this walk, or I shall return tomorrow, and never revisit this spot again.'

'Oh, Captain Broughton, how should we ever manage to live without you?'

'Very well,' he said; 'up to the end of this walk I can bear it all;—and one word spoken then will mend it all.'

During the whole of this time she felt that she was ill-using him. She knew that she loved him with all her heart; that it would nearly kill her to part with him; that she had heard his renewed offer with an ecstasy of joy. She acknowledged to herself that he was giving proof of his devotion as strong as any which a girl could receive from her lover. And yet she could hardly bring herself to say the word he longed to hear. That word once said, and then she knew that she must succumb to her love for ever! That word once said, and there would be nothing for her but to spoil him with her idolatry! That word once said, and she must continue to repeat it into his ears, till perhaps he might be tired of hearing it! And now he had threatened her, and how could she speak it after that? She certainly would not speak it unless he asked her again without such threat. And so they walked on again in silence.

'Patty,' he said at last. 'By the heavens above us you shall answer me. Do you love me?'

She now stood still, and almost trembled as she looked up into his face. She stood opposite to him for a moment, and then placing her two hands on his shoulders, she answered him. 'I do, I do, I do,' she said, 'with all my heart; with all my heart—with all my heart and strength.' And then her head fell upon his breast.

Captain Broughton was almost as much surprised as delighted by the warmth of the acknowledgment made by the eager-hearted passionate girl whom he now held within his arms. She had said it now; the words had been spoken; and there was nothing for her but to swear to him over and over again with her sweetest oaths, that those words were true—true as her soul. And very sweet was the walk down from thence to the parsonage gate. He spoke no more of the distance of the ground, or the length of his day's journey. But he stopped her at every turn that he might press her arm the closer to his own, that he might look into the brightness of her eyes, and prolong his hour of delight. There were no more gibes now on her tongue, no raillery at his London finery, no laughing comments on his coming and going. With downright honesty she told him everything: how she had loved him before her heart was warranted in such a passion; how, with much thinking, she had resolved that it would be unwise to take him at his first word, and had thought it better that he should return to London, and then think over it; how she had almost repented of her courage when she had feared, during those long summer days, that he would forget her; and how her heart had leapt for joy when her old friend had told her that he was coming.

'And yet,' said he, 'you were not glad to see me!'

'Oh, was I not glad? You cannot understand the feelings of a girl who has lived secluded as I have done. Glad is no word for the joy I felt. But it was not seeing you that I cared for so much. It was the knowledge that you were near me once again. I almost wish now that I had not seen you till tomorrow.' But as she spoke she pressed his arm, and this caress gave the lie to her last words.

'No, do not come in tonight,' she said, when she reached the little wicket that led up the parsonage. 'Indeed you shall not. I could not behave myself properly if you did.'

'But I don't want you to behave properly.'

'Oh! I am to keep that for London, am I? But, nevertheless, Captain Broughton, I will not invite you either to tea or to supper tonight.'

'Surely I may shake hands with your father.'

'Not tonight—not till—. John, I may tell him, may I not? I must tell him at once.'

'Certainly,' said he.

'And then you shall see him tomorrow. Let me see—at what hour shall I bid you come?'

'To breakfast.'

'No, indeed. What on earth would your aunt do with her broiled turkey and the cold pie? I have got no cold pie for you.'

'I hate cold pie.'

'What a pity! But, John, I should be forced to leave you directly after breakfast. Come down—come down at two, or three; and then I will go back with you to Aunt Penelope. I must see her tomorrow.' And so at last the matter was settled, and the happy Captain, as he left her, was hardly resisted in his attempt to press her lips to his own.

When she entered the parlour in which her father was sitting, there still were Gribbles and Poulter discussing some knotty point of Devon lore. So Patience took off her hat, and sat herself down, waiting till they should go. For full an hour she had to wait, and then Gribbles and Poulter did go. But it was not in such matters as this that Patience Woolsworthy was impatient. She could wait, and wait, and wait, curbing herself for weeks and months, while the thing waited for was in her eyes good; but she could not curb her hot thoughts or her hot words when things came to be discussed which she did not think to be good.

'Papa,' she said, when Gribbles' long-drawn last word had been spoken at the door. 'Do you remember how I asked you the other day what you would say if I were to leave you?'

'Yes, surely,' he replied, looking up at her in astonishment.

'I am going to leave you now,' she said. 'Dear, dearest father, how am I to go from you?'

'Going to leave me,' said he, thinking of her visit to Helpholme, and thinking of nothing else.

Now there had been a story about Helpholme. That bedridden old lady there had a stalwart son, who was now the owner of the Helpholme pastures. But though owner in fee of all those wild acres and of the cattle which they supported, he was not much above the farmers around him, either in manners or education. He had his merits, however; for he was honest, well to do in the world, and modest withal. How strong love had grown up, springing from neighbourly kindness, between our Patience and his mother, it needs not here to tell; but rising from it had come another love—or an ambition which might have grown to love. The young man, after much thought, had not dared to speak to Miss Woolsworthy, but he had sent a message by Miss Le Smyrger. If there could be any hope for him, he would present himself as a suitor—on trial. He did not owe a shilling in the world, and had money by him—saved. He wouldn't ask the parson for a shilling of fortune. Such had been the tenor of his message, and Miss Le Smyrger had delivered it faithfully. 'He does not mean it,' Patience had said with her stern voice. 'Indeed he does, my dear. You may be sure he is in earnest,' Miss Le Smyrger had replied; 'and there is not an honester man in these parts.'

'Tell him,' said Patience, not attending to the latter portion of her friend's last speech, 'that it cannot be,—make him understand, you know—and tell him also that the matter shall be thought of no more.' The matter had, at any rate, been spoken of no more, but the young farmer still remained a bachelor, and Helpholme still wanted a mistress. But all this came back upon the parson's mind when his daughter told him that she was about to leave him.

'Yes, dearest,' she said; and as she spoke, she now knelt at his knees. 'I have been asked in marriage, and I have given myself away.'

'Well, my love, if you will be happy—'

'I hope I shall; I think I shall. But you, papa?'

'You will not be far from us.'

'Oh, yes; in London.'

'In London.'

'Captain Broughton lives in London generally.'

'And has Captain Broughton asked you to marry him?'

'Yes, papa—who else? Is he not good? Will you not love him? Oh, papa, do not say that I am wrong to love him?'

He never told her his mistake, or explained to her that he had not thought it possible that the high-placed son of the London great man shall have fallen in love with his undowered daughter; but he embraced her, and told her, with all his enthusiasm, that he rejoiced in her joy, and would be happy in her happiness. 'My own Patty,' he said, 'I have ever known that you were too good for this life of ours here.' And then the evening wore away into the night, with many tears but still with much happiness.

Captain Broughton, as he walked back to Oxney Colne, made up his mind that he would say nothing on the matter to his aunt till the next morning. He wanted to think over it all, and to think it over, if possible, by himself. He had taken a step in life, the most important that a man is ever called on to take, and he had to reflect whether or no he had taken it with wisdom.

'Have you seen her?' said Miss Le Smyrger, very anxiously, when he came into the drawing-room.

'Miss Woolsworthy you mean,' said he. 'Yes, I've seen her. As I found her out I took a long walk and happened to meet her. Do you know, aunt, I think I'll go to bed; I was up at five this morning, and have been on the move ever since.'

Miss Le Smyrger perceived that she was to hear nothing that evening, so she handed him his candlestick and allowed him to go to his room.

But Captain Broughton did not immediately retire to bed, nor when he did so was he able to sleep at once. Had this step that he had taken been a wise one? He was not a man who, in worldly matters, had allowed things to arrange themselves for him, as is the case with so many men. He had formed views for himself, and had a theory of life. Money for money's sake he had declared to himself to be bad. Money, as a concomitant to things which were in themselves good, he had declared to himself to be good also. That concomitant in this affair of his marriage, he had now missed. Well;

he had made up his mind to that, and would put up with the loss. He had means of living of his own, though means not so extensive as might have been desirable. That it would be well for him to become a married man, looking merely to that state of life as opposed to his present state, he had fully resolved. On that point, therefore, there was nothing to repent. That Patty Woolsworthy was good, affectionate, clever, and beautiful, he was sufficiently satisfied. It would be odd indeed if he were not so satisfied now, seeing that for the last four months he had declared to himself daily that she was so with many inward asseverations. And yet though he repeated now again that he was satisfied, I do not think that he was so fully satisfied of it as he had been throughout the whole of those four months. It is sad to say so, but I fear—I fear that such was the case. When you have your plaything how much of the anticipated pleasure vanishes, especially if it have been won easily!

He had told none of his family what were his intentions in this second visit to Devonshire, and now he had to bethink himself whether they would be satisfied. What would his sister say, she who had married the Honourable Augustus Gumbleton, gold-stick-in-waiting to Her Majesty's Privy Council? Would she receive Patience with open arms, and make much of her about London? And then how far would London suit Patience, or would Patience suit London? There would be much for him to do in teaching her, and it would be well for him to set about the lesson without loss of time. So far he got that night, but when the morning came he went a step further, and began mentally to criticize her manner to himself. It had been very sweet, that warm, that full, that ready declaration of love. Yes; it had been very sweet; but—but—; when, after her little jokes, she did confess her love, had she not been a little too free for feminine excellence? A man likes to be told that he is loved, but he hardly wishes that the girl he is to marry should fling herself at his head!

Ah me! yes; it was thus he argued to himself as on that morning he went through the arrangements of his toilet. 'Then he was a brute,' you say, my pretty reader. I have never said that he was not a brute. But this I remark, that many such brutes are to be met with in the beaten paths of the world's high highway. When Patience Woolsworthy had answered him coldly, bidding him go back to London and think over his love; while it seemed from her

479

manner that at any rate as yet she did not care for him; while he was absent from her, and, therefore, longing for her, the possession of her charms, her talent, and bright honesty of purpose had seemed to him a thing most desirable. Now they were his own. They had, in fact, been his own from the first. The heart of this country-bred girl had fallen at the first word from his mouth. Had she not so confessed to him? She was very nice,—very nice indeed. He loved her dearly. But had he not sold himself too cheaply?

I by no means say that he was not a brute. But whether brute or no he was an honest man, and had no remotest dream, either then, on that morning, or during the following days on which such thoughts pressed more thickly on his mind—of breaking away from his pledged word. At breakfast on that morning he told all to Miss Le Smyrger, and that lady, with warm and gracious intentions, confided to him her purpose regarding her property. 'I have always regarded Patience as my heir,' she said, 'and shall do so still.'

'Oh, indeed,' said Captain Broughton.

'But it is a great, great pleasure to me to think that she will give back the little property to my sister's child. You will have your mother's, and thus it will all come together again.'

'Ah!' said Captain Broughton. He had his own ideas about property, and did not, even under existing circumstances, like to hear that his aunt considered herself at liberty to leave the acres away to one who was by blood quite a stranger to the family.

'Does Patience know of this?' he asked.

'Not a word,' said Miss Le Smyrger. And then nothing more was said upon the subject.

On that afternoon he went down and received the parson's benediction and congratulations with a good grace. Patience said very little on the occasion, and indeed was absent during the greater part of the interview. The two lovers then walked up to Oxney Colne, and there were more benedictions and more congratulations. 'All went merry as a marriage bell', at any rate as far as Patience was concerned. Not a word had yet fallen from that dear mouth, not a look had yet come over that handsome face, which tended in any way to mar her bliss. Her first day of acknowledged love was a day altogether happy, and when she prayed for him as she knelt beside her bed there was no feeling in her mind that any fear need disturb her joy.

I will pass over the next three or four days very quickly, merely saying that Patience did not find them so pleasant as that first day after her engagement. There was something in her lover's manner—something which at first she could not define—which by degrees seemed to grate against her feelings. He was sufficiently affectionate, that being a matter on which she did not require much demonstration; but joined to his affection there seemed to be—; she hardly liked to suggest to herself a harsh word, but could it be possible that he was beginning to think that she was not good enough for him? And then she asked herself the question—was she good enough for him? If there were doubt about that, the match should be broken off, though she tore her own heart out in the struggle. The truth, however, was this,—that he had begun that teaching which he had already found to be so necessary. Now, had any one essayed to teach Patience German or mathematics, with that young lady's free consent, I believe that she would have been found a meek scholar. But it was not probable that she would be meek when she found a self-appointed tutor teaching her manners and conduct without her consent.

So matters went on for four or five days, and on the evening of the fifth day, Captain Broughton and his aunt drank tea at the parsonage. Nothing very especial occurred; but as the parson and Miss Le Smyrger insisted on playing backgammon with devoted perseverance during the whole evening, Broughton had a good opportunity of saying a word or two about those changes in his lady-love which a life in London would require—and some word he said also—some single slight word, as to the higher station in life to which he would exalt his bride. Patience bore it—for her father and Miss Le Smyrger were in the room—she bore it well, speaking no syllable of anger, and enduring, for the moment, the implied scorn of the old parsonage. Then the evening broke up, and Captain Broughton walked back to Oxney Colne with his aunt. 'Patty,' her father said to her before they went to bed, 'he seems to me to be a most excellent young man.' 'Dear papa,' she answered, kissing him. 'And terribly deep in love,' said Mr. Woolsworthy. 'Oh, I don't know about that,' she answered, as she left him with her sweetest smile. But though she could thus smile at her father's joke, she had already made up her mind that there was still something to be learned as to her promised husband before she could place herself altogether in his hands. She would ask him whether he thought himself liable to injury from this proposed marriage; and though he should deny any such thought, she would know from the manner of his denial what his true feelings were.

And he, too, on that night, during his silent walk with Miss Le Smyrger, had entertained some similar thoughts. 'I fear she is obstinate', he had said to himself, and then he had half accused her of being sullen also. 'If that be her temper, what a life of misery I have before me!'

'Have you fixed a day yet?' his aunt asked him as they came near to her house.

'No, not yet; I don't know whether it will suit me to fix it before I leave.'

'Why, it was but the other day you were in such a hurry.'

'Ah—yes-I have thought more about it since then.'

'I should have imagined that this would depend on what Patty thinks,' said Miss Le Smyrger, standing up for the privileges of her sex. 'It is presumed that the gentleman is always ready as soon as the lady will consent.'

'Yes, in ordinary cases it is so; but when a girl is taken out of her own sphere—'

'Her own sphere! Let me caution you, Master John, not to talk to Patty about her own sphere.'

'Aunt Penelope, as Patience is to be my wife and not yours, I must claim permission to speak to her on such subjects as may seem suitable to me.' And then they parted—not in the best humour with each other.

On the following day Captain Broughton and Miss Woolsworthy did not meet till the evening. She had said, before those few ill-omened words had passed her lover's lips, that she would probably be at Miss Le Smyrger's house on the following morning. Those ill-omened words did pass her lover's lips, and then she remained at home. This did not come from sullenness, nor even from anger, but from a conviction that it would be well that she should think much before she met him again. Nor was he anxious to hurry a meeting. His thought—his base thought—was this; that she would be sure to come up to the Colne after him; but she did not come, and therefore in the evening he went down to her, and asked her to walk with him.

They went away by the path that led by Helpholme, and little was said between them till they had walked some mile together. Patience, as she went along the path, remembered almost to the letter the sweet words which had greeted her ears as she came down that way with him on the night of his arrival; but he remembered nothing of that sweetness then. Had he not made an ass of himself during these last six months? That was the thought which very much had possession of his mind.

'Patience,' he said at last, having hitherto spoken only an indifferent word now and again since they had left the parsonage, 'Patience, I hope you realize the importance of the step which you and I are about to take?'

'Of course I do,' she answered: 'what an odd question that is for you to ask!'

'Because,' said he, 'sometimes I almost doubt it. It seems to me as though you thought you could remove yourself from here to your new home with no more trouble than when you go from home up to the Colne.'

'Is that meant for a reproach, John?'

'No, not for a reproach, but for advice. Certainly not for a reproach.'

'I am glad of that.'

'But I should wish to make you think how great is the leap in the world which you are about to take.' Then again they walked on for many steps before she answered him.

'Tell me, then, John,' she said, when she had sufficiently considered what words she would speak;—and as she spoke a dark bright colour suffused her face, and her eyes flashed almost with anger. 'What leap do you mean? Do you mean a leap upwards?'

'Well, yes; I hope it will be so.'

'In one sense, certainly, it would be a leap upwards. To be the wife of the man I loved; to have the privilege of holding his happiness in my hand; to know that I was his own—the companion whom he had chosen out of all the world—that would, indeed, be a leap upward; a leap almost to heaven, if all that were so. But if you mean upwards in any other sense—'

'I was thinking of the social scale.'

'Then, Captain Broughton, your thoughts were doing me dishonour.'

'Doing you dishonour!'

'Yes, doing me dishonour. That your father is, in the world's esteem, a greater man than mine is doubtless true enough. That you, as a man, are richer than I am as a woman is doubtless also true. But you dishonour me, and yourself also, if these things can weigh with you now.'

'Patience,—I think you can hardly know what words you are saying to me.'

'Pardon me, but I think I do. Nothing that you can give me— no gifts of that description—can weigh aught against that which I am giving you. If you had all the wealth and rank of the greatest lord in the land, it would count as nothing in such a scale. If—as I have not doubted—if in return for my heart you have given me yours, then—then—then, you have paid me fully. But when gifts such as those are going, nothing else can count even as a make-weight.'

'I do not quite understand you,' he answered, after a pause. 'I fear you are a little high-flown.' And then, while the evening was still early, they walked back to the parsonage almost without another word.

Captain Broughton at this time had only one more full day to remain at Oxney Colne. On the afternoon following that he was to go as far as Exeter, and thence return to London. Of course it was to be expected, that the wedding day would be fixed before he went, and much had been said about it during the first day or two of his engagement. Then he had pressed for an early time, and Patience, with a girl's usual diffidence, had asked for some little delay. But now nothing was said on the subject; and how was it probable that such a matter could be settled after such a conversation as that which I have related? That evening, Miss Le Smyrger asked whether the day had been fixed. 'No,' said Captain Broughton harshly; 'nothing has been fixed.' 'But it will be arranged before you go.' 'Probably not,' he said; and then the subject was dropped for the time.

'John,' she said, just before she went to bed, 'if there be anything wrong between you and Patience, I conjure you to tell me.'

'You had better ask her,' he replied. 'I can tell you nothing.'

On the following morning he was much surprised by seeing Patience on the gravel path before Miss Le Smyrger's gate immediately after breakfast. He went to the door to open it for her, and she, as she gave him her hand, told him that she came up to speak to him. There was no hesitation in her manner, nor any look of anger in her face. But there was in her gait and form, in her voice and countenance, a fixedness of purpose which he had never seen before, or at any rate had never acknowledged.

'Certainly,' said he. 'Shall I come out with you, or will you come upstairs?'

'We can sit down in the summer-house,' she said; and thither they both went.

'Captain Broughton,' she said—and she began her task the moment that they were both seated—'You and I have engaged ourselves as man and wife, but perhaps we have been over rash.'

'How so?' said he.

'It may be—and indeed I will say more—it is the case that we have made this engagement without knowing enough of each other's character.'

'I have not thought so.'

'The time will perhaps come when you will so think, but for the sake of all that we most value, let it come before it is too late. What would be our fate—how terrible would be our misery, if such a thought should come to either of us after we have linked our lots together.'

There was a solemnity about her as she thus spoke which almost repressed him,—which for a time did prevent him from taking that tone of authority which on such a subject he would choose to adopt. But he recovered himself. 'I hardly think that this comes well from you,' he said.

'From whom else should it come? Who else can fight my battle for me; and, John, who else can fight that same battle on your behalf? I tell you this, that with your mind standing towards me as it does stand at present you could not give me your hand at the altar with true words and a happy conscience. Is it not true? You have half repented of your bargain already. Is it not so?'

He did not answer her; but getting up from his seat walked to the front of the summer-house, and stood there with his back turned upon her. It was not that he meant to be ungracious, but in truth he did not know how to answer her. He had half repented of his bargain.

'John,' she said, getting up and following him so that she could put her hand upon his arm, 'I have been very angry with you.'

'Angry with me!' he said, turning sharp upon her.

'Yes, angry with you. You would have treated me like a child. But that feeling has gone now. I am not angry now. There is my hand;—the hand of a friend. Let the words that have been spoken between us be as though they had not been spoken. Let us both be free.'

'Do you mean it?' he asked.

'Certainly I mean it.' As she spoke these words her eyes were filled with tears in spite of all the efforts she could make to restrain them; but he was not looking at her, and her efforts had sufficed to prevent any sob from being audible.

'With all my heart,' he said; and it was manifest from his tone that he had no thought of her happiness as he spoke. It was true that she had been angry with him—angry, as she had herself declared; but nevertheless, in what she had said and what she had done, she had thought more of his happiness than of her own. Now she was angry once again.

'With all your heart, Captain Broughton! Well, so be it. If with all your heart, then is the necessity so much the greater. You go tomorrow. Shall we say farewell now?'

'Patience, I am not going to be lectured.'

'Certainly not by me. Shall we say farewell now?'

'Yes, if you are determined.'

'I am determined. Farewell, Captain Broughton. You have all my wishes for your happiness.' And she held out her hand to him.

'Patience!' he said. And he looked at her with a dark frown, as though he would strive to frighten her into submission. If so, he might have saved himself any such attempt.

'Farewell, Captain Broughton. Give me your hand, for I cannot stay.' He gave her his hand, hardly knowing why he did so. She lifted it to her lips and kissed it, and then, leaving him, passed from the summer-house down through the wicket-gate, and straight home to the parsonage.

During the whole of that day she said no word to anyone of what had occurred. When she was once more at home she went about her household affairs as she had done on that day of his arrival. When she sat down to dinner with her father he observed nothing to make him think that she was unhappy, nor during the evening was there any expression in her face, or any tone in her voice, which excited his attention. On the following morning Captain Broughton called at the parsonage, and the servant-girl brought word to her mistress that he was in the parlour. But she would not see him. 'Laws miss, you ain't a quarrelled with your beau?' the poor girl said. 'No, not quarrelled,' she said; 'but give him that.' It was a scrap of paper containing a word or two in pencil. 'It is better that we should not meet again. God bless you.' And from that day to this, now more than ten years, they have never met.

'Papa,' she said to her father that afternoon, 'dear papa, do not be angry with me. It is all over between me and John Broughton. Dearest, you and I will not be separated.'

It would be useless here to tell how great was the old man's surprise and how true his sorrow. As the tale was told to him no cause was given for anger with anyone. Not a word was spoken against the suitor who had on that day returned to London with a full conviction that now at least he was relieved from his engagement. 'Patty, my darling child,' he said, 'may God grant that it be for the best!'

'It is for the best,' she answered stoutly. 'For this place I am fit; and I much doubt whether I am fit for any other.'

On that day she did not see Miss Le Smyrger, but on the following morning, knowing that Captain Broughton had gone off,—having heard the wheels of the carriage as they passed by the parsonage gate on his way to the station,—she walked up to the Colne.

'He has told you, I suppose?' said she.

'Yes,' said Miss Le Smyrger. 'And I will never see him again unless he asks your pardon on his knees. I have told him so. I would not even give him my hand as he went.'

'But why so, thou kindest one? The fault was mine more than his.'

'I understand. I have eyes in my head,' said the old maid. 'I have watched him for the last four or five days. If you could have kept the truth to yourself and bade him keep off from you, he would have been at your feet now, licking the dust from your shoes.'

'But, dear friend, I do not want a man to lick dust from my shoes.'

'Ah, you are a fool. You do not know the value of your own wealth.'

'True; I have been a fool. I was a fool to think that one coming from such a life as he has led could be happy with such as I am. I know the truth now. I have bought the lesson dearly—but perhaps not too dearly, seeing that it will never be forgotten.'

There was but little more said about the matter between our three friends at Oxney Colne. What, indeed, could be said? Miss Le Smyrger for a year or two still expected that her nephew would return and claim his bride; but he has never done so, nor has there been any correspondence between them. Patience Woolsworthy had learned her lesson dearly. She had given her whole heart to the man; and, though she so bore herself that no one was aware of the violence of the struggle, nevertheless the struggle within her bosom was very violent. She never told herself that she had done wrong; she never regretted her loss; but yet—yet!—the loss was very hard to bear. He also had loved her, but he was not capable of a love which could much injure his daily peace. Her daily peace was gone for many a day to come.

Her father is still living; but there is a curate now in the parish. In conjunction with him and with Miss Le Smyrger she spends her time in the concerns of the parish. In her own eyes she is a confirmed old maid; and such is my opinion also. The romance of her life was played out in that summer. She never sits now lonely on the hillside thinking how much she might do for one whom she really loved. But with a large heart she loves many, and, with no romance, she works hard to lighten the burdens of those she loves.

As for Captain Broughton, all the world knows that he did marry that great heiress with whom his name was once before connected, and that he is now a useful member of Parliament, working on committees three or four days a week with zeal that is indefatigable. Sometimes, not often, as he thinks of Patience Woolsworthy a smile comes across his face.

ANTHONY GARSTIN'S COURTSHIP

By Hubert Crackanthorpe

I

A stampede of huddled sheep, wildly scampering over the slaty shingle, emerged from the leaden mist that muffled the fell-top, and a shrill shepherd's whistle broke the damp stillness of the air. And presently a man's figure appeared, following the sheep down the hillside. He halted a moment to whistle curtly to his two dogs, who, laying back their ears, chased the sheep at top speed beyond the brow; then, his hands deep in his pockets, he strode vigorously forward. A streak of white smoke from a toiling train was creeping silently across the distance: the great, grey, desolate undulations of treeless country showed no other sign of life.

The sheep hurried in single file along a tiny track worn threadbare amid the brown, lumpy grass: and, as the man came round the mountain's shoulder, a narrow valley opened out beneath him—a scanty patchwork of green fields, and, here and there, a whitewashed farm, flanked by a dark cluster of sheltering trees.

The man walked with a loose, swinging gait. His figure was spare and angular: he wore a battered, black felt hat and clumsy, iron-bound boots: his clothes were dingy from long exposure to the weather. He had close-set, insignificant eyes, much wrinkled, and stubbly eyebrows streaked with grey. His mouth was close-shaven, and drawn by his abstraction into hard and taciturn lines; beneath his chin bristled an unkempt fringe of sandy-coloured hair.

When he reached the foot of the fell, the twilight was already blurring the distance. The sheep scurried, with a noisy rustling, across a flat, swampy stretch, over-grown with rushes, while the dogs headed them towards a gap in a low, ragged wall built of loosely-heaped boulders. The man swung the gate to after them, and waited, whistling peremptorily, recalling the dogs. A moment later, the animals reappeared, cringing as they crawled through the bars of the gate. He kicked out at them contemptuously, and mounting a stone stile a few yards further up the road, dropped into a narrow lane.

Presently, as he passed a row of lighted windows, he heard a voice call to him. He stopped, and perceived a crooked, white-bearded figure, wearing clerical clothes, standing in the garden gateway.

'Good-evening, Anthony. A raw evening this.'

'Ay, Mr. Blencarn, it is a bit frittish,' he answered. 'I've jest bin gittin' a few lambs off t'fell. I hope ye're keepin' fairly, an' Miss Rosa too.' He spoke briefly, with a loud, spontaneous cordiality.

'Thank ye, Anthony, thank ye. Rosa's down at the church, playing over the hymns for tomorrow. How's Mrs. Garstin?'

'Nicely, thank ye, Mr. Blencarn. She's wonderful active, is mother.'

'Well, good night to ye, Anthony,' said the old man, clicking the gate.

'Good night, Mr. Blencarn,' he called back.

A few minutes later the twinkling lights of the village came in sight, and from within the sombre form of the square-towered church, looming by the roadside, the slow, solemn strains of the organ floated out on the evening air. Anthony lightened his tread: then paused, listening; but, presently, becoming aware that a man stood, listening also, on the bridge some few yards distant, he moved forward again. Slackening his pace, as he approached, he eyed the figure keenly; but the man paid no heed to him, remaining, with his back turned, gazing over the parapet into the dark, gurgling stream.

Anthony trudged along the empty village street, past the gleaming squares of ruddy gold, starting on either side out of the darkness. Now and then he looked furtively backwards. The straight open road lay behind him, glimmering wanly: the organ seemed to have ceased: the figure on the bridge had left the parapet, and appeared to be moving away towards the church. Anthony halted, watching it till it had disappeared into the blackness beneath the churchyard trees. Then, after a moment's hesitation, he left the road, and mounted an upland meadow towards his mother's farm.

It was a bare, oblong house. In front, a whitewashed porch, and a narrow garden-plot, enclosed by a low iron railing, were dimly discernible: behind, the steep fell-side loomed like a monstrous, mysterious curtain hung across the night. He passed round the back into the twilight of a wide yard, cobbled and partially grass-grown, vaguely flanked by the shadowy outlines of long, low farm-buildings. All was wrapped in darkness: somewhere overhead a bat fluttered, darting its puny scream.

Inside, a blazing peat-fire scattered capering shadows across the smooth, stone floor, flickered among the dim rows of hams suspended from the ceiling and on the panelled cupboards of dark, glistening oak. A servant-girl, spreading the cloth for supper, clattered her clogs in and out of the kitchen: old Mrs. Garstin was stooping before the hearth, tremulously turning some girdle-cakes that lay roasting in the embers.

At the sound of Anthony's heavy tread in the passage, she rose, glancing sharply at the clock above the chimney-piece. She was a heavy-built woman, upright, stalwart almost, despite her years. Her face was gaunt and sallow; deep wrinkles accentuated the hardness of her features. She wore a black widow's cap above her iron-grey hair, gold-rimmed spectacles, and a soiled, chequered apron.

'Ye're varra late, Tony,' she remarked querulously.

He unloosened his woollen neckerchief, and when he had hung it methodically with his hat behind the door, answered:

'"Twas terrible thick on t' fell-top, an' them two bitches be that senseless.'

She caught his sleeve, and, through her spectacles, suspiciously scrutinized his face.

'Ye did na meet wi' Rosa Blencarn?'

'Nay, she was in church, hymn-playin', wi' Luke Stock hangin' roond door,' he retorted bitterly, rebuffing her with rough impatience.

She moved away, nodding sententiously to herself. They began supper: neither spoke: Anthony sat slowly stirring his tea, and staring moodily into the flames: the bacon on his plate lay untouched. From time to time his mother, laying down her knife and fork, looked across at him in unconcealed asperity, pursing her wide, ungainly mouth. At last, abruptly setting down her cup, she broke out:

'I wonder ye hav'na mare pride, Tony. For hoo lang are ye goin' t' continue settin' mopin' and broodin' like a seck sheep? Ye'll jest mak yesself ill, an' then I reckon what ye'll prove satisfied. Ay, but I wonder ye hav'na more pride.'

But he made no answer, remaining unmoved, as if he had not heard.

Presently, half to himself, without raising his eyes, he murmured:

'Luke be goin' South, Monday.'

'Well, ye canna tak' oop wi' his leavin's anyways. It hasna coom't that, has it? Ye doan't intend settin' all t' parish a laughin' at ye a second occasion?'

He flushed dully, and bending over his plate, mechanically began his supper.

'Wa dang it,' he broke out a minute later, 'd'ye think I heed the cacklin' o' fifty parishes? Na, not I,' and, with a short, grim laugh, he brought his fist down heavily on the oak table.

'Ye're daft, Tony,' the old woman blurted.

'Daft or na daft, I tell ye this, mother, that I be forty-six year o' age this back-end, and there be some things I will na listen to. Rosa Blencarn's bonny enough for me.'

'Ay, bonny enough—I've na patience wi' ye. Bonny enough—tricked oot in her furbelows, gallivantin' wi' every royster fra Pe'rith. Bonny enough—that be all ye think on. She's bin a proper parson's niece—the giddy, feckless creature, an she'd mak' ye a proper sort o' wife, Tony Garstin, ye great, fond booby.'

She pushed back her chair, and, hurriedly clattering the crockery, began to clear away the supper.

'T' hoose be mine, t' Lord be praised,' she continued in a loud, hard voice, 'an' as long as he spare me, Tony, I'll na see Rosa Blencarn set foot inside it.'

Anthony scowled, without replying, and drew his chair to the hearth. His mother bustled about the room behind him. After a while she asked:

'Did ye pen t' lambs in t' back field?'

'Na, they're in Hullam bottom,' he answered curtly.

The door closed behind her, and by and by he could hear her moving overhead. Meditatively blinking, he filled his pipe clumsily, and pulling a crumpled newspaper from his pocket, sat on over the smouldering fire, reading and stolidly puffing.

II

The music rolled through the dark, empty church. The last, leaden flicker of daylight glimmered in through the pointed windows, and beyond the level rows of dusky pews, tenanted only by a litter of prayer-books, two guttering candles revealed the organ pipes, and the young girl's swaying figure.

She played vigorously. Once or twice the tune stumbled, and she recovered it impatiently, bending over the key-board, showily flourishing her wrists as she touched the stops. She was bare-headed (her hat and cloak lay beside her on a stool). She had fair, fluffy hair, cut short behind her neck; large, round eyes, heightened by a fringe of dark lashes; rough, ruddy cheeks, and a rosy, full-lipped, unstable mouth. She was dressed quite simply, in a black, close-fitting bodice, a little frayed at the sleeves. Her hands and neck were coarsely fashioned: her comeliness was brawny, literal, unfinished, as it were.

When at last the ponderous chords of the Amen faded slowly into the twilight, flushed, breathing a little quickly, she paused, listening to the stillness of the church. Presently a small boy emerged from behind the organ.

'Good evenin', Miss Rosa', he called, trotting briskly away down the aisle.

'Good night, Robert', she answered, absently.

After a while, with an impatient gesture, as if to shake some importunate thought from her mind, she rose abruptly, pinned on her hat, threw her cloak round her shoulders, blew out the candles, and groped her way through the church, towards the half-open door. As she hurried along the narrow pathway that led across the churchyard, of a sudden, a figure started out of the blackness.

'Who's that?' she cried, in a loud, frightened voice.

A man's uneasy laugh answered her.

'It's only me, Rosa. I didna' think t' scare ye. I've bin waitin' for ye, this hoor past.'

She made no reply, but quickened her pace. He strode on beside her.

'I'm off, Monday, ye know,' he continued. And, as she said nothing, 'Will ye na stop jest a minnit? I'd like t' speak a few words wi' ye before I go, an tomorrow I hev t' git over t' Scarsdale betimes,' he persisted.

'I don't want t' speak wi' ye: I don't want ever to see ye agin. I jest hate the sight o' ye.' She spoke with a vehement, concentrated hoarseness.

'Nay, but ye must listen to me. I will na be put off wi' fratchin speeches.'

And gripping her arm, he forced her to stop.

'Loose me, ye great beast,' she broke out.

'I'll na hould ye, if ye'll jest stand quiet-like. I meant t' speak fair t' ye, Rosa.'

They stood at a bend in the road, face to face quite close together. Behind his burly form stretched the dimness of a grey, ghostly field.

'What is't ye hev to say to me? Hev done wi' it quick,' she said sullenly.

'It be jest this, Rosa,' he began with dogged gravity. 'I want t' tell ye that ef any trouble comes t'ye after I'm gone—ye know t' what I refer—I want t' tell ye that I'm prepared t' act square by ye. I've written out on an envelope my address in London. Luke Stock, care o' Purcell and Co., Smithfield Market, London.'

'Ye're a bad, sinful man. I jest hate t' sight o' ye. I wish ye were dead.'

'Ay, but I reckon what ye'd ha best thought o' that before. Ye've changed yer whistle considerably since Tuesday. Nay, hould on,' he added, as she struggled to push past him. 'Here's t' envelope.'

She snatched the paper, and tore it passionately, scattering the fragments on to the road. When she had finished, he burst out angrily:

'Ye cussed, unreasonable fool.'

'Let me pass, ef ye've nought mare t'say,' she cried.

'Nay, I'll na part wi' ye this fashion. Ye can speak soft enough when ye choose.' And seizing her shoulders, he forced her backwards against the wall.

'Ye do look fine, an' na mistake, when ye're jest ablaze wi' ragin',' he laughed bluntly, lowering his face to hers.

'Loose me, loose me, ye great coward,' she gasped, striving to free her arms.

Holding her fast, he expostulated:

'Coom, Rosa, can we na part friends?'

'Part friends, indeed,' she retorted bitterly. 'Friends wi' the likes o' you. What d'ye tak me for? Let me git home, I tell ye. An' please God I'll never set eyes on ye again. I hate t' sight o' ye.'

'Be off wi' ye, then,' he answered, pushing her roughly back into the road. 'Be off wi' ye, ye silly. Ye canna say I hav na spak fair t' ye, an', by goom, ye'll na see me shally-wallyin this fashion agin.

Be off wi' ye: ye can jest shift for yerself, since ye canna keep a civil tongue in yer head.'

The girl, catching at her breath, stood as if dazed, watching his retreating figure; then starting forward at a run, disappeared up the hill, into the darkness.

III

Old Mr. Blencarn concluded his husky sermon. The scanty congregation, who had been sitting, stolidly immobile in their stiff, Sunday clothes, shuffled to their feet, and the pewful of school children, in clamorous chorus, intoned the final hymn. Anthony stood near the organ, absently contemplating, while the rude melody resounded through the church, Rosa's deft manipulation of the key-board. The rugged lines of his face were relaxed to a vacant, thoughtful limpness, that aged his expression not a little: now and then, as if for reference, he glanced questioningly at the girl's profile.

A few minutes later the service was over, and the congregation sauntered out down the aisle. A gawky group of men remained loitering by the church door: one of them called to Anthony; but, nodding curtly, he passed on, and strode away down the road, across the grey upland meadows, towards home. As soon as he had breasted the hill, however, and was no longer visible from below, he turned abruptly to the left, along a small, swampy hollow, till he had reached the lane that led down from the fell-side.

He clambered over a rugged, moss-grown wall, and stood, gazing expectantly down the dark, disused roadway; then, after a moment's hesitation, perceiving nobody, seated himself beneath the wall, on a projecting slab of stone.

Overhead hung a sombre, drifting sky. A gusty wind rollicked down from the fell—huge masses of chilly grey, stripped of the last night's mist. A few dead leaves fluttered over the stones, and from off the fell-side there floated the plaintive, quavering rumour of many bleating sheep.

Before long, he caught sight of two figures coming towards him, slowly climbing the hill. He sat awaiting their approach, fidgeting with his sandy beard, and abstractedly grinding the ground beneath his heel. At the brow they halted: plunging his hands deep into his pockets, he strolled sheepishly towards them.

'Ah! good day t' ye, Anthony,' called the old man, in a shrill, breathless voice. ''Tis a long hill, an' my legs are not what they were. Time was when I'd think nought o' a whole day's tramp on t' fells. Ay, I'm gittin' feeble, Anthony, that's what 'tis. And if Rosa here wasn't the great, strong lass she is, I don't know how her old uncle'd manage;' and he turned to the girl with a proud, tremulous smile.

'Will ye tak my arm a bit, Mr. Blencarn? Miss Rosa'll be tired, likely,' Anthony asked.

'Nay, Mr. Garstin, but I can manage nicely,' the girl interrupted sharply.

Anthony looked up at her as she spoke. She wore a straw hat, trimmed with crimson velvet, and a black, fur-edged cape, that seemed to set off mightily the fine whiteness of her neck. Her large, dark eyes were fixed upon him. He shifted his feet uneasily, and dropped his glance.

She linked her uncle's arm in hers, and the three moved slowly forward. Old Mr. Blencarn walked with difficulty, pausing at intervals for breath. Anthony, his eyes bent on the ground, sauntered beside him, clumsily kicking at the cobbles that lay in his path.

When they reached the vicarage gate, the old man asked him to come inside.

'Not jest now, thank ye, Mr. Blencarn. I've that lot o' lambs t' see to before dinner. It's a grand marnin', this,' he added, inconsequently.

'Uncle's bought a nice lot o' Leghorns, Tuesday,' Rosa remarked. Anthony met her gaze; there was a grave, subdued expression on her face this morning, that made her look more of a woman, less of a girl.

'Ay, do ye show him the birds, Rosa. I'd be glad to have his opinion on 'em.'

The old man turned to hobble into the house, and Rosa, as she supported his arm, called back over her shoulder:

'I'll not be a minute, Mr. Garstin.'

Anthony strolled round to the yard behind the house, and waited, watching a flock of glossy-white poultry that strutted, perkily pecking, over the grass-grown cobbles.

'Ay, Miss Rosa, they're a bonny lot,' he remarked, as the girl joined him.

'Are they not?' she rejoined, scattering a handful of corn before her.

The birds scuttled across the yard with greedy, outstretched necks. The two stood, side by side, gazing at them.

'What did he give for 'em?' Anthony asked.

'Fifty-five shillings.'

'Ay,' he assented, nodding absently.

'Was Dr. Sanderson na seein' o' yer father yesterday?' he asked, after a moment.

'He came in t' forenoon. He said he was jest na worse.'

'Ye knaw, Miss Rosa, as I'm still thinkin' on ye,' he began abruptly, without looking up.

'I reckon it ain't much use,' she answered shortly, scattering another handful of corn towards the birds. 'I reckon I'll never marry. I'm jest weary o' bein' courted—'

'I would na weary ye wi' courtin',' he interrupted.

She laughed noisily.

'Ye are a queer customer, an' na mistake.'

'I'm a match for Luke Stock anyway,' he continued fiercely. 'Ye think nought o' taking oop wi' him—about as ranty, wild a young feller as ever stepped.'

The girl reddened, and bit her lip.

'I don't know what you mean, Mr. Garstin. It seems to me ye're might hasty in jumpin' t' conclusions.'

'Mabbe I kin see a thing or two,' he retorted doggedly.

'Luke Stock's gone to London, anyway.'

'Ay, an' a powerful good job too, in t' opinion o' some folks.'

'Ye're jest jealous,' she exclaimed, with a forced titter. 'Ye're jest jealous o' Luke Stock.'

'Nay, but ye need na fill yer head wi' that nonsense. I'm too deep set on ye t' feel jealousy,' he answered, gravely.

The smile faded from her face, as she murmured:

'I canna mak ye out, Mr. Garstin.'

'Nay, that ye canna. An' I suppose it's natural, considerin' ye're little more than a child, an' I'm a'most old enough to be yer father,' he retorted, with blunt bitterness.

'But ye know yer mother's took that dislike t' me. She'd never abide the sight o' me at Hootsey.'

He remained silent a moment, moodily reflecting.

'She'd jest ha't' git ower it. I see nought in that objection,' he declared.

'Nay, Mr. Garstin, it canna be. Indeed it canna be at all. Ye'd best jest put it right from yer mind, once and for all.'

'I'd jest best put it off my mind, had I? Ye talk like a child!' he burst out scornfully. 'I intend ye t' coom t' love me, an' I will na tak ye till ye do. I'll jest go on waitin' for ye, an', mark my words, my day 'ull coom at last.'

He spoke loudly, in a slow, stubborn voice, and stepped suddenly towards her. With a faint, frightened cry she shrank back into the doorway of the hen-house.

'Ye talk like a prophet. Ye sort o' skeer me.'

He laughed grimly, and paused, reflectively scanning her face. He seemed about to continue in the same strain; but, instead, turned abruptly on his heel, and strode away through the garden gate.

IV

For three hundred years there had been a Garstin at Hootsey: generation after generation had tramped the grey stretch of upland, in the spring-time scattering their flocks over the fell-sides, and, at the 'back-end', on dark, winter afternoons, driving them home again, down the broad bridle-path that led over the 'raise'. They had been a race of few words, 'keeping themselves to themselves', as the phrase goes; beholden to no man, filled with a dogged, churlish pride—an upright, old-fashioned race, stubborn, long-lived, rude in speech, slow of resolve.

Anthony had never seen his father, who had died one night, upon the fell-top, he and his shepherd, engulfed in the great snowstorm of 1849. Folks had said that he was the only Garstin who had failed to make old man's bones.

After his death, Jake Atkinson, from Ribblehead in Yorkshire, had come to live at Hootsey. Jake was a fine farmer, a canny bargainer, and very handy among the sheep, till he took to drink, and roystering every week with the town wenches up at Carlisle. He was a corpulent, deep-voiced, free-handed fellow: when his time came, though he died very hardly, he remained festive and convivial to the last. And for years afterwards, in the valley, his memory lingered: men spoke of him regretfully, recalling his quips, his feats of strength, and his choice breed of Herdwicke rams. But he left behind him a host of debts up at Carlisle, in Penrith, and in almost every market town—debts that he had long ago pretended to have paid with money that belonged to his sister. The widow Garstin sold the twelve Herdwicke rams, and nine acres of land: within six weeks she had cleared off every penny, and for thirteen months, on Sundays, wore her mourning with a mute, forbidding grimness: the bitter thought that, unbeknown to her, Jake had acted dishonestly in money matters, and that he had ended his days in riotous sin, soured her pride, imbued her with a rancorous hostility against all the world. For she was a very proud woman, independent, holding her head high, so folks said, like a Garstin bred and born; and Anthony, although some reckoned him quiet and of little account, came to take after her as he grew into manhood.

She took into her own hands the management of the Hootsey farm, and set the boy to work for her along with the two farm servants. It was twenty-five years now since his uncle Jake's death: there were grey hairs in his sandy beard; but he still worked for his mother, as he had done when a growing lad.

And now that times were grown to be bad (of late years the price of stock had been steadily falling; and the hay harvests had drifted from bad to worse) the widow Garstin no longer kept any labouring men; but lived, she and her son, year in and year out, in a close parsimonious way.

That had been Anthony Garstin's life—a dull, eventless sort of business, the sluggish incrustation of monotonous years. And until Rosa Blencarn had come to keep house for her uncle, he had never thought twice on a woman's face.

The Garstins had always been good church-goers, and Anthony, for years, had acted as churchwarden. It was one summer evening, up at the vicarage, whilst he was checking the offertory account, that he first set eyes upon her. She was fresh back from school at Leeds: she was dressed in a white dress: she looked, he thought, like a London lady.

She stood by the window, tall and straight and queenly, dreamily gazing out into the summer twilight, whilst he and her uncle sat over their business. When he rose to go, she glanced at him with quick curiosity; he hurried away, muttering a sheepish good night.

The next time that he saw her was in church on Sunday. He watched her shyly, with a hesitating, reverential discretion: her beauty seemed to him wonderful, distant, enigmatic. In the afternoon, young Mrs. Forsyth, from Longscale, dropped in for a cup of tea with his mother, and the two set off gossiping of Rosa Blencarn, speaking of her freely, in tones of acrimonious contempt. For a long while he sat silent, puffing at his pipe; but at last, when his mother concluded with, 'She looks t' me fair stuck-oop, full o' toonish airs an' graces,' despite himself, he burst out: 'Ye're jest wastin' yer breath wi' that cackle. I reckon Miss Blencarn's o' a different clay to us folks.' Young Mrs. Forsyth tittered immoderately, and the next week it was rumoured about the valley that 'Tony Garstin was gone luny over t' parson's niece.'

But of all this he knew nothing—keeping to himself, as was his wont, and being, besides, very busy with the hay harvest—until one day, at dinner-time, Henry Sisson asked if he'd started his courting; Jacob Sowerby cried that Tony'd been too slow in getting to work, for that the girl had been seen spooning in Crosby Shaws with Curbison the auctioneer, and the others (there were half-a-dozen of them lounging round the hay-waggon) burst into a boisterous guffaw. Anthony flushed dully, looking hesitatingly from the one to the other; then slowly put down his beer-can, and of a sudden, seizing Jacob by the neck, swung him heavily on the grass. He fell against the waggon-wheel, and when he rose the blood was streaming from an ugly cut in his forehead. And henceforward Tony Garstin's courtship was the common jest of all the parish.

As yet, however, he had scarcely spoken to her, though twice he had passed her in the lane that led up to the vicarage. She had given him a frank, friendly smile; but he had not found the resolution to do more than lift his hat. He and Henry Sisson stacked the hay in the yard behind the house; there was no further mention made of Rosa Blencarn; but all day long Anthony, as he knelt thatching the rick, brooded over the strange sweetness of her face, and on the fell-top, while he tramped after the ewes over the dry, crackling heather, and as he jogged along the narrow, rickety road, driving his cartload of lambs into the auction mart.

Thus, as the weeks slipped by, he was content with blunt, wistful ruminations upon her indistinct image. Jacob Sowerby's accusation, and several kindred innuendoes let fall by his mother, left him coolly incredulous; the girl still seemed to him altogether distant; but from the first sight of her face he had evolved a stolid, unfaltering conception of her difference from the ruck of her sex.

But one evening, as he passed the vicarage on his way down from the fells, she called to him, and with a childish, confiding familiarity asked for advice concerning the feeding of the poultry. In his eagerness to answer her as best he could, he forgot his customary embarrassment, and grew, for the moment, almost voluble, and quite at his ease in her presence. Directly her flow of questions ceased, however, the returning perception of her rosy, hesitating smile, and of her large, deep eyes looking straight into his face, perturbed him strangely, and, reddening, he remembered the quarrel in the hay-field and the tale of Crosby Shaws.

After this, the poultry became a link between them—a link which he regarded in all seriousness, blindly unconscious that there was aught else to bring them together, only feeling himself in awe of her, because of her schooling, her townish manners, her ladylike mode of dress. And soon, he came to take a sturdy, secret pride in her friendly familiarity towards him. Several times a week he would meet her in the lane, and they would loiter a moment together; she would admire his dogs, though he assured her earnestly that they were but sorry curs; and once, laughing at his staidness, she nicknamed him 'Mr. Churchwarden'.

That the girl was not liked in the valley he suspected, curtly attributing her unpopularity to the women's senseless jealousy. Of gossip concerning her he heard no further hint; but instinctively, and partly from that rugged, natural reserve of his, shrank from mentioning her name, even incidentally, to his mother.

Now, on Sunday evenings, he often strolled up to the vicarage, each time quitting his mother with the same awkward affectation of casualness; and, on his return, becoming vaguely conscious of how she refrained from any comment on his absence, and appeared oddly oblivious of the existence of parson Blencarn's niece.

She had always been a sour-tongued woman; but, as the days shortened with the approach of the long winter months, she seemed to him to grow more fretful than ever; at times it was almost as if she bore him some smouldering, sullen resentment. He was of stubborn fibre, however, toughened by long habit of a bleak, unruly climate; he revolved the matter in his mind deliberately, and when, at last, after much plodding thought, it dawned upon him that she resented his acquaintance with Rosa Blencarn, he accepted the solution with an unflinching phlegm, and merely shifted his attitude towards the girl, calculating each day the likelihood of his meeting her, and making, in her presence, persistent efforts to break down, once for all, the barrier of his own timidity. He was a man not to be clumsily driven, still less, so he prided himself, a man to be craftily led.

It was close upon Christmas time before the crisis came. His mother was just home from Penrith market. The spring-cart stood in the yard, the old grey horse was steaming heavily in the still, frosty air.

'I reckon ye've come fast. T' ould horse is over hot,' he remarked bluntly, as he went to the animal's head.

She clambered down hastily, and, coming to his side, began breathlessly:

'Ye ought t' hev coom t' market, Tony. There's bin pretty goin's on in Pe'rith today. I was helpin' Anna Forsyth t' choose six yards o' sheetin' in Dockroy, when we sees Rosa Blencarn coom oot o' t' 'Bell and Bullock' in company we' Curbison and young Joe Smethwick. Smethwick was fair reelin' drunk, and Curbison and t' girl were a-houldin' on to him, to keep him fra fallin'; and then, after a bit, he puts his arm round the girl t' stiddy hisself, and that fashion they goes off, right oop t' public street—'

He continued to unload the packages, and to carry them mechanically one by one into the house. Each time, when he reappeared, she was standing by the steaming horse, busy with her tale.

'An' on t' road hame we passed t' three on' em in Curbison's trap, with Smethwick leein' in t' bottom, singin' maudlin' songs. They were passin' Dunscale village, an't' folks coom runnin' oot o' houses t' see 'em go past—'

He led the cart away towards the stable, leaving her to cry the remainder after him across the yard.

Half-an-hour later he came in for his dinner. During the meal not a word passed between them, and directly he had finished he strode out of the house. About nine o'clock he returned, lit his pipe, and sat down to smoke it over the kitchen fire.

'Where've ye bin, Tony?' she asked.

'Oop t' vicarage, courtin'', he retorted defiantly, with his pipe in his mouth.

This was ten months ago; ever since he had been doggedly waiting. That evening he had set his mind on the girl, he intended to have her; and while his mother gibed, as she did now upon every opportunity, his patience remained grimly unflagging. She would remind him that the farm belonged to her, that he would have to wait till her death before he could bring the hussy to Hootsey: he would retort that as soon as the girl would have him, he intended taking a small holding over at Scarsdale. Then she would give way, and for a while piteously upbraid him with her old age, and with the memory of all the years she and he had spent together, and he would comfort her with a display of brusque, evasive remorse.

But, none the less, on the morrow, his thoughts would return to dwell on the haunting vision of the girl's face, while his own rude, credulous chivalry, kindled by the recollection of her beauty, stifled his misgivings concerning her conduct.

Meanwhile she dallied with him, and amused herself with the younger men. Her old uncle fell ill in the spring, and could scarcely leave the house. She declared that she found life in the valley intolerably dull, that she hated the quiet of the place, that she longed for Leeds, and the exciting bustle of the streets; and in the evenings she wrote long letters to the girl-friends she had left behind there, describing with petulant vivacity her tribe of rustic admirers. At the harvest-time she went back on a fortnight's visit to friends; the evening before her departure she promised Anthony to give him her answer on her return. But, instead, she avoided him, pretended to have promised in jest, and took up with Luke Stock, a cattle-dealer from Wigton.

V

It was three weeks since he had fetched his flock down from the fell.

After dinner he and his mother sat together in the parlour: they had done so every Sunday afternoon, year in and year out, as far back as he could remember.

A row of mahogany chairs, with shiny, horse-hair seats, were ranged round the room. A great collection of agricultural prize-tickets were pinned over the wall; and, on a heavy, highly-polished sideboard stood several silver cups. A heap of gilt-edged shavings filled the unused grate: there were gaudily-tinted roses along the mantelpiece, and, on a small table by the window, beneath a glass-case, a gilt basket filled with imitation flowers. Every object was disposed with a scrupulous precision: the carpet and the red-patterned cloth on the centre table were much faded. The room was spotlessly clean, and wore, in the chilly winter sunlight, a rigid, comfortless air.

Neither spoke, or appeared conscious of the other's presence. Old Mrs. Garstin, wrapped in a woollen shawl, sat knitting: Anthony dozed fitfully on a stiff-backed chair.

Of a sudden, in the distance, a bell started tolling. Anthony rubbed his eyes drowsily, and taking from the table his Sunday hat, strolled out across the dusky fields. Presently, reaching a rude wooden seat, built beside the bridle-path, he sat down and relit his pipe. The air was very still; below him a white filmy mist hung across the valley: the fell-sides, vaguely grouped, resembled hulking masses of sombre shadow; and, as he looked back, three squares of glimmering gold revealed the lighted windows of the square-towered church.

He sat smoking, pondering, with placid and reverential contemplation, on the Mighty Maker of the world—a world majestically and inevitably ordered; a world where, he argued, each object—each fissure in the fells, the winding course of each tumbling stream—possesses its mysterious purport, its inevitable signification . . .

At the end of the field two rams were fighting; retreating, then running together, and, leaping from the ground, butting head to head and horn to horn. Anthony watched them absently, pursuing his rude meditations.

. . . And the succession of bad seasons, the slow ruination of the farmers throughout the country, were but punishment meted out for the accumulated wickedness of the world. In the olden time God rained plagues upon the land: nowadays, in His wrath, He spoiled the produce of the earth, which, with His own hands, He had fashioned and bestowed upon men.

He rose and continued his walk along the bridle-path. A multitude of rabbits scuttled up the hill at his approach; and a great cloud of plovers, rising from the rushes, circled overhead, filling the air with a profusion of their querulous cries. All at once he heard a rattling of stones, and perceived a number of small pieces of shingle bounding in front of him down the grassy slope.

A woman's figure was moving among the rocks above him. The next moment, by the trimming of crimson velvet on her hat, he had recognized her. He mounted the slope with springing strides, wondering the while how it was she came to be there, that she was not in church playing the organ at afternoon service.

Before she was aware of his approach, he was beside her.

'I thought ye'd be in church—' he began.

She started: then, gradually regaining her composure, answered, weakly smiling:

'Mr. Jenkinson, the new schoolmaster, wanted to try the organ.'

He came towards her impulsively: she saw the odd flickers in his eyes as she stepped back in dismay.

'Nay, but I will na harm ye,' he said. 'Only I reckon what 'tis a special turn o' Providence, meetin' wi' ye oop here. I reckon what ye'll hev t' give me a square answer noo. Ye canna dilly-dally everlastingly.'

He spoke almost brutally; and she stood, white and gasping, staring at him with large, frightened eyes. The sheep-walk was but a tiny threadlike track: the slope of the shingle on either side was very steep: below them lay the valley; distant, lifeless, all blurred by the evening dusk. She looked about her helplessly for a means of escape.

'Miss Rosa,' he continued, in a husky voice, 'can ye na coom t' think on me? Think ye, I've bin waitin' nigh upon two year for ye. I've watched ye tak oop, first wi' this young fellar, and then wi' that, till soomtimes my heart's fit t' burst. Many a day, oop on t' fell-top, t' thought o' ye's nigh driven me daft, and I've left my shepherdin' jest t' set on a cairn in t' mist, picturin' an' broodin' on yer face. Many an evenin' I've started oop t' vicarage, wi' t' resolution t' speak right oot t' ye; but when it coomed t' point, a sort o' timidity seemed t' hould me back, I was that feared t' displease ye. I knaw I'm na scholar, an' mabbe ye think I'm rough-mannered. I knaw I've spoken sharply to ye once or twice lately. But it's jest because I'm that mad wi' love for ye: I jest canna help myself soomtimes—'

He waited, peering into her face. She could see the beads of sweat above his bristling eyebrows: the damp had settled on his sandy beard: his horny fingers were twitching at the buttons of his black Sunday coat.

She struggled to summon a smile; but her under-lip quivered, and her large dark eyes filled slowly with tears.

And he went on:

'Ye've coom t' mean jest everything to me. Ef ye will na hev me, I care for nought else. I canna speak t' ye in phrases: I'm jest a plain, unscholarly man: I canna wheedle ye, wi' cunnin' after t' fashion o' toon folks. But I can love ye wi' all my might, an' watch over ye, and work for ye better than any one o' em—'

She was crying to herself, silently, while he spoke. He noticed nothing, however: the twilight hid her face from him.

'There's nought against me,' he persisted. 'I'm as good a man as any one on 'em. Ay, as good a man as any one on 'em,' he repeated defiantly, raising his voice.

'It's impossible, Mr. Garstin, it's impossible. Ye've been very kind to me—' she added, in a choking voice.

'Wa dang it, I didna mean t' mak ye cry, lass,' he exclaimed, with a softening of his tone. 'There's nought for ye t' cry ower.'

She sank on to the stones, passionately sobbing in hysterical and defenceless despair. Anthony stood a moment, gazing at her in clumsy perplexity: then, coming close to her, put his hand on her shoulder, and said gently:

'Coom, lass, what's trouble? Ye can trust me.'

She shook her head faintly.

'Ay, but ye can though,' he asserted, firmly. 'Come, what is't?'

Heedless of him, she continued to rock herself to and fro, crooning in her distress:

'Oh! I wish I were dead! . . . I wish I could die!'

—'Wish ye could die?' he repeated. 'Why, whatever can't be that's troublin' ye like this? There, there, lassie, give ower: it 'ull all coom right, whatever it be—'

'No, no,' she wailed. 'I wish I could die! . . . I wish I could die!'

Lights were twinkling in the village below; and across the valley darkness was draping the hills. The girl lifted her face from her hands, and looked up at him with a scared, bewildered expression.

'I must go home: I must be getting home,' she muttered.

'Nay, but there's sommut mighty amiss wi' ye.'

'No, it's nothing . . . I don't know—I'm not well . . . I mean it's nothing . . . it'll pass over . . . you mustn't think anything of it.'

'Nay, but I canna stand by an see ye in sich trouble.'

'It's nothing, Mr. Garstin, indeed it's nothing,' she repeated.

'Ay, but I canna credit that,' he objected stubbornly.

She sent him a shifting, hunted glance.

'Let me get home . . . you must let me get home.'

She made a tremulous, pitiful attempt at firmness. Eyeing her keenly, he barred her path: she flushed scarlet, and looked hastily away across the valley.

'If ye'll tell me yer distress, mabbe I can help ye.'

'No, no, it's nothing . . . it's nothing.'

'If ye'll tell me yer distress, mabbe I can help ye,' he repeated, with a solemn, deliberate sternness. She shivered, and looked away again, vaguely, across the valley.

'You can do nothing: there's nought to be done,' she murmured drearily.

'There's a man in this business,' he declared.

'Let me go! Let me go!' she pleaded desperately.

'Who is't that's bin puttin' ye into this distress?' His voice sounded loud and harsh.

'No one, no one. I canna tell ye, Mr. Garstin . . . It's no one,' she protested weakly. The white, twisted look on his face frightened her.

'My God!' he burst out, gripping her wrist, 'an' a proper soft fool ye've made o' me. Who is't, I tell ye? Who's t' man?'

'Ye're hurtin' me. Let me go. I canna tell ye.'

'And ye're fond o' him?'

'No, no. He's a wicked, sinful man. I pray God I may never set eyes on him again. I told him so.'

'But ef he's got ye into trouble, he'll hev t' marry ye,' he persisted with a brutal bitterness.

'I will not. I hate him!' she cried fiercely.

'But is he *willin'* t' marry ye?'

'I don't know . . . I don't care . . . he said so before he went away . . . But I'd kill myself sooner than live with him.'

He let her hands fall and stepped back from her. She could only see his figure, like a sombre cloud, standing before her. The whole fell-side seemed still and dark and lonely. Presently she heard his voice again:

'I reckon what there's one road oot o' yer distress.'

She shook her head drearily.

'There's none. I'm a lost woman.'

'An' ef ye took me instead?' he said eagerly.

'I—I don't understand—'

'Ef ye married me instead of Luke Stock?'

'But that's impossible—the—the—'

'Ay, t' child. I know. But I'll tak t' child as mine.'

She remained silent. After a moment he heard her voice answer in a queer, distant tone:

'You mean that—that ye're ready to marry me, and adopt the child?'

'I do,' he answered doggedly.

'But people—your mother—?'

'Folks 'ull jest know nought about it. It's none o' their business. T' child 'ull pass as mine. Ye'll accept that?'

'Yes,' she answered, in a low, rapid voice.

'Ye'll consent t' hev me, ef I git ye oot o' yer trouble?'

'Yes,' she repeated, in the same tone.

She heard him draw a long breath.

'I said 't was a turn o' Providence, meetin' wi' ye oop here,' he exclaimed, with half-suppressed exultation.

Her teeth began to chatter a little: she felt that he was peering at her, curiously, through the darkness.

'An' noo,' he continued briskly, 'ye'd best be gettin' home. Give me ye're hand, an' I'll stiddy ye ower t' stones.'

He helped her down the bank of shingle, exclaiming: 'By goom, ye're stony cauld.' Once or twice she slipped: he supported her, roughly gripping her knuckles. The stones rolled down the steps, noisily, disappearing into the night.

Presently they struck the turf bridle-path, and, as they descended silently towards the lights of the village, he said gravely:

'I always reckoned what my day 'ud coom.'

She made no reply; and he added grimly:

'There'll be terrible work wi' mother over this.'

He accompanied her down the narrow lane that led past her uncle's house. When the lighted windows came in sight he halted.

'Good night, lassie,' he said kindly. 'Do ye give ower distressin' yeself.'

'Good night, Mr. Garstin,' she answered, in the same low, rapid voice in which she had given him her answer up on the fell.

'We're man an' wife plighted now, are we not?' he blurted timidly.

She held her face to his, and he kissed her on the cheek, clumsily.

VI

The next morning the frost had set in. The sky was still clear and glittering: the whitened fields sparkled in the chilly sunlight: here and there, on high, distant peaks, gleamed dainty caps of snow. All the week Anthony was to be busy at the fell-foot, wall-building against the coming of the winter storms: the work was heavy, for he was single-handed, and the stone had to be fetched from off the fell-side. Two or three times a day he led his rickety, lumbering cart along the lane that passed the vicarage gate, pausing on each journey to glance furtively up at the windows. But he saw no sign of Rosa Blencarn; and, indeed, he felt no longing to see her: he was grimly exultant over the remembrance of his wooing of her, and over the knowledge that she was his. There glowed within him a stolid pride in himself: he thought of the others who had courted her, and the means by which he had won her seemed to him a fine stroke of cleverness.

And so he refrained from any mention of the matter; relishing, as he worked, all alone, the days through, the consciousness of his secret triumph, and anticipating, with inward chucklings, the discomforted cackle of his mother's female friends. He foresaw without misgiving, her bitter opposition: he felt himself strong; and his heart warmed towards the girl. And when, at intervals, the brusque realization that, after all, he was to possess her swept over him, he gripped the stones, and swung them almost fiercely into their places.

All around him the white, empty fields seemed slumbering breathlessly. The stillness stiffened the leafless trees. The frosty air flicked his blood: singing vigorously to himself he worked with a stubborn, unflagging resolution, methodically postponing, till the length of the wall should be completed, the announcement of his betrothal.

After his reticent, solitary fashion, he was very happy, reviewing his future prospects, with a plain and steady assurance, and, as the week-end approached, coming to ignore the irregularity of the whole business: almost to assume, in the exaltation of his pride, that he had won her honestly; and to discard, stolidly, all thought of Luke Stock, of his relations with her, of the coming child that was to pass for his own.

And there were moments too, when, as he sauntered homewards through the dusk at the end of his day's work, his heart grew full to overflowing of a rugged, superstitious gratitude towards God in Heaven who had granted his desires.

About three o'clock on the Saturday afternoon he finished the length of wall. He went home, washed, shaved, put on his Sunday coat; and, avoiding the kitchen, where his mother sat knitting by the fireside, strode up to the vicarage.

It was Rosa who opened the door to him. On recognizing him she started, and he followed her into the dining-room. He seated himself, and began, brusquely:

'I've coom, Miss Rosa, t' speak t' Mr. Blencarn.'

Then added, eyeing her closely:

'Ye're lookin' sick, lass.'

Her faint smile accentuated the worn, white look on her face.

'I reckon ye've been frettin' yeself,' he continued gently, 'leein' awake o' nights, hev'n't yee, noo?'

She smiled vaguely.

'Well, but ye see I've coom t' settle t' whole business for ye. Ye thought mabbe that I was na a man o' my word.'

'No, no, not that,' she protested, 'but—but—'

'But what then?'

'Ye must not do it, Mr. Garstin . . . I must just bear my own trouble the best I can—' she broke out.

'D'ye fancy I'm takin' ye oot of charity? Ye little reckon the sort o' stuff my love for ye's made of. Nay, Miss Rosa, but ye canna draw back noo.'

'But ye cannot do it, Mr. Garstin. Ye know your mother will na have me at Hootsey . . . I could na live there with your mother . . . I'd sooner bear my trouble alone, as best I can . . . She's that stern is Mrs. Garstin. I couldn't look her in the face . . . I can go away somewhere . . . I could keep it all from uncle.'

Her colour came and went: she stood before him, looking away from him, dully, out of the window.

'I intend ye t' coom t' Hootsey. I'm na lad: I reckon I can choose my own wife. Mother'll hev ye at t' farm, right enough: ye need na distress yeself on that point—'

'Nay, Mr. Garstin, but indeed she will not, never . . . I know she will not . . . She always set herself against me, right from the first.'

'Ay, but that was different. T' case is all changed noo,' he objected doggedly.

'She'll support the sight of me all the less,' the girl faltered.

'Mother'll hev ye at Hootsey—receive ye willin' of her own free wish—of her own free wish, d'ye hear? I'll answer for that.'

He struck the table with his fist heavily. His tone of determination awed her: she glanced at him hurriedly, struggling with her irresolution.

'I knaw hoo t' manage mother. An' now,' he concluded, changing his tone, 'is yer uncle about t' place?'

'He's up the paddock, I think,' she answered.

'Well, I'll jest step oop and hev a word wi' him.'

'Ye're . . . ye will na tell him.'

'Tut, tut, na harrowin' tales, ye need na fear, lass. I reckon ef I can tackle mother, I can accommodate myself t' parson Blencarn.'

He rose, and coming close to her, scanned her face.

'Ye must git t' roses back t' yer cheeks,' he exclaimed, with a short laugh, 'I canna be takin' a ghost t' church.'

She smiled tremulously, and he continued, laying one hand affectionately on her shoulder:

'Nay, but I was but jestin'. Roses or na roses, ye'll be t' bonniest bride in all Coomberland. I'll meet ye in Hullam lane, after church time, tomorrow,' he added, moving towards the door.

After he had gone, she hurried to the backdoor furtively. His retreating figure was already mounting the grey upland field. Presently, beyond him, she perceived her uncle, emerging through the paddock gate. She ran across the poultry yard, and mounting a tub, stood watching the two figures as they moved towards one another along the brow, Anthony vigorously trudging, with his hands thrust deep in his pockets; her uncle, his wideawake tilted over his nose, hobbling, and leaning stiffly on his pair of sticks. They met; she saw Anthony take her uncle's arm: the two, turning together, strolled away towards the fell.

She went back into the house. Anthony's dog came towards her, slinking along the passage. She caught the animal's head in her hands, and bent over it caressingly, in an impulsive outburst of almost hysterical affection.

VII

The two men returned towards the vicarage. At the paddock gate they halted, and the old man concluded:

'I could not have wished a better man for her, Anthony. Mabbe the Lord'll not be minded to spare me much longer. After I'm gone Rosa'll hev all I possess. She was my poor brother Isaac's only child. After her mother was taken, he, poor fellow, went altogether to the bad, and until she came here she mostly lived among strangers. It's been a wretched sort of childhood for her—a wretched sort of childhood. Ye'll take care of her, Anthony, will ye not? . . . Nay, but I could not hev wished for a better man for her, and there's my hand on 't.'

'Thank ee, Mr. Blencarn, thank ee,' Anthony answered huskily, gripping the old man's hand.

And he started off down the lane homewards.

His heart was full of a strange, rugged exaltation. He felt with a swelling pride that God had entrusted to him this great charge—to tend her; to make up to her, tenfold, for all that loving care, which, in her childhood, she had never known. And together with a stubborn confidence in himself, there welled up within him a great pity for her—a tender pity, that, chastening with his passion, made her seem to him, as he brooded over that lonely childhood of hers, the more distinctly beautiful, the more profoundly precious.

He pictured to himself, tremulously, almost incredulously, their married life—in the winter, his return home at nightfall to find her awaiting him with a glad, trustful smile; their evenings, passed together, sitting in silent happiness over the smouldering logs; or, in summer-time, the midday rest in the hay-fields when, wearing perhaps a large-brimmed hat fastened with a red ribbon, beneath her chin, he would catch sight of her, carrying his dinner, coming across the upland.

She had not been brought up to be a farmer's wife: she was but a child still, as the old parson had said. She should not have to work as other men's wives worked: she should dress like a lady, and on Sundays, in church, wear fine bonnets, and remain, as she had always been, the belle of all the parish.

And, meanwhile, he would farm as he had never farmed before, watching his opportunities, driving cunning bargains, spending nothing on himself, hoarding every penny that she might have what she wanted . . . And, as he strode through the village, he seemed to foresee a general brightening of prospects, a sobering of the fever of speculation in sheep, a cessation of the insensate glutting, year after year, of the great winter marts throughout the North, a slackening of the foreign competition followed by a steady revival of the price of fatted stocks—a period of prosperity in store for the farmer at last . . . And the future years appeared to open out before him, spread like a distant, glittering plain, across which, he and she, hand in hand, were called to travel together . . .

And then, suddenly, as his iron-bound boots clattered over the cobbled yard, he remembered, with brutal determination, his mother, and the stormy struggle that awaited him.

He waited till supper was over, till his mother had moved from the table to her place by the chimney corner. For several minutes he remained debating with himself the best method of breaking the news to her. Of a sudden he glanced up at her: her knitting had slipped on to her lap: she was sitting, bunched of a heap in her chair, nodding with sleep. By the flickering light of the wood fire, she looked worn and broken: he felt a twinge of clumsy compunction. And then he remembered the piteous, hunted look in the girl's eyes, and the old man's words when they had parted at the paddock gate, and he blurted out:

'I doot but what I'll hev t' marry Rosa Blencarn after all.'

She started, and blinking her eyes, said:

'I was jest takin' a wink o' sleep. What was 't ye were saying, Tony?'

He hesitated a moment, puckering his forehead into coarse rugged lines, and fidgeting noisily with his tea-cup. Presently he repeated:

'I doot but what I'll hev t' marry Rosa Blencarn after all.'

She rose stiffly, and stepping down from the hearth, came towards him.

'Mabbe I did na hear ye aright, Tony.' She spoke hurriedly, and though she was quite close to him, steadying herself with one hand clutching the back of his chair, her voice sounded weak, distant almost.

'Look oop at me. Look oop into my face,' she commanded fiercely.

He obeyed sullenly.

'Noo oot wi 't. What's yer meanin', Tony?'

'I mean what I say,' he retorted doggedly, averting his gaze.

'What d'ye mean by sayin' that ye've *got* t' marry her?'

'I tell yer I mean what I say,' he repeated dully.

'Ye mean ye've bin an' put t' girl in trouble?'

He said nothing; but sat staring stupidly at the floor.

'Look oop at me, and answer,' she commanded, gripping his shoulder and shaking him.

He raised his face slowly, and met her glance.

'Ay, that's aboot it,' he answered.

'This'll na be truth. It'll be jest a piece o' wanton trickery!' she cried.

'Nay, but 't is truth,' he answered deliberately.

'Ye will na swear t' it?' she persisted.

'I see na necessity for swearin'.'

'Then ye canna swear t' it,' she burst out triumphantly.

He paused an instant; then said quietly:

'Ay, but I'll swear t' it easy enough. Fetch t' Book.'

She lifted the heavy, tattered Bible from the chimney-piece, and placed it before him on the table. He laid his lumpish fist on it.

'Say,' she continued with a tense tremulousness, 'say, I swear t' ye, mother, that 't is t' truth, t' whole truth, and noat but t' truth, s'help me God.'

'I swear t' ye, mother, it's truth, t' whole truth, and nothin' but t' truth, s'help me God,' he repeated after her.

'Kiss t' Book,' she ordered.

He lifted the Bible to his lips. As he replaced it on the table, he burst out into a short laugh:

'Be ye satisfied noo?'

She went back to the chimney corner without a word. The logs on the hearth hissed and crackled. Outside, amid the blackness the wind was rising, hooting through the firs, and past the windows.

After a long while he roused himself, and drawing his pipe from his pocket almost steadily, proceeded leisurely to pare in the palm of his hand a lump of black tobacco.

'We'll be asked in church Sunday,' he remarked bluntly.

She made no answer.

He looked across at her.

Her mouth was drawn tight at the corners: her face wore a queer, rigid aspect. She looked, he thought, like a figure of stone.

'Ye're not feeling poorly, are ye, mother?' he asked.

She shook her head grimly: then, hobbling out into the room, began to speak in a shrill, tuneless voice.

'Ye talked at one time o' takin' a farm over Scarsdale way. But ye'd best stop here. I'll no hinder ye. Ye can have t' large bedroom in t' front, and I'll move ower to what used to be my brother Jake's room. Ye knaw I've never had no opinion of t' girl, but I'll do what's right by her, ef I break my sperrit in t' doin' on't. I'll mak' t' girl welcome here: I'll stand by her proper-like: mebbe I'll finish by findin' soom good in her. But from this day forward, Tony, ye're na son o' mine. Ye've dishonoured yeself: ye've laid a trap for me—ay, laid a trap, that's t' word. Ye've brought shame and bitterness on yer ould mother in her ould age. Ye've made me despise t' varra sect o' ye. Ye can stop on here, but ye shall niver touch a penny of my money; every shillin' of 't shall go t' yer child, or to your child's children. Ay,' she went on, raising her voice, 'ay, ye've got yer way at last, and mebbe ye reckon ye've chosen a mighty smart way. But time 'ull coom when ye'll regret this day, when ye eat oot yer repentance in doost an' ashes. Ay, Lord 'ull punish ye, Tony, chastize ye properly. Ye'll learn that marriage begun in sin can end in nought but sin. Ay,' she concluded, as she reached the door, raising her skinny hand prophetically, 'ay, after I'm deed and gone, ye mind ye o' t' words o' t' apostle—"For them that hev sinned without t' law, shall also perish without t' law.'"

And she slammed the door behind her.

A LITTLE GREY GLOVE

By George Egerton (Mary Chavelita [Dunne] Bright)

The book of life begins with a man and woman in a garden and ends—with Revelations.

OSCAR WILDE

Yes, most fellows' book of life may be said to begin at the chapter where woman comes in; mine did. She came in years ago, when I was a raw undergraduate. With the sober thought of retrospective analysis, I may say she was not all my fancy painted her; indeed now that I come to think of it there was no fancy about the vermeil of her cheeks, rather an artificial reality; she had her bower in the bar of the Golden Boar, and I was madly in love with her, seriously intent on lawful wedlock. Luckily for me she threw me over for a neighbouring pork butcher, but at the time I took it hardly, and it made me sex-shy. I was a very poor man in those days. One feels one's griefs more keenly then, one hasn't the wherewithal to buy distraction. Besides, ladies snubbed me rather, on the rare occasions I met them. Later I fell in for a legacy, the forerunner of several; indeed, I may say I am beastly rich. My tastes are simple too, and I haven't any poor relations. I believe they are of great assistance in getting rid of superfluous capital, wish I had some! It was after the legacy that women discovered my attractions. They found that there was something superb in my plainness (before, they said ugliness), something after the style of the late Victor Emanuel, something infinitely more striking than mere ordinary beauty. At least so Harding told me his sister said, and she had the reputation of being a clever girl. Being an only child, I never had the opportunity other fellows had of studying the undress side of women through familiar intercourse, say with sisters. Their most ordinary belongings were sacred to me. I had, I used to be told, ridiculous high-flown notions about them (by the way I modified those considerably on closer acquaintance). I ought to study them, nothing like a woman for developing a fellow. So I laid in a stock of books in different languages, mostly novels, in which women played title roles, in order to get up some definite data before venturing amongst them. I can't say I derived much benefit from this course. There seemed to be as great a diversity of opinion about the female species as, let us say, about the salmonidae.

My friend Ponsonby Smith, who is one of the oldest fly-fishers in the three kingdoms, said to me once: Take my word for it, there are only four true salmo; the salar, the trutta, the fario, the ferox; all the rest are just varieties, subgenuses of the above; stick to that. Some writing fellow divided all the women into good-uns and bad-uns. But as a conscientious stickler for truth, I must say that both in trout as in women, I have found myself faced with most puzzling varieties, that were a tantalizing blending of several qualities. I then resolved to study them on my own account. I pursued the Eternal Feminine in a spirit of purely scientific investigation. I knew you'd laugh sceptically at that, but it's a fact. I was impartial in my selection of subjects for observation—French, German, Spanish, as well as the home product. Nothing in petticoats escaped me. I devoted myself to the freshest *ingenue* as well as the experienced widow of three departed; and I may as well confess that the more I saw of her, the less I understood her. But I think they understood me. They refused to take me *au sérieux*. When they weren't fleecing me, they were interested in the state of my soul (I preferred the former), but all humbugged me equally, so I gave them up. I took to rod and gun instead, *pro salute animae*; it's decidedly safer. I have scoured every country in the globe; indeed I can say that I have shot and fished in woods and waters where no other white man, perhaps ever dropped a beast or played a fish before. There is no life like the life of a free wanderer, and no lore like the lore one gleans in the great book of nature. But one must have freed one's spirit from the taint of the town before one can even read the alphabet of its mystic meaning.

What has this to do with the glove? True, not much, and yet it has a connection—it accounts for me.

Well, for twelve years I have followed the impulses of the wandering spirit that dwells in me. I have seen the sun rise in Finland and gild the Devil's Knuckles as he sank behind the Drachensberg.

I have caught the barba and the gamer yellow fish in the Vaal river, taken muskelunge and black-bass in Canada, thrown a fly over *guapote* and *cavallo* in Central American lakes, and choked the monster eels of the Mauritius with a cunningly faked-up duckling. But I have been shy as a chub at the shadow of a woman.

Well, it happened last year I came back on business—another confounded legacy; end of June too, just as I was off to Finland. But Messrs. Thimble and Rigg, the highly respectable firm who look after my affairs, represented that I owed it to others, whom I kept out of their share of the legacy, to stay near town till affairs were wound up. They told me, with a view to reconcile me perhaps, of a trout stream with a decent inn near it; an unknown stream in Kent. It seems a junior member of the firm is an angler, at least he sometimes catches pike or perch in the Medway some way from the stream where the trout rise in audacious security from artificial lures. I stipulated for a clerk to come down with any papers to be signed, and started at once for Victoria. I decline to tell the name of my find, firstly because the trout are the gamest little fish that ever rose to fly and run to a good two pounds. Secondly, I have paid for all the rooms in the inn for the next year, and I want it to myself. The glove is lying on the table next me as I write. If it isn't in my breast-pocket or under my pillow, it is in some place where I can see it. It has a delicate grey body (suède, I think they call it) with a whipping of silver round the top, and a darker grey silk tag to fasten it. It is marked 5-3/4 inside, and has a delicious scent about it, to keep off moths, I suppose; naphthaline is better. It reminds me of a 'silver-sedge' tied on a ten hook. I startled the good landlady of the little inn (there is no village fortunately) when I arrived with the only porter of the tiny station laden with traps. She hesitated about a private sitting-room, but eventually we compromised matters, as I was willing to share it with the other visitor. I got into knickerbockers at once, collared a boy to get me worms and minnow for the morrow, and as I felt too lazy to unpack tackle, just sat in the shiny armchair (made comfortable by the successive sitting of former occupants) at the open window and looked out. The river, not the trout stream, winds to the right, and the trees cast trembling shadows into its clear depths. The red tiles of a farm roof show between the beeches, and break the monotony of blue sky background. A dusty waggoner is slaking his thirst with a tankard of ale. I am conscious of the strange lonely feeling that a visit to England always gives me. Away in strange lands, even in solitary places, one doesn't feel it somehow. One is filled with the hunter's lust, bent on a 'kill', but at home in the quiet country, with the smoke curling up from some fireside, the mowers busy laying the hay in swaths, the children tumbling under the trees in the orchards, and a girl singing as she spreads the clothes on the sweetbriar hedge, amidst a scene quick with home sights and sounds, a strange lack creeps in and makes itself felt in a dull, aching way. Oddly enough, too, I had a sense of uneasiness, a 'something going to happen'. I had often experienced it when out alone in a great forest, or on an unknown lake, and it always meant 'ware danger' of some kind. But why should I feel it here? Yet I did, and I couldn't shake it off. I took to examining the room. It was a commonplace one of the usual type. But there was a work-basket on the table, a dainty thing, lined with blue satin. There was a bit of lace stretched over shiny blue linen, with the needle sticking in it; such fairy work, like cobwebs seen from below, spun from a branch against a background of sky. A gold thimble, too, with initials, not the landlady's, I know. What pretty things, too, in the basket! A scissors, a capital shape for fly-making; a little file, and some floss silk and tinsel, the identical colour I want for a new fly I have in my head, one that will be a demon to kill. The northern devil I mean to call him. Some one looks in behind me, and a light step passes upstairs. I drop the basket, I don't know why. There are some reviews near it. I take up one, and am soon buried in an article on Tasmanian fauna. It is strange, but whenever I do know anything about a subject, I always find these writing fellows either entirely ignorant or damned wrong.

After supper, I took a stroll to see the river. It was a silver grey evening, with just the last lemon and pink streaks of the sunset staining the sky. There had been a shower, and somehow the smell of the dust after rain mingled with the mignonette in the garden brought back vanished scenes of small-boyhood, when I caught minnows in a bottle, and dreamt of a shilling rod as happiness unattainable. I turned aside from the road in accordance with directions, and walked towards the stream. Holloa! someone before me, what a bore! The angler is hidden by an elder-bush, but I can see the fly drop delicately, artistically on the water. Fishing upstream, too! There is a bit of broken water there, and the midges dance in myriads; a silver gleam, and the line spins out, and the fly falls just in the right place. It is growing dusk, but the fellow is an adept at quick, fine casting—I wonder what fly he has on—why, he's going to try downstream now? I hurry forward, and as I near him, I swerve to the left out of the way. S-s-s-s! a sudden sting in the lobe of my ear. Hey! I cry as I find I am caught; the tail fly is fast in it. A slight, grey-clad woman holding the rod lays it carefully down and comes towards me through the gathering dusk. My first impulse is to snap the gut and take to my heels, but I am held by something less tangible but far more powerful than the grip of the Limerick hook in my ear.

'I am very sorry!' she says in a voice that matched the evening, it was so quiet and soft; 'but it was exceedingly stupid of you to come behind like that.'

'I didn't think you threw such a long line; I thought I was safe,' I stammered.

'Hold this!' she says, giving me a diminutive fly-book, out of which she has taken a scissors. I obey meekly. She snips the gut.

'Have you a sharp knife? If I strip the hook you can push it through; it is lucky it isn't in the cartilage.'

I suppose I am an awful idiot, but I only handed her the knife, and she proceeded as calmly as if stripping a hook in a man's ear were an everyday occurrence. Her gown is of some soft grey stuff, and her grey leather belt is silver clasped. Her hands are soft and cool and steady, but there is a rarely disturbing thrill in their gentle touch. The thought flashed through my mind that I had just missed that, a woman's voluntary tender touch, not a paid caress, all my life.

'Now you can push it through yourself. I hope it won't hurt much.' Taking the hook, I push it through, and a drop of blood follows it. 'Oh!' she cries, but I assure her it is nothing, and stick the hook surreptitiously in my coat sleeve. Then we both laugh, and I look at her for the first time. She has a very white forehead, with little tendrils of hair blowing round it under her grey cap, her eyes are grey. I didn't see that then, I only saw they were steady, smiling eyes that matched her mouth. Such a mouth, the most maddening mouth a man ever longed to kiss, above a too-pointed chin, soft as a child's; indeed, the whole face looks soft in the misty light.

'I am sorry I spoilt your sport!' I say.

'Oh, that don't matter, it's time to stop. I got two brace, one a beauty.'

She is winding in her line, and I look in her basket; they *are* beauties, one two-pounder, the rest running from a half to a pound.

'What fly?'

'Yellow dun took that one, but your assailant was a partridge spider.' I sling her basket over my shoulder; she takes it as a matter of course, and we retrace our steps. I feel curiously happy as we walk towards the road; there is a novel delight in her nearness; the feel of woman works subtly and strangely in me; the rustle of her skirt as it brushes the black-heads in the meadow-grass, and the delicate perfume, partly violets, partly herself, that comes to me with each of her movements is a rare pleasure. I am hardly surprised when she turns into the garden of the inn, I think I knew from the first that she would.

'Better bathe that ear of yours, and put a few drops of carbolic in the water.' She takes the basket as she says it, and goes into the kitchen. I hurry over this, and go into the little sitting-room. There is a tray with a glass of milk and some oaten cakes upon the table. I am too disturbed to sit down; I stand at the window and watch the bats flitter in the gathering moonlight, and listen with quivering nerves for her step—perhaps she will send for the tray, and not come after all. What a fool I am to be disturbed by a grey-clad witch with a tantalizing mouth! That comes of loafing about doing nothing. I mentally darn the old fool who saved her money instead of spending it. Why the devil should I be bothered? I don't want it anyhow. She comes in as I fume, and I forget everything at her entrance. I push the armchair towards the table, and she sinks quietly into it, pulling the tray nearer. She has a wedding ring on, but somehow it never strikes me to wonder if she is married or a widow or who she may be. I am content to watch her break her biscuits. She has the prettiest hands, and a trick of separating her last fingers when she takes hold of anything. They remind me of white orchids I saw somewhere. She led me to talk; about Africa, I think. I liked to watch her eyes glow deeply in the shadow and then catch light as she bent forward to say something in her quick responsive way.

'Long ago when I was a girl,' she said once.

'Long ago?' I echo incredulously, 'surely not?'

'Ah, but yes, you haven't seen me in the daylight,' with a soft little laugh. 'Do you know what the gipsies say? "Never judge a woman or a ribbon by candle-light." They might have said moonlight equally well.'

She rises as she speaks, and I feel an overpowering wish to have her put out her hand. But she does not, she only takes the work-basket and a book, and says good night with an inclination of her little head.

I go over and stand next to her chair; I don't like to sit in it, but I like to put my hand where her head leant, and fancy, if she were there, how she would look up.

I woke next morning with a curious sense of pleasurable excitement. I whistled from very lightness of heart as I dressed. When I got down I found the landlady clearing away her breakfast things. I felt disappointed and resolved to be down earlier in future. I didn't feel inclined to try the minnow. I put them in a tub in the yard and tried to read and listen for her step. I dined alone. The day dragged terribly. I did not like to ask about her, I had a notion she might not like it. I spent the evening on the river. I might have filled a good basket, but I let the beggars rest. After all, I had caught fish enough to stock all the rivers in Great Britain. There are other things than trout in the world. I sit and smoke a pipe where she caught me last night. If I half close my eyes I can see hers, and her mouth, in the smoke. That is one of the curious charms of baccy, it helps to reproduce brain pictures. After a bit, I think 'perhaps she has left'. I get quite feverish at the thought and hasten back. I must ask. I look up at the window as I pass; there is surely a gleam of white. I throw down my traps and hasten up. She is leaning with her arms on the window-ledge staring out into the gloom. I could swear I caught a suppressed sob as I entered. I cough, and she turns quickly and bows slightly. A bonnet and gloves and lace affair and a lot of papers are lying on the table. I am awfully afraid she is going. I say—

'Please don't let me drive you away, it is so early yet. I half expected to see you on the river.'

'Nothing so pleasant; I have been up in town (the tears have certainly got into her voice) all day; it was so hot and dusty, I am tired out.'

The little servant brings in the lamp and a tray with a bottle of lemonade.

'Mistress hasn't any lemons, 'm, will this do?'

'Yes,' she says wearily, she is shading her eyes with her hand; 'anything; I am fearfully thirsty.'

'Let me concoct you a drink instead. I have lemons and ice and things. My man sent me down supplies today; I leave him in town. I am rather a dab at drinks; I learnt it from the Yankees; about the only thing I did learn from them I care to remember. Susan!' The little maid helps me to get the materials, and *she* watches me quietly. When I give it to her she takes it with a smile (she *has* been crying). That is an ample thank you. She looks quite old. Something more than tiredness called up those lines in her face.

* * * * *

Well, ten days passed, sometimes we met at breakfast, sometimes at supper, sometimes we fished together or sat in the straggling orchard and talked; she neither avoided me nor sought me. She is the most charming mixture of child and woman I ever met. She is a dual creature. Now I never met that in a man. When she is here without getting a letter in the morning or going to town, she seems like a girl. She runs about in her grey gown and little cap and laughs, and seems to throw off all thought like an irresponsible child. She is eager to fish, or pick gooseberries and eat them daintily, or sit under the trees and talk. But when she goes to town—I notice she always goes when she gets a lawyer's letter, there is no mistaking the envelope—she comes home tired and haggard-looking, an old woman of thirty-five. I wonder why. It takes her, even with her elasticity of temperament, nearly a day to get young again. I hate her to go to town; it is extraordinary how I miss her; I can't recall, when she is absent, her saying anything very wonderful, but she converses all the time. She has a gracious way of filling the place with herself, there is an entertaining quality in her very presence. We had one rainy afternoon; she tied me some flies (I shan't use any of them); I watched the lights in her hair as she moved, it is quite golden in some places, and she has a tiny mole near her left ear and another on her left wrist. On the eleventh day she got a letter but she didn't go to town, she stayed up in her room all day;

twenty times I felt inclined to send her a line, but I had no excuse. I heard the landlady say as I passed the kitchen window: 'Poor dear! I'm sorry to lose her!' Lose her? I should think not. It has come to this with me that I don't care to face any future without her; and yet I know nothing about her, not even if she is a free woman. I shall find that out the next time I see her. In the evening I catch a glimpse of her gown in the orchard, and I follow her. We sit down near the river. Her left hand is lying gloveless next to me in the grass.

'Do you think from what you have seen of me, that I would ask a question out of any mere impertinent curiosity?'

She starts. 'No, I do not!'

I take up her hand and touch the ring. 'Tell me, does this bind you to any one?'

I am conscious of a buzzing in my ears and a dancing blurr of water and sky and trees, as I wait (it seems to me an hour) for her reply. I felt the same sensation once before, when I got drawn into some rapids and had an awfully narrow shave, but of that another time.

The voice is shaking.

'I am not legally bound to anyone, at least; but why do you ask?' she looks me square in the face as she speaks, with a touch of haughtiness I never saw in her before.

Perhaps the great relief I feel, the sense of joy at knowing she is free, speaks out of my face, for hers flushes and she drops her eyes, her lips tremble. I don't look at her again, but I can see her all the same. After a while she says—

'I half intended to tell you something about myself this evening, now I *must*. Let us go in. I shall come down to the sitting-room after your supper.' She takes a long look at the river and the inn, as if fixing the place in her memory; it strikes me with a chill that there is a goodbye in her gaze. Her eyes rest on me a moment as they come back, there is a sad look in their grey clearness. She swings her little grey gloves in her hand as we walk back. I can hear her walking up and down overhead; how tired she will be, and how slowly the time goes. I am standing at one side of the window when she enters; she stands at the other, leaning her head against the shutter with her hands clasped before her. I can hear my own heart beating, and, I fancy, hers through the stillness. The suspense is fearful. At length she says—

'You have been a long time out of England; you don't read the papers?'

'No.' A pause. I believe my heart is beating inside my head.

'You asked me if I was a free woman. I don't pretend to misunderstand why you asked me. I am not a beautiful woman, I never was. But there must be something about me, there is in some women, "essential femininity" perhaps, that appeals to all men. What I read in your eyes I have seen in many men's before, but before God I never tried to rouse it. Today (with a sob), I can say I am free, yesterday morning I could not. Yesterday my husband gained his case and divorced me!' she closes her eyes and draws in her under-lip to stop its quivering. I want to take her in my arms, but I am afraid to.

'I did not ask you any more than if you were free!'

'No, but I am afraid you don't quite take in the meaning. I did not divorce my husband, he divorced *me*, he got a decree *nisi*; do you understand now? (she is speaking with difficulty), do you know what that implies?'

I can't stand her face any longer. I take her hands, they are icy cold, and hold them tightly.

'Yes, I know what it implies, that is, I know the legal and social conclusion to be drawn from it—if that is what you mean. But I never asked you for that information. I have nothing to do with your past. You did not exist for me before the day we met on the river. I take you from that day and I ask you to marry me.'

I feel her tremble and her hands get suddenly warm. She turns her head and looks at me long and searchingly, then she says—

'Sit down, I want to say something!'

I obey, and she comes and stands next the chair. I can't help it, I reach up my arm, but she puts it gently down.

'No, you must listen without touching me, I shall go back to the window. I don't want to influence you a bit by any personal magnetism I possess. I want you to listen—I have told you he divorced me, the co-respondent was an old friend, a friend of my childhood, of my girlhood. He died just after the first application was made, luckily for me. He would have considered my honour before my happiness. *I* did not defend the case, it wasn't likely—ah, if you knew all? He proved his case; given clever counsel, willing witnesses to whom you make it worth while, and no defence, divorce is always attainable even in England. But remember: I figure as an adulteress in every English-speaking paper. If you buy last week's evening papers—do you remember the day I was in town?'—I nod—'you will see a sketch of me in that day's; someone, perhaps he, must have given it; it was from an old photograph. I bought one at Victoria as I came out; it is funny (with an hysterical laugh) to buy a caricature of one's own poor face at a news-stall. Yet in spite of that I have felt glad. The point for you is that I made no defence to the world, and (with a lifting of her head) I will make no apology, no explanation, no denial to you, now nor ever. I am very desolate and your attention came very warm to me, but I don't love you. Perhaps I could learn to (with a rush of colour), for what you have said tonight, and it is because of that I tell you to weigh what this means. Later, when your care for me will grow into habit, you may chafe at my past. It is from that I would save you.'

I hold out my hands and she comes and puts them aside and takes me by the beard and turns up my face and scans it earnestly. She must have been deceived a good deal. I let her do as she pleases, it is the wisest way with women, and it is good to have her touch me in that way. She seems satisfied. She stands leaning against the arm of the chair and says—

'I must learn first to think of myself as a free woman again, it almost seems wrong today to talk like this; can you understand that feeling?'

I nod assent.

'Next time I must be sure, and you must be sure,' she lays her fingers on my mouth as I am about to protest, 'S-sh! You shall have a year to think. If you repeat then what you have said today, I shall give you your answer. You must not try to find me. I have money. If I am living, I will come here to you. If I am dead, you will be told of it. In the year between I shall look upon myself as belonging to you, and render an account if you wish of every hour. You will not be influenced by me in any way, and you will be able to reason it out calmly. If you think better of it, don't come.'

I feel there would be no use trying to move her, I simply kiss her hands and say:

'As you will, dear woman, I shall be here.'

We don't say any more; she sits down on a footstool with her head against my knee, and I just smooth it. When the clocks strike ten through the house, she rises and I stand up. I see that she has been crying quietly, poor lonely little soul. I lift her off her feet and kiss her, and stammer out my sorrow at losing her, and she is gone. Next morning the little maid brought me an envelope from the lady, who left by the first train. It held a little grey glove; that is why I carry it always, and why I haunt the inn and never leave it for longer than a week; why I sit and dream in the old chair that has a ghost of her presence always; dream of the spring to come with the May-fly on the wing, and the young summer when midges dance, and the trout are growing fastidious; when she will come to me across the meadow grass, through the silver haze, as she did before; come with her grey eyes shining to exchange herself for her little grey glove.

THE WOMAN BEATER

By Israel Zangwill

I

She came 'to meet John Lefolle', but John Lefolle did not know he was to meet Winifred Glamorys. He did not even know he was himself the meeting-point of all the brilliant and beautiful persons, assembled in the publisher's Saturday Salon, for although a youthful minor poet, he was modest and lovable. Perhaps his Oxford tutorship was sobering. At any rate his head remained unturned by his precocious fame, and to meet these other young men and women—his reverend seniors on the slopes of Parnassus—gave him more pleasure than the receipt of 'royalties'. Not that his publisher afforded him much opportunity of contrasting the two pleasures. The profits of the Muse went to provide this room of old furniture and roses, this beautiful garden a-twinkle with Japanese lanterns, like gorgeous fire-flowers blossoming under the white crescent-moon of early June.

Winifred Glamorys was not literary herself. She was better than a poetess, she was a poem. The publisher always threw in a few realities, and some beautiful brainless creature would generally be found the nucleus of a crowd, while Clio in spectacles languished in a corner. Winifred Glamorys, however, was reputed to have a tongue that matched her eye; paralleling with whimsies and epigrams its freakish fires and witcheries, and, assuredly, flitting in her white gown through the dark balmy garden, she seemed the very spirit of moonlight, the subtle incarnation of night and roses.

When John Lefolle met her, Cecilia was with her, and the first conversation was triangular. Cecilia fired most of the shots; she was a bouncing, rattling beauty, chockful of confidence and high spirits, except when asked to do the one thing she could do—sing! Then she became—quite genuinely—a nervous, hesitant, pale little thing. However, the suppliant hostess bore her off, and presently her rich contralto notes passed through the garden, adding to its passion and mystery, and through the open French windows, John could see her standing against the wall near the piano, her head thrown back, her eyes half-closed, her creamy throat swelling in the very abandonment of artistic ecstasy.

'What a charming creature!' he exclaimed involuntarily.

'That is what everybody thinks, except her husband,' Winifred laughed.

'Is he blind then?' asked John with his cloistral *naïveté*.

'Blind? No, love is blind. Marriage is never blind.'

The bitterness in her tone pierced John. He felt vaguely the passing of some icy current from unknown seas of experience. Cecilia's voice soared out enchantingly.

'Then, marriage must be deaf,' he said, 'or such music as that would charm it.'

She smiled sadly. Her smile was the tricksy play of moonlight among clouds of faëry.

'You have never been married,' she said simply.

'Do you mean that you, too, are neglected?' something impelled him to exclaim.

'Worse,' she murmured.

'It is incredible!' he cried. 'You!'

'Hush! My husband will hear you.'

Her warning whisper brought him into a delicious conspiracy with her. 'Which is your husband?' he whispered back.

'There! Near the casement, standing gazing open-mouthed at Cecilia. He always opens his mouth when she sings. It is like two toys moved by the same wire.'

He looked at the tall, stalwart, ruddy-haired Anglo-Saxon. 'Do you mean to say he——?'

'I mean to say nothing.'

'But you said——'

'I said "worse".'

'Why, what can be worse?'

She put her hand over her face. 'I am ashamed to tell you.' How adorable was that half-divined blush!

'But you must tell me everything.' He scarcely knew how he had leapt into this role of confessor. He only felt they were 'moved by the same wire'.

Her head drooped on her breast. 'He—beats—me.'

'What!' John forgot to whisper. It was the greatest shock his recluse life had known, compact as it was of horror at the revelation, shamed confusion at her candour, and delicious pleasure in her confidence.

This fragile, exquisite creature under the rod of a brutal bully!

Once he had gone to a wedding reception, and among the serious presents some grinning Philistine drew his attention to an uncouth club—'a wife-beater' he called it. The flippancy had jarred upon John terribly: this intrusive reminder of the customs of the slums. It grated like Billingsgate in a boudoir. Now that savage weapon recurred to him—for a lurid instant he saw Winifred's husband wielding it. Oh, abomination of his sex! And did he stand there, in his immaculate evening dress, posing as an English gentleman? Even so might some gentleman burglar bear through a salon his imperturbable swallow-tail.

Beat a woman! Beat that essence of charm and purity, God's best gift to man, redeeming him from his own grossness! Could such things be? John Lefolle would as soon have credited the French legend that English wives are sold in Smithfield. No! it could not be real that this flower-like figure was thrashed.

'Do you mean to say——?' he cried. The rapidity of her confidence alone made him feel it all of a dreamlike unreality.

'Hush! Cecilia's singing!' she admonished him with an unexpected smile, as her fingers fell from her face.

'Oh, you have been making fun of me.' He was vastly relieved. 'He beats you—at chess—or at lawn-tennis?'

'Does one wear a high-necked dress to conceal the traces of chess, or lawn-tennis?'

He had not noticed her dress before, save for its spiritual whiteness. Susceptible though he was to beautiful shoulders, Winifred's enchanting face had been sufficiently distracting. Now the thought of physical bruises gave him a second spasm of righteous horror. That delicate rose-leaf flesh abraded and lacerated!

'The ruffian! Does he use a stick or a fist?'

'Both! But as a rule he just takes me by the arms and shakes me like a terrier a rat. I'm all black and blue now.'

'Poor butterfly!' he murmured poetically.

'Why did I tell you?' she murmured back with subtler poetry.

The poet thrilled in every vein. 'Love at first sight', of which he had often read and often written, was then a reality! It could be as mutual, too, as Romeo's and Juliet's. But how awkward that Juliet should be married and her husband a Bill Sykes in broad-cloth!

II

Mrs. Glamorys herself gave 'At Homes', every Sunday afternoon, and so, on the morrow, after a sleepless night mitigated by perpended sonnets, the love-sick young tutor presented himself by invitation at the beautiful old house in Hampstead. He was enchanted to find his heart's mistress set in an eighteenth-century frame of small-paned windows and of high oak-panelling, and at once began to image her dancing minuets and playing on virginals. Her husband was absent, but a broad band of velvet round Winifred's neck was a painful reminder of his possibilities. Winifred, however, said it was only a touch of sore throat caught in the garden. Her eyes added that there was nothing in the pathological dictionary which she would not willingly have caught for the sake of those divine, if draughty moments; but that, alas! it was more than a mere bodily ailment she had caught there.

There were a great many visitors in the two delightfully quaint rooms, among whom he wandered disconsolate and admired, jealous of her scattered smiles, but presently he found himself seated by her side on a 'cosy corner' near the open folding-doors, with all the other guests huddled round a violinist in the inner room. How Winifred had managed it he did not know but she sat plausibly in the outer room, awaiting newcomers, and this particular niche was invisible, save to a determined eye. He took her unresisting hand—that dear, warm hand, with its begemmed artistic fingers, and held it in uneasy beatitude. How wonderful! She—the beautiful and adored hostess, of whose sweetness and charm he heard even her own guests murmur to one another—it was her actual flesh-and-blood hand that lay in his—thrillingly tangible. Oh, adventure beyond all merit, beyond all hoping!

But every now and then, the outer door facing them would open on some newcomer, and John had hastily to release her soft magnetic fingers and sit demure, and jealously overhear her effusive welcome to those innocent intruders, nor did his brow clear till she had shepherded them within the inner fold. Fortunately, the refreshments were in this section, so that once therein, few of the sheep strayed back, and the jiggling wail of the violin was succeeded by a shrill babble of tongues and the clatter of cups and spoons. 'Get me an ice, please—strawberry,' she ordered John during one of these forced intervals in manual flirtation; and when he had steered laboriously to and fro, he found a young actor beside her in his cosy corner, and his jealous fancy almost saw *their* hands dispart. He stood over them with a sickly smile, while Winifred ate her ice. When he returned from depositing the empty saucer, the player-fellow was gone, and in remorse for his mad suspicion he stooped and reverently lifted her fragrant finger-tips to his lips. The door behind his back opened abruptly.

'Goodbye,' she said, rising in a flash. The words had the calm conventional cadence, and instantly extorted from him—amid all his dazedness—the corresponding 'Goodbye'. When he turned and saw it was Mr. Glamorys who had come in, his heart leapt wildly at the nearness of his escape. As he passed this masked ruffian, he nodded perfunctorily and received a cordial smile. Yes, he was handsome and fascinating enough externally, this blonde savage.

'A man may smile and smile and be a villain,' John thought. 'I wonder how he'd feel, if he knew I knew he beats women.'

Already John had generalized the charge. 'I hope Cecilia will keep him at arm's length,' he had said to Winifred, 'if only that she may not smart for it some day.'

He lingered purposely in the hall to get an impression of the brute, who had begun talking loudly to a friend with irritating bursts of laughter, speciously frank-ringing. Golf, fishing, comic operas—ah, the Boeotian! These were the men who monopolized the ethereal divinities.

But this brusque separation from his particular divinity was disconcerting. How to see her again? He must go up to Oxford in the morning, he wrote her that night, but if she could possibly let him call during the week he would manage to run down again.

* * * * *

'Oh, my dear, dreaming poet,' she wrote to Oxford, 'how could you possibly send me a letter to be laid on the breakfast-table beside *The Times*! With a poem in it, too. Fortunately my husband was in a hurry to get down to the City, and he neglected to read my correspondence. ('The unchivalrous blackguard,' John commented. 'But what can be expected of a woman beater?') Never, never write to me again at the house. A letter, care of Mrs. Best, 8A Foley Street, W.C., will always find me. She is my maid's mother. And you must not come here either, my dear handsome head-in-the-clouds, except to my 'At Homes', and then only at judicious intervals. I shall be walking round the pond in Kensington Gardens at four next Wednesday, unless Mrs. Best brings me a letter to the contrary. And now thank you for your delicious poem; I do not recognize my humble self in the dainty lines, but I shall always be proud to think I inspired them. Will it be in the new volume? I have never been in print before; it will be a novel sensation. I cannot pay you song for song, only feeling for feeling. Oh, John Lefolle, why did we not meet when I had still my girlish dreams? Now, I have grown to distrust all men—to fear the brute beneath the cavalier . . . '

* * * * *

Mrs. Best did bring her a letter, but it was not to cancel the appointment, only to say he was not surprised at her horror of the male sex, but that she must beware of false generalizations. Life was still a wonderful and beautiful thing—*vide* poem enclosed. He was counting the minutes till Wednesday afternoon. It was surely a popular mistake that only sixty went to the hour.

This chronometrical reflection recurred to him even more poignantly in the hour that he circumambulated the pond in Kensington Gardens. Had she forgotten—had her husband locked her up? What could have happened? It seemed six hundred minutes, ere, at ten past five she came tripping daintily towards him. His brain had been reduced to insanely devising problems for his pupils—if a man walks two strides of one and a half feet a second round a lake fifty acres in area, in how many turns will he overtake a lady who walks half as fast and isn't there?—but the moment her pink parasol loomed on the horizon, all his long misery vanished in an ineffable peace and uplifting. He hurried, bare-headed, to clasp her little gloved hand. He had forgotten her unpunctuality, nor did she remind him of it.

'How sweet of you to come all that way,' was all she said, and it was a sufficient reward for the hours in the train and the six hundred minutes among the nursemaids and perambulators. The elms were in their glory, the birds were singing briskly, the water sparkled, the sunlit sward stretched fresh and green—it was the loveliest, coolest moment of the afternoon. John instinctively turned down a leafy avenue. Nature and Love! What more could poet ask?

'No, we can't have tea by the Kiosk,' Mrs. Glamorys protested. 'Of course I love anything that savours of Paris, but it's become so fashionable. There will be heaps of people who know me. I suppose you've forgotten it's the height of the season. I know a quiet little place in the High Street.' She led him, unresisting but bemused, towards the gate, and into a confectioner's. Conversation languished on the way.

'Tea,' he was about to instruct the pretty attendant.

'Strawberry ices,' Mrs. Glamorys remarked gently. 'And some of those nice French cakes.'

The ice restored his spirits, it was really delicious, and he had got so hot and tired, pacing round the pond. Decidedly Winifred was a practical person and he was a dreamer. The pastry he dared not touch—being a genius—but he was charmed at the gaiety with which Winifred crammed cake after cake into her rosebud of a mouth. What an enchanting creature! how bravely she covered up her life's tragedy!

The thought made him glance at her velvet band—it was broader than ever.

'He has beaten you again!' he murmured furiously. Her joyous eyes saddened, she hung her head, and her fingers crumbled the cake. 'What is his pretext?' he asked, his blood burning.

'Jealousy,' she whispered.

His blood lost its glow, ran cold. He felt the bully's blows on his own skin, his romance turning suddenly sordid. But he recovered his courage. He, too, had muscles. 'But I thought he just missed seeing me kiss your hand.'

She opened her eyes wide. 'It wasn't you, you darling old dreamer.'

He was relieved and disturbed in one.

'Somebody else?' he murmured. Somehow the vision of the player-fellow came up.

She nodded. 'Isn't it lucky he has himself drawn a red-herring across the track? I didn't mind his blows—*you* were safe!' Then, with one of her adorable transitions, 'I am dreaming of another ice,' she cried with roguish wistfulness.

'I was afraid to confess my own greediness,' he said, laughing. He beckoned the waitress. 'Two more.'

'We haven't got any more strawberries,' was her unexpected reply. 'There's been such a run on them today.'

Winifred's face grew overcast. 'Oh, nonsense!' she pouted. To John the moment seemed tragic.

'Won't you have another kind?' he queried. He himself liked any kind, but he could scarcely eat a second ice without her.

Winifred meditated. 'Coffee?' she queried.

The waitress went away and returned with a face as gloomy as Winifred's. 'It's been such a hot day,' she said deprecatingly. 'There is only one ice in the place and that's Neapolitan.'

'Well, bring two Neapolitans,' John ventured.

'I mean there is only one Neapolitan ice left.'

'Well, bring that. I don't really want one.'

He watched Mrs. Glamorys daintily devouring the solitary ice, and felt a certain pathos about the parti-coloured oblong, a something of the haunting sadness of 'The Last Rose of Summer'.

It would make a graceful, serio-comic triolet, he was thinking. But at the last spoonful, his beautiful companion dislocated his rhymes by her sudden upspringing.

'Goodness gracious,' she cried, 'how late it is!'

'Oh, you're not leaving me yet!' he said. A world of things sprang to his brain, things that he was going to say—to arrange. They had said nothing—not a word of their love even; nothing but cakes and ices.

'Poet!' she laughed. 'Have you forgotten I live at Hampstead?' She picked up her parasol.

'Put me into a hansom, or my husband will be raving at his lonely dinner-table.'

He was so dazed as to be surprised when the waitress blocked his departure with a bill. When Winifred was spirited away, he remembered she might, without much risk, have given him a lift to Paddington. He hailed another hansom and caught the next train to Oxford. But he was too late for his own dinner in Hall.

III

He was kept very busy for the next few days, and could only exchange a passionate letter or two with her. For some time the examination fever had been raging, and in every college poor patients sat with wet towels round their heads. Some, who had neglected their tutor all the term, now strove to absorb his omniscience in a sitting.

On the Monday, John Lefolle was good-naturedly giving a special audience to a muscular dunce, trying to explain to him the political effects of the Crusades, when there was a knock at the sitting-room door, and the scout ushered in Mrs. Glamorys. She was bewitchingly dressed in white, and stood in the open doorway, smiling—an embodiment of the summer he was neglecting. He rose, but his tongue was paralysed. The dunce became suddenly important—a symbol of the decorum he had been outraging. His soul, torn so abruptly from history to romance, could not get up the right emotion. Why this imprudence of Winifred's? She had been so careful heretofore.

'What a lot of boots there are on your staircase!' she said gaily.

He laughed. The spell was broken. 'Yes, the heap to be cleaned is rather obtrusive,' he said, 'but I suppose it is a sort of tradition.'

'I think I've got hold of the thing pretty well now, sir.' The dunce rose and smiled, and his tutor realized how little the dunce had to learn in some things. He felt quite grateful to him.

'Oh, well, you'll come and see me again after lunch, won't you, if one or two points occur to you for elucidation,' he said, feeling vaguely a liar, and generally guilty. But when, on the departure of the dunce, Winifred held out her arms, everything fell from him but the sense of the exquisite moment. Their lips met for the first time, but only for an instant. He had scarcely time to realize that this wonderful thing had happened before the mobile creature had darted to his book-shelves and was examining a Thucydides upside down.

'How clever to know Greek!' she exclaimed. 'And do you really talk it with the other dons?'

'No, we never talk shop,' he laughed. 'But, Winifred, what made you come here?'

'I had never seen Oxford. Isn't it beautiful?'

'There's nothing beautiful *here*,' he said, looking round his sober study.

'No,' she admitted; 'there's nothing I care for here,' and had left another celestial kiss on his lips before he knew it. 'And now you must take me to lunch and on the river.'

He stammered, 'I have—work.'

She pouted. 'But I can't stay beyond tomorrow morning, and I want so much to see all your celebrated oarsmen practising.'

'You are not staying over the night?' he gasped.

'Yes, I am,' and she threw him a dazzling glance.

His heart went pit-a-pat. 'Where?' he murmured.

'Oh, some poky little hotel near the station. The swell hotels are full.'

He was glad to hear she was not conspicuously quartered.

'So many people have come down already for Commem,' he said. 'I suppose they are anxious to see the Generals get their degrees. But hadn't we better go somewhere and lunch?'

They went down the stone staircase, past the battalion of boots, and across the quad. He felt that all the windows were alive with eyes, but she insisted on standing still and admiring their ivied picturesqueness. After lunch he shamefacedly borrowed the dunce's punt. The necessities of punting, which kept him far from her, and demanded much adroit labour, gradually restored his self-respect, and he was able to look the uncelebrated oarsmen they met in the eyes, except when they were accompanied by their parents and sisters, which subtly made him feel uncomfortable again. But Winifred, piquant under her pink parasol, was singularly at ease, enraptured with the changing beauty of the river, applauding with childish glee the wild flowers on the banks, or the rippling reflections in the water.

'Look, look!' she cried once, pointing skyward. He stared upwards, expecting a balloon at least. But it was only 'Keats' little rosy cloud', she explained. It was not her fault if he did not find the excursion unreservedly idyllic.

'How stupid,' she reflected, 'to keep all those nice boys cooped up reading dead languages in a spot made for life and love.'

'I'm afraid they don't disturb the dead languages so much as you think,' he reassured her, smiling. 'And there will be plenty of love-making during Commem.'

'I am so glad. I suppose there are lots of engagements that week.'

'Oh, yes—but not one per cent come to anything.'

'Really? Oh, how fickle men are!'

That seemed rather question-begging, but he was so thrilled by the implicit revelation that she could not even imagine feminine inconstancy, that he forebore to draw her attention to her inadequate logic.

So childish and thoughtless indeed was she that day that nothing would content her but attending a 'Viva', which he had incautiously informed her was public.

'Nobody will notice us,' she urged with strange unconsciousness of her loveliness. 'Besides, they don't know I'm not your sister.'

'The Oxford intellect is sceptical,' he said, laughing. 'It cultivates philosophical doubt.'

But, putting a bold face on the matter, and assuming a fraternal air, he took her to the torture-chamber, in which candidates sat dolefully on a row of chairs against the wall, waiting their turn to come before the three grand inquisitors at the table. Fortunately, Winifred and he were the only spectators; but unfortunately they blundered in at the very moment when the poor owner of the punt was on the rack. The central inquisitor was trying to extract from him information about Becket, almost prompting him with the very words, but without penetrating through the duncical denseness. John Lefolle breathed more freely when the Crusades were broached; but, alas, it very soon became evident that the dunce had by no means 'got hold of the thing'. As the dunce passed out sadly, obviously ploughed, John Lefolle suffered more than he. So conscience-stricken was he that, when he had accompanied Winifred as far as her hotel, he refused her invitation to come in, pleading the compulsoriness of duty and dinner in Hall. But he could not get away without promising to call in during the evening.

The prospect of this visit was with him all through dinner, at once tempting and terrifying. Assuredly there was a skeleton at his feast, as he sat at the high table, facing the Master. The venerable portraits round the Hall seemed to rebuke his romantic waywardness. In the common-room, he sipped his port uneasily, listening as in a daze to the discussion on Free Will, which an eminent stranger had stirred up. How academic it seemed, compared with the passionate realities of life. But somehow he found himself lingering on at the academic discussion, postponing the realities of life. Every now and again, he was impelled to glance at his watch; but suddenly murmuring, 'It is very late,' he pulled himself together, and took leave of his learned brethren. But in the street the sight of a telegraph office drew his steps to it, and almost mechanically he wrote out the message: 'Regret detained. Will call early in morning.'

When he did call in the morning, he was told she had gone back to London the night before on receipt of a telegram. He turned away with a bitter pang of disappointment and regret.

IV

Their subsequent correspondence was only the more amorous. The reason she had fled from the hotel, she explained, was that she could not endure the night in those stuffy quarters. He consoled himself with the hope of seeing much of her during the Long Vacation. He did see her once at her own reception, but this time her husband wandered about the two rooms. The cosy corner was impossible, and they could only manage to gasp out a few mutual endearments amid the buzz and movement, and to arrange a *rendezvous* for the end of July. When the day came, he received a heart-broken letter, stating that her husband had borne her away to Goodwood. In a postscript she informed him that 'Quicksilver was a sure thing'. Much correspondence passed without another meeting being effected, and he lent her five pounds to pay a debt of honour incurred through her husband's 'absurd confidence in Quicksilver'. A week later this horsey husband of hers brought her on to Brighton for the races there, and hither John Lefolle flew. But her husband shadowed her, and he could only lift his hat to her as they passed each other on the Lawns. Sometimes he saw her sitting pensively on a chair while her lord and thrasher perused a pink sporting-paper. Such tantalizing proximity raised their correspondence through the Hove Post Office to fever heat. Life apart, they felt, was impossible, and, removed from the sobering influences of his cap and gown, John Lefolle dreamed of throwing everything to the winds. His literary reputation had opened out a new career. The Winifred lyrics alone had brought in a tidy sum, and though he had expended that and more on despatches of flowers and trifles to her, yet he felt this extravagance would become extinguished under daily companionship, and the poems provoked by her charms would go far towards their daily maintenance. Yes, he could throw up the University. He would rescue her from this bully, this gentleman bruiser. They would live openly and nobly in the world's eye. A poet was not even expected to be conventional.

She, on her side, was no less ardent for the great step. She raged against the world's law, the injustice by which a husband's cruelty was not sufficient ground for divorce. 'But we finer souls must take the law into our own hands,' she wrote. 'We must teach society that the ethics of a barbarous age are unfitted for our century of enlightenment.' But somehow the actual time and place of the elopement could never get itself fixed. In September her husband dragged her to Scotland, in October after the pheasants. When the dramatic day was actually fixed, Winifred wrote by the next post deferring it for a week. Even the few actual preliminary meetings they planned for Kensington Gardens or Hampstead Heath rarely came off. He lived in a whirling atmosphere of express letters of excuse, and telegrams that transformed the situation from hour to hour. Not that her passion in any way abated, or her romantic resolution really altered: it was only that her conception of time and place and ways and means was dizzily mutable.

But after nigh six months of palpitating negotiations with the adorable Mrs. Glamorys, the poet, in a moment of dejection, penned the prose apophthegm, 'It is of no use trying to change a changeable person.'

V

But at last she astonished him by a sketch plan of the elopement, so detailed, even to band-boxes and the Paris night route *via* Dieppe, that no further room for doubt was left in his intoxicated soul, and he was actually further astonished when, just as he was putting his hand-bag into the hansom, a telegram was handed to him saying: 'Gone to Homburg. Letter follows.'

He stood still for a moment on the pavement in utter distraction. What did it mean? Had she failed him again? Or was it simply that she had changed the city of refuge from Paris to Homburg? He was about to name the new station to the cabman, but then, 'letter follows'. Surely that meant that he was to wait for it. Perplexed and miserable, he stood with the telegram crumpled up in his fist. What a ridiculous situation! He had wrought himself up to the point of breaking with the world and his past, and now—it only remained to satisfy the cabman!

He tossed feverishly all night, seeking to soothe himself, but really exciting himself the more by a hundred plausible explanations. He was now strung up to such a pitch of uncertainty that he was astonished for the third time when the 'letter' did duly 'follow'.

* * * * *

'Dearest,' it ran, 'as I explained in my telegram, my husband became suddenly ill'—('if she *had* only put that in the telegram,' he groaned)—'and was ordered to Homburg. Of course it was impossible to leave him in this crisis, both for practical and sentimental reasons. You yourself, darling, would not like me to have aggravated his illness by my flight just at this moment, and thus possibly have his death on my conscience.' ('Darling, you are always right,' he said, kissing the letter.) 'Let us possess our souls in patience a little longer. I need not tell you how vexatious it will be to find myself nursing him in Homburg—out of the season even—instead of the prospect to which I had looked forward with my whole heart and soul. But what can one do? How true is the French proverb, 'Nothing happens but the unexpected'! Write to me immediately *Poste Restante*, that I may at least console myself with your dear words.'

The unexpected did indeed happen. Despite draughts of Elizabeth-brunnen and promenades on the Kurhaus terrace, the stalwart woman beater succumbed to his malady. The curt telegram from Winifred gave no indication of her emotions. He sent a reply-telegram of sympathy with her trouble. Although he could not pretend to grieve at this sudden providential solution of their life-problem, still he did sincerely sympathize with the distress inevitable in connection with a death, especially on foreign soil.

He was not able to see her till her husband's body had been brought across the North Sea and committed to the green repose of the old Hampstead churchyard. He found her pathetically altered—her face wan and spiritualized, and all in subtle harmony with the exquisite black gown. In the first interview, he did not dare speak of their love at all. They discussed the immortality of the soul, and she quoted George Herbert. But with the weeks the question of their future began to force its way back to his lips.

'We could not decently marry before six months,' she said, when definitely confronted with the problem.

'Six months!' he gasped.

'Well, surely you don't want to outrage everybody,' she said, pouting.

At first he was outraged himself. What! She who had been ready to flutter the world with a fantastic dance was now measuring her footsteps. But on reflection he saw that Mrs. Glamorys was right once more. Since Providence had been good enough to rescue them, why should they fly in its face? A little patience, and a blameless happiness lay before them. Let him not blind himself to the immense relief he really felt at being spared social obloquy. After all, a poet could be unconventional in his *work*—he had no need of the practical outlet demanded for the less gifted.

VI

They scarcely met at all during the next six months—it had, naturally, in this grateful reaction against their recklessness, become a sacred period, even more charged with tremulous emotion than the engagement periods of those who have not so nearly scorched themselves. Even in her presence he found a certain pleasure in combining distant adoration with the confident expectation of proximity, and thus she was restored to the sanctity which she had risked by her former easiness. And so all was for the best in the best of all possible worlds.

When the six months had gone by, he came to claim her hand. She was quite astonished. 'You promised to marry me at the end of six months,' he reminded her.

'Surely it isn't six months already,' she said.

He referred her to the calendar, recalled the date of her husband's death.

'You are strangely literal for a poet,' she said. 'Of course I *said* six months, but six months doesn't mean twenty-six weeks by the clock. All I meant was that a decent period must intervene. But even to myself it seems only yesterday that poor Harold was walking beside me in the Kurhaus Park.' She burst into tears, and in the face of them he could not pursue the argument.

Gradually, after several interviews and letters, it was agreed that they should wait another six months.

'She *is* right,' he reflected again. 'We have waited so long, we may as well wait a little longer and leave malice no handle.'

The second six months seemed to him much longer than the first. The charm of respectful adoration had lost its novelty, and once again his breast was racked by fitful fevers which could scarcely calm themselves even by conversion into sonnets. The one point of repose was that shining fixed star of marriage. Still smarting under Winifred's reproach of his unpoetic literality, he did not intend to force her to marry him exactly at the end of the twelve-month. But he was determined that she should have no later than this exact date for at least 'naming the day'. Not the most punctilious stickler for convention, he felt, could deny that Mrs. Grundy's claim had been paid to the last minute.

The publication of his new volume—containing the Winifred lyrics—had served to colour these months of intolerable delay. Even the reaction of the critics against his poetry, that conventional revolt against every second volume, that parrot cry of over-praise from the very throats that had praised him, though it pained and perplexed him, was perhaps really helpful. At any rate, the long waiting was over at last. He felt like Jacob after his years of service for Rachel.

The fateful morning dawned bright and blue, and, as the towers of Oxford were left behind him he recalled that distant Saturday when he had first gone down to meet the literary lights of London in his publisher's salon. How much older he was now than then—and yet how much younger! The nebulous melancholy of youth, the clouds of philosophy, had vanished before this beautiful creature of sunshine whose radiance cut out a clear line for his future through the confusion of life.

At a florist's in the High Street of Hampstead he bought a costly bouquet of white flowers, and walked airily to the house and rang the bell jubilantly. He could scarcely believe his ears when the maid told him her mistress was not at home. How dared the girl stare at him so impassively? Did she not know by what appointment—on what errand—he had come? Had he not written to her mistress a week ago that he would present himself that afternoon?

'Not at home!' he gasped. 'But when will she be home?'

'I fancy she won't be long. She went out an hour ago, and she has an appointment with her dressmaker at five.'

'Do you know in what direction she'd have gone?'

'Oh, she generally walks on the Heath before tea.'

The world suddenly grew rosy again. 'I will come back again,' he said. Yes, a walk in this glorious air—heathward—would do him good.

As the door shut he remembered he might have left the flowers, but he would not ring again, and besides, it was, perhaps, better he should present them with his own hand, than let her find them on the hall table. Still, it seemed rather awkward to walk about the streets with a bouquet, and he was glad, accidentally to strike the old Hampstead Church, and to seek a momentary seclusion in passing through its avenue of quiet gravestones on his heathward way.

Mounting the few steps, he paused idly a moment on the verge of this green 'God's-acre' to read a perpendicular slab on a wall, and his face broadened into a smile as he followed the absurdly elaborate biography of a rich, self-made merchant who had taught himself to read, 'Reader, go thou and do likewise,' was the delicious bull at the end. As he turned away, the smile still lingering about his lips, he saw a dainty figure tripping down the stony graveyard path, and though he was somehow startled to find her still in black, there was no mistaking Mrs. Glamorys. She ran to meet him with a glad cry, which filled his eyes with happy tears.

'How good of you to remember!' she said, as she took the bouquet from his unresisting hand, and turned again on her footsteps. He followed her wonderingly across the uneven road towards a narrow aisle of graves on the left. In another instant she has stooped before a shining white stone, and laid his bouquet reverently upon it. As he reached her side, he saw that his flowers were almost lost in the vast mass of floral offerings with which the grave of the woman beater was bestrewn.

'How good of you to remember the anniversary,' she murmured again.

'How could I forget it?' he stammered, astonished. 'Is not this the end of the terrible twelve-month?'

The soft gratitude died out of her face. 'Oh, is *that* what you were thinking of?'

'What else?' he murmured, pale with conflicting emotions.

'What else! I think decency demanded that this day, at least, should be sacred to his memory. Oh, what brutes men are!' And she burst into tears.

His patient breast revolted at last. 'You said *he* was the brute!' he retorted, outraged.

'Is that your chivalry to the dead? Oh, my poor Harold, my poor Harold!'

For once her tears could not extinguish the flame of his anger. 'But you told me he beat you,' he cried.

'And if he did, I dare say I deserved it. Oh, my darling, my darling!' She laid her face on the stone and sobbed.

John Lefolle stood by in silent torture. As he helplessly watched her white throat swell and fall with the sobs, he was suddenly struck by the absence of the black velvet band—the truer mourning she had worn in the lifetime of the so lamented. A faint scar, only perceptible to his conscious eye, added to his painful bewilderment.

At last she rose and walked unsteadily forward. He followed her in mute misery. In a moment or two they found themselves on the outskirts of the deserted heath. How beautiful stretched the gorsy rolling country! The sun was setting in great burning furrows of gold and green—a panorama to take one's breath away. The beauty and peace of Nature passed into the poet's soul.

'Forgive me, dearest,' he begged, taking her hand.

She drew it away sharply. 'I cannot forgive you. You have shown yourself in your true colours.'

Her unreasonableness angered him again. 'What do you mean? I only came in accordance with our long-standing arrangement. You have put me off long enough.'

'It is fortunate I did put you off long enough to discover what you are.'

He gasped. He thought of all the weary months of waiting, all the long comedy of telegrams and express letters, the far-off flirtations of the cosy corner, the baffled elopement to Paris. 'Then you won't marry me?'

'I cannot marry a man I neither love nor respect.'

'You don't love me!' Her spontaneous kiss in his sober Oxford study seemed to burn on his angry lips.

'No, I never loved you.'

He took her by the arms and turned her round roughly. 'Look me in the face and dare to say you have never loved me.'

His memory was buzzing with passionate phrases from her endless letters. They stung like a swarm of bees. The sunset was like blood-red mist before his eyes.

'I have never loved you,' she said obstinately.

'You—!' His grasp on her arms tightened. He shook her.

'You are bruising me,' she cried.

His grasp fell from her arms as though they were red-hot. He had become a woman beater.

BIBLIOBAZAAR

The essential book market!

Did you know that you can get any of our titles in large print?

Did you know that we have an ever-growing collection of books in many languages?

**Order online:
www.bibliobazaar.com**

Find all of your favorite classic books!

Stay up to date with the latest government reports!

At BiblioBazaar, we aim to make knowledge more accessible by making thousands of titles available to you- *quickly and affordably*.

Contact us:
BiblioBazaar
PO Box 21206
Charleston, SC 29413

Made in the USA
Coppell, TX
05 October 2022